THE HUNGARIAN REVOLUTION

"There are times, men, and events about which only history can pass a final judgement; contemporaries and individual observers may write only what they have seen and heard."

LIVY

A White Book

THE
HUNGARIAN
REVOLUTION

The Story of the October Uprising as Recorded in Documents,
Dispatches, Eye-Witness Accounts,
and World-wide Reactions

Edited by Melvin J. Lasky

Published for the
CONGRESS FOR CULTURAL FREEDOM
by
FREDERICK A. PRAEGER
NEW YORK 1957

This documentation of the Hungarian Revolution

is humbly dedicated to the

writers, poets, scholars, intellectuals,

to the intelligentsia of Hungary,

who one day will write their own story

Editor's Note

*1. "White Book," according to the Oxford Dictionary, is a translation from the medieval Latin (*LIBER ALBUS*), and is defined there as "a book of official records or reports bound in white." Being neither bound in white nor official in any way, this volume is thus technically not quite that. But in a more general and widely-accepted sense the "whiteness" (or whatever the color, for the historical archives know also of blue, brown, yellow, and black books) has come to refer to certain qualities of authenticity and completeness in documentary presentation. It is to be hoped, therefore, that this "white book" on the Hungarian Revolution will be accepted as a fairly objective and comprehensive record of one of the great events of contemporary history. The documentation is based on Hungarian sources, leaflets, broadcasts, as well as dispatches of foreign correspondents and eyewitness accounts; the material has been gathered from many languages and parts of the world. Some of the original, previously unpublished documents will, we trust, throw some new light on the course of the Budapest uprising, and perhaps it is not too much to hope that many readers will get, possibly for the first time, a full, clear, and many-sided view of events.*

Soviet and Communist points of view (orthodox and unorthodox) have been included along with Western accounts. If they have not come off better in the relative proportions, the fault lies not in our editorial bias but in their repetitiousness and their single-minded reluctance to depart from one familiar note in reportage and commentary.

It is obvious that our intention has not been to make a dry-as-dust collection of documents for file, but to tell a story. The editor admits that he has made the effort not merely to "edit" these pages but to "compose" them. The attempt has been made here to catch history on the wing, to observe a revolution and a war with a thousand eyes. From the beginnings of the uprising on October 23rd in Budapest till the brutal Soviet counter-attack at daybreak on Sunday, November 4th, we have wanted to plunge the reader into an almost minute-by-minute unfolding of demonstrations, meetings, political crises, street-fighting, personal adventure and human tragedy. It has been our hope not only to compile the facts, but to find a form and a way to catch the color and the sound as well as the deeper meanings of the Hungarian Revolution.

2. As the reader will note, a substantial amount of Hungarian radio broadcasting from official Governmental (Gero, Nagy, Kadar) programs as well as from independent revolutionary stations, temporarily in command of a wave-length in the provinces, has been included. These have been monitored and recorded in translation by the British Broadcasting Corporation and Radio Free Europe (Munich and New York); some newspaper bureaus and foreign correspondents have also collected such messages. All of them have been generous with their material, and their assistance is gratefully acknowledged. (The complete BBC SUMMARIES are only available in mimeographed form; R.F.E. has published in New York a paperbound selection from its monitoring.) No translations, we regret, are completely or consistently adequate, and we have tried, to some extent, to improve on their readability and accuracy. But there is, sad to say, no UNIVAC for rendering shades of meaning in felicitous phrasing. On the eve of the Soviet military intervention of November 4th, PRAVDA expounded angrily on the relations between Premier Imre Nagy and the so-called "counter-revolution;" the NEW YORK TIMES referred to his "tolerance" and BBC to his "direct connivance." This obviously important word in Russian emerged, on check, as "POPUSTITELSTWO," which is rather closer to "non-intervention," and this is how we have excerpted the PRAVDA document. Here, as in other more basic matters involving the larger interpretation of events, we have made the effort, within the limits of human bias, not to impose any theses of our own. Scholars, statesmen, and political analysts have already offered personal views on the relationship between "Budapest and Suez," on Hungarian "extremism," on "basic Soviet strategy," on the varying historic responsibilities of Tito, Mindszenty, Mikoyan, Gomulka, Eden, and Dag Hammarskjold. A sampling of these have been included to illustrate some aspects of world opinion during the Hungarian crisis. Needless to say, the careful and thoughtful reader, pondering on cause and effect in the light of a many-sided documentation, may find many of these proferred theories untenable. In this, as in many other respects, our hope has been to shed some light and let the reader find his own way.

3. The documentary sources have been treated with the usual caution prescribed by historical scholarship. Where passages have been omitted there is the familiar (...) indication. (In some cases, in the interests of compactness, there has been some minor condensation.) Throughout we have attempted to give the exact source of the published text. In the day-to-day accounts, where it is not otherwise stated, the text belongs to the day in question. It has not obviously been possible in all matters to establish the precise hour of a broadcast, nor to include a report cleanly here rather than there. Historical events cannot always be recorded with chronometric accuracy. Meetings and battles often fall between dusk and dawn, and correspondents' references to "last night" and "this morning" become difficult to decipher even allowing for the time differences between Budapest and London, Paris, and New York. Where personal eyewitness accounts were recorded at a later date (because of censorship or interrupted communications), I have thought it appropriate to publish them under their original Budapest date-line to indicate their first-hand character as primary sources.

4. A word about the spelling of Hungarian names and places. There is, alas, no standard way of translation (and transliteration), and the renderings as they have occurred in the material of a half-dozen languages and twice as many editorial styles and proof-reading habits are varied and often confusing. Some reports carry over all the accents (Mátyás Rákosi, János Kádár); some do not. Some documents employ the umlauted vowels (Petőfi Club); others change it to Petoefi, others omit it altogether. Similarly in the Anglicisation of surnames, and especially first names: so that the philosopher Lukacs

is sometimes György and sometimes Gyoergy; in Yugoslav sources he appears as Djherdji, in German as Georg, in French Georges and in English simply as George. Except in certain extreme cases we have not, therefore, made the attempt to coordinate all the variations and divergences. It will surely be no surprise that Máleter Pál is none other than Col. Paul Maleter, the revolutionary commander, and we trust no one will by mystified by Ernö Gerö who also appears as Erno Gero (and sometimes even as Ernoe Geroe).

As our Hungarian friends have reminded us, the Hungarian language is "half-Finno-Ugrian and half 'Mongolian' in origin," is "dry in tone, with polysyllabic words which tend to monotony on account of their basic phonetic rule," and "with a music which contrasts to that of European languages as the drum to the violin" (Paul Ignotus). For the drumming inconsistencies and variations in spelling of names and places we can only ask the reader's patience and understanding.

5. The editor's gratitude should be expressed to Professor Hugh Seton-Watson who kindly agreed to write an introduction to help put in focus the flickering kaleidoscopic character of a thousand quick-moving scenes; and to François Bondy (who is preparing the French edition of this book) for the epilogue which chronicles events through the winter of 1956–57. The international offices of the Congress for Cultural Freedom have assisted in the location of material, and thanks are due to Jørgen Schleimann in Paris for his patient research. Above all I am obliged to my friend Harold Hurwitz in Berlin who cut and clipped and pasted and edited with me for long days and nights. Without him this book might have been finished a little earlier; but it would have been poorer without his admirable fussiness.

6. As these lines are being written, on the ill-starred 109th anniversary of Louis Kossuth's "March Days," reports are still coming in from Hungary of a government, weak and uncertain, trying to cope with unrest, resistance and revolutionary opposition. One can only hope, in the words of the philosopher, that those who remember the past are not condemned to repeat it ...

15 MARCH 1957   M. J. L.

CONTENTS

I

THE HISTORICAL BACKGROUND
1945–1956

"It is one thing to write like a poet, and another thing to write like an historian. The poet can tell or sing of things, not as they were but as they ought to have been, whereas the historian must describe them, not as they ought to have been, but as they were, without exaggerating or suppressing the truth in any particular."

CERVANTES

"The knowledge of the past, the record of truths revealed by experience, is eminently practical, is an instrument of action, and a power that goes to the making of the future."

LORD ACTON

"History is only in part a matter of 'fact'. Collect the 'facts' of the French Revolution! You must go down to Hell and up to Heaven to fetch them . . ."

G. M. TREVELYAN

HUNGARY 1945—1956

An Introduction by Hugh Seton-Watson

Hungary has had three major revolutions in her modern history—in 1848, 1918, and 1956. The Revolution of 1848 was a rising of the nation against foreign rule, in a pre-industrial age: it was a movement of landed gentry, intellectuals and peasants. The Revolution of 1918 was a rising of the industrial working-class against the old social order; but armed conflict with neighbouring nations (Rumanians, Slovaks and Serbs) turned it into a national movement, and for a time, though its leaders were communists, gave it the support of officers, bureaucrats and intellectuals. In the Revolution of 1956 the social and national factors were fused: it was a rising of the workers against exploitation, of the intellectuals against thought-control, and of the whole nation against the Soviet imperialists.

The Communist regime created by Mátyás Rákosi, which was overthrown in October 1956, was the result of the occupation of Hungary by the Soviet Army in 1944-5. Soviet occupation followed defeat in the Second World War (Hungary was Hitler's last ally in the field), and the collapse of a fascist reign of terror organised by Hitler's last disciples. To understand the Rákosi regime, one must begin by considering the cause of Hungary's involvement in the war and the nature of Hungarian Fascism.

Hungary joined the Axis in order to regain as much as possible of the territory which she had lost in 1920. The historic Kingdom of Hungary had been a multi-national state. The original Magyars came from the Eurasian steppes to Central Europe in the 9th century. They have preserved their language, which is not Indo-European; racially they became mixed with the Slavs and Rumanians who lived in the Danube valley and the Carpathians before their arrival. St. Stephen, the first Christian King of Hungary,

declared: *Regnum unius linguae uniusque moris imbecille et fragile est.* Racial intolerance was not regarded as a virtue in the Middle Ages. After the Turks had conquered Hungary in 1526, and then been expelled at the end of the following century, the country's ethnic composition became still more complicated. But the birth of modern nationalism in the nineteenth century affected not only the Magyars but also the Slovak, Rumanian, Croatian, and Serbian subjects of Hungary. Louis Kossuth the revolutionary leader of the Magyars in 1848, ignored the national claims of these other peoples: consequently they supported the Habsburgs in repressing the Revolution. When Hungary obtained something approximating to "Dominion Status" under the Compromise of 1867 with Austria, the Budapest governments had another chance to win the loyalty of the non-Magyar peoples. Again the opportunity was missed. Slav and Rumanian nationalism became an increasingly serious danger not only to Hungary but to the whole Austro-Hungarian Monarchy. When the Monarchy was defeated in war in 1918, the nationalities broke away from Hungary and joined the new Republic of Czechoslovakia and the greatly expanded kingdoms of Rumania and Yugoslavia.

Hugh Seton-Watson is Professor of Russian History at the University of London. Like his distinguished father, he has been a life-long student of East European affairs. His published works include "Eastern Europe Between the Wars" (1945), "The East European Revolution" (1950), "The Decline of Imperial Russia" (1952), "The Pattern of Communist Revolution" (1953).

The revolutionary government of Hungary in October 1918 tried to win the nationalities by offering the autonomy which the old regime had refused. But now the nationalities were as intransigent as the Magyar rulers had been. Their determination to secede, and to take with them large areas inhabited by Magyars, was one of the main factors which caused power to pass into the hands of the Communists in Budapest. The short-lived Hungarian Red Army was in the end overpowered by the Rumanians. The peace treaty of Trianon not only gave the nationalities independence from Hungary, but also transferred about one third of the Magyar nation (3 million persons) under foreign rule. This was bitterly resented by all Magyars. It is of course true that the discontented included landowners who had been deprived of estates, and bureaucrats who had given up jobs in the lost territories. But the repudiation of Trianon was more than the revolt of privileged classes: it was the profound feeling of a whole nation. Undoubtedly however, this national feeling benefited the old ruling class and the political right-wing. Nationalist indignation was used to divert effort from internal social reform. In foreign policy, Hungary sought any protector who would espouse her irredentist cause. The first patron to appear was Benito Mussolini; the second, Adolf Hitler. By associating herself with the Axis, Hungary recovered territory from Slovakia in 1938, Ruthenia in 1939, part of Transylvania from Rumania in 1940, and the Bácska from Yugoslavia in 1941. The price of the last acquisition was, first to allow Hitler's troops to pass through Hungary to attack the Yugoslavs, and three months later to join Nazi Germany in war against the Soviet Union.

Association with the Axis inevitably strengthened Fascism within Hungary. It has often been asserted that Hungarian fascism was a creation of landowners and capitalists. But this is not true. The dominant political outlook of Hungarian landowners, up to 1944, was a sort of Whiggish liberalism. They were reactionaries in social policy, but they preached and practised a large measure of personal political freedom. As for the capitalists, they were mostly Jews, and naturally disliked Fascism and Nazism.

In any case the power of the Hungarian landowners has been exaggerated. Certainly they were supreme in the countryside, both economically and politically. But the government of the country, and the determination of its policies, were largely in the hands of a bureaucratic middle class, many of whose members were children or descendants of landed gentry, but who had little connection left with the villages. The growth of industry in the 1930's also drew Magyars—as opposed to Jews or members of the German ethnical minority—into business. Here they found themselves in competition with the older business class which was largely Jewish, and this provided a strong new motive for anti-semitism. The Hungary of 1867—1918, whatever its faults in other fields, had shown a remarkable toleration to Jews. Certainly there were Magyars who expressed dislike of Jews on vague religious or cultural grounds; but Jewish citizens enjoyed equality before the law, in practice as well as in theory. The first anti-Jewish violence appeared in the White Terror of 1919—1920, which followed the defeat of the communist revolution. But in the 1930's economic causes revived it, and it was deliberately fostered by fascist groups and by agents of Nazi Germany.

It was in the growing middle class of Magyar bureaucrats, and to some extent among intellectuals and the new business element, that Hungarian fascism had its main strength. These were the strongholds of fascism: the odd aristocrat, or half-Jewish capitalist of fascist sympathies was an exception. Fascism also had a certain mass base. Some Hungarian fascists agitated for a land reform, and so won some popularity with the peasants. There were also fascists among miners and factory workers. The Hungarian fascists were thus a strong force, and they had an important influence on the intellectual and moral climate of Hungarian political life from the mid-1930's onwards. But they remained in opposition until the last months of Hitler's war.

The Hungarian regime between the world wars, associated with the name of Admiral Horthy, who as Head of State took the title of Regent for a King who never returned, was certainly reactionary, and its methods were often cruel, but it was not fascist. Even the demagogic General Gömbös, Prime Minister from 1932 to 1936, who dearly loved fascist phrases and rhetoric, rejected anti-semitism. Later governments introduced half-hearted measures of economic discrimination against Jews in order to please Hitler. But these were not harshly executed. It must be admitted that the oligarchic reactionary rulers of Hungary during the Second World War preserved greater liberties for their subjects, even for Social Democrats, than the rulers of any other country in Hitler's Europe, neutral Switzerland and Sweden of course excepted. This came to an end with the direct military occupation by the German Army in March 1944. The government which followed, a curious mixture of Germanophile generals, time-serving bureaucrats and real fascists, dishonoured Hungary by deporting to German extermination camps about 600,000 Jews, about half of whom were from Trianon Hungary and half from the territories recovered between 1939 and 1941. It is only fair to say that Horthy tried to prevent this, and that in October 1944 he made a last, pathetically ineffective, attempt to bring his country out of the war, as King Michael had done in Rumania two months earlier. The Nazis deposed him, and installed a puppet regime under the most radical of all the fascist leaders, Ferenc Szálassi. For a few months this man subjected Hungary to a reign of terror. But now the war was drawing to an end. In the spring of 1945, after a terribly destructive siege, Budapest was taken by the Soviet Army, and the Germans were driven out of the whole country. Szálassi's forces fled with them. Nazi executioners were replaced by the liberating Soviet Army, which soon distinguished itself by the thoroughness with which it robbed and raped the defenceless population.

Under Soviet Russian Occupation

In 1945 Hungary was completely at the mercy of the Soviet conquerors. Many factories were destroyed, and many of the rest were idle for lack of materials or labour. Agricultural work had been interrupted by war, and a large part of the livestock had been slaughtered or driven westward by the retreating Germans. The administration had ceased to function. Many civil officials and still more army officers had fled to German territory. There was a nominal Hungarian government, led by General Béla Miklos, who had obeyed Horthy's order in October 1944 to surrender to the Russians. It was recognised by the Soviet, United States, and British governments. But in fact the only real authority was the occupying Soviet army. It could have imposed any regime that it wished.

But at this moment the Soviet leaders did not set up a Communist regime. It is true that they brought with them a number of Hungarian Communists who had been in exile in Russia, of whom the two most important were Mátyás Rákosi and Ernö Gerö. These men at once proceeded to reorganise the Communist Party, which can hardly be said to have existed in Hungary since 1919. At most it was a tiny conspiratorial sect, which in 1944 had conducted a little, brave, but ineffective underground activity against Hitler. Its main

leader inside Hungary was a young man named László Rajk. This small organisation was now taken over by Rákosi and his emigré team. They rapidly enlisted all the recruits they could find, mainly opportunists and careerists, with a large sprinkling of Fascists hoping to save their skins. But Moscow's official policy at this time was the "Grand Alliance" in foreign policy and the "Popular Front" in internal politics. It was therefore premature to hand full power to the Communist Party. Rather, it was necessary to have in Hungary a coalition of democratic parties. These had to be rebuilt, or built for the first time, and each had to have its own organisation. The Soviet authorities therefore encouraged, and even practically helped, the available political leaders to set up their machinery, side by side with the Communists.

Potentially the most important was the *Smallholders Party*, which drew its support from the peasants, who formed slightly more than half the population of Hungary. Between the wars this party had not been very successful, because until 1939 the ballot had been open in rural constituencies, and the gendarmes had always effectively stopped political propaganda, other than that of the government party, in the villages. The Smallholder leaders were mostly intellectuals of the middle class, their views varying from liberal conservatism to semi-socialist radicalism. During the war the peasant influence within the party had somewhat increased with the foundation of the Peasant Union, a part-economic and part-political organisation headed by Ferenc Nagy.

The second party, with a smaller mass base but a longer history and better organisation, was the *Social Democratic Party*. Founded in 1892, it had little opportunity of parliamentary influence under the restricted franchise before the First World War. In 1918 military defeat and the political collapse of the old regime swept the Social Democrats to power, but almost at once they were crippled by the split which gave birth to the Communist Party. During the Communist regime of March-August 1919 the party was reunited, but under Communist leadership. After the White Terror had given way to the respectable oligarchy of Count Bethlen (Premier, 1921—1931), the Social Democratic Party, once more shorn of its Communist wing, was able to operate legally again. There was now universal suffrage, and with a secret ballot in Budapest the Socialists were able to return a few members to parliament. The trade unions were under strong socialist influence. The Social Democrats enjoyed political freedom under the Horthy regime right up to the German occupation of March 1944. In the first post-war years four factions could be discerned in the party. The right wing, led by Károly Peyer, corresponded roughly in its views to the British Labour Party. The centre, led by Anna Kéthly and Antal Bán, might be compared with the left wing of British Labour. It was in favour of co-operation with the Communists, but believed that Social Democrats should remain a separate party. The left, which included the post-1944 head of the party, Arpád Szakasits, favoured fusion with the Communists. Finally the fourth group consisted of agents of the Communist Party or the Soviet government, such as György Marosán, who later figured in the Kádár quisling "government".

A third party, small but interesting, was the *National Peasant Party*. It was derived from a group of young intellectuals who in the 1930's had attracted attention by their carefully documented and moving studies of the condition of the Hungarian peasantry. Like the Russian Narodniki of the 1870's who had "gone to the people", these writers had lived among the peasants and had got to know the human side of the problem as well as the statistics of land distribution or grain production. They were known as "the village-explorers." They were socialists and revolutionaries, but not Marxists. Later they became split, one wing became quite subservient to the Communists, while the rest simply retired from political life. In October 1956, however, most of these men reappeared as active revolutionaries, and formed the nucleus of the new "Petöfi Party".

Together with the creation of party organisations in 1945 went the rebuilding of a state machine. A National Council composed of representatives of the four parties served as a temporary parliament, and there were local councils similarly composed at a lower level. At all levels the Communists had greater power than their numbers or popularity could justify, but it would be too much to say that they controlled the machinery of government. However even at this stage they paid special attention to the newly created police force and to the Ministry of the Interior, in which they placed their men in key positions. They also did their best to arrange that those entrusted with important positions by the other parties should be persons subservient to the Communist Party, and even to push their own agents into leading positions in those parties. Here they had some success, especially with the

Social Democrats. But on the whole the three other parties at this stage were genuinely independent. It was clear to all that the Soviet Army was master of the country, and no wise person dared publicly to criticise Bolshevik Russia. But it was still hoped that Hungary would be left internal freedom, and that when the peace treaty was signed the Soviet Army would retire.

One of the first acts of the coalition government was a sweeping land reform. Though carried out in a hurry, and in unfavourable economic conditions, it was welcomed by the peasants and by all persons of democratic convictions. It was indeed long overdue. The domination of the agricultural scene by a small number of landowners, with immense personal power over the peasants, was an intolerable anachronism in the 20th-century. There had been no substantial redistribution of land in 1919, and the victory of the old ruling class over the Communists had postponed reform indefinitely. On the eve of the Second World War, less than 1% of owners of land possessed slightly less than 50% of the arable land. The agricultural population of Hungary included a rural proletariat of more then 3 million persons, consisting of estate servants, landless agricultural labourers, dwarf holders, and tenants. Under the 1945 reform about four-and-a-half million acres of arable land were distributed among 660,000 peasant families. Holdings of less than 20 acres, which in the 1930's had only about one third of the arable land of the country, now constituted 65 %. The Minister of Agriculture responsible for the reform was a Communist returned from Moscow, Imre Nagy. The Communists were determined to claim for their party the credit expected from the reform. It is doubtful whether they had much success, but Nagy personally did win some popularity.

The economic situation was disastrous. To the ravages of war were added plundering by the invaders, the cost of maintenance of the Soviet Army of Occupation, and the formal reparations claims under the peace treaty. The Soviet authorities were able to interpret the armistice clauses to their own advantage, and vast quantities of goods were removed. The result of these various factors was the worst inflation known in financial history. Money was valueless. The urban population lived from mid-1945 to mid-1946 on the verge of starvation. The reconstruction of Budapest was in effect performed by slave labour; but it was a slavery which the whole population accepted as a patriotic duty. By the summer of

1946 the factories were working again, and the harvest was fairly good. In August a new currency was introduced. For this heroic period of reconstruction too the Communists, and especially their economic boss Gerö, tried to take the credit. But it was the achievement not of a party but of the whole nation. And if the Communists' Soviet bosses had been less exacting, it would have been completed sooner.

In October 1945 a free parliamentary election was held, the first in Soviet-occupied Europe.[1] The Smallholders Party had an absolute majority of the votes (57%), while the Social Democrats and Communists each had 17% and the National Peasants 7%. But the majority party was not allowed to form a homogeneous government. The Soviet commander, Marshal Voroshilov, had only given his consent to an election based on free competition between the parties on condition that all agreed to maintain the coalition. Moreover the Smallholders were obliged to give the key post of Minister of Interior to a Communist, first to Imre Nagy and soon afterwards to László Rajk.

Despite the presence of the Soviet Army, the sinister maneuvers of the Communists, and the economic hardships, the year 1946 was also a time of freedom and of promise. The peasants were freed of the large estates, and there was hope of a new prosperous agriculture based on the patient labour of millions of smallholders and the natural wealth of the Hungarian earth. The workers were freed of the capitalists, and hoped for a new socialist industrial society in which they would be the leading force. The intellectuals were freed of the mental strait-jacket of the oligarchic and the Fascist eras; they could express and develop their social and political ideas, and could hope for a new flowering of Hungarian literature and art. All who believed in friendship with the neighbouring small nations, fellow-victims with Hungary of Hitlerism, now hoped that after decades of sterile nationalism and small-state imperialism on all sides, a new era would begin. The events of 1945 could hardly be described as a Revolution in the sense of 1848 or 1918, for their origin was occupation by a foreign Power rather than insurrection from within. But there was a passionate desire for a new life, a powerful explosion of new social and intellectual forces, a great promise of better

things to come. No one who visited Hungary in these months could fail to note it.

Yet every one of these hopes was betrayed. Agriculture was neglected and the peasants treated as enemies. The workers were placed under a new yoke, of Communist managers more exacting than the old capitalists. Intellectual liberty lasted only a year or two, and was replaced by totalitarian dogma. The sincere desire of the Hungarians for friendship with their neighbours was spurned. None were more chauvinist than the Czechs and Slovaks, in whom for many years Hungarian democrats had placed special hopes. They looked for the spirit of the great President Thomas Masaryk, but they found that the spirit of Horthy had moved from Budapest to Prague. As for the "liberating" Power, it was not interested in "friendship". Hungary was to become another Soviet colony, another Uzbekistan. In 1945 many Hungarians who were not Communists hoped that the Soviet liberators would help them make the revolution their country needed. Instead the Soviet conquerors destroyed the revolution which Hungarians had tried to make.

Towards One-Party Dictatorship

The Soviet and Communist offensive against the beginnings of Hungarian democracy reached its climax in 1947. The main object of attack was the Smallholders Party. Already in the previous year the Communists had forced this party to expel some of its most courageous parliamentary members. The security police manufactured a treason conspiracy to compromise the leadership. In February 1947 the party's Secretary-General, Béla Kovács, was arrested by Soviet MVD troops and disappeared. The resistance of the real peasant representatives was broken, and a few fellow-travelling intellectuals were pushed into leading positions in the party by Communist pressure. The same was done to the National Peasant Party. Several prominent figures in both parties escaped abroad.

Communist propaganda made much of the argument that the Smallholders were a "reactionary party" because former fascists supported them. It is of course possible that fascists, and perhaps still more, persons of right-wing views, had voted for the party in 1945. It is also undoubtedly true that fascist toughs not only voted for, but became members of, the Communist Party, and were welcomed in it. But the character of a party is determined not by its casual voters but by its whole membership and

---

[1] The only other example was in Czechoslovakia in May 1946, and in this case there was no Soviet Army in the country. The courage of the Hungarian voters in the presence of the Soviet troops was all the more impressive.

organisation. The Smallholders were a thoroughly democratic party, representing the peasants who formed more than half the Hungarian nation. The Communists could not endure that such a party should possess an absolute majority of the seats in Parliament. The only element of truth in Communist assertions that the Smallholders Party was "conspiring" is that some of its members were talking of using their parliamentary majority to end the coalition and form an homogeneous government. In any democratic country, such action is perfectly constitutional. This is in fact what happened in the summer of 1947 in France and Italy; the Communists were expelled from the government coalitions, which continued to rule without them, with the necessary constitutional majority. This would have happened in Hungary too if the Soviet Army had not been there. It is sometimes suggested in the West that the Communists in Eastern Europe showed themselves more intelligent than their democratic rivals, because they outmaneuvered them in the coalitions: the clever Communists proved more than a match for their stupid partners. This is said especially of Rákosi in Hungary. But it is not true. Certainly Rákosi is a clever man. But his partners were not stupid, and he did not deceive them. They knew perfectly well what his aims were. They could not prevent him, because they had no power. He could rely on the Soviet Army for help. The fate of Béla Kovács was the decisive proof. Later the Communists themselves admitted this. Rákosi boasted in 1952 that he had dealt with his partners one by one, cutting them off "like slices of salami." Jozsef Révai, another leading Communist, stated in 1949: "Our force was multiplied by the fact that the Soviet Union and the Soviet Army were always there to support us with their assistance."[2]

In 1948 the Communists finally subdued the only other important political party, the Social Democrats. Already in 1946 the old leadership of the party had been removed by persons willing to cooperate closely with the Communists. But there were differences as to the degree of cooperation. Most of the leaders, and the great majority of the active members, insisted on keeping their party organisation independent, while a minority advocated "fusion" with the Communist Party, which in practice could only mean seizure by the Communist bosses of the whole organisation of the fifty-year old socialist party. The opponents of "fusion", Antal Bán and Anna Kéthly, were defeated by the intrigues of the Communist agents within their party, supported by the terror of the Communist-controlled security police, and were expelled from it in February 1948. In June "fusion" took place. It is interesting to note that the champions of "fusion" lived to learn their errors. Arpád Szakasits after a brief period as President of the Republic, was arrested. Even the Soviet agent György Marosán spent some years in prison.

Hungary now had a one-party totalitarian regime. The security police had the same vast powers as in the Soviet Union. The formal structure of the Hungarian state was adapted to the Soviet model. All means of communication, from broadcasting to the school-room, were used for Marxist-Leninist indoctrination and the glorification of Hungary's imperial master, Joseph Stalin.

The Communist Party itself was not safe from persecution. The breach between Yugoslavia and the Soviet Union in the summer of 1948 was followed by a campaign against "nationalist deviation" throughout Eastern Europe. In Hungary the chosen victim was László Rajk. Whether Rajk had in fact especially close connections with Tito is uncertain. It is certain that he was never in exile in Moscow, that he played some part in resistance inside Hungary in 1944, that he did not belong to Rákosi's "Muscovite" band, and that Rákosi disliked him. At his public trial in September 1949 Rajk confessed to various quite unbelievable crimes, and was hanged. Of all the East European treason trials, that of Rajk came closest to the Soviet models of 1936-1938.

The execution of Rajk was accompanied by a purge in the party, and this continued for several years afterwards. The victims included numerous Communists who had had no connection with Rajk, and several of the left-wing Social Democrats who had betrayed their party to the Communists in 1948. Among the first was the Communist János Kádár, and among the second the renegade socialist György Marosán, both of whom reappeared in sinister roles in November 1956. An impression of the scope of the purge at the highest level of the party can be obtained from the turnover in membership of its Central Committee. Of 92 persons who were elected members of the Central Committee at the party congresses of 1948 and 1951, 46 had been removed by 1954. This is a turnover of 50%, higher than in any other East European Communist party

---

[2] As Antal Ban has recorded in *"The Curtain Falls"* (London, 1951): "Pushkin, then the Soviet Ambassador in Hungary, once remarked in the presence of the writer: 'We have shed our blood for Hungary and we do not want to loosen our grip on her.'"

except that of Czechoslovakia. The purge was spread out in time, for of the 46 removals 20 took place between 1948 and 1951 and 26 between 1951 and 1954.

Totalitarianism

Communist treatment of the peasants followed the Soviet model, though at a slower pace. Hungary offers exceptionally favourable conditions for intensive small farming and peasant cooperatives. The large estates were well adapted to cereal production, but small holdings could do better with more valuable crops—fruit, vegetables, meat, and dairy produce. Processing industries could have excellent opportunities. Hungary has far better physical conditions than Denmark, and could build up an excellent export trade in both fresh and canned foodstuffs. This would have required encouragement to peasant initiative, and state aid to genuine cooperatives, to be run by the peasants themselves. But all this is incompatible with Communism. According to Stalinist dogma, peasants are enemies. The only long-term solution is to transform them into agricultural workers, and agriculture itself into a complex of large industrial enterprises, organised according to factory discipline. Until this is possible, the peasants must be held down by physical force and exploited economically. They must pay for the process of industrialisation. Above all no peasant initiative must be tolerated, least of all any cooperative initiative. Collective farms, based on the model of the Soviet *kolkhoz*, which is first and foremost a political coercive institution, an instrument of party rule, must be introduced. Collectivisation of agriculture was announced as an aim of policy in Hungary in July 1948. By 1952 about 30 % of Hungary's arable land was in either collective farms or state farms. The general level of agricultural output remained backward, and an obstinate struggle continued between the passive resistance of the peasants and the repressive measures of the government. Not only the peasants, but the whole nation suffered from this dogmatic policy, which deprived Hungary's economy of a source of great potential wealth.

The government's main effort went into industry. Here results were undoubtedly achieved, but at high cost. Capital goods industry, especially engineering and chemicals, received dogmatic priority over consumers' goods. In the bauxite and oil industries the Soviet government had a direct share through the "joint companies", formed in 1945, to which the Soviet "contribution" consisted of confiscated "German assets". Later the Soviet authorities claimed special rights in the development of uranium ore in Hungary. Soviet trade policies accentuated economic exploitation by fixing prices that underrated Hungarian and overrated Soviet goods. In 1951 the targets of the Hungarian First Five Year Plan were increased by 60 % (from 51 milliard florint to 85 milliard), as part of the increase of heavy industry throughout the Soviet bloc in connection with the Korean War. The burden was borne both by the peasantry and by the workers. The extent to which the standard of living declined during these years cannot be accurately measured from the few ambiguous figures that were published. There is no doubt however that the workers suffered great hardship, with long hours, ruthless pressure for higher output per hour, and wages of low purchasing power. The trade unions existed, as in the Soviet Union, not to protect the workers against their employers, but to impose on the workers the will of their masters, the bosses of the Communist Party. By the end of 1952 a good deal of new industrial

One Example

There was only one organisation over which our Party had control from the very first, and which never was influenced by the political coalition: that was the A.V.H. [the Political Police] . . . We maintained firm control of it from the moment of its creation, and we made certain of it as a safe weapon in our fight . . .

*

In their own countries, in the so-called "free world," how often have they used tanks against the working people and the unemployed, tear-gas, weapons, bludgeons, hundreds and thousands of policemen, gendarmes, and soldiers against those who only ask for more bread? You can't open a single capitalist picture magazine without being confronted with sensational photos of such incidents. What wouldn't the "Voice of America" give to be able to cite just one example of tanks being used against the masses in a socialist country, one example where it had been necessary to use tanks and arms the way it occurs every day in countries of the so-called "free world?" . . .

Matyas Rakosi (29 February 1952)

capacity had been created, and the numbers and level of skill of the industrial working class had notably increased, but the national economy was in a desperate state.

Intellectual and religious freedom were crushed. The Communists prided themselves on their achievements in education. The number of university and technological students enormously increased, and these were mostly children of workers or peasants, who would have found it very difficult to get a higher education under the pre-1945 regime unless they were quite exceptionally able. This extension of opportunity is a real achievement. The quality of the education they received is an open question, but in the physical sciences and technology at least it was usually good. The Communists set themselves the task of creating a new "toiling intelligentsia" to replace the narrower educated class of the past, and judged by the numbers educated their efforts were successful. They hoped that this new intellectual elite of worker and peasant origin would be the most loyal element of the nation. They spared no efforts to indoctrinate them with Marxism-Leninism. Indoctrination took place also in the schools. Not a single Hungarian child escaped it.

The results disappointed the rulers in October 1956.

Religion was, of course, denounced by the whole propaganda apparatus. Religious instruction was gradually eliminated from the schools. The churches were allowed to perform religious ceremonies, but were excluded from any social activity. The most dramatic conflict between government and church was the arrest of the Catholic Primate, Cardinal Mindszenty. The Cardinal never concealed his dislike of the Communists. During the war he had bravely opposed the German Nazis and the Hungarian Fascists. After 1945 he denounced the Communists. He was also a passionate Hungarian nationalist, and was bitterly indignant when the government accepted the restoration in the peace treaty of the Trianon frontiers. In the summer of 1948 the nationalisation of church schools brought the conflict between him and the regime to an acute stage. He was arrested in December, accused of treason, and brought to trial aften five weeks of torture and isolation in prison. He confessed to the charges made against him, and was condemned to life imprisonment. Two years later Archbishop Groesz, the leading Catholic bishop after the Cardinal's removal, was also arrested, tried and confessed. The Protestant

Exploitation

There were two major ruses for depriving the workers even of the miserable wages they were supposed to be paid. One was the system of Peace Loans. This was supposed to be voluntary but actually every form of pressure was employed to extort from every worker a minimum of about 12 per cent of his total income. Those who refused to pay were pilloried and later dismissed or even arrested. The second ruse was the institution of "voluntary" shifts for various patriotic reasons. Between April 1950 and February 1951 there were eleven so-called competitions in Hungarian industry, all of which meant an increased tempo of work for no material benefit: (1) In memory of the liberation of Hungary; (2) In honour of May 1st; (3) In memory of the introduction of local councils; (4) Korea week; (5) Constitution day; (6) Tenth anniversary of Rákosi's release from jail; (7) Completion of the 1950 plan before the deadline; (8) In honour of the Council election; (9) Thirty-third anniversary of the Russian October Revolution; (10) Stalin's birthday; and (11) In honour of the second Hungarian Communist Party Congress.

To drive the exhausted, plundered and desperate worker yet further, there were a large number of movements "for the promotion of Stakhanovism and increased productivity." Here are a few samples: (1) The Korabelnikova movement. The aim of this was to complete one day's work using material saved during the previous month. (2) The Kovaliov movement. This meant "the close co-operation of technicians with manual workers in the promotion of labour competitions." (3) The Nazarova movement and (4) The Panin movement. These are too complicated to explain: the first aim at machine maintenance, the second at increased productivity. (5) The Kuznietrov movement. This movement was launched in conjunction with the thrift drive. As many workers as possible were required to fight "for the care of tools and their repair." (6) The Gazda movement. This was a simple magyarised version of (1), probably because Hungarian workers could not pronounce Korabelnikova ... *George Mikes, The Hungarian Revolution (Andre Deutsch, London, 1957)*

churches too were purged of their outstanding leaders, replaced by more pliant persons.

Rakosi and Nagy

A new period began in July 1953. This was a result of the death of Stalin, the riots in Pilsen, the East German rising, and the fall of Beria. Rákosi gave up the Premiership to Imre Nagy, and contented himself with the post of First Secretary of the party, over which he firmly maintained his grip. Nagy announced a new and milder policy. This coincided with the milder regime promised in the Soviet Union by Stalin's successors. In this "New Course" Hungary went further than any other East European country. More attention was paid to the needs of agriculture, and peasants were allowed to leave collective farms. Where a majority of members wished to dissolve a collective farm, they were allowed to do so. It appears that in the following months about one tenth of the farms made use of this right. Nagy also released from prison many of those arrested during the purges of the preceding years. He allowed the families who in 1951 had been deported from Budapest to return. This was less helpful than it seemed, for these people —mostly members of the former bourgeoisie— found that their apartments and possessions were occupied by persons who refused to give them up. But at least they had the right to leave their place of exile. Nagy also reduced the pace of industrial development and promised to pay more attention to consumers' goods. The economic results of the Nagy policy were not very substantial, but the generally milder political atmosphere was welcome. It was however only reluctantly accepted by Rákosi, presumably under pressure from Moscow. He awaited his opportunity to reverse the trend. This came with the fall of Malenkov in the Soviet Union in February 1955. On 18 April it was announced that Nagy had been removed from the Central Committee of the Party as well as the Premiership. His agricultural policy was stated to have been wrong, and a programme of further collectivisation was announced. Nagy was also accused of having underrated the importance of heavy industry and of having built up the People's Front (a mass organisation completely controlled by the Communist Party) as a rival to the Party itself. As Nagy's successor in the Premiership Rákosi

chose a young and obedient follower named András Hegedüs.

Rákosi's new supremacy did not last long. Already the reconciliation between Khrushchov and Tito in the summer of 1955 was an ominous sign, for he could have no doubt of Tito's hostility. The denunciation of Stalin and of the "personality cult" at the Soviet party's 20th Congress in February 1956 was a further blow. Rákosi fought hard. He even had the effrontery to announce that the Rajk trial had been a "miscarriage of justice," and to denounce the "personality cult," while he himself, the organiser of the trial and the object of the cult, remained in power. But eventually, on 18 July, he had to give up his position as First Secretary. He was however able to secure the appointment as his successor of his closest collaborator Ernö Gerö, second only to himself in Stalinist rigidity and subservience to Soviet policy.

The removal of Rákosi was immediately brought about by Soviet orders. Mikoyan himself was in Budapest when it was announced. It was also undoubtedly a result of pressure by Tito. But internal forces in Hungary had played their part. The most active element were the intellectuals, and especially a number of Communist writers within the officially sponsored Writers' Association. Writers released from prison during Nagy's Premiership exercised a large influence behind the scenes. The Petöfi Club (named after the revolutionary poet who had played a leading part in 1848) was formed during the Nagy period. It provided a forum for literary discussions which soon took a political character, and which drew in many younger people, including university students. At the Petöfi Club the demand for the return of Nagy to power was openly expressed. During the summer political criticism increased in the Hungarian press, especially in the organ of the Writers' Association, *Irodalmi Újság*. In September the Writers' Association held its congress, and elected a new Committee. The exponents of the party line, who had managed the Association in the past, were not re-elected, and several persons who had recently emerged from prison became members. At the end of the month came the public reinterment of Rajk, attended by a vast crowd, which was clearly less concerned to pay homage to the former Minister of the Interior, responsible in his day for many acts of violence and injustice, than to express its opposition to the regime still in power. Then in mid-October came the crisis in Poland, which provided the immediate occasion for action.

Revolution Against Communism

The events of the Revolution which followed, are described in the rest of this book. It may be useful to conclude with some general comments.

The Hungarian Revolution of 1956 has some obvious points of resemblance to that of 1848. In both cases the first action came from the intellectuals. The students of 1956 were treading in the steps of Petöfi.

The Revolution of 1956 also ended in the same way as that of 1848-9, with the re-establishment of a hated regime by Russian military force. A hundred years ago this took longer: the Austro-Hungarian war lasted ten months, the Russian intervention three, while the whole revolution and war of 1956 was over in less than one month. Things move faster in the twentieth century. After 1849 it took 18 years to convince the Habsburgs that it was impossible to restore the past: this process is unlikely to last as long in our time. One important difference between 1849 and 1956 is in the behaviour of the Russians. Tsar Nicholas I was a reactionary despot, but he was an honourable and comparatively humane man. His troops fought only against Hungarian soldiers, and prisoners of war were not maltreated. The Austrians committed atrocities after the Russians were gone, and hanged some of the prisoners whom the Russians had handed over. In 1956 the Russian commanders executed prisoners, massacred civilians and treacherously arrested Hungarians generals whom they had invited to negotiate. They did not leave the activities to the Kádár puppet government: they preferred to undertake them themselves.

The neighbouring small nations did not fight against Hungary in 1956 as they had done in 1848-9 and in 1919. Certainly the Hungarians gave them no excuse, for during these weeks there was no sign of nationalist claims against Slovaks, Serbs or Rumanians. On the contrary repeated appeals for friendship and help were heard. An unconfirmed report states that the Soviet leaders asked the Rumanian government to send forces against Hungary and that it refused on the ground that it could not count on the obedience of its army. Student demonstrations took place in some Rumanian cities, both in Transylvania and in the Old Kingdom, ant it seems that there was

some unrest among workers in Bucharest. The Yugoslav government expressed sympathy for Nagy in the first days, then justified the second Soviet intervention. In Czechoslovakia there was no sign of activity. At least these countries did not join in the repression.

In 1849 Kossuth sent representatives to West European capitals to beg for help, but the West did nothing. Here at least in 1956 the parallel is exact. The difference is in the relationship of the Western governments to Russia. In 1849 the Tsarist and Habsburg régimes were distasteful to Western statesmen, but they were certainly legitimate governments, conventionally correct in their international behaviour, and they did not threaten Western security. In 1956 the Soviet government is the declared enemy of the West, seeking permanently, by every means available, and in every part of the world, to destroy Western and democratic interests and ultimately liberal democracy itself. Moreover Western spokesmen have often declared their sympathy for the peoples of Eastern Europe; yet in the crisis they did nothing for them. This is not of course to say that Western propaganda had incited the Hungarian people to rise in arms. This it never did. The myth of "Western incitement" is designed to secure a scapegoat. This is needed both by the Communists themselves and by various right-wing groups in Western Europe who hope to make their own terms with the Soviet Union at the expense of others. The truth is that the Hungarian Revolution was a result of Hungarian conditions, and that it was abandoned not by Western radio broadcasting stations but by Western governments.

A special feature of the 1956 Revolution is the part played by the working class. The workers were slower to move than the intellectuals, but once they were fully engaged they showed themselves very stubborn. It was the workers who provided the main fighting forces in Budapest, stiffened of course by army units. The last centres of organised fighting were the great industrial centres—Csepel island and Dunapentele. It is ironical that the latter, a new steel plant founded with Soviet equipment, had been named Sztálin-város as a symbol of Hungary's enslavement to Soviet Russia. After military resistance had ended, the workers in factories and mines continued strikes and passive resistance. Throughout the winter 1956-57 resistance still continued.

If the disparity between the strength of the combatants is taken into account, one may say that the effort of the Hungarian workers is the greatest single effort of resistance ever made by an industrial working class against an oppressor. It surpasses the Paris Commune, the St. Petersburg Soviet of 1905, or the Viennese fighting of 1934. It is equally true that the Soviet government has shown itself more systematically, ferociously and consciously "anti-working-class" than any capitalist government in history. The Budapest Workers' Councils are historical heirs to the Russian Soviets, but the Soviet government is a monstrously distorted and inflated offspring of Nicholas II's.

The Soviet story that there was "counter-revolution" in Hungary is a myth. The suggestion that great landowners and capitalists were plotting to recover their properties is ridiculous. Landowners and capitalists are strong only as long as they possess wealth: once this is gone they lose all power and influence and can do nothing. In Hungary in 1956 they did nothing. Fascism might have been a more serious danger, for Fascism has its roots in the masses; in a country with Hungary's past one might have expected an outbreak of fascism and anti-semitism. But the remarkable fact is that no such outbreak occurred. Some members of the security police were lynched. The correspondent of the Polish Communist *Nowa Kultura* estimated the victims in Budapest at 80. Though these men had for years subjected thousands of their compatriots to unspeakable tortures and humiliations, one must still deplore lynchings. To compare them with the White Terror of 1919 is however absurd. The correct parallel is the mob violence to which some dozens of Tsarist Okhrana men fell victims in the February Revolution of 1917. It is also worth stressing that Cardinal Mindszenty, released by the freedom-fighters, showed himself no "reactionary" seeking vengeance, no "chauvinist" denouncing neighbour nations, but a Christian patriot pleading for the unity of the nation and peace with neighbours great and small.

The well-known political names which reappeared in October were the Smallholders' leader Béla Kovács (who had been allowed to return from Russia some months before the Revolution) and the Social Democrat Anna Kéthly. Both enjoyed great popularity in Hungary. Some of the intellectuals of the National Peasant Party also reappeared under a new name as the Petofi Party. But essentially the Revolution was the work of the younger generation, of new forces

which would have crystallised into new political shapes if the Soviet imperialists had allowed them to develop freely.

Though the Revolution was crushed in blood, and the vanquished nation is inundated with lies and calumny, it has shown two immensely encouraging facts. One is that indoctrination of youth with lies does not work. Orwell's "1984" is only a nightmare. The Hungarian students, children of workers and peasants, saw the truth for themselves. It was they who led the Revolution. The second is that a totalitarian régime can be overthrown by its own subjects. Totalitarianism, with its one party, its omnipresent propaganda, its scientifically planned torture, its elevation of moral relativism into absolute dogma, is a more formidable enemy than a nineteenth-century dictatorship. Yet it too is no stronger than the will and loyalty of those who execute its orders.

Truth

Budapest

It should be the writer's prerogative to tell the truth. To criticise anybody and anything. To be sad. To be in love. To think of death. Not to ponder whether light and shadow are in balance in his work. To believe in the omnipotence of God. To deny the existence of God. To doubt the correctness of certain figures in the Five Year Plan. To think in a non-Marxist manner. To think in a Marxist manner even if the thought thus born is not yet among the truths proclaimed to be of binding force. To find the standard of life low even of people whose wages do not yet figure among those to be raised. To believe something unjust that is still officially maintained to be just. To dislike certain leaders. To depict troubles without finding the means of remedying them. To consider ugly the New York Palais, declared a historic building, irrespective of the fact that millions have already been spent on it. To notice that the city is falling to ruins since there is no money to repair the buildings. To criticise the way of life, the way of speaking, and the way of working of certain leaders ... To like Sztalinváros. To dislike Sztalinváros. To use an unusual style. To oppose the Aristotelian dramaturgy. To insist on Aristotelian dramaturgy ... etc. etc. Who would deny that a short while ago many of those things were strictly forbidden and would have entailed punishment? ... But today, too, they are just tolerated and are not really allowed ...

JULIUS HAY *(June 1956)*

Within a few days nothing was left of the totalitarian régime of Rákosi and Gerö. Only foreign intervention crushed the Revolution. Totalitarianism has been overthrown once, and it will be overthrown again.

The most important effects will be felt in Russia itself. The three social groups which made the Hungarian Revolution were the intellectual youth, the workers, and the army. It is these three groups that form the weakest points in Soviet society. Since October 1956 there have been stormy political meetings in Moscow university, political discontent in Moscow factories, and mutinous incidents and desertions in the Soviet occupation forces in Hungary. Soviet soldiers are workers or peasants, brought up in school on Marxist historical mythology, with its tales of heroic workers fighting their oppressors on the barricades. In Hungary this has been not legend but reality, with the Soviet worker-soldiers shooting at working-class women in food queues, arresting leaders of Workers' Councils, and suppressing strikes. The Soviet soldiers know very well what they have been doing, and the story is already spreading in Russia. Since Beria fell, the Soviet police has lost the power it had over the army, the power to segregate and intern and indoctrinate troops returning from the West. The truth is beginning to spread in Russia, and Russian students and workers and soldiers are beginning to express their thoughts. This was inconceivable while Stalin lived. A new process has begun.

The Hungarian Revolution may prove to have been Bolshevism's 1905.

II

THE PRELUDE

"...*Keep your patience proud;*
The bitter toil shall not be lost,
The rebel thought unbowed ...

The heavy-hanging chains will fall,
The walls will crumble at a word;
And Freedom greet you in the light,
And brothers give you back the sword."

PUSHKIN

"*I call revolution the conversion of all hearts and the raising*
of all hands in behalf of the honour of man."

KARL MARX

"*Magyars, rise, your country calls you!*
Meet this hour, whate' er befalls you!
Shall we free men be, or slaves?
Choose the lot your spirit craves!"

SANDOR PETOFI

PRELUDE

"The Long Years of Terrorism and Misery"

Budapest

With many thousands of others, I was arrested by the Hungarian secret police (AVO) in the summer of 1949. It was the time when Stalin and his henchmen started to kill off thousands of their followers as part of a ludicrous propaganda drive against Tito. It was also the time when, in Hungary, they started to arrest the Social Democratic leadership and the outstanding non-Muscovite Communists.

I believed then that we would be able to assert our innocence. But I soon found out that our fate was worse than if we had been guilty, because we had nothing to give away in the torture chambers. I was thrown into an icy cold cellar cubicle three yards by four. There was a wooden plank for a bed, and a bright naked electric light glared in my face day and night. Later, it was a great relief to return to this bleak place.

Now I am going to find out the secret of those rigged trials, I thought, when they took me for my first hearing. Two AVO officers questioned me in turn from 9 a.m. till 9 p.m. Then I had to type my life story till 4 a.m. The rest of the 24 hours I had to spend walking up and down in the cubicle because I was not permitted to sleep. This went on for three weeks. The only sleep I got was a few minutes when the guard was slack. The "hearings" soon became tortures. The AVO officers wanted us to invent crimes for ourselves because they knew we were innocent. I won't describe the tortures. There are so many ways to cause piercing pain to the human body. There were days when we were tossed about on a stormy ocean of pain. The torments alone did not make us "confess." Sleeplessness, hunger, utter degradation, filthy insults to human dignity, the knowledge that we were utterly at the mercy of the AVO— all this was not enough. Then they told us they would arrest our wives and children and torment them in front of us. We heard women and children screaming in adjacent rooms. Was this a put-up job for our benefit? I still don't know.

After the first period of torture we were sent back to our solitary cellars for some weeks to "rot away for a while." Now we were tormented by the intense cold, by the glaring bulb and the four walls which threatened to collapse on us. We had to be awake 18 hours a day. There were no books, no cigarettes, only thousands of empty minutes. Our fear now was insanity. Our heads were whirling, we imagined sounds and colours. Some of us had a nightmarish feeling of being drowned. Our emaciated bodies and feverish brains produced eerie visions and hallucinations. Is it a wonder that many of us had no sound judgment, no willpower to resist our tormentors? This torture made some confess. Others went insane, or were clubbed to death. A few held out. I could not bring myself to "confess"—that UNO and the World Federation of United Nations Associations was an imperialist spy and sabotage organisation; that the Hungarian UNA, of which the late Michael Karolyi was president and myself secretary-general, conspired to overthrow the "people's democracy."

After a period of "rotting," a new period of torments started. And so it went on for 13½ months.

When at last I signed a ludicrous statement prepared by my tormentors, I was regularly collapsing three or four times a day and had lost more than thirty pounds. I had to confess that John F. Ennals, secretary-general of WFUNA, was my "spy chief" and that I handed him spy reports in Budapest daily from 1947 till the time of my arrest in 1949. During this period Ennals spent only three days in Budapest. He was either at the Geneva headquarters or touring the five continents. When I repeatedly pointed this out to the AVO they said: "Never mind. No word of it will leak out. Your trial will be kept secret."

"But why tell a lie if it will be kept secret? Whom do you want to mislead?" I asked.

"That's none of your business," I was told.

I had to learn my confession by heart, and the trial was rehearsed several times. The AVO told me I would be sentenced to 15 years. They were right. In addition, my home and library were confiscated. I spent exactly five years and one week in prison, completely isolated from the outside world, having fewer rights and far worse treatment than any murderer. Then, in 1954, when Premier Nagy released thousands, the Hungarian Supreme Court finally declared our innocence. But Stalin's No. 1 Hungarian henchman, Rakosi, was still the Party boss and wanted to liquidate Nagy, who tried to end the regime of terrorism.

After our legal rehabilitation, those of us who had been Party members were offered Party "rehabilitation," too. I was a Party member from 1947 till 1949. Out of several thousands, three of us declared that our conscience did not permit us to rejoin the Party. Party headquarters then started a financial drive against me, in an attempt to force me to change my mind. It was then I discovered that in the total tyranny invented by Stalin, a politician, a writer, or scientist has only one choice: "You become either a bloodstain or a louse."

We politicians, authors, and scientists knew Rakosi and his gang meant to get rid of us. We knew it was either our heads or theirs. We had to loosen Rakosi's grip on the Party and State machinery, dissolve AVO, and inspire resistance in the people. That task was not easy. The long years of terrorism and misery had made them lose hope. We tried to show by our acts of defiance that there was hope.

The Writers' Association revolted first. Communists and non-Party poets and novelists achieved freedom from censorship for their weekly paper, *Literary Gazette*, ["Irodalmi Ujsag"] which soon became the banner of resistance and liberty. We attacked the Rakosi regime and its record. In a long series of articles we told how he and his gang wrecked our country morally, culturally and economically. Our weekly was attacked all the time by the official Party daily, was confiscated on occasions. But its popularity was such that Rakosi did not dare to suppress it. People fought for it when it appeared on the streets.

Early this year the Communists held their XXth Party congress, at which they paid lip service to democratic rights. Exploiting the possiblities, we intensified our resistance. The famous Petofi Circle of the university youth was founded.

In early summer, I risked writing about the mass-murders committed by Rakosi and demanded, as the first step in our drive against the AVO, that its former head, General Farkas, should be arrested and tried for murder. But he was only cashiered as a general and expelled from the Party. In September, Party headquarters accused me of inciting revolt. At the yearly Congress of the Writers' Association, I answered the charge.

"That's true—I have spoken and written against terror and injustice. Is that a crime? Even if it were, could I now be punished for it? General Farkas is a mass murderer—yet he is only cashiered and expelled from the Party. You cannot cashier me, like Farkas, because I am not a general. You cannot expel me, because I am not a party member. If loss of rank or expulsion from the Party is all you are willing to do against a murderer—even a mass murderer—what possible punishment can you threaten us writers with?"

I'd like to make it clear that I speak about my role only as an example of how we writers behaved. To give instances about the brave fight of those who stayed behind would mean their instant arrest.

Insecurity

The inquisitor from Budapest came often to see me at Felsopeteny. He told me that I could improve my status if I would only co-operate. "Why are you so stubborn?" he asked me. He talked about the alleged increased standard of living of the Hungarian people. He praised their leaders, telling me the country was in the hands of experienced, excellent men. He tried to convince me the domestic situation couldn't be better.

The AVO gave me a radio that played only the Bolshevik station in Budapest, and each day sent me the two Communist newspapers, "Szabad Nep" and "Magyar Nemzet." Then one day I was told that George Parragi, editor of "Magyar Nemzet," would be brought to me. A long time ago he had been a Catholic journalist, but since then had become a Communist stooge. I refused to see him.

On another occasion they gave me a list of priests who wanted to visit me. From their own newspapers and the radio, I had heard the names of these priests and knew them as collaborators. I would not see them.

Underneath all of this it was easy to see an ill-concealed insecurity. Because of this I was not surprised when the AVO man from Budapest announced that Andrew Hegedus, at that time Prime Minister of Hungary, wanted to talk to me.

"Why do all these people come?" I asked. Do you not know you can get wine only once from a grape? I have been squeezed of everything. The only thing I have left is my honor. This I will not give."

I did not see Hegedus.

The Mindszenty Story, N. Y. Herald Tribune (Paris), 16 December 1956

By this time the ground was prepared for our revolt. It was prepared by the long years of terrorism and misery, by the very low living standard, by the new tactics of Moscow in allowing freer speech and writing.

On October 23 we wanted only to demonstrate. There were no preparations for an armed revolt. As we marched that afternoon none of us had any idea that our people could be involved in a desperate fight within a few hours. The armed revolt was started by the AVO and the Russians when they fired on peaceful demonstrators. After the first shots the people filled the streets and the years of suffering made us unanimous in our feelings and demands. We were unable to stop fighting. It was freedom or death.

George Paloczi-Horvath, Daily Herald (London),
11 December 1956

An American Writes from Budapest

Budapest, in July

Since my last letter to you, and especially during the weeks I have been in Hungary, the situation has been changing profoundly.

The events that started in Moscow with the de-Stalinization program have now more than ever begun to have an influence here, and events are travelling at such a pace that I certainly will not venture to predict. They found their climax in the meeting at the Petofi Club on the night of June 27. The Petofi meeting was staged, of course, by the regime. It was one of the series of meetings that have been held to broaden the base of Communist Party support. From the beginning I felt that the Petofi Club meetings were a considerable expression of dissent, that they must constitute a minor revolution by themselves. In view of the total number of meetings the man arranging them is probably the most overworked man in the Government; he organized approximately ten meetings in a month's time; all of them were done by invitation; they were all held in the same hall; and they all had to be "managed" and "controlled."

Just a word about the Petofi Club. It is made up of a group of not very well-known intellectuals. Obviously the Club is a regime device to hold "free expression" meetings, and in the past it had no standing whatsoever. It is formally attached to the DISZ (which is the workers' youth federation) but this seems to be only a kind of holding-company device. The idea, of course, was to draw back into the Party fold many people who had lost standing. This was in line with "breezes" that are coming from Moscow . . .

The first meeting at the Petofi Club was held on May 30th, a meeting of economists; two days later the Institute of Literary History reappraised their mistakes. On June 4th the shortcomings of Hungarian scientific history were dealt with; this was a more remarkable meeting than earlier ones. It was attended mostly by students and addressed by Elizabeth Andics (a professor of history at the University of Budapest and head of the Peace Movement), a real fire-breathing communist. She began by saying, "We have made a lot of mistakes in the last ten years concerning Hungarian history." At this, there were cat-calls and shouts: "Haven't we!", "Why don't you name them?" She tried to continue, "In fact, we made some very severe mistakes." There were shouts — "Why don't you tell us exactly what they are?" This went on through the evening, and the meeting finally broke up in total confusion because she couldn't go on with her speech.

On June 14th the philosophers convened at the Petofi Club, with George Lukacs, Hungary's leading Marxist philosopher, deploring the "assembly line production of philosophers." Next day school teachers met, and on June 17th, former college staff members who had been dismissed by Revai. On June 19th, the meeting of former partisans was convened at which Mrs. Rajk spoke. Then on June 21st the Hungarian-Soviet Society and the Institute of Political Science and Jurisprudence combined to invite Budapest lawyers and officials of the Judiciary to meet and criticize a number of things: slowness in rehabilitating Social Democrats, the continued evasion of the Hungarian Constitution by constantly appointing instead of electing judges, the inadequate compensation for property expropriated be the State, etc..

Another meeting of some interest was held by the Hungarian Musicians Federation. A delegation headed by Hungary's foremost living composer, 72-year-old Zoltan Kodaly, demanded that steps be taken to stop the deterioration in Hungarian musical life. But the Petofi Club meeting on June 19th, which was addressed by Mrs. Rajk, set the stage for what was to happen on the night of June 27th.

This was a meeting of so-called partisans, former underground-workers, "freedom fighters" and, in general, former illegal communists, some of whom had been purged from the Party and were now personally invited to this meeting. Mrs. Rajk requested permission to speak. She was very bitter, saying she did not want to be made a "hero" for what had happened to her husband. She only wanted the people who had murdered him thrown out of office. She said that prisons in Communist Hungary were a disgrace to a People's Democracy, that prison conditions had been much better under the Horthy regime! During the time she was in jail herself, she was permitted neither visitors nor packages or mail. For years she was separated from her baby child, and she thought these conditions were a disgrace and ought to be changed. When she finished speaking, she was given an ovation. The audience stood up to applaud her. There were about 2,000 people in the audience (about a third of them were army officers) . . .

Rajk's Widow

Budapest

A tall, gaunt woman, her face deeply lined, strode to the speaker's stand. She was Mrs. Laszlo Rajk, wife of the former Foreign Minister of Hungary who had been executed in 1949. Rajk had "confessed" under torture of being a Titoist, but as he was led to the gallows he had cried: "Long live the People's Democracy of Hungary!" Rajk and his wife, who was jailed at the same time, were both "rehabilitated" recently.

"Comrades," she began, "there are no words with which to tell you what I feel facing you after cruel years in jail, without a word, a crumb of food, a letter, or a sign of life reaching me from the outside, living in despair and hopelessness. When they took me away I was nursing my five-month-old infant. For five years I had no word of my baby."

Turning directly toward the white-faced functionaries on the rostrum, she said:

"You not only killed my husband but you killed all decency in our country. You destroyed Hungary's political, economic, and moral life. Murderers cannot be rehabilitated: they must be punished!

"Where," she asked the audience, "were the members of the party while these things were happening? How could they allow such degeneration to take place without rising in wrath against the guilty?"

Choking with emotion, she said that the nadir of the party's immorality had been reached when Rajk was executed, and she demanded a party housecleaning. "Comrades," she cried, "stand by me in this fight!"

Then the unbelievable happened. Along with the audience, the Communist officials on the rostrum stood and gave the widow Rajk a standing ovation . . .

Leslie Bain, *The Reporter* (New York), 4 October 1956

Word spread about Mrs. Rajk speaking her mind. It was the strongest attack on the regime that had yet been made by anyone of prominence. In Budapest everybody was talking about it. When the Petofi Club meeting assembled on June 27th there had been a crowd waiting since 4:30 in the afternoon.

This particular meeting was called for the purpose of rehabilitating several hundred so-called "bourgeois" newspaper-men who had lost their jobs as the result of various Stalinist decrees. Marton Horvath, the editor of *Szabad Nep*, was to address the meeting, and two other Communist newspaper-men were to act as chairmen. The Petofi Club has been meeting in a small theater on the Vaci Utca, which has about 800 seats. The meeting was scheduled for 7 p.m., but the house was full at 4:30, and crowds continued to arrive in such numbers that ushers (entry only by invitation) finally shrugged their shoulders and let anybody in. People sat in the aisles, and wherever there was space. The hallway was so crowded that, arriving late, Horvath himself hardly managed to get in.

Horvath made a short, nervous, introductory speech. He said that this meeting was called for the purpose of "self-criticism," which he was going to indulge in, and criticism by anyone else who wanted to make it, so that the Party could be examined by writers and newspapermen in the light of XXth Congress decisions. After that, the meeting went on until 3:30 in the morning. It was one of the hottest days of the year. The air became absolutely humid. By universal consent there was no smoking. There was also no eating or drinking. Nobody left the room for nine hours . . .

The meeting was quite orderly at first. Speeches were made and were applauded, but later on things got out of control. Yet, during those nine hours, Hungarians, perhaps for the first time since the beginning of communism, really were able to say what they pleased! And hearing others say it, they took courage, so that in the end almost everyone felt he had his say. The first one to speak in the discussion was Tibor Dery, a well-known novelist and a Party member. He was an illegal communist during the Horthy days, but he has not always gotten along with the Party, and as recently as a year ago, one of his novels was condemned because it presented "too sympathetic" a portrait of a bourgeois professor. Dery began by commenting that much had been heard about censorship in general, and that he thought it was time that "we got down to cases." "Take Marton Horvath here, the editor of *Szabad Nep*. He doesn't stand for himself at all, and sometimes it's hard to tell whether he even stands for the Party. One day he's extreme right, and other days extreme left; one never knows where he stands." Then he moved on to the case of Joszef Revai, the former Minister of Culture: "he knows what he says isn't the truth, but he goes ahead and says it anyway." And as for Joszef Darvas, the present Minister of Culture, "He's afraid of himself. That's all there is to be said about him." And then he asked the rhetorical question: "What is the source of all our troubles?" And his answer was, "There is no freedom. I hope there will be no more police terror. I am optimistic, and I hope that we will be able to get rid of our present leaders. Let us bear in mind that we are allowed to discuss these things only with permission from above. They think it's a good idea to let some steam off an overheated boiler. We want deeds and we want the opportunity to speak freely!" Then Dery said: "We've been fighting and struggling for so many things, but we've forgotten the main thing. That is *humanism*."

The next speech was by Tibor Merai, the novelist. "We need a purification from top to bottom and from bottom to top. Fresh wind must not be rationed into little gentle breezes." Then he attacked Mihaly, the Deputy Minister of Culture: "How is it that he's been made a professor of journalism at the University? He's already got ten jobs."

Alexander Fekete, another journalist, who had arrived on the Moscow plane a few hours before, addressed the meeting. A few hours before leaving Moscow he had spoken with the highest Yugoslav and Russian officials and party members and, with regard to the "cultural revolution" in Budapest, they had told him: "If you want it, you journalists have got to make it yourselves."

Then a young physicist named Janossy spoke. He had been at Trinity College in Dublin, doing research on atomic physics, and on his return to Budapest in 1949 to visit his mother, he was kept there. He is now one of the regime's best physicists. "The fact is, it's impossible to get information ... The Togliatti speech was only partly published in Budapest; much was left out. Only from Western radio stations could we get the full text of Khrushchev's speech. Western broadcasts are also being jammed. Western newspapers must be allowed to reach this country!" ...

Gyorgy Nemesz listed the names of 50-odd journalists who had been restricted or put in prison, and he remarked that out of 52 journalists who worked for *Szabad Nep* in 1951 only six still had their jobs.

Probably the most direct attack on Rakosi was made by Peter Kuczka, a gifted young poet. Kuczka said, "The sign of good journalists is not a car, a chauffeur, and the privilege to shop in a special store. He must write the truth. But in our country, truth must not contradict the party line. In 1949 Rakosi said that Rajk was a 'Titoist,' and in 1955 he said Rajk was a 'palace provocateur.' This year he calls Rajk a 'comrade.' The masses have lost confidence, not in the Party, but in its leaders. It should be a tragedy of one, or two men instead of a whole nation. Truth can be disseminated where there is freedom. We demand a free press! It is even guaranteed us by the Constitution. What kind of press is it, when Imre Nagy is attacked in *Szabad Nep* and then doesn't get space to defend himself in the same paper? When we can get nowhere the full text of the Khrushchev speech!" ...

So it went all night. Hearing the speeches the people took heart themselves. The meeting became more and more disorderly. Pretty soon persons speaking on the stage were being talked back to by the audience. It became very difficult to make sense out of what took place. Some exchanges are rather remarkable. Horvath got up to defend the regime and was shouted down three times. In reply he remarked: "Don't insult the Party!" Someone got up and shouted, "We are the Party!" Another time someone said: "Let's take Rajk's corpse out of the ditch and give him a funeral!" And then somebody shouted: "How is it that we call this the Sandor Petofi Club? Petofi fought for freedom of the press." And then somebody jumped up and added—"Which we don't have!" Then Horvath said, "That's right." And someone else said, "You're telling us? You're the editor of *Szabad Nep*." And he shrugged his shoulders.

So, you see, the atmosphere inside was very infectious. Probably the greatest point of sedition from the government's point of view was when a bunch of people in the audience stood up in

---

"Don't Tell Me It Is Worse In Africa"

Don't talk to me about space ships,
a trip to the moon or Mars,
about life in the atomic age ...

We live like this. In darkness, in mud,
*   far away ...*

We too are "heroes" all of us

who, crowded into tiny rooms,
chew pumpkin seeds and lie around like
*   garbage.*

Don't tell me it is worse in Africa.
I live in Europe, my skin is white.
Who will embrace me to make me feel
*   that I am human?*

Karoly Jobbagy, Csillag (Budapest), April 1956

applauding some speech and called, "Down with the regime! Long Live Imre Nagy!"

That was as far as they went.

Of course, word had already gotten around Budapest that night. Two hours after the meeting started the Vaci Utca was blocked with crowds of people, several thousand in the street. Upon somebody's order, loudspeakers were strung up so that the people in the street heard it all too. The next day there was an atmosphere in Budapest that had not been felt there for a long time. The events of the night before had, in a way, electrified the town, and people were talking of nothing else. Many people said to me that this was "the second Hungarian revolution," that this was "the way things were going to be from now on." Other people who were a little more cautious said that for the first time people had spoken up, and as yet (a day or two later, at least) they weren't in jail for it . . .

On Sunday morning came the *Szabad Nep* stricture—the Central Committee scolding the people for having "gone too far." People felt that if the Poznan incidents had not given the regime the opportunity to tie the two things together they might not have been in a position to issue this reproach, for what had happened at the Petofi Club on Wednesday night had such wide-spread popular approval. The effect of Poznan has been to make most people extremely worried in Hungary. They felt that they had only begun to get their own liberalization, and that Poznan might bring complete reaction all over again.

People always ask, "How long is *this* going to go on?" Everybody knows what "this" means without saying it. If you tell them that it will probably go on for quite a while, they despair. I told one man that it might go on for five or ten years; he shrugged his shoulders and said, "My God, I am forty years old. Ten years is too long. It's not worth it . . ."

The last time I had been in Budapest foreign diplomatic people were debating whether Rakosi

would last; the odds were that he would. Now Hungarians are openly discussing Rakosi and there is no argument: they are all saying that Rakosi has to go, that this is the minimum of what the people would stand for. This is the sort of talk I hear from mechanics in garages and middle-class people and hotel-porters—anybody whom I could manage to take aside and talk to for a bit. This doesn't mean at all that Rakosi is going. The best guess in Budapest is that unless Tito, in his last visit to Moscow has absolutely insisted that Rakosi has to go, he will remain.

The Tito visit was followed with exceptional interest in Hungary. First of all it was attended by a riddle: Why is Tito like a foot-ball? The answer is: first we blew him up, then we kicked him around, and now we chase him . . . It is quite evident that Tito is very popular in Hungary.

A diplomat who is close to the Communists and has their confidence told me that the Russians were quite satisfied with Rakosi's new line, that he was not going as far as they were going in Poland, but that he was still doing enough so that he couldn't be accused of doing nothing. As far as the Russians are concerned Rakosi is reliable, loyal, and able. In short, from the Russian viewpoint it's rather generally agreed that he is indispensable. At the moment Rakosi is in Moscow. There are lot of rumours about why he is there.

A word about Imre Nagy. He had his 60th birthday a few weeks ago and it turned into a remarkable demonstration of confidence from unexpected quarters. First of all, Suslov was in town from Moscow and made an unexpected call on Nagy that afternoon to "pay his respects." Secondly, almost every eminent writer in the country was there. He was told that, collectively, they felt a very great debt to him because it was he who, by standing up to Rakosi, had given them inspiration for the Writers' Revolt. In fact they felt that his courage was "greater than Tito's" when standing up to Stalin since he, Nagy, was within Rakosi's reach.

Rakosi is universally detested and despised in and out of his party. But although Nagy has a certain stubborn popularity with some of the people who associated with him personally and with the public who remember that brief, short-lived breathing period that he gave them, I wonder whether he is popular in general. His regime ended on a very negative note . . . It is quite generally agreed that the Russians will never place enough confidence in him to permit him to come back as Prime Minister. Any candidate must be approved by the Russians, and the government fell apart so dangerously during Nagy's last days that the Russians would never permit him to be returned to power again . . .

Personal Letter by Simon Bourgin, U.S. Journalist, 5 July 1956

— *"How Can I Be Brave?"* —

I am not worthy of praise.
Believe me, my friend, it chills my bones
When you praise my courage.

I am not a tiger; I am human being,
My worn heart is a nest of fears.
Believe me: I am frightened. I am frightened.

I am a human being, I live like a human being,
How can I be brave?
I fear only that I may be worthless.
Of this I am more afraid than of death.

        Zoltan Zelk, *Irodalmi Ujsag* (Budapest), 5 May

Rakosi Goes, Gero Stays

HONORABLE CENTRAL COMMITTEE!

I request the Central Committee to relieve me of the post of First Secretary of the Central Committee and of my membership in the Politburo. One of the reasons for my request is that I am in my 65th year and that my illness, with which I have now been suffering for 2 years with growingly aggravated effect, hinders me from discharging the work devoling upon the First Secretary of the Central Committee ...

As regards my condition of health, I have been suffering hypertension for the past 2 years, my blood pressure is rising, and a few days ago the physicians sent to the Politburo a report from which I would like to quote one sentence: "We do not in any way consider Comrade Rakosi's present condition as satisfactory and consequently we ask for the most urgent intervention so as to prevent a deterioration of his condition."

My comrades frequently mentioned in the past two years that I do not visit the factories as often as I did in the past. They were right, the only thing they did not know is that this was due to the deterioration of my health. My state of health began to tell on the quality and amount of work I was able to perform, a fact that is bound to cause harm to the Party in such an important post. So much about the state of my health.

A regards the mistakes that I committed in the field of the "cult of personality" and the violation of socialist legality, I admitted them at the meetings of the Central Committee in June, 1953, and I have made the same admission repeatedly ever since. I have also exercised self-criticism publicly.

After the 20th Congress of the CPSU and Comrade Khrushchev's speech it became clear to me that the weight and effect of these mistakes were greater than I had thought and that the harm done to our Party through these mistakes was much more serious than I had previously believed.

These mistakes have made our Party's work more difficult, they diminished the strength of attractiveness of the Party and of the People's Democracy, they hindered the development of the Leninist norms of Party life, of collective leadership, of constructive criticism, and self-criticism, of democratism in Party and state life, and of the initiative and creative power of the wide masses of the working class.

Finally, these mistakes offered the enemy an extremely wide opportunity for attack. In their totality, the mistakes that I committed in the most important post of Party work have caused serious harm to our socialist development as a whole.

It was up to me to take the lead in repairing these mistakes. If rehabilitation has at times proceeded sluggishly and with intermittent breaks, if a certain relapse was noticed last year in the liquidation of the cult of personality, if criticism and self-criticism together with collective leadership have developed at a slow pace, if sectarian and dogmatic views have not been combated resolutely enough — then for all this, undoubtedly, serious reponsibility weighs upon me, having occupied the post of the First Secretary of the Party ...

MATYAS RAKOSI
Szabad Nep (Budapest), 19 July

It would be a grave mistake not to draw a lesson from the Poznan provocation as regards our situation and our tasks. As a matter of fact, the enemy openly mentions — more than one imperialist paper and radio station did mention — that the enemy aims at having "Hungarian Poznans." Hungry pigs dream of acorns! ...

Touch wood, no Poznan has occurred in Hungary, although one imperialist radio station boastfully described the Petofi Circle events [of June 27] as a "little Poznan". There were sound features in the Petofi Circle and several of the motions made there should be taken to heart, as was clearly stated in the June 30 resolution of the Central Committee. The Petofi Circle included many honest people, loyal to the Party and to our People's Democracy, among them not a few Communists who cherish the Party, are unquestionably loyal to socialism, are good Hungarian patriots as well as adherents of proletarian internationalism. At the same time, however, it must also be said that in and around the Petofi Circle a second political center began to form, which challenged the nation's only real political center, the Central Committee of the Hungarian Workers Party. It is beyond doubt that this [challenge] had an organized character ...

In addition, it must be noted — though this is by no means of decisive importance — that the central leadership of DISZ, or more accurately its executive committee, erred when it permitted guidance of the Petofi Circle to slip from its hands. It was a serious mistake to permit the direction of *Szabad Nep* and of the press in general to slip out of our hands, and we did not guide our broadcasting properly, which, naturally, caused no small confusion among our cadres, activists, members, and honest workers who cling to the Party and support our People's Democracy ...

ERNO GERO
Szabad Nep (Budapest), 19 July

"What the Future Will Bring"

Budapest, in August

It is only about two months since my last letter from Budapest. Changes are great and rapid. I am sure they will continue. Things are improving. By this I mean not living conditions, but the "climate." One Party member told me the AVO was no longer following through on personal denunciations. A very common greeting in Budapest today is "When did you get out of jail?" More people are getting passports than ever before. The deportees have been permitted to return to Budapest; this concerns between ten-and-twenty thousand people, many of them Jews. There are thousands of foreigners in Budapest and in Hungary compared with only a few dozen some months ago. No attention is paid to where I go or whom I talk to. A man who runs a State Enterprise told me that he had been instructed to hire people for their "ability" rather than on the basis of whether or not they belong to the Party or what kind of "political friends" they have. This is a minor revolution and he told me that it is going on in a good many other state enterprises ... But the Petofi Club meetings have not been continued. The events that culminated in the meeting on June 27th, for which the participants were sharply censored by the Party, more or less ran their course. That was the climax and that period was over. One other meeting was scheduled first for July 29th, was then postponed to August 5th, and now it has been postponed until October on the grounds that "many people are on vacation." ...

The first Danube steamer excursion to Vienna carried about 300 Hungarian writers and film people. Individually, if not collectively, this has had a most remarkable effect. I have heard a great deal about it. Someone remarked: "No wonder the regime has an Iron Curtain. No wonder they prevent us from seeing things like Vienna!" It was a complete and total shock—so much prosperity, so much relaxation, so much luxury. After they came back many writers couldn't work; their whole life had been changed in many ways. A few went through periods of "hating" their families whom they loved because the thought of them had prevented defecting in Vienna when they had a chance to do so ... Now a kind of camaraderie has grown up among those who had been "outside."

Many of these changes reflect the fact that Rakosi is gone and it is pretty well agreed that he is gone for good. He must realize it himself. I was told that he wept when he got on the plane at the Budapest airport to go to Russia, and there were even some reports that he was put on the plane by force. He was seen at a French legation party shortly before he left office; he looked shrunken, emaciated, and worn. Somebody who

knew him told me that the only other time he has ever seen Rakosi lose his poise was upon Stalin's death; this really shook him, the loss of his "closest and oldest friend." At the meeting of the Presidium which resulted in his "resignation" [18 July], Rakosi, himself, is said to have provoked the issue by demanding that some 400 people associated with the Petofi Club should be jailed because they had "opposed the Party." Mikoyan was present at this meeting. Mikoyan disagreed. He argued that these people had not opposed the Party but merely the leadership. Rakosi is said to have pressed the issue and a call was made to Moscow. After the appeal to Khrushchev, Rakosi's retirement was announced.

It is pretty obvious that Imre Nagy is on his way in. This would have been unthinkable a few months ago; then Rakosi was regarded as "indispensable." But many things have changed, and apparently the Russians, who previously would not have countenanced Nagy, now are reconsidering. Recently Nagy was called to Gero and asked if he would take a cabinet post on the government's terms. This would, of course, have implied his recanting his previous "mistakes." Nagy declined. Everyone is convinced that if he simply waits, he will be returned to power on his own terms. It is also believed that the Russians installed Gero as a temporary stop-gap, simply because they only wanted to go half-way at this time, and that if they went directly from Rakosi to Nagy, the shock would be so great and the loss in prestige for Communism so sharp that the consequences might be far too damaging. Apparently Suslov's visit to Nagy on his 60th birthday two months ago had a special point.

I have been "authoritatively" told that Gero naturally will "have to go," and probably within a few months. The economic system cannot work on the basis of the concessions which have been made. Pressure will be renewed. After all, the government has satisfied neither the intellectuals, the peasants, nor the workers. Nagy's popularity is enormous. He is applauded even when he walks in the streets ...

It is said that the next man, if it is not Nagy,—that is, if there is another stopping-off point in the direction of Nagy—will be Janos Kadar. On the other hand, someone else remarked: "How could it possibly be Kadar? Rakosi was a brilliant revolutionist. Gero is an able administrator. But what is Kadar?"

Someone who knew a great deal about Hungary suggested to me, on my last trip, that the Yugoslavs would never consent to Nagy's return to any position of power because communism in Hungary had almost collapsed when he was the Prime Minister, and that while the Yugoslavs did not like Rakosi, they did not want to see the communist system break up. I don't know, but I daresay that the Russians will never let things get as far as they did under Nagy without switching back in the other direction.

Now when I talk to Hungarians about what the future will bring, curiously enough I hear lots of talk about "free elections." This is very remarkable because everyone talks about them but there isn't anything very solid to go on. Many Hungarians also tell me that they think new personalities are somehow going to emerge from these elections; but they won't say who they might be or how one can really get free elections. People in the government have been talking privately and informally about the possibility of putting two or three candidates on an electoral list, instead of one, even though all would stand for the same thing. There is a chance that this will be done. But people think the events I described are leading to free elections. One has to write this with a smile, but it is talked about so much that it is probably something one shouldn't smile about...

Personal letter by Simon Bourgin, U. S. Journalist,
31 August 1956

Writers, Lies, and Truth

Budapest, in September

I want to speak clearly. In the evolution of democracy the first step is this: citizens outside the Party, including writers, should not have to applaud things with which they do not agree. To make anyone do so is unfair and unworthy of man. But to force a writer to do so is to make him sick in spirit, for a writer's element, his *profession*, is to tell truth. (And if he does not tell the truth he is only a slave or a paid scribbler.)

The second step is to allow people to be silent if they wish—either for their personal reasons or because they do not agree with official government opinion. The man who cannot or does not wish to take part in politics should not be forced to do so. A writer should thus be allowed to remain silent without starving to death. A writer who is valuable to literature and not politically dangerous can help to give pleasure or to instruct the nation. He should not be hindered from publishing and marketing his work.

Many of our writers are faced with this unhealthy dilemma, not only those who speak, but those who are silent. If, for personal reasons a man does not speak out, that is his right. But if we prevent him from speaking out, we are guilty of a crime.

Thus I believe that the third step is simply to allow writers to say and think what they feel. With more or less success, this is what we are trying to do...

There are writers who adapt themselves. The political powers then imagine that these writers have no other concern but to serve or amuse them. Sometimes, however, these entertainers slap the tyrants so hard that the smack resounds forever... There is an old truth which says that the prisoner is cleverer than his jailor, for the prisoner concentrates fully on one thing only, his freedom, whereas the jailor has to think about a thousand things. That is why it is advisable to reduce the number of prisoners, particularly the intelligent and thoughtful prisoners. Citizens should be able to think as free men, for the thinking of the entire people thereby becomes sounder...

The great Hungarian poets—and, in general, all the great poets of the world—were men who were endowed with a deep sense of community... At the moment, the situation is not simple. As far as writing is concerned, it is no easy matter to support the government—and it never was, except perhaps during the brief period of the common struggle of revolutionary writers and political revolutionaries in their efforts to establish a new world... An ideological literature is justified. What would be left for men who did not take their stand on a people or on a class or on a community, and who did not believe in an idea? Abstract humanism is not worth much. I can be a humanist only in my own community, where I have the roots of my being.

That, of course, is not a program; it is only the expression of my feeling. In any case, our General Assembly ought even now to be giving the example of a future functional democracy so that writers may truly become the forerunners of social progress...

Peter Veres, Irodalmi Ujsag (Budapest), 22 September

... We have come to the point where the most essential problem — in my opinion the most essential question of today's general assembly [Writers Association] — this is the question of telling the truth. The best Communist writers after much trouble, grave errors, and bitter spiritual struggle, have decided that never, under any conditions, will they ever write lies in the future. Let us declare sincerely that this was the basic cause of the battles and humiliations in recent years. The real reason of our clashes was that we took an Oath of Truth, and certain influential persons — not understanding literature's real role in society, and forgetting that the Party also demands its members to tell the truth! — blamed us for this. And here we want to promise that, in the future, we shall never be linked to those who, considering lies as indispensable means of politics, want also to force them on literature. We know how extremely difficult it is to write the truth. This requires courage, talent, knowledge, and many other things. The late Bertold Brecht wrote a study on this subject ... We know how difficult it is to be a writer ...

Our Assembly will only fulfill its purpose if everything we do is moved by the following sense: We, Hungarian writers, irrespective of party attachment or philosophical conviction, must pledge our words together to the truth. It is the profession of writers to tell the truth. Today they are witnesses, tomorrow judges, in the immense process for the rights and happiness of Man. It is a painful and shameful fact that, during the tragic years of schematic literature, the writers of the truest outlook, the Communist writers, participated in Machiavellian deviations. But they suffered bitterly in this atmosphere of lies. They paid for their faults with the loss of inspiration and standards. And with something else, too ... As we became less truthful and worse writers, we also became worse Marxists and worse Communists. ...

I was fifteen years old when I realized for the first time, upset by the horrors of the First World War, that the Rights of Man could only be enforced on the basis of an endlessly wise philosophy, radiating immense strength. This philosophy is Marxism. During the four decades that have passed, the Marxist philosophy became the basis of my whole way of thinking, the guiding force of my life. Recent years, however, and its spiritual torment, taught me that even the wisest philosophical basis is unable to protect us automatically from faults, from deviations, even from sins and dishonesty. Even a Marxist has to fight daily for the truth against himself as well as against others.

My whole literary activity represents this fight for truth, standing on the truest of all bases, but still exposed to a thousand errors. And, reciprocally, I learned to know many writers who were, in my opinion, in philosophical error, but nevertheless came, in the performance of everyday literary duties, very often nearer to truthfulness than I ... My conviction is, therefore, that during the evolution of our literature a manyfold intertwining will occur, a genuinely national unification of our literature ...

If I may be permitted to conclude on a subjective note I will admit how pleased I am by the almost symbolic fact that on the two stages of the National Theater tomorrow morning the the rehearsals of two Hungarian plays will begin. One is *"Galilei,"* the other *"The Truth of Gaspar Varro."* Both had been postponed by a cultural policy that is now ended ...

Julius Hay, Irodalmi Ujsag (Budapest), 22 September

Tito, the Soviets, and Hungary

Pula, Yugoslavia

... As you know, Khrushchev came over here on a holiday [19 September 1956]. On that occasion we had talks here and many more in Belgrade. Since I and comrades Rankovic and Pucar were invited to go to Crimea, we went there [27 September] and resumed the talks. We realized that it would be rather difficult to do anything since the Soviet leaders had different viewpoints as to other countries; they looked on their relations with other countries, with Poland, Hungary and others, from a wrong and defective angle. Still, we did not take this too tragically because we saw that this was not the attitude of the entire Soviet leadership, but only of a part of it which to some extent had imposed its standpoint on the others. We saw that this attitude was imposed by those people who took and still take Stalinist positions, but that there was still a possibility that within the leadership of the Soviet Union, through an internal evolution, those elements would triumph which favour a stronger and more rapid development in the direction of democratization, abandonment of all Stalinist methods, and the creation of new relations through new foreign policies among socialist countries. From certain signs, as well as from conversations, we could see that these elements were not weak, that they were strong, but that this internal process of development in the progressive direction, in the direction of abandoning Stalinist methods, was also hindered by certain Western countries which, by their propaganda and ceaseless repetition of the need to "liberate" those countries, have been interfering in their internal affairs and thwarting a rapid development and improvement of relations among those countries. The Soviet Union maintains, in view of the fact that this interference in internal affairs has assumed rather extensive proportions through radio propaganda, the dispatch of materials by ballons etc., that unfortunate consequences might result if it completely abandoned these countries, or if, for example, they were to be given the status enjoyed by Yugoslavia. They fear that in those countries reactionary forces might then triumph. In other words, this means that they lack sufficient confidence in the internal revolutionary forces in these countries. In my opinion, this is erroneous, and there lay the roots of all subsequent errors resulting from insufficient confidence in the socialist forces of those peoples ...

When we were in Moscow, we also talked about Poland, Hungary and other countries. We declared that Rakosi's regime, and Rakosi himself, had no qualifications whatsoever to lead the Hungarian state and to bring about national unity, but that, on the contrary, there could only be very grave consequences.

Unfortunately, Soviet comrades did not believe us. They said that Rakosi was an old revolutionary, that he was honest, and so forth. It is true, he is old, but that is not sufficient. That he is honest, I could not say, since I know him — especially after Rajk's trial and all the other things. As far as I am concerned, these are the most dishonest people in the world. The Soviet comrades stated that he was a clever man, that he would succeed, and that they did not know anyone else whom they could rely upon in that country. Just because our state and Party policy is opposed to interference in the domestic affairs of other countries, and in order to avert another conflict with the Soviet comrades, we were not insistent enough with the Soviet leaders for the removal of a team like that of Rakosi and Gerö.

When I went to Moscow there was great surprise that I did not travel via Hungary. It was precisely because of Rakosi that I did not want to pass through Hungary. I said that I would not go through Hungary even if it would have meant making the trip three times shorter.

When stronger and stronger dissatisfaction began to appear in the ranks of Hungarian Communists themselves, and when they demanded that Rakosi should go, Soviet comrades realized that it could not go on like this and they agreed to his removal. But they made a mistake by not also allowing the removal of Gerö and other Rakosi followers who had compromised themselves in the eyes of the people. They made it a condition that Rakosi would go only if Gerö remained. This was wrong because there was no difference between Gerö and Rakosi. Gerö followed the same policy and was as guilty as Rakosi.

Well, comrades, what could we do now? We saw that things were not going well. When we were in Crimea Gerö was "accidentally" there and we met him "accidentally". We had talks with him [30 September]. Gerö condemned the earlier policy and said that it was wrong to have slandered Yugoslavia; in short, he repented in sackcloth and ashes and asked us to establish good relations, promising to make amends for all previous mistakes and that the past would never be repeated. We wanted to show that we were not vindictive, that we are not narrow-minded, and so we agreed to talk with Gerö and an Hungarian Party delegation which was to come to Yugoslavia. We wanted to establish relations with the Hungarian Workers Party, because we hoped that by not isolating the Hungarian Party, we could more easily influence their proper internal development ...

Marshal Tito, Borba (Belgrade), 16 November 1956

Laszlo Rajk Reinterred, Imre Nagy Rehabilitated

On October 3 the Central Committee of the HWP announced that it had reached a decision to pay "last respects worthy of militants and revolutionaries ... to comrades who, as a result of political trials in past years, have been innocently condemned and executed, and who have already been rehabilitated earlier by the Party's Central Committee and reinstated in their Party membership" (*Szabad Nep*, October 4).

On October 6, 1956, there took place the ceremonial reinterment of Laszlo Rajk, Lt. Gen. Gyorgy Palffy, Tibor Szonyi, and Andras Szalai, the chief victims of the purge trials of 1949. The deeper meaning of this macabre ritual was conveyed by an editorial in *Szabad Nep* ("The Nation's Painful, Silent Tribute to Its Great Deceased," *Szabad Nep*, October 7):

> ... The silent demonstration of the hundreds of thousands of mourners was a pledge not only that we will preserve the pure memories [of the four dead leaders] but will also remember the dark practices of tyranny, lawlessness, slander, and defrauding of the people ... The people stood honor guard at the biers ... The silent demonstration began. Is it possible to give an account of this, on the basis of consecutive impressions of the facts, the events? It is not! ... No, it is not possible to speak of mourning when we describe the procession [of thousands upon thousands]. People were numbed not only by a deep sense of grief ... but by burning hatred, by the memory that these comrades, these men were executed as enemies of the fatherland, of the people! We were led to believe – and we were willing to believe – the slanders about you! Forgive us for this, comrades!

On the same day on which tribute was paid to these Hungarian victims of Stalinism, Erno Gero, Janos Kadar, Istvan Hidas, and Zoltan Szanto (the last three were on their way back from the Congress of the Chinese CP) held discussions with A. I. Mikoyan and M. A. Suslov in Moscow. (*Szabad Nep*, October 7).

On October 12 the arrest of Gen. Mihaly Farkas, former Minister of Defense, for having violated "socialist legality" was announced.

On October 14, a Hungarian delegation under the leadership of Erno Gero departed to Yugoslavia to formalize the terms of friendly cooperation between the two countries and Communist Parties. On the same day, the reinstatement of the Party membership of Imre Nagy was made public.

National Communism and Popular Revolt in Eastern Europe (Columbia University Press, New York, 1956)

Honorable Comrades:

Budapest, 4 October 1956

I follow the imperative voice of my Communist convictions and attachment to the Party by discarding personal interest, prestige considerations, and resentment as I am again turning to the Party. In writing this letter I was above all prompted by my anxiety for the unity of the Party and by a desire to be able to work as soon as possible in the ranks of the Party and shoulder to shoulder with members of the Party, on the many and arduous tasks of building socialism for the country's prosperity and the peaceful and happy life of our working people, which require every effort of the Party and the firm and loyal stand of every Party member.

At the same time, when the great tasks arising from the July 1956 resolution of the Central Committee and, last but not least, the thwarting of the calculations of the enemies of our People's Republic absolutely demand the ideological, political, and organizational unity of the Party, and also on this basis the national rallying of the broadest democratic forces, my unclarified Party status and the uncertainty steadily growing around this affairs aggravate the Party's unity of action and divide the forces of the Party and democracy precisely at the moment when grave economic and political tasks must be solved under the direction of the Party. In such a situation the cause of Party unity is a paramount and decisive question. I wish to establish that I regard Party unity based on the teachings of Marxism-Leninism and the principles of democracy within the Party as the basic conditions for the Party's success. Therefore I would consider it culpable if the struggle within the Party around the so-called Imre Nagy affair were to sharpen and become an obstacle to the strengthening of Party unity and the firm united policy of the Party when this obstacle could be and can be overcome by settling my affair.

I want to stress emphatically that in the interest of settling my Party status I will do everything in my power that is compatible with my Marxist-Leninist convictions and principles and with my Communist and human honor.

As I have already said in several memoranda, I deem it necessary to restate that

   (a) I am in agreement with the Party's main political line, as determined by the resolutions of June, 1953, of the Central Committee and by the Third Party Congress, that industry, agriculture, and the entire national economy should be placed on the foundations of socialism in the spirit of Marxism-Leninism in accordance with the special conditions existing in Hungary;

   (b) I am in agreement with the Leninist principle of democratic centralism on the basis of which I recognize Party decisions as binding on me even if I partly or wholly disagree with them;

   (c) I am agreement in principle with those aims of the Central Committee resolution of July, 1956, which lead that Party along the road of socialist democratism in the spirit of the 20th Congress of the CPSU. Although I hold

a different opinion of several points of the resolution, I consider the resolution to be binding on me and I will fight for its realization.

I consider it absolutely indispensable that the accusations made in the past in connection with my political and ideological activity should be properly discussed before a leading Party forum in public, and, should ideological clarification make it necessary, simultaneously with the rectification of the accusations which proved to be unfounded, I for one am ready to admit the truly existing mistakes.

I am convinced that my case must be settled both in the interest of Party unity and the success of the political and economic tasks. I must emphasize this all the more because my expulsion from the Party took place in violation of democracy within the Party and of the Party statutes and was un-Partylike. I was prompted by this conviction when I sent several memoranda to leading Party organizations and when I turned to the Party committee of my former primary Party organization.

On the basis of all this I feel that my place is in the Party, where I have spent nearly 40 years, and in the ranks of which I have struggled to the best of my ability, either with arms in hand, or by work, words, or pen for the cause of the people, Fatherland, and socialism. I ask the Central Committee to examine my Party affairs again and to return my rights of Party membership so that in this way, with the termination of my Party affair, the successful solution of the tasks facing the Party and the country may also be promoted.

With Communist Greetings

Imre Nagy

Szabad Nep (Budapest), 14 October

The Politburo has discussed Comrade Imre Nagy's letter of October 4 asking for readmission to the Party. The Politburo has resolved:

(1) To annul the resolution of November, 1955, expelling Comrade Imre Nagy from the ranks of the Party because the political mistakes he had committed did not justify his expulsion from the Party. The personal bias of Comrade Matyas Rakosi played a considerable part in bringing about the expulsion. Taking all this into consideration, the Politburo restores Party member rights to Comrade Imre Nagy.

(2) It recommends that the Central Committee should shortly discuss the still open problems of the affair, and throw light on the mistakes actually committed by Comrade Imre Nagy and on the overstatements and incorrect findings in the previous Party resolution.

These arrangements will make it possible for the Central Committee to clear up and conclusively close the matter in a principled manner.

Szabad Nep (Budapest), 14 October

"People Refuse to Live in the Old Way"

Belgrade

Vlajko Begovic, Director of the Yugoslav Institute of International Politics and Economy, was in Budapest from 10th to 17th October to give several lectures, at the invitation of the Economic Institute of the Hungarian Academy of Sciences, on Yugoslavia's experiences in socialist economics. His notes on his impressions are contained in a three-part article, entitled "On the Eve of the Rising in Budapest", carried by *Borba* on 17th, 18th and 19th November...

Begovic quotes the letter he wrote from Budapest on 14 October to Veljko Vlahovic (Chairman of the committee for International Relations of the Socialist Federation of Working People of Yugoslavia):

"... people refuse to live in the old way, nor can the leadership govern in the old way. Conditions for an uprising have been created. Who will lead it when the working class is disoriented, and the Party lags behind events and has lost authority over the masses?..."

Tanjug, Yugoslav News Agency (Belgrade), 18 November

Budapest, in October

In the monumental, although slightly neglected building of the School of Economics, I was received by the Deputy Rector, Apro Hass, who took me to the hall where professors and student representatives were waiting. This school is one of the most active centres of political life in Budapest. My visit immediately turned into a conference. Just as in "Csepel," I was asked an endless stream of questions: about our Yugoslav economic and political studies, about self-government in universities, about our agrarian policy, our relations with the USA, my assessment of contemporary capitalism, the possibility of directing an economy without centralized planning, etc. etc....

The composition of this group of people was characteristic. Most of them were former party and state officials who had been dismissed, persecuted, and even imprisoned. In introducing me Apro Hass pointed out, in humorous way, what their former situations had been... One of them was Imre Vajda, formerly a member of the Politburo and chairman of the Planning Commission... Hass himself is an old Party member, a collaborator of Varga. He had come to the school after having been driven out of political life. He introduced to me a very young man named Kovacs by saying: "This is our Party Secretary. He and about twenty others have been sent to this school to make us toe the political line and to inform the higher-ups about our work. But they all share our views now." Which means they are supporters of Nagy, seeking a radical change of the existing

system, democratization and the dismissal of Rakosi's men from the Party and the Government. With pride, they told me that Nagy was also a professor at the School, that he was certain to be rehabilitated, and that they were very hopeful that he would return to the leadership of the country.

Discussion with them was a very lively affair. I felt they had a correct approach to the problems affecting Hungary. Socialism was close to their hearts. They believed that within the Party progressive forces are developing. Out of 800,000 Party members — who Rakosi turned into mechanical performers for executing decisions passed by the leadership—they claim about 30,000 were taking an active part in the struggle for democratization. I asked them why they always took the conclusions of the [Russian] 20th Congress as a point of departure when explaining something, even though in another country [Yugoslavia] a Party had drawn these conclusions earlier? In reply, they said they needed to have a legal platform to begin their struggle for democratization... My friends were especially embittered by the sterile way political economy had to be taught, divorced from reality... Something that is contrary to common sense was being affirmed in the name of Marxism and Leninism.

They neither have confidence in their State nor in the Party leadership, and considerable distrust has accumulated against the Soviet political leadership because of its stubborn support for Rakosi. One of them said to me: "We Hungarians, just like you Yugoslavs, have many reasons, much justification to despise Stalinism."

... I expected a sharply-worded discussion with the people from the State and Party apparatus... But I was surprised when a huge majority approved those standpoints. A minority took more or less the following attitude: certain of your principles are completely new to us, quite different from our conception of the economic system under Socialism, and for this reason it is impossible for us to discuss this matter now... The lecture took an hour-and-a-half, and I answered questions for the next three hours. The next day we resumed for an additional five hours... They also voiced criticisms. They were especially worried because the existing system made it particularly difficult to raise the standard of living, because industrial plants could not use their full capacity, and because they had great difficulties in the countryside.

One has the impression that, in the eyes of these leading economic cadres, the existing economic system has been compromised in the fullest sense of the word, that they have lost confidence in it, and that they are trying to discover a way out as soon as possible... They were anxious to change the system as soon as possible, but the leadership was so slow that its own people had begun to lose faith in it.

I called on the Planning Commission and talked to its chairman Berei. About 3,000 people, a large proportion of them experts, are employed there producing tons of paper in a waste of time and energy. By such stiff centralisation and minute planning, the independent activity of enterprises and the initiative of the working people are hampered and a more rapid economic development is being thwarted. Berei is fairly satisfied with such methods; the only change he is contemplating is a reduction of the number of indices. In his opinion, such methods constitute truly socialist, scientific planning. Every other method is no planning at all ...

Questions

When Jozsef Horvath, chairman of the shop committee [Matyas Rakosi Works], opened the meeting, one could sense that something unusual was about to happen at the Csepel Martin Furnace ... When the opening report came to a close a whole "forest" of hands went up.

From the comments it was clear that the workers were troubled by a problem not on the agenda, a problem which was not even mentioned [in the talks].

"We have been discussing it for months," said stove-builder Ferenc Vincze in an annoyed voice. "The fact that our system of wage computation is very complicated. We never know on what basis our earnings rise or fall!"

When Chairman Horvath rose to speak the workmen eagerly watched for what he would have to say concerning the matter.

"What everybody is interested in," [Horvath] started, "is why the other fellow gets two thousand forint when he himself gets one thousand forint, whereas he would do better to work harder."

"That's not true, we do our best," could be heard from several workers.

"Never before has anyone so harshly attacked the wage computation system," roared Horvath.

"But are we right? Answer this question!" a voice interrupted.

"I am speaking now!" shouted Horvath. "When I finish, you, Comrade, may ask for the floor."

"If in Parliament questions can be asked while a Minister is speaking, then we cannot be forbidden to do the same, because we have a right to ask questions," declared Foreman Lengyel ...

Nepszava (Budapest), 8 August

I also visited the deputy Prime Minister Istvan Hidas, where I also met the second deputy Prime Minister, Joszef Mekis. Hidas is responsible for the economy. I was already acquainted with his writings on economic matters. They were the well-known old stiff conceptions ... But Hidas had begun to realize that the existing set-up could not survive much longer. He said every change made to satisfy requests by enterprises and local authorities would lead to other changes, and he concluded that it would be necessary to change the entire economic system. His problem was how to replace it, with what kind of system? He was fearful of starting a new road. And, to tell the truth, this was not easy for him to do, for until now he had known only one system, the theory and practice of the USSR. That system of economic management has created people who, when a change is necessary, feel quite helpless.

Then we turned to Stalinism ... Both Hidas and Mekis faced a dilemma. Hidas said that there were three viewpoints on Stalinism. One viewpoint was upheld by the Soviet Union and Hungary, the second one by China (as he had learned during his recent trip to Peking) and the third was the Yugoslav interpretation. He declared himself unable to discuss the matter, because, as he put it: "You, Yugoslavs, are in a different, far more favourable position. You have thought about it a great deal, you have discussed the matter and possess a whole arsenal of arguments to support your stand, while I feel unprepared and helpless. We have not yet discussed these things in the Party." He indicated how good it was that now it was possible for communists from the two countries to exchange views so frankly, without any fears or reservations. In his opinion that was real progress.

I also wanted to meet high-ranking political leaders from the Central Committee and was informed that Erno Gero, would receive me. I met Gero for the first time in 1935, and I met him again in Berlin this year ... I was anxious to hear his views on the situation in Hungary.

He told me immediately that he had been informed about my lecture at the Institute of Economics, that it was a good thing to exchange views on such matters, but that he disagreed with some of my views. I could not learn from him on which points we differed. Instead of a reply, he lectured me about the need for a deeper study of Marxism-Leninism, and he asked whether I had read the new Soviet textbook on political economy. I answered in the affirmative and said that I did not think much of it. "But have you read the new, second edition?"

This political leader drew his knowledge from such a textbook.

With great care I tried to tell him something about my impressions of "Csepel" and the Budapest Town Council. I talked about the political situation, about the lack of political activity and political engagement of the working class, the danger of the Party lagging behind events. But Gero maintained that a certain awakening among the masses was noticeable, that I had been unable to investigate the situation and the problems thoroughly enough. He spoke about the line endorsed at the July Plenum of the Central Committee which maped out a road for slow and steady progress. He was the only Hungarian with whom I was unable to establish close contact and to speak frankly about current problems ...

The people were aware of their problems, trying by all means to discover a solution ... They could, more or less, discern the road to be taken ... But as soon as one contacted persons in higher positions, one saw they had a vaguer picture of the situation and were confused by abstract conceptions of Marxism-Leninism. And here, in the Central Committee, with the First Secretary of the Party, it was as if darkness prevailed ... The more these dogmatic interpreters abandoned the principles of Marx and Lenin and distorted Socialism, the more they talked about Marxism and Leninism ...

I went to the cemetery where Rajk and his comrades were buried. At the Central Cemetery, in the vicinity of Kossuth's Mausoleum, the four graves were covered with wreaths ... Those 300,000 people who attended the funeral and all those who still come to place flowers, are they not closely bound to the workers' movement and the cause of Socialism? The leadership of the Hungarian Workers' Party does not know how to approach those people, to show them understanding, to lead and help them to follow a correct road to a better life. Instead they wish to drive them along a road which they will and can not take. They are simply provoking their opposition.

One part of the leading party cadres had been ruined by the Stalinist system, by bureaucratization and isolation from the people, while the other part, which offered resistance, was removed from political and social life, imprisoned or physically liquidated. Dozens of members of the Central Committee were either killed or scheduled for liquidation between 1948 and Stalin's death. Few, very few, real working-class leaders have survived who are fit to lead ... The situation is extremely serious.

Vlajko Begovic, Borba (Belgrade), 18—19 November

"The Spirit of 1848"

Events in Poland naturally accelerated the reform movement that had developed inside the Petofi Circle and the associations of writers and journalists. But, having been in Budapest end of September, I can certify that neither the leaders of the Petofi Circle nor the writers and journalists were considering an insurrection, because they thought that a peaceful transformation of the régime was possible. On my return [to Paris] I wrote in *L'Express* on 12 October:

"Democratisation is inevitable and irresistible. Neither Rakosi nor the Russians, nor anybody else, can reverse this trend without risking an insurrection greatly surpassing the events in Poznan. ..."

Thomas Schreiber, Gauche Européenne (Paris), December 1956

Budapest

Szabad Nep and *Magyar Nemzet* hailed the appearance of a new literary magazine *Nagyvilag* (The Wide World). *Szabad Nep* says that the magazine will be an *"effective weapon against provincialism and dogmatism"*, and would help to develop Hungarian national culture *"together with world culture instead of in isolation from it ..."*

In an article Gyorgy Lukacs said that "one of the most important tasks for the new magazine is to prove that Hungarian readers are not children who need a teacher but adults aware of their reponsibilities." The first number also included poems by Dylan Thomas, essays by Hemingway, Bertold Brecht, Roger Martin du Gard and Bernard Shaw.

Hungarian News Agency, 18 October

The Cultural and Critics Branch of the Journalists Union met on 19th October and passed a resolution demanding a new Press Law which would guarantee full freedom of criticism and immunity for journalists. The Chinese principle —*"Let every flower bloom and every bird sing"*— should apply in cultural life. In a telegram to the Politburo the journalists expressed their pleasure at the talks between the Hungarian and Yugoslav Parties and Imre Nagy's readmission to the Party. ...

Hungarian News Agency, 19 October

In view of the country-wide interest in the debates of the Petofi Circle, and in the debates arranged by writers and by the Kossuth Club, the PPF National Council had decided to publish the speeches made at these debates in 20,000 copies. The most interesting speeches will be issued in 60,000 copies. ...

Hungarian News Agency, 19 October

It is impossible to ignore that, in recent years, young people were not supposed to think, indeed

"Don't Look Back . . ."

Belgrade

A delegation of the Hungarian Workers Party was in Yugoslavia October 15–22 . . .

The members of the delegation were—Erno Gero, the First Secretary of the Central Committee of Hungarian Workers Party, and Antal Apro, Andras Hegedus, Janos Kadar, and Istvan Kovacs, all members of the Politburo . . . The Representatives of the Communist League of Yugoslavia and of the Hungarian Workers Party conducted talks in a spirit of friendship, frankness and mutual understanding . . .

Borba (Belgrade), 24 October

Zagreb

The delegation of the Hungarian Workers Party arrived here this morning [19 October]. During a 2-hour talk Erno Gero and Polit-buro-members Andras Hegedus and Janos Kadar asked numerous questions regarding the role of the workers councils and the trade unions in the factories. At the end of the talk Erno Gero expressed his thanks for the in-formation . . . Erno Gero wrote in the Visitor's Book . . . At 5 p.m. the Hungarian political leaders went to see the Museum of the People's Revolution . . .

Borba (Belgrade), 20 October

Belgrade

The Yugoslav Party accepted the offer that a Party delegation headed by Gero should come to Yugoslavia. In Hungary our men heard hundreds of remarks of dissatisfaction at Gero's visit. But because we did not want anyone to say that we were interfering in the internal affairs of Hungary, we glossed over all these remarks and considerations, holding then, as we do today, that it is the internal affair of every Party whom it will have in its leadership. Today when our "errors" in re-spect to Hungary are being aired, we must say that not even Gero's stay in Yugoslavia can be numbered among our sins. Gero probably thought that his visit would be sufficient to compensate for the authority he had lost. However, reality has shown that authority is acquired in one's own country, in one's own working class, among one's own people, and not in other countries, even though it might be Yugoslavia . . .

Veljko Vlakovic, Borba (Belgrade), 15 November

A Yugoslav Film Week will be organized in Hungary during the beginning of No-vember. On that occasion, the film "Blood-Stained Road," one of the most successful Yugoslav films, as well as the films "Don't Look Back, My Son" and "Bad Money," will be shown . . .   *Politika (Belgrade), 20 October*

they were not even supposed to dance or amuse themselves. They were intended only to show enthusiasm, to acclaim, and produce.

All this must be said because the events of these days truly reflect the real face of our youth. When you open the youth paper, *Szabad Ifjusag,* you are simply startled by the ardour of the debates. Without exaggeration we may say that these days our youth has become one great debating forum. The students' parliament is in session, university students are engaged in lively discussions, young technicians are conferring, and youth parliaments are meeting in the factories.

We have no time even to enumerate the large number of national problems, the questions which young people are now discussing with such a very great sense of responsibility. But one thing is certain: the youth of Hungary, whose maturity was so often called in question in the past, have now proved their intellectual and ideological maturity beyond doubt.

It is no mere slogan when we say that these days our youth has proved itself a worthy suc-cessor of the youth of March 1848. It marches in the van of progress and national rejuvena-tion . . .   *Radio Kossuth, 19 October*

This morning university lecturers held an extraordinary conference at which Albert Konya, the Minister of Education, made several an-nouncements . . . Compulsory instruction of Rus-sian language in the universities will cease. Students will be allowed to choose for themselves which language they wish to learn . . . National defence training will be reexamined, and in this connection talks will be held with representatives of the Ministry of National Defence . . . Up to now our scholarship students went mostly to the USSR and the People's Democracies. In the future, we shall send scholarship students to Western countries as well . . .

Radio Kossuth, 19 October

The Minister of Justice has offered Laszlo Rajk's widow the sum of 200,000 forints as partial compensation for the material damage sustained by the Rajk family and the imprisonment of Mrs. Rajk . . . Mrs. Rajk made the following state-ment: "I am a librarian, and I earn a salary. Since August I have been receiving a pension, after the murder of my innocent husband . . . I therefore donate this sum to the People's Col-leges and the education of the needy. . . . The years of terror cannot be paid for. Let this money help those who will remedy our mistakes."

Radio Kossuth, 19 October

Szeged undergraduates and high-school students held a meeting in the University's great lecture hall yesterday. More than 1,000 students attended the meeting. All speakers demanded the rehabilitation of the Pedagogical Academy of Szeged, branded as "Rightist deviationist" by the sectarian political leadership. The students also demanded the reinstatement of two of their professors ...

Radio Kossuth, 19 October

At a meeting of leading officials in Veszprem, which intellectuals also attended, it was decided to set up a "Bacsanyi Circle" ... A committee is to prepare the first debate ... A Petofi Circle was set up in Keszthely. A similar circle is to be set up in Zalaegerszg. ...

Radio Kossuth, 20—21 October

Budapest

A withdrawal of Soviet troops from Hungary and the release of Joseph Cardinal Mindszenty were demanded by speakers in an open meeting last week-end in Gyor. The meeting, which was held in the Jokai Theatre, was described to-day by the newspaper *Gyor-Sopronmegyei Hirlap* as "the first entirely free public and outspoken debate" since 1948.

Presiding at the meeting in Gyor was Gyula Hay, who won the Kossuth Prize for literature. He was one of the leading members of the Communist authors' group that voiced a demand a year ago for artistic freedom and he declared three

Demands

Budapest

The students of the Engineering University called a "parliament" for October 22 ... Long before the appointed time, 4000 students crowded the big hall.

Professor Istvan Pribeky returned to the university about 5 p.m. To his astonishment, standing under the staircase by the side entrance to the hall, he heard impassioned speeches still being made, punctuated by cheers and clapping ... A student jumped on the platform and shouted, "The truth is that the Russians exploit us worse than a colony!" The 4000 students crammed in the hall howled their approval.

Now the university Communist Party secretary pushed his way on the rostrum and tried to say that the Russians were Hungary's friends and liberators. He was hustled out of the hall ... Then, at last, one student shouted, "We want to be rid of the Russians!" The roar of approval was deafening. The Communist Party's "agitprop" ... grabbed the microphone and tried to defend the Russians. She was whistled down and pushed out of the hall. Then the Communist dean climbed on the rostrum and insisted that the students give him a hearing. He, too, was howled down ...

Someone shouted, "We must have our views printed!" "No, we must have them broadcast!" ... Pribeky offered to drive three students to the radio in his car – he had a small Italian Topolino. When he passed by the National Museum, which is only a few hundred yards distant from the Radio Building, Pribeky stopped the car and said, "Now let me see those demands of yours." He read them. "Your can't take this mess to the studio ... Let's reduce them to ten points which matter." In his car, Professor

Pribeky compressed the thirty suggestions of the students into ten points ...

Pribeky took the three students to the entrance of the Radio Building, and they went in with their ten demands. Soon they were back, very angry. "The radio people will only broadcast five of our demands ... They will not broadcast that the Russians must get out, that our uranium must remain in Hungary, that Rakosi must be tried, and so on. What are we to do?"

Pribeky drove them back to the university where the student's parliament was still on ... There was great indignation over the failure of the radio people to cooperate. At 9 p.m. one of the students suggested over the loudspeaker, "If the radio won't broadcast our demands, let's go to Nagy." ...

Professor Pribeky drove the three students to Nagy's villa, situated on a hill, the Rozsadomb, on the outskirts of Budapest. The village was surrounded by secret policemen ... "He can't see you tonight; he's very tired," one AVO man said ... "Maybe he'll see you tomorrow ..."

At the Engineering University the students concentrated on one problem: how to publicize their demands. The periodical of the Communist students organisation, DISZ, agreed to print eight points, but not the demands that the Russians should get out, and that free and secret elections be held. This concession was not good enough for the students ... They rang up all the universities of Budapest and asked all typewriters to go into action. "Type one top copy and four carbons." ... Batches of the demands were taken to every factory in and around Budapest ... pinned up on walls ... tied to trees ...

Judith Listowel, *Saturday Evening Post* (Philadelphia), *5 January 1957*

weeks ago that "a writer must be free to think like a Marxist or a non-Marxist."

The meeting was said to be the first time that the withdrawal of the Soviet troops from Hungary had been publicly advocated. Lajos Simon, another member of the group of rebellious writers, said the Russians were welcome guests in Hungary, but the presence of military units no longer was necessary.

"We live in an era of big changes", Mr. Hay said. "These began in the Soviet Union with Stalin's death. In Hungarian-Soviet relations, this change is unfortunately hardly noticeable, although it is quite obvious that no sound political relations could develop between Stalin's Soviet Union and Rakosi's Hungary." ...

The author continued: "Yugoslavia has succeeded in protecting her complete independence and Poland and China are on the way to developing a special way to build socialism based on national characteristics and the past of these countries. We must strive to develop this useful practice also in our country. That depends on us."

As for the abolition of Soviet bases in Hungary, he said, this would be part of an independent domestic and foreign policy that he hoped would be developed more vigorously in the wake of the current Belgrade talks between Hungarian and Yugoslav delegations.

As for the release of Cardinal Mindszenty from his long imprisonment, Dr. Hay said he did not believe in religion but disapproved of administrative interference with it ...

Mr. Hay explained that the expulsion some months ago from the Communist party of Tibor Dery and Tibor Tardos, two Hungarian writers who had condemned the Rakosi regime, "was intended to intimidate the authors and was also the preamble of a trial of Imre Nagy, which was to have been arranged. ... Fortunately the 'manager' is no longer able to 'arrange the play' ..."

John MacCormac, New York Times, 23 October

Our ears are unaccustomed to the sharper tones of democracy. It depends on us whether these debates acquire the character of an opposition, or whether they become a great intellectual force furthering the development of the country ... If, in one particular clash of opinions ... incorrect bourgeois-democratic views triumph, it is only we who are to blame for withdrawing instead of arguing ...

Szabad Nep (Budapest), 21 October

The leadership of the Petofi Club met tonight. ... They proposed to the Politburo that, in view of the country's present situation, it should call a meeting of the Central Committee. Comrade Imre Nagy should be included in the preparatory work ... The Party and Government should elaborate a positive program for the solution of the country's economic and social problems ...

Radio Kossuth, 22 October

A meeting of 400 students at the Lorand Eotvos University in Budapest on 22 October decided to set up a "15th March Circle". Speakers at the meeting said that undergraduates must march shoulder-to-shoulder with young workers and peasants and suggested that delegations should visit Budapest factories immediately ...

Hungarian News Agency, 23 October

... There is hardly room enough for so many guests in the big room. Among neighbors, people from Tapolca, Szeged, Budapest, we found the most popular guest of this year's wine harvest in Badacsony, Imre Nagy. He had visited the research institute and from there came over with the director Geza Biro ... for a glass of old wine ...

Radio Kossuth, 22 October

The youth of two Budapest universities held extraordinary meetings today. The fervent spirit of March [1848] swept over the auditorium of the Technical University of Architecture. From the galleries and staircase, thousands of young people shouted their approval or disapproval of some important points of the draft resolution, which is still being debated at this very moment ...

After the debate, the meeting decided with a sweeping majority, and with a minimum of opposition, to secede from DISZ [Hungarian Communist Youth League] and to set up an Association of University Youth. The meeting is still in progress.

The students of the Budapest University of Economics are also holding a mass meeting ...

One of the mass meeting's greatest moments was when it expressed solidarity with Polish comrades and declared their struggle was an example to be followed ...

Radio Kossuth, 22 October

III

REVOLUTION
AND COUNTER-REVOLUTION

"Hate is a passion all tyrants are bound to arouse; but contempt is often the cause by which tyrannies are actually overthrown."

ARISTOTLE

"Whoever becomes the ruler of a free city and does not destroy it, can expect to be destroyed by it, for it can always find a motive for rebellion in the name of liberty and its ancient usages, which are forgotten neither by lapse of time nor by benefits received; and whatever one does or provides, so long as the inhabitants are not separated or dispersed, they do not forget that name and those usages, but appeal to them at once in every emergency."

MACHIAVELLI

"From the beginning till the end there is here only one hero—the people..."

MICHELET

23 OCTOBER

Petofi Circle's Ten Demands

Budapest

The leadership of the Petofi Circle has passed the following resolution at its meeting:

1. In view of the present situation in Hungary we propose that the Central Committee of the Workers [Communist] Party should be convened with the minimum possible delay. Comrade Imre Nagy should take part in the preparatory work of this session.

2. We consider it necessary that the Party and Government should reveal the country's economic situation in all sincerity, revise the second Five-Year Plan directives, and work out a specific constructive program in accordance with our special Hungarian conditions.

3. The Central Committee and the Government should adopt every method possible to ensure the development of socialist democracy, by specifying the real functions of the Party, asserting the legitimate aspirations of the working class and by introducing factory self-administration and workers' democracy.

4. To ensure the prestige of the Party and of the state administration, we propose that Comrade Imre Nagy and other comrades who fought for socialist democracy and Leninist principles should occupy a worthy place in the direction of the Party and the Government.

5. We propose the expulsion of Matyas Rakosi from the Party Central Committee and his recall from the National Assembly and the Presidential Council. The Central Committee, which wishes to establish calm in the country, must offset present attempts at a Stalinist and Rakosi-ite restoration.

6. We propose that the case of Mihaly Farkas be tried in public in accordance with socialist legality.

7. The Central Committee should revise resolutions it passed in the period which has just elapsed — resolutions which have proved wrong and sectarian — above all the resolutions of March 1955, the December 1955 resolution on literature, and the 30 June 1956 resolution on the Petofi Circle. We propose that the Central Committee should annul these resolutions and draw the proper conclusions as to the persons concerned.

8. Even the most delicate questions must be made public, including the balance sheets of our foreign trade agreements and the plans for Hungarian uranium.

9. To consolidate Hungarian-Soviet friendship, let us establish even closer relations with the Soviet Party, State and people, on the basis of the Leninist principle of complete equality.

10. We demand that at its meeting on 23 October the DISZ Central Committee should declare its stand on the points of this resolution and adopt a resolution for the democratisation of the Hungarian Youth Movement.

Hungarian News Agency

"A Silent Demonstration"

Budapest

At the students' meetings held in the universities of Budapest on 22nd October it was decided that young people should arrange a silent demonstration on the afternoon of 23rd October to express their deep sympathy and agreement with events in Poland. The young people concerned passed a resolution pledging themselves not to permit any sort of provocation or anarchistic manifestation and to make sure that this demonstration of sympathy would take place in a spirit of socialist democracy, order, and discipline.

University youth will meet before the house of the Writers' Association at two thirty this afternoon.

Radio Kossuth

"With Caution?"

Budapest

In the past our youth was prevented from making its voice heard in national as well as in its own affairs. We are well aware that the DISZ laboured under terrible shortcomings ... In past years much justified dissatisfaction lay buried in the souls of young people. It is no wonder that now ... they are raising their voices. Those who now demand that our youth express its opinion with caution and calm restraint ignore historical developments and the specific situation of the Hungarian youth movement. They ignore the state of mind of Hungarian youth ...

Szabad Nep (Budapest), 23 October

Ban — No Ban

Budapest

[Gypsy music was interrupted] A communique: In order to assure public order, the Ministry of the Interior is not permitting any public meetings and demonstrations until further notice.

László Piros, Minister of the Interior

Addressing a meeting of the students of the Polytechnical University, Mihaly Fekete, Deputy Minister of the Interior announced that the ban on the proposed students' march had been lifted. He added that employees and Communists in his Ministry "rallied to the side of honest Hungarians in the interests of a change."

[A musical program was interrupted at 14 : 23]: Lázló Piros, Minister of the Interior, has withdrawn the ban imposed on public meetings and demonstrations.

The First Secretary of the Central Committee of the Hungarian Workers' Party, Comrade Erno Gero, will speak tonight at 8 p.m.

Radio Kossuth

The Polish Example

Budapest

We have watched with deep concern at first, but later with growing reassurance and pleasure the developments in Poland. ... It is worthwhile for us to examine this because there are many people among us who have become too accustomed to the old order and who think that democratization at such revolutionary speed is bound to bring on relaxation of law and order and the ascendancy of counter-revolutionary forces. Changes in Poland prove exactly the opposite. Information from Poland is unanimous in stressing that the unity of the Polish people has never been as firm and that never has there been so unanimous or enthusiastic support of the Communist Party and its leaders. The lesson to be drawn is that if the Communists and the Party's leading organisations take into consideration the real situation, if they turn frankly to all strata of the working population and champion their claims, the result will be unparalleled unity and confidence ....

Szabad Nep (Budapest), 23 October

Peter Veres Addresses the Demonstration

Budapest

University students gathered in front of the Petofi statue in Pest shortly before 15 : 00 hrs. They sang the "Kossuth Hymn" and carried banners inscribed *"Long Live the Youth of Poland"*, *"For Freedom in the Spirit of the Friendship between Bem and Kossuth"* ... The demonstrators, including a number of well-known professors, carried Hungarian and Polish national flags. The actor Imre Sinkovits recited Petofi's *„Arise Hungarians!"* Then he read the students' demands.

The group which had been demonstrating at the Petofi statue in Pest then marched to the Bem statue in Buda, where they were joined by nearly 800 students and teaching staff members from the Petofi Military Academy, as well as others from the Polytechnical University, the Agricultural University, and the High School of Physical Education. The students wore cockades in the national colours. National flags were distributed from lorries.

Peter Veres, President of the Writers' Association, then read a seven-point resolution passed by his Praesidium ...

"We have arrived at an historic turning point. In this revolutionary situation we shall not be able to acquit ourselves well unless the entire Hungarian working people rallies as a disciplined camp. The leaders of the Party and Government have so far failed to present a workable program. Responsible for this are those persons who, instead of expanding socialist democracy, are still obstinately organising themselves to restore Stalin's and Rakosi's regime of terror in Hungary. We Hungarian writers have formulated seven points, the demands of the Hungarian nation:

1. We want an independent national policy based on the principle of socialism. Our relations with all countries, and particularly with the USSR and the people's democracies, should be regulated on the basis of the principle of equality. We demand a review of treaties and economic agreements between States in the spirit of the equality of rights for the nations involved.

2. An end must be put to national minority policies which disturb friendship between peoples. We want true and sincere friendship with our allies — the USSR and the people's democracies. This can only be realised on the basis of Leninist principles.

3. We demand a clear disclosure of the country's economic situation. We shall not be able to emerge from this crisis unless all workers, peasants, and intellectuals can play their proper part in the political, social, and economic administration of the country.

4. Factories must be directed by workers and technicians. The present humiliating system of wages and norms, and the disgraceful condition of social security benefits, etc. must be reformed. The trade unions must truly represent the interests of the Hungarian working class.

BUDAPEST 1956

Matyas Rakosi   Erno Gero   Imre Nagy

Andras Hegedus   Janos Kadar

Mayor Joszef Kovago · Minister Anna Kethly · Major-General Bela Kiraly

Zolton Tildy

Laszlo Rajk

Imre Nagy

Josef Broz-Tito   Erno Gero

Col. Pal Maleter

Cardinal Mindszenty

5. Our peasant policy must be established on a new basis. Peasants must be given the right to decide their own fate freely. Political and economic conditions for free membership in co-operatives must finally be created. The present system of deliveries to the State and of taxation must gradually be replaced by an system ensuring free socialist production and exchange of goods.

6. If these points are to be realized there must be changes of structure and of personnel in the leadership of the Party and Government. The Rakosi clique is seeking a restoration, and it must be removed from our political life. Imre Nagy, a pure and brave Communist, who enjoys the confidence of the Hungarian people and all those who have systematically fought for socialist demo-cracy in recent years, must be given the posts they deserve. At the same time, a resolute stand must be made against all counter-revolutionary attempts and aspirations.

7. The development of the situation demands that the PPF [Patriotic People's Front] should assume the political representation of the working classes of Hungarian society. Our electoral system must correspond to the demands of socialist democracy. The people must elect their representatives in parliament, in the Councils, and in all autonomous organs of administration by free, secret ballot."

Hungarian News Agency

Ideologues and Marseillaise

Budapest

I have been the witness today of one of the great events of history. I have seen the people of Budapest catch the fire lit in Poznan and Warsaw and come out into the streets in open rebellion against their Soviet overlords. I have marched with them and almost wept for joy with them as the Soviet emblems in the Hungarian flags were torn out by the angry and exalted crowds. And the great point about the rebellion is that it looks like being successful.

As I telephone this dispatch I can hear the roar of delirious crowds made up of student girls and boys, of Hungarian soldiers still wearing their Russian-type uniforms, and overalled factory workers marching through Budapest and shouting defiance against Russia. "Send the Red Army home," they roar. "We want free and secret elections." And then comes the ominous cry which one always seems to hear on these occasions: "Death to Rakosi." Death to the former Soviet puppet dictator—now taking a "cure" on the Russian Black Sea Riviera—whom the crowds blame for all the ills that have befallen their country in 11 years of Soviet puppet rule.

Leaflets demanding the instant withdrawal of the Red Army and the sacking of the present Government are being showered among the street crowds from trams. The leaflets have been printed secretly by students who "managed to get access," as they put it, to a printing shop when newspapers refused to publish their political programme. On house walls all over the city primitively stencilled sheets have been pasted up listing the 16 demands of the rebels.

But the fantastic and, to my mind, really super-ingenious feature of this national rising against the Hammer and Sickle, is that it is being carried on under the protective red mantle of pretended Communist orthodoxy. Gigantic portraits of Lenin are being carried at the head of the marchers. The purged ex-Premier Imre Nagy, who only in the last couple of weeks has been read-mitted to the Hungarian Communist Party, is the rebels' chosen champion and the leader whom they demand must be given charge of a new free and independent Hungary. Indeed, the Socialism of this ex-Premier and—this is my bet—Premier-soon-to-be-again, is no doubt genuine enough. But the youths in the crowd, to my mind, were in the vast majority as anti-Communist as they were anti-Soviet—that is if you agree with me that call-ing for the removal of the Red Army is anti-Soviet.

In fact there was one tricky moment when they almost came to blows on this point. The main body of students and marchers had already as-sembled outside their university in front of the monument to the poet-patriot Petofi who led the 1848 rebellion against the Austrians. Suddenly a new group of students carrying red banners ap-proached from a side street. The banners showed them to be the students of the Leninist-Marxist Institute, which trains young teachers of Com-munist ideology and supplies many of the puppet rulers' civil servants.

The immediate reaction of the main body, I noticed, was to shout defiance and disapproval of the oncoming ideologists.

But they were quickly hushed into silence and the ideologues joined in the march with the rest of them, happily singing the *Marseillaise* ...

Sefton Delmer, Daily Express (London), 24 October

Interrupted Meeting

Budapest

At 14.00 hrs., the Central Committee of the DISZ [Hungarian Communist Youth League] opened its sixth session. The Central Committee approved demonstrations of Budapest youth in sympathy with the Polish People's Republic. It then decided to participate in the demonstration, and the meeting was therefore interrupted, to be resumed after the demonstration. The Committee requested university students and other youth participating in the demonstrations to prevent any attempts at provocations. A resolution was passed to send Polish youth a telegram of appreciation.

Radio Kossuth

"The People of Bem and Kossuth"

Budapest

National flags, red-white-and-green badges on the lapels of the youth, the Kossuth Song, the Marseillaise, the Internationale, — this is how we would characterize in colour and in slogans the new March 15th celebration in autumnal Budapest. This afternoon a great youth demonstration took place in our capital. Perhaps for you, Hungarians who are living abroad, this is a surprise, but here at home we who are participating in the wonderful fermentation which during the past weeks showed itself in passionate meetings and newspaper articles, we have counted on this. Ever since this February — we might even say since June, 1953 — workers, peasants, officials, students, writers, journalists, are demanding more and more loudly that our country's economic and political life be put on a real socialist basis, demanding that it be cleansed from the many crimes and mistakes with which Matyas Rakosi, Mihaly Farkas, and others, defiled the holy ideals of socialism.

During the past days, meeting followed meeting at our universities, where youth approved demands to reform the government under the leadership of Imre Nagy...

There were Universities where demands were listed in 12 points, others in 20 points, but everywhere it was done with a level head and a warm heart.

Today the University students of Budapest demonstrated. Although at noon the Minister of Interior prohibited all demonstrations, the Political Committee of the Hungarian Workers' Party changed this decision. Doctors, students of the Technical Faculty, philosophers, lawyers, economists, and students of other faculties, demonstrated, led by professors and leaders of the Hungarian Workers' Party.

At first they were only a few thousand, but then by-standers, soldiers, young high-school students, tram-car conductors joined them, and the mass soon numbered tens of thousands. The street resounded with slogans. The people of Father Bem and of Kossuth marched hand in hand.

"We want new leaders! ... We trust Imre Nagy! ... Long live the People's Army!" The shouting booms in the streets. The windows of the houses open. There is an air of freedom again on the streets of Budapest ...   *Radio Szabadság*

Nagy Confers

Budapest

The youth of Budapest this afternoon marched to the parliament building. In the evening Comrade Imre Nagy addressed them. Comrade Imre Nagy is at present conferring with youth delegates and several Deputies.   *Radio Budapest (22.00)*

When Imre Nagy appeared, he was cheered, but when he began his speech with the salutation, "Dear Comrades", he was whistled down. Nagy told them the historical situation was complicated and everyone should go home and wait for developments. The whistling started again ... "Why do you whistle at me?" Someone shouted, "We do not whistle at you, but at your words." There was a long, dramatic silence and then Nagy asked everyone to sing the national anthem, leading the singing himself.

At this high point of patriotic emotion, messengers came with the news that Gero was talking on the radio ...   *Time (New York), 7 January 1957*

Young Marxists vs. "Red Fascists"

Budapest

The revolution which broke out on the 23rd October on Joseph-Bem-Square started off as a peaceful manifestation. The students' demands, summed up in sixteen points and distributed in the streets of Budapest in the form of leaflets, were those of impatient revolutionary youth.

Certain observers insist on the essentially nationalistic characteristics of the manifestations. Incontestably the presence of the Soviet Army on Hungarian territory, the visible outward signs of foreign occupation (there was no practical difference between Soviet and Hungarian uniforms), rekindled the flame of Hungarian nationalism which had never been extinguished. But it was not only a question of nationalism; the students of Budapest also wanted true socialism.

It was for free independent Socialism that young Hungarians began the struggle against the only armed fascists who on the night of the 23rd October still wished to save their government: the red fascists of the political police, appointed to safeguard the last vestiges of the Stalinist government.

Numerous eye-witnesses have affirmed that at the beginning of the revolution the insurgents *had no arms*. It was only after Gero's menacing and disastrous speech on his return from Belgrade that the State Police (which must not be confused with the "AVO", or political police) joined the students and distributed arms to them in front of the Hungarian radio broadcasting house in Sandor-Brody Street. Next morning the entire Budapest garrison officers, non-commissioned officers and soldiers, joined the students and opened armament depots to them.

The officers responsible were nearly all of them Communists and not "fascist agents or Horthyist officers." The Army's revolt was a result of the turn of events which took place during the night on the banks of the Danube in the neo-Gothic building which overlooks Parliament.

On the second floor an extraordinary meeting of the Central Committee of the Workers' Party, presided over by Gero, took place at 22.30. Thanks to a personal report by one of the participants, it is possible to give a detailed account of this historic meeting. Assessing the situation, Gero began by trying to convince his colleagues of the necessity of a Soviet intervention, as the "popular forces" (*népi erök* in Hungarian; this is the title he gave to the political police) were being overwhelmed and the government was in danger. Janos Kadar and then Gyula Kallai (another Titoist who had just been released from prison) replied that the only way to avoid catastrophe was for Gero to resign immediately. Istvan Hidas (Vice President) and Laszlo Piros (Home Secretary) violently opposed this suggestion. Piros referred to Imre Nagy and his friends as "accomplices of the fascists who are at the moment sweeping through the capital ..."

The youth, meanwhile, were in the midst of their all-too-specific struggle against Soviet armoured cars and political police for the abstract ideas of "liberty" and "democracy". They had no leader, no definite programme; they only felt that their courage would guide them.

Budapest's youth, which filled the streets of the capital on 23rd October, was joined by the entire population. By "youth" we mean all citizens from 14 to 30 years of age—students, apprentices of the Csepel and Ujpest factories, and school-boys. The young people who began the manifestation of 23rd October were mainly led by students, including scholars of economics and those of the Lenin Institute. Thus, that afternoon those who demanded that the programme of democratisation and "desatellisation" be accelerated, were precisely those young persons who were best informed about politics ... Most of them were members of the Communist Party, and they continued as Marxists. It was they who started the Revolution, with the support of writers and Communist journalists.

Intellectuals were thus at the source of this Revolution, as in 1848. A few hours later some of the workers of Budapest joined the insurgents ... Often, under the leadership of the local secretary of the Communist Party, workers assembled in groups and then left together to fight the enemy ...

Thomas Schreiber, Le Monde (Paris), 4 December

Erno Gero's Speech

Budapest

Dear Comrades, Beloved Friends, Working People of Hungary!

... Of course we want a socialist democracy and not a bourgeois democracy. In accord with our Party and our convictions, our working class and people are jealously guarding the achievements of our people's democracy, and they will not permit anyone to touch them. We shall defend these achievements under all circumstances from whichever quarter they may be threatened. Today the chief aim of the enemies of our people is to shake the power of the working class, to loosen the peasant-worker alliance, to undermine the leadership of the working class in our country and to upset their faith in its party, in the Hungarian Workers' Party. They are endeavouring to loosen the close friendly relations between our nation, the Hungarian People's Republic, and other countries building socialism, especially between our country and the socialist Soviet Union. They are trying to loosen the ties between our party and the glorious Communist Party of the Soviet Union, the party of Lenin, the party of the 20th Congress.

They slander the Soviet Union. They assert that we trade with the Soviet Union on an unequal footing, that our relations with the Soviet Union are not based on equality, and allege that our independence has to be defended, not against the imperialists, but against the Soviet Union. All this is a barefaced lie — hostile slanders which do not contain a grain of truth. The truth is that the Soviet Union has not only liberated our people from the yoke of Horthy fascism and German imperialism, but that even at the end of the war, when our country lay prostrate, she stood by us and concluded pacts with us on the basis of full equality; ever since, she has been pursuing this policy.

There are people who want to create a conflict between proletarian internationalism and Hungarian patriotism. We Communists are Hungarian patriots. We were patriots in the prisons of Horthy fascism and in the difficult years of underground work and illegality ... We declare that we do everything in our power to build up socialism in our country ... on a Marxist-Leninist basis—which we have in common with other socialist countries—at the same time taking into account the peculiarities of our country, its economic and social situation, and Hungarian traditions. Yet, while we proclaim that we are patriots, we also energetically state that we are not nationalists. We are waging a constant fight against chauvinism, anti-Semitism and all other reactionary, anti-social and inhuman trends and views. Therefore, we condemn those who try to spread the poison of chauvinism among our youth, and who use the democratic freedom which our state has assured the working people for nationalistic demonstrations.

However, not even this demonstration shakes the resolution of our party to proceed on the road of developing socialist democracy. We are patriots but at the same time we are also proletarian internationalists.

Our relations with the Soviet Union and all other countries building socialism are based on the fact that our parties — leading parties in our respective countries — are inspired by the teachings of Marxism-Leninism, that we love our people and respect all other peoples, and that we follow the principle of complete equality and non-interference in each other's affairs, while at the same time, we give friendly mutual aid to each other. We help each other in order to further the progress of socialism in our countries and the victory of the lofty ideals of socialism in the whole world ...

The unity of the Party is always a great necessity. Without unity our Party would have been unable to defy the murderous terror of Horthy fascism for a quarter of a century. Without the unity of our Party and the working class, the people's democracy could not have triumphed in our country and the working class allied to the laboring peasantry could not have gained power. This unity, the unity of the Party, working class and working people, must be guarded as the apple of our eye. Let our Party organisations oppose with discipline and complete unity any attempt to create disorder, nationalistic well-poisoning, and provocation.

Worker-Comrades, Workers! We must put it frankly: the question now is whether we want a socialist democracy or a bourgeois democracy. The question is: do we want to build socialism in our country or to make a hole in the building of socialism and then open the door for capitalism? The question is: do you allow the power of the working class and the worker-peasant alliance to be undermined, or will you stand up resolutely, disciplined, and in complete unity with our entire working population, to defend the worker's power and the achievements of socialism? ...

Radio Kossuth

"Down with Gero!"

Budapest

The Hungarian police fired tonight on a crowd assembled before the Budapest radio building ...

The shooting incident came when a crowd gathered before the headquarters of the Budapest radio and became restive. It shouted: "Down with Gero!"

The crowd sent a delegation into the building. Shortly afterward flares were sent up from the roof of the radio headquarters. Five trucks filled with armed soldiers appeared and tried to make their way through the crowd. The crowd refused to give way and the trucks left.

The crowd waited. When the youth delegation failed to emerge from the building the crowd began to press against the doors. This was the signal for the political police to throw tear bombs. Apparently these were not effective and firing began.

Previously the demonstration had been disciplined and peaceful. The police made no attempt to interfere. One meeting held across the Danube in Buda, the right bank of Budapest, numbered nearly 10,000 persons. Among them were 500 officers and soldiers.

The red-white-and-green of Hungary's national colors waved in the air and ornamented every buttonhole. The flags were supplemented by banners inscribed with slogans, such as *"Do Not Stop Half Way: Away with Stalinism"*, *"Independence and Freedom"*, *"We Want New Leaders: We Put Our Trust in Imre Nagy"* and *"Hurrah for the Poles"*.

As the demonstrators marched this evening past the Hungarian Parliament, crowned with its illuminated star, they shouted: "Put out the red star." An hour later the star had been extinguished and the Parliament buildings were draped with the Hungarian national flag.

The demonstrations began after students held meetings at noon at universities in Budapest.

Office workers from Pest, the city's left bank, quickly attached themselves to the students, as did passers-by ... Gatherings were held in a half dozen public squares, generally before a statue of a national hero.

At every meeting a list of resolutions was distributed. They expressed hatred of Mr. Rakosi and resentment over Hungary's relations with the Soviet Union. The resolutions demanded:

Withdrawal of Soviet troops from Hungary in accordance with the 1947 peace treaty and publication of Hungary's trade agreements and reparation payments to the Soviet Union ...

A reshuffling of the Government with Mr. Nagy as leader and an open trial of Mr. Rakosi ...

Restoration of Hungary's traditional national emblem and her traditional Army uniforms instead of the present Soviet-style dress.

Destruction of a giant Stalin statue in a Budapest square. In the course of the demonstrations, the marchers in fact tried, though without success, to tear down the statue.

Attached to the list of resolutions was a statement that the Government had refused to permit them to be printed or broadcast.

It was announced that a mass meeting would be held at the Polytechnical University tomorrow to give further consideration to the resolutions.

John MacCormac, New York Times, 24 October

The Battle of the Radio Building

Budapest

In the early evening of 23 October enthusiastic students had demonstrated at the Bem statue, in front of the parliament building, and also in front of the radio building. They were disciplined, orderly demonstrators. Employees of the radio station greeted them with the Hungarian national flag from the balcony. A deputation went to see the management and made requests. Agreement was reached on several points. When the delegates appeared on the balcony they were prevented from talking to the crowd by irresponsible hooligans who intermingled with the crowd in increasing numbers. The delegates were not even listened to.

Stones were thrown at the windows of the radio building. The crowd attacked the mobile recording van which was in readiness to make a recording of the delegation's visit. Another car was burnt. At this stage most of the students and young workers left the scene in groups. From the Koerut (Ring Road) new groups and, later on, armed hooligans arrived. Somewhere they had broken the gates of a barracks and got hold of weapons. The crowd now broke the gate of the radio building. The guards tried to keep them off with water hoses, at the same time trying to extinguish the flames of the burning car. When this was of no avail they were compelled to use tear gas. The situation was becoming more and more acute, minute by minute.

The windows of the building were broken by the crowd and people climbed through the fence. They had armed themselves with bricks from a nearby building site and did much damage. The slogan now was: "Occupy the radio". The guards fired shots into the air. The guards then tried to repel the attack without harming the attackers but the crowd fired more and more shots. The first victim was a major of the State Security authority. During the first hours six soldiers were shot dead. But the security guards did not fire. There was a state of siege in the radio building but transmissions went out undisturbed.

Later on, two lorries arrived with armed hooligans. They occupied nearby buildings and fired at the studio. Then, and only then, as a last resort — after many guards had been killed and innumerable ones had been wounded — did they receive the order to return the fire. The attackers, in possession of automatic pistols and hand grenades, intensified their assault more and more. In the mad fire of bullets, the workers of the radio managed to broadcast. When the mob broke into the building the radio workers prevented the provocateurs from succeeding in silencing Radio Kossuth.

As you can hear, dear listeners, the program of Radio Kossuth is somewhat different from the scheduled program, but the Hungarian radio — Radio Kossuth — is on the air. No counter-revolutionary hordes, not even well organised counter-revolutionaries can silence it. Our studio has suffered great damage. Many a security guard has died a hero's death. The workers of the radio stood in the fire of bullets, often in the fire of machine-gun bullets, but not in vain. Already in the small hours of this morning we were on the air and have been on the air all day. This is Radio Kossuth Budapest.

Gyoergy Kalmar, Radio Kossuth, 24 October

Violence, Arms, Barricades

Budapest

The revolt began as a series of demonstrations that remained peaceful until about 10:30 o'clock Tuesday evening. The trouble began in front of the Budapest radio station when a delegation that had entered it to request the broadcasting of its "sixteen points" was arrested by political policemen who were guarding the building.

The crowd demanded their release and tried to storm the doors. At first the policemen tried to drive the demonstrators back with tear gas. Then they opened fire, killing one demonstrator and wounding several others.

When this correspondent arrived at midnight the radio station had been stormed. Its lower floors had been occupied by the demonstrators.

while the political police held the upper ones. A group of students had mounted a balcony in front of the building, hung out Hungarian flags and Hungary's pre-Communist national emblem.

A military command car that had been set on fire burned with dense smoke and a rubbery stench. The air in the narrow street in front of the station reeked of tear gas, which was reinforced by an occasional bomb hurled from the upper floors by the political policemen.

Trucks filled with Hungarian soldiers stood by, but their occupants were taking no action.

Shortly before midnight seven heavy Hungarian tanks rumbled into the area. Some of the demonstrators fled. But the leading tank displayed the national flag, its crew cheered the demonstrators and numbers of them mounted it to shake hands with the soldiers. One youth shouted: "Come on, the army is with us!" and the crowd surged forward again to invest the building.

It was obvious that the army was refusing to make common cause with the political police. An hour later several insurgents were observed with tommy guns in their hands. They said they had obtained them from the soldiers.

Meanwhile, the crowd was beginning to grow more violent. It threw up barricades at street intersections. These were flimsy affairs made of park benches but they were guarded by youths with tommy guns.

At one intersection the crowd overturned the automobile of a state official. It seemed for a moment as if an American car would share that fate, but the crowd grew good-humored when it realised that the car was being driven by a Western newspaper man.

At 1:30 a.m. Wednesday the crowd stormed the plant of *Szabad Nep*, principal Communist newspaper. They brought with them the body of a dead demonstrator wrapped in a national flag.

The newspaper had just issued a one-page extra edition condemning the political police force for having opened fire on the demonstrators at the radio station.

Meanwhile, other insurgents stormed a Soviet bookstore, threw books into the street and set fire to them. The headquarters of the Soviet-Hungarian Friendship Society was wrecked ...

John MacCormac, New York Times, 27 October

Stalin Falls
Nickelsdorf

The 5,000 students who were meeting in front of the Petofi Monument in Budapest were joined shortly after dusk by thousands of workers and others. The great crowd then marched to the Stalin monument. Ropes were wound round the statue's neck, and, to cheers, the crowd attempted to topple the statue. But it would not budge. They finally managed to melt Stalin's knees by using welding torches.

When the body of the statue broke apart and his legs crashed on the ground, the crowd started shouting. "Russians go home, Russians go home." They also shouted "Away with Gero", "Long live Nagy," and "Give us back the Church."

[When the 24-foot Stalin monument was erected on the grounds of the Budapest City Park in 1951, a Roman Catholic church had to be demolished to make enough space for its huge concrete base.

It is inscribed with the words *"A Nagy Sztáliniak a hálás Magyar Nép"* (To the great Stalin, from the grateful Hungarian people). The sculptor was Kistaludi-Strobl.]

With hammers, iron pipes, and various other tools, the crowd cut and broke the monument into countless pieces. Several demonstrators told me they wanted a souvenir of that — Stalin. While the Stalin Monument was being attacked, another crowd stormed the building of the Congress of Trade Unions, broke a huge Red Star from the roof, and threw it to the pavement. Police were standing by but made no attempt to interfere.

I have never seen more determination in the faces of a crowd ... I'm sure they were all ready to risk their lives for their cause ...

An Austrian Eye-Witness, Manchester Guardian, 25 October

"Ozymandias"
Budapest

... As to Stalinism itself, the best symbol of its fate is the bronze memorial to the late dictator on the Stalin Square. Demonstrators wrenched off the huge metal monument ... and dragged it like a strange sacrificial animal down the street, howling with joy. Two jagged bronze feet, each the size of a man, are all that remains now on the pedestal.

Gordon Shepherd, Daily Telegraph (London), 27 October

The Politburo in Crisis
Budapest

19:30: At today's session, the Politburo of the Central Committee of the Hungarian Worker's Party decided the next meeting of the Central Committee will convene on 31 October 1956. The agenda will be: (1) the political situation and tasks of the Party-speaker, Erno Gero. (2) Organisational questions.

20:23: [The previous announcement was declared "erroneous".] At today's session, the Politburo ... decided that the next session of the Central Committee will convene in the next few days ...

22:22: Dear Listeners, you now hear a special announcement — The Politburo ... called on the Central Committee to meet immediately in order to discuss the present situation and the tasks to be carried out.

24:00: At today's session, the Politburo . . . decided to convene a meeting of the Central Committee for this very evening. The meeting is now in progress.

08:23: The Hungarian News Agency reported that the Central Committee had been in session all night and announced the results of new Politburo and Central Committee elections.

Radio Kossuth and Hungarian News Agency, 23—24 October

Nagy as "Prisoner"

Budapest

When young Hungarian blood was already flowing, Sandor Erdei and Laszlo Benjamin and I decided to call on the potentates then in power in an attempt to bring them to their senses and demand that they should not allow Hungarian youth to be fired on. In vain. They did not interrupt their deliberations. What did the life of hundreds or thousands of students and workers, or that of a nation matter to them? They just carried on with their discussions. Woolly-minded writers had no business to poke their noses into their affairs. We sent in the demand of the Writers' Association that they should hand over power to those who enjoyed the affection of the people and that they should not order firing on the people. For an hour and a quarter — from 22.30 to 23.45 — we waited and waited. For a second we saw Istvan Kovacs and Joszef Revai emerge with frightened faces . . .

Finally, we were admitted to Andras Hegedus' room. He told the lie that a fascist counter-revolution had broken out which they would quell by arms. Should they not be strong enough to do it, they would call in Soviet troops. He said all this when, on their orders, the university students marching in Sandor Street were already being murdered; when the calling-in of Soviet troops was already a fait accompli. He said that smilingly, like someone who had already thought out the devilish plan together with his accomplices of trying to shield behind Imre Nagy. But we could not see Imre Nagy, and could not talk to him. He was then indeed a prisoner. We only saw his son-in-law, Ferenc Janosi, who had been persecuted and deprived of his military rank, hanging about lonely and haggard in the waiting room, and who was panic-stricken about his fate. Thus, on the night of the revolution, we returned to the Writers' Union, when death on caterpillar tracks—the tanks—was roaring in the streets of Budapest, and when it was in fact Andras Hegedus and Erno Gero who were at the controls of the tanks, guns, and machine guns.

Zoltan Zelk, Free Radio Kossuth (31 October)

Taking Power in Debrecen

A woman, who later fled, described the revolution in Debrecen . . . the second largest provincial city in Hungary, with a population of about 140,000. It lies near the Rumanian border and is the economic and cultural center of Eastern Hungary . . . Meetings were held everywhere in the university. Demands in twenty points were compiled and submitted to the city's Party committee on 22 October. The Party functionaries did not risk raising objections, and the youths impatiently awaited the newspaper with the publication of their demands.

They read the 23 October edition of *Neplap* eagerly . . . the otherwise so despised party organ . . . but found that their theses had been tampered with. They decided to demonstrate before the local Party building at 11 o'clock that very morning.

At 11 a.m. Debrecen was entirely peaceful and orderly. Only a group of university students, with national colors, marched by the ancient church, turned into Bishop Balthasar Street, and stopped across the way from the Party headquarters. The students waved the *Neplap* in their hands and shouted "You've broken your promise! You've changed our demands! We want them printed . . ." Soon the functionary Kulesar appeared on the balcony. He spoke very confidently. The alterations of the twenty points were just printer's errors and had nothing to do with the Party. The Party supported the students' declaration fully and unconditionally . . . After Kulesar retired, the students had a short discussion. Then they formed two groups. One went to the large rail-car manufacturing plant to invite the workers to a joint demonstration in the main street at 5 p.m.; the other went directly to the Party print-shop to make sure that the newspaper printed their demands correctly . . .

I was walking from the Cathedral to the main square and heard a steady murmur coming from the center of town. I began to hurry along, noticing that from all sides people were coming on to the main street. I couldn't get any nearer . . . There were already about 2000 persons. The trolleys stopped, blocked by the crowd. The cars seemed strange: their red stars were missing. Here and there I heard the voice of a news-vendor, and in all hands I saw copies of the new edition of *Neplap* with the right twenty points . . . Indi-

viduals shouted: "Long live the 15th of March!...
Long live the free press!... Long live Poland!..."
Suddenly all eyes were fixed on the former Tisza
Palace, now the seat of the railroad management.
Two or three youngsters were on the roof. They
began to take down the red star. Everyone became
very silent... And I knew the revolution had
begun. When the hated star fell and broke, a
joyful shout went up... Then the Hungarian
anthem was sung... The crowd pushed forward
and in half-an-hour the star on the City Hall was
down... Windows were open everywhere; people
shouted happily. Red-white-green flags flew from
almost every house... Some had a hole in the
middle...

Toward 7 p.m. the revolutionaries moved slowly
and with dignity into Kossuth Square. They
wanted to march to the police headquarters to
take down the last official red star in town. The
crowd was growing larger all the time... I could
hardly see the head of the column. Suddenly there
were shots and cries from up front. The police
had opened fire on the unarmed crowd. The word
spread quickly that a man had been killed and
three wounded... Shot after shot... I went
home.

The next day I learned that there had been no
"fighting" since the people had no arms at all. A
man whom I knew myself, an elderly shoemaker,
had been killed... On the police headquarters the
last red star remained, for a time, undamaged. But
on the same day the Revolutionary Committee
was created. The city government was taken over
by freedom-fighters. Then the last red star in
Debrecen fell...   *Neue Zürcher Zeitung, 29 January 1957*

Interviews with Students

Vienna

The student demonstrations were planned not
on Tuesday, but on Monday night, October 22, in
the collegium of the Polytechnic Institute, in the
King's Castle in Buda. A student who took part
gave me the following account: —

"After dinner on Monday night, the 1,500 students in our collegium were suddenly called to a
meeting in the hall. The Army colonel who lived
above us in the King's Castle and taught military
science at the Polytechnic Institute told us that a
demonstration was being planned for the following day. We were to demonstrate our sympathy
for Poland through a march to the statue of Josef
Bem—the Polish general who led the Hungarians
during the revolution of 1848. This was to be our
symbol of protest against the present Government."

The student said it was a long and controversial
meeting, and lasted until 1 a.m. Together with the
colonel, the students framed 14 demands, which
the mass student demonstration was to submit to
the Government. At first the demands were
moderate, but as the meeting progressed they became more radical. The first five finally emerged
as frankly political demands. They called for: —

(1) A central congress of the Communist Party
to elect a new leadership; (2) Imre Nagy to replace Hegedus as Premier; (3) continued friendship
with the Soviet Union, but on a new basis;
(4) withdrawal of Soviet troops from Hungary;
(5) the holding of free elections.

Some of the rest dealt with economic questions,
and the others concerned the re-establishment of
academic freedom in Hungary

During the night these demands were printed
by the Polytechnic students for distribution at the
mass meeting in the university park on the following day. Also, all cars passing the park were
stopped and the passengers handed copies.

The same student, who was corroborated by
others, told me about the course the meeting took
on Tuesday: —

"It commenced about noon. About 1,500 were
present, including the officer candidates from the
Military Technical Academy. This military participation was particularly noticeable, and the
crowd grew rapidly as student delegations from the
law, agricultural, and medical faculties in other
parts of the city arrived. Several workers' delegations from factories nearby in Buda also took part.

"The same colonel presided over the meeting,
and was assisted by professors and student
leaders. He began by saying that the Minister of
the Interior had refused permission for a request
to demonstrate, and suggested we send a delegation now to get that permission.

"A group of 10 professors, students, and a few
workers was dispatched at 2.15, but returned in
half an hour without having succeeded. They
brought instead the Assistant Minister of the
Interior, who began to address us with the usual
empty words. We whistled and shouted, and the
colonel joined in ridiculing him. Finally, we voted
to demonstrate anyway, and at 3 p.m. we began
our march along the bank of the Danube."

From this point onwards, the initial organisation began to be superseded by the weight of
outsiders joining the procession. Another of the
participants told me: —

"I am sure they wanted us to demonstrate for
reforms of the regime, not for its overthrow.
When this began to happen we were branded
'counter-revolutionaries.' However, once it began,
there was no stopping.

"Just as we left the university park word passed
around that the bulk of the medical students
were demonstrating across the river at the monument to Petofi—the Hungarian national poet—

hero of the revolution of 1848. We decided we would join them after our demonstration."

Most of these students got no farther than the Parliament building, for by the time they swarmed into Kossuth Square there was already a large crowd of students and others assembled. Some merged with the crowd in calling for Imre Nagy, others continued on to the Petofi Monument, others dispersed to different parts of the city to demonstrate, and still others went back to the university. All semblance of unified organisation disappeared.

When Mr. Nagy finally did appear on the Parliament steps, he left the crowd unsatisfied by his guarded remarks. As one student said to me: "He was only a private citizen now, and was afraid to answer our demands because of Gero ... At the same time, we did not push our demands for the removal of Premier Hegedus in favour of Nagy, for fear of armed intervention by the Government."

A 17-year-old girl who studied at the electrical technical school in Budapest spoke of her aims that afternoon: "I joined the crowd in front of the Parliament at 4.30 that afternoon. For weeks we had been talking about reforms—at first educational, and then more and more political and economic. We were peaceful. We only wanted to better the lot of the students. No one thought it would end in revolution. We sang our national anthem and then put out the Red Star which shone on the top of the Parliament."

In the disordered events which ensued, the riots on front of the radio station that evening mark a decisive turn in the road from protest to outright revolt. After it became known that the station was crowded with AVH men and that the director had refused permission to a student delegation to broadcast their expanded demands, the station became a central rallying point for all the separate demonstrations throughout the city.

Workers who had finished for the day, students, and, generally, civilians of all types pushed their way through the streets. Trucks were used to transport people from all over the city to the station, the simple call "to the radio station" being enough to jam the empty trucks with willing demonstrators.

A young architect who responded to the call,

and who subsequently became my interpreter and guide among his fellow Hungarian exiles, described the sence as follows: —

"By 10 p.m. the people, by their sheer weight, were pushing in the doors of the station. At first the AVH tried to disperse us with tear-gas, and then to keep us away by a united charge with bayoneted rifles held crossways. We resisted by tripping and kicking them. Then, for fear of their lives, they began shooting. It was terrible—innocent people were killed because they could not move in the crowd. It was the last blow.

"Some of the people had small sporting rifles which they had taken from the officers of Mohosz —the Hungarian Voluntary Defense Federation, a military sports organisation sponsored by the Communist Party. They returned the AVH fire as best they could.

"Then two trucks of soldiers arrived from Buda across the river, but neither officers nor soldiers fired on the people. No order was given, and the soldiers remained in the trucks. They began slipping their guns over the side of the trucks into our outstretched hands.

"I took a machine-gun and began firing it at the AVH in the station windows. By 11 a.m. the next day the crowd had occupied the radio station but it was totally destroyed by then."

So, revolution and bloodshed began in earnest. What had commenced as an organised student demonstration for reform of the regime snowballed in a matter of hours into a mass revolt against the system itself. All participants with whom I talked agreed that the sympathy of the Army was never in doubt. The young architect, who spent the next six days on the rooftops against the AVH, put it this way: —

"Some Army units, especially their officers who were revolutionary at heart, wanted to remain neutral at first, for they feared we could not succeed. Such hesitation could not last, however, for they hated Communism—and the AVH particularly—as much as we. By Wednesday morning the Government had to call for Soviet help, for all its internal supports—except the hated AVH— had collapsed."

George Sherman, The Observer (London), 11 November

24 OCTOBER

"What Has Happened in One Night?..."

Budapest

Dear Listeners, we wish you good morning! Listen, please, to our morning broadcast. We now read an announcement:

Fascist reactionary elements have started an armed attack against our public buildings and have also attacked our police. In the interest of restoring order, and until further notice is given, we announce that it is forbidden to hold any meetings, rallies, and parades. Police units have been issued orders to act with the full force of the law against violators of this order.

We repeat our announcement... [04 : 30]

Attention, Attention, Attention

The Ministry of Interior of the Hungarian People's Republic addresses the population of Budapest. The suppression of looting counter-revolutionary groups is still under way. We ask the population not to leave home before 9 a.m. except in case of urgent business... [06 : 30]

Attention! Attention! The dastardly armed attack of counter-revolutionary gangs during the night has created an extremely serious situation. The bandits have broken into factories and public buildings and have murdered many civilians, members of the national defence forces, and fighters of the State security organs. The Government was unprepared for these bloody and dastardly attacks, and has therefore applied for help to the Soviet formations stationed in Hungary under the terms of the Warsaw Treaty. In compliance with the Government's request, the Soviet formations are taking part in the restoration of order. The Government appeals to the inhabitants of the capital to remain calm, to condemn the bloody havoc of the counter-revolutionary gangs, and to support everywhere Hungarian and Soviet troops maintaining order. The liquidation of the counter-revolutionary gangs is the most sacred cause of every honest Hungarian worker, of the people, and of the fatherland. At this moment, we are concentrating all our strength on this task... [09 : 00]

National independence, friendship with the Soviets on a basis of mutual respect and complete equality—yesterday afternoon university youth began its demonstration with these correct ideas.

Yes, these ideas were really correct and wise! What has happened to them in one night? What happened to the beautiful patriotic thoughts? What have the misled youths and the counter-revolutionary bandits, hiding in their tanks, done to the beautiful patriotic thoughts?

Shooting in the streets accompanied by our national anthem! Plundering the slaughter-house accompanied by the waving of red-white-green banners! The shooting in the sick-ward of the clinic on the Ulliciut, and an assault on the Kozert accompanied by the "Talpra Magyar" [Hungarian revolutionary poem]! Is this Hungarian independence? Robbing. Plundering. Shedding workers' blood under cover of the sacred ideas of national independence and sovereignty. These are no patriots! These are black scoundrels or misled adolescents. The soldiers and workers who come to disarm them are the true patriots. We greet them and the Soviet soldiers rushing to their aid. Let the population of our capital help them everywhere!

Radio Kossuth

"Chronology"

Vienna

A curious chronological fact has been noticed here. It would seem that the first Soviet tanks went into action at 4.30 a.m. yesterday, but it was not until 8.30 a.m. that it was announced that the Government had invoked Soviet military assistance. The radio had been making almost continous announcements... *The Times (London), 26 October*

Tanks, Jets

Nickelsdorf

Travellers reaching this Austrian border town said that heavy artillery was in operation and several Budapest buildings were burning when they left the Hungarian capital today. Tanks were reported to have ringed Budapest along a perimeter 25 miles outside the capital and there were said to be at least 350 persons dead, including soldiers.

The travellers said Hungarian police and troops did not appear to be taking any action against the rioters, but were looking on the scene with detachment. Most of the soldiers had torn off the Communist badges from their caps. An Austrian eye-witness of the rising said:

"I woke up this morning to the sound of machine-gun fire and explosions which sounded like artillery. The trams weren't running. The fighting was taking place along the Korut and Voerös Boulevards, and most of the side streets were blocked by tanks. Early in the morning a large number of jet fighters flew over and repeatedly opened fire at groups of civilians who were demonstrating. I couldn't see whether the fighters were Russian or Hungarian.

"When I left the city by car at noon I saw a great number of dead soldiers and civilians on the streets. Driving was extremely dangerous since shooting was still going on ..."

Reuters and United Press, 25 October

New Prime Minister

Budapest

An important announcement follows [08 : 13]: The Central Committee of the Hungarian Workers' Party at its meeting on 24th October 1956 has elected the following members: Comrades Ferenc Donath, Geza Losonczy, Gyorgy Lukacs, Ferenc Munnich, and Imre Nagy.

Members of the newly elected Politburo: Comrades Antal Apro, Sandor Gaspar, Erno Gero, Andras Hegedus, Janos Kadar, Gyula Kallai, Karoly Kiss, Jozsef Kobol, Gyorgy Marosan, Imre Nagy and Zoltan Szanto.

Alternate members of the Politburo: Comrades Geza Losonczy and Sandor Ronai.

The Central Committee has confirmed Comrade Erno Gero as First Secretary.

Secretaries of the Central Committee: Comrades Ferenc Donath, Janos Kadar and Gyula Kallai.

The Central Committee recommends that the Presidential Council of the People's Republic elect Comrade Imre Nagy as Chairman of the Council of Ministers and Comrade Andras Hegedus as First Deputy Chairman.

The Central Committee has instructed the Politburo to draft without delay its recommendations for the solution of the tasks confronting the Party and the nation.

Attention, attention! We repeat the announcement:

Imre Nagy became the new Prime Minister and Andras Hegedus his first deputy.

Radio Kossuth

Nagy: "Cease Fighting!"

Budapest

Here is Imre Nagy [noon]:
People of Budapest, I announce that all those who cease fighting before 14.00 to-day, and lay down their arms in the interest of avoiding further bloodshed, will be exempted from martial law. At the same time I state that as soon as possible and by all the means at our disposal, we shall realise, on the basis of the June 1953 Government program which I expounded in Parliament at that time, the systematic democratization of our country in every sphere of Party, State, political and economic life. Heed our appeal! Cease fighting, and secure the restoration of calm and order in the interest of the future of our people and nation. Return to peaceful and creative work!

Hungarians, Comrades, my friends! I speak to you in a moment filled with responsibility. As you know, on the basis of the confidence of the Central Committee of the Hungarian Workers' Party and the Presidential Council, I have taken over the leadership of the Government as Chairman of the Council of Ministers. Every possibility exists for the Government to realise my political program by relying on the Hungarian people under the leadership of the Communists. The essence of this program, as you know, is the far-reaching democratization of Hungarian public life, the realisation of a Hungarian road to socialism in accord with our own national characteristics, and the realisation of our lofty national aim: the radical improvement of the workers' living conditions.

However, in order to begin this work—together with you—the first necessity is to establish order, discipline and calm. The hostile elements that joined the ranks of peacefully demonstrating Hungarian youth, misled many well-meaning workers and turned against the people's democracy, against the power of the people. The paramount task facing everyone now is the urgent consolidation of our position. Afterwards, we shall be able to discuss every question, since the Government and the majority of the Hungarian people want the same thing. In referring to our great common responsibility for our national existence, I appeal to you, to every man, woman, youth, worker, peasant, and intellectual to stand fast and keep calm; resist provocation, help restore order, and assist our forces in maintaining order. Together we must prevent bloodshed, and we must not let this sacred national program be soiled by blood.

The Hungarian Government is preparing for peaceful and creative work. The Government is determined not to allow itself to be diverted from the road of democratisation, from realising a pro-

Portrait of Imre Nagy

Even during the many years he spent in Moscow as a Communist refugee Hungary's new Premier, Imre Nagy, was regarded as a strange sort of Communist by his comrades. Their puzzlement about him was expressed by the nickname they gave him: "kulak," the Russian word meaning a rich peasant of the sort Stalin exterminated in the early thirties. Mr. Nagy's Communist comrades called him "kulak" because in background, appearance and tastes he reminded them of the rich, solidly bourgeois peasants they had known in Hungary. A burly 6-foot 200-pounder, he never made any secret of his fondness for good food, good drink, good clothes.

Walking down the streets of Moscow he looked like a prosperous Hungarian peasant dressed in his Sunday best and on his way to church, rather than what he was: the Hungarian Communist party's farm expert on his way to his job as a specialist at the Soviet Agrarian Institute.

When he returned to Budapest with the Red Army in 1944 and had become one of Hungary's chief rulers, he continued his strange ways. He let his daughter marry a practicing Protestant minister. He liked to sit in Budapest cafés and discuss politics or the merits of different Hungarian football teams.

His wife, whom he married more than thirty-five years ago, was the daughter of a village clerk.

As early as 1945 Mr. Nagy's friends knew that he was politically "peculiar" and perhaps even dangerous. Though he had spent more than a quarter of his life in the Soviet Union and had become a Soviet citizen about 1930, he told his friends in Budapest that it was not necessary for Hungary to follow the Soviet Union in every respect.

This was arrant heresy, but then in the early post-war period trained Hungarian Communists were too few and far between to permit the luxury of purging them.

Imre Nagy — pronounced Imreh Nodge — was born in 1896 in a peasant family with strong religious faith of the stern Calvinist variety. As a young man he aspired to become a locksmith and was a locksmith's apprentice until World War I, when he entered the Austro-Hungarian Army. Captured by the Russians and taken home with them, he fought with the Bolsheviks in the Civil War and then went home to try to establish "workers' and peasants' rule" in his homeland.

There followed a quarter of a century where his life paralleled that of many another East European professional revolutionary. He played a minor role in the short-lived Communist Hungarian Government of Bela Kun and then went underground as a Communist organizer until he had to flee to the Soviet Union in 1929. In Moscow he continued to study Hungarians conditions and watched Stalin transform the Soviet Union with force and violence.

Back in Hungary after World War II he was the architect of the early post-war land reform, breaking up the large estates and giving small parcels to peasants and farm laborers. As a good Communist he took over the secret police for a time and harried anti-Communists. But always in the back of his head there apparently was hope that a Hungarian path to socialism could be reached...

New York Times, 25 October

From 1947 to 1953 he was Speaker of the Hungarian Parliament and a member of the central committee. On July 5, 1953, after the fall of Rakosi and failure of the "Russian" policy of emphasis on heavy industry and neglect of agriculture, Mr. Nagy was elected Prime Minister.

On February 20, 1955, Budapest radio announced that Mr. Nagy, who had not been seen in public since January 25, was seriously ill with coronary thrombosis and would not be able to return to work until April. On February 27 his son was relieved of his post as chief deputy Minister in the Ministry of Popular Culture. The previous week Szabad Nep had laid greater emphasis on the development of heavy industry in Hungary than at any time since June, 1953, when Mr. Nagy's "new course," with its emphasis on light industry and food production, was introduced.

On March 9 the central committee of the Hungarian Workers' Party condemned Mr. Nagy for "rightist deviation," though a careful distinction was drawn between the party decisions on the new course and Mr. Nagy's implementation of them.

Press attacks then followed thick and fast, most of them accusing Mr. Nagy of having caused a crisis by his neglect of heavy industry. Mr. Rakosi, then first secretary of the party, joined in the fray, and on April 18, 1955, Mr. Nagy was dismissed from his post by a unanimous vote of the National Assembly on the joint proposal of the party committee and the Government.

The Times (London), 25 October

gram corresponding with the interests of the Hungarian people and discussed with the broad masses of the people. We do not want to pursue a policy of revenge but of reconcilation. For this reason the Government has decided that all those who voluntarily and immediately lay down arms and cease fighting will not be subjected to summary prosecution, as is the case with groups which have so far surrendered.

Workers! Defend the factories and machines. This is your own treasure. He who destroys or loots harms the entire nation. Order, calm, discipline—these are now the slogans; they come before everything else.

Friends! Hungarians! I will soon announce in detail the program of the Government, and it will be debated in the National Assembly which will meet soon. Our future is at stake. Before us lies the great road of raising our national standards. Line up behind the Government. Ensure peace, the continuation of peaceful and creative labour, so that every worker of our country can work undisturbed for his own and his family's future. Stand behind the Party, stand behind the Government! Trust that we have learned from the mistakes of the past, and that we shall find the correct road for the prosperity of our country.

Radio Kossuth

"Murder, Arson, Death"
Budapest

The Council of Ministers of the Hungarian People's Republic has ordered that martial law should be applied throughout the country to acts calculated to overthrow the People's Republic and to acts of revolt, incitement, appeal and conspiracy to revolt, murder, manslaughter, arson, possession of explosives, crimes committed with explosives, indirect crimes, the use of force against the official authorities, the use of force against private individuals and the illegal possession of arms. Crimes in the categories coming under summary jurisdiction are punishable by death. This order comes into force immediately.

(Signed)   *Imre Nagy,*
Chairman of the Council of Ministers.
Radio Kossuth

A "Fait Accompli"
Budapest

Igazsag, the paper of the revolutionary Honved army and youth, describes in a report how and by whom Imre Nagy was terrorised. The reporter says that the Soviet troops had already been called in and martial law proclaimed when Imre Nagy become Premier. Thus, he was confronted with a *fait accompli* and for days could not master the situation. Even on Friday the Hegedus-Gero-clique still wanted to make Nagy sign a pre-dated letter calling on the Soviet troops to help crush the uprising. Naturally, Nagy would not sign the letter...

Free Radio Kossuth (31 October)

In the Factories
Budapest

Imre Nagy's address has been re-broadcast over the loudspeaker systems of many factories. Order has been completely restored at the Csepel iron and metallurgical works, and the counter-revolutionary groups outside the factory are also dispersing. According to the Party Committee of the "Red Star" tractor works, there is no trouble there. At the Lang engineering works, there were about 48—50 workers present around noon. They welcomed the Premier's speech. At the Ganz wagon works, a factory guard was organised at dawn. Both the guard and the workers welcomed the Government's announcement with joy. At the Klement Gottwald works, the majority of the workers are absent from the workshops. Those present heard Comrade Nagy's speech over the loudspeakers...

Radio Kossuth

Misgivings in Belgrade
Belgrade

Throughout the afternoon Yugoslavs on Belgrade's main street have been jostling around vendors of special editions of the evening paper carrying news of the day's events in Hungary. Rarely before has there been such excitement, and each new batch of papers has been sold within a few minutes of the sellers' first cries of: "Latest events in Budapest."

The violent storm which burst over the heads of the Hungarian Communist leaders almost as soon as they arrived home yesterday morning from their talks with Marshal Tito, has taken the Yugoslavs as much by surprise as certainly it did Mr. Gero and his politburo colleagues. In circles close to official sources there is a marked reluctance to comment on this turn of events; such comment as is being ventured suggests a certain anxiety that things might be "going too far," and that in such a situation "all the parties might be trying to turn it to their advantage."

The example of Yugoslavia has shown that there are limits set for "democratization" and "liberalization" under Communist régimes; and there are misgivings here that events in Hungary —and also in Poland—have taken a turn in which ultimately the influence and authority of the Communist Party and systems themselves might encounter serious challenge.

The Times (London), 25 October

Tito on Gero
Belgrade

...Things had already gone rather far, further than we knew, and Gero's visit to Yugoslavia and our joint declaration could no longer help. People in Hungary were absolutely against the Stalinist elements still in power; they asked for their removal and a turn to the road of democratization. When the Hungarian delegation headed by Gero returned to their country, Gero found himself in a difficult position and again showed his previous face. He called those hundreds of thousands of demonstrators, who at that time were still demonstrating, a gang and insulted almost the whole nation. Imagine how blind he was, what kind of a leader he was! At such a critical moment, when everything boils and when the whole nation is discontented, he dares to call that nation a gang, among whom a great number, and perhaps a majority were communists and young people. This was enough to blow up the powder-keg. Conflicts took place.

The point now is not to examine who fired the first shot. Gero called the army. It was a fatal mistake to call Soviet troops at the time when demonstrations were still going on. To call upon troops of another country to give lessons to the people of one's own country, even if shooting takes place, is a great mistake. This made the people even more furious and this is how a spontaneous uprising came about...

Marshal Tito, Borba (Belgrade), 16 November

Moscow's First Reaction

Budapest

Late in the evening of October 23 underground reactionary organizations attempted to start a counter-revolutionary revolt against the people's regime in Budapest.

This enemy adventure had obviously been in preparation for some time. The forces of foreign reaction have been systematically inciting anti-democratic elements for action against the lawful authority.

Enemy elements made use of the student demonstration that took place on 23 October to

Troops

According to the Warsaw agreement, Soviet intervention would have been justified only in case of foreign aggression on Hungarian territory. The only foreign aggressor on Hungarian territory, however, was the Soviet Union itself. Against this foreign intervention, military aid from the other parties to the treaty would have been justified. For reasons which can be understood but not approved, the other signatory powers did not extend any aid to Hungary...

It was well-known some units of the Soviet forces had been mobilized even during the first weeks of October 1956, when the discontent and resentment of the Hungarian people were beginning to manifest themselves more and more clearly.

On October 20 and 21, 1956, the Soviet Union set up floating bridges at Zahony on the Russian-Hungarian border. On the night of October 23—24, at 1 a.m., the first Russian motorized units crossed the Hungarian border. At that time, no mention was made of the Warsaw Pact. Then, no references were made to any Soviet obligations under this Pact...

Anna Kethly, Memorandum to the United Nations Commission on Hungary (1957)

bring out into the streets groups previously prepared by them, to form the nucleus of the revolt. They sent agitators into action who created confusion and tried to provoke mass disorder.

A number of governmental buildings and public enterprises were attacked. The fascist thugs who let themselves go began to loot shops, break windows in houses and institutions, and tried to destroy the equipment of industrial enterprises. Groups of rebels who succeeded in getting hold of arms caused bloodshed in a number of places.

The forces of revolutionary order began to repel the rebels. On orders of the reappointed Premier Imre Nagy martial law was declared in the city.

The Hungarian Government asked the USSR Government for help. In accordance with this request, Soviet military units, which are in Hungary under the terms of the Warsaw treaty, helped troops of the Hungarian Republic to restore order in Budapest. In many industrial enterprises workers offered armed resistance to the bandits who tried to damage and destroy equipment and to mount armed guards.

By the end of the day on 24th October the enemy adventure was liquidated. Order was restored in Budapest. Speaking on 24th October over the radio, the Chairman of the Council of Ministers Imre Nagy called on the whole people to maintain calm and order.

The attempts of the counter-revolutionaries to find supporters in Debrecen and some other towns met with no success.

The Central Committee of the Hungarian Workers' Party and the Government are receiving telegrams from all parts of the country in which Hungarian workers express their wrathful indignation at the criminal action of the counter-revolutionaries and assure the Party and Government of their readiness to defend staunchly the people's democratic regime against any enemy attempts and to strengthen friendship with the Soviet Union and with all Socialist countries.

Tass (Moscow), 24 October

Workers Join Students

Budapest

It was 4 a.m. when the first Soviet tanks and armored cars arrived in the city. Overnight another series of events had occurred. Workers in the suburbs had held meetings and drawn up demands generally in line with those of the students. To these had been added several specific points about factory-management councils and general increases in wages. At dawn the workers began marching into the city. Only about fifteen hundred of them were armed. All the rest had nothing but their bare hands and flags. No one was in command. Whoever spoke the loudest or made the most sense was obeyed. Impromptu committees and delegations formed, but the general impression was of huge convergent masses chanting slogans such as "Down with Gerö!" "Punish the murderers!" "We want Nagy!" Later in the morning, another cry was taken up that was heard all through the subsequent days: "Out with the Russkies!"

All through this second day furious battles raged. On one side were seventy Soviet tanks, fifty armored cars, and small arms and automatic weapons. On the other were twenty-five thousand students and nearly two hundred thousand workers steadily pouring in from outlying districts. The rebels had at this time about four thousand small arms. To escape the wildly shooting Soviets and AVH men, the insurgents broke into small groups and occupied strategic corner buildings. Some entrenched themselves in military barracks. But still there was no central command, and each rebel unit operated on its own. This lack of organization contributed largely to the heavy casualties. No one plotted this revolt. It just happened.

Leslie B. Bain, The Reporter (New York), 15 November

A Communist Correspondent Has Difficulties

Budapest

I was not an eyewitness of the start of the revolution in Budapest on October 23. I have pieced together the account which follows from those who were, both Hungarians and a British Communist, Charles Coutts, English editor of *World Youth*, who had lived in Budapest for three years.

It began with a students' demonstration, partly to show the students' sympathy for the people of Poland, who that weekend, through Gomulka and the Central Committee of the Polish United Workers' Party, had resoluted rebuffed an attempt by an unprecedented delegation of Soviet leaders to get tough with them. This sturdy assertion of independence captured the imagination of the Hungarians, and the student orators who addressed the demonstration from the statue of Josef Bem, a Polish general who helped lead the Hungarians in 1849, recalled the words of Petofi:

Our battalions have combined two nations,
And what nations! Polish and Magyar!
Is there any destiny that is stronger
Than these two when they are united?

...The crowds which had gathered outside the radio station to ask that the students' demands be broadcast were fired on by A.V.H. men, 300 of whom were in the building. This was, without question, the spark that turned peaceful demonstrations ("the quiet and orderly behaviour of the marchers was impressive," Coutts had telephoned the *Daily Worker*) into a revolution ...

Where did the arms come from that found their way so speedily into the hands of the workers and students of Budapest? According to Kádár (*Daily Worker*, November 20) there were "hidden arms" on the Szabadsaghegy (Liberty Hill), and the young people had been told at midday, before the demonstration, to go to a "certain place" where they would find them. This version of the arming of the people side-steps the whole question of the attitude of the Hungarian People's Army. The troops in Budapest, as later in the provinces, were of two minds: there were those who were neutral and there were those who were prepared to join the people and fight alongside them. The neutral ones (probably the minority) were prepared to hand over their arms to the workers and students so that they could do battle against the A.V.H. with them. The others brought their arms with them when they joined the revolution. Furthermore, many sporting rifles were taken by the workers from the factory armouries of the Hungarian Voluntary Defence Organisation. The "mystery" of how the people were armed is no mystery at all. No one has yet been able to produce a single weapon manufactured in the West.

The Hungarian Stalinists, having made two calamitous mistakes, now made a third—or rather, it would be charitable to say, had it thrust on them by the Soviet Union. This was the decision to invoke a non-existent clause of the Warsaw Treaty and call in Soviet troops. This first Soviet intervention gave the people's movement exactly the impetus needed to make it united, violent and nation-wide. It seems probable, on the evidence, that Soviet troops were already in action three or four hours before the appeal, made in the name of Imre Nagy as his first act on becoming Prime Minister. That is debatable, but what is not debatable is that the appeal was in reality made by Gero and Hegedus; the evidence of this was later found and made public. Nagy became Prime

Minister precisely twenty-four hours too late, and those who throw mud at him for making concessions to the Right in the ten days he held office should consider the appalling mess that was put into his hands by the Stalinists when, in desperation, they officially quit the stage.

With Nagy in office it would still have been possible to avert the ultimate tragedy if the people's two demands had been met immediately —if the Soviet troops had withdrawn without delay, and if the security police had been disbanded. But Nagy was not a free agent during the first few days of his premiership. It was known in Budapest that his first broadcast were made— metaphorically, if not literally—with a tommy-gun in his back . . .

My second dispatch from Budapest, telephoned on November 2, dealt with the causes of the revolution and with how it broke out in Budapest. The dispatch consisted entirely of an interview with Charles Coutts. Except for a short "intro" of my own, everything in it was taken down as Coutts told it, while we sat together at breakfast that Friday morning in the Duna Hotel . . .

When the dispatch was received there was a half-hearted attempt to dismiss Coutts as "politically naive." George Matthews, assistant general-secretary of the Communist Party, who was standing in at the *Daily Worker* in place of the editor, J. R. Campbell, at that time in Moscow, blue-pencilled the dispatch to ribbons. I gather there was a certain amount of feeling about this among the staff. After all, Fryer might have got drunk, or had a nervous breakdown, or temporarily lost his political bearings and balance. But here was old Charlie Coutts, whom everyone knew as a reliable, level-headed man, backing him up . . .

For instance, Coutts quoted a Hungarian Communist Party member who said to him during the fighting: "The feeling here is like that May Day in 1947, when we danced in the streets." This was omitted. So was a passage about the "revolt of the intellectuals." So was a statement that "the Communist Party had ceased to be a Communist Party —it had become an organ of the State and nothing else," backed up by what honest Communists had told him: "Ours is not a Communist Party. You can't change anything."

Particularly significant was the cutting-out of Coutts' statement that the security police was deliberately created by a dominant clique inside the Party, the people who had returned from the U.S.S.R.: Rakosi, Farkas, and Gero, and that this dominant clique, "incapable of independent thought, relied on the thinking of the Soviet Communist Party, right or wrong. They felt that if the Soviet Party made a turn, then they had to make a turn."

The *Daily Worker* also deleted Coutts' considered opinion that there was no reason for calling in Soviet troops on October 24, other than the concern of Gero and the other leaders to save their skins and their positions. "They were not called in to restore order nor to defend Socialism," he told me. His description of how forty A.V.H. men trapped in the Budapest Party headquarters were captured and hanged and of how thirteen and fourteen-year-olds were fighting with machine-guns and tommy-guns was also left out. Coutts told me how Freedom Fighters said to him: "It is better to die than live as they have made us live." The *Daily Worker* thought that this, too, had better be withheld from its customers. Finally, Coutts' forecast of the emergence, for the first time in eight years, of "a real Communist Party in Hungary, not a Party run by professional politicians and bureaucrats but led by those Communists who have remained true to principle and have suffered for it"—this, too, fell victim to "normal editing." Readers can judge for themselves how far this was in fact "normal editing and subbing," and how far it was the result of a deliberate decision by Party leaders afraid to let the whole distressing, shocking and—for them— dangerous truth be known . . .

Peter Fryer, Hungarian Tragedy (London, 1956)

"Lies"

Budapest

I learned about the dramatic meetings of the Central Committee from a very good source . . . At the first one none of the new members of the CC participated, neither Imre Nagy (who had been asked to take part) nor Geza Losonczy or the others . . . So this first session was dominated by the purest Stalinist spirit. Not without some protests, Gero had pushed through the appeal to Soviet troops and the proclamation of martial law.

The extent to which he acted on his own initiative, or on orders, is as open question. In any case, with Machiavellian cunning, Gero and his

---

Marxism

"*A people which enslaves others forges its own chains.*"   KARL MARX

"*The victorious proletariat can force no blessings of any kind upon any foreign nation without undermining its own victory by so doing.*"   FREDERICK ENGELS

"*If Finland, if Poland, if the Ukraine break away from Russia, there is nothing bad about that. Anyone who says there is, is a chauvinist. It would be madness to continue the policy of Tsar Nicholas . . . No nation can be free if it oppresses other nations.*"   V. I. LENIN

Quoted in Peter Fryer, Hungarian Tragedy (Dobson), London, 1956

"friends" decided at the same time to hang on Nagy the office of Prime-Minister in order to discredit him from the beginning.

Later in the night, the Central Committee met again in a second session with Nagy and his friends now attending. While the AVO was firing murderous salvos in the crowds, they carried on a confused discussion. The Gero-clique, still a majority, insisted that Nagy include reliable Stalinists in his government. The debate soon became turbulent and Kadar supported Nagy, whom he later would replace. But Nagy still remained a kind of hostage. Nothing clear or definite came out of the discussion, and the hastily adopted final resolution carried a Rakosi stamp.

When news spread about the Soviet intervention, most of our older friends, particularly those with some political experience, were convinced that all resistance would be useless from now on. What could unarmed Hungarian students and workers do against Russian armed force? "Foreign arms arriving by parachute" existed only in the imagination of Soviet propagandists...

During the night of 24 October, the offices of the Hungarian News Agency on Nap Hill had the appearance of a besieged building. Blankets camouflaged the windows. Everywhere there were bottles wrapped in rags. The editors sat under their desks, still arguing fiercely. "How could Nagy have appealed to the Russians?" "Had he really?" The short declaration he made on the radio had seemed peculiar; his voice seemed to show nervousness; there was something wrong somewhere.

The first thing we did was to decide to stop giving the radio any service; it just kept on spreading lies. On the other hand, we tried the impossible, to inform Imre Nagy about the actual situation in the country, just as our correspondents in the provinces reported it hour by hour.

In Rakosi's Hungary, the political and eco-nomic leaders of the country—all told about 200 persons—had a special telephone network which wasn't tied up with Central. Through this secret line, the "K-line" as it was called, we tried to reach Imre Nagy. It was impossible. The Prime-Minister's special line was controlled by the Stalinists. Then we tried to contact Kadar. Another failure. A female voice answered for him, and when we told her that in the Miskolc region the AVO slaughtered a crowd, she exclaimed, "Lies!" and hung up.

Only on the following morning were we able to get a connection with a Minister. As a matter of fact, he called us. It was Kossa, one of the Government's Stalinists. He scolded us bitterly for one of our items announcing that in Debrecen a revolutionary committee had taken power and was absolute master of the situation. Even at this moment the Stalinists expected others to lie and were still lying to themselves...

Dezso Kosak, Franc-Tireur (Paris), 18 December

Fraternization, Desertion

Vienna

Austrian travellers report that the situation in the Hungarian capital is still hard to define. While part of the Soviet troops are fighting the revolutionaries, others are fraternizing with the Hungarian population. It is very difficult to estimate the number of victims.

Reports say further: "Many Soviet soldiers tore out the hammer-and-sickle from their flags and carried red flags without Soviet insignia. The population of Gyor, near the Austrian border, tore down from the buildings the enormous red stars that have been put up all over Hungary. Many buildings in the Hungarian capital are still in flames. In Pest Hungarian troops are said to have destroyed twelve Soviet tanks. In certain districts of Budapest Soviet soldiers have been deserting to the revolutionaries." *Neue Zürcher Zeitung, 27 October*

"An Atmosphere of Revolution"

Budapest

On Wednesday, from early morning until night-fall, an atmosphere of revolution reigned over the city.

Tanks were rattling through the streets along with trucks with steel-helmeted soldiers armed with sub-machine guns. There were overturned cars and barricades.

The question that puzzled both the demonstrators and Western observers was on whose side the Hungarian Army stood. Some signs indicated that the soldiers were on the demonstrators' side. A column of tanks roared along the Budapest Boulevard toward the besieged radio building. The crowd cheered enthusiastically and the crew of the tanks waved back, with national flags unfold-ed on their turrets. Many young Hungarians were given a ride on the top of the tanks.

It appeared the army either sided with the youth or remained neutral. The tanks and trucks drove into the narrow streets surrounding the radio building, site of the fighting between the youths and unarmed A.V.H. soldiers earlier that evening. They stopped there but did not seem to interfere in what happened. The streets around the radio building appeared to be a battlefield. Streets and doorways were packed with young demonstrators, including many women, cursing the A.V.H. and hailing the army. Opposite the building an army passenger car was burning. About a dozen of the youth leaders climbed the first floor balcony of the radio station with a huge Hungarian flag and remained there while the windows of the second and third floors were packed with uniformed A.V.H. soldiers. All windows of the building had been smashed earlier.

While I was there between 11 p.m. and midnight the A.V.H. refrained from harsher methods and only a few tear gas bombs were thrown occasionally. But many young men on the street showed sub-machine gun bullets to Western newsmen. Many told contradictory stories of earlier fighting around the building. How the fighting actually started is still a mystery. But it is safe to assume that the crowd either wanted to occupy the radio station or became enraged when a delegation that had entered was apparently prevented from returning. "Yes, we want to get in and tell the world the truth over the air," a young woman told me with tears running down her cheeks. The tears rolled because of tear gas bombs. While a car was burning and a machine gun was rattling, the crowd shouted abuse at the A.V.H. and cheered the soldiers... On some corners the mob took over complete control, especially as no policemen or soldiers or A.V.H. men were to be seen, except the troop concentrations around the radio building. There were also primitive barricades of overturned benches and roadblocks on Stalin Road, and neighboring streets. At a corner of Stalin Road a huge government passenger car had been overturned and used as a roadblock.

About 2 o'clock in the morning I made a last stroll in the city.

Most of the young people I talked with maintained that the overwhelming majority of the soldiers supported them in one way or another. There were, for instance, reports that the students and other elements got their sub-machine guns and ammunition from the soldiers.

On Wednesday, when the Government announced that it had to call in Soviet troops because it was "not prepared," the revolution of the previous night changed into war. It is understood that the Soviet soldiers moved into the town at 4 o'clock in the morning. A printed leaflet that was

pushed into my hand Tuesday night said among other things that eight Hungarians, including an army major and an army captain, were killed in the battle for the radio building. The official version broadcast Wednesday said the A.V.H. had opened fire only when eight of their men had been killed. The broadcast stressed, more and more emphatically, that it was counter-revolutionary elements, fascists, and the like, that did the fighting against the soldiers and A.V.H. men, aiming at the overthrow of the regime...

Endre Marton, Associated Press, 25 October

Disruption

Belgrade

Communications between the Hungarian capital and other European centers were completely disrupted. The closing of the Austrian-Hungarian border early today caused a heavy traffic jam on both sides of the frontier. Trains bound for Budapest did not reach their destination and private automobiles once inside the country were turned back by Hungarian tanks within twenty miles of Budapest.

Telephone operators in Vienna, Belgrade and London informed prospective callers that all lines to Budapest were closed.

Elie Abel, New York Times, 25 October

A Sniper

Budapest

A succession of Soviet tanks, armored cars and infantry bombarded for hours a whole block of buildings around Engels Square beside the British legation, in one of which one lone Hungarian sniper had hidden himself. Two tanks and a field-piece kept up a steady fire while three others dashed up and down the street. At the end of all this could be heard a single but heroic "pop" as the lone sniper fired back from his hidden retreat. And in the middle of it a civilian calmly strolled across the line of fire with his brief case under his arm... *John MacCormac, New York Times, 27 October*

"Unconditional Surrender"

Budapest

In a few minutes it will be two o'clock. Those who surrender before 14:00 will be exempt from martial law.

Attention! Attention!

We request that our listeners place their radio sets in the windows. We want to inform counter-revolutionaries and those who were misled that if they surrender before two o'clock they will be exempt from martial law...

According to orders issued, armed groups causing disturbances will be exempt from the summary jurisdiction law which implies the death

penalty—if they lay down their arms by 14:00. In view of the fact that this announcement may have escaped the notice of some insurgent groups, the Government has postponed the surrender deadline to 18:00. Those who do not avail themselves of this last opportunity will not escape the fate they deserve. Members of the groups which are still carrying on sporadic fighting must come to their senses. Stop the futile bloodshed and put out a white flag to indicate unconditional surrender...

Twelve minutes to go! All those who have attacked the State of the workers with arms have only 12 more minutes to avail themselves of the magnanimity of our Government and to escape a summary trial and the death penalty. Those who fail to lay down their arms by 18:00 today and continue to murder and plunder and to fight against the State of the Hungarian workers cannot hope for mercy...

News bulletin [20:00]: — Heavy fighting is still in progress in front of the building of the Party Committee in Budapest City District No. 13 and near the Robert Karoly Square Barracks. A reactionary group armed with machine pistols, machine-guns, hand grenades and other weapons is trying to occupy these two buildings. Workers of the district, under the leadership of the District Party Committee and together with considerable armoured army formations, are fighting heroically for the second day running and have already disarmed a counter-revolutionary group after sharp attacks.   *Radio Kossuth*

The Cradle Will Rock

Budapest

The workers of the Csepel Works have sent us the following letter: "Dear Comrade, the workers of the Csepel Iron and Metallurgical Works profoundly denounce the reactionary attack ... Our workers disarmed the provocateurs and chased them out ... Fellow-workers! Hungarian mothers and fathers! Call back your children so that this unnecessary bloodshed can be stopped!"...

Young intellectuals, Hungarian students! We appeal to you in the tragic hours, in the difficult situation of our nation, in the name of the Petofi Circle ...

Fellow-sportsmen, dear friends! Allow me to convey in these grave hours the sentiments and thoughts of the entire Hungarian sporting community, the outstanding sportsmen preparing for the Olympic Games, and the members of the Hungarian international football team. We know each other well, as we have always been together whenever Hungarian sportsmen and women have competed for the glory of the Hungarian tricolor. The honour of our country and a great many future successes of our sportsmen are now at stake. We do not want to shed one another's blood; we want to create a better and happier life for Hungarian youth. Our sports life stands on the threshold of gigantic tests. How uplifting it would be, and how happy we should feel if the Hungarian national flag were again to be hoisted on the mast of victory in Melbourne! ...

Jozsef Groesz, Archbishop of Kalocsa, has made the following statement in connection with the shocking events in Budapest: "The attitude of the Catholic Church is open and clear. We condemn massacre and destruction. Members of our flock know this. I therefore hope confidently that believers will not take part in such activities. Set an example ..."

The parents of Laszlo [last name unintelligible], 17-year-old, have been notified that their son is taking part in the fighting. His mother has had a nervous breakdown. If he wishes to see his mother alive he should go home immediately ...

Sorry, but the Children's Hour has been cancelled. Do not be angry, children, that you have to go to sleep to night without your bed-time stories ...   *Radio Kossuth*

Kadar: "With Burning Anger"

Budapest

Workers, comrades! The demonstration of university youth, which began with the formulation of, on the whole, acceptable demands, has swiftly degenerated into a demonstration against our democratic order; and under the cover of this demonstration an armed attack has broken out. It is only with burning anger that we can speak of this attack by counter-revolutionary reactionary elements against the capital of our country, against our people's democratic order and the power of the working class. Towards the rebels who have risen with arms in their hands against the legal order of our People's Republic, the Central Committee of our Party and our Government have adopted the only correct attitude: only surrender or complete defeat can await those who stubbornly continue their murderous, and at the same time completely hopeless, fight against the order of our working people ...

At the same time we are aware that the provocateurs, going into the fight surreptitiously, have been using as cover many people who went astray in the hours of chaos, and especially many young people whom we cannot regard as the conscious enemies of our regime. Accordingly, now that we have reached the stage of liquidating the hostile attack, and with a view to avoiding further bloodshed, we have offered and are offering to those misguided individuals who are willing to surrender on demand, the opportunity of saving their lives and their future, and of returning to the camp of honest people.

The fight is being waged chiefly by the most loyal units of our People's Army, by the members of our internal security forces and police, who are displaying heroic courage, and by former partisans with the help of our brothers and allies, the Soviet soldiers. Yet this fight is at the same time a political fight in which our Party and our working class constitute the major force.

Janos Kadar, Radio Kossuth [20:45]

"Welcome with Affection ..."

Budapest

Several listeners here turned to us with the question, "explain under what conditions and with what task did the Soviet units come to Budapest?" We will answer our listeners' question as follows: These Soviet units are stationed in Hungary in accordance with the Warsaw Pact. On Tuesday, the enemies of our people turned the demonstration of university youth into an organized counter-revolutionary provocation; with their armed attacks they endangered order and threatened the life of the people throughout the country. Conscious of its responsibility and to restore order and security, the Hungarian government requested that Soviet troops help to control the murderous attacks of counter-revolutionary bands. These Soviet soldiers are risking their lives in order to defend the peaceful population in our capital and the peace of our nation.

After order is restored, the Soviet troops will return to their bases. Workers of Budapest! Welcome with affection our friends and allies!

Radio Kossuth

The Proletariat

Vienna

The workers, as a distinct, unified, social force. did not make their weight felt until Wednesday. They mingled in the demonstrations and riots on the Tuesday night, but during that day most had stayed in the factories — unaware of what was happening.

A 28-year-old refugee who had fought alongside these workers tersely summed up their role in the revolution: "The young workers were the power of the revolution. The students began it, but when it developed they did not have the numbers or the ability to fight as hard as those young workers."

A 21-year-old worker in the huge United Electric factory in Ujpest — an industrial suburb of Budapest — described how his factory joined the revolt:

"On Tuesday we worked, but we talked as we worked. We talked about wages, about the results of the writers' meeting. We had printed copies, and knew what they meant when they said it was impossible to go on in this way. We could not live on what we got from our work. After work we saw the students demonstrating, and joined in.

"On Wednesday morning the revolt began in our factory. It was unorganised and spontaneous. If it had been organised, the A.V.H. would have known and stopped it before it started. The young workers led the way and everyone followed them."

He paused, and then added thoughtfully: "Yes, it was the young workers who made the revolution against Communism—the workers on whom the whole system was supposed to be based."

Then he continued his description of what happened that morning: "We usually began work at 7 a.m. Those of us who came by train from outlying districts waited in the factory as usual for the other workers to arrive. Just before 7 a.m. a truck filled with young workers with arms arrived at the gate. When one began to shoot at the red star on top of the factory a member of the management gave orders for the doors to be closed.

"We were now divided into two groups — those inside and those outside. We who were inside broke into the Mohosz offfce and took the sporting rifles. A Communist woman leader tried to stop us by putting a guard over the rifles. It was no good, everyone — including the foremen — was united. With the guns we broke out of the factory and everyone marched into the city.

"When we first acted, we had no communication with anyone. We were not in touch with other factories. But as we marched, more and more workers joined us, some with arms. On the corner of Rakoczy street, a university student began to organise us into small groups and instruct us in the slogans to shout. Then we marched to the American Legation, where we demonstrated ..."

George Sherman, The Observer (London), 11 November

The Countryside

Kecskemet

We crossed the frontier at 4 p.m.... We took a woman with us. We asked her what she thought about events. She said: "It is a good thing that Nagy came. We trust him. But it could have happened without bloodshed. It should not have happened this way. Why has bloodshed been necessary?"

After several kilometers we entered Szegedin. People are excited. They are standing in their doorways, talking. We saw the first troops with rifles, but there is complete law and order. There were some demonstrations yesterday, mostly students, but everything passed calmly.

When we left Szegedin we met the first tanks; we ourselves were excited seeing such a great number of tanks. It was dangerous driving. We could hardly make headway. We imagined that it would take three hours to reach Budapest, but the journey lasted longer. So we went to Kecskemet ... In a restaurant, to our great surprise, a band was playing. About twenty couples were dancing. It means that there were uprisings only in Budapest.

We proceeded towards Budapest though, the journey was very rough. When we reached the suburbs we found out that it was impossible to get into town. Persons we met told us we would not manage to get through ...

When we saw that we could not get into Budapest we went to a village. There, however, we could not get any accomodations. People were frightened of the roaring tanks ... One could see nobody in any of the villages we passed through. People stayed inside and locked the doors ... Tanks were along the roads ...

Vlado Teslic, Borba (Belgrade) 26, 30 October

The Attack on "Szabad Nep"

Budapest

Szabad Nep, the newspaper of the Hungarian Workers' Party, did not appear on Wednesday ... Events led to circumstances in which the paper could not be published. Various delegations called at the editorial office in the afternoon. They had presented resolutions and voiced various demands, but the members of the staff succeeded in calming them.

In the evening hours the substance and tone of the demands presented by the delegations changed. The more sober young people who were members of these delegations ... said "We didn't want this." Then they went out to the street and tried to calm the crowd. But they came back in a desperate hurry and said "the provocateurs have gotten the upper hand."

The situation changed radically after 10 p.m. The demonstrators were mostly different men from those of the evening and afternoon. This could be seen from their attitude. After 10 o'clock one could hear only the howling of counter-revolutionaries and misguided young people on the square in front of *Szabad Nep.* They demanded that *Szabad Nep* should publish an appeal for a general strike.

Then the siege of the *Szabad Nep* building began. The provocateurs attacked with stones and smashed the building's windows and the glass panels of its entrance one after another. But up to the last minute the editorial staff did not give up hope of publishing the paper; the workers of the printing office continued their work in a disciplined manner.

The attackers forced their way into the building around midnight. They set fire to the *Szabad Nep* bookshop, tore up books and set them on fire. While some were destroying everything in the shop, several attackers climbed to the sixth floor of the building and tore down the red star. Then the armed attackers demanded that the staff should hand over the building's loudspeaker system. This the staff refused to do, but the attackers found it and broadcast inciting and seditious slogans and appeals to the square below.

The crowd advanced yard by yard further into the building, breaking, smashing and looting.

A woman stepped out of a room. She belonged to the demonstrators, but they thought she was a member of the editorial staff and shot her dead. The members of the editorial staff retreated to the printing works. The printers were printing the last pages of the paper. The attackers, who had by then occupied the whole building, found the entrance to the printing works as well. There they found the brave and loyal workers of the paper. It was due to the calm attitude of the printers and journalists that the demonstrators were unable to destroy the valuable machines.

For hours they committed unbridled excesses in the building. The journalists and printers did not leave their posts, but made preparations for publishing the paper. Armed fights broke out several times round the building and there was no hope of delivering *Szabad Nep* to the readers. The printers and workers of the paper started work again this morning, and *Szabad Nep* will appear on the streets again towards noon. It will carry reports about the events of the last two days, about which it was prevented from giving an account ... *Radio Kossuth, 25 October [08:38]*

"Master of the Situation"

Budapest

We shall now read a communique on the situation prevailing at midnight: The situation has further improved. The armed attackers are increasingly isolated. However, in some places they have begun new actions. They are carrying out surprise attacks in groups of two or three.

The Party and Government are making every effort to restore order as soon as possible ... More and more factories are starting work and it is planned to investigate streetcar tracks immediately in order to prepare to restore service on certain lines. Further bloodshed is senseless. The Government demands most categorically that armed aggressors cease their resistance, that they surrender or throw away their arms. The Government is master of the situation ... *Radio Kossuth*

25 OCTOBER

"After the Dreadful Day"

Budapest

Communiqué on the situtaion at 4 a. m.: The situation has improved considerably since the issue of last night's communiqué ...

The fight at the radio station has not yet completely come to an end. A small number of those who occupied the studios have not complied with the surrender conditions. There is shooting going on. Operations to clear the studios completely will start after daybreak.

There are still small groups of people who wander about the streets or take up positions in doorways. Taking advantage of the dark of night and the dim light of dawn, they are still firing. Small groups of Hungarian military and security forces are carefully combing the city to clear it of these attackers. Daylight will help this work ... Only common criminals are now resisting in order to continue robberies and excesses.

The Party and Government are firmly in control of the situation. The Budapest Party and City Council have appealed to the people of Budapest to resume work after 6 a. m. quietly and in a disciplined manner. They have also asked that workers not be transported to factories and offices in trucks, because some counter-revolutionary groups are trying to escape by lorry, and also because this form of transport might provide opportunity for provocative acts.

There will be no school today ...

People of Budapest, Comrades! The counter-revolutionary gangs have mostly been liquidated. However, it is possible that, attempting to escape, small groups may try to take cover in some houses. Our armed forces are continuing with the final liquidation of counter-revolutionary groups. The Budapest Party Committee and the Budapest City Council appeal to the people, for their own sake, to try to prevent the entry of these elements into their houses. They suggest that tenants' committees should organise gate-guards to prevent armed elements from hiding in apartment houses.

Communiqué (6 a. m.): On the orders of the Council of Ministers of the Hungarian People's Republic, the Army, the State Security authority and the armed workers' guards, assisted by Soviet troops, have liquidated an attempted counter-revolutionary *coup d'état* during the night of 24th—25th October. The counter-revolutionary forces have been dispersed, and only here and there are small armed groups and isolated snipers still active. The Government appeals to the population to start traffic, trams, trolleybuses, and buses—wherever possible. Workers must resume work! Let factories produce and offices and enterprises function! ... Shops must open at the usual time ...

Dear village listeners,

This morning you will not hear your regular program, for events in Budapest have prevented our editors and co-workers from preparing their programs. Budapest wakes up again after this dreadful day and begins anew its constructive work ... Now peace is needed, above all. Nobody should believe false reports. The radio will inform its listeners of the true situation just as it has done so far. In all likelihood some rebels will try to flee to the country. Nobody should let themselves be fooled by provocateurs. The new government will bring the peasantry the prosperity they have desired so long ...

I instruct all military personnel who, for one reason or another, have been separated from their units to report to the commanding officers of their unit areas without delay, not later than 12:00 hrs. ...

(signed)   *Col. Gen. Istvan Bata,*
Minister of Defense

Radio Kossuth

Curfew

Budapest

Although the restoration of order is making good progress in Budapest, certain irresponsible elements in small groups are trying to create disturbances and are even firing shots. Government security forces are making a vigorous stand against such occurrences. We advise the population in their own interest not to go out into the streets unless absolutely necessary.

We again draw the attention of the people of Budapest to the fact that untit further notice a curfew is in force between 18:00 and 06:00 hrs. The front doors of houses must be locked during the hours of curfew.   *Radio Kossuth (10:47)*

The Shooting in Parliament Square

Budapest

It turned out that last night's shooting [24 Oct.] was more than a mopping-up operation. At 10 a.m. a crowd of about 2,000 men and women, waving flags and shouting, "This is a peaceful demonstration!" passed in front of the United States Legation toward the near-by Parliament building. They greeted the United States flag, waving from the Legation building, with beaming faces. The marchers waved their hats and some shouted: "Why don't you help us?"

Then an amazing thing happened. Two huge Soviet tanks and an armored car drove up packed with young Hungarians fraternizing with the Russian soldiers. All were smiling uneasily. Other tanks and also a number of Soviet guns were mounted at various corners of the huge Gothic Parliament building. The demonstrators sent a three-member delegation into the building, which houses the office of Premier Imre Nagy. While waiting the return of their delegation, they shouted slogans such as "Down with Gero!" and "Release our prisoners!" The Russians remained friendly but kept away from the crowd and prevented the demonstrators from reaching a gate leading to the Premier's office.

I took cover in a doorway and, looking out, saw a tank firing wildly. Then three armored cars drove up packed with Soviet soldiers, but they aimed their guns toward the sky before they fired. How many became the victims of the shooting in Parliament Square today could not be ascertained. I saw a body of a woman lying under the arcades of the Ministry of Agriculture, opposite the Parliament building, and three other bodies lying on the street car track.

When I revisited the scene in the afternoon the bodies had been taken away. One eyewitness said there were about two to three hundred dead on this square but figures naturally are exaggerated sometimes in such critical times. I could not see a single Hungarian soldier, neither army nor security police. At least in this area all the work was done by Soviet troops. The crowd shouted, "The radio is telling lies!" The Budapest radio is the only operating medium of public information—no newspapers have been printed for two days—and it frequently has called the rebels "counter-revolutionary," "reactionary elements," "fascists" and "armed gangs". I cannot know, of course, what the political sentiments of the crowd at the Parliament building were but it is a fact that none of them had arms.

I was present when a truck with a few Hungarian frontier guards was halted at a corner near the Parliament building and a young man in the crowd discovered that there were firearms in the truck.

"Go and get them!" said one of the soldiers.

"No, our weapon is the flag," said a middle-aged man who seemed to be in command of the unit ...   *Endre Marton, Associated Press, 25 October*

"The Workers Are Being Murdered"

Budapest

It looked Wednesday as if the intervention of Soviet troops, who had been called in at 4.30 o'clock that morning, had quelled the revolt. The Soviet forces had eighty tanks, artillery, armored cars and other equipment of a variety normally possessed only by a complete Soviet mechanized division. The insurgent Hungarian students and workers at no time had more than small arms furnished by sympathizing soldiers of the Hungarian Army.

What revived the revolt was a massacre ...

Since only a few minutes earlier Soviet tank crews had been fraternizing with insurgents, it is possible that the massacre was a tragic mistake. The most credible version is that the political policemen opened fire on the demonstrators and panicked the Soviet tank crews into the belief that they were being attacked.

But in any case when the firing subsided Parliament Square was littered with dead and dying men and women. The total number of casualties has been estimated at 170. This correspondent can testify that he saw a dozen bodies.

Far from deterring the demonstration, the firing embittered and inflamed the Hungarian people. A few minutes later and only a few blocks from the scene of the massacre, the surviving demonstrators reassembled in Szabadsag (the word means liberty) Square. When trucks filled with Hungarian soldiers drove up and warned the demonstrators that they were armed, the leader of the demonstrators brandished a Hungarian flag and replied: "We are armed only with this, but it is enough".

On a balcony above appeared an elderly Hungarian clad in pyjamas and a dressing gown and clasping a huge flag. He threw it down to the demonstrators.

Another man mounted a ladder to tear down the Soviet emblem from the "Liberty" monument in "Liberty" square. It was erected in 1945 by the Russians with forced Hungarian labor.

A crowd assembled before the United States legation in the square and shouted: "The workers are being murdered, we want help."

Finally Spencer Barnes, Chargé d'Affaires, told them that their case was one for decision by his Government and the United Nations, not for the local staff. The British Minister had received a deputation and given it the same message.

Among those watching this demonstration was a furtive figure clad in a leather coat. Suddenly someone identified him rightly or wrongly as a member of the hated AVO, the Hungarian political police. Like tigers the crowd turned on him, began to beat him and hustled him into a courtyard. A few minutes later they emerged rubbing their hands with satisfaction. The leather-coated figure was seen no more.

During all these activities and while Soviet tanks continued to race through near-by streets firing their fusillades, the crowd never ceased shouting: "Down with Gero!" Less than an hour later the radio announced that Mr. Gero had been replaced by Janos Kadar, former Interior Minister and second secretary of the party...

The massacre before the Parliament occurred in a mysterious circumstance for which no explanation has been forthcoming.

Known is the fact that the crews of three Soviet tanks began to fraternize with the insurgents shortly before noon in front of the Astoria Hotel. They shouted that they did not want to fire on unarmed Hungarian workers.

They let a score of the demonstrators climb on their tanks and drove them to Parliament Square. This correspondent saw the Soviet soldiers there laughing and waving to the crowd of hundreds that had collected. But only a minute later from a few blocks in the distance he heard a violent cannonade and saw at the end of the street another Soviet tank firing in the direction of the crowd...

That the Soviet forces suffered at least one casualty was demonstrated Wednesday morning when a Soviet soldier, bleeding from an abdominal bullet wound, was carried into the dining room of the Duna Hotel for treatment. He was bandaged by a Western physician.

A few hours later a Soviet armored car was set on fire near Engels Square. A worker told this correspondent that some Soviet tanks had been attacked with "Molotov cocktails," made, according to the Russian recipe, out of winebottles filled with gasoline.

John MacCormac, New York Times, 27 October

"Slander"

The demonstrators' got as far as the Parliament building, which was protected by Soviet tanks. The demonstrators did not shoot, because they had no arms; and the Soviet soldiers did not fire. When the people stopped in front of the Parliament building, machine guns opened fire from the rooftop of the building opposite, showering the people with bullets and mercilessly mowing them down. When the Soviet soldiers saw this, they immediately moved their tanks forward, and their fire silenced the machine-guns on the rooftops. Dozens of people were killed on the spot, and many others were wounded. This is the work of counter-revolution.

Western propaganda took advantage of the massacre for slanders, by saying that the Soviet soldiers caused the bloodshed, and this for no other purpose than to incite the Hungarian people against the Soviet Army. The truth, however, is that the Soviet soldiers by firing silenced the machine-guns of the counter-revolution which sowed death among the Hungarian people.

B. Konieczny, Rude Pravo (Prague), 11 November

"Purpose of the Provocation"

Budapest

There were forces which still hoped to give the people a thrashing and so bring the Rakosi-Gero group back to power, and these forces engineered the provocation in front of the Parliament building on Thursday, October 25.

According to Charles Coutts, [British Communist editor] whom I met a week later, and who still had the details of the whole turmoil very fresh in his mind, a big and completely unarmed demonstration had started from Rákóczi út, carrying the national flag and black flags in honour of the dead. On the way to Parliament Square they met a Soviet tank. The tank stopped, a soldier put his head out, and the people in the front of the crowd began to explain they were unarmed and were engaged in a peaceful demon-

stration. The soldier told them to jump on the tank; a number of them did so, and the tank set off to the demonstration—"and I have a photograph of this", said Coutts.

Entering Parliament Square they met another Soviet tank which had been sent to fire on them, and this tank, too, turned and joined the demonstration. In the square were three more Soviet tanks and two armoured cars. The crowd went right up to them and began to talk to the soldiers. The Soviet commandant was saying: "I have a wife and children waiting for me in the Soviet Union. I don't want to stay in Hungary at all", when suddenly from the roof-tops there were three salvoes of gun-fire. Some of the people ran to the sides of the square for shelter. Others were told by the Russians to shelter behind the tanks.

Some thirty people were left lying on the square either dead or wounded, including a Soviet officer. Tanks and cars opened fire on the roof-tops.

"It is still not clear to me who it was that began the shooting", Coutts added. "It is more than likely they were security police." More than likely. And the provocation served its purpose: to prevent fraternisation, and to start the story that Soviet troops had opened fire on unarmed demonstrators. If the Soviet withdrawal had begun on October 24 instead of one week later, better still if the Soviet Army had never entered the fight, and if the A.V.H. had been disarmed and disbanded on October 24, much bitterness and suffering could have been prevented...

Peter Fryer, *Hungarian Tragedy* (London, 1956)

Janos Kadar

The new leader of Hungary's Communists is well acquainted with terror since he has in turn been a jailer of anti-Communists and a victim of Communist jailers. He is a man who has been moved by a single passion for five years — to destroy Matyas Rakosi, the leader of the Working People's (Communist) Party, who put him in jail in April 1951, and kept him there until late 1953. It was the strength of this passion that enabled Mr. Kadar to survive the purge and then to emerge so steeled in mind and body that within three years he had driven his enemy into exile and had himself won the seat of power...

The measure of the man is the skill with which Mr. Kadar rose from prisoner to party chief. Released, still in semi-disgrace, in late 1953, he was given a relatively minor job as party chief in Budapest's Thirteenth District, an area with factories and workers' residences. In that ward he built up his own machine and his influence and prestige soon spread elsewhere.

By last spring and early summer, he was so powerful that he was one of the key figures behind the scenes in the intrigues that culminated in Mr. Rakosi's resignation last July. Formal recognition of his role came at the Central Committee's July meeting, which elected him to the Politburo. His return to power parallels that of Wladyslaw Gomulka, Poland's new party leader.

There is both irony and justice in Mr. Kadar's appearance at this critical moment when Hungarian Communists looked for a symbol of national communism to placate the country's rebels. He was, after all, the Minister of Interior and head of the secret police in 1949 when Laszlo Rajk, one of Hungary's Communist leaders, was tried and executed on charges of national communism

and Titoism. But this factor in his career is more than counter-balanced by his jail terms and other elements.

Janos Kadar (pronounced Yanosh Kahdahr) is a genuine home-grown Hungarian Communist, not a man who lived much of his life in Moscow and was trained there, like Mr. Rakosi and the new Premier, Imre Nagy. At 44, he represents a new and younger generation of Communists. Born in a village near the Yugoslav border, he became a locksmith as a youth. A slight German accent in his speech reflects the mixed Swabian and Hungarian population of his native village.

It was through the trade unions that Mr. Kadar became a member of the illegal Communist youth movement in the Thirties, and it was in the harsh conditions of underground work before and during World War II that he came to political maturity. He has not forgotten that in these difficult years his elders had the relative comfort of Moscow.

Even his anti-Communist opponents consider him an effective and moving public speaker. "Don't make a mistake", one of those opponents said yesterday, "Kadar is not eloquent. But his utter sincerity, his complete belief in what he is saying come through in his speeches, even as he stumbles sometimes and has trouble finding just the right word to express his thoughts."

Mr. Kadar is regarded as a "tough man". As deputy chief of Budapest's police immediately after World War II, and then in the Ministry of Interior, he showed no mercy toward communism's opponents in Hungary. His toughness is showing itself now as he helps lead the fight to put down the remaining resistance in the country. But after his experience, in jail and out of jail, for the last five years, he may be moved to be tough toward Russians and Hungarians alike...

New York Times, 26 October

Gero Goes to "Unreserved Joy"

Budapest

Meeting today, 25th October, the Central Committee of the Hungarian Workers' Party relieved Comrade Erno Gero of the post of First Secretary of the Central Committee. The Politburo has appointed Janos Kadar First Secretary of the Central Committee. After the Politburo meeting, Comrades Janos Kadar and Imre Nagy will make statements on the radio. Hungarians! Raise the National Flag over your houses! [12 : 33] ...

A few minutes ago, we announced the Politburo's decision. According to reports from our correspondents, the people of Budapest received the news with joy. In Angyalfold, workers embraced and kissed each other. The people have hoisted the National Flag on their houses. Cheers echo everywhere. The same unreserved joy is being reported from the Great Ring Road, from the Museum Boulevard, and from other quarters of the city. The National Anthem and the Marseillaise are being played ...   *Radio Kossuth*

"Huis Clos"

Appeal to the Population of Budapest!

With regard to the fact that shootings were reported in several parts of the capital this morning, we ask the population to stay at home in the interest of its own safety, and only to go out if it is absolutely necessary. We call on the janitors to keep the doors of the houses locked.

Radio Kossuth

Broadcast by Kadar

Budapest

Hungarian workers, dear comrades! The Politburo of our Party has entrusted me with the post of First Secretary of the Central Committee in a grave and difficult situation. There is not much time today for talking; therefore I just want to say a few brief words.

The grave situation in which we find ourselves is characterised by the fact that various elements are mixed up in it. The demonstration of a section of the youth, which started peacefully in accordance with the aims of the overwhelming majority of the participants, degenerated after a few hours, in accordance with the intentions of anti-democratic and counter-revolutionary elements which had joined it, into an armed attack against the State power of the people's democracy. It was in this grave situation that a decision had to be made.

In complete unity the leadership of our Party decided that the armed attack against the power of our People's Republic must be repelled by all possible means. The power of the working people —the working class and the peasantry—embodied in the People's Republic is sacred to us, and must be sacred to all who do not wish to re-impose the old yoke on the neck of our people, the rule of the capitalists, bankers and big estate-owners ...

Comrades, the Central Committee of the Party proposes to the Government that, after the restoration of order, the Government should conduct negotiations with the Soviet Government in a spirit of complete equality between Hungary and the Soviet Union, of fraternal co-operation and internationalism, in order to arrive at an equitable and just settlement for both parties of the issues between the two socialist countries ...

Radio Kossuth

Broadcast by Nagy

Budapest

Working people of Hungary! During the past few days our country has lived through tragic events. Counter-revolutionaries and provocateurs, small in number, have launched an armed attack against the order of our People's Republic, which attack has been supported by part of the workers of Budapest because they were desperate about the situation of the country. This bitterness has been aggravated by the political and economic mistakes of the past, the remedying of which was imperatively demanded by the condition of the country and the general desire of our people. Under my direction the new Party leadership and the Government are resolved to draw the most far-reaching conclusions from these tragic events.

Soon after order is restored the National Assembly will meet. At this session I shall submit an all-embracing and well-founded program of reforms. This program will embrace all important problems of our national life. The implementation of this program demands that the Government be reshuffled on the basis of a revived PPF [Patriotic People's Front], rallying within its ranks the broadest democratic forces of the nation. The immediate cessation of fighting and the restoration of calm and order are absolutely indispensable for the realization of this program. And so is the resumption of production. I appeal to the working people of the country and all true patriots to promote this with all means at their disposal.

As Chairman of the Council of Ministers I hereby announce that the Hungarian Government is initiating negotiations on relations between the Hungarian People's Republic and the

Soviet Union, concerning, among other things, the withdrawal of Soviet forces stationed in Hungary, on a basis of Hungarian-Soviet friendship and proletarian internationalism, and also on a basis of equality between Communist Parties and socialist countries, and on a basis of national independence.

I am convinced that Hungarian-Soviet relations resting an these principles will provide a firm foundation for sincere and true friendship between our peoples, for our national progress and our socialist future.

The Soviet troops whose intervention in the fighting was necessitated by the vital interests of our socialist order will be recalled immediately after peace and order are restored.

Towards those who took up arms but not with the intention of overthrowing our people's democratic regime, if they immediately stop fighting and surrender their arms — towards all young people, workers, and Honveds who do this — the Government will show magnanimity in a spirit of understanding and reconciliation, and it will not institute penal proccedings against them.

At the same time, in the interest of workers who love peace and order, and to defend our people's democratic system, we shall apply the rigour of the law against those who continue armed action, incitement, and plunder.

I especially warn our working people against irresponsible alarmists and rumour-mongers, whose harmful activity is one of the greatest obstacles to the restoration of peace and order.

I am filled with deep grief over every drop of blood shed by innocent working people who fell during these tragic days. Let us put an end to the tragic fighting and senseless bloodshed.

Hungarian men and women, friends, comrades! Under the leadership of the Party let us set out along a new road of peaceful and creative work, of building a better, more beautiful and socialist future for our people. *Radio Kossuth*

Troops, Rebels, Russians

Munich

In the absence of reliable reports that whole Army units have joined the insurgents, the order broadcast this morning by General Bata, the Minister of Defence, instructing all military personnel in Budapest "who have fcr any reason been separated from their units" to report not to their units but to area commanders seems to suggest that many units may no longer exist as such or that they are now a long way from where they were when the fighting started.

A further order specifying certain assembly points in Budapest for men who are now in the capital, but who were not originally stationed there, suggest that some Army units may have come to Budapest from the provinces to take part in the fighting. Since it now seems fairly well established that the Government called in Soviet but not Hungarian troops from the provinces — because it feared that its own Army might join the rising — it seems evident that this appeal is directed to Hungarian units which came to Budapest of their own will to help the insurgents.

The announcement by Mr. Nagy, the new Premier, that Soviet troops would withdraw from the fighting as soon as peace and order were restored does not help much, for it implies a determination to rely on the Russians to the very end, and this can only increase popular resentment at the present stage as well as leave a legacy of bitterness for the future.

The Government must have been aware of these factors and, while unable to forgo the continued use of Soviet troops because their immediate withdrawal would lead to the immediate end of the Communist regime, it has tried to regain some popularity through Mr. Nagy's announcement that it would ask in due course for the withdrawal of all Russian forces from Hungary.

Although the first announcement that Mr. Nagy would speak was made in the morning, the speech was not broadcast until a quarter past three, and it must have been preceded by much argument among the leaders as to whether they should promise the withdrawal of Soviet troops. On the one hand, it must have seemed that this would be welcomed by the people. But on the other it must have been clear that the Government could not afford to deprive itself very soon — if ever — of Soviet protection, and there may have been those in the leadership who thought that a promise palpably incapable of fulfilment could only aggravate the situation.

Also, if any Soviet advisers took part in the Government deliberations—as is only too likely— they may have objected to the publication of a promise which, when it becomes known to the people of the other satellite countries, would lead to popular pressure for the withdrawal of Soviet troops from the whole of Eastern Europe ...

Both in Hungary and in Poland anti-Russian feeling has played a major part in bringing about the recent developments. Whether or not there is an end to the present troubles, this feeling will persist and can at the slightest provocation again be vented in a violent form. If a dozen or so years of "loving the Russians" propaganda has been unable to eradicate it, the present intervention of Soviet troops in Hungary is bound to make the hatred of the Russians more intense— and not in Hungary alone ...

Victor Zorza, Manchester Guardian, 26 October

A Yugoslav Report
Kecskemet

We were unable to reach Budapest. We only reached the suburbs. What we report we learned here or were told by eye-witnesses ... Probably several thousand people lost their lives or were seriously injured. At some places where fighting occured, in front of the building of the Ministry of Defense, which was attacked by armed groups on three occasions during the day in an effort to capture it, there are great piles of dead. Similarly in front of the building of Budapest Radio and other public buildings.

Thousands of people have obtained arms by disarming soldiers and militiamen. Some of these soldiers and militiamen have been fraternizing with the embittered and dissatisfied masses. They are said to have broken into some barracks; the Budapest arms factory was taken; machine-guns, and even light artillery, appeared in streets. According to eyewitness reports, the authorities are paralysed, unable to stop the bloody events ...

The armed masses, who were already in a delirium, broke into individual buildings, into factories, and then followed the attack on institutions. There was a general mixture: communists, embittered people, and fascist elements were all together. The spirits were high. Fire was set to a part of the building of *Szabad Nep*, and the paper has not appeared for two days. This morning fire was set to the National Museum in the centre of the city. We are told many buildings are still burning; many factories have been damaged. Generally, eyewitnesses report, some parts of Budapest look like a city after fierce street-fighting in a real war.

Although fascist elements have also been taking part in the uprisings, this has not been a counter-revolution. Rather this has been a protest against attitudes which had blocked the efforts of the working class towards socialist democracy. The less the leadership was prepared to meet the workers' demands, the more bitter the people became, and this finally culminated in the Budapest events. Danger of a counter-revolution had existed, because fascist elements created trouble. But this danger has, in the main, been overcome now ...

Djuka Julius, Politika (Belgrade), 26 October

Leaflets, Pamphlets, Demands

Budapest

At 4 p.m., pamphlets were distributed signed by "Hungarian Workers and University Students." They read: "We summon all Hungarians to a general strike. As long as the Government fails to grant our demands and until the murderers are called to account, we shall answer the Government with a general strike. Long live the new Government under the leadership of Imre Nagy."

At 6 p.m. a one-sheet newspaper was issued from the printing plant of the Hungarian Army. It had been occupied by the political police but apparently reoccupied by the Army. It was an Army officer who threw hundreds of copies from an upper window to a crowd waiting for them below. The sheet repeated the sixteen demands that had been formulated by Tuesday's peaceful demonstrators, which the Government had refused to print or broadcast ...

John MacCormac, N. Y. Times, 27 October

Budapest

One of the worst massacres of the last three days happened when Russian tanks opened fire without any clear reason on a crowd of passive and unarmed people in the Parliament Square yesterday. The total dead here alone is put at over 100. Women and children were among the dozens mown down. Ambulances had removed the bodies when I drove by three hours later but some bloodstains were still on the pavement.

A few minutes later I witnessed a scene which showed well enough the part Hungarian army units are playing in the uprising. It took place in the army printing press in the Bajesy Bilinski Street.

This had been seized on Wednesday by the political police forces of the regime and had been recently retaken by military rebels. From the windows and balconies officers in uniform were hurling to cheering crowds below copies of a manifesto which had just been rolled off inside. It spoke in the name of the "Provisional Revolutionary Hungarian Government," and demanded the immediate end of martial law, the disarming of the political police, and Hungary's withdrawal from the Warsaw Pact under the terms of which Soviet troops are stationed in the country.

Neither this rebel leaflet nor any other I have seen so far openly demands the end of any form of Communist rule in Hungary. This is probably because the word Communism has lost here any specific meaning.

But the demand also printed on this sheet for "genuine democratic government" told its own language. So did the roars of assent from the crowd as they read the smeared and crumpled leaflets under the headlamps of cars.

Gordon Shephard, Daily Telegraph (London), 27 October

Copies have reached Vienna of a leaflet bearing the imprint of the Army Printing Press in Budapest ...

"We swear by the corpses of our martyrs that we shall win freedom for our country in these critical times. The leaders of the Party and Government have been concerned only with preserving their power. What kind of leadership is this which takes hesitant steps solely under pressure from the masses? ...

"Their arbitrary actions have exacted enough sacrifices in the past 10 years. Now they have brought in the Soviet Army to suppress the Hungarian revolution.

"Citizens, we demand:

1. A new provisional revolutionary Army and national Government, in which will be represented the leaders of youth in revolt;

2. The immediate ending of martial law;

3. The immediate cancellation of the Warsaw Agreement; the immediate and peaceful withdrawal of Soviet troops from the motherland;

4. The heads of those who are really responsible for the bloodshed; the release of the captured and a general amnesty;

5. A true democratic basis for Hungarian Socialism; meanwhile the Hungarian Army to assume responsibility for order and disarm the security police.

"Without that, the danger of further bloodshed remains. We shall continue the demonstrations till final victory, but we must remain calm. We condemn all anarchy and destruction. Comrades, Imre Nagy and Janos Kadar are members of the new revolutionary Army Government. There has been enough bloodshed."

(Signed)   *"The New Provisional Revolutionary Hungarian Government and the National Defence Committee."*

The Times (London), 27 October

Hay: "Nagy is our Man"

Budapest

I was with you and marched with you arm in arm through the streets of Budapest. We marched to the Petofi statue under the National Flag and the Kossuth Crest, and from there to Kossuth Square. I have been fighting together with you for years, for a new and youthful art and literature, for honour, for youth, for truth, for the people. I know you, and I know that you are honest patriots, that every breath of yours is true. If need be I am willing to bear witness before any tribunal in the world and declare: It is not these young people who are the guilty ones! Let them not be punished!

But there will be no need for such testimony. Radical changes have taken place in the Government and Party leadership. Our most important demands have been fulfilled. Imre Nagy is our man. His program is our program. Janos Kadar has learned in Rakosi's prison what it is that Hungarian youth must be protected against. With Gero's replacement those forces against which you had to be shielded are leaving their positions of command. Your patriotic feelings have been understood.

You need not fear retaliation. But there is no time to lose. With the utmost urgency we must change to peaceful methods. Let fighting stop immediately. Even peaceful demonstrations are not suitable means at this time because they can be misconstrued. Let the merciless, uncompromising, and democratic battle of ideas and thoughts begin. Here our representatives, the youth and the young in spirit, will win a splendid and resounding victory! Guard your lives now! Your country will be in sore need of you in the new Hungary now liberating itself from tyranny. This is the message of your loving old friend, Gyula Hay.

Radio Kossuth (18 : 45)

On the Streets

Budapest

The tone of the radio changed significantly today, and Premier Nagy's last appeal in fact was directed to "soldiers, young men, young workers and everyone who is still fighting," almost begging them to stop.

In Buda, on the right bank of the Danube, things were much quieter although a small group of rebels found refuge on the the rocky side of Gellert Hill. They were hunted by a Soviet helicopter.

Shops were closed yesterday. Some state-run groceries opened today for a few hours and long queues were formed with people waiting for bread and other foodstuffs. There were neither buses, nor trams, nor taxis and only a few passenger cars. The situation was slightly better this morning until fighting flared up again after 10 a.m. Very few buses and trams were in operation. They were too few to carry everyone to the factories and offices, though the Government had asked everyone repeatedly the day before through the radio to return to work.

All bridges were immediately blocked by Soviet tanks when they entered the city at 4 a.m. Wednesday. There were as many as six or more on one bridge. They usually permitted pedestrians to go through, and occasionally some cars. How many Soviet troops were brought to Budapest could not be ascertained, but there are a remarkable number of huge T-34 tanks. I counted more than fifty when I passed them Wednesday afternoon parked near the Parliament building. Most of the Russian soldiers seemed very young. The same applies to the rebels. Most of them are students and young workers. Some arrived in oilstained overalls at Tuesday's demonstrations.

The demonstrators showed amazing courage. I saw them boldly going straight toward tanks and guns with only a flag in their hands and demonstrating against far superior forces ranging from tanks to submachine guns.

What the outcome of all this will be remains anybody's guess. Premier Nagy took over and he signed an order introducing martial law that doubtless harmed his former immense popularity. But so far I have not heard a single shout against him.

But as to the question of who actually is in overall command of the rebels, the answer obviously must be that no one seems to be. That is the unanimous belief of the few Westerners, diplomats and newsmen who toured the city on both days of what must be termed a war.

But the greatest thing doubtless is that Premier Nagy has promised to negotiate with the Soviet Union the withdrawal of Soviet troops from Hungary.

That was point No. 1 of the demands of the youth.

Earlier today I toured the neighbourhood of the big block of red brick houses on Madach Square, site of heavy fighting Wednesday. The picture was frightful indeed, resembling the grim days after the siege of the city in 1945. Shiny passenger cars with Austrian and other foreign license plates in front of the Astoria Hotel had broken windshields. All the windows of the hotel were smashed and big holes, unmistakably made by gunfire gaped on the walls of various buildings. All the streets around are strewn with debris. Cables and trolleys dangle down into the street. Shops are burned out. All this is the remains of the fighting Wednesday afternoon, which appeared to Western observers watching events from the windows of the British Legation as a war between tanks, machine guns and infantry on the one side and a handful of snipers on the other. The beautiful museum near the radio station and the Astoria Hotel caught fire Wednesday and was still burning today.

As I was sending this dispatch late tonight from Buda, the most peaceful part of Budapest, machine guns and other weapons could be heard roaring somewhere in the city. Steel-helmeted police stood in front of the battered Astoria Hotel. There was dead silence around the radio buildings. Streets were dark. Two Hungarian and eight Soviet tanks towered in the fog...

Endre Marton, Associated Press, 26 October

Nagy and the Russians: "Betrayal"?

...Soviet chiefs Mikoyan and Suslov flew into Budapest, ousted Geroe as party boss, and acceded to Nagy's assumption of the premiership in fact as well as in name. An account of the precise circumstances surrounding these moves was later furnished to a Western correspondent by a high Hungarian official reportedly present at the meeting of Mikoyan and Suslov with Geroe. (The official who revealed these details was not identified by name, presumably for security reasons; see Leslie Balogh Bain, "Witness Tells How Soviet Dictated to Budapest Reds," *The Evening Star*, Washington, D. C., October 31, 1956.) Though the account cannot by its nature be verified, its interesting details accord with the steps taken on that day. According to the source, Mikoyan and Suslov flew into a rage at Geroe; Mikoyan berated him for having "stampeded" Moscow into an ill-advised commitment of Soviet troops through his "exaggerated and distorted" picture of the situation. Suslov followed up with the "suggestion" that Geroe resign at once. When Geroe protested, citing Moscow's earlier position that he was needed to hold the party together, Mikoyan re-

portedly replied angrily, "the party already has fallen apart, thanks to your incredible blunders." The Soviet leaders then summoned Janos Kadar, purged under Rakosi and Geroe, and informed him that he would succeed Geroe as First Secretary of the party. The now unuseful Geroe was taken away in protective custody. Next, Mikoyan and Suslov agreed that Nagy should announce a series of "concessions," in particular promising withdrawal of Soviet troops from the city of Budapest and a review of Soviet-Hungarian treaties. By then the rebellion had become nation-wide revolt.   *Raymond L. Garthoff, "The Tragedy of Hungary,"*
Problems of Communism, Jan.—Feb. 1957

London

...Nagy's supposed betrayal of the revolution: I cannot, even today, disclose my sources, but it is certain that my informant knew what was going on, and I have no reason to doubt that he told me the truth.

Suslov and Mikoyan continued their talks with Nagy and Kadar. Nagy wanted to broadcast to the nation telling them that it was not he but

Gero who had declared martial law and called the Russians in. He believed such a statement was an essential preliminary to the restoration of order, but the two Russains disagreed with him, and "advised" him to refrain from such a statement. Nagy, however, remained adamant, repeating that he would not be able to restore order and confidence in himself without making his previous role quite clear. The Russians, still unconvinced, reminded Nagy that order would easily be restored by Russian tanks. They had no doubts on that score and, indeed, it was quite reasonable to suppose that the people of Budapest would not even attempt to defy the might of two Russian armoured divisions. Once order had been restored, Mikoyan continued, the Russians would leave the country, provided certain conditions were fulfilled.

The Russian leaders now left for Moscow and Nagy prepared to make his broadcast. Two Russian officers belonging to a counter-espionage unit appeared in civilian clothes and asked to see his script. Having read it, they ordered Nagy to delete all references to Gero having called in the Russians. Nagy refused once again, whereupon the Russians drew revolvers and repeated their order. Nagy still refused to obey and tried to strike away the hand pointing the gun at him. A scuffle followed between the two young officers and the elderly Prime Minister. There could be only one result, and Nagy had to agree to refrain from clearing himself of the charges. While he was making his broadcast, the two Russian officers stood behind him, their hands deep in their pockets. In all Western reports of Mr. Nagy's first broadcast, it was remarked that he seemed to be speaking under great stress and with deep emotion. The reasons for his emotion were not known. The Russians also requested him to sign a statement to the effect that he had, in fact, called them in and proclaimed martial law. This Nagy refused to do, in spite of threats ...

The speech had only one meaning for his listeners: he did not disclaim responsibility for calling the Russians in and that seemed to mean that he was, in fact, responsible for it ...

Had Nagy been allowed to tell the truth, perhaps he could have brought the situation under control and retained the people's confidence, which indeed he was to regain a few days later when he did reveal the true facts ...

George Mikes, "The Hungarian Revolution" (London, 1957)

Reactions: Moscow, New York, London, Warsaw

Moscow

Mr. Shepilov, the Foreign Minister, was quoted to-night by Belgian journalists who attended a reception in the Kremlin for the Belgian Prime Minister, M. Van Acker, and Foreign Minister, M. Spaak, as having said in reply to questions: —

"We can see a very complex movement taking place (in Hungary). There has been discontent for many different reasons. There have been difficulties in the material situation of the population. There have been bureaucratic methods of administration, and there is a demand from the people for democratization.

"In these last few days there were demonstrations, above all by students and youths. There have been forces which have tried to profit by these demonstrations with an aim hostile to the people. Some can say they were counter-revolutionary elements. These forces organized meetings, and provoked disorders prepared a long time ago. It seems that they had the objective of making themselves masters of certain establishments, above all the radio and such places.

"The Government was obliged to employ force to re-establish order. It appealed to the Army and the security organs. As there was a danger that these events might disorganize the life of the country, the Government appealed for the aid of Soviet troops."

Earlier Mr. Shepilov contrasted the situation in Hungary with that in Poland. "There have been difficulties, but the Polish people know how to deal with the situation," he said.

Reuters, 25 October

New York

President Eisenhower said to-day that the United States Government "deplores the intervention of Soviet military forces" in Hungary.

The President issued a statement on the situation in Hungary after arriving here by train from Washington for a major election campaign address to-night. His statement followed a telephone conference with Mr. Dulles.

After stating that the United States "deplores the intervention," General Eisenhower said that under the provisions of the peace treaty those forces "should have been withdrawn." He stated that the presence of such forces in Hungary "as is now demonstrated, is not to protect Hungary against armed aggression from without but rather to continue an occupation of Hungary by the forces of an alien Government for its own purposes ..."

The President added: "The heart of America goes out to the people of Hungary." The United States "considers the developments in Hungary as being a renewed expression of the intense desire for freedom long held by the Hungarian people."

Demands made by Hungarian students and working people "clearly fall within the framework of those human rights to which all are entitled and which are offered in the Charter of the United Nations, and which are specifically guaranteed to the Hungarian people by the treaty of peace to which the Governments of Hungary and the allied and associated Powers, including the Soviet Union and the United States, are parties."

Reuters, 25 October

London

Mr. Leslie Fry, British Minister in Budapest, radioed messages to London throughout yesterday giving the Foreign Office the latest developments. It is clear that up to Thursday night the Hungarian insurgents were confident that they had succeeded in overthrowing the existing regime. It was this confidence that led to the massacre in Budapest's Parliament Square ...

Mr. Fry reported that heavy fighting continued throughout Thursday night ...—particularly in the Gellert Hill area. (Here Hitler's S.S. fought on to the death against the advancing Russians in 1945. The steep hill makes it difficult ground for tanks.)

The district surrounding the British Legation is quiet. The American Legation is cut off from the outside world altogether.

On Thursday some 2,000 rebels arrived outside the British Legation. About 50 went inside to state their case to Mr. Fry. They demanded that Hungary's case should be taken up by the United Nations. They argued that the Warsaw Pact, under which the Communists claim the Russian troops were invited in, applies only to external aggression.

Diplomatic sources in London state that in fact the Russian troops moved against the insurgents four hours before Imre Nagy took over as Prime Minister and four and three-quarter hours before his broadcast inviting Russian action.

Daily Mail (London), 27 October

Warsaw

Thousands of young people demonstrated in the streets of Warsaw tonight in an outburst of feeling against the Soviet Union and of sympathy with Hungarians trying to throw off the Soviet yoke.

For a short while, it appeared that the demonstrations might get out of hand. But swift sympathetic handling of the situation by interior security troops prevented an explosion of violence.

New York Times, 25 October

Radio Free Miskolc: "Regardless of Comrade Nagy's Answer..."

Miskolc

End the massacre of Hungarians in Budapest! Do not believe deceptions! Let them withdraw Soviet troops from Hungary! Strike! ...

We have had enough—enough of the autocracy of certain leaders. We too want socialism, but according to our own special Hungarian conditions, which reflect the interests of the Hungarian working class and the Hungarian nation, and our most sacred national sentiments.

We demand that all persons who compromised themselves by the cult of personality be eliminated immediately ...

We demand that those Communists and non-Communists be given the most important positions in Government and Party life who, in following the principles of proletarian internationalism, honor above all else our Hungarian national traditions and our thousand-year history.

We demand the revision of the institutions of the state security authority and the elimination immediately of all leaders and functionaries who are compromised ...

We demand a public trial of Mihaly Farkas before an independent court, regardless whether this trial may reflect on individuals currently holding important office.

With regard to the grave errors committed in the field of planned economy we demand the immediate dismissal of the responsible leaders of the planning offices.

We demand an increase of real wages.

We believe our demands will be realized when our parliament ceases to be an electoral machine, and the members of parliament cease being yes-men.

We demand that March 15th be proclaimed a national holiday, and we also demand that October 6th be a national memorial day.

Radio Free Miskolc

Budapest

Led by the First Secretary of the Party Committee of the County Borsod, a workers' delegation called on Comrade Nagy. Imre Nagy listened to the delegation, and, through them, sent the County's workers a message that he was in agreement with their suggestions and proposals and would undertake to carry them out. He would shortly form a new Government, a PPF Government. As regards the composition of the Government, he would give the greatest consideration to the wishes and proposals of the people. These, too, would be embodied in the new Government's program. He would shortly submit its program to the National Assembly.

Comrade Nagy expressed thanks for the trust of the workers of Diosgyor and Miskolc and the population of the County as conveyed by the delegation. He said that this, too, would give him strength in his work. He asked for their support in the implementation of the Government's program. He asked them to continue work because the Government needed production in order to raise the standard of living. He expressed his conviction that the people of Borsod would give him their support. He asked them to continue to ensure order and calm in the County.

Radio Kossuth

Miskolc

The Committee of the Workers' Council of Greater Miskolc and the Party Committee, regardless of the answer made by Comrade Imre Nagy, have decided to maintain the demands submitted in the resolution of the working people of Borsod County and Miskolc as long as they are not fulfilled.

Our proclamation issued to the workers in connection with these demands, which bears the Kossuth arms, consists of five points:

(1) We demand that the Soviet Army shall leave the country at once. (2) A new Hungarian Government. (3) The right to strike. (4) Complete amnesty for Hungarians who have participated in the revolution. (5) As long as these demands are not met, the people of Borsod County and Greater Miskolc will remain on strike, with the exception of railways, mining, health services, public supply, electric power and the press.

We ask the population of Borsod County to conduct themselves in accordance with the above message, to follow attentively the resolutions of the Workers' Council of Greater Miskolc which will be made known by the radio and in the press, and to observe them under all conditions in a disciplined manner and without provocation.

We also announce that public supply and public utilities are operating 100 per cent. We will not tolerate any strikes in these fields.

The people should keep calm. Working people should under all conditions go to their places of work and await with discipline the resolutions of the Council, all the while safeguarding public property and personal security. If they do not appear at their places of work their wages will suffer ...

Young workers and students! Conduct yourself in a disciplined manner. Do not offer any cause for interference by the authorities. We are able to assert our demands without bloodshed. In the attainment of their ends you can furnish the people of Budapest the greatest aid if you carry on the strike in a disciplined manner and if you do not demonstrate unnecessarily. Do not commit any provocation or any sabotage, because the only thing we would achieve by that would be the weakening of our common forces.

Assist us and do not give way to ill-considered enthusiasm and student romanticism! We are not cowards but we cannot be irresponsible either. We understand your anxieties on account of the events in Budapest, but we are anxious for you too. The country needs not heroic dead but honest working citizens ...

In the interest of insuring the withdrawal of Soviet troops, we have sent a telegram to the Council of Ministers. Have confidence in us! We have been elected by the workers and not by the government!

... The workers council furthermore requests leaders of enterprises and plants to elect their representatives to these councils with the utmost urgency, without regard for Party affiliation.

Radio Free Miskolc [01 : 10]

Secret Radio
Vienna

A secret radio is broadcasting calls for "a new Government in the spirit of Bela Kun and Laszlo Rajk." Bela Kun was dictator of Hungary after the First World War. Foreign Minister Rajk was executed as a "Titoist" in 1949 ...

Lawrence Davis, Daily Express (London), 26 October

"Broadcasting the Truth"
Vienna

News of the revolution first seems to have spread from Budapest and other cities by way of workers who lived outside the cities, by broadcasts against the rebels over the Government radio, and by improvised radios set up by the insurgents.

A radio and television student told me how he had used his knowledge in Budapest. "On Wednesday morning students in trucks brought arms to the university in Buda. Our polytechnic collegium could not get any, however, for the A.V.H. locked us in.

"When I went home in the afternoon I made a short-wave set, and began broadcasting our 14 demands. I stated that the Government had refused to accept them.

"During the following days I broadcast all morning the general opinion of the people, in contrast to what the Government 'Kossuth' radio was saying. As time went on, the Government's line came closer to the line of the people. They could not resist the pressure in the streets.

"When I was not broadcasting, I walked unarmed around the streets of Budapest to see what was happening. I talked to people; I watched the fighting; I saw young girls throw 'Molotov cocktails' at Russian tanks. Then, I broadcast to the world the truth, that we were not the counterrevolutionaries the Government said, but rather, the whole Hungarian people fighting for our freedom."

George Sherman, The Observer (London), 11 November

26 OCTOBER

"Mopping Up the Remnants"

Budapest

The Council of Ministers of the Hungarian People's Republic appeals to the inhabitants of Budapest not to go out into the streets all day today. This measure is necessary because early this morning the mopping-up of the remnants of armed revolutionary groups has begun throughout the area of the capital. The restoration of order is in progress. There will be no work today in factories, except for public utilities—gas, electricity and water, the telephone exchanges, food factories, and bakeries—which must supply the population without interruption. Those employed in enterprises of this type must carry identification papers, since they may be challenged in the streets. The Council of Ministers relies on the discipline and patriotism of the inhabitants of Budapest, who can best promote the restoration of order by helping the resumption of peaceful, constructive work.

Radio Kossuth [04 : 30]

Budapest

During the night from Thursday to Friday the guns thunder. Machine-gun and carbine shots ring out. Underneath the windows of my hotel room 20 to 25 Soviet tanks drive past. From the south, from the direction of the large working-class quarter of Csepel, one can hear dull booms— artillery fire. It is shortly before midnight. Curfew since 6 p.m. In spite of that youths and civilians, pistols in their hands, slink along the walls.

I spoke with some of the rebel leaders. They are Communists. They are thinking on the lines of a kind of a popular front. They are burning patriots, steeled in battles, who want no return to the old feudal state of affairs. They want the Hungarian way to Socialism.

5 a.m. The battle goes on with undiminished force. It is not possible to make sure just exactly where clashes are continuing. No one is to be seen on the streets any more.

7 a.m. The battles continue, undiminished, as day breaks. Heavy tanks move towards Csepel, gunfire becomes heavier and heavier.

At 10 a.m., as I complete this first report from Budapest, heavy clashes are raging in Soroksar

(in the south of the city) on Boraros Square. The Soviets are shooting into houses there. In Csepel the workers have dug themselves in. Leaflets are being distributed demanding the resignation of Nagy, as he is a "traitor" ...

Eugen-Géza Pogany, Deutsche Presse Agentur, 27 October

Budapest

As our listeners have already been informed on the radio, the inhabitants of Budapest wishing to buy food have been given permission by the Government to go out into the streets from 10:00 to 15:00. The Ministry of the Interior wishes to emphasise that troops engaged in mopping-up operations will fire on anyone with a weapon in his hand. Nobody is allowed on the streets after 15:00. No traffic across the bridges will be allowed all day.

Radio Kossuth [10 : 00]

"A War"

Budapest

What began here Tuesday as a demonstration turned that same night into a revolt and yesterday became a war that was still raging today.

It is war by Soviet troops and Hungarian political policeman against the mass of the Hungarian people. The war is being waged on behalf of the Soviet Union and in support of the Hungarian Communist Government, which would fall in ten minutes if it were not for the presence of Soviet tanks in Budapest.

The Soviet troops were called in by the Hungarian Government while it still was dominated by Erno Gero, who had succeeded Matyas Rakosi ... Imre Nagy, for whose appointment as Premier the insurgent masses had been calling, did not take office until after the invitation to the Soviet troops had been sent, although by doing so he countenanced it.

Mr. Gero's removal from power did not occur until Mikhail A. Suslov, a member of the Soviet Presidium, and Anastas I. Mikoyan, a Soviet First Deputy Premier, who had successively visited Hungary when the fall of Mr. Rakosi was imminent, arrived in Budapest yesterday for a brief visit.

As late as last night the insurgents still were calling for a democratic government headed by Mr. Nagy, but one that would accede to demands that no Communist regime anywhere had yet accepted. But they were saying that Mr. Nagy already had demonstrated he was no Gomulka ...

The trouble seems to be that Hungary has no Communist, who like Mr. Gomulka would have courage to defy the Soviet leaders. The only alternative mentioned during the last few days has been Bela Kovacs, former leader of the Smallholders Party who was imprisoned by the Russians when he tried to defy them in 1948. But his advent would mean the end of communism in Hungary and no one believes the Soviet leaders would allow that.

On this fourth day of the revolt, it shows no sign of subsiding. Last night the firing was heavier than ever.

This correspondent counted forty-seven Soviet tanks as they passed along the Danube in the direction of Csepel Island, which contains the greatest aggregation of industry in Hungary. There was fighting last night in the hills of Buda across the river, although Buda previously had been quiet.

John MacCormac, New York Times, 27 October

What Happened in Magyarovar

Magyarovar

This is a little town about ten kilometres away from the Austrian border. The bodies of eighty-two people are lying side by side in the chapel of the cemetery. I counted them one by one, and stopped in front of each of them. ... Nearly all of them were very young, as far as I could judge. The smell of blood, mingled with the scent of the flowers which the population had brought, pervaded the cemetery chapel. Here lay 82 martyrs who made one of the most glorious pages of history and who demonstrated the insurrection in one of Hungary's provincial towns ... They had made up a large group of people who were heading for the barracks of the security police in order to throw out the occupants. There were almost a thousand of them, mainly students and workers from local bauxite factories who had been on strike for four days. The policemen awaited the attack, sheltered in small trenches which had been dug in front of the barracks. When the group approached, an officer, hands over his head, walked towards the group to negotiate. The crowd stopped. The officer exchanged a few words and shook hands with some of the men whom he knew personally, as he lived in Magyarovar himself. He even embraced two or three of them. Then he returned to his men and fellow officers— thirty in all. He took out his pistol and as the demonstrators approached he fired into the air. This was the signal for the massacre. The thirty armed soldiers standing behind their machine guns unexpectedly opened fire on the crowd, which was in no way prepared for such foul play. It had all happened within a split-second. Numerous students and workers doubled up and collapsed. Cries of terror and horror rose to the skies of Magyarovar. The blood ran from victims' torn flesh. The roar of powerful grenades thrown by the security police joined the rattle of machine guns. Bits of human flesh were strewn all around the site of this mass slaughter. This horrifying massacre was witnessed by some of the terrorized population, who had first thought that the occupants of the barracks would give themselves up without any blood being spilled ...

The survivors had gone to ask for reinforcements. When they returned to the barracks, the latter seemed deserted. Only three officers remained, and they were all trying to escape. One of them had thrown himself from the window of the third floor. His body landed on the pavement and parts of his brains had squirted out of his open skull ... the two others were captured. The crowd threw itself upon them. They were beaten until their bodies were mere sanguinary objects. Then they were split into pieces as if this had been the work of wild animals.

Bruno Tedeschi, Il Giornale d'Italia (Rome), 30 October

Magyarovar

"We are not cruel", said someone who spoke English to me, "but the women and children killed by grenades must be avenged" ...

The head of the committee explained the insurgent attitude to me. "Three times", he said, "the Government has acted too late. If Nagy had been appointed Prime Minister only one day sooner, nothing would have happened, or at most a few demonstrations. For while we want democracy and freedom, we also want socialism. If Nagy had not called in the Russian troops everything would have returned to normal on the first day because we had confidence in his government. If Gero had been expelled from the Communist Party twenty-four hours earlier, there would have been no need to appeal to the Russians. If Gero, when speaking on the radio, had not described us as 'terrorists' and 'fascists', if the Government had understood our claims, the revolt would have ceased immediately. Unluckily the Government took a day too long to realize that we were neither fascists nor terrorists. The

Massacre

Vienna

Your Correspondent was able to cross into Hungary from the Austrian frontier town of Nickelsdorf, on the main Vienna—Budapest road, and go on about 10 miles to the town of Magyarovar. In Magyarovar on Friday morning, some 80 people were killed and about 100 wounded when a detachment of A. V. H. (State secret police) opened fire on a large unarmed crowd of demonstrators who had gone to their barracks on the outskirts of the town to tear down the red star . . .

The people of Magyarovar took their revenge. Of the four officers of a detachment of A. V. H. about 20 strong, one was killed on the spot. The three others took refuge in a cellar of the barracks. One of the three, said to have been the commander, escaped. The others were killed in the afternoon. One was lynched; the other was hanged from a plane tree in the Lenin Ut, one of the main streets of the town.

The demonstration in Magyarovar followed what, from accounts reaching here, is the standard pattern of the protest of the Hungarian people. About 10 o'clock in the morning a crowd assembled in the centre of the town and set out for the barracks with the intention of replacing the red star by the Hungarian red, white, and green tricolour. By the time the crowd reached the barracks it appears to have numbered several thousand — by some accounts, most of the population of the town, which numbers 22,000, was there . . .

In front of the barracks the crowd sang the national anthem and other Hungarian patriotic songs. This part of the proceedings was described to your correspondent by a middle-aged professional man who had been there. Speaking quietly and with evident truthfulness, he said: "The A. V. H. opened fire with machine-guns and flung hand-grenades. They gave no warning. People were mown down. It was an entirely peaceful demonstration. We wanted only to remove the star."

After describing how the A. V. H. officers were killed he added: "What will happen now is in God's hands, but we want freedom for Hungary." A woman who joined in the conversation said: "I was in Budapest two days ago. It was the same there as here yesterday. The people demonstrated peacefully, shouting: 'Down with the red star!' and 'Out with the Russians'."

Magyarovar and the surrounding countryside are now in the hands of a national committee of 20, representing the workers and the young people of the town. The committee has turned out the previous Communist administration and has its headquarters in the town hall, which is also the seat of the county administration. There are no Russian troops in or about Magyarovar. The nearest appeared to be in Gyor (Raab).

A member of the committee said: "We do not regard ourselves as counter-revolutionaries, but the new Government must base its policy on the wishes of the people. We have shown here what we think of the old system and want a free and independent Hungary controlled by a Government that does not rely on foreign armed support. We are willing to support the new Government, but it must show its spirit before we trust it fully." . . .

In Magyarovar, we were first shown the tree in the Lenin Ut on which the A. V. H. officer was hanged. The twigs on one of the branches were torn. There was a big splash of blood on the kerb. Ironically enough, the street signs bearing Lenin's name had not been removed. A Hungarian who had joined the group was hoisted up by two others so that he could be photographed taking down one of the shields. As he pulled it off the old name of the street could be seen on the reserve side.

From there we were taken to the cemetery, the main walk of which, thickly lined with plane trees, was crowded with mourners. In a mortuary, the bodies of six men and three women were lying on the floor, the blood still unwashed on their wounds. From their clothing all seemed to be working-class people. Some had tiny bunches of flowers on their breasts. Outside two other corpses lay on biers.

In the main hall of a chapel near by, hung with black curtains and with an altar at the far end, 14 bodies lay on the floor. Behind the curtains on the left were the bodies of two women and one man on the floor; behind the curtains on the right, the body of a young man. Two other bodies here were in coffins. One was a young woman: the other was a child of about 18 months. "Send out the news of this," said the man who lifted the lid of the child's coffin to show the lightly shrouded corpse.

The Times (London), 29 October

Russians had begun firing. The civil war turned into a patriotic war of Hungarians against Russians. We do not want the Russians in our country. They are taking the uranium from our mines and exploiting our mineral resources. The whole army joined our ranks and even the communists fought at our side. On the first day the democrats fought against the Stalinists. Then, after the Russians had fired, the whole army and population, whatever their party, spontaneously reacted against the foreign troops. We are not organized. We have no chief. We have no arms. The revolt broke out of itself without any preparation."

That is what the insurgents of Magyarovar told me. They want free elections, democracy, a representative government, freedom for all parties, a general amnesty, the trial of the Stalinist leaders. The departmental committees controlled by the insurgents (at Gyor, Raab, Komaron, etc.) have submitted claims, summarized in a dozen or so items, and often contradictory No mention is made therein of altering the political structure; the economic reforms and social achievements are questioned by no one ...

Giorgio Bontempi, Il Paese (Rome), 28 October

"No Such Thing"

Pecs

This is Radio Pecs. We notify the inhabitants of the City and County that there is no such thing as a revolutionary committee. All that has happened is this. One or two irresponsible elements, posing as a revolutionary committee, broke into the studio in the evening hours and had an announcement read.

(Signed) *Gyorgy Bradacs, Head of the Baranya County District of the Ministry of the Interior*

Attention, attention! We now read an important announcement. Attention, attention. Curfew! Curfew! Until further notice in the area of the City of Pecs, I order curfew until six a. m. It is forbidden to be in the streets and squares.

(Signed) *Gyorgy Bradacs, Colonel*

Radio Pecs [02 : 20]

The resistance groups Kinizsy and Zriny, should report and keep in contact! Until further instructions, the direction of the attack remains unchanged. *Radio Free Baranya (Pecs) [11 : 45]*

In the West

Vienna

Travellers who reached Nickelsdorf to-night said that the rebellion has spread to the provinces. All of Western Hungary is said to be in rebel hands.

Two Resistance radios, apparently giving military orders, have been heard. One is at Miskolc and another at Pecs, a coal-mining town near the Jugoslav border, where the miners have joined a general strike called by the rebels. The strike has halted all rail traffic.

Daily Telegraph (London), 27 October

Nagy Accepts Borsod Demands

Budapest

Comrade Imre Nagy has adopted the demands of the people from Borsod. A workers' delegation from Borsod County headed by Rudolf Földvári came to Prime Minister Imre Nagy. The people from Borsod published a very important proclamation which — among other things — sharply and energetically condemned the policy which brought the country into this grave crisis. The proclamation establishes that the workers of Borsod want socialism and that they will suppress "any possible attempt at restoration". They enumerated 21 demands.

Among other things they demand: a public trial for Mihály Farkas and his associates; the revision and publication of foreign trade agreements; the correction of grave faults in the planned economy and the replacement of the persons responsible.

They demand that our national treasure, uranium ore, should be utilized according to the interest of the Hungarian people.

In matters concerning the living standard of the people the workers of Borsod demand that basic wages be raised and that the concealed price rise be stopped, that the age limit for pensions be lowered, pensions and family allowances be raised. They demand the elimination of taxes for childlessness, the granting of railway-fare reductions, increased housing construction, and support for the building of small houses.

Further they said: we agree with the socialist road in agriculture, but we demand that reorganization be conducted with full observance of the voluntary principle and with consideration for the interests of the peasantry and their national characteristics.

On political matters they completely agree with the political changes in Poland under Gomulka; they condemn the "yes-men" of the Hungarian Parliament and demand that Soviet troops be withdrawn from the territory of Hungary by January 1st at the latest ...

To the workers of Borsod and Miskolc Comrade Imre Nagy replied that he agreed with every point of the demands and would implement them. Tonight, or tomorrow morning, a new Government would be formed, a Patriotic People's Front Government. As to the composition of the Government, he would give the utmost consideration to the wishes, demands and suggestions of public opinion. In his new Governmental program Comrade Imre Nagy will embody these demands, and he will soon submit them to the National Assembly. Imre Nagy explained that in certain matters the demands could even be surpassed.

Nagy pointed out that the confidence of the workers lends strength to his work but he requested the following from the workers of Borsod: that they help and support him in carrying out the Government program, which fully agrees with their demands. They should see to it that production be resumed as soon as possible because Government measures to raise the standard of living call for more and more production. This should be the first step in support of the Government by workers of Miskolc, Diosgyoer and the entire county of Borsod. This support, comrade Nagy said, he was convinced would be forthcoming. He then said that Miskolc and Borsod had reason to be proud of the fact that there had been no disturbances and provocations there. He asked the people of Miskolc and Borsod to see that this should be so in the future, that they should ensure order in the factories ...

Radio Kossuth [13:00]

Communist Declarations

Budapest

Since the two world wars our country has not experienced days as tragic as these. A fratricidal battle is raging in the capital city of our country. The number of injured is estimated to run into thousands, and of the dead into hundreds. An immediate end must be put to the bloodshed. The Central Committee therefore announces the following measures:

1. A recommendation ... for the election of a new national Government. This Government shall make good without fail the mistakes and crimes of the past ... The Central Committee, led by Comrade Imre Nagy, is presenting recommendations regarding members of a Government to be formed on the basis of the broadest national foundations.

2. The new Government shall start negotiations with the Soviet Government, on the basis of independence, complete equality and non-interference in internal affairs, to settle relations between our countries. As a first step towards this end, after the restoration of order, Soviet troops will immediately return to their bases. Complete equality between Hungary and the Soviet Union corresponds with the interests of both countries, because only on that basis can a truly fraternal, unbreakable Hungarian-Soviet friendship be built. It is on that basis that relations between Poland and the Soviet Union are now being reshaped. [Note: in a repetition of the text of this statement in a Budapest broadcast at 21:00 this reference to relations between Poland and the Soviet Union was omitted.]

3. The Central Committee deems correct the election of Workers' Councils in the factories through the intermediary of the trade union organs ...Wage increases must be implemented ...

4. The Government shall grant an amnesty to all those who have taken part in the armed battles, with the sole condition that they lay down their arms immediately, or by 22:00 tonight at the latest.

5. The Central Committee and the Government leave no room for doubt regarding their standpoint on socialist democracy, but at the same time they are firmly resolved to defend the achievements of our People's Democracy and not to relinquish anything in the cause of socialism ... It warns those who raise their arms against the power of our People's Republic and fail to lay down weapons within the time limit fixed: they shall be annihilated without mercy.

6. Immediately after order has been restored we shall set about elaborating all the changes to be made ...

We need peace and order so that not a single life should be lost from now on, so that parents and children, married couples and lovers may find each other again, and so that we can heal the wounded and console those who mourn. We need order and peace so that work can be resumed ...

Hungarian soldiers! Stand in the vanguard of establishing order. It is in you that the population of the capital places confidence. Leave no room for provocation. Clear the streets of those fishing in troubled waters.

In these fateful days great tasks await Communists. Let them meet and talk with the people sincerely. Let them talk, straight to the hearts of the truly patriotic people. Let them explain events and reassure the people. With an adult sense of responsibility let them tell the youth: what you have rightly asked for, you have attained!

The Party's top leadership is almost completely new. Just how new is this Party leadership? It suffices to say that all three Secretaries — Janos Kadar, Ferenc Donath and Gyula Kallai — have for years been prisoners of Rakosi-type despotism; as victims of faked trials they spent years in prison from which they only recently have been released. If anyone knows that the old road must not be taken it is they. Let Communists explain that whoever seeks to spread distrust against these men and to set the people against them helps everybody except the people ...

Radio Kossuth

The Government in Despair

Munich

Although only at noon today Radio Budapest said that Mr. Nagy would try to negotiate a [Soviet] withdrawal by January 1, the promise was not repeated in the Central Committee's declaration broadcast in the afternoon. Nor, incidentally, was it mentioned in Moscow radio's summary of Mr. Nagy's speech or in any other East European reports on the situation in Hungary, except in those put out by the official Polish news agency ...

The rebel radio at Miskolc rejected the promises Mr. Nagy had made in a broadcast reply to demands by the workers of Borsod County, and reiterated the rebels' demands, including the right to strike, and called for the continuation of the present strike until such time as the demands were met. It announced the formation of a "workers' council" for the Greater Miskolc area and called upon the population to cooperate with it.

It would seem that what the Hungarian people desire most, next to moral support, would be a reference of the whole matter to the United Nations. The use of Soviet troops in Hungary may lend itself to some form of action there. The whole matter is likely to be aggravated, possibly in the near future, by the apparent success of the rebels, which, if it continues, will require the bringing of considerable Soviet reinforcements into Hungary.

The obvious danger is that the revolt may spread to the other satellite countries and thus threaten to knock not only Hungary but the whole of Eastern Europe out of the Soviet bloc. It would appear to serve the Soviet interest much better to arrive at some accommodation with the rebels, as indeed they have done in the case of Gomulka, in order to stop the rot, or the fighting, from spreading.

The Nagy Government is still in no mood to surrender to the rebels, but this evening a new trend was discernible in Budapest Radio broadcasts. It looked as if, by agreeing to treat with workers' committees representing various industrial areas, by stating irrevocably that the Government "accepts all their demands" — while taking care not to name them — and by recommending the further formation of such committees in other areas, the Government was trying to take the wind out of the rebels' sails.

These are the tactics of a desperate group of people now representing what must have become a very small minority of the Hungarian population. Indeed, it is by no means certain that the Government remains in Budapest. Certainly the broadcasts that claim to come from Budapest Radio — which seems to have been wrecked in the fighting — do not come from the centre of Budapest. In the past few days, the radio has given its telephone number to listeners — so that parents may send messages to be broadcast to their sons — and these numbers proved to be those of buildings in outlying parts of the city ...

The one object that certainly does remain in the hands of the Government is the Budapest Radio transmitter, located some way out of the city. If only the rebels had first attacked the transmitter site and not the building which housed the studios, the whole course of the revolution might have been different ...

Victor Zorza, Manchester Guardian, 27 October

A Polish Correspondent Reports

Budapest

Our pilot taxis the plane to the airport building. I can make out a group of people near a blue bus, with white flags and red crosses; we have brought medicine and blood plasma ... In the distance we hear machine-guns. A heavy tank drives in; from another side an armored car; soldiers with red-starred helmets jump out and surround our plane. Light machine-guns pointed at us. The soldiers' faces are covered with dirt; they are unshaven and sweating. My heart beats. Why are they pointing their weapons at me? An officer in a leather coat leaps out from the tank and explains that they have come to ensure the security of the plane ... I look at the faces of the Soviet soldiers. I see not only tiredness on their faces, not only the burden of days spent in fighting and under fire, but their eyes express insecurity, something uncomfortable, something which suggests how ill at ease they feel in their present role. It is not only my impression; my friend R. feels it too: the Russian uncertainty, and the stiff silent hatred of a group of Hungarians ...

We had left Warsaw convinced that Hungary had become peaceful, and here before reaching Budapest, we hear about the war, about "front lines". We hear shooting. E. takes me aside towards a young woman in a dark blue coat over a white nurse's uniform. The woman speaks slowly, but with obvious emotion: "You are a journalist — you simply don't have the right to lie! It is a lie that fascist and counter-revolutionaries are fighting in the city. We are fighting, our nation is fighting, for *real* democracy, for *real* socialism, for freedom and independence! You will be convinced about this yourself. Our aims are the same as those which your own nation put forward."... The woman (a surgeon, as I learned later) goes off into the Red Cross bus. A big black motor-car of our Polish Embassy is waiting for us; we follow the bus. There is deadly silence in our car.

In front of us is the road to Budapest. At the Soviet post, heavy weapons, several nests of machine-guns. All the soldiers are in position, with their fingers on the trigger. An officer with a small machine-gun and several soldiers come forward with their guns pointing at us: "From the Polish Embassy?" — He takes a rapid look at the passengers. We can proceed. Two kilometres further at a cross-road, we are stopped again. Another armed checkpoint: "*Lengyel* (Pole)?" Friendly smiling faces. "Poles are friends, Poles are brothers." This happens again and again before our car enters the streets of a workers' suburb.

Long walls of empty factories. Little houses in front of which a few people hover, ready to hide. Something uncanny in the air. An atmosphere which I cannot yet define. Is it horror, fear, hatred, or despair? ... Behind the iron gates of one of the industrial works, a group of armed people. They explain that they are workers, revolutionaries who are defending their factories ... At one of the insurgent posts, we are advised to take a longer road because on the Ullei Street there is heavy fighting going on between Hungarian soldiers, defending their barracks, and Soviet tanks ... From windows and balconies, heavy wet flags are drooping, white-green-red, and also black colours of mourning. The symbol of freedom and the symbol of death, the price of freedom.

The national flags have a jagged hole in the middle. A few days ago there was a coat of arms there. Why? ... The answer is cruel but I must face it. The coat of arms which was cut out was the symbol of a régime which was not a régime of freedom and of human happiness, although these aims presided at its birth. I don't know the details; I canot yet give a full analysis of the past ten or twelve years in Hungary, but I know that it was a cruel period. I know that Stalinist terror broke human minds and hearts, I know that freedom was transformed into slavery, truth into falsehood and hypocrisy. I know that the noblest of all ideas has been polluted with mud and blood, and that crimes were hidden by hollow phrases.

The system which was proudly called "people's democracy" had infinitely less in common either with people or with democracy than in any country. I know about this from many personal accounts, from deeply anguished letters of Hungarian friends; I know it from the tears of the widow of Laszlo Rajk; I feel it from the terrifying

coldness of these flags with the hole in the middle ... Here is the square, spacious and empty, with high houses on all sides. In the middle, a block of granite with two enormous bronze boots on it, and above them a fluttering white-green-red flag. There is something deeply moving in the sight which contains the tragedy and the greatness of these days. I see it as the symbol of the Hungarian revolution ... This happened during the evening of the 23rd, when the crowd, enraged at the criminal murder of young people by the AVO troops, seized arms. Those who called for democracy, freedom, socialism, were murdered by police machine-guns ...

It is not easy to write about all this. For so many years I believed in a good which did not exist, in a nobility which turned out to be only depravity, in a greatness which was nothing but vileness. To understand now does not ease one's conscience. The pain, the anguish, the anger is all the greater ... Thus the people smashed the statue, breaking the symbol of slavery and wild oppression and crime. The statue resisted ... But the man of bronze fell ... This is the fall of a new Bastille. Here on its ruins, we see the flag of freedom which opens the road towards the future of a socialism freed from lies and vices, from a system which falsely paraded as socialism. We have only one thought: the tanks should vanish as soon as possible from this road. Those tanks should after all, be defending freedom and not strangling it with gun-fire.

Another turn, a street full of autumn trees, a street named after Gorki. What would you say, Comrade Maxim: "*Man — how proud a word*"?

One thing emerges from all the chaotic information—the whole nations is on the side of the insurgents. The division is clear: the nation on one side, and on the other, the Stalinist faction of the Government and the AVO. There are thousands of Communists among the insurgents. The Hungarian Army is either neutral or takes the side of the revolution. The workers have occupied their own plants. The whole working class youth and the students are on the barricades. The Soviet Army was called in by Gero.

"It would be criminal to call us fascists, or counter-revolutionaries", shouts T. on the telephone; T. is a Communist, an intellectual, a man of great heart and keen mind. In the voice of R. there is a pained sadness and anguish. "I fought in Spain, I fought in the underground against Hitler, and now I am called a counter-revolutionary. Judge for yourself." ...

I shall have to get more details. But one thing is certain: one cannot talk to one's own nation in the language of guns, and foreign guns, at that, when the nation demands the recognition of its inalienable rights to freedom and justice ...

E. puts on the radio. The Wagnerian music irritates us; suddenly there is a slow tired voice.

The words sound like a prayer. The poet Tamasi calls it "Hungarian Prayer". The theme? "What had to happen, happened ... We were thirsty, but instead of clear water, we were given mud to drink. We must find our own way of life in democracy and national independence. Only a government which expresses the will of the nation can bring peace again to the wounded toilers of Hungary ..."

An old Hungarian woman says: "Nobody will lay down arms until we are sure that Soviet forces will evacuate. Everybody says that, communists and non-communists, the young and the old. These are Hungarian affairs and only Hungary can deal with them ..."

Marian Bielicki, Po Prostu (Warsaw), 25 November

"Life Itself Has Decided ..."

Budapest

The resolution of the Central Committee about forming Workers' Councils is not the outcome of a few hours' debate. This resolution has been ripening for many months ... Debates were conducted ... Now life itself has decided this question. We cannot say yet that the details of the new system of management by the workers are completely clear. We have to collect experience; life has to show us the most suitable forms for workers' management in our country. ... The Central Committee of our Party and the newly elected political committee have deep confidence in our working class ...

Radio Kossuth

How to Surrender, and Other Advice

Budapest

Today's Party and Government resolutions grant an amnesty to those who lay down their arms by 22:00 this evening. As regards the execution of the resolution, the HQ of the Government Forces has issued the following statement: Those fighting in formations or groups should notify their intention to surrender by hoisting a white flag. They must put down their arms in one place and line up on the spot indicated by Government troops. Individual fighters should notify their intent to surrender by throwing away their arms and raising their hands. We repeat that the final time-limit for laying down arms is 22.00 this evening. [17:34]

Members of the armed forces, soldiers, armed workers, Comrades! ... In the spirit of reconciliation, and prompted by the desire that the severity of the law should not punish any misguided but well-meaning people, the Government has extended the amnesty to everyone who will lay down his arms by 22.00 today. Treat those who lay down their arms humanely. Let them go home after they have surrendered. But, after the time limit expires, deal annihilating blows to all those who continue the armed fight against the people's power. May your heroic struggles to protect the peace and freedom of our people succeed. We will be with you with all the warmth of our hearts, in the hour of decisive action. [20:08]

The Central Committee of the Hungarian Workers' Party and the Council of Ministers of the People's Republic.

It is becoming increasingly difficult to mislead the honest people. In this serious situation every honest worker, every patriotic youth, every Communist has a new task before him: join the Workers' Councils that have been formed. Lose no time in forming in every factory, every building, committees to maintain order. Do all you can to prevent further bloodshed. Publicise the amnesty decree, and convert those who still hesitate. Every minute is precious. The fatherland needs the life of every worker. [20:45]

The Budapest Party Committee of the Hungarian Workers' Party

There may be some who think that the amnesty decree proves the weakness of the Government. No, this is not so. Although we dislike threats and do not approve of a policy of intimidation we have to say that those who do not obey kind words, those who do not find the amnesty decree sufficient will feel the force centered in the hands of the Government. We repeat: end bloodshed, stop the fight! This is our main endeavor and our common interest! Hungarians, accept the amnesty decree. You still have 16 minutes. Lay down your arms! [21:44]

Young people! The writer Gyula Hay sends you this message. I have had many fine and sensible replies to the message I sent you yesterday, and I feel that it is my duty to speak again. I am addressing you, my dear children, you who have seized arms because you were permeated with patriotic ideals and because your heart was full ... There are dreadful moments ahead — moments of destruction — for all who fail to understand that the armed phase of the struggle has ended. The fight for the same aims must now go on with other, peaceful weapons. The hands of the clock are merciless in their advance. Time is nearly up. There are only some 10 minutes to go. If you wish, all life is in front of you. Courage is needed not only for death: it is necessary for life as well. A heroic life is worth more than an unnecessary death. We are waiting for you with open arms. Let us build the new country together. This is the message of your loving old friend, the writer Gyula Hay. [21:50] *Radio Kossuth*

Russians
Turin

Signor Mario Rossi, conductor of the Italian Symphony Orchestra, who left Budapest on Friday, said: "All eye-witnesses agree absolutely that Russian troops as well as Hungarians joined the insurgents." Russian tanks were in action against Russian tanks in the capital's streets, he added. *News Chronicle (London), 29 October*

"Choking Hate"
Budapest

From what I have seen and been told already there is no doubt that the spearhead of the revolt was in units of the Hungarian Regular Army itself. The Kossuth academy, the Hungarian officers' training school, went over *en bloc* to the rebels.

Others, like the Hadik Barracks, were taken by force, but after half-hearted resistance. Several military commanders are said to have shown themselves "benevolently neutral" by taking no part, but offering the rebels free pick of their arsenal. Three independent eye-witnesses told me how they had seen Hungarian officers distributing arms to the civilian demonstrators. The rebels had also been in possession of some Soviet-type tanks, whose number is put conservatively at about a dozen. One which roared down the Danube embankment with its turrets open was piled high with civilians throwing out patriotic leaflets.

But all accounts of tank incidents are blurred by the problem of identification. The entire armoured element of one Soviet mechanised division, numbering more than 150 tanks, is thought to have been called in with other Russian troops. In an attempt to disguise the detested Soviet presence, Hungarian flags have been hung on many of their tanks. In other cases Hungarian tanks are filled with Russian crews. The rebels seem to have only one clear way of identifying themselves. This is to fly Communist flags with the hammer and sickle slashed away to leave a ragged hole in the middle. Rumours that some Russian troops fraternised with the rebels and taught them how to fire from Soviet tanks are probably wishful thinking, arising from this identification muddle.

It seems fair to say that in some cases the Soviet troops appeared reluctant to carry out their unpleasant job. Yet in other cases their hastiness or wilful brutality have caused needless slaughter ...

This is the most impossible thing to convey out of the tragic Budapest scene yet the most important, the choking hate of the ordinary people against their present masters and the Russians who protect them. For these three days and nights, under the cloak of a military revolt with which they were mostly unconnected, they have been able to give vent to this hate.

The worst side of this hatred is a still unshaken joy and hope at seeing anything Western. A dozen or more times driving around Budapest my car has been hemmed in by passers-by, shouting in English, German, or Hungarian "For God's sake tell the truth about these massacres!" and "Do they know in the West what these Russians are doing?"

One man, thrusting an old Hungarian blade through the car window, cried: "This is our only weapon. When are you going to help us?"

Gordon Shepherd, Daily Telegraph (London), 27 October

Demands From Miskolc
Miskolc

The Students' Parliament of Miskolc worded their demand as follows at the joint meeting held on October 26, 1956:

1. We support the resolutions of the University youth.

2. We demand the immediate and unconditional withdrawal of Soviet troops from Hungary.

3. We demand the immediate liberation of Hungarian war and other prisoners from the Soviet Union.

4. We demand that the former servants of the Rakosi dictatorship be expelled from the government and brought to trial.

5. We demand a people's trial for those responsible for the intervention of Soviet troops and for decreeing summary jurisdiction.

6. We demand the immediate revocation of the Warsaw Treaty and of any other secret military agreements.

7. We demand the rejection of the Soviet loan offer.

8. Our country should become a member of the Danubian Federation proposed by Kossuth.

9. We demand amendments to the constitution and the re-establishment of the Kossuth coat of arms.

10. We demand that our national resources be returned to Hungarian hands.

11. We demand that our country should not join forces with any foreign power, that we remain neutral.

12. We demand that AVH and Police torturers be brought before tribunals.

13. We demand the reorganization of agriculture on the basis of sound economic principles and the abolition of compulsory deliveries.

14. We demand that instruction in the Russian language become a matter of individual choice.

15. We demand the abolition of norms and the just settlement of wages.

16. We demand that the 15th of March become a national holiday and the 6th of October a day of National Mourning.

17. We demand that October 23rd, the first day of our national fight for freedom, become a national holiday.

18. In the schools the teaching of history should be independent of day-to-day politics.

(Signed)   *The Student Parliament of Miskolc High-Schools*

Radio Free Miskolc

"The Price of Peace"

Budapest

On the fourth day, peace seemed near. Nagy had guaranteed amnesty. The last remnants of the first student bands surrendered. They considered that their demands had been met. So too, with some minor exceptions, did the workers from the surburbs. Practically all the citizens' groups that had been engaged in the fight started preaching and practicing cease-fire.

Up to then, at the height of battle the Soviet forces numbered 310 tanks, half of them heavy, 250 armored combat vehicles, and ten thousand men. What there was of the rebellion in the provinces was confined to meetings passing resolutions that were sent to Nagy and organizing local administration. One exception was Magyarovar, a small township between Gyor and the Austrian border, where the local AVH opened fire and the ensuing massacre claimed eighty-five lives.

Popular pressure exacted more and more concessions from the government, and the price of peace continued to rise. There was still some firing by groups fighting independently of any line of command. By Saturday, the fifth day, accurate counting was possible. The rebel army could still count on about eight thousand fighters, while another thirty thousand could be mobilized on short notice. Still the rebels had no leaders

and not much of a program beyond "Out with the Russkies!" and "Down with the AVH!"

Leslie B. Bain, The Reporter (New York), 15 November

Soviet Policy Split?

London

All the evidence suggests that the Soviet leaders —taken aback by the crises in Poland and Hungary—are still discussing what their basic policy in eastern Europe should be. Some members of the Praesidium are all too likely to blame Mr. Khrushchev for having promised too much too soon to the satellite régimes, and for having brought trouble for Russia with all his encouraging talk about "different roads to Socialism." He and others exaggerated the loyalty of the satellite peoples to their régimes and to Russia.

Now there are rumours of splits in the Praesidium. It is probably nearer the truth to say that most of the leaders are divided in their own minds as they weigh the advantages and disadvantages of letting "liberalization" go forward. But, from what is known of the men and of their recent words, it would seem that Mr. Molotov, Mr. Kaganovich, and Mr. Suslov have the gravest doubts about the new road, and they may have Marshal Voroshilov and even Mr. Malenkov leaning to their side.

On the other side have been Mr. Khrushchev, Mr. Shepilov, Mrs. Furtseva, and Mr. Kirichenko —the newer leaders—joined for a good part of the way, at any rate, by Mr. Bulganin and Mr. Mikoyan. Then there are the military leaders, Marshal Zhukov, and Marshal Koniev, whose interest is to see that no policy weakens the military potential of eastern Europe. This interest should incline them to a moderate policy.

Views change in a changing situation. Mr. Khrushchev himself was alarmed by the Polish programme, and then took a prudent and accommodating line. The Praesidium has now to consider the effects of Poland and Hungary together.

Special Correspondent, The Times (London), October 26

Washington, London, Moscow, Berlin and the UN

New York

An American spokesman at United Nations headquarters said his country was consulting with friendly nations on the feasibility and advisability of referring the Hungarian crisis to the United Nations. The United Nations mission here was in constant touch with the State Department, and a decision was expected to be taken soon.

If decided upon, action could possibly be taken under Chapter VII of the United Nations Charter, relating to "threats to the peace, breaches of the

peace, and acts of aggression," or it could come within the purview of Chapter VI relating to the pacific settlement of disputes likely to endanger the maintenance of international peace and security.

There are also the basic principles of the Charter relating to human rights and self-determination, and the use of Russian troops against the Hungarian people might be regarded as a violation of these principles. The sole justification for the presence of Russian troops on Hungarian soil—now that Austria is unoccupied and there is no need to preserve military lines of communication—would appear to be the Warsaw pact, which provides for mutual defence of Soviet Russia and her east European allies. But to invoke this pact as a justification for using Russian occupation forces against a popular uprising in Hungary would be comparable to suggesting that British or American forces stationed in a N.A.T.O. country should be used against similar demonstrations by the people of that country.

However that may be, it is known that western representatives at the United Nations are examining the possibility of bringing Russia to book for her armed intervention in Hungary. Even if no urgent complaint to the Security Council is made, there is still the chance that the matter may be inscribed on the agenda of the forthcoming session of the General Assembly on November 12.

The Times (London), 27 October

London

The British Government has been approached by the United States on the question of raising the developments in Hungary at the United Nations, and particularly the question of the intervention of Soviet forces in the fighting. The French Foreign Minister also told a luncheon of the Foreign Press Association in Paris yesterday that the matter was under discussion between the three Western Powers.

Unless it can be established that the Soviet forces have intervened in Hungary without being asked to do so by the Hungarian authorities, it is not yet clear under what article of the United Nations Charter the question could be raised.

A request was made by demonstrators in Budapest on Thursday to the British Minister that their case should be taken up by the United Nations. A Foreign Office spokesman said that about two thousand demonstrators had arrived outside the legation, and that about fifty of them managed to get inside. The Minister, Mr. Leslie Fry, had gone down to see them, and a representative of the demonstrators had asked him to tell the world that the demonstrations had been entirely peaceful until the unjustified shooting by the security police had begun.

The demonstrators had claimed that the Warsaw Pact, which was given as the excuse for the intervention of the Soviet troops, provided for Soviet assistance only in the case of attack from abroad. This, they claimed, was an internal affair and they asked that the matter should be taken up the United Nations. Mr. Fry replied that he was doing his utmost to keep the British Government informed of events, and he assured them that he would try to act as a faithful reporter. The demonstrators had then left for the American Legation. . . .

Diplomatic Correspondent, Manchester Guardian, 27 October

Washington

The State Department disclosed today that the United States was consulting with Britain, France and other friendly governments on "the feasibility and advisability of bringing the situation in Hungary before the United Nations."

This was revealed by Lincoln White, the State Department spokesman. Officials said later that the United States was making no proposals, but was exploring various possibilities. Mr. White said that among the questions under consideration was that of the legality of the presence of Soviet troops in Hungary under the Warsaw Pact. Statements by President Eisenhower and Secretary of State Dulles on this point have appeared to be in conflict.

The Warsaw Pact of May 14, 1955, is a Soviet version of the North Atlantic Treaty Organization. Under the pact's provisions, Soviet troops have remained in Hungary, a member nation, to "safeguard" her security. The view in the State Department is that there is little doubt that the troops have a right to be there. But a question might be raised about the legitimacy of their use to put down an internal rebellion. Even this raised a problem, however. The Soviet troops are being used at the request of the Hungarian Government. There is little effort in Washington to deny that United States forces abroad could be used in the same way if there were a Communist-led revolution in, say, Italy. In 1944 and 1945, for example, British troops, at the request of the Athens Government, fought Communist rebels in Greece. Furthermore, any possible United Nations approach is at the moment clouded by French threats to use force in Morocco and Tunisia to protect Europeans there.

Edwin L. Dale Jr., New York Times, 27 October

Berlin

The political upheavals in Poland and Hungary, directed so clearly against Stalinism, continue to produce the typically Stalinist echoes in East Germany. The Communist press here, in particular, is trying so hard to pretend that nothing unorthodox is happening that it has become the laughing stock of East Berlin.

For example, the evening newspaper which is known to have been confiscated on Monday for publishing uncensored extracts of Mr. Gomulka's speech, brought out a new version described as "the authorized text". A Communist official seriously suggested to your Correspondent that it might have taken five days to have the speech properly translated.

Similarly, *Neues Deutschland*, which yesterday loudly acclaimed Mr. Gero's "confirmation" as First Secretary of the Hungarian party, mentioned his removal from this post in an embarrassed whisper among the minor news items. . . .

The electrical apparatus works in East Berlin, which still bears the name of J. V. Stalin, has sent a message to a similar works in Warsaw expressing solidarity with the Polish working class. Another East German factory has sent an almost identical message to the Hungarian Government.

The Times (London), 27 October

Moscow

The Moscow radio reported tonight an official Budapest statement admitting that fighting was still raging in Hungary. The Moscow radio and the Soviet press had reported for two days "the failure of the anti-popular venture in Budapest."

The Moscow radio also announced the offer of amnesty to the Hungarian rebels. A news item in Moscow's regular night broadcast said "the Government is master of the situation." It asserted that "more and more concerns are going back to work."

But it did not mention the demand by Hungarian workers' delegations that Soviet troops in Hungary be withdrawn immediately or the promise by Premier Imre Nagy that he would negotiate for the withdrawal of the troops.

Earlier, the Moscow radio had mentioned for the first time that there was an uprising in Hungary and said then that it was over.

Reuters, 26 October

"A City of Mourning"

Budapest

Tonight Budapest is a city of mourning. Black flags hang from every window. For during the past four days thousands of its citizens fighting to throw off the yoke of Russia have been killed or wounded. Budapest is a city that is slowly dying. Its streets and once-beautiful squares are a shamble of broken glass, burnt-out cars and tanks, and rubble. Food is scarce, petrol is running out.

But still the battle rages on. For five hours this morning until a misty dawn broke over Budapest I was in the thick of one of the battles. It was between Soviet troops and insurgents trying to force a passage across the Danube.

Two of the rebels into whose ranks I literally wandered died in the battle, one of them in my arms. Several were wounded. Tonight, as I write this dispatch, heavy firing is shaking the city, which is still sealed off from the rest of the world.

To get here I drove through endless Russian check points and through fighting that has now killed thousands of civilians.... Where formerly the trams ran, the insurgents have torn up the rails to use as anti-tank weapons. At least 30 tanks have been smashed so far, many with Molotov cocktails. Their burnt-out skeletons seem everywhere, spread on both sides of the Danube. Even trees have been dug out as anti-tank barricades. Burned-out cars are used by the rebels at every street corner, but still the Soviet tanks are rumbling through the city. There are at least 50 still in action, together with armoured cars and troop carriers. They fire on anything, almost at sight.

At the moment I can hear, like thunder rolling in the distance, the sound of their 85 mm. guns. They are battling for some objective which sounds about a quarter of a mile away. The Chain Bridge probably. The insurgents have plenty of ammunition, stored in a central dump, but it is all for automatic weapons and the making of Molotov Cocktails.

Travelling around the city is a nightmare, for no one knows who is friend or foe, and all shoot at everybody. There is no doubt now the revolt has been far more bloody than the official radio reports suggested. Casualties number many thousands. The Russian are just unloosing murder at every street corner.... I owe my life to a young girl insurgent who, speaking a little English, helped me to safety after the Russians had opened fire on my car.

It took me three hours to drive from the border to the outskirts of Buda, the hilly part of Budapest. Twice on the way I was stopped by Soviet troops. But each time I persuaded them to let me through. I made for the Chain Bridge that spans the Danube. In front of the bridge stood a barricade of burned out tramcars, a bus, old cars, and uprooted tramlines. It was at least the 50th barricade of its kind I had seen since I entered the city. As I drove towards it, lights full on and the Chain Bridge on my left, heavy firing started from the centre of the bridge. Machine-gun bullets whistled past the car. Then, when some heavier stuff began falling I switched off the lights, jumped out and crawled round to the side.

It was foggy. For ten minutes the firing, in a desultory fashion, went on. Then I heard a whispered voice—a woman's. She spoke first in German, crawled round to where I was crouching, then in halting English told me to get back in my car. She herself, walking, crouched by the car, guided me into a side street. Then, together, we darted back to the road-block.

I found nine boys there, their average age about 18. Three wore Hungarian uniform, but with the hated Red Star torn off. Others wore red, green, and white armbands, the national colours of Hungary. All had sub-machine guns. Their pockets were filled with ammunition. The girl, whose name I discovered was Paula, had a gun too.

Half-way across the bridge I could see the dim outlines of two Soviet tanks. For an hour they fired at us. But never a direct hit — a shell smashed straight through the bus. One of the boys was killed instantly. I tried to help a second boy who was hurt, but he died five minutes later. The shelling went on. We crouched under cover and only splinters hit us. The rebels kept up machine-gun fire all the time. Paula was wounded in the arm, but not seriously. I helped her dress it with one of my handkerchiefs.

"Now you see what we are fighting against", said Paula. She was wearing slacks, bright blue shoes, and a green overcoat.

"We will never give in — never", she said. "Never until the Russians are out of Hungary and the AVH (she pronounced it Avo) is dissolved".   *Noel Barber, Daily Mail (London), 21 October*

An Empire Erupts

London

The Hungarians have added a tragic rider to the Polish example. Though the anti-Russian tradition there has not such deep roots, in such bitter soil, in Hungary as in Poland, there are similarities in the recent history of the two countries. The people of both these Catholic countries are preponderantly hostile to communism; in both, economic pressure has combined with political recalcitrance to produce an explosive mood... But while the Poles—who contrived even in Stalin's lifetime to hold no major state trials—were first on the road towards a relative freedom when the Stalinist fetters began to be removed, the Hungarian rulers, constrained by their own past actions, put up a long and obdurate resistance to the pressures from below. It was only in July that Mr. Rakosi, representative of the hated past, relinquished the party leadership to Mr. Gero, who in turn was suspected of also trying to apply the brakes... Mr. Nagy, the former premier, disgraced because, like Mr. Malenkov, he had paid too much attention to consumer goods, was brought back only when the government was in extremis. By then the spark from Warsaw had ignited the explosive mixture; no course of action remained for a communist regime but to call in the Soviet military fire brigade. Not until that had been done was Mr. Gero deprived of the party leadership. Would swifter action have averted the conflagration? The question is one which the Soviet rulers have to answer for themselves....

To change the mechanics of an empire from coercion to co-operation—even if the co-operation is limited to the communist elect in each country—is a revolutionary change. When the Moscow Politbureau precipitately sent four of its leading members to Warsaw on October 19, Mr. Molotov may still have been dreaming nostalgically of good old Stalin's days, or repeating, in a new context, Pushkin's words of over a century ago:

Tell me: how soon will Warsaw
Proudly lay down the law for us?
Whither shall we withdraw our fortresses?
Beyond the Bug, to Vorskla or Odessa?...

Belatedly, the Soviet leaders grasped the gravity of what was going on. Faced with one of their dead master's victims, they had also inherited the burden of his crimes... They could have taken counsel from Lenin's dictum that

oppressed people are sensitive to nothing as much as to the feeling of equality and to violations of that equality ... particularly by their proletarian comrades.

But the blunder had already been committed; and it may well have played its part in precipitating events in Budapest. Back home again, the Soviet leaders had little leisure to digest their Polish lesson; they have yet another crisis to face ...

Where extravagant hopes perhaps were raised in the West by the Polish insubordination, the agony of Budapest will have come as a cold shower. It is plain that no communist regime will be allowed to collapse without a struggle: mass desertions from the communist block are not in sight. Not even the Poles, with their appetite for domestic experiment, are likely to demand much freedom in shaping their foreign policy; they are in no position to do so. This is not the end. Events still march, and men may still rise or fall. But the statesmen of the West will have to face the question, when the dust has settled, whether a more genuinely national communist government, even if propped by Soviet power, is not preferable to a mere puppet of Moscow. And if their answer is yes, they may well have to encourage such men as Mr. Gomulka—or even Mr. Nagy—on their road to a limited independence, by helping them in their economic difficulties. And, looking further ahead, they will have to consider, too, what can be done to give Germany's eastern neighbours some limited freedom of action in foreign policy by reassuring them about the danger of German expansion, a threat which always weighs upon them ... Without these decisions, the West may have to sit supine watching Communism at grips with itself.

The Economist (London), 27 October

27 OCTOBER

"Life Will Be More Beautiful"

Budapest

Enough bloodshed! Enough ransacked streets! We would love to know whether our children, whether our relatives are still alive. We would love to be together again ... We would love to enjoy life again. We would like not to fear death any longer ... In Hungary, after order has been restored, life will be more beautiful, more human, more Hungarian than it ever was before ... The realization of these plans is guaranteed by the new government, which is national and democratic and is led by Imre Nagy ... Those who accept Hungary's new democratic government will cease fighting immediately, but those who continue fighting, who still choose the way of bloodshed, do not want the democratic revival of the country; they are giving support to the return of landlords, of bankers, of the Esterhazys, and of the Weissmanfreds ...

[7:00]

Yesterday evening 80 weapons were surrendered to the Budapest garrison troops. Several hundred armed persons ceased fighting and surrendered their arms to Government forces around the radio building. According to reports from various parts of the city, last night was quieter than the previous one. In the 5th city district only distant shots were heard. In the 9th there was shooting by armed fighters from some houses during the night. There was less firing in the 10th district. In the 11th, Soviet tanks were shot at from the University of Agriculture and an exchange of fire developed. According to reports from the 11th district, Workers Councils are being set up one after the other. Workers Guards are protecting the factories. A provisional Workers Council has been formed in the Csepel automobile works, where workers have made arrangements to guard the factory. There was no shooting around the plant. Liquidation is still in progress of groups still fighting after expiration of the amnesty deadline at 22:00 hours ...

[7:29]

The inhabitants of Budapest and several provincial towns have drawn our attention to the fact that armed groups in the capital and elsewhere are distributing leaflets containing statements purporting to emanate from the Government and other organs. These are causing confusion. We have been authorized to announce that they are forgeries. The population should not give credence to any leaflets which do not correspond to the spirit of the declaration of Comrade Imre Nagy and the resolution of the Central Committee, and the announcements which the Central Committee has already published ...

[10:00]

A Workers Council has been formed in the Budapest Omnibus Works, and has started work immediately. It has procured food for the workers, and has passed on, or will pass on, the large quantities in its possession to hospitals and clinics.

Workers Councils have been set up in County Csongrad, in most of the factories in Szeged and Hodmezoevasarhely, and in County Heves. Similar reports have come in from the Bekescsaba Clothing Factory and the Machinery Works; from the Nyiregyhaza railway station and tobacco factory; and from the factories in Dunapentele ...

[15:06]

A three-member delegation from Inota and the surrounding district has called on Premier Nagy, bringing 16 wagons of food for Budapest. The delegates handed the Premier the demands of the workers of the Inota aluminium works, backed by the workers and engineers of the "7th November" power station. They will tell the people of Inota that the Government, as Comrade Imre Nagy has put it, agrees with most of their demands. The other points are still under consideration. On their return in a few days time, the delegation will report on the results of its journey. A similar delegation, from the "Duna" Iron works, called yesterday, and received the same reply from the Government ...

Radio Kossuth

Imre Nagy's New Government

Budapest

[10:55] Attention! Attention! Please keep listening. In a few minutes we will transmit a very important communiqué ...

The Presidential Council of the Hungarian Republic, on the recommendation of the Central Committee of the Hungarian Workers' Party and the Praesidium of the National Council of the Patriotic People's Front, has elected the new Government of the Hungarian People's Republic.

The composition of the Government is as follows:

President of the Council	IMRE NAGY	[Communist]
Deputy Presidents	ANTAL APRO	[Com.]
	JOSZEF BOGNAR	[former Small Holder-Party]
	FERENC ERDEI	[former Nat'l Peasant Party]
Ministers of State	ZOLTAN TILDY	[SH-Party & former President of Hungary]
	MIKLOS RIBIANSZKY	[SH-Party]
Mining & Electricity	SANDOR CZOTTNER	[Com.]
Produce Collection	ANTAL GYENES	[Com.]
Internal Trade	SANDOR TAUSC	[Com.]
Interior	FERENC MUNNICH	[Com.]
Health	PROF. ANTAL BABICS	[Com.]
Food Industry	RESZO NYERS	[Com.]
Construction	ANTAL APRO	[Com.]
Agriculture	BELA KOVACS	[former SH-Party General Secretary]
Defence	KAROLY JANZA	[Com.]
Justice	ERICH MOLNAR	[Com.]
Metallurgy & Machine Industry	JANOS CSERGO	[Com.]
Light Industry	MRS. JOZSEF NAGY	[Com.]
Communications & Post	LAJOS BEBRICS	[Com.]
Foreign Affairs	IMRE HORVATH	[Com.]
Foreign Trade	JOSZEF BOGNAR	[SH-Party]
Popular Culture	PROF. G. LUKACS	[Com.]
Education	ALBERT KONYA	[Com.]
Finance	ISTVAN KOSSA	[Com.]
Urban & Rural Development	FERENC NASZVAL	[Com.]
Chemical Industry	GERGELY SZABO	[Com.]
Central Planning Board	ARPAD KISS	[Com.]

For the time being the Ministry of State Control is not being filled.

After being sworn in the new National Government took office immediately. *[11:18]*

Radio Kossuth

Tanks, Bombs, and Youth

Budapest

Again I tried to get through to the Kilian Barracks, this time with success. Dozens of destroyed tanks shot to pieces, ruined houses, corpses, mark the neighborhood of the Budapest Alcazar. Behind its thick walls stand soldiers, students, young workers, remarkable youngsters. I am introduced to a tall, impressive looking officer, the commander of these 1200 men. He introduces himself as "Colonel Acs". What he said to me then, while still fighting, he would later repeat again as a celebrated hero, for this "Colonel Acs" was actually the legendary Pal Maleter. "For us there is only one alternative", he said in accent-free German. "Either we win, or we fall. There is no third possibility. We have confidence in Imre Nagy, but we will lay down our weapons only to regular Hungarian troops, and we will put ourselves at the disposal of the new government immediately if it is really a Hungarian government."

After this quick visit, I went to the hospital where the wounded from the Kilian Barracks lay, young boys and girls who had gambled courageously with their lives for the freedom of their country. How often in the last years, seeing youngsters in the West gadding about without ideals, have I asked myself what will become of this youth? And now here, severely wounded, some in agony, two and three to a hospital bed, lie kids who could be a Franzl from Ottakring, or a Poldl from Prater Park. No, this youth is not lost. They have high ideals.

In the same hospital, another incident: the head physician leads me to the bed of a little boy, a small, pitiful figure, with long dishevelled blond hair falling over his face, white as chalk. "Is he badly wounded?" I whispered. The doctor answered, "Not at all."

"What's he doing in the hospital?" I ask astonished. "The boy is totally exhausted. With a machine-gun he defended, all by himself, an important street intersection for four days, only taking a break now and then to fetch food and new munition. He fought four sleepless days and nights, and now he's completely out with exhaustion." The boy's name was Jancsi; he is thirteen years old ...

Eugen-Géza Pogany, „Ungarns Freiheitskampf"
Vienna, 1957)

Budapest

"We knew we were strong and the government was weak," said Peter ... When word reached the [Kilian] barracks that Russian tanks were coming, the colonel [Pal Maleter] ordered complete quiet. The tanks came close to the barracks wall, but no one stirred. Some infantry appeared and shot up the building, but the Freedom Fighters did not return the fire. Finally there were 20 tanks, some 75 infantrymen, a truck, and an armored car outside the barracks. "Colonel Maleter came and looked down," recalls Peter Szanto. "He picked up a small nitroglycerin bottle and threw it at the truck. The truck disappeared in one big roar. Then we all threw nitroglycerin bottles and benzine and used machine pistols on the infantry. It was a fine trick. We killed the infantry, got the truck, the armored car, and four of the tanks in about five minutes."

After that, morale at the barracks was sky-high. When citizens called up to report the presence of Russian tanks or the whereabouts of the AVH, the Freedom Fighters forayed out to do battle ...   *Time Magazine (New York), 7 January*

Budapest

Gabor, who was 22 years old, was the "Commander" of 1,500 young men of about the same age ... Their headquarters had been set up in the building of a chemical experimental centre, a sturdy, thick-walled structure which provided a certain security ... Gabor had discovered in the building some bottles of nitroglycerin, which were probably intended for laboratory experiments. He told me that his find had reminded him of the French film *The Wages of Fear* ...

He made arrangements to have the bottles, which contained 15 litres of the powerful explosive, carefully transported to insurgent headquarters at the Korvin Cinema, a few feet from Ulloi Ut Street ... Powerful bombs were fabricated with the help of students and chemists ... Consequently, in that quarter the insurgents were able to attack the tanks by hurling at them bottles containing nitroglycerine which tore huge and ghastly holes in the steel walls. I myself saw these holes; they could not have been made by the machine guns or the cannons used by the insurgents.

... "Sandor died in 'Villanyi Ut' when the Soviet tanks arrived. He was a little hero. The rest of us were hiding behind the main entrance of a building, waiting for the tanks to go by. We were armed with automatic pistols and lots of grenades. The tanks came from the south, from beyond the Danube, by way of Szabadszag Bridge. There were five of us. Sandor was the youngest. He was 16 years old. His father was dead, and he lived with his mother. We wanted him to go home, but he showed his tri-coloured armband: 'It was my mother who sewed it on. I'm staying.'

"The firing began, first in scattered flurries, then with increasing intensity. Suddenly we heard the rattling of the tank-bands. A tank was approaching. It could not be far off. The Russians were coming from Bela Bartok Avenue. They tried to take rather wide streets so as to avoid the danger of jets of petrol. We were all livid. Sandor was yellow. Of what use were our weapons against the T-34's? Even the grenades were useless. Suddenly the tanks charged. There were five of them. 'We'll each take one,' said Jeza, who was the oldest of us. Sandor slipped to the corner where the grenades were stored. He returned with a batch of six held together by a string. 'I'm waiting for them,' he said. When the tanks passed in front of us, Sandor went out alone.

"I saw him run behind the tank and try to get up from behind. He actually succeeded without attracting the attention of the Russians. He lifted his batch of grenades and tossed them on the platform, then jumped and ran back to us. When I turned to look at the tank again I saw that the grenades had rolled to the ground. 'Sandor,' I cried, 'come back, come back fast!' I can still see his face. He had certainly heard me. His eyes were wet with tears. He picked up the grenades, climbed on to the tank and threw the lot of them at the tower. There was a blinding flash, a horrible explosion. We all threw ourselves to the ground to avoid the splinters. I didn't want to look. Sandor was dead." ...

Bruno Tedeschi, Il Giornale d'Italia (Rome), 18 November

"The Confidence of Us All ..."

Budapest

A new national Government, headed by Comrade Imre Nagy, has taken the oath, pledging to lead the country out of the tragic situation into which it was plunged by political neglect and faults of the past ... This is a beautiful and immense task ...

Listening to the list of Ministers, one asks first whether or not this Government will be able to cope with the job it faces? During the past years every one of the Ministers proved that he or she is a Hungarian patriot who loves the Nation and the people. Often they were slandered for speaking out for our common cause. But this Government is not only willing, it is capable of realizing our great objectives. Its members are experienced politicians who proved they were qualified statesmen during the difficult post-liberation years. Their prestige is based on the success of their activities. The Government is capable of accomplishing the tasks ahead because it feels the support of the whole population ...

This Government is also capable of solving its problems because its leaders represent truth, socialist democracy, national independence, and equal rights ...

Hungarians know Comrade Imre Nagy as a politician who proved in 1953 that he has consistently rejected a policy of bureaucratic centralism ...

The composition of the new Government proves that many honest and capable Hungarian politicians have returned to the place they deserve to occupy after years of neglect. Thus, the nation has given them satisfaction, but their return to public life is also a source of satisfaction to the nation, because the persons now heading the Government enjoy the confidence of us all ...

Radio Kossuth

"With Joy, But—"
Miskolc

The workers of Borsod Country and the Workers Council of the County and of the town of Miskolc have declared that they greet with joy the formation of a new Government, but will continue the strike until our demands, and above all the one concerning the withdrawal of Soviet troops, are fulfilled. The Council counts on you to strike in a disciplined manner. Hold out! Victory is near!

Radio Free Miskolc

"Shocked by the News"
Pecs

We have just received the following telegram: In these critical days the workers of Pecs Mav [Hungarian railroad] headquarters stand as one man behind the reorganized central leadership and behind Comrade Nagy, fighting for the realization of an independent and democratic Hungary.

Bu we were greatly shocked by news over our radio that the new government has oppointed Lajos Bebrics as Minister of Communications and Postal Service — that same Bebrics who introduced an arbitrary, terroristic system on the railroads. In these critical times, as always we want to preserve peace, and therefore we demand that Bebrics be dismissed immediately for violating laws and decrees. We demand that a minister be appointed who does not find pleasure in arbitrary measures but fights courageously for the interests of railroad men and for realizing a socialist order in our enterprises ...

Radio Free Pecs

Miskolc Holds Out

Miskolc

For two days the town of Miskolc has been under the leadership of the Workers Council and the Students Parliament. The Workers Council has taken over control of the garrison and the police. The demands of the Workers Council and the students have been made known publicly by radio and press — our 21 points as well as the University's 11 points. As you know, the County Strike Committee has also called on all plants in the County to strike, with the exception of the post, transport, communications, food supplies and health services, and the power plants.

The Government still does not comply with our demands, and particularly with our most important demand that Soviet troops be withdrawn at once. In yesterday's message the Government said: "Let order be restored and the Soviet troops will be withdrawn to their bases." The workers of Borsod County adhere to the stand they have taken and demand the immediate with-

drawal of Soviet troops. Soviet troops are to stop military operations at once and are to start withdrawing from our country immediately. Only then will there be order. Only then will Borsod County stop the strike. The entire working class of Borsod County sticks as faithfully now as two days ago to this, our primary demand.

The fact that in Miskolc and in Borsod County there have not been any large-scale disturbances is primarily due to our good and honest working class, which is patriotic to the bone. Let us be proud of this! Let us continue to avoid disturbances. Let us help our workers guards maintain order, but by means of the strike, let us also continue to seek the immediate fulfilment of our demands ...

Dear Hungarian President: We inform you that yesterday the Workers Council took over power in Borsod County in every respect. The Army and police are under control of the Workers Council. Soviet troops are displaying a neutral attitude and are not interfering in our affairs. The Workers Council adopts as its own all your demands and stands for amnesty of all Hungarians who have participated in the revolution. Stalinist provocateurs who yesterday shot into the crowd have felt the just punishment of the people.

Dear fighting Hungarian brethren: We are supporting your demands. We are fighting for the immediate withdrawal of Soviet troops. We have contacted the Russian command about this matter, so that they can discuss it with their superior command in Moscow and leave the country at once. In the meantime, the Soviet Army is displaying a passive attitude ...

[signed] *The Workers Council of Borsod County*
Radio Free Miskolc

Insurgents Hold Western Border

Vienna

Anti-Communist rebels appeared today to be firmly in control of the western part of Hungary. The region adjoins Austria from the Danube to the southern plains, where Austria, Hungary and Yugoslavia meet. Along the 160-mile Austrian-Hungarian border neither Hungarian soldiers wearing the Communist red star insignia nor Soviet troops were reported seen.

However, Soviet forces were being moved to the rear of the rebels facing the Austrian-Hungarian border, according to information received by Austrian military authorities. In particular, strong Soviet tank units were reported concentrating in the area between Gyor and Komarom, south of the Danube. The railroad and main highway between Vienna and Budapest traverse this area.

A broadcast monitored here at 6 p.m. purporting to originate from the "Free Station" of Gyor, said Soviet troops in that area had given assurances they would not take any actions against the local population unless attacked. The broadcast added that during a mass meeting in Gyor's main square orators demanded weapons in order to be able to bring aid to the insurgents in Budapest. The broadcast also reported that Vac, Hatvan and Szolnok to the north and northeast of Budapest had proclaimed themselves "free towns."

The insurgents entrenched on the Leitha River less than forty miles from here claim to be in continuous contact by telephone with other "fighters for freedom" in Budapest ... Only at Lockenhaus, an Austrian village not far from the Hungarian town of Sopron, was firing heard this afternoon. It sounded like light artillery ... Sopron itself was reported controlled by the insurgents. The streets of that town were said to be patrolled by groups of three, consisting of one soldier, one worker and one student. Sopron's statue of Stalin was said to have been toppled from its pedestal ...

Railroad service in the Hungarian border area has come to a standstill. All international traffic via the Hungarian frontier station and railroad hub, Hegyeshalom, is suspended. The town of Hegyeshalom is understood to be ruled by a Revolutionary Committee. When this body first had its communications put on official billboards yesterday, local security police tore them down. However, later yesterday all military and police forces placed themselves at the disposal of the insurgents. Also cooperating with them are reported to be the officers and soldiers of a new block of barracks near Hegyeshalom. The insurgents' general strike order was rigidly observed in the entire Hegyeshalom district ...

Hungarians living near the border appeared to have high hopes that the West would intervene if Soviet forces attacked the rebels in the western part of the country. Hungarian railroad men expressed confidence that it would take the Russians several days to move reinforcements from Poland and Rumania into Hungary because railroad connections between eastern Hungary and neighboring countries were clogged by cars of sugar beets. ...

Paul Hofmann, New York Times, 28 October

Couriers

Vienna

The question of organisation and communication between revolutionary groups in the country and in Budapest is complicated, just because revolution means confusion and disorder while a new order fights to emerge from the old. A young Budapest worker who had papers showing he had been a courier between revolutionary committees in Gyor and Budapest could only tell me vaguely about their organisation and liaison.

"I was a courier for the Central Revolutionary Committee of Budapest, but I don't know how many people were on it. I never saw them all, and their numbers changed constantly. At first, it was composed of high school and university students, but later soldiers and young workers were admitted. I think all were elected by lower committees, which had been elected by individual organisations of students, soldiers and workers.

"I was in one group of eight couriers, and we were constantly travelling. The Russians never interfered, but we sometimes had trouble with Hungarian soldiers who did not know us. Groups of couriers operated between Budapest and the provincial cities, so that the capital received and sent at least two couriers a day to each city.

"Although the connections existed, Budapest did not give orders to other revolutionary centres.

This was not possible, for conditions were different everywhere. However, I do know that the Revolutionary Committee of 10 in Gyor did look to Budapest for guidance and new slogans. ...."

George Sherman, The Observer (London), 11 November

A Revolutionary Committee Meets

Magyarovar

The revolutionary committee was meeting in what might have been a library, with a massive but modern bookcase, a tall stove faced with brown glazed tiles, and a grandfather clock. The room was full of cigarette smoke. Everywhere there were young men wearing their colours, either as armbands or in their buttonholes, and with tommy-guns slung on their shoulders; they said they were going to fight in Budapest. They reminded me of a poem about some other revolutionaries:

I have met them at close of day
Coming with vivid faces
From counter or desk among grey
Eighteenth-century houses.

The spokesman of the committee had, in one way, the stamp of a man in revolt. He was wearing the classic, heavy military-style raincoat, even though it was a warm evening. But he was agreeable and cheerful. He said he was an engineer and belonged to no party, although he had been in prison on some political charge. It did not seem to have hardened him. The chairman of the committee was a slightly built man, considerably older and with a two days' growth of grey beard. He was wearing a crumpled grey alpaca jacket with, underneath it, a rather grubby leather jerkin and an unbuttoned shirt. He, too, had a sense of humour, although of a less evident kind. He seemed tired. Nowhere in either of these two men was there any sign of self-importance, at least that I could see at the time. Nor was there anything conspiratorial about them or any of their friends.

There was no sign anywhere of the professional revolutionary.

They told me that their committee, which was in touch with others of its kind in the area and elsewhere, represented all political parties. It included, they said, some Communists, although whether these were perhaps ex-Communists I could not discover, the interpretation of their Hungarian and German was a little inflexible. But this was clear, that the committee is keeping order, that there is no effective opposition to it now, that it organises supplies of food and that there are the rudiments of a bus service being run by it. It is also in touch with similar committees elsewhere and gets something like intelligence reports from them. I rather doubt if these are really accurate ... The committee said that the Russians in Budapest had laid down their arms, but Budapest radio, still controlled by the authorities, suggests that, if anything, the opposite is true ... The young men with tommy-guns from Magyarovar will be testing the truth of these different stories in a stern way.

It is hard to sum up these men quickly. The lynching of the policeman who fired on the crowd shows perhaps that there are deeper hatreds at work than I was shown. But I do know that they feel earnestly about what they are doing and that they feel warmly towards the West. All that we few journalists had done was to go and see them, but when we left they kissed us on the cheeks; it might, in other circumstances, have seemed a rather forced gesture.

Ivor Jones, The Listener (London), 1 November

Functions of Workers Councils

Budapest

The Trade Union Council Praesidium recommends that workers and employees embark on the introduction of worker-management in factories, workshops, mines and everywhere else. They should elect Workers Councils.

(1) Regarding the functioning of the Workers' Councils, we recommend that members should be elected by all workers of the factories, workshop, or mine in question. A meeting called to carry out the election should decide the method of elec-

tion. Recommendations for Workers Council membership should be presented, as a general rule, by the works council or by a worker who commands respect. Depending on the size of the enterprise, the Worker Councils should generally consist of 21—71 members, including proportionate representation of every group of workers. In factories employing less than 100 workers, all workers may be included in the Workers Council.

(2) The tasks of the Workers Councils: A Workers Council shall decide all questions con-

nected with production, administration and management of the plant. Therefore: (a) it should elect from among its own members a council of 5—15 members, which in accordance with direct instructions of the Workers Council, shall decide questions connected with the management of the factory — it will hire and fire workers, economic and technical leaders; (b) it will draw up the factory's production plan and define tasks connected with technical development; (c) the Workers Council will choose the wage-system best suited to conditions peculiar to the factory, decide on the introduction of that system as well as on the development of social and cultural amenities in the factory; (d) the Workers Council will decide on investments and the utilisation of profits; (e) the Workers Council will determine the working conditions of the mine, factory, etc.; (f) the Workers Council will be responsible to all the workers and to the State for correct management.

At present the principal task of the Workers Councils is to effect and ensure order, discipline and production. With the help of all the workers, their electors, the Workers Council should defend the factory, the source of their livelihood.

On this basis of the aforesaid, the Präsidium of the TU Council recommends the setting up of Workers' Councils.

(Signed)   *The Praesidium of the National Trade Union Council.*

Radio Kossuth

Defiant Groups Hold Out

Budapest

The Hungarian uprising has now reached its third, and potentially its bloodiest, stage. It began nearly a week ago with unarmed student demonstrations. When these grew into a popular tumult a military revolt, which had probably been planned long in advance within certain units of the Hungarian Regular Army, was superimposed upon them. As far as Budapest is concerned, this semi-organised military action seems to have been subdued by Soviet tanks. Fighting continued in the city, though on a reduced and more sporadic scale. The severest actions have been on the hills of Buda, near the island of Csepel, south of the city, at an intersection of the Stalin road in the middle of the capital, and at the Maria Theresia Barracks. Here a group of students and soldiers rejected four successive orders to surrender. They were flattened by guns of the Soviet T 34 and T 54 tanks, firing at point-blank range.

The Russians are using their heavy tanks purely as extermination squads. They rumble from one district to another, flattening every house where even one sniper's rifle is heard or suspected. Moscow may restore "order" by these means, but it will never quell the fresh waves of hate which every new action sets up.

Of the dozens of moving incidents I have seen in the streets the most pathetic sight was the action of a little Hungarian boy, aged about eight or nine. He clambered into a Soviet tank and poured a little can of petrol on to its tracks in an attempt to start a blaze. It is hard to think of any Communist Government reshuffle which will pacify this spirit.

From the régime's standpoint the main threat has now passed back to mostly unarmed mass demonstrators, who, having smelt blood and sensed their enormous moral power in the past few days, are even more determined than they were a week ago.

Typical of this latest phase are a few hundred students and workmen who were reported today to be barricaded behind stone and rubble barriers in the two main squares of Buda. As far as is known on this side of the river they have hardly any arms or food. They face certain extermination as and when the Russians choose to open fire. Yet they have rejected surrender appeals across the barricades, even when made by friendly soldiers of the Hungarian Army. Their answer was: "We will stay here and die if necessary until the Russians agree to leave our homeland."

Similar outbursts of fanatical patriotism are reported from all over the country. In the Eastern provinces a sort of peasants' guerilla war is said to have broken out, with the rebels going for their local enemies with shotguns, or even in mediaeval style with scythes and pitchforks. At Tatabanya the colliers are reported to be on strike and preparing an unarmed protest march on the beleaguered capital. Regional revolutionary com-

Candy and Flowers

Budapest

It is difficult, if not altogether impossible, to convey any notion of these people's fighting gallantry. Wherever the rebels were students and workers, there was not a single case of looting. Shop windows without glass were filled with desirable goods, yet nothing was touched. An incident I saw will illustrate this. Windows from a candy store and an adjacent flower shop were smashed and the sidewalk was littered with candy boxes. All these boxes were replaced in the glassless windows, but the flowers strewn about were gathered and placed on the bodies of dead rebels.

Leslie B. Bain, The Reporter (New York), 15 November

mittees have been set up in Sopron and Hegye-shalom, on the Western frontier.

In all cases the main targets of hate have been the Russian troops and the AVO, or political police. Thus in this third stage the Red Army, which has hitherto concentrated its efforts almost entirely on the capital, is now forced to disperse them on a hundred or more smaller punitive actions in the countryside. This is not the same direct threat to the régime's seat of power as was put up in Budapest a few days ago by sections of the Hungarian Army. But the cumulative damage to the Russian cause may be greater in the long run.

One can now truly speak of an active national revolt, stretching from Neusiedler Lake, in the West, to the Transylvanian Mountains in the East. In an attempt to stifle this revolt before news of it can reach the outside world Red Army reinforcements have poured into Hungary in strength over the weekend. They came across the Rumanian and Russian borders. Two of the new units have been identified for certain by military observers here. One is a complete armoured regiment transferred from Timisoara, in Western Rumania. The other is a mortar battalion which has come in direct from Russia across Hungary's narrow strip of frontier with the Soviet Union. I saw rocket batteries from the mortar battalion in action against rebel targets on the Buda hills. Of the two Soviet Army divisions stationed permanently in Hungary only one is known for certain to have been committed in the Budapest fighting. The other is presumably dealing with local actions which have now broken out in other provinces.

One thing is certain. Nowhere does the Soviet command trust any Hungarian Army unit, whatever its alleged loyalties. One rebel told me that even some of the "loyal" Hungarian tanks fighting under Russian orders had been allowed only two rounds of ammunition for warning shots. At least one senior Hungarian Army commander is reported to have paid with his life for siding with the rebels. His name is given as Gen. Kis, and he is said to have been shot out of hand by the Russians for refusing to order his troops to fire on demonstrators.

Meanwhile, as Red Army reinforcements have poured in from the East, the discredited Communist leadership in Budapest has fought to save its skin by roping itself to its former opponents.

Gordon Shepherd, Daily Telegraph (London), 29 October

The Soviet Troops

Nickelsdorf

The attitude of Soviet troops in Hungary differs from place to place, reported a member of the rebel forces in Nickelsdorf on the Austrian border. In many areas the Red Army soldiers are exercising obvious restraint. In Raab (Gyor) in West Hungary on Saturday there was a strong concentration of Soviet troops, who did not attack the insurgents, not even to defend themselves when demonstrators pelted them with stones. The Hungarian informant also said that near Gran regular Hungarian Army tank units handed over their vehicles to the revolutionaries...

Neue Zürcher Zeitung, 29 October

Budapest

The Ministry of Defence has issued the following communiqué: The Town Council of Baja rang up the Ministry of Defence this afternoon and asked for information about the rumour that Soviet troops are engaged in large-scale military operations in Budapest. Are these rumours true? The Ministry of Defence informs inquirers that they are not. By this morning the bulk of the armed groups was liquidated. Military action is now confined to a few nests. It is true that Soviet troops have helped, and are helping very much in liquidating groups which have attacked the workers' power. In many places, however, insurgents trapped in larger buildings have asked to be allowed to lay down arms to Hungarian People's Army units, and their request has been granted. As the military activities are subsiding, formations of the Hungarian army are gradually taking over the task of maintaining order everywhere. If those armed groups which are still resisting do not lay down their arms after being summoned to do so by the Hungarian army units, they will be completely liquidated. ...

Radio Kossuth

Miskolc

Radio Miskolc has called on the Hungarian authorities to grant political asylum to all Soviet soldiers who left their units during the last few days and sided with the freedom figthers, adding that there were many Soviet soldiers who would claim political asylum if granted it.

Radio Vienna

London

Reports reaching London supported the Hungarian Nationalists' claim that they hold the five towns of Gyor, Sopron, Szentgotthard, Magyarovar and Miskolc. ...

Soviet tanks entering the country by-passed Miskolc. They were prevented, at least temporarily, from crossing the River Tisza at Szolnok by Nationalists, who threatened to blow up the bridge. ...

Russian formations based in Rumania are now known to be engaged in the fighting. Some of their troops are among the wounded in the hospitals.

Some Russian soldiers are believed to have thrown in their lot with the Nationalists. The trade union paper *Nepszava*, which carried two Nationalist manifestos on Friday, demanded among other things "political asylum for Soviet fighting men who have come over to support our people." ...

Diplomatic Correspondent, Daily Telegraph (London),
29 October

Budapest

Lazlo and his friends heard Radio Budapest, in rebel hands on Oct. 27, tell all factories to set up workers' councils. Lazlo was one of 14 elected by secret ballot at his mill. "I thought to myself, 'My God! What is happening? Are we really practising democracy?' I felt like crying."

"There were happy meetings everywhere," says Lazlo. Everything went well until the day that the Soviet army attacked again. The workers got 6,000 rifles from the Hungarian army, but when 37 Soviet tanks and armored cars suddenly descended on Vac, there was no resistance.

The Russians had no food, and the Vac people gave them bread and a little meat, for which the soldiers were grateful. Says Lazlo: "Our people were not afraid of the Russians, and talked to them. Some of the Russians thought they were in East Germany and that they would soon meet American 'fascists' who had invaded the country. Other troops thought they were in the Suez Canal zone. Our people explained what was going on and what the Hungarian objectives were and what the Russians had done in Budapest. There was one captain who listened to all of this. He got redder and redder. We thought he was angry at us. Suddenly he threw his hat down and said: 'Bulganin and Khrushchev would rape their own mothers!' He was very angry, but not with us."

Time Magazine (New York), 7 January

Unorthodox Communist Reactions

London

I know a former Communist — he eventually left the Party in disgust — who was appalled by what he found during a lengthy stay in Eastern Europe as a journalist. On his return to Britain he went to see Harry Pollitt, then general secretary of the Communist Party, and told him everything that had distressed him. Pollitt's reply was: "My advice to you is to keep your mouth shut." The day is over when Communists will follow such advice. Never again shall we keep our mouths shut. The *Daily Worker* sent me to Hungary, then suppressed what I wrote. Much of what I wrote was concealed even from my colleagues. Both as a Communist and as a human being I believe it my duty to tell the truth about the Hungarian revolution...

I wrote in my first, unpublished, dispatch:

After eleven years the incessant mistakes of the Communist leaders, the brutality of the State Security Police, the widespread bureaucracy and mismanagement, the bungling, the arbitrary methods and the lies have led to total collapse. This was no counter-revolution, organised by fascists and reactionaries. It was the upsurge of a whole people, in which rank-and-file Communists took part, against a police dictatorship dressed up as a Socialist society — a

police dictatorship backed up by Soviet armed might.

I am the first Communist journalist from abroad to visit Hungary since the revolution started. And I have no hesitation in placing the blame for these terrible events squarely on the shoulders of those who led the Hungarian Communist Party for eleven years — up to and including Erno Gero. They turned what could have been the outstanding example of people's democracy in Europe into a grisly caricature of Socialism. They reared and trained a secret police which tortured all — Communists as well as non-Communists — who dared to open their mouths against injustices. It was a secret police which in these last few dreadful days turned its guns on the people whose defenders it was supposed to be.

I wrote this under the immediate impact of a most disturbing and shattering experience, but I do not withdraw one word of it. Much of the rest of the dispatch was never received in London because the call was cut off after twenty minutes, and the first ten had been taken up by three different people giving me contradictory instructions as to the "line" I should take. Mick Bennett insisted on reading me a long extract from a resolution of the Central Committee of the Polish United Workers' Party. I had had enough of resolutions.

I had seen where eleven years of terror and stupidity had led Hungary, and I wanted to tell the readers of the *Daily Worker* the plain unvarnished truth, however painful it might be. But the readers of the *Daily Worker* were not to be told the truth. The day after I had sent this dispatch they were reading only about "gangs of reactionaries" who were "beating Communists to death in the streets" of Budapest. The paper admitted in passing that "some reports claimed that only identified representatives of the former security police were being killed." Next day Hungary disappeared altogether from the *Daily Worker's* front page...

Peter Fryer, Hungarian Tragedy (London, 1956)

New York

The Daily Worker, New York Communist newspaper, terms the use of Soviet troops in Hungary "deplorable" today and calls for the end of the fighting in that country ... The editorial says, "the delay of the Hungarian Communists in developing their own path played into the hands of the counter-revolutionaries" ... After asserting the Soviet troops in Hungary had been used at the request of the Hungarian Government, the editorial added its only note of protest —"which does not, however, in our view, make the use of Soviet troops in Hungary any the less deplorable."

New York Times, 28 October

Moscow & Friends on the "Evil Rebellion"

Moscow

It is clear from the latest reports from Hungary that the calculations of the counter-revolutionary insurgents are suffering failure. The newly formed Hungarian Government headed by Imre Nagy is master of the situation in the country. The Hungarian Workers' Party and the Government of the Republic are doing everything possible to restore order as quickly as possible.

During the last few days bourgeois propaganda has been spreading naked lies about the situation in Hungary and has kept silent about the main thing: the fact that a counter-revolutionary putsch flared up in Hungary and that its organisers began to overthrow the people's power, the very people's power which had been won with such great difficulty by the Hungarian workers in the struggle against fascism.

The events of the last days in Budapest leave no doubt that the forces which started the counter-revolutionary putsch were anti-national forces deeply hostile to the cause of building socialism in Hungary. Moreover, those forces have very close and direct ties with abroad.

In his report from Vienna the other day the UP correspondent wrote that the participants in the insurrection against the people in Hungary were well-armed. This is a matter of a well-trained and armed underground. At present, bourgeois organs of the Western press prefer to keep silent about who is organising and financing subversive actions against countries of the Socialist camp. But it is already clear to the whole world that the US. Congress annually appropriates 100 million dollars for this shady business. And last summer the USA appropriated an additional 25 million dollars to intensify subversion in the People's Democracies. But is this all? Remember that the great campaign for sending off balloons with inflammatory propaganda was organised

from West German territory by imperialist agents. Remember how many dirty and provocative rumours are spread every day by the so-called "Radio Free Europe", which is financed by American dollars. If we added to this, direct diversionary and spying activities by Western Intelligence organisations in these countries, it becomes even clearer who the real initiator is of the anti-people's putsch in Hungary.

Reactionary insurgents played on temporary economic difficulties. For their dark purposes they used various shortcomings in the work of the Hungarian State apparatus and individual instances where revolutionary legality had been violated. The enemies of the People's Democracy did not shrink from anything. As the Polish paper *Trybuna Ludu* points out, peaceful demonstrations of the Hungarian population were joined by organised counter-revolutionary elements who were ready to turn the mood of the Hungarian public against the most sacred cause — the cause of socialism.

As a result of the armed outbreak by reactionary putschists a situation arose in Hungary which involved the question of defending the democratic conquests of the Hungarian working people. In order to protect these sacred gains from the designs of the counter-revolutionary insurgents, the Government of the Hungarian People's Republic appealed for help to the Soviet Union. At the request of the Hungarian Government, Soviet troops took part in repulsing the sallies of armed reactionaries and in establishing order and peace.

All honest men are convinced that the working people of Hungary will find strength and courage to give the reactionary putschists a deserving rebuff and to safeguard the peaceful construction of their free motherland.

Antoly Sherstyuk, Radio Moscow

Sofia

The Polish and Hungarian people know well that nobody but the Soviet Army liberated them from the German-Fascist yoke, that after the war the USSR protected their national interests and independence from the attempts of the Western imperialists and helped them to take the road to Socialism ... To break with the USSR is to jeopardize ... their free existence, national independence and their state sovereignty.

Rabotnichesko Delo (Sofia), 27 October

Bucharest

In these difficult hours ... only international reactionary circles are openly jubilant over what has happened. ... But they forget that in this very way they expose their complicity in this bloody adventure. Meanwhile imperialist propaganda is trying very hard to mislead world public opinion on the character, aims, and course of this evil rebellion. ...

Scinteia (Bucharest), 28 October

Lukacs, Gero, Kovacs, Nagy

Budapest

I consider it of great importance that a Government has been formed representing every shade and stratum of the Hungarian people that wants progress and socialism. It was a great mistake of the previous regime to become isolated from those creative elements with whose help the Hungarian road to socialism could have been successfully taken. The main task of the new Government is to make a most radical break with narrow-minded and petty trends, and to make use of every sound popular initiative, so that every true Hungarian can look upon the socialist fatherland as his own. The task of the Ministry of People's Culture is the realisation of these principal aims in the sphere of culture. The Hungarian people have an exceptionally rich tradition in almost every field of culture. We do not want to build socialism out of air; we do not want to bring it into Hungary as an imported article. What we want is that the Hungarian people work out, organically, and by long, glorious and successful work, a socialist culture worthy of the Hungarian people's great and ancient achievements, and which, as a socialist culture, can place Hungarian culture on even broader foundations with even deeper roots. ...

Prof. George Lukacs, Radio Kossuth

Budapest

According to one report, Erno Gero, the Stalinist Hungarian Communist party secretary, who was displaced soon after the revolt began by the "Titoist" Janos Kadar, is now in Russia. He is said to have been taken back to Moscow by the Kremlin's "riot squad", headed by Messrs. Mikoyan and Suslov, who paid a 24-hour visit to Budapest on Thursday. If true, it is more than likely that this was no mere consultation visit but a decision to remove Gero from the Hungarian scene until tempers have calmed down, and possibly for ever.

He may thus have joined in exile in Russia his old friend and co-Stalinist, Mr. Rakosi, whose

fall from power last July was the massive stone which set the present landslide in motion. ...

Gordon Shepherd, Daily Telegraph (London), 29 October

Budapest

In view of the fact that the Hungarian Workers' Party alone cannot conduct the affairs of the country I consider the formation of a coalition Government necessary. This circumstance requires the restoration of peace and order. It is clear that the task of the new Government will consist not only in managing the country's affairs but also in fulfilling the will of the people. To do this, it is necessary that the population show discipline, condemn looting, and defend the property of the people. ...

Bela Kovacs, Hungarian News Agency

Budapest

By chance I meet two prominent authors who played a major role in the writers' revolt ... They lead me into the archives of the parliament, where I get to see, as the first foreigner, a document of historical significance: the proof that it was not Imre Nagy who had asked the Russians for Soviet military intervention against the Hungarian insurgents. The original document is actually signed "Imre Nagy" but not with his own written signature. There where it should stand is type-written, fine and clean: Nagy Imre m. p.

Eugen-Géza Pogany, Ungarns Freiheitskampf (Vienna, 1956)

Closed Doors

Budapest

The City Council of Budapest appeals to porters of blocks of flats and chairmen of Tenants' Committees in Budapest to make sure that front doors are kept permanently locked. The curfew is in force because certain groups of the dispersed armed insurgents are disturbing order in the streets and firing in certain places; and because thieves are also active. Therefore front doors must be kept locked.

Radio Kossuth

"Taking the Future Into Our Own Hands"

Gyor

This is Radio Free Gyor speaking. We shall gave a short evaluation of today's events.

The just fight of the people is progressing with long strides toward complete victory. Even if we limit ourselves to the position of radio, we can see this. Yesterday we were alone in broadcasting, until evening ... when the people of Magyarovar won the radio station, and Radio Masonmagyarovar joined us. Thus we had two powerful radio stations from which to broadcast as Radio Free Gyor. ... In the late afternoon we warmly welcomed the workers of the powerful Szombathely radio station, who have joined us in transmitting our programs. This evening we can therefore tell our listeners that Radio Free Gyor is transmitting, to almost the entire Dunantul [Western Hungary]: to Gyor, Komarom, Vas, and Apso Zala Counties. We are informing more than half the Dunantul about the situation and the achievements of the people's true fight. We assume that in other Hungarian towns the situation today is similar. The people have taken the direction of our future into their own hands ...

We can surely say that there also [in Budapest] the true battle of the nation will soon be won. Among the outstanding events of the day is the change in the behavior and mood of Soviet troops all over the country. Seeing that here it is a question of the people's just fight for freedom, Soviet soldiers declared: "Do not hurt us and we shall not hurt you. We shall be glad to be able to return home at last". ...

Not only in Gyor but in the whole district, in all western Dunantul, our sturdy Honveds are standing guard, arms in hand, over our nightly rest. Let us rest, dear listeners, we have need of a night's repose, for until order is entirely restored we must guard the results so far achieved. ...

Radio Free Gyor

"Waiting for Instructions"

Budapest

Last night the *Szabad Nep* building was bombarded by Soviet tanks. Why? Because yesterday its editorial expressed the timid opinion that the accusation "counter-revolution" was somewhat exaggerated. At this, Stalinists in the Party leadership decided *Szabad Nep* had joined the revolution! The Stalinists alarmed the Soviet commander and obtained agreement from the War Ministry. Tanks fired at the first floor, then at the third floor. Only after delegates from the newspaper managed to explain to the Soviet officers that there must have been some mistake—they were firing at the official organ of the Central Committee of the Hungarian Communist Party—did the tanks withdraw ...

The editor-in-chief of *Szabad Nep* received us in his office which, by some miracle, was saved. Many people, cut off from their homes, were sleeping in the room. The editor explained: "There was no counter-revolution. The crimes of the A.V.H. and a false evalution of the situation offended the whole nation and brought about a nation-wide revolution. The Party does not exist. All its leaders can rely on is the apparatus. Real Communists turned away from the leadership and the ideology it represented. The abyss between the leadership and the nation has become definitive since the moment of the Soviet intervention ... We must tell the masses the whole truth."

"Are you doing that in your newspaper?"

The editor hangs his head and after a moment's silence answers: "We are the organ of the Central Committee. We are waiting for instructions."

Marian Bielicki, Po Prostu (Warsaw), 2 December

Miskolc

The Hungarian people have lost confidence in some men in Imry Nagy's government ...

Soviet troops should stop fighting as soon as possible and leave Hungary. The people of Budapest want to shake off the Rakosi spirit. Workers, students and soldiers march together against the bad memories of recent times. The Gero-Rakosi line completely lost the people's confidence, and, seeing that they were no longer masters of the situation, they called in the Soviet troops. Blood has run in streams and the bitterness of the people has turned into a revolutionary rage. Shall Russia again trample Hungarian liberty in the mud, as she did in 1848?

Hungarians, fellow patriots: in the last few days something has been born, that did not exist before. No, no, a thousand times no, say Miskolc, Pecs, Gyor, and all Borsod County: *Hungarian freedom has not been lost!* Today Imre Nagy has the people's confidence. But is this enough? Guns are still firing in Budapest. How can Hungarians wish that Soviet troops disarm our freedom-fighters? The new Government should not lean on foreign arms. Let them lean on the people. There is no need for foreign weapons. ...

Hungarians do not want to kill Hungarians. The people have spoken their judgment with arms. Soviet troops should be sent home and no more Hungarian blood should be shed in Budapest. Imre Nagy should have the courage to get rid of politicians who can only lean on weapons used to suppress the people. No more Hungarian blood should be shed in this country. Soviet troops should leave the country without delay. Freedom, order, and independence for this country! ...

Radio Free Miskolc

28 OCTOBER

"From the Hearts of the People"

Budapest

We do not agree with those who summarily dismiss the events of the past few days as a counter-revolutionary fascist attempt at a coup d'état. We have followed developments attentively and are fairly well informed about the various movements. On the basis of this we establish the following as facts.

The events started with the demonstration by Budapest university and college youth. The young people of Budapest expressed a feeling arising from the bottom of the hearts of the entire people, and a noble and warm passion. We must realise at last that a great national democratic movement has developed in our country, a movement which united and welded together our people as a whole, which was forced by the tyranny of the past years to remain unter the surface, but which started to burn with high flames when touched by the first breeze of freedom in the past few months. This movement expressed the workers' claim to become genuine masters in the factories. This movement expressed the human claim of the peasantry to be freed from the constant uncertainty of existence, from unwarranted vexations, and to be able to live their lives as individual or co-operative peasants according to their inclinations or desires. The struggle waged by Communist and non-Party intellectuals for the freedom of constructive work and the moral purity of our system has strengthened this movement. It was love of country which gave this people's movement its greatest strength, warmth and passion, even with the prospect of death. The demand for the equality and independence of the country is as all-embracing as the mother tongue which we speak.

It is an eternal shame that there were Communists in leading positions who did not understand the language of their own people. What has saved the Party's honour was that even under Rakosi's tyranny there were Communists — and their number grew steadily so that they gradually became the majority — who understood, as revolutionaries do, the faster and faster passionate throb of the nation's heart and stood at the head of that struggle which is leading the country towards socialism on a Hungarian and democratic oath. This passion, which carries away a whole nation only once in a century, this passion carried away Budapest's university and working-class youth on 23rd October.

To the many, mostly correct, demands voiced during the demonstrations we must now add one thing. We must find out what factors and what persons are responsible for the fact that this mighty and patriotic demonstration was soiled by blood, and that it became the beginning of the most horrible fracticidal fight . . .

Armed fights started in various points in the city. It is important to point out that after this, as well as on the second and third days of the fighting, demonstrators appeared before public buildings shouting such slogans as: "We want independence and freedom. We are not fascists" . . . It is also true that minor looting was done only by those bad and infamous elements who wormed themselves into the ranks of the demonstrators, but we were able to see in many places that the articles were untouched behind the broken shop windows. All this shows that it cannot be said that after the outbreak of the armed conflict counter-revolutionaries fought on one side and units loyal to the regime on another. The truth is that among the fighting insurgents there were, at the beginning, a very large number of honest patriots, including Communists, who up to that time did not see that socialist democracy was adequately guaranteed. The tragic event cannot blind us to such an extent as to lose sight of the truth. We cannot regard those university students from the working, peasant and intellectual classes and young working men who form the bulk of the insurgents as enemies of the People's Democracies . . .

The reason for the lessening of the strength of the resistance was not due exclusively, nor even in the first place, to the Soviet troops, but to the fact that a large number of insurgents, realising that the satisfying of their democratic demands was guaranteed, availed themselves of the possibilities offered by the amnesty, from

Thursday on, and laid down their arms. It is characteristic of the mentality of these democratic strata that, after laying down their arms, some of them joined with Hungarian soldiers and policemen in restoring order ...

It would, however, be a distortion of truth if we kept silent about the fact that bad elements also took part in the demonstration from the very beginning ...

For this reason and in order to avoid bloodshed on a larger scale, and not because we are led by revengeful hatred, we appeal with sober and calm words to those who, merely misled and carried away, are still fighting, to cut themselves off from counter-revolutionaries ... and to lay down their arms. They may count on the magnanimity of our National Government. But this is the 12th hour in which they can turn back on the road leading to counter-revolution.

First, the National Government has already fulfilled the essential demands of our people. Second, further demands such as the removal of Soviet troops, were accepted by the Government as its own, and it will begin negotiations in this respect parallel with the restoration of order ...

Szabad Nep (Budapest), 28 October

"Marginal Characters"

Budapest

By Saturday, the fifth day, accurate counting was possible. The rebel army could still count on about eight thousand fighters, while another thirty thousand could be mobilized on short notice. Still the rebels had no leaders and not much of a program beyond *"Out with the Russkies!"* and *"Down with the AVH!"*

The masses of embattled students and workers never became a mob, but from time to time there appeared a few groups of marginal characters who gathered on street corners and started yelling "Exterminate the Jews!" Several cases of hard liquor were freely distributed and many people got drunk.

Nothing like this happened where either students or workers were assembled, but there was enough anti-Semitism around during subsequent days to present a distinct danger signal in a country which only recently had gone through several years of intense Jew hating and which had maintained an official anti-Semitic policy since 1919. During the fifth and sixth days I saw four people attacked and beaten because they may have been Jews. Not severely, but nevertheless their clothes were torn and they were bleeding. The slogan was that Rakosi, Gero and Mihaly Farkas — three Jews — were responsible for all the misery that had descended on the country. Still, during the first six days of the revolt these episodes could be considered both sporadic and exceptional.

Here and there, wherever a group started rioting, a few individuals seemed inclined to strike a note of extreme nationalism. I even wondered at times whether these nationalist elements had a supreme command. I did my best to find it, but I never succeeded in obtaining any convincing evidence. Yet the nationalist tide kept rising. A close associate of Nagy admitted on Saturday, the fifth day, that the revolt was beyond the control of those who had started it. Nagy decided that a final bid should be made. He advanced a program: The revolt was to be declared a national patriotic uprising and was to be handled as such. Again, he proposed an amnesty for all rebels and dissolution of the AVH, and promised the early withdrawal of all Soviet troops from Budapest and negotiations with Moscow for removal of all Soviet troops from Hungarian soil ...

Leslie B. Bain, The Reporter (New York), 15 November

Writers' Appeal in England

London

Several hundred people, including the leading writers of the Polish, Hungarian and other emigré groups in London, attended the meeting yesterday in the Denison Hall, Vauxhall Bridge Road, to pay homage to Hungary. The meeting, which was open to the public, was organised by "artists, writers, and members of the liberal professions of varied political creeds, but united in their belief in the Rights of Man."

The platform included Countess Judith Karolyi, Miss Rose Macaulay, Mr. Arthur Koestler, Mr. George Mikes, Mr. J. B. Priestley, Mr. Henry Green, and M. Zoltan Szabo. After measured and thoughtful speeches from George Mikes and Professor Hugh Seton-Watson, and a short, sharp explosion by Mr. Priestley, a resolution was passed declaring that:

> *"The news of what is happening in Hungary has filled each and every one of them [the artists, writers, etc. of the meeting] with anguish, guilt, and hope: anguish for a battle so bravely fought, guilt for the bloodshed which we could not prevent, and yet hope because the thirst for freedom has once again, as in 1848, proved inextinguishable. In this anguish, guilt and hope, even at this distance — across so many frontiers — lies the brotherhood of man. We therefore resolve to try to repay our debt to those who sacrificed their lives so nobly in the streets of Budapest, we resolve to do all in our power to defend man's birthright to freedom, that is his right to be ruled by men of his own nation and governed by men of his own choice: his right to consent or refuse, his right to be master of his own destiny."*

Manchester Guardian, 29 October

Armed Clashes and "Cease-Fire"

[06:00] Communiqué by the Military Command: Budapest has been quiet during the night. There have been no armed clashes. Negotiations have begun between armed resisters and army representatives at the requests of the insurgents ...

[07:20] Budapest was quiet yesterday and last night except for the activity of a few armed groups. At the Moscow Square point of fighting, army negotiators have concluded a cease-fire agreement with the rebels after several preliminary talks last night. The rebels asked for time to consider the conditions for laying down arms until 07:00. Despite the truce which they proposed and agreed to, insurgents fired on Soviet patrols during the night ... Eight Soviet soldiers were wounded. In accordance with the truce, Soviet soldiers did not return the snipers' fire ...

[11:00] Attention! Attention! A message to resisters in the Kilian Barracks and Corvin District by two negotiators: We have transmitted your answer to the Commanders of the Soviet and Hungarian troops. They consider your conditions unacceptable. In their opinion the new Hungarian government, listed in the copy of *Szabad Nep* we left with you to read, represents the interests of the whole Hungarian people and will fulfill the most important demands that are contained in the 16 points. This is also our conviction.

Dear friends. You know us well, one of us was your physician, and we ask you with the good faith you always experienced on our part to believe us ... You will be granted full amnesty after laying down your weapons and you will then freely return to your homes ...

[13:20] The Government of the Hungarian People's Republic orders an immediate general cease-fire to stop further bloodshed and ensure peaceful development. It instructs the armed forces that they should only fire if attacked.

(Signed) Imre Nagy, President of the Council of Ministers

[14:25] Firing has stopped. We would like to believe and we feel certain that this unfortunate civil war will be ended now and that no more shots will be fired on the streets of Budapest.

The true cause of the recent dramatic events are eight years of Stalinism in Hungary, the wild raging of despotism which was then followed by restoration ... What was the actual reason for the warfare of past days in Budapest? Delay. Temporizing. Not understanding the real, the actual situation, and disregarding the will of the people ... Peace can be built up on those demands which, as has been promised by Imre Nagy, will be realized by the new government. The food supply in the capital has improved, shops are again open, the government has sent new supplies of goods, a cease-fire was announced. Thus the hour of activity has begun, but the tempo must be stepped up. In order to do that no weapons are needed ...

[15:03] The Council of Ministers issued the order for a general cease-fire. Thereafter the Ministers of Defense and Interior commanded the troops to cease-fire immediately. The Ministers of Defense and Interior want to draw attention to the fact that this order must be carried out in a fully disciplined and responsible manner. After the cease-fire, armed forces must return to their bases and await further instructions. The order concerning cease-fire was signed by Karoly Janza, Minister of Defense, and Ferenc Munnich, Minister of Interior.

To the questions of our listeners who live in the country we wish to declare that the cease-fire order refers to the entire country and to all groups in our country.   *Radio Kossuth*

"Every Street Is a Cemetery"

Budapest

Premier Nagy has surrendered to all the demands of Hungary's freedom rebels — and told the Russian troops to quit Budapest immediately. ... Nagy's surrender offer, made only a few hours before the United Nations debated Hungary, could bring peace after six days of bitter fighting.

... I believe that the rebels will parley if, as promised, the AVH is liquidated — and hope that the Russians will leave the country later. But who is to speak for them in a city where no man treads the street without the fear of a bullet? The revolt would have long since ended if the Red Army had not been here.

Meanwhile, as I write this in the dying city of Budapest, fresh Soviet troops, brought in from Poland, are fighting hand-to-hand street battles with the freedom fighters. Three more columns of Russian troops are on their way to the capital- one from Poland, one from Russia, and one from Rumania. The bridges that span the Danube are alive with infantry — and, a new departure, artillery. Not satisfied with 75 mm tank guns, the Soviets have put six or eight pieces of artillery on each of the major bridges. There is desolation everywhere and fighting lasted all day yesterday in Buda, just across the Margaret Bridge.

It is clear now that the Russians grossly under-estimated the qualities of the freedom fighters. Tanks have got them nowhere in the narrow streets of Budapest, where almost every window is draped with a gigantic black crêpe flag. But with the infantry it is going to be tougher. These new troops are clearly battle-scarred veterans, and the mood is changing. This morning down one deserted, smashed-up street where the fighters had even torn up stones, I saw a Soviet tank trundle by dragging the bodies of four Russian soldiers. Whenever they felt like it the tank crew blasted open a window or house. It was their way of showing revenge.

This morning I tried to cross the Margaret Bridge to Margit Square, where rebels had fought desperately for 12 hours yesterday. No sooner had my car — with a Union Jack on one side and a white flag on the other — moved on to the bridge than the Russians opened fire on me. I backed, and then walked halfway across on foot, a flag in one of my upheld arms. They stopped me halfway across and I soon saw why.

In the middle was a three-ton-lorry, and round it — like icing on a wedding cake — the road was covered with flour. Two bodies lay by its side — the driver and his mate. Ostensibly they had been bringing flour into the city. But the Russians found a cache of arms hidden and shot them out of hand.

Lined up by the bridge were 15 trucks of Soviet infantry. I could not pass, so I went back to the car and drove along the river — despite the curfew — to Stalin Bridge. Here I managed to get across, helped by packets of American cigarettes. It was guarded by Hungarians. I made my way through the back streets to Margit Square, where a scene of such desolation lay before me that I just can't describe it. Nearby is a railway siding, and the rebels had somehow dragged out four complete railway passenger carriages and turned them over to form a gigantic tank-trap. One was smashed to firewood and halfway up it — looking as silly as broken tanks always do — lay a Soviet tank, half burned out. Behind the barricade hundreds of fighters waited in pouring rain. The whole square was literally — and I mean literally — torn to pieces. Every stone that could be taken from the road and pavements had been pickaxed to use for shelter walls. In one corner is a large café. Every single chair was smashed. Hardly a shop window was left and even above the cracks of riflefire was the echo of the old days of the blitz — the crashing of broken glass.

The city itself dies slowly and gallantly, but every street is a cemetery — every home a weep-ing one. The killed run into thousands, the wounded have no hospital space.

And the Soviets are advancing towards Buda-pest in force. The column from Poland came in via Kosice, and had its first brush at Miskolc.

They detoured the city after meeting large de-monstrations. The last report I had of them they had reached Hatvan. There were many trucks of infantry. The column from the Soviet Union has entered via Debrecen and reached the city of Szolnok. Troops from Rumania are also in Szolnok.

Everywhere people ask me one thing: "When is help coming?"

"Please, anything — even one gun," a girl begged me.

"Can't the British help — we are fighting for the world," said another.

It makes me ill, unable to reply.

There are tears all the way, and I feel terribly that if the Russians win the Hungarians are going to feel a thousand times worse the disappointment experienced by the East Germans in their rising in 1953 ...

What makes the situation so difficult is that though the Government has agreed to most of the demands of the fighters there is no leader with whom authority can deal. Government speakers can only plead on the radio. But each group of fighters fights separately. The Russians have de-liberately and calculatingly kept the fight alive, and now — unless pressure comes from outside — they must reduce the country.

Once out of Budapest, it is a different story. I am luckier than most correspondents, for I have a fast car, and, by now, a sizable quantity of petrol stacked away.

Later I toured the country, and it is clear that the rebels control a belt from west to east along the Austrian frontier about 30 miles deep into Hungary. Everywhere in this belt the AVH has been disarmed or shot.

The rebels have two radio stations and the hospitals and public works. There are no Russians there at all — I have covered all this territory. They have even unaccountably withdrawn from Gyor, perhaps to lend help in Budapest. Yester-day I saw no Russians west of Komarom, which is 25 miles beyond Gyor on the Vienna-Budapest road. There I saw a column of Soviet tanks — presumably withdrawing from Gyor. How can it be anything else but just a question of time, if the Soviet troops go in?

If Budapest were subjected, the heart would go out of the country, and then it might be easy for the Soviets to win victory against the boys and girls who are fighting for liberty in this stricken land. In Budapest it could still go on for a few days. It is a sort of "Warsaw", with a gun at every corner. I am pretty hardened to the sight of war, but this is terrible.

These kids, with clotted blood sticking to the bandages around their arms and heads, fighting tanks — and now artillery — with sub-machine guns and home-made grenades!

Noel Barber, Daily Mail (London), 29 October

Gyor and the Revolution "From Below"

Gyor

I reached Gyor about 9.30 p.m. [27 Oct.], booked in at the Voros Csillag (Red Star), hotel, and shouldered my way through the crowds of people still standing about and holding discussions in the square outside the Town Hall, the seat of the Gyor national committee. The word 'national' was not intended to imply that this body arrogated to itself any authority outside its own region; such committees called themselves indifferently "national" or "revolutionary". In their spontaneous origin, in their composition, in their sense of responsibility, in their efficient organisation of food supplies and of civil order, in the restraint they exercised over the wilder elements among the youth, in the wisdom with which so many of them handled the problem of Soviet troops, and, not least, in their striking resemblance at so many points to the soviets, or councils of workers', peasants' and soldiers' deputies, which sprang up in Russia in the 1905 revolution and again in February 1917, these committees, a network of which now extended over the whole of Hungary, were remarkably uniform. They were at once organs of insurrection — the coming together of delegates elected by factories and universities, mines and Army units — and organs of popular self-government, which the armed people trusted. As such they enjoyed tremendous authority, and it is no exaggeration to say that until the Soviet attack of November 4 the real power in the country lay in their hands.

Of course, as in every real revolution "from below", there was "too much" talking, arguing, bickering, coming and going, froth, excitement, agitation, ferment. That is one side of the picture. The other side is the emergence to leading positions of ordinary men, women and youths whom the A.V.H. dominion had kept submerged. The revolution thrust them forward, aroused their civic pride and latent genius for organisation, set them to work to build democracy out of the ruins of bureaucracy. "You can see people developing from day to day", I was told.

Both sides of the picture could be studied in the Gyor Town Hall. There were deputations arriving here, delegations departing there. There was noise and bustle and, outside on the balcony during most of next day, constant speech-making. At first glance one might have seen only flags, armbands, rifles slung over shoulders, a jostling throng of people in room after room; or heard only uproar and argument and jangling telephone bells. But each room had its point of rest: one or two calm, patient figures engaged in turning near-chaos into something like order, sorting things out, soothing the hasty tempers of men who badly needed sleep, organising, advising, building an apparatus to prevent, above all,

hunger and demoralisation. These were the leaders — some of them Communists who had at last found the revolution of their dreams, some of them Socialists, many of them indifferent to political distinctions, since all Hungary was now united around two simple demands that even the children of six were shouting. Here was a revolution, to be studied not in the pages of Marx, Engels and Lenin, valuable though these pages may be, but happening here in real life before the eyes of the world. A flesh and blood revolution with all its shortcomings and contradictions and problems — the problem of life itself. As they took me to see the president and vice-president of this committee not yet forty-eight hours old I caught sight of a portrait of Lenin on the wall, and I could almost fancy his shrewd eyes twinkling approvingly ...

The president, Gyorgy Szabo, a metal-worker, was a tall figure in a shiny blue suit, the inevitable red, white and green ribbon in the buttonhole. But the real personality of the committee was its vice-president, Attila Szigeti, an M.P. for the National Peasant Party (a party that had long been a dormant ally of the Communists: a few days later it renamed itself the Petofi Party.) Szigeti looked for all the world like an English academic, with his stoop, his untidy hair, his Sherlock Holmes pipe, his bulging briefcase tucked under his arm and his swift, quizzical, appraising glance. His and Szabo's main efforts that Saturday and Sunday were devoted to calming the hotheads among the youth. From all over the county delegates had been coming to demand trucks for a grandiose "march on Budapest", where fighting between Hungarians and Russians was reported to be still going on. This would clearly have been folly. The national committee, in touch with the Nagy Government by railway telephone, had information that a Soviet withdrawal from the capital was only a matter of two or three days. For young people with rifles and tommy-guns to converge on Budapest would prejudice Nagy's delicate negotiations. I watched Szabo and Szigeti arguing with each fresh delegation, convincing them that their exuberance could only prejudice the success of the revolution, and that such trucks as were available must be used to carry food to the people of Budapest ...

By 11 p.m. on the Saturday night over a dozen journalists of different nationalities had arrived in Gyor, and Szigeti agreed to give a Press conference. He made no bones about his committee's broad support for the Nagy Government, "but there are things which the Nagy Government has not yet said." The basis of the committee was a people's front. They wanted complete independence and the withdrawal of Soviet troops. It was true that Nagy was a Communist, "but he is a clean man and an honest man." The next step was to persuade people to start work again ...

It was in Gyor too, that I met a group of Communists for the first time and was able to have a long talk with them. They were members of a theatrical and puppet theatre company ... It was from them I heard how the Soviet troops at Gyor had been neutralized. On Wednesday Soviet tanks and armoured cars had patrolled the town. Youths had catcalled and thrown apples, and one soldier had levelled his gun as if to fire, but his colleagues had knocked his arm down. Then the Russians disappeared to their camp a few kilometres away. By Friday there was news of foraging parties at nearby farms, and the national committee decided to send a delegation to the Soviet commander with the following proposal: that if the Russians would promise to stay away from the town and not fire on people the national committee would supply them with food. That promise, said my Communist friend who had been on the delegation, had been kept.

The Communist Party district organisation had fallen to pieces, but that Sunday, as I changed pound notes for forints at the Ibusz office opposite the hotel, the clerk obligingly translated for me a proclamation by the entirely new district committee — "all Nagy men" — printed prominently in the local paper that morning. (The slogan by the title-piece was no longer "Proletarians of all countries unite!" but "For an independent, democratic Hungary!") The local Party statement declared complete support for the two main demands: abolition of the A.V.H. and the withdrawal of Soviet troops.

Peter Fryer, Hungarian Tragedy (London, 1956)

Soviet Commander Protests, Thanks
Gyor

We read now the statement of the Soviet Military Commander of Gyor: "We will not interfere in your national political affairs ... I think that the rising of the Hungarian people against the oppressive leaders is just ..."

According to the Commander's statement, certain elements got into this movement who are practically anarchists; they wouldn't agree with any regime. "I think the Hungarian people is strong enough to maintain its achievements and to constrain these elements to obedience. The commander feels very sorry that a few provocateurs incite againgst Soviet soldiers. They were stoned and spat at, although for their part they do not wish to interfere, not even by their presence, with the life of the town. The Commander begs the population of Gyor and its sober citizens to curb the dangerous elements, all the more so because he himself has experienced the most friendly attitude in the past. In the past women in the families of many Soviet and Hungarian

soldiers were on very friendly terms, and also the members of both armies befriended each other in many cases. Their children played on the same play-grounds. The Commander thanks gratefully for the considerate behaviour of the citizens of Gyor who even yesterday, without a request from the Russians, asked them about their material needs and offered to give them 40 liters of milk for their children. They are in no need ... In connection with the Gyorszentivany affair the commander said the following: "I have investigated the affair personally, but I could not establish any transgression." In spite of that he asked us that in case we observe any irregularity we should inform him immediately. They would punish any kind of excess most severely. As an example he mentioned the open trial that passed sentence against a Soviet soldier im January 1956. He was sentenced to 23 years in the penitentiary because he assaulted a child in Gyor. Hearing of this severe sentence even the child's mother asked for leniency. The Hungarian people may be assured that the Soviet State and the Soviet Army will punish even the slightest Soviet excess most severely!

When we parted, the Soviet Military Commander told me that he was leaving with the best impressions and asked us to tell this to the inhabitants of Gyor by press and radio. He assured us repeatedly the Soviet troops are making no preparations whatsoever for an attack, because they believe the peace of the world is at least at important as the peace of Gyor.   *Radio Free Gyor*

No Agreement with Soviet Troops
Gyor

What did Veszprem people who visited us say about the situation in Veszprem? At present the situation is calm in Veszprem, but, they say, most probably new fights will begin because they could not come to an agreement with the Soviet troops. So they must be prepared for all eventualities. ...

Radio Free Gyor

In an AVH-Headquarters
Gyor

On the floor we find, in a pile of torn and partly burned documents, the register of the Security Police for the year 1951. Page after page is filled with names, professions, and addresses of political prisoners. 699 names for this year alone. Next to most of the names there is the remark *"Transferred"* ... and then the name of another prison. Only opposite a single name in this whole book-keeping of ruined destinies is there the remark "Discharged." The record of prisoners is a catalogue of workers, drivers, waiters, mechanics, office employees—a grey mass of little people, 699 names in one year alone, in the political prison of Gyor. But Hungary has 14 provinces, and every province has a political prison ...

Adolph Rastén, Politiken (Copenhagen), 29 October

Freedom-Fighters . . .

. . . and Hungarian Patriots

Soviet Tanks Arrive in Budapest   *Death of an AVO Man*

Gyor Between "Moderates" and Revolutionaries

Gyor

Tonight, while a crowd of 1,200 demonstrated noisily before the City Hall, the National Committee forced its president, a Communist, to inform Budapest of the prevailing sentiments in northwest Hungary.

Reluctantly, Attila Szigeti, a stout florid party leader, picked up the telephone in his crowded office and dictated an urgent message to the Nagy Government. Other committee members breathed down his neck. Mr. Szigeti's blond walrus mustache heaved and twitched as if to strangle the treasonable words. He told Budapest that the people and his committee demanded that a date for free elections be announced immediately and that the elections must be held "within two or three months." He listed the other demands: an immediate cease-fire by the Soviet forces surrounding Budapest and prompt evacuation of the Soviet forces from Hungary.

"We want a clear answer to-night," he shouted. From the balcony outside members of the committee tried to pacify the crowd.

Ludwig Pocsa, who had been town clerk in the old regime and was now back at his post, told Western reporters this crowd was quiet compared with the mob that surrounded City Hall yesterday, clamoring for guns and for trucks to transport them to Budapest.

"Enough of communism, enough of the Russians," the crowd yelled. "We want a new government in Budapest."

Mr. Pocza informed correspondents that the committee was dissatisfied with Mr. Szigeti's leadership. "He was the No. 2 Communist in Gyor," said Mr. Pocza, "and naturally we cannot trust him completely. He is too moderate."

Mr. Szigeti said he was too busy to talk with reporters. His secretary, a wistful Hungarian intellectual in a shiny blue suit, said, "La situation — elle est tragique."

"Pay no attention to him," growled a committee man. "He is half a Communist."

The committee's demands were, of course, sheer bravado. Gyor would be defenseless against Soviet tanks.

But the city semed in no mood to consider the probable grim consequences of further anti-Soviet demonstrations. The only expression of Gyor was conveyed by a man in a soiled trenchcoat who plucked the correspondent's arm and whispered: "The Russians are moving 200 to 300 tanks into Hungary from the East. We just heard it on the railway telegraph. It's official."

Outside the crowd surrounded the correspondents yelling: "Why doesn't America send us guns? What is the United Nations doing to help us?"

Gyor is on the main highway between Budapest and Vienna. Army trucks, their hoods covered with white sheets on which red crosses had been painted, passed through the city en route to Budapest loaded with medical supplies from the frontier. ...

This city of 60,000, base of the huge Wilhelm Pieck wagon factory, makers of locomotives and railway cars, was in revolutionary mood, Throughout the day crowds filled the square before the City Hall demanding assurances from the National Committee.

Gyor is the seat of one of the four insurgent radio stations. But officials said the transmitter was weak and could be heard not more than forty kilometers from the city. They said no one believed the Budapest radio.

"Three-fourths of Hungary is free," said Mr. Pocza. "Only Budapest awaits liberation. The secret-police rules Budapest only because Russian tanks are there."

Homer Bigart, New York Times, 30 October

Szigeti in Command: Marching on Budapest?

Gyor

Here, just as at Magyarovar, the "Avos" fired on the crowd and their resulting anger drove the whole population into the insurgent camp. After they had put the police to flight, the rebels occupied the radio building and began broadcasting their appeals and their demands on the government ...

Our taxi was immediately surrounded by a large, curious, and excited crowd. Everyone wanted to speak to us and the few people who had a rudimentary knowledge of foreign languages translated the most contradictory statements. Some said that the Russians were savages; others asserted that they had helped the population without firing a single shot. While they claimed that the war was won, they also feared the morrow. Here the truth has a thousand faces ...

Sitting at his desk I saw Attila Szigeti, a man of thirty-five, tall, distinguished, blond, and bespectacled. He was speaking to Budapest on the phone in the act of negotiating with the government on behalf of the insurgents. He presented it with the following ultimatum: that if Nagy did not offer the most substantial guarantees before 8 p. m., the revolutionaries of Gyor would march on the capital.

Szigeti was perfectly calm. Although his life might have been hanging by a thread, he showed not the slightest trace of emotion. Perhaps this was the result of his personal prestige; his authority over the insurgent leaders was perfectly obvious. At that movement he was presiding over a "military" meeting. In that little room he was surrounded by three Honved officers and a civilian representing the committee ...

At the frontier we were greeted with cheering news; a cease-fire had come to Hungary. The bloody fighting was over. Here, in this provincial backwater, we had lived through days similar to that of 25 July 1943 in Italy and accompanied, just as in Italy, by the threat of a new 8th of September. It was a Hungarian 25 July, similar to ours because of the agitated and uncertain atmosphere. But there will be no 8th of September here. There will be no war! ...

Giorgio Bontempi, Il Paese (Rome), 29 October

Gyor

The county's National Council was formed from representatives of the former coalition parties. In Vas county, the National Committee has power; police and army are carrying out its orders. In its first declaration the National Committee summoned the Budapest government to conclude a cease-fire agreement with the Commander of the Soviet troops in Hungary on a reciprocal basis. Furthermore, the Hungarian government should request the Soviet government to declare to the world without delay that Soviet troops stationed in Hungary will be withdrawn from Hungary by the first of January 1957 at the latest — fully and definitively. In addition to this the Vas National Council declared in its statement addressed to the government that it will not consider any government truly "national" unless it accepts these two points.

The Commander of Soviet troops in Szombathely has taken note of the decisions of the National Council, but declared that he will defend the Soviet soldiers, the members of their families, their buildings and monuments, against any provocation. Therefore, the National Committee calls on the workers and the population of the country, in order to avoid bloodshed, to preserve its calm and to refrain from demonstrations of any kind.

The National Council of County Vas, Radio Free Gyor

Gyor

In the name of the Dunantul, the Gyor County National Council calls on Premier Imre Nagy to take further steps. He is summoned to issue instructions, at the latest by 20:00 on the 28th of October, to stop fighting. In fulfilling this demand he should request the commander-in-chief of the Soviet troops to cease fire. We transmit these demands by radio [12:15] and we expect Imre Nagy's personal answer by 20:00 at the latest ...

Radio Free Gyor

On The Austrian Frontier

Gyoergy Szabo, spokesman for the newly formed National Council in control of Western Hungary, said they had proclaimed this four-point programme: a democracy of the Western type; free formation of parties of all kinds; free elections; an armistice and the withdrawal of Russian troops.

Szabo said Attila Szigeti, the Council's chairman, phoned Premier Nagy with the ultimatum. He told him: "Tens of thousands of Nationalists at Gyor, 67 miles from Budapest, were ready to march."

Would the rebels accept Western aid? No, said Szabo. But he asked for a ten-kilowatt radio station "to send messages to the Hungarian people." Now the rebels have a 500-watt station.

Jeffrey Blyth, Daily Mail (London), 29 October

A Jugoslav in Szeged

Horgos

The worker Kis Karol says that peace and order prevail in Szeged. Only two days ago demonstrators marched along the streets. One person was killed. That was the only bloodshed reported from this university centre with a population of over 120,000. Stalin's memorial has been removed from the main square. A delegation of workers from the local factory called on the Prime-Minister Imre Nagy, presenting their request for the introduction of workers' management in enterprises. The delegation expressed its conviction to the Premier that on Monday normal work will be resumed in all factories. A railway man added that all workers agreed to start work on Monday. He said that in all large factories of Szeged Workers Councils have been elected ... The workers are enthusiastic about this novelty.

Furthermore, we have learned that regular lectures will be resumed in schools and faculties. The railwayman declared that in numerous villages as well as in Szeged it is not yet quite clear what the rebels in Budapest and elsewhere want ...

In Kecskemet peace and order were reported until yesterday. Then, all of a sudden, a group of about 450 rebels who had escaped from Budapest penetrated the place, broke into a prison and set free about 300 prisoners. Yesterday, last night and today Hungarian army units are constantly clearing the place of these armed groups. It is believed that the situation will be soon normal in Kecskemet ...

J. Pjevic, Borba (Belgrade), 29 October

Nagy Denies "Counter-Revolution", Announces Soviet Agreement

Budapest

People of Hungary! Last week, bloody events followed, one after another, with tragic rapidity. The fateful consequences of the horrible mistakes and crimes of the past decade are unfolding before us in the painful events which we are witnessing and in which we are participants. During our thousand-year-old history fate was not sparing in scourging our people and nation, but such a shock as this has perhaps never before afflicted our country.

The Government rejects the view that sees the present formidable popular movement as a counter-revolution. Without doubt, as always happens at the time of great popular movements, in the last few days, evil-doers seized the chance of committing common crimes. It also occured that reactionary, counter-revolutionary elements joined the movement and tried to make use of events for overthrowing the people's democratic system. But it is also indisputable that in this movement, a great national and democratic movement embracing and unifying all our people. unfolded itself with elementary force. This movement has the aim of guaranteeing our national independence and sovereignty, of advancing the democratization of our social, economic and political life, for this alone can be the basis of socialism in our country.

The grave crimes of the preceding era released this great movement. The situation was aggravated even further by the fact that up to the very last the leadership was unwilling to break totally with its old and criminal policy. This, above all, led to the tragic fratricidal fight in which so many people are dying on both sides.

In the midst of the fighting was born a Government of democratic national unity, independence and socialism, which has become the genuine means for expressing the people's will. This is the firm resolve of the Government: The new Government, relying on the strength and control of the people, and in the hope that it will obtain the full confidence of the people, will immediately begin to realize the people's just demands ...

The Government wants to rely, first of all, on the militant Hungarian working class but, naturally, it wants to rely also on the entire Hungarian working people.

The Government strongly supports the worker, peasant and student youth and university students, their activity and initiative; great scope should be secured for them in our purified political life, and it will do its best to see that young people starting their careers should enjoy as good a financial situation as possible. The Government will support the new democratic autonomous bodies created on the initiative of the people and will endeavour to integrate them into the State administration.

In the interest of avoiding further bloodshed and ensuring a peaceful clarification of the situation, the Government has ordered an immediate and general cease-fire. It has instructed the armed forces to open fire only if attacked. At the same time it appeals to all those who took up arms to refrain from all fighting activity and to surrender their arms without delay. For maintaining order and restoring public security, a new security force has been created, at once, from units of the police and Honveds, as well as from the armed platoons of the workers and youth.

The Hungarian Government has come to an agreement with the Soviet Government that Soviet troops will immediately begin their withdrawal from Budapest and, simultaneously with the establishment of the new security forces, will leave the city's territory.

The Hungarian Government is initiating negotiations to settle relations between the Hungarian People's Republic and the Soviet Union, including the question of the withdrawal of Soviet troops stationed in Hungary. All this is in the spirit of Soviet-Hungarian friendship, equality among socialist countries and national independence.

After the restoration of order we are going to organise a new and single state police force and we shall abolish the State Security Authority. No one who took part in the armed fighting need fear further reprisals.

The Rhythm of Events

Rapid ideological evolution is a phenomenon characteristic of all serious revolutionary crises. Minds and events move ahead at dizzying speed. Within a period of two weeks Budapest lived through "F e b r u a r y", "O c t o b e r" and "J u l y." In the course of those frightful weeks, the world watched in amazement an unfolding of all revolutionary ideas, even those that were thought to be most antiquated, from Blanqui to Sorel. One could give a course in the history of socialist ideas and methods merely by relating the successive episodes of this Hungarian Revolution. Unity of time and place, which had seemed an artifice of classical tragedy, governed the rhythm of the events. The Winter Palace, Kronstadt and Barcelona followed upon each other with the speed of special editions of a popular newspaper ...

Ignazio Silone, L'Express (Paris), 2 December

The Government will propose to the National Assembly that the national emblem should again be that of Kossuth and that the 15th March should again be declared a National Holiday.

People of Hungary! In these hours of bitterness and conflict, people are prone to see only the black side of our history during the last 12 years, but we must not allow ourselves to entertain such an unjust view of things. These 12 years mark historic achievements, both lasting and ineffaceable, which have been attained by Hungarian workers, peasants and intellectuals under the leadership of the Hungarian Workers' Party. In this force, the spirit of sacrifice and creative work, our revived people's democracy has the best guarantee of Hungary's future. *[17:23]*

Radio Kossuth

"A Different Interpretation"
Budapest

The Government program has been announced. ... Why have these just demands not been met earlier? Why was it necessary for thousands and thousands to resort to arms? Why did honest and good patriots have to kill each other? This is the essence of our great national tragedy!

Not so long ago there were men at the helm who were not only unworthy, but who are mainly responsible for the tragedy. Their responsibility lies in their indifference and in their contempt for the will of the people. The tragedy is that it was only possible to sweep those people away by the wrath of the people growing into open struggle. All that happened in Budapest and elsewhere in the country last week can and must be interpreted in this spirit.

It is our duty to admit that until a few days ago the Hungarian radio had long been giving a different interpretation.

What shape do we think the implementation of the recent Government statement will take? The statement condemns those wrong views which called the present powerful popular movement "counter-revolutionary" ...   *Radio Kossuth*

Demanding the Truth
Gyor

The city of Gyor's provisional National Council with the agreement of the people in the country note with sorrow that Radio Kossuth is not fulfilling its duty of informing the people in these dramatic times. For this reason, the city of Gyor's provisional Council demands that the government give Radio Kossuth to the Hungarian writers so that they may fulfil the task of informing the nation. They demand that for truth and the realization of the peoples' just demands this be carried out.
Radio Free Gyor

Party Remnant Approves
Budapest

The Central Committee approves the declaration made today by the Government of the Hungarian People's Republic. It calls on every member and every organization of the Party to help carry out everything contained in this declaration.

In view of the exceptional situation, the Central Committee has passed on its mandate to lead the party — which it received from the 3rd Party Congress — to a new Party Praesidium of six members. Its chairman is comrade Janos Kadar. The members are Antal Apro, Karoly Kiss, Ferenc Munnich, Imre Nagy, Zoltan Szantho.

The mandate of the Party Praesidium is valid until the 4th Party Congress, which is to be convened as soon as possible.

In its work the Praesidium is relying on the Central Committee and the Politburo.
Radio Kossuth

Appeal to Soviet Army
Miskolc

In order to calm public opinion we inform you that brutalities, orders and deeds against the people were only committed by the personnel of the county's main department for state security. The county's Workers Council should immediately initiate action against these persons.

We read now the appeal of Miskolc workers and students to the Soviet Army ... Here is the translation of the Russian text:

Officers and soldiers! We appeal to you not to fight against your brothers, the Hungarian workers, students, and youths. Our people did not revolt against you, but for the achievement of legal demands. Our interests are identical. We and you are all fighting together for a better socialist life. Don't be simple tools in the crushing of the Hungarian people's justified fight!

The Workers and Students of Miskolc.
Radio Free Miskolc

"Citizens Guards"
Miskolc

This afternoon a Citizens Guard was formed at the headquarters of the Workers Council. The security of persons and property of the working population of Nyiregyhaza is in the hands of the Citizens Guard, consisting of policemen, students, and soldiers. This afternoon talks were also conducted in Nyiregyhaza between the Workers Council and the Soviet Command. As a result Russian military formations have promised to withdraw from Nyiregyhaza and not to station themselves in the town.
Radio Free Miskolc

Sceptical Miskolc: "With a Grain of Salt"

Miskolc

A short time ago was read the announcement of the Workers Council and the Students Parliament of Borsod County to the Workers Councils of the country. Meanwhile Imre Nagy has spoken to the people of the country on the wavelength of Radio Kossuth. Hundreds of thousands have heard this speech. Now the radio of the county's Workers Council will also inform you about the speech of Imre Nagy. We agree with most of his statements and applaud them since they more or less reflected the demands of the people of Borsod County.

In his speech Imre Nagy emphasized that the Government relies on the support of the Hungarian workers, peasants, intellectuals, and students fighting for freedom. We emphasize: we are counting on the Government's realization without delay of everything which Imre Nagy has announced in tonight's speech and all that he has promised in the name of the Government ... At the beginning of his speech Imre Nagy said that there has been no example of such a fight for freedom in the history of the Hungarian people. Then he referred to the views that the present powerful people's movement constitutes a "counter-revolution" ...

As Imre Nagy has said, this great movement was caused by the grave faults of the past historic era ... Imre Nagy said that it was chiefly this which led to the tragic fratricidal war and to the death of so many patriots on both sides. Since we listened to the speech of Imre Nagy attentively, we immediately wondered at this point: *How could there have been patriots on both sides?* The people of Miskolc, for example, think that the true Hungarian patriots were in the ranks of the peacefully demonstrating students and workers, and *not* among the AVH bandits who shot at a defenseless crowd. We believe that this flaw in the speech of Imre Nagy was due to the government being uninformed.

Then, Imre Nagy stated that in the battles there was formed a government of democratic national unity, independence, and socialism, which will truly express the will of the people. It is the opinion of the working people of Borsod that it is really high time that Imre Nagy's government express the will of the people by deeds as soon as possible. The Government promises that it will rely on the strength and the control of the people and hopes to win the full confidence of the people. The strength of the people will back Imre Nagy if his Government will immediately start to fulfill the justified demands of the people, without any delay.

The working population of Borsod county admits that the severe economic situation has worsened in consequence of the past days' fighting. The government of Imre Nagy can, however, count above all on the working class, but also on the entire population, if all is done to meet the people's demands ...

In his speech Imre Nagy announced that in order to end all bloodshed and to restore order, the Government has ordered an immediate cease-fire. It commanded soldiers only to fire in case they were attacked. At the same time it called on all who were bearing arms to hand these over immediately. All we have to add to this is that here in Borsod County those workers, policemen and soldiers who have arms will only fire at those who start armed action against the interests of the people. They are watching over order and the security of the people of Borsod. By the cease-fire, we mean that we will answer shooting by shooting back.

As Imre Nagy reported, the Hungarian government has negotiated with the Russian government for the immediate withdrawal of Russian troops from Budapest, simultaneously with the establishment of new troops for preserving order. We want to add something to this; we are only partly satisfied by this report. The working people of Borsod County do not only want the withdrawal of Soviet troops from Budapest; but desire that they withdraw completely from Hungary and go home. We are very sorry that Imre Nagy in his speech only mentioned Budapest ...

The working people of Borsod County will take Imre Nagy's speech this evening with a grain of salt. We are behind the government of Imre Nagy and support it with all our strength, but only if he proves with facts and immediate action that this government is really serving the people's interests and wants to act, now and in the future.

Radio Free Miskolc

"Ruszki Haza!"

Budapest

A motorcar ride of 25 miles into Budapest, and a long walk into the heart of the city. October 28th, the fifth day.

Soviet tanks taking out their dead; Soviet tanks blockading the grey factory districts of Kispest; the rumble of small arms fire from somewhere unidentified; then, towards the Danube, where the great boulevards lie, the chaotic signs of street fighting lately over — shipwrecked tramcars, smashed barricades, chalk scrawls — *"Ruszki Haza!"* Russians Go Home — the remains of one of Stalin's twelve-foot legs, Red Cross lorries, black flags of mourning, people walking carefully peering round corners ...

Basil Davidson, Times of India (Bombay), 24 November

"*When You Have Lied Too Much . . .*"

Budapest

In a small crowd in front of a tobacco shop, nobody was even trying to buy more than one or two packages of cigarettes. I asked, "why not?" "It's very simple," an elderly woman explained. "Everything will be all over now; another day's fighting and Soviet troops will withdraw. Nagy has promised. There are even rumours that the AVO is going to be dissolved."

But a young man interrupted her: "Who will believe him? He's just taking us in."

Soon everyone had joined in the discussion. For them the main question was: "Should we believe Nagy or not?" Opinions varied, but most people thought Nagy should be trusted . . .

Will Nagy be able to regain the confidence of the nation, which only last Tuesday considered him its leader . . .

A. told me that Nagy had decided to break with the Stalinists . . . We decided to go to the Central Committee together . . . We were not allowed in, but a young girl, probably a secretary, came out to speak with us: The Central Committee is still in session, but its decisions will probably be favourable. Nagy seems determined to act energetically. "And high time too!" she added with a sigh, "otherwise we'll all be drowned in this chaos." We asked her what was happening in the countryside. Nobody knew exactly, but one thing was certain: the revolutionaries controled a large part of the country. Some of the revolutionary leaders promised Nagy their support if he fulfil their essential demands: to withdraw Soviet forces, disband and disarm the A.V.H., and rid the government of people compromised by their Stalinist past . . .

From an armoured car two soldiers threw out packages of newspapers. Nobody picked them up. Everybody waited for the armoured car to drive off. But then only a few people responded. One young man gathered up several copies, shouted

something, and tore them to bits. Then everybody did the same thing, even though these fresh copies of *Szabad Nep* have replaced (in their upper left hand corner) the old star with the new Kossuth emblem. I recalled the face of the editor as he talked to me about his article about the necessity for truth. Does he know what is now happening to his newspaper? . . .

The young man shouted: "Don't read this slop! Whatever Communists print serves the Russians and not the Hungarians. That's why *their* soldiers are distributing Communist newspapers. The Kossuth emblem is just a pretext . . ."

I asked almost desperately. "But why don't you even read it?"

Somebody answered: "Even if it is the truth, it comes too late. It cannot find its way to human hearts. When you have lied too much, nobody will believe you . . ."

I spent the night with Hungarian friends. In the room more than thirty people were sprawled about on improvised couches. I knew some of them. The small man next to me was a steel worker; another was a skilled worker in the shipyards; there was also a plumber, a bookkeeper, and a young medical student . . .

I asked them: "But what do you really want? What are you fighting for?" About fifteen people answered my question. The answers were different, but the essential themes were the same: a free and independent Hungary, a country in which nobody will land in prison just because of a bureaucrat's fancy. They want a Hungary free of 75,000 irresponsible armed A.V.H. agents. They want a Hungary where you can talk freely to one's neighbour, without being afraid that he might be a police informant. They want a Hungary where power will belong to the people, and not to a small elite abusing the slogans of socialism.

Did they want socialism?

The steel worker answered fiercely: "We want justice, freedom, truth. If socialism doesn't give that to us, we don't want socialism."

Each word I felt as a reproach . . . These people identified the system in which they live with socialism. The shipworker then said: "We are going to build our own socialism." But the bookkeeper was sceptical: "Ideas are beautiful, but people are capable of spoiling everything."

"We are not going to allow anybody to spoil anything now," protested the medical student.

"And fascism," I ask, "aren't you afraid of fascism?"

Everybody shouted, but I understood the words of the student: "Nobody wants fascism . . . We won't allow it." . . .

Marian Bielicki, Po Prostu (Warsaw), 9 December

"*A Little Fresh Air*"

Vienna

One of the boys I talked to in Vienna, used a particularly imaginative parable: "People say we live behind the Iron Curtain," he said. "This is not quite true. We lived in a tin. As long as a tin is hermetically closed, it's all right. But then during Imre Nagy's first Premiership they pierced the tin and let in a little bit of fresh air. You know what happens to a tin when a little fresh air gets into it? . . . Everything inside gets rotten."

This is true. It is also the complete history of Communist indoctrination . . .

George Mikes, The Listener (London), 27 December

"We Will Fight On Until —"

Nickelsdorf

In the bus half-a-dozen men were sitting in ragged clothes, red-eyed and weary, their unshaved faces stubbled with several days' growth. One wore a blood-stained bandage around his head. And then there was a pretty blonde seventeen-year old girl who loaded Red-Cross boxes, doing the work of two, with revolutionary enthusiasm for four.

While jolting along all were arguing with one another. What had the revolution achieved? Nothing? Everything? Could Communist Nagy remain prime minister? Or should all those who had been tied up with the regime for the past eleven years make way for a provisional government until free elections could be held? Should all political prisoners be freed? Should the Communist Party be banned? Or should it remain in power as the exponent of a national Hungarian socialism? And the basic question: Should the Russian soldiers — of whom there are an estimated 80,000 in Hungary — be attacked with any weapon that happens to be at hand, with scythes or tanks, or should one leave them alone? On each question these Hungarians held basically different views.

When much later we arrived at Raab [Gyor], I stood in front of city hall as a group of young students — none could have been older than twenty — stepped out on the balcony. One of them shouted down at the thousand people gathered in the square: "Whatever the national committees may decide, we, the youth of Hungary will fight until our beloved land is freed from Soviet yoke, until the Communist party is no longer the despotic master of the country, until all those have gone who are responsible for our 11-year misery, until truly free and secret elections, held under the control of the United Nations, make a government possible which is elected by and for the people!" The words of the young student were followed by long lasting applause.

When we approached Veszprem — north of the Plattensee — two trucks with Soviet troops came towards us. The Russians were holding on to their machine pistols and were staring gloomily into the street. A few kilometers further we suddenly saw tanks, artillery and soldiers in prepared positions on both sides of the street ... A Soviet officer stopped us. He got into the bus, saw the Red-Cross supplies and motioned us to go on. Three minutes later we ran into Hungarian positions. Here we stopped and asked for the officer-in-charge. He explained that they had an agreement with the Russians: "If you won't shoot, we won't." ...

Ten minutes later we arrived in Veszprem. At the City Hall I was introduced to the chairman of the National Revolutionary Committee for Veszprem County one of the ten Hungarian administrative districts west of the Danube. He said that like most of West Hungary, his city was quiet. Almost everywhere, the army, police, and the local authorities had joined the revolution last Tuesday. Only the secret police had caused difficulties.

In Veszprem, after disarming members of the secret police — which was done without bloodshed — the revolutionaries unlocked a special prison for political prisoners. The chairman of the revolutionary committee said: "I was there myself. We found eight men in the subterranean cells. Among them were three Yugoslavs. They were mental and physical wrecks. One of them could not speak because — it seemed — his tongue had been torn out."

The chairman told how in several places the Russians had come to an amicable understanding with Hungarian troops. He explained to me that most Soviet units were dependent on Hungarian food supplies. Then the chairman put a car and a driver at my disposal.

We left Veszprem. The driver, who knew the area well, suggested a short cut. We were driving almost cross-country, when a Soviet motorized patrol spotted us almost at the same time as we him. The Russian jumped down and opened fire on our car with his submachine gun. He must have been a poor marksman. Only two bullets hit the car. Suddenly his machine pistol went silent. My driver lowered the rifle in his hand; for all the clatter of the machine pistol, I had not heard him shoot, but I saw the Russian crumple and fall. We got back into the car and drove off at top speed.

In every town through which we passed, as soon as it became known that "people from outside" were there — we were given enthusiastic hand-shakes. Newspaper and revolutionary proclamations were pressed into my hand. "Demands of the soldiers of Rajka", "the 15-point program of the miners of Dudar", etc. ...

Peter Howard, Reuters, Süddeutsche Zeitung (Munich),
30 October

History

Budapest

The Government has instructed the Minister of Education without delay to withdraw from circulation all history text-books. In other text-books, all passages impregnated with the spirit of the personality-cult must be rectified by teachers in the course of instruction.   *Radio Kossuth*

"Birth of a New State Power"

Budapest

Radio Free Gyor has just demanded dissolution of the Warsaw Pact and free secret elections. [15:30].   *Radio Kossuth*

Gyor

Headed by Te Andras, a miner, the miners of Balinka sent a delegation of seven to Radio Free Gyor. [17:43] They have also formed their own Workers Council and said the miners are keeping order and discipline. However, they are watching events in Budapest with concern and that is why they asked that their demands be transmitted through Radio Free Gyor to the Hungarian government and Imre Nagy. Their first demand is that Imre Nagy call on the Russian troops in Hungary to begin their withdrawal carrying white flags.

How do the miners see the future? In their opinion the future social system of Hungary should be decided by free elections that are perfectly clean and without compulsion. They have nothing against the Communist Party running beside other Parties in these elections; the people will decide which party has its confidence.

The delegation, which represents 30,000 miners, proposed to Imre Nagy that he should begin negotiations with delegates of the Budapest insurgents to form a common Government...

Until these demands are met the miners of Balinka and its district are not prepared to produce a single spade-full of coal ... *Radio Free Gyor*

Miskolc

An appeal to Hungarian Workers Councils and freedom fighters! Debrecen, Szeged, Hatvan, Szekesfehervar, Pecs, Szombathely, Gyor, Mosonmagyarovar, Szolnok, Nyiregyhaza and all Workers Councils, freedom fighters and youth of the country! [18:40]

We workers, students, and armed forces under the leadership of the Miskolc Workers Council and Student Parliament:

1. We demand a new provisional government, truly democratic, sovereign and independent, which will fight for a free and socialist country, excluding all ministers who had served in the Rakosi régime.

2. Such a government can be created only through general and free elections. Since under present conditions we cannot achieve this, we propose that Imre Nagy form a temporary government with only the most essential ministries... There is no need whatever to have 22 ministers and three deputy prime ministers.

3. The first act of this new, free and independent, temporary government, based on a coalition of the Patriotic People's Front and of the Hungarian Workers Party, shall be the immediate withdrawal of Soviet troops from our country — not only to their bases but back to their own country, to the Soviet Union.

4. The new Government shall include in its program and fulfill the demands of all Workers Councils, factories and Student Parliaments.

5. The new state power shall possess only two kinds of armed forces: the police and the Honveds. The AVH is to be abolished.

6. After the withdrawal of Soviet troops the abolition of martial law and full amnesty for all freedom fighters and all patriots who have in any form participated in the uprising.

7. General elections in two months with several parties participating.

In the above, let us all adopt a common attitude. So far this attitude seems to be shared by all; it is by no means the same as that of the present government which is relying on a foreign power. Let us seek every means of contact with one another in the interest of presenting our views, especially by radio.

Pecs, Gyor, Mosonmagyarovar, Miskolc, Debrecen and Nyiregyhaza and other towns are by now in possession of radio stations. We suggest contact on 42 and 43 metres short-wave. Miskolc will signal on these wave-lenghts every second even-numbered hour. This message is important in order to keep our stations from interfering with each other.

Our friends and patriots: we await your suggestions! With utmost urgency let us develop joint points of view and then call on the present Government to resign. Let us form a new Provisional Government under the leadership of Imre Nagy in order to realize our demands.

All of you! — call on Soviet troops, in Russian, not to fight for the suppression of the Hungarian people's legitimate struggle for liberty! We want to regard the Soviet Union as our friend, but we want to be independent ourselves. We do not want to be at war with them ...

We demand that Gero and his criminal accomplices be held responsible.

The Workers Council and Student Parliament of Borsod County

Radio Miskolc

Budapest

The fact is that at last we have a government which constructs its program not on illusions and rigid dogma, but on the desires of the people ... The People's Councils which are being created all over the country illustrate the birth of the new state power. These new People's Councils, which under different names but with quite similar aims, are being created every day in all cities, districts, counties and villages. [20:25]

Radio Kossuth

Sunday Session of the UN Security Council

New York

Not since June, 1950, has the Security Council been called into an emergency Sunday session to urge the condemnation of an act of war. But yesterday the United States, Britain, and France, abandoning their inclination to let the Hungarian rebellion advertise its heroic course a little longer, asked the Council to meet at once to consider "the action of foreign military forces in Hungary in violently repressing the rights of the Hungarian people."

It took two-and-a-half hours before lunch yesterday for Mr. Henry Cabot Lodge, Sir Pierson Dixon, and M. Cornut-Gentille of France to compose their letter of complaint, which M. Cornut-Gentille — who is the President of the Council — acted on by calling the Council meeting this afternoon at 4 p.m. The letter cites Article 34 of the Charter as its enabling clause:

> *"The Security Council may investigate any dispute or any situation which might lead to international friction or give rise to a dispute in order to determine whether the continuance of the dispute or situation is likely to endanger the maintenance of international peace and security."* ...

The rebellion is called, in the three-Power letter, a "situation" and neither the Soviet Union nor its supporting satellite armies or police forces is identified as "a party to the dispute", which under the Charter, may not vote in any debate about it. The three Western delegates saw no hope that the Russians would accept such a stigma, and it might only have taunted them into writing a violent counter-charge.

They are likely to do so as it is, for last night the Moscow Radio, *Pravda* and *Izvestia* were mobilised to launch the version that "imperialist circles in the U.S., U.K. and W. Germany are interfering in the affairs of Socialist countries."

The three active Powers give as the main cause of their complaint the Soviet violation of yet another treaty to which it is a signatory: namely, the 1947 Treaty of Paris (the peace treaty with Hungary), under which the "fundamental freedom of assembly, the press, and worship" were guaranteed to the Hungarians.

The Soviet Union cannot prevent the mere placing of the Allied protest on the agenda. But it can, and surely will, veto any action, or condemnation, that the Council might take. The Russians learned the lesson of a lifetime from the last frantic call for a Sunday meeting. In June 1950, they were sulking in a dignified boycott of the Security Council, and Mr. Truman and Mr. Acheson were able to alert the Council and get a majority vote against the Korean aggression before the Russians could fly out of retirement and land in N.Y. Today they are here, and the veto is poised for the downstroke.

Alistair Cooke, Manchester Guardian, 28 October

Washington

In view of Russia's veto, which is certain to be cast against any sanctions or hostile resolution, the Security Council can do no more than express its moral condemnation of the repressive measures being applied in Hungary. The three Western Governments are resolved to place the majority of the Security Council firmly on record in opposition to Russia's conduct as they seek to isolate and discredit the Soviet Union before world opinion ...

Echoes of Mr. Dulles' unfortunate references to the Warsaw Pact last week again were heard when Mr. Zador, the Hungarian legation's first secretary, was summoned yesterday to the State Department to receive a protest from Mr. Robert Murphy, deputy Under-Secretary of State, on Russia's intervention in Hungary and on the broken communications between the American legation in Budapest and the outside world.

Mr. Zador informed Mr. Murphy that the use of Soviet forces was "quite legal under the Warsaw Pact." He also said that Russian troops were stationed in Hungary "just like American troops are in West Europe." He claimed that a "riot" had occured in Hungary. It soon became known from Mr. Zador's conversations with reporters that Mr. Murphy regarded the interview as an unsatisfactory one because the State Department had received no clear answer to its question whether Hungary had requested military support from the Soviet forces. Mr. Zador insisted that Hungary's internal affairs are the concern neither of the United States nor of the U.N....

The official American reply came not from Mr. Murphy but from Mr. Lodge as Ambassador to the United Nations. Mr. Lodge said:

"The situation in Hungary has developed in such a way as to cause deep anxiety and concern throughout the world. Available information indicates that the people of Hungary are demanding the fundamental rights and freedoms affirmed in the Charter of the United Nations and secured to them by the Hungarian peace treaty.

"They are being subjected to violent repressive measures by foreign military forces and they are reported to be suffering very heavy casualties.

UN Debate

MR. SOBOLEV (U.S.S.R.): *What then is the true purpose of the United States, United Kingdom and French Governments in raising the question of the internal situation in Hungary in the Security Council? In our view, the purpose of their action is to give further encouragement to the armed rebellion which is being conducted by a reactionary underground movement against the legal Hungarian Government. Is such a step consistent with normal diplomatic relations between sovereign Governments? Of course not ...*

It is a provocative step intended in reality not to maintain international peace and security but to foment criminal activities by elements of a fascist type in Hungary and to exacerbate the international situation ...

MR. BRILEJ (Yugoslavia): *We are confident, however, that the Hungarian Government and the Hungarian people will find a solution to the present difficulties in conformity with the best interests of their country. We do not, therefore, view with favour the bringing of its item, "The situation in Hungary", before the Security Council.*

MR. SOBOLEV: *... the meeting has proceeded so quickly — and I blame myself for this— that I failed to draw your attention to the fact that I wanted to make a procedural proposal before the authors of the letter made their substantive statements. I wanted to propose that in accordance with rule 33 of the rules of procedure we should postpone discussion of this question for a certain period, say, three or four days, in order to enable all members of the Council, including, more particularly, the Soviet delegation, to obtain all the necessary information on this matter ...*

MR. PRESIDENT: *So far, however there is every reason to believe that the foreign intervention was spontaneous and that it occured before any appeal was made by the Hungarian Government. Moreover, that appeal was not made until after the night of 23 to 24 October, when the Soviet troops intervened. There was therefore no justification in the Warsaw Treaty for their intervention, for according to article 4 of that Treaty its members are allied against foreign aggression only; it could certainly be invoked by the Hungarians against the Russians, but not by Hungarians against Hungarians ...*

UN Verbatim Record, Security Council, 28 October

The members of the United Nations clearly have a deep interest in this situation and cannot remain indifferent to it. They must assert their serious concern and consider how best they might discharge the obligations which they have assumed under the Charter."

Max Freedman, Manchester Guardian, 29 October

The tremendous public interest aroused by the Hungarian crisis was shown to-day by crowds outside United Nations headquarters. Over 1,000 persons paraded up and down the avenue, some carrying Hungarian and American flags, others placards and banners denouncing the "Kremlin butchers".

At the outset of the meeting it became clear that Russia would do all she could to prevent the western proposal from being inscribed on the council's agenda ...

M. Cornut-Gentille then proposed the adoption of the draft agenda, namely, "The situation in Hungary" and the three western Powers' letter. Mr. Sobolev thrice objected to this, and asked the sponsors of the item to state their justification for it. As they remained silent ... Mr. Sobolev was driven to state his case against it ...

The motion for adoption of the agenda was accepted by nine votes to one (Russia), with one abstention (Yugoslavia). There followed a move by Russia to defer consideration of the subject for three or four days "to watch events and see how they went". This was defeated with only one vote in favour, nine votes against it, and one abstention. The council then turned to the substantive debate on the western proposal, which is certain to have the support of most members.

At this stage the president of the council announced that he had received from the permanent representative of Hungary, Mr. Peter Kos, a request on behalf of his country to be allowed to take part on behalf of his Government in the council's debate ...

Earlier to-day Hungary had also addressed a letter to the Secretary-General of the United Nations categorically protesting against the placing on the agenda of the council any question concerning the domestic affairs of Hungary as amounting to "a serious violation of the sovereignty of the Hungarian People's Republic" and in contradiction with the principles of the United Nations Charter." There being no objection from any member of the council, the Hungarian representative was invited to take his place at the table with the right to speak but not to vote on the question before the council.

M. Cornut-Gentille who, speaking in the capacity of representative of France, said that while his country did not wish to encourage the rebels, whoever they were, to pursue ideological aims contrary to those of their country and people, she did maintain that the internal affairs of every country should be settled by that country alone. The sovereignty of the Hungarian people should be restored as soon as possible.

There followed in succession the spokesmen of half a dozen other countries, members of the Security Council, all of whom, with the exception of the Soviet Russian spokesman, condemned the use of Soviet troops to repress the wishes of the Hungarian people.

The Times (London), 29 October

Mr. Sobolev asserted that Britain, the United States, and France had brought in "inventions about violations of human rights in Hungary" in order to justify in some way the campaign against Hungary and other people's democracies. The tears shed by Messrs. Dixon, Lodge, and Cornut-Gentille are crocodile tears," he declared. In "foisting" on the Security Council the consideration of "false accusations" about human rights in Hungary, the United States, Britain, and France were seeking to divert world public opinion from the true facts. "Well known," said Mr. Sobolev, "are the facts of the refusal of rights to the Algerian people. We may ask why the British Government refuses to allow the exercise of Cypriot freedom and suppresses by armed might all attempts of Cypriot patriots to raise their voice and defend their rights. Then there are the recent events in Singapore."

The council adjourned the debate to a date to be decided by the council's president.

Reuters, 29 October

Dulles Offers Aid
Dallas, Texas

Secretary of State Dulles offered U.S. economic aid to Soviet satellites tonight to tide them over the period of economic readjustment that must come if they gain some independence from Moscow.

In a major address on foreign policy, which he delivered here before the Dallas Council on World Affairs, Mr. Dulles emphasized that his offer was not conditional "upon the adoption by these countries of any particular form of society." In the next sentence Mr. Dulles sought to reassure the Soviet Union. He asserted that the United States had "no ulterior purpose in desiring the independence of the satellite countries" and that it did not look upon these nations as "potential military allies."

New York Times, 28 October

Western Attitude
London

The warning that the Soviet Union would fight to maintain its control of Eastern Europe has affected the attitude of the British Government, and possibly of other Western Governments, toward intervention in Hungary.

Direct Western intervention in the conflict between the Hungarian rebels and the Russian forces, in the opinion of authoritative sources, would certainly lead to harsher punitive measures by the Soviet Union in Hungary and elsewhere in the satellite countries. In view of the Soviet warning, such intervention could also lead to war.

Drew Middleton, New York Times, 2 October

"— and a Great Feeling of Guilt ..."

Nickelsdorf

Then a girl, the only one in a crowd of rebels, took up the tale. "To-day is my seventeenth birthday," she said, a little bashfully, with just a hint of pride in her voice. Seventeen and she was one of the rebels who were defying the massive might of the Soviet Army. Seventeen, and she had just come from the town of Gyor, sixty or so kilometres from the frontier, where, someone else told us, 80 members of the Security Police had been "liquidated" by the workers; where, she announced proudly, "we put up a ladder against the Russian memorial, threw a noose round the Red Star on top of it, and pulled it down.

She was 17, but the Budapest youths who had attacked Russian tanks with bare hands were younger. Many were now dead. "What is your estimate of our casualties?" she asked. "Estimates vary from 200 to ..." Perhaps the journalist who was replying was going to say 10,000, a figure that has been mentioned in some reports. But would it be fair to the girl? The thousands of dead, however few or many of them there were,

had been her compatriots, her comrades in arms. Why name a possibly wild figure?

But her question had been purely rhetorical. She drew herself up to her full height, a look of steel came into her blue eyes. "I must tell you that the dead must be counted not in hundreds but in many, many thousands," she said. "What is the feeling of the Hungarian people about the sacrifices they are making," another journalist asked. "They believe that by thus drawing the attention of the world to what is happening they will compel the Russians to get out," she said, and without pausing, asked: "And what is the feeling of the British people?" We all hesitated. No one was anxious to reply ...

Haltingly one of the reporters began to frame an answer. "First, amazement." Then a pause ... "Second ... admiration." Then quickly, desperately, as if he wanted to withdraw each word as soon as he had uttered it: "And a great feeling of guilt." The girl came back like a flash: "There is much to feel guilty for" ...

Victor Zorza, Manchester Guardian, 29 October

29 OCTOBER

"We Salute the Victorious Dawn . . ."

Budapest

If today, we should listen only to our hearts, then confronted with Imre Nagy's declaration we could only say this: why was he not given this opportunity earlier, why was it not understood sooner that for years, though silenced, the entire nation had a passionate desire which can no longer be stifled now — that Hungary should be truly Hungarian, that our emblem should be a national one, that the 15th of March should be a great national holiday, that Soviet troops should be withdrawn from Hungarian territory, that the justified claims of the workers should be realised, that instead of pretty words and promises the Government should secure a better life, that harassments should cease and an end should be put to forcible collectivisation, redivision of land, etc.? Why did we have to wait so long? Why did the remnants of the Rakosi clique dare, even during these last terrible days, to hamper and make more difficult this evolution? How much blood of true Hungarian patriots had to be sacrificed for this. But if we do not listen only to the voice of our heart we have to speak of other things first. We have to say that essentially the claims of the Hungarian people have been met and all possibilities for progress given.

The withdrawal of Soviet troops from Budapest began in the evening of 28th October — as Imre Nagy informed the country — and this is the first step towards their return to their bases, then to their final evacuation from national territory. The Government is going to dissolve the State Security organisation and create a unified and democratic police force. Thus, the two principal causes of the justified bitterness of the patriots, Communist and non-Party Hungarians, which drove youth's fighting spirit to the extreme, will belong to the past. Without doubt these are the two most important passages in Imre Nagy's speech . . .

This splendid victory of Hungarian youth is also a triumph in the country's struggle and recognition of the justice of our cause. Without them and without their cooperation one cannot restore order and assure the future of Hungary. It is only with them, above all, because this youth has proved that it is capable of heroic acts, that they loved the homeland more than their lives and because they proved that they truly represent the interests of the nation and the broad masses of the people. This youth has proved its political maturity, its incredible sense of responsibility towards the people and country, it proved that it represents a political force capable of becoming a leading force, a dynamic force for which there is no substitute, not only today but also in future struggles for the progress of the country.

This will remain so because from the first moments of the demonstration and fighting they repeatedly declared on innumerable occasions, and proved it during the fighting, that they did not want to seize the power of the people, that they were not fascists or counter-revolutionaries or plunderers. It is very important to state this clearly in face of all the slanders and lies, deliberate or unwitting, which have hitherto been spread. It is very important above all for the country to see clearly the true face of this university and workers' youth which showed themselves the worthy heirs of their ancestors of 1848. It is important also because, in fact, counter-revolutionary groups and looters have tried and are trying to join them to attack the people's power. One cannot dismiss this affair by a wave of the hand. These groups could inflict much damage, shed much blood, commit atrocities, and if we are not on our guard they may well stain the actions of our revolutionary youth . . .

It is with the youth alone one can create order in the country . . . For those who have not yet found the evidence of this, let them just go out into the streets and see for themselves. Many of these students or young workers, who, a few hours ago, were still fighting, are now on lorries bringing in provisions from the countryside for the population of Budapest, helping with the distribution on the market, nursing the wounded, bringing food and cigarettes to them, donating blood, and doing all they can . . .

What we now need is that the achievements should be consolidated and developed. True, although there are people who disapprove of the nomination of this or that Minister, the people have confidence in the new National Government, but of this we shall speak when we are "at peace", when work was been resumed. Enough of endless quarrelling. In peace and calm we can speed up the present evolution. The question is to increase salaries and low-grade pensions, to create workers councils, and introduce university reform. To realise all this we need peace and tranquility, the workers councils, the national committees of students, and revolutionary democratic organisations.

Having put an end to the rule of the Rakosi clique, the people are now really taking the country into their own hands ... Don't let us inflict new wounds. Let us treasure all that remains ... It is true that there is still much to be done; but we can solve this by peaceful means. The elite of the Hungarian people is really and truly united in the fight to achieve the country's independence, and to secure our freedom, for the full democratisation of the country, and the final and complete elimination of arbitrariness. We have no doubt that it will be united and determined in guarding the country's future. Dawn is breaking over the Hungarian fatherland. We salute this dawn with the vigilant eyes of an adult and victorious nation ...   *Szabad Nep (Budapest), 29 October*

Visit to a Revolutionary Headquarters

Western Hungary

It was an amazing spectacle. There were no rooms, there were no walls, there were no secrets. I stood inside the big gate and gazed. At first nobody paid any attention to me. Everyone was too busy. And the sight was made fantastic by the fact that all of them — men, women and children — were all dressed in their carefully-preserved national costumes, the soldiers in their old uniforms, hidden away all this time with the old national flags in attics. I felt ashamed to be intruding into the busy and intent activity of this emergency headquarters, where everybody had a job to do and carried his life in his hands.

"Please come and see the Colonel. He is expecting you." At the sound of a gentle, woman's voice I looked round and saw a young girl, dressed in a man's uniform, hand grenades in her belt, and a "guitar" — a tommy-gun — in her hand. She took me into one of the great barns where the military had set up their committee. The Colonel was there — but dressed in civilian clothes: a grey-haired regular officer, now helping to direct a revolution of workers and students, of women and children. And he turned out to be an old friend ... We had not met for more than twenty years. It was he who had heard of my arrival at the frontier and arranged for me to come through.

It was from him that I heard the latest reports of the rising. He had no doubt as to where the loyalty of the Army lay. You must know, he said, that we would all rather die than surrender. "Look at this crowd—look at them carefully! All they want is to be free. There's hardly a man or a woman here who knew any of the others before. And yet they work together as though they'd been together for years. Students, miners, factory workers, writers, soldier—and all the rest. Nobody cares where anybody comes from. Catholics, Protestants, Jews—here they all are, and because first they're Hungarians, they know exactly what they want. There's no need for discussion. There's hardly any need for orders."

Lajos Lederer, The Observer (London), 25 November

Heroes, Martyrs, and the "AVO"

Budapest

Those, however, who are still shooting at random, even today, and attacking peaceful people — there were many instances of it in City District No. 11 — besmirch the objectives of this great national movement and turn the population against themselves. The people of Albertfalva said they were glad to have a workers' battalion. The people of Hungary are able to protect their country from those who disturb the peace ...

Radio Kossuth

Miskolc

In Miskolc three days ago the State Security forces fired on unarmed demonstrators. Today the whole population attended the funeral of the demonstrators who died as heroes ...

Hungarian News Agency

Miskolc

Since October 26th, there has been no end to funerals ... Rakosi! Gero! Other oppressors of the people! Can you see the gravestones? ... Answer! Because the people will find you wherever you are hiding ... We shall not be annihilated ... We have swept back the dirty tide ... that has brought you to the surface ... and here, at the graves of Hungarian martyrs, we declare firmly that the day of liberty has come ...

Radio Free Miskolc

Gyor

Dear listeners, a four-member delegation of faculties of the Sopron University, representing professors and students, has arrived in Gyor. They represent 1,600 young students and will present their demands. The first point is that further bloodshed should be stopped. In order to do that the Government should withdraw without delay requests by which it attacked our insurgents. In accordance with the peace treaty it shall take steps in order that Soviet armed forces may be withdrawn from Hungary in the shortest possible time. Many demands of Sopron students agree with the demands of trade unions, the Petofi Circle, etc. But the demands of Sopron youth call the attention of the country to very many correct things. They too want a free and democratic Hungary with all power concentrated in the hands of the people. They stated that they do not agree with the present composition of Parliament and Government, and therefore do not believe them suitable to draw up a new electoral law. They demand that a new parliament should be formed from representatives of town and village national councils; this provisional assembly should then immediately take adequate measures and also elaborate a new electoral law. They demand a revision of all our relations with the Soviet Union and full compensation for damages which were caused by our dependency on the Soviet Union.

They do not agree with that part of Imre Nagy's address yesterday in which he announced that the AVO will be disbanded. They demand that the Government announce that the AVO has been disbanded.

Radio Free Gyor

Budapest

The Minister of the Interior has abolished all special police organs invested with special rights. He has also abolished the State Security Authority (AVO). There will be no need for such an organisation in our democratic public life. No formation belonging to any kind of State Security organ is now on duty in the streets of Budapest. Those now serving in our State police force, which is being reorganised, are people who are in no way responsible for past crimes.

Radio Kossuth (16:57)

Nagy – "One of Us?"

On Tuesday evening, in front of the Parliament ... the entire crowd demanded Imre Nagy. Not only this crowd of one hundred thousand, but the entire Hungarian people trusted Imre Nagy as a man who would represent its interests.

Since then, this confidence has weakened day by day. Today, the entire population is by no means behind Imre Nagy; people feel disappointed in him. This disappointment was caused by mistakes, just as it was a mistake when Radio Free Europe broadcast that it was Imre Nagy who had called in the Soviet troops. Soviet troops were called in by Andres Hegedus on Tuesday night. He said so himself to the Writers' delegation of which Laszlo Benjamin was a member. Imre Nagy was fooled and outwitted by the treacherous Gero clique which issued orders in his name and behind his back. He was cut off from the people. He was not informed truthfully about the revolution. Then when he learned the truth and discovered what was going on in the street, he was isolated and not permitted to act. On Wednesday morning, at 6 o'clock, the Writers Association phoned Imre Nagy to ask him what measures he intended to take. It was only then that Imre Nagy learned that he was Prime Minister!

By then, Soviet troops had already arrived in Budapest, as we all know; it is impossible that he could have called them in. The people thus knew that he was Prime Minister before he knew it himself. The radio kept announcing in his name orders of which he knew nothing. His honour and his name were defiled. We have been fooled. Just as we should be fooled again if the regime of the traitorous Gero clique had not come to an end.

The Dangerous Moment

It is not always by going from bad to worse that a nation is driven to revolution. It often happens that a nation which has suffered without complaint, almost as if it were insensible to the most oppressive of laws, will suddenly reject them with violence at the first sign of alleviation. A régime which a revolution has destroyed is often much better than the one which preceded it, and experience suggests that the most dangerous moment for an evil government is usually when it begins to reform itself. Only great ingenuity can save a prince who undertakes to give relief to his subjects after long oppression. The sufferings that are endured patiently, as being inevitable, become intolerable the moment it appears that there might be an escape. Reform then only serves to reveal more clearly what still remains oppressive and now all the more unbearable; the suffering, it is true, has been reduced, but one's sensitivity has become more acute.

ALEXIS DE TOCQUEVILLE, "L'ANCIEN RÉGIME ET LA RÉVOLUTION" (1856),

Quoted in Le Monde (Paris), 30 October

But the reign of this group, alien to our nation, is over ... And now we shall learn whether we will be disillusioned by Imre Nagy or not. It will now be demonstrated whether Imre Nagy is one of us or not. Within a day his orders will show this. Yesterday, in the first speech he made freely, he announced among other things that Soviet troops would immediately be withdrawn from Budapest. If he continues to act in this spirit, then we were right when we said that Imre Nagy was a true Hungarian, a man of our revolution ...

Egyetemi Ifjusag (University Youth), 29 October

Program of the Hungarian Intellectuals

Budapest

The Revolutionary Committee of Hungarian Intellectuals was formed on 28th October in the Central Building of the Lorand Eoetvoes University of Sciences, Budapest. The Committee united every organisation of intellectuals — writers, artists, scientists and university students alike. The Committee then issued the following appeal to the Nation's population ...

Praise to all who, sword in hand, fought against the enemy's overwhelming superiority, and praise to the man in the street who, unarmed, fought against tanks and machine-guns! Our thanks go to those Soviet soldiers who refused to raise their arms against the Hungarian people.

Hungarians! We proudly face the world's judgment ... The power of our country is, at last, in the hands of the people. Our youth, our army, our police, the worker councils, and the peasants have fought side by side. Together, we have the strength to organise our life, independent, free, and democratic. This is the reason why we appeal to our heroic fighters, to the young workers and peasants, to the students, the members of the Petofi circle, and to the members of the peoples' colleges, to enroll in the national guard so that, along with the army, the police force and the workers councils, they may safeguard order and security in our country. We trust that our claims will be satisfied by peaceful means, and that there will reign perfect understanding between our government and the workers councils under the combined protection of the national guard and other patriotic formations. We will not stand for, and are ready to fight against, any attempts tending to restore Stalinism or bring about a counter-revolution.

Hungarians! We may disagree on certain problems, but we all agree as regards our principal claims. Here is the program that we propose to submit to our government:

(1) The immediate settlement of our relations with the Soviet Union. The withdrawal of Soviet troops from Hungarian territory.

(2) The immediate cancellation of all commercial contracts with foreign countries which are prejudicial to the interests of our national economy. The country must be informed as to the nature of these commercial contracts, including those covering uranium and bauxite exports.

(3) General and secret elections. The candidates must be nominated by the people.

(4) Industrial plants and mines must really become the property of the workers. Factories and land are to remain the people's property and nothing is to be given back either to capitalists or big landowners. Factories must be managed by freely elected workers councils. The government must protect the craftsmen's and small tradesmen's right to do business.

(5) The ruthlessly exploitative norm schemes now in effect must be abolished. Low salaries and pensions must be increased as far as economically possible.

(6) The union must really defend the interests of the working classes and their leaders are to be elected freely. Working peasants may create their own associations for protecting their interests.

(7) The government must guarantee free agricultural production and help small landowners and cooperatives formed voluntarily. The hated system compelling delivery of produce must be abolished.

(8) Peasants who have sustained losses by the enforcement of collectivisation must be done justice and receive compensation.

(9) Absolute freedom of press and assembly must be guaranteed.

(10) October 23, the day our nation's uprising against oppression began, shall be declared a national holiday.

In the name of the Hungarian Intellectuals' Revolutionary Committee:

(Signed)

The Students Revolutionary Committee: Istvan Prozsar, Jozsef Molnar, Janos Varga.

The Hungarian Writers Association: Sandor Erdei, Secretary General, Gyulo Sipos, Tibor Merai.

The Hungarian Press Association: Sandor Haraszti, Miklos Vasarhelyi, Ivan Boldizsar, Sandor Fekete.

The Fine Arts Association: Laszlo Bencza, Jozsef Somogyi.

The Hungarian Musicians Association: Endre Szervanszky, Pal Jardanyi.

The University Professors: Tamas Nagy, Mate Major, Ivan Kadar, Gyorgy Markos.

On behalf of the peoples' colleges: Laszlo Kardos, Otto Toekes.

The Petofi Circle: Gabor Tanczos, Balazs Nagy.

MEFESZ: Gyorgy Liebik.

Szabad Nep (Budapest), 29 October

Writers at the Microphone

Budapest

It was the Revolutionary Council in Gyor that first asked to hear from the Hungarian writers. The echo of this demand spreads until the whole country wants to hear 'from those who first opposed the tyranny, cruelty and dogmatism, who fought for those reforms for which our nation has been shedding its blood these last five days. Hungarian writers are now standing at the microphone, relating their thoughts, asking their questions. Their words, born in the heat of battle, let them be heard!

First a poem by Laszlo Benjamin, recited by Gyorgy Bassa:

> *... What will happen to us?*
> *Is there no freedom but in the grave?*
> *No answer. There is only blood,*
> *And the tears of mourning ...*

The next poem is by Lajos Tamasi, recited by the poet ...

> *... There is red blood on the streets of Pest ...*
> *Enthusiasm, patriotic feeling, and then ...*
> *Whom do you shoot at, you fallen ministers?*
> *AVO and tanks will not protect you,*
> *Blood reddens your hands, Erno Gero,*
> *What handwork do you know but murder ...*

The next is by Zoltan Zelk, recited by Gyorgy Bassa ...

> *... Bless the living, God bless the dead,*
> *For out of our blood will come*
> *A new resurrection ...*

An essay by Ferenc Karinthy, read by himself ...

> *"... Only one thing is as certain as the death around us, and that is that the Soviet troops must leave. All say that ..."*

Finally a poem by Istvan Rosi ...

> *... And so we dare to tear down idols.*
> *Throw open all windows, you who were prisoners ...*

Radio Kossuth

A "Suspicious" Yugoslav Feels "Uneasy"

Budapest

Today at last we succeeded in getting into Budapest ... We have been trying to do so in vain for the last four days.

Our first impressions of the capital ... It looks like war time ..., everything seems like the situation on a battlefield immediately following a cease-fire ...

In Ferencvaros, the well-known suburb of Budapest, a part of the capital which suffered serious damage in the last few days, tanks were to be seen left and right; several buildings were damaged. Next to the Hungarian colors black banners were also flying on each house ...

Suddenly we noticed two or three young men with rifles. They were in plain clothes carrying a tricolor ... We were ordered by one of them to stop. The young man asked for our papers. He then pointed to the dead bodies and destroyed arms.

The young man warned us of the danger in which we were and offered to help us get out ... He took us to a half-demolished house in a street where young men with rifles and tricolors were seen. The house was also full of armed young men and girls. A woman was preparing coffee. The young man said: "These are Yugoslav journalists."

One of the Hungarians who had come along with us addressed the young man as "Comrade".

They said in reply: "Here, we're not in the habit of using such greetings."

This sounded suspicious. Only then could we realize that we were not among civil guards appointed by the Government but in a group of rebels. They immediately started to talk about their bravery, about the number of tanks des-

troyed. First, they wanted to take us to the first floor, to the Headquarters, but they changed their mind and took us to the first aid station instead.

This was a small room in which we were met by five or six doctors who started to discuss things with us ... First of all, they stated that as long as Soviet troops are stationed in Budapest and Hungary they would not give up fighting. Of course, there were various people there and different comments were made. The arguments given by some were quite correct. Some were boastful and used reactionary slogans too often.

A young man — he could not have been more then sixteen — had a bunch of onions. He explained that on Tuesday, when it all had broken out, he had bought a kilo of onions for his mother; later on, he kept the onions for luck. He boasted about his bravery and wanted to give the impression of being politically a very mature man. Actually, he held no conceptions and was unable to say just what was at stake.

As soon as we realized where we were we began to feel uneasy. When we were about to leave, a kind of commander, in plain clothes and unarmed, apologized and asked for our papers. We produced our passports and explained how we got there. He excused himself again, questioned us, and let us go. One man with him unbuttoned my coat, touched my overcoat and said that there was no need to question me any more as it was obvious who I was and where I came from. To tell the truth, the material of my overcoat appealed to him.

When we walked out in the street we became aware of machine-guns in the windows of neighbouring houses. Young men were also on the alert there. One can presume that they could not feel exactly at ease, but, luckily, there was no firing at that time. We went back to our car. They even suggested escorting us "to the other side" ... We returned without any difficulty along the main road leading to the centre of the city and soon reached our destination. The situation was quite normal there. People were busy and moved quickly in the street. Many shops were opened. It was getting dark already and it was necessary to look for accommodations.

Those are my first impressions of Budapest.

Vlado Teslic, Borba (Belgrade), 30 October

Striking for "the Democratic Revolution"

Budapest

A delegation of the National Council of Gyor came to Budapest to see if there really was a cease-fire in the capital and returned satisfied that the Government expected order to be restored. ...

Radio Kossuth

Gyor

We have learned that ... Soviet troops have started to withdraw from the capital ... Troops leaving Budapest have already passed through Szekesfehervar ... Do not provoke Soviet troops during this move so that armed clashes are avoided. ...

Radio Free Gyor

Budapest

Shops in Laszlo Kelemen Street, the Fasor and the Hidegkuti Road are open. People are queuing and shopping. There is not much to buy: fat, oil, flour and other essential foodstuffs are already sold out. But the people are helping each other. A woman in the queue offers her neighbour a bit of fat so that the children can have something hot to eat ... Another woman pointed out to me the Kossuth coat-of-arms on the front page of *Szabad Nep* and kissed it ... "This is what our sons have fought for."

At Szena Square I met some armoured cars. People stop. The faces reflect determination and excitement. They look at the buildings which had been shelled with guns, at the cars which had been turned upside down ... We met Soviet soldiers on our way. People asked me: "Why are they still here? Comrade Nagy said yesterday that they would withdraw to their bases." People rightly remark that Budapest is not a base ...

Radio Kossuth

A statement: The Hungarian Frontier Guard sincerely supports the splendid struggle of the Hungarian people for the restoration of our national existence, freedom and independence ... We assure the whole nation that the Frontier Guard, in close unity with the People's Army and the armed militia, is firmly guarding the true power of the people, order, and, above all, the inviolability of Hungary's frontiers. We identify ourselves with the democratic revolution ...

Radio Kossuth

Budapest

The drivers of lorries which had brought gifts of food from Szolnok to the City Districts V and VII ... said that they were glad to be bringing food to the revolutionary capital after the tragic days it had lived through, but their pleasure would have been even greater had they also been able to relate that they had met Soviet formations leaving Budapest. ...

Radio Kossuth

Gyor

Contrary to the announcements of Radio Budapest, we inform you that the people of Budapest are still fighting to obtain their freedom ... [At a meeting] attended by representatives of the Workers Councils of Pecs, Dorog, Tokod, Tatabanya, Tata and Miskolc, we passed a resolution: We shall fulfill our desire for immediate withdrawal of the Russians from the country with the help of one weapon — that means, with a strike! The Councils vowed that they would not produce coal until the last Soviet division has left Hungary. The youth of Gyor will not work until the last Soviet division has left Hungary. Now I speak to the youth of Gyor. Support our strike until we have won! ... Strike for an independent and free Hungary!

Radio Free Gyor

Watching the Russian Retreat

Budapest

Soviet tanks and troops crunched out of this war-battered capital today carrying their dead with them. They left a wrecked city where the stench of death already rises from the smoking ruins to mingle with a chill fog from the Danube River. I arrived here from Warsaw by plane, car and foot, walking the last five miles ...

No sooner were we on the road north to Budapest than we ran into a massive southbound Soviet convoy headed by two armored cars. Ten T-54 tanks, their Red stars still visible through the grime of gunpowder, oil and blood, waddled behind, leaving Budapest behind. Then came numerous motorcycles and trucks. On the back of one tank lay the corpse of a Soviet soldier, his eyes staring vacantly back at the Hungarian capital. Other bodies were in the trucks. The Russian tankmen in their black crash helmets looked tired and grim. They were retreating for the first time since they steam-rollered out of mother Russia into central Europe during World War II. Whether they are moving on order from Moscow is not known.

A Hungarian peasant spat on one tank as it passed him an arm's length away. The Russian crew did not notice. Hatred literally oozed from the Hungarians who silently lined the roadsides watching the Soviets evacuate Budapest. The Russians were nervous but alert. They manned their 100 millimeter tank cannon which were zeroed at the horizontal for firing straight ahead if necessary. And they held tightly to the handles of machine-guns mounted in the tank cockpits and on truck tops.

Soon we came across the first signs of fighting. Huge cannon holes punctured workers' houses. Windows were shattered. A strange music filled the air—the tinkling of broken glass being trod on, driven on, swept aside. Telephone and high tension wires hung crazily and tangled like wet spaghetti as if a hurricane had passed through. We reached a railroad crossing. The crossing gates appeared ridiculous, they were so unnecessary. No trains would be running on that railroad for some time. Sleeping cars had been turned over as roadblocks. Their sides were stitched with machine-gun bullets as if a giant sewing machine had methodically worked them up and down, zigzagged and came back for a final floral touch.

Now we ran into convoys of Hungarian trucks pressed into duty as ambulances and flying Red Cross flags. The doctors looked like butchers, so blood-spattered were their once-white aprons. Trucks passed full of moaning wounded. Then a truck with a large sign proclaiming *"Dead Bodies."* The stench now was overpowering and as we neared the city the acrid smell of cordite also assailed our nostrils.

We were now in the Budapest suburbs, and more and more Soviet troops and tanks could be counted hurrying the wrong way. I counted at least 60 Red Army tanks in one convoy. They looked like circus elephants lumbering one behind the other, twitching from side to side as their heavy steel trucks slipped on debris or an oil slick. "Budapest city limits," the sign said, and with it came the distant chattering of machine-guns. An impressive-looking Soviet tankman blocked the road and waved us into a detour. "Mopping up" operations were still going on. A tank gun coughed in the distance and a split

second later came a muffled concussion that pressured the eardrums. The crack of rifles sounded from snipers who would prefer to die rather than give up.

The street now was so littered I had to abandon the car. I began walking ... There was Rakoczi Street, one of the main thoroughfares, leading down to the bank of the gently flowing Danube. A Soviet tank was roaring down the street and I jumped quickly into a doorway ... Hungarian women completely ignored the tank except for looks of such cold hatred that the emotion must have penetrated the steel side like x-rays ...

The curfew is till in force from 3 p.m. until 10 a.m. but people did not seem to be taking much notice of it. Reports circulated here that rebels in the West of Hungary were marching on Budapest. The reports could not be confirmed here ...

It is doubtful if the Soviets have ever churned up such hatred, anywhere, anytime.

A. J. Cavendish, United Press, 29 October

Budapest

In accordance with an agreement reached with leaders of Budapest resistance groups, the insurgents are beginning to hand over their arms to Hungarian troops relieving Soviet units. Within 24 hours after they hand over their arms, the withdrawal of Soviet units from Budapest will begin. ....   *Radio Kossuth*

Attention, attention! Units of the Hungarian People's Army tonight began replacing Soviet troops in Budapest's 8th District. This will guarantee the withdrawal of Soviet troops. At dawn Soviet troops will evacuate the area agreed on with the command of the resisters. At mine o'clock the resisters will lay down their arms. The replacement and undisturbed withdrawal of Soviet troops are necessary to enable the Soviet troops to continue to evacuate the capital during the day in accordance with the plan fixed in the agreement on their gradual withdrawal from Budapest. I call upon every true patriot to support the Hungarian People's Army in carrying out this task successfully and to the satisfaction of the population of Budapest and the whole country.

(Signed) Lt.Gen. Karoly Janza, Defence Minister of the Hungarian People's Republic.

Radio Kossuth

Munich

To-night in an attempt to persuade the freedom fighters of Budapest that it has acceded to their most important demand — for the withdrawal of Soviet troops from the city — the Government announced that the withdrawal would begin twenty-four hours after the insurgents had handed over their arms. To many of the freedom fighters this can only mean that they are being asked to disarm and to abandon themselves to the tender mercies of the Russians — if only for twenty-four hours — whom they have fought with such fury for a week.

Later the Gyor Radio announced that the fighting in Budapest was definitely continuing, "contrary to the claims of Budapest Radio," and that people of the capital were "still fighting to obtain their freedom with arms in their hands."

Therefore at a meeting representing most of the Revolutionary Councils of Western Hungary and some of Eastern Hungary, a resolution was adopted calling for a general strike throughout the country in support of their demands for the immediate withdrawal of the Russians from the whole of Hungary. Though no mention was made of carrying out their threat to march on Budapest, this may yet come. ...

Victor Zorza, Manchester Guardian, 30 October

Between Scepticism and Dismay

Budapest

The seventh day of the Hungarian revolution has dawned with Soviet soldiers still patrolling the Budapest streets despite a promise by Hungary's new Government that they would be withdrawn. The Government had qualified its announcement yesterday with the condition "as soon as order has been completely restored."

As far as could be learned, armed resistance in Budapest has ceased, even in the Maria Theresa barracks in Ulloi Ut, which was holding out late yesterday. But that order can ever be completely restored in Budapest as long as the Russians are here seems unlikely because of the fears and propaganda with which the Soviet troops seem to be filled.

At 10 o'clock last night, for instance, a Soviet soldier guarding an area known as Szent Istvan Ut shot and seriously wounded Noel Barber, London Daily Mail correspondent. Mr. Barber had been making a tour of inspection to get the public's reaction to Premier Imre Nagy's announcement that there would be no further firing and that the insurrection had been recognized by this Government as not a counter-revolution but revolution provoked by crimes committed by previous Communist regimes. ...

The truth appears to be that, ever since they have been brought into this Hungarian capital, Soviet troops have been trigger-happy. This is less surprising in view of the statements some have made to Russian-speaking Hungarians that they have been told that the Hungarians were fascists and that United States troops could be expected in Budapest.

It would seem that the Hungarian Government, which called in the Russians, is in the position of a Frankenstein faced by his monster. The right wing of the Hungarian Communist party seems to have won control of it over the faction led by Erno Gero, Stalinist, who had replaced Matyas Rakosi—whose protegé he had been—as party chief, only to be ousted himself. Not only has the party said that this has been a revolution to create independent, free Hungary but its organ, *Szabad Nep,* has found it necessary to defend it against the charge that it was "fascist or counter-revolutionary."

But the questions remain: Can the Government get the Russians out of Budapest now and can it ever get them out of Hungary? Will the Soviet be ready to surrender control of Hungary's uranium?

The news that the United Nations Security Council had adjourned without even adopting a resolution about Hungary appeared to come as a shock to those in Budapest who heard it this morning on their radios.

All along the revolutionaries have voiced dismay over failure of the West, and particularly of the United States, to give them any real help. They still have a touching reverence for everything American, but it seems doubtful that this will last much longer. Yesterday in Budapest a father held his child up to see and touch the United States flag with which the windshield of this correspondent's car was draped. But an English-speaking member of another knot of insurgents uttered the nearest thing to a reproach yet heard.

"You know, we have been rather disappointed that you have not helped us," he said.

Asked if he wanted a world war, he replied: "Not that, but tell me, if China could send volunteers to Korea, why could not the United States send some to help us?" ...

A mother in Moritz Zsigmund Square said yesterday with a sigh: "I am frantic with worry about my two children. I can't tie them up in the house. They want to be with their schoolmates. Such babies against tanks." A man pointed to two boys about 12 years old and said: "You know kids like this have been to the barricades for five days now."

The revolutionaries with whom we talked seemed utterly objective and clear-headed. They deplored the fact that they had had "no organization and therefore no leaders." They recognized that the Hungarian Army had been on the whole neutral though it had given them some small arms. ...

"The political police have been worse than the Russians," a rebel said bitterly.

The revolutionaries were sceptical that the political police ever would be disbanded, despite the promise made by Premier Nagy.

Though the revolutionaries said further armed resistance in Budapest had been made impossible by the calling in of new Soviet forces, they insisted that no Hungarian Government could ever enforce compliance with its decrees unless it ordered the Russians out of Hungary. ...

John MacCormac, New York Times, 30 October

Between Hate and Pride

Budapest

From the military point of view Hungary is now back precisely where she started a week ago, with the difference that the Red Army garrison, which had always been stationed only in the countryside, is now nearly four divisions strong instead of two. Reports from the eastern frontiers suggest that Russian forces are still moving into Hungary despite all the conciliatory moves announced in Budapest yesterday.

Even Hungarian anti-Communists I have spoken to admit the speech by Mr. Nagy, the Prime Minister, last night had a ring of sincerity. But it is argued that even if his intentions are as honest as those of any discredited Communist in present day Hungary can be, he still faces two big obstacles in living up to them. One is the opposition of some of his party colleagues still known to be bitterly hostile to any form of genuine coalition rule. The other is the Kremlin's reluctance to abandon its military grip on Eastern Europe as a whole.

Until Hungary is allowed to secede from the Warsaw Pact, which virtually binds her to a permanent Soviet garrison, little hope is felt on the military front. And on this vital point the régime has not even dared to raise hopes, let alone make promises. ...

Meanwhile Budapest is returning to a stunned semblance of its normal self. The shops have reopened. The first street-sweepers are at work clearing some of the numberless mounds of brick and glass splinters. ... Occasional gun-fire has been heard in the city during the past 12 hours. There is still a general tension, from which new flare-ups may at any moment spring.

In any case, as I reported yesterday, it is in the Hungarian provinces that widely-scattered rebel movements are now at their most defiant, and it is not known what the Red Army may feel compelled to do there to "restore order." ...

The rebel activity at Veszprem is particularly impressive, since this province, north of Lake Balaton, is the seat of the permanent Soviet garrison. There are signs that the Russian troops themselves are becoming increasingly uncomfortable in their role. Some of them have told Russian-speaking Hungarians that the Soviet orders of the day, which preceded the advance on Budapest, alleged that a "Fascist revolution aided by Western troops" had to be put down in the city. Instead, they have been blasting from street barricades soldiers from a Communist army side by side with young students and workers. The hate which has welled up against them must have penetrated the thickest Mongolian skull. One or two cases of Russian looting have been reported, but in general there have been no excesses. It is likely that all Soviet troops are under strict orders to be on their best behaviour when not actually occupied with exterminating rebels.

The moral discipline and loyalty of the Budapest population have been astounding to anyone who knows them, and remarkable by any standards. There has been an unwritten law, obeyed throughout the city, that no plundering should take place. In one street I saw watches and fountain pens lying untouched in a smashed shop window. Another food-shop with an empty display counter had the notice "Goods not plundered but removed inside for safety." ... The people have taken a fierce pride in disproving the lies put out by Radio Budapest last week that the capital was "a prey to looters and rioters."

Gordon Shepherd, The Daily Telegraph (London), 30 October

Moscow Views: Shepilov, Zhukov, "Pravda"

Moscow

At tonight's reception in the Turkish Embassy, the Soviet Foreign Minister Shepilov and the Minister of National Defence, Marshal Zhukov, replied to questions put to them by foreign journalists in connection with the latest events in Hungary.

Asked whether the Soviet government has received a message sent by the Austrian government about the cease-fire, Minister Shepilov replied that he heard about it over the radio. He went on to say that the Soviet troops have already stopped firing, and if the insurgents cease fire and if there is no danger, Soviet troops would withdraw from Budapest.

Speaking about the causes of events in Hungary, Shepilow said that there are circles who wish to improve the work of the state administration and also the welfare of the people. One cannot deny the fact, Shepilov went on to say, that there were bureaucratic manifestations in the past. One must satisfy the demands of workers, peasants and intellectuals for the improvement of the situation.

Shepilov said that it is a well-known fact that there were counter-revolutionary elements and criminals, who were also referred to in the declaration of the Hungarian government; they were the first to take up arms. According to Shepilov, they had long prepared themselves to do that.

Asked whether the Soviet troops will withdraw, Shepilov replied: "The sooner the activity of anti-national and anti-democratic elements stops, and if there is no danger, the sooner would the Soviet troops withdraw."

Asked what he could say about Nagy's statement that he would demand that Soviet troops definitely withdraw from Hungary, Shepilow replied: "I have said all that I have to say about that".

The Minister of Defence, Marshal Zhukov, also replied to questions of journalists.

Asked whether Soviet troops started action in Hungary because they were asked by the Hungarian government to do so, Marshal Zhukov replied: "Yes".

Asked whether the Soviet troops in Hungary suffered heavy losses, the Marshal replied: "No".

Replying to a remark made by journalists that in the Security Council today there was mention of new Soviet troops having been sent to Hungary, Marshal Zhukov said that no new Soviet troops had been sent to Hungary in the course of the last 24 hours nor in the course of the last 64 hours either. He said that there were enough Soviet troops in Hungary to proffer aid. However, Zhukov said, the situation in Hungary is improving. A government has been formed which is enjoying our support and the support of the Hungarian people.

Asked what he could say about the statement made by the Hungarian Prime Minister Nagy about the formation of new armed forces composed of workers, Zhukov replied that this fact shows that the Hungarian government is relying on the working class.

Asked whether the Soviet troops will definitely withdraw from Hungary, as was said by the Hungarian Prime Minister Nagy, Zhukov said that he could not reply on behalf of the government to this question. . . .

Asked by the journalists whether the Warsaw Pact included a clause according to which one country should lend support to the other not only in case of danger from abroad, but also with regard to internal problems, Zhukov replied that the stipulations of the Warsaw Pact in some statements and in the writing of the western press have been wrongly interpreted and that the provisions of the Warsaw Pact also apply to internal aid.

At the end of the conversation with the journalists, Zhukov said that agreement should be reached on the disbandment of NATO and the Warsaw Pact.

T. Popovski, Borba (Belgrade), 30 October

Moscow

What happened in Hungary? Comrade Janos Kadar characterized these events in his October 25 radio speech as follows: ". . . The leadership of our party unanimously decided that all possible measures should be taken to repel the armed outbursts against our people's democratic system . . ." Comrade Imre Nagy speaking over the radio the same day, also indicated that "a handful of counter-revolutionary instigators staged an armed attack against the regime of our People's Republic, and this attack was supported by some sections of the Budapest working people who were dissatisfied with the situation in Hungary."

This anti-popular adventure was the result of prolonged subversive activity conducted by the

"The Stupid Level"

Because Fascist elements participated in the struggle in Hungary at the end of October and beginning of November, and tried to exploit it for their own purposes, some observers have tried to deny the national and popular character of the struggle as a whole. One is reminded of Lenin's reply to those Marxists who in 1916 disapproved of the Easter Rebellion in Ireland because of the variety of groups taking part in it.

Lenin then wrote: "The Russian Revolution of 1905 was a bourgeois-democratic revolution. It consisted of a series of battles in which a l l the discontented classes, groups and elements of the population participated. Among these there were masses imbued with the crudest prejudices, with the vaguest and most fantastic aims of struggle; there were small groups which accepted Japanese money, there were speculators and adventurers, etc. Objectively, the mass movement broke the back of Tsarism and paved the way for democracy; for that reason the class-conscious workers led it." And he went on to put it to his comrades that "if, on the one hand, we were to declare and repeat in a thousand keys that we were 'opposed' to all national oppression, and, on the other hand, we were to describe the heroic revolt of the most mobile and intelligent section of certain classes in an oppressed nation against its oppressors as a 'putsch,' we would be sinking to the stupid level . . ." (The Discussion on Self-Determination Summed Up)

New Statesman & Nation (London), 29 December

imperialist powers with the criminal intent of destroying the people's democracies and restoring the capitalist system in these countries. While the countries of the socialist camp fight consistently with all the power at their command for peaceful coexistence of states with different social and economic systems, for the reduction of international tension and for the strengthening of international co-operation, the imperialist circles of the United States, England, Western Germany, and certain other countries are making every effort to interfere in the affairs of the socialist countries through provocations, subversive activity, and the organization of a counter-revolutionary underground ...

Events in Hungary made it crystal clear that a reactionary counter-revolutionary underground, well-armed and thoroughly prepared for decisive action against the people's government, had been organized with outside help. This is borne out by the fact that the rebels acted according to a plan laid out in advance and were led by people experienced in military affairs, namely by officers of the Horthy regime. ...

"*Nomina perdidimus rerum*"

The worst tyranny of all is that of words. In order to start learning to think honestly once again, we must first tidy up our language. Believe me, that's not easy. For example, why the devil do we keep referring to the Russian army as the "Soviet" army? In reality, the Soviets disappeared from Russia as early as 1920, and the only soviets that exist in the world at present are precisely the Hungarian revolutionary committees! And they are soviets in the most genuine sense of the word, open, elementary and improvised forms of the people's power in a country where autocracy has prevented the organizing of political parties.

This means that the term "Soviet soldier" involves the same kind of historical reminiscense as, for example, the seventeenth-century uniforms still in use among the Italian carabinieri. Nevertheless, in order to be understood by everybody, we too are forced to abide by the current and distorted meaning of words; for example, we have to write: "the Soviet troops against the Hungarian insurgents," whereas the simplest respect for accuracy would oblige us to write, "the Russian imperialist troops against the soviets of Hungary." That's how things stand: "Nomina perdidimus rerum" — we have lost the names of things. What a godsend for those who enjoy fishing in troubled waters ...

Ignazio Silone, l'Express (Paris), 7 December

Bourgeois propaganda is now trying to present the working people as the pioneers of the armed rising. But surely there is not a single honest person who would dare to equate the Hungarian working people with those people who barbarously set fire to the National Museum and directed their automatic rifles and machine guns against the firemen and soldiers who tried to save art treasures belonging to the Hungarian people? Who would dare to put Hungarian workers on a par with those who burned books in the streets of Budapest, thus reviving a spectacle of medieval obscurantism and Hitlerite vandalism? ...

Trybuna Ludu, the Polish United Workers' Party newspaper, comments on the events in Hungary as follows: "Unfortunately, organized counter-revolutionary elements, ready to turn the sentiments of the Hungarian public against the most sacred cause — the cause of socialism — infiltrated the peaceful demonstrations of the Hungarian population. These elements circulated unbridled nationalistic and anti-Soviet demagogic slogans and drew upon the reservoir of the politically backward strata of society. A very dangerous situation resulted which was a threat to the socialist conquests of the Hungarian working people and of the people's system." ...

Pravda (Moscow), 28 October

A Polish Comment

Warsaw

The events in Hungary are shaking the conscience of every honest man in Poland. The fratricidal struggle lasting now for several days, and the heavy casualties caused by it, have cast a shadow of mourning over our land.

Many of us are asking ourselves the dramatic question: How has it come about that under the conditions of people's rule a considerable part of the Hungarian people has come out armed in opposition?

We repeat ... although, as usually happens in mass movements, irresponsible and in some cases reactionary elements joined in action, they do not constitute the backbone of such long-lasting and intense struggles.

The answer to the question posed should not be sought in a simplified version about "alien agencies," nor in looking for counter-revolution at every step ...   *Trybuna Ludu (Warsaw), 28 October*

Soviet Omissions

London

The following [omissions], among others, may be noted in Soviet [home-front radio and press] coverage so far: (i) The full scope of the use of, and any opposition to or requests for the withdrawal of Soviet armed forces; (ii) *Szabad Nep's* criticism of *Pravda's* suggestion that the revolt was imperialist-instigated; (iii) Nagy's promised pro-gramme of democratic reform; (iv) emergence of any anti-Soviet trend in Hungary or the satellites generally (Soviet friendship was still the motif in general propaganda on and to the satellites); (v) any form of central leadership and organisa-tion among the insurgents, or negotiations between insurgent representatives and the Nagy Government. (The term "uprising" has been avoided in Moscow radio's reporting in favour of "mutiny" or "insurrection" (*mjatjezh*) and later "putsch" (*puch*); terminology has throughout re-inforced the characterisation of the revolt as "anti-popular" and alien.) BBC *Summary, 2 November*

Reply to Pravda: "The Sun is Rising..."

Budapest

The latest issue of *Pravda* carries a dispatch from its own correspondent about the events in Hungary. Its title is: *"The Collapse of the Anti-Popular Adventure in Hungary"*. This is an error. The events in Budapest were neither anti-popular, nor an adventure; nor was there a collapse. For five days bombs exploded and machine-guns were in action, spreading death. This city, torn by fate, shed blood and suffered for five days. But despite hundreds of deaths, the ideals of true patriotism and democracy were burning in every heart. The loudest slogans were those of socialist democracy and not those of counter-revolution. The revolu-tionary people of Buda and Pest want a people's freedom and a life without arbitrariness, without terror and without fear. They want more bread and national independence. Is this what *Pravda* calls an adventure against the people? Something did collapse; that was the rule of the anti-popular Rakosi-Gero clique.

The *Pravda* article further states that the action of the people of Pest and the revolt were instigated by the subversive work of British and American imperialists. We must sincerely say: the whole of the one-and-a-half million population of Budapest are hurt and insulted by the *Pravda* statement. In body or in spirit the great majority of the po-pulation of Budapest were present at the Tuesday demonstrations. In their minds or their sentiments they agreed with the basic patriotic and demo-cratic aims of the great popular uprising. The sanguinary, tragic, but at the same time elevating fight, lasting for five days, was not instigated by any sort of subversion. It was caused — alas — by our own faults and crimes. Our most important fault was that we had not protected the sacred fire inherited from our great ancestors: our na-tional independence.

In 1848 the Youth of March asked: What does the Hungarian nation want? The answer was given in the first of the Twelve Points of Petofi and his friends: the independence of the nation. At last let us speak openly. Today, again, this is the first answer and the first demand! Hungary must be a free and independent country and she should live in peace and friendship with her neigh-bour the USSR on this basis! This is what we have fought for and this is what we want. This is what writers and journalists — fighting with their pens — want; this is what was demanded by the engineers, workers and peasants, by the demon-strating students, by the insurgents and by the Prime Minister of the country. A heavy stone rolled from our hearts when the new Government and the new leadership of the Party espoused this demand. From behind the dark clouds the sun is rising — red in colour because bathed in blood — but it is the sun of liberty and peace.

And here is another comment on the deplorable *Pravda* article. True, the evil fratricide has been raging for many days. Now we believe that it is at last over. It will be necessary to punish: to punish those who, clinging to their power and frightened for their lives, instigated the battle and ordered fire to be opened on the defenceless people in front of Parliament. Criminal elements who, freed from prisons, rode on the waves of the revolution, must also be punished. Yes, it will be necessary to punish. But this is quite different from what *Pravda* calls "liquidation". Today nobody could — and now nobody wants to — liquidate the fight of the Hungarian people. This fight has borne fruit — precious and dear — the victory of the ideals of freedom. And now at last it will bring on to a soil bathed in blood the si-lencing of arms, a beautiful peace, the ending of bloody fights and the beginning of new construc-tive work.

Ferenc Molnar, Szabad Nep (Budapest), 29 October

End of the "Stalin Road"

Budapest

The executive committee of the municipal council decided to rename Stalin Road the "Street of Hungarian Youth"; the Stalin Bridge, Arpad Bridge, and the Stalin Square will be called "Gyorgy Dozsa Square" from now on ...

Radio Kossuth

30 OCTOBER

"Not Insurgents, But Fighters for Freedom!"

Budapest

This morning Budapest awoke in mild October sunshine. People were walking about in the vast Square of Heroes. All vehicles are flying the Hungarian tricolors. A few Soviet armored vehicles roared by. No shooting was heard. A man distributed newspapers in the street; people snatched them ... At a street-corner they gathered around a policeman. There were lively discussions. Everyone carries one or two newspapers. These are the latest editions calling for the withdrawal of Russians and free elections ...

Some shop-windows are riddled with bullets, but shoes, or candy, have remained untouched. Not a single factory is working; yet no one is short of food. "Such is this revolution, such are these people. And above all they are not thieves ..."—a student told me. I asked him whether this applied to those who were still holding some districts by armed force. "Of course," he said, and he gave the following illustration. This morning these so-called "plunderers" took a group of people caught stealing to the police, with posters on which was written: "We are thieves and brigands" ...

We called on the commander of the city police ... The news came that insurgents had attacked the Municipal Party Headquarters. The Colonel shrugged his shoulders in resignation ...

Then we started towards the Danube to Etves University. The headquarters of the students is there. A tricolor sentinel is in front of the building ... Armed young people are running up and down. We entered the printing room. Students are running off mimeographs, putting the question to Imre Nagy: "Let him say who called in Soviet troops!"

We are received by a member of the Presidium of the Committee. He told us they are strong enough so that when the Russians withdraw, he is convinced they will be able to maintain law and order. He too is a Communist. He assures me that socialist accomplishments are not at all threatened. "We are able to stop any attempt to restore the old order. We are convinced that we can gather into our organisation all those who are still fighting. They are not fascists," he said.

In another room there is an elderly man, a captain, and a middle-aged civilian. The civilian is a representative of former Horthy officers and he came with the suggestion that they, too, as an organisation, should be included in the National Guard. The old man is a Writers' representative serving as liaison to students and the police. He rejects steadily the proposal of the Horthy follower. "We do not want to restore Horthy's Hungary, just as we do not want Stalin back."

I ask about the insurgents ... The captain corrects me—"Not insurgents, but fighters for freedom." ...

In one street we are stopped by young men with rifles. The are fearless. In our car is a young man with a machine-gun. The driver shows the permit of the "Students' Revolutionary Committee". The young men smile, salute, and let us go on ...   *Vlado Teslic, Borba (Belgrade), 31 October*

Sopron

Hungary's seven-day battle for freedom has reached a critical stage. I spent last night at the headquarters of the Liberation Forces of Western Hungary some 50 miles from here, and heard disturbing reports brought by student couriers from Budapest this morning. One spoke of two Rumanian infantry divisions crossing the Hungarian border in support of Soviet reinforcements which arrived from Rumania during the weekend ...

It seems certain that Russian military operations, which in the early days were confused by political and tactical issues, are now running according to a well-directed and ruthless plan. The reported statement of Mr. Shepilov that Soviet troops will be withdrawn from Budapest only after the rebels "have surrendered" is taken here very seriously. Only the total and united support of the Hungarian Army could change the present situation, and this is not yet forthcoming. Though the regular army has, in the past few days, in large numbers, and in various parts of the country, sided with the Liberation figthers, and has nowhere fought against them, no major decision by the army as a whole has been taken to support the people's fight ...

It is difficult to see how this tremendous human struggle will now resolve itself. The concessions made by the new Government of Mr. Nagy are far-reaching, and even one-third of them would have satisfied the Hungarian people a week ago. So they might today, if only the people did not feel that once they lay down their arms the promises made would not be kept. There is no one here who dares to accept them.

I still see the same fire and determination in young and old, in man and woman, as I did in the first hours when I arrived in Hungary a few days ago. There is no sign of fatigue, and I have met no one with a thought of compromise or surrender. But there is great anxiety about the fate of Budapest here tonight. If all resistance there ends, it will be a terrible blow. Without outside military help—which they know today they cannot obtain—they know also that their ultimate fate is the same. Their hope that Moscow would withdraw when the Kremlin knew where the majority of the Hungarian people stood is steadily waning.

Lajos Lederer, Observer Foreign News Service (London),
30 October

Soviet Withdrawal

Budapest

Ministry of National Defence announcement: As reported earlier, the withdrawal from Budapest of Soviet troops opposing armed groups is in full progress. Units of the Hungarian Army, the police and armed Workers and Youth detachments are taking over the job of maintaining order. Armed groups which are still resisting will cease fighting at 9 a. m. and immediately take part in the restoration of peace and order. We will continue to inform you systematically about the withdrawal of Soviet troops from Budapest ...

Radio Kossuth

Victory Appears Near

Budapest

The Hungarian people seem to have won their revolution. Soviet troops are now leaving Budapest and apparently are also leaving Hungary. This afternoon Janos Kadar, chief of the Hungarian Communist party, former President Zoltan Tildy, leader of the Smallholders party, and Ferenc Erdei, representing the former National Peasant party, broadcast to the people a promise to hold free elections, to proclaim Hungary a neutral country, and to insist on the immediate departure of Soviet troops. In other words all the parties in Hungary, even the Communist party, have united in a common front against the Soviet Union and in favor of a return of democracy ...

This was an eleventh-hour grant of the demands on which the revolutionaries have insisted ever since their demonstration a week ago turned into a revolt. It was made after the insurgents had stormed the headquarters of the political police in Republic Square in Pest this afternoon, burned down the Communist party headquarters in Buda, and set fire to every Communist bookshop in the city.

During the storming of the political police headquarters Jean-Pierre Petrazzini, photographer for the magazine *Paris Match*, received a burst of machine-gun fire in the stomach and leg while Tim Foote, photographer for *Life*, was slightly wounded in the hand. They were fired on by A.V.H. tanks. Not long afterward a number of political police, who had been captured by the revolutionaries, paid for their resistance with their lives. Tonight the A.V.H. appealed to the Hungarian Writers Association, which started the revolutionary movement, to intervene for their 10,000 members. They said they were willing to surrender in return for an amnesty. Whether the public in its present mood of fierce hatred will be willing to consent to this is highly doubtful.

Mr. Tildy broadcast tonight an order that all political prisoners who had not already been freed by the revolutionaries be immediately released.

The Government has also ordered that the compulsory collection of produce from Hungarian farmers be canceled. This means the end of the Communist agricultural system. This was followed by an instruction from the Revolutionary Council to the Army and police to send delegates from their revolutionary councils (this was the first revelation that such bodies existed) to a meeting to be held in the Ministry of Defence at 2 o'clock tomorrow morning. The radio also announced that the third motorized formation of the Hungarian army would replace the Soviet troops leaving Budapest.

The last group of the Hungarian insurgents who had been holding out in the Maria Theresia barracks for six days stopped fighting at 8 o'clock this morning. They did not surrender but merely emerged from the building they had defended with incredible bravery against Soviet tanks, artillery, armored cars and infantry. They did not lay down their arms and said they were ready to resume fighting if the Russians did not leave Budapest today.

This correspondent when he drove down Ulloi Ut at 9 o'clock this morning saw havoc that was not surpassed by any of his experiences as a correspondent in World War II. The barracks, renamed Kilian, a 200-year-old building with massive walls, had stood up under the constant battering by Soviet tanks and artillery. Not only that but there was evidence in burned-out Soviet tanks and armored cars as well as in the bodies of twenty Soviet soldiers that lay still unburied in the shattered street, that its defenders had given as good as they got...

As I drove carefully up the street, steering past broken glass, broken telegraph wires, unexploded shells, unexpended ammunition and the corpses of Soviet troops, the car was immediately surrounded by a crowd of youthful insurgents. Their faces were gray with exhaustion, their young chins were covered with a week's beard, but their spirit was still indomitable.

"We greet you in the name of the Hungarian freedom fighters," said one of them in German, when we had disclosed our identity. He said he had been in the barracks since October 23...

"When did you surrender?" he was asked. He drew himself up. "We never surrendered," he said, "The Russians went away and we came out."

It was unnecessary to ask him if the rebels had laid down their arms. He had a submachine gun slung over his shoulder and a pistol in his belt. Near him stood another partisan similarly armed and with two hand grenades stuck in his waistband. A boy who could not be more than 10 years old stood holding at the ready a rifle as tall as himself. Beside him was a 15-year-old girl with a submachine gun and a forage cap on her head, who looked on the brink of absolute exhaustion. She tried to tell my wife in Hungarian what it had been like to fight with no sleep and little food for five long days. Our German-speaking informant confirmed that the defenders of the barracks had been under the command of a lieutenant colonel of the Hungarian Army but he said only a few of them had been soldiers. Their commander, he said, was still in the barracks. "We were armed with rifles, tommyguns, grenades and Molotov cocktails," he continued. "We got a lot of them from dead Russians. The Russian tanks used to attack us in the night and go away in the morning."

At this juncture a youthful partisan with an armband and an air of command advised us to withdraw our car. "Get out," he said, "we don't like some of the people around here. We have some scores to settle." Some of his clear-headed lieutenants directed us to safety down a side street. As we turned down it a rattle of tommygun fire only a few yards down Ulloi Ut reinforced the wisdom of his command. The air was electric. Obviously anything could happen and might happen.

In the side street we passed a surgical clinic whose chief surgeon said that forty dead and about 500 wounded had been carried into his clinic alone from the barracks fighting. He said Sovict troops had shot up the clinic and even its operating theater. When we left Ulloi Ut to get this story off by courier five Russian tanks were still posted only 500 yards from the barracks. It seemed obvious that the situation in Budapest would remain explosive until and unless the Russians leave.

Near the Technical University building where the revolution had its inception A.V.H. soldiers at 10 o'clock this morning shot at a crowd that had gathered before the building. Later an A.V.H. captain tried to make a run for it, He was captured by the crowd and hanged from a lamppost.

In Roeck Szilard Street in District VIII a crowd of children, 12-to-14 years old, quietly surrounded a Soviet tank that was standing there. Suddenly several of them jumped on the tank, one of them produced a pistol and shot into it, and the rest stole the machine gun of the Russian driver. Then they fled down the street under a hail of fire from other Russian tanks.

At 10 o'clock thousands marched in mass demonstration toward the Kilian barracks. They carried black flags to commemorate those who had died there and shouted, "Whoever is a Hungarian join us."

In the Rokus Hospital, the central hospital of Budapest, lie 500 wounded. One, a major of the Hungarian Army from the Petofi Academy Military School, said that all the cadets had joined in the revolution as early as last Tuesday. They fought chiefly in Buda, where they suffered heavy casualties but also inflicted them on the secret police.

Premier Imre Nagy walked this morning from Communist party headquarters to Parliament. He was attended by two policemen wearing their new uniforms and followed by a truckload of policemen.

John MacCormac, *New York Times*, 31 October

Kilian Barracks

Budapest

Kilian Barracks is the 200-year-old building in which Colonel Maleter ... and soldiers of the Hungarian Army's Labour Corps have been successfully staging a miniature Stalingrad against the Russians. I got into the barracks myself a couple of hours later and had a talk there with the colonel ... He was indignant when I told him people outside were saying he had surrendered.

"Who says that? The lying radio, I suppose. We have not surrendered, and if our demands are not granted we shall carry on our fight until they are." ...

Colonel Maleter told me he had given his demands to a Hungarian officer admitted to the barracks after the Russians had withdrawn: —

1. If the Government of Imre Nagy accepts and fulfills our demands, we and the other army units shall support the Government.

2. Greater Budapest must be evacuated by the Red Army by this evening and the rest of Hungary by November 15.

3. We Freedom Fighters will not surrender our arms but, with the rest of the army, we shall take over police powers to assure peace and good order until a new police has been organised to replace the present one.

4. The honour and patriotism of the Freedom Fighters must be publicly confirmed by the Government and the Government must publicly confirm its approval of their uprising.

"Do you think Imre Nagy and his Government are going to accept all those demands?" I asked.

Said the colonel, smiling grimly: "Yes, I think they will."

Sefton Delmer, Daily Express (London), 31 October

Nagy Confirms . . .

Budapest

On behalf of the Council of Ministers of the Hungarian People's Republic, I acknowledge and confirm the formation today of the Preparatory Committee of the Revolutionary Armed Forces consisting of representatives of those who took part in the revolutionary fighting, representatives of the Army and police, and of armed forces of workers and the youth which are in the process of formation. The Revolutionary Committee will form new armed forces from among these elements. With their assistance it will restore the domestic peace of our country and create conditions for the implementation of the Government programs proclaimed on the 28th and 30th of October. The Revolutionary Armed Forces Committee will operate until a new Government is formed by general and secret elections and takes office.   *Radio Kossuth*

Nagy Breaks with One-Party System

Budapest

Here is Prime Minister Imre Nagy [*14:28*]:

Hungarian workers, soldiers, peasants and intellectuals! The constantly widening scope of the revolutionary movement in our country, the tremendous force of the democratic movement has brought our country to a cross-road. The National Government, in full agreement with the Presidium of the Hungarian Workers' Party, has decided to take a step vital for the future of the whole nation, and of which I want to inform the Hungarian working people.

In the interest of further democratization of the country's life, the cabinet abolishes the one-party system and places the country's Government on the basis of democratic cooperation between coalition parties as they existed in 1945. In accordance with this decision a new national government — with a small inner cabinet — has been established, at the moment with only limited powers.

The members of the new Cabinet are Imre Nagy, Zoltan Tildy, Bela Kovacs, Ferenc Erdei, Janos Kadar, Geza Losonczy and a person whom the Social Democratic Party will appoint later.

The government is going to submit to the Presidential Council of the People's Republic its proposition to appoint Janos Kadar and Geza Losonczy as Ministers of State.

This Provisional Government has appealed to the Soviet General Command to begin immediately with the withdrawal of Soviet troops from the territory of Budapest. At the same time, we wish to inform the people of Hungary that we are going to request the Government of the Soviet Union to withdraw Soviet troops completely from the entire territory of the Hungarian Republic.

On behalf of the National Government I wish to declare that it recognizes all autonomous, democratic, local authorities which were formed by the revolution; we will rely on them and we ask for their full support.

Hungarian brothers, patriotic citizens of Hungary! Safeguard the achievements of the revolution! We have to re-establish order first of all! We have to restore peaceful conditions! No blood should be shed by fratricide in our country! Prevent all further disturbances! Assure the safety of life and property with all your might!

Hungarian brothers, workers and peasants: Rally behind the government in this fateful hour! Long live free, democratic and independent Hungary!   *Radio Kossuth*

Zoltan Tildy

Budapest

Dear listeners! Now Minister of State Zoltan Tildy is going to speak to you:

Hungarian brethren! The will of the nation and the national revolution have conquered . . . I stand before the microphone deeply moved. I haven't written down my speech. It may therefore be disjointed. But I greet, I embrace Hungary's dear youth, my heart overflowing with warmth . . . The National Government will bury those who died a hero's death in the struggle with full military honours. It will take care of the wounded and will make provision for their recovery and for the members of their families with the greatest national generosity. In this connection I ask the representatives of the fighting University youth to send their delegates to me at the Parliament building. I am expecting them and so is Premier Imre Nagy. We shall also charge them with an official mission, namely, to form National and University militia to safeguard order ...

I announce now a few measures that have been taken. I inform the country that the Government relieves Peter Kos of his post as representative of Hungary at the UN and will send a new delegation to the UN; this delegation will represent the views of this Government. I also announce that the crop delivery system, which has borne so heavily on the peasantry, will be abolished today. I am convinced that from now on Hungary's farming population will provide more supplies for urban dwellers and urban workers than before.

Hungarian brethren! The radio, too, will become the radio of the Hungarian nation. We shall see to it that mistakes and errors committed in the past are not repeated in the future ...

I am convinced that the peoples and leaders of the Soviet Union will see, once they negotiate with a free and not a humiliated nation and its representatives, how different our relationship will be, how much greater the mutual understanding, respect and affection ...

Now an appeal to the leaders of my own Party in Budapest and in the Provinces — those leaders of the Independent Smallholders' Party who have been hardened in long political battles, who are still alive, who were neither intimidated nor swayed from their convictions by tyranny and terror, and who have always held the country's independence next to their hearts. These leaders, in Budapest and the provinces, should immediately take in hand the reorganisation of the Party. Let them again freely call the Hungarians into their own Party, let them call on the Hungarian farmers and those who feel as we do. Let us urgently set up the Party's organisations on a firm basis. That, too, will contribute to restoring order and safeguarding the nation's future. I await all those brethren with whom I fought and so often suffered through the long years ...

Radio Kossuth

Ferenc Erdei

Budapest

Now the First Deputy Minister of the Council of Ministers, Ferenc Erdei, is going to speak to you:

The victory of the revolution must now be defended with unmistakable determination above all against those who would like to reverse it. But it also has to be defended against those who would like to drown it in anarchy or to turn it against the vital interests of and rights attained by our people ...

For this reason I call on all my Peasant Party colleagues to mobilise the followers of the Party, revive its organisations, and line up for the final defense of the national revolution and of order. Let them co-operate with the other coalition Parties, the revolutionary organisations of the youth, and fight in the vanguard for the creation of the new order of Hungarian life ...

Radio Kossuth

Janos Kadar

Budapest

My fellow-workers, working brethren, dear comrades! Moved by the deep sense of responsibility to spare our nation and working masses further bloodshed, I declare that every member of the Presidium of the Hungarian Workers' Party agrees with today's decisions by the Council of Ministers. As for myself, I can add that I am in whole-hearted agreement with those who spoke before me, Imre Nagy, Zoltan Tildy and Ferenc Erdei. They are my acquaintances and friends, my esteemed and respected compatriots.

I address myself to the Communists, to those Communists who were prompted to join the Party by the progressive ideas of mankind and socialism, and not by selfish personal interests — let us represent our pure and just ideas by pure and just means.

My comrades, my fellow workers! Bad leadership during the past years has cast on our Party the shadow of great and grave burdens. We must fully rid ourselves of these burdens, of all accusations against the Party. This must be done with a clear conscience, with courage and straightforward resolution. The ranks of the Party will thin out, but I do not fear that pure, honest and well-meaning Communists will be disloyal to their ideals. Those who joined us for selfish personal reasons, for a career or other motives will be the ones to leave. But, having got rid of this ballast and the burden of past crimes by certain persons in our leadership, we will fight, even if to some extent from scratch, under more favourable and clearer conditions for the benefit of our ideas, our people, our compatriots and country.

I ask every Communist individually to set an example, by deeds and without pretense, a real example worthy of a man and a Communist, in restoring order, starting normal life, in resuming work and production, and in laying the foundations of an ordered life. Only with the honour thus acquired can we earn the respect of our other compatriots as well.   *Radio Kossuth*

"The Lie Has Been Evicted"

DEAR LISTENERS! *We are opening a new chapter in the history of the Hungarian Radio. For many years now the radio was nothing else but an instrument for disseminating propaganda and lies. Its main task was to carry out orders received from above and day and night it did nothing else than spread mendacities on all wavelengths. Even during the last days, in the hour of our nation's rebirth, this radio was compelled to continue spreading lies, although the struggle, which in the streets was being fought to regain liberty and national independence, was also going on within the walls of this station. Here too it was triumphant! All those who have broadcast lies from this station in the past have been evicted and have nothing more to do with the Hungarian radio. From this hour our radio is going to be entitled to carry the names of Kossuth and Petofi. The people speaking into these microphones are for the most part new men. From now on you will hear new voices speaking on the old wavelengths. From now on, in the messages sent from this station you will hear the truth, as the old oath goes "the whole truth, and nothing but the truth!"*

We, the workers of this radio station, are but a small part of this country's life, but we are asking you, dear listeners, to have confidence in us and to give us all the attention which a working Hungarian deserves. We wish to be, from now on, the spokesmen of the entire Hungarian revolutionary movement. We are going to carry from now on the true voice of the Hungarian people to this country as well as to the whole wide world! Several former leading members of our staff as well as several correspondents of the station have been dismissed.

(signed)   THE REVOLUTIONARY COMMITTEE
OF THE HUNGARIAN RADIO

Free Radio Kossuth [15:06]

TO THE YOUNG GIRL WITH RED HAIR

I would like to speak to you, to clasp your hand, to learn your name and then to ask: Where did you find strength to summon a courage that has stunned us all? It was on Tuesday night that we first saw you, in the crowd of demonstrators enjoining the radio station to broadcast the demands of the revolutionary youth. You signaled to us where we were sitting at the windows, powerless, appealing to us for help. We were inside the building, but our hands were tied. The directors of the station categorically refused to publicize any text that was not dictated to them by superior authority. Your delegation barely succeeded in getting an audience; they hardly condescended to speak to you— they could hardly bring themselves to talk even to us any more. And—let this be understood—for them to hear the will of the people was out of the question.

So I only know you as a young girl with red hair. Your face was burning with rage when you finally burst into our place. But first, I must tell the world that it was not you who had started the fighting. We were inside the radio building, and we saw and heard everything. You proclaimed your demands with increasing force, while inside the building we tried to convince our bosses to listen to you. They refused. Not your voice but that of Erno Gero resounded over the radio with one of the most shameful speeches of our time.

The demonstrators—and you among them—protested when you heard these unspeakable words. You demanded an end to broadcasts of this kind. And at that moment troops of the security police inside the building threw tear-gas bombs at you ... You tried then to get into the building; the commander of the AVH ordered a bayonet attack. We were on the second floor, over the entrance door, and we heard the first screams of the wounded ... A salvo was shot into the air, the guns were levelled point-blank. And the harvest of death began.

We cried out, and we tried to restrain the AVH, imploring them not to shoot. But this caste has been raised by the regime, and its blindness knew no limits. And then you too found arms. We did not see how it happened because we were pushed back and locked up in the editorial offices.

The siege began. It was the first and one of the most dramatic of the revolution. It was long after midnight. It was perhaps almost two-thirty in the morning when you finally broke into the building. And you, young girl with fiery red hair, were the first to enter. Your face was burning with the excitement of battle. In one hand, you carried our beloved tri-colored flag, in the other the weapon of liberty.

We, who saw you then, we will never forget you.

All the thirst of a nation for freedom was burning in you.

May all your battles end thus, in victory! We want to know you, to clasp your hand, and to thank you for having given us a free Hungarian radio.   SZABAD MAGYAR RADIO,

Organ of the Revolutionary Comittee, Free Radio Kossuth

A "Counter-Government"?

Demonstrators during the past few days have demanded the foundation of a "counter-Government". This morning Attila Szigeti, President of the town's National Council, went to the Wagon-Works where the Workers' Council was in special session. A large crowd again demanded the formation of a "counter-Government". The atmosphere was very heated. During the meeting a messenger announced that a "limited" Cabinet had been formed within the Government. He read the declarations made by the members of the Government. The Workers' Council gave a very favourable reception to the news of the Government re-shuffle, the recall of the Hungarian representative to the UN, and the promise of elections with multiple lists. Stormy cheers met statements that followed on the radio. This afternoon representatives of all the Revolutionary Councils of Transdanubia will assemble at Gyor...

Hungarian News Agency

At 17.30 it was announced that the Workers Council of the Gyor railway wagon factory had appealed to all workers to remain calm, and not to listen to demagogues and provocateurs advocating the setting up of a counter-Government, "since this would give foreign Powers an excuse to intervene."

BBC Summary

Budapest

Every Government pronouncement in recent days has fallen short of the demands of the masses. Every announcement has been greeted by the man in the street with the remark: "Why didn't this come yesterday?" The statements by the leaders of the democratic parties have at last made known something that the people has been awaiting for days: until free and democratic elections take place, power must be vested in the democratic coalition parties. After the creation of an inner Cabinet, there remains the justified and still valid demand that all those Ministers who failed in the past to serve the people's interests... at last be relieved of their posts. The latest pronouncements strengthen the belief that this, too, will happen soon. Until the joyful promise of free elections can be implemented, it is essential, now that leaders of the democratic parties, who have been pushed into the background for so long, have spoken, that the local leaders and the masses should also have their say. Their place is in the Revolutionary Committees and Workers' Councils...

Free Radio Kossuth

"Dual Power"

Budapest had a Government of sorts to-day. But Hungary had none. While order has more or less been restored to the capital a state of anarchy without violence seems to reign in the countryside.

The present National Communist Prime Minister, Mr. Imre Nagy, has an even chance of clearing all Soviet troops out of this city in the next 48 hours. But he then faces the even greater task of getting his authority accepted by the various rebel committees "ruling" in the provinces. How far he gets with this task in the next few days will decide not only his own fate but that of the Hungarian uprising as a whole.

I understand from a high Government source close to Mr. Nagy that he has persuaded delegations from nearly all the leading provincial committees to come to Budapest to negotiate with him. Most of them arrived here in secret yesterday and to-day. Discussions are now believed to be going on in Budapest's bullet-scarred Gothic Parliament. This is at present the Prime Minister's headquarters. Mr. Bela Kovacs, the staunch anti-Communist and former leader of the Smallholders' party, who is a member of the Nagy Government ... agreed by telephone to join the Administration on condition that the Communist party abandoned the idea of trying to govern Hungary by itself.

The main problem now is to reconcile the different complexions of the provincial rebel groups. Some are just National Communists. But in others strong Socialist or Roman Catholic peasant trends predominate. None has an outstanding leader, and none has any clear programme except to get Russian troops out of the country and to secure more internal liberty. One likely outcome is that some provincial leaders will join a National Government concentration and take over minor portfolios now held by Budapest nominees. Mr. Nagy seems hard to replace at the moment, for he seems to be the only man who can negotiate with both Russians and rebels with some hope of success...

Mr. Mikoyan, a Russian Deputy Prime Minister, is reported to have arrived again in Budapest yesterday. Even if partial evacuation of the Russians is agreed upon, the achievement of a peaceful withdrawal will be the principal problem...

The civil war can easily flare up again unless the detested Soviet uniforms disappear rapidly and completely from the street scene. Nearly all the rebels still have their arms and, quite apart from the Russians, there are thousands of old Hungarian scores to be paid off.

Gordon Shepherd, Daily Telegraph (London), 31 October

Parties on the New Political Scene

Budapest

The National Peasant Party had been re-established. A temporary organisational committee will issue a report on 31 October. The Party's central organ *Szabad Szo* will be published under the editorship of Pal Szabo. The Party's national HQ is at 8 Dorottya Street, Budapest V...

We now read a letter sent to us by Ferenc Erdei, Minister of State: "Several fellow-members of the former Peasant Party have criticised the fact that it was I who made the appeal for re-organisation of the National Peasant Party. I feel it my duty to state that my simple reason was that I took part in initiating and making this decision, and I alone was in a position to make the relevant announcement. Of course, this does not mean that I intend in any way to influence the reorganisation of the National Peasant Party." ...

Zoltan Tildy, Minister of State, has asked the former staff of *Kis Ujsag* to visit him at his office in the Parliament Building with a view to re-publishing the paper ...

The National Office of the Independent Small-holders Party has resumed its activities in its former offices at No. 1 Semmelweiss Street, Budapest ...

The Hungarian Social Democratic Party was re-formed in the offices of *Nepszava* this afternoon. The Prime Minister has agreed to a request by Anna Kethly, Gyula Klemen and Jozsef Komuves to return to the Party its former main office and the *Nepszava* printing works and publishing house. To the Prime Minister's request that the Party should participate in the Coalition Government, Social Democratic representatives declared that this would be decided by the Social Democratic Party after it had been re-established ...

Janos Kadar, the Chairman of the Hungarian Workers' Party, announces that the reorganization of the Party has already begun. In spirit, policy, structure and personal, the rejuvenated Party will bring about a complete break with the mistakes of the past. Only persons who bear no responsibility for the crimes of the past can become Party members ...   *Free Radio Kossuth*

Russians Are Going, Russians Are Coming

Budapest

Communiqué of the Minister of National Defence: As a result of the heroic revolution for the social and national rebirth of the country, I have concluded an agreement with the Command of the Soviet Armed Forces concerning the order of withdrawal of these troops from Budapest. According to this agreement, all Soviet troops stationed in Budapest will have begun to withdraw at 16:00 on 30 October. This withdrawal will be completed according to schedule by dawn on 31 October. Parallel with the withdrawal of Soviet troops, I order the concentration of certain units of the People's Army. Units of the People's Army, the police and the National Guard together will assume charge of the maintenance of order. ...

(Signed)   General Karoly Tanza

Hungarian News Agency

Our message [said a delegate of the Hungarian oil workers] is that we shall not produce one single drop of oil for Soviet tanks. We shall not deliver oil until we receive an answer from the Government, or preferably from Imre Nagy personally, to the question: who gets the oil we produce?

We wish to draw the Government's attention to the fact that if the answer is that oil will be used for the needs of the Freedom Fighters and their vehicles, we personally want to be convinced of the authenticity of the statement.

Q: If you do not receive a guarantee from the government in this respect, what will you do then?

A: In that case we shall immediately stop the production of all oil wells in a common agreement with the oil miners of Nagylengyel and Baza-karettye.

Q: What influence would this have on the future situation?

A: This paralysing of the oil wells would mean that we would never be able to maintain our oil reserves. The loss would involve many billions. Therefore we request the government to give full consideration to their answer ... Our Csepel friends certainly do not want Soviet tanks attacking the Hungarian people with the use of Hungarian fuel. We demand an immediate answer ...

Radio Free Gyor

The following news has been forwarded to us from the village of Csaroda in Szatmar County:

Since the night of 23/24 October, the Soviet Army has been moving several formations into our country. This we personally witnessed in Berigsurany. According to the latest announcements of the Government after the cease-fire the Soviet troops will be withdrawn from Budapest. Why is it necessary then to march in new Soviet troops. We demand immediate action to prevent the further entry of Soviet troops and to see to it they begin with drawing from Budapest immediately. The Government must inform the population of the truth. It must keep its promise. Only this can secure order in the country ...

Radio Free Miskolc

Just now it has been announced from Kisvárda that many thousand tanks with light and heavy arms are pouring into our country. Motorized infantry is advancing towards Nyiregyhaza. New Russian units! Marshal Zhukov, do you know of this? You must know! ... I should like to respect your word. I can only respect you if by tonight the noise of these troops can not be heard in Nyiregyhaza and does not wake me from restless dreams ... *Mikles Fodor, for the Borsod County Workers Council* ...   *Radio Free Miskolc*

At 19:00 it was stated that the station had received a telephone message from the postal inspector at Zahony to the effect that the infiltration of Soviet troops near Beregsurany had ceased, and that "enormous numbers" of Soviet troops were leaving the country at Zahony ...

BBC Summary, Free Radio Petofi

A correspondent in Nyiregyhaza was reported to have rung up "a few minutes ago" and to have said that "the withdrawal of Soviet troops from Hungary is going on without interruption throughout Nyiregyhaza" *[19.40]*. Soviet tanks stopped in the central square and their crews asked for the road to Zahony. *[19.50]* ...

BBC Summary, Radio Free Miskolc

A resolution adopted by the National Air Defence Command:

1. All Soviet armed formations stationed in Hungary to begin the evacuation of Hungary at once.

2. Soviet formations stationed in Budapest, which constantly violate the cease-fire, to be withdrawn from Budapest within 12 hours. Soviet injured left behind to be looked after in the same way as Hungarian casualties until their complete recovery or safe transfer.

3. Following the Hungarian Government's statement, the declarations of the Soviet Ambassador and Military Attaché on the immediate withdrawal of Soviet troops should be broadcast. Should this not take place, the Air Forces of the People's Army will make an armed stand in support of the demand of the entire Hungarian working people.

4. Notice of termination should be given regarding all military and economic agreements concluded by Governments preceding the Government led by Comrade Nagy, because the previous Governments acted in a way alien to the people and under outside pressure.

With the people through fire and water!

(Signed)   All Members of the National Air Defence Command.

Free Radio Kossuth, 31 October [02:05]

Hegedus, the Warsaw Pact, and the UN Charter

Miskolc

Repeatedly Soviet leaders have referred to the Warsaw Pact in connection with the demands made during the last days. ... Hence I wish to remark: it has become evident to the whole world, and furthermore the present Hungarian government has acknowledged that the persons who allegedly were delegated to conclude the Warsaw Pact, Andras Hegedus, Janos Boldocki, Istvan Bata are "enemies of the Hungarian people and traitors to the nation". They were the representatives of the personality-cult in Hungary—something also condemned by the Soviet government—and they are Rakosi's greatest accomplices. Let us now quote from a speech by Andras Hegedus on May 11, 1955:

"The Hungarian people and government attach great significance to the new endeavour of the Soviet Union which aims to restore complete independence to Austria and the Austrian people in the interest of peace in Europe." ...

Two weeks later, on May 25, 1955, in his so-called ratification speech before the Parliament Hegedus emphasized the following:

"The Pact we have signed corresponds fully with the aims and principles of the UN Charter, and in every respect it is in accordance with the principle of respecting the independence and sovereignty of all states and with the principle of non-interference in their internal affairs."

At the very same ratification session Rakosi emphasized the following:

"All over the world, all those who consider peace as the greatest guarantee of their future welcomed the Warsaw Pact with great relief. The Soviet Union's firm will for peace and her courageous initiative made it possible to solve the Austrian question and with this to return independence and freedom to the Austrian people."

Five-and-a-half months later the same Andras Hegedus does not agree with his own people's fight for freedom. Five-and-a-half months later that Hungarian working-class, working peasantry and intelligentsia whom this Andras Hegedus, this traitor, referred to, have swept him away with elementary strength. Obviously, after this the question arises as to whether the Hungarian people concluded the Warsaw Pact or whether Andras Hegedus did so—Hegedus, the agent of Matyas Rakosi!

We read with amazement that in the course of ratification Hegedus declared that the Pact corresponds with the principles of the UN Charter, with non-interference in internal affairs of another country and with respect for the independence and sovereignty of other States ... Hegedus also declared that if any of the States that signed the Pact should be the object of armed aggression then, according to the UN Charter, all other States must help the attacked. ...

In the present situation the Soviet Union has severely violated the Warsaw Pact, and the Charter of the UN as well. It is not true that the present struggle—certain circles call it a "counter-revolution"—was started by imperialists. Lenin taught, and his thesis still applies, that revolutions cannot be exported or imported. Accordingly, we cannot call the present revolution an imported counter-revolution. It is not counter-revolution. It has been the dynamic explosion of the people's suppressed longing for freedom.

Spokesman for the Borsod Workers Council and Student Parliament

Radio Free Miskolc

Nagy Discusses, Persuades

Budapest

We spent the whole afternoon, waiting in front of Imre Nagy's office. There was very great excitement. Meetings were held one after another, by the Government, the Executive of the Party Central Committee and representatives of various political parties ...

Imre Nagy's associates told us that the Government was in a very difficult position, because, among other things, most people believe that Imre Nagy had called in the Soviet troops and decreed martial law. Today's statement by Imre Nagy clearly showed that this happened before he had taken over ... Imre Nagy and the members of the "inner cabinet" went to a large hall where delegations from all districts of Hungary were waiting. There, a very lively discussion developed. There was quite a lot of disagreement. Re-

presentatives were also present from those districts which up until now have taken positions against the Imre Nagy Government, or which have not given him their confidence, representatives of the Gyor District for example. Finally, after numerous explanations during which demands were made for withdrawal of Soviet troops, first from Budapest and then from the entire Hungarian territory, the district representatives unanimously supported the Government of Imre Nagy as it is today, and they promised to assist in carrying out its tasks.

Djuka Julius, Politika (Belgrade), 31 October

Foreign Affairs

Budapest

The Revolutionary Committee of the Ministry of Foreign Affairs has decided: (1) No time should be lost in elaborating the basic principles of an independent Hungarian foreign policy; accordingly the foreign policy of the Hungarian People's Republic must be placed on a new basis. (2) We condemn the declaration made by Peter Kos, the Hungarian UN representative at the session of the Security Council in connection with the situation in Hungary and we demand his immediate recall from the UN. (3) We demand the recall and replacement of heads and members of the Foreign Ministry and missions abroad who were alien to the people and who represented and still represent the treasonable policy of the anti-national Rakosi-Gero clique. (4) The workers of the Foreign Ministry declare that they will take part with all their energy in assuring order and the development of peaceful life in Budapest. (5) Finally, the Revolutionary Committee of the Foreign Ministry calls on workers of the Ministry to turn up at their offices on Wednesday morning.

Hungarian News Agency

Shifting Moscow Line

Moscow

Current reports from all over Hungary indicate that the working people are backing the new Government and approve its program. Even the Western correspondents, whose sensational reports give a completely distorted picture, have to acknowledge that the overwhelming majority of the population stands for the consolidation and development of the popular democratie regime, for the strongest friendship with all the socialist countries and first of all with the USSR.

I said "overwhelming majority" because there is a minority of counter-revolutionary elements who have broken completely with the people, but have hitched themselves to the popular movement in Hungary in an effort to capitalise on the situation and overthrow the popular democratic regime. The provocations and outrages of the

counter-revolutionary minority are what led to
bloodshed. ... Evidently, certain Western leaders
responsible for implementing the so-called liberation policy drew a lesson from the events in
Poland where the efforts to frame a mass provocation failed. They therefore decided to make up
for that failure in Hungary. No wonder the ringleaders of the Hungarian emigré organisations
darted about Western Europe, as reported in the
U.S. Press, organising and preparing the uprising
of the counter-revolutionary underground. ...

Andreyev, Radio Moscow, 30 October

London

The bewildering speed with which events subsequently unrolled in Budapest was reflected in
Pravda's assurance to its readers (October 30)

that the Nagy Government (which Soviet troops
and tanks were to overthrow five days later) had
won the support of the Hungarian workers. The
fact that Nagy had asked for the withdrawal of
Soviet troops was tactfully omitted. On the same
day, a well-known Soviet writer, Georgi Gulya,
admitted in *Literaturnaya Gazeta* that "much per-
plexity" had accumulated in Hungary during the
Rakosi régime, and suggested that the rebellion
had been essentially democratic. He had a special
word of praise for the Budapest writers in some
of their demands, for they had not on the whole
set themselves in opposition to the "People's Democracy" as such. This cautious appraisal suggests, perhaps, that some Soviet writers may have
hoped for a "Polish" solution....

Soviet Survey (London), January 1957

Soviet Declaration on Satellites

Moscow

In the process of the rise of the new system
and the deep revolutionary changes in social
relations there were not a few difficulties, un-
solved problems and downright mistakes, including mistakes in the relations among the Socialist
states—violations and errors which demeaned the
principles of equality in relations among Socialist
states ...

As recent events have shown, the need has
arisen for an appropriate declaration of the position of the Soviet Union on the mutual relations
between the USSR and other Socialist countries,
particularly in the economic and military spheres ...

It is known that, in accordance with the
Warsaw Treaty and governmental agreements,
Soviet units are stationed in the Hungarian and
the Rumanian Republics ...

With a view to insuring the mutual security of
the Socialist countries, the Soviet Government is
ready to review with the other Socialist countries
which are members of the Warsaw Treaty the
question of the Soviet troops stationed on the territory of the above-mentioned countries.

In so doing the Soviet Government proceeds from
the principle that the stationing of troops of another
member state of the Warsaw Treaty takes place
on the basis of an agreement between all its participants and not only with the agreement of that
state, on the territory of which, at its request, these
troops are stationed or are planned to be stationed ...

The course of events has shown that the working people of Hungary, who achieved great progress on the basis of the people's democratic
order, are rightfully raising the question of the

need to eliminate serious defects in the field of
economic construction, of improving further
the material well-being of the population and of
combating bureaucratic distortions in the state
apparatus.

However, this just and progressive movement
of the working people was soon joined by forces
of black reaction and counter-revolution, which
are trying to take advantage of the discontent of
part of the working people in order to undermine the foundations of the people's democratic
system in Hungary and to restore there the old
landlords' and capitalists' order.

The Soviet Government, like the whole of the
Soviet people, deeply regret that the development
of events in Hungary has led to bloodshed. At the
request of the Hungarian People's Government,
the Soviet Government consented to the entry
into Budapest of Soviet Army units for the purpose of assisting the Hungarian People's Army
and Hungarian government agencies to establish
order in the city.

Since it considers that the further presence of
Soviet Army units in Hungary can serve as a
cause for even greater aggravation of the situation,
the Soviet Government has given instructions to
its military command to withdraw the Soviet
Army units from Budapest as soon as this is considered necessary by the Hungarian Government.

At the same time, the Soviet Government is
ready to enter into corresponding negotiations
with the Government of the Hungarian People's
Republic and other participants of the Warsaw
Treaty on the question of the presence of Soviet
troops on the territory of Hungary ...

Pravda (Moscow), 31 October

Neighbors

Miskolc

Slovaks! Rumanians! Serbians! Blood is flowing from our wounds and you are silent. We are fighting for liberty and you call us Fascists. Rakosi's colleagues, who were not Hungarians, but enemies of our country, said the same thing ... We see that you too are groaning under the yoke we wish to throw off. Now foreign interests want to incite you against us. We have every confidence that you will not believe their lies ... We have proposed a Socialist State form which will guarantee the free development of our people and stop the clash between East and West. We are fighting for you, too, for peace, for Socialist truth, for the guarantee of the free development of our peoples. Help us in our fight!

Radio Free Miskolc

Bucharest

Rumanian security authorities were reported to have arrested leaders of scattered demonstrations among Transylvanian Magyars. The Magyars, a Hungarian minority in Rumania, were understood to have demonstrated in sympathy with their kinsmen in Hungary. ...

Both Rumania and Soviet Army units stationed in the Magyar Autonomous Region and other parts of Transylvania are being reinforced heavily....

There are persistent reports of student outbreaks against the regime in Cluj and other tcwns of western Rumania. The demonstrators are also understood to include workers and farmers.

Gheorghe Gheorghiu-Dej, First Secretary of the Rumanian Communist party, Premier Chivu Stoica and other leaders returned unexpectedly yesterday afternoon from their official visit to Yugoslavia. ... They must deal with serious minority problems, chief among which is the undoubted sympathy of the large Magyar community in this country for the Hungarian nationalists.

Scinteia, organ of the Rumanian Workers (Communist) party, appealed yesterday for minority loyalty in the present situation. Meanwhile Rumanian officials are seeking to minimize the importance of the Hungarian situation. However, in their remarks to United States diplomats and to this correspondent, Rumanian authorities have conceded the "democratizing" nature of the changes in Hungary and Poland.

Welles Hangen, New York Times, 30 October

Mikoyan "Accepts Everything"

New York

On October 30th, in the Parliament building, General Pal Maleter, commanding officer of all Hungarian armed forces, reported in my presence to the government that Soviet armored units were crossing in large numbers our border in the North-East. In the ensuing discussion we agreed not to disclose this in releases to the press as long as the government had the opportunity to take up this question with the Soviet ambassador. By recalling this I wish to prove that all actions of the Nagy government were carefully deliberated with due consideration for the prestige of the Soviet Union. The government sought to avoid any break, and to solve all problems by peaceful means. For this reason, the news bulletin dealing with the new Soviet troop movements was broadcast only the next day ...

On October 30, I was present when Mr. Mikoyan, member of the Soviet politbureau, put through a telephone call to one of the Ministers of State of Imre Nagy's government. He expressed his wish of meeting the Minister. The meeting took place on hour later and lasted for some 60 minutes. Before his departure I advised the Minister of State to find out from Mr. Mikoyan what the Soviet's attitude was towards the multiparty system and the withdrawal from the Warsaw Pact, and what

stand the Soviet Union intends to take concerning the evacuation of its troops from Hungary. Further, whether the decisions of the government will be accepted.

The Minister of State returned from the meeting in a happy mood, saying: "He accepted everything."

Considering this, I am in a position to declare that competent Soviet circles were not only fully informed about the most minute details of all developments in Hungary's politics, but were actually in concurrence with these.

Statement of Mr. Joszef Koevago, former Mayor of Budapest, United Nations Special Committee, 28 January 1957.

The 23rd October was the greatest day in the history of our people. After fighting ceased and after the Soviet Army had begun to withdraw, Comrades Kadar and Munnich met the commanders and representatives of the armed units of revolutionary youth and, after talks lasting three hours, they decided to form, on behalf of the youth of City District No. 9, the Revolutionary Youth Committee of the Kilian Barracks, Tompa Street, Corvin Square, Tuezolto Street and Berzencey Street, thus roughly the freedom-fighters of districts 8 and 9. This was the first step towards the creation of order, public safety, peace and an independent Hungarian Republic. It has been agreed that the revolutionary armed youth, together with the Revolutionary Committee of the Army Command, shall take over the duty of safeguarding the personal safety and property of the peaceful population in the 8th and 9th City Districts. We, the leaders of the armed groups, have made this decision because certain notorious elements and bandits are jeopardising the results which we have achieved at the cost of heavy sacrifice in blood.

Further it has been agreed to dismiss from service all armed AVH members and to guard public buildings by Army units aided by the Committee of Revolutionary Youth. The Revolutionary Committee calls on all freedom fighters in the country and in Greater Budapest to unite forces ...

Free Radio Kossuth [22:41]

Transdanubian Pressure

Gyor

The Transdanubian National Council, which has been set up at Gyor has called for a neutral Hungary. About 400 delegates from the National Councils of Transdanubia met in Gyor on 30th October. In the course of the meeting, which lasted until midnight, Attila Szigeti, Chairman of the Gyor National Council, warned against any steps which might threaten the achievements of the revolution. He spoke against the idea of setting up a "Counter-Government" and was opposed to the continuation of the armed struggle, which had become pointless. In the course of the meeting, the majority decided to continue the strike until the Government had satisfied the revolutionary demands. ... The Transdanubian National Council took note of the pledge given by army units in Papa, Gyor, Tata, and Zalaegerszeg that they would defend the people against all foreign attacks, even if they received orders to the contrary.

The Transdanubian National Council will initiate negotiations with the Government on the following demands: (1) The Government must hold general elections by secret ballot with the participation of several parties after the departure of the Soviet troops, but not later than January 1957; (2) The Government must set up local organs for maintaining order with the approval of the competent National Councils; (3) Until a new National Assembly is convened, all appointments of colonels and other senior officers must be approved by a Central National Council, which has yet to be set up; (4) The freedom fighters must be represented in the new Government; (5) The Government must proclaim Hungary's neutrality in the UN; (6) The Government must guarantee freedom of speech, freedom of the Press, freedom of assembly, and freedom of religion.

The Transdanubian National Council will not recognise the Government unless these demands are satisfied.   *Hungarian News Agency*

Escape

Budapest

According to a report from Vienna, news had reached the Austrian frontier that Erno Gero and Andras Hegedus had escaped from Hungary to the Soviet Union on the night of 30th October. The former Minister of the Interior, Laszlo Piros, had gone with them. ...   *Free Radio Kossuth*

School

Miskolc

Youth is yearning with all its heart for school and learning. Therefore it asks the miners and the farmers that even during sit-down strikes they should produce enough for teaching to be carried on during the winter. ...

The Gyorgy Millian School, Radio Free Miskolc

The Cardinal

Budapest

Dear listeners! We interrupt our gramophone program to read an important announcement: Zoltan Tildy, Minister of State, has received a workers' delegation. He told them he thought it desirable that Cardinal Jozsef Mindszenty, the Primate, should return to Esztergom and, by discharging his functions as Primate, take part in the noble struggle which counts on every true patriot in these historic days ...

Free Radio Kossuth

Statement by Dr. Ivan Lukacs, Chairman of the National Committee of the District of Retsag (County Nograd): On 30th October at 22.05 a Retsag Army unit liberated Mgr. Jozsef Mindszenty, Primate of Hungary, from his prison at Felsoepeteny where he has spent one year short of three days. His eight years of incarceration are now ended. The victorious Hungarian revolution has ended his sufferings. The population of Retsag were the first to greet the freed Primate, who has never wavered, either morally or physically. Mgr. Mindszenty replied to the greetings with the words: "My sons, I shall carry on where I left off eight years ago ..."

The Primate spent 20 minutes at the Retsag presbytery, where he conferred in a friendly way with those present and gave his blessings. He then left for his home in Buda ...

Hungarian News Agency

149

Mindszenty's Liberation

The months of summer and early fall, 1956, dragged slowly on. But toward the end of October there came a sudden change. I heard on the radio that the workers and students had started demonstrations, but no details were given. I was isolated . . .

Then on Oct. 24 the radio was taken away and the newspapers stopped. The guards became silent. There was a week of total isolation. The tension could be felt every time I saw one of the guards. Then, on Oct. 30, they broke their silence. Their leaders came into my room. They asked me to come with them. My life was threatened, they said.

"But who threatens me?" I asked.

"The mob," was all the AVO man would say.

"I won't go," I answered him. "If it is the will of God that I should die here, here I will die. But I will not move."

The officers were puzzled. They spoke briefly among themselves. Then one of them asked almost timidly: "Would you go if we used force — just token force? For example, we could touch your arm as a symbol of force. Then would you go?"

"No," I answered them.

At this they hardened. They were afraid. They grabbed at me and started to pull me from the chair. I resisted. They were still pulling at me when one of the guards downstairs rushed up to say that a Russian-style armored car was coming up the driveway to the house. The officers ran to the window. A few minutes later, John Horvath, head of the Government's Office of Church Affairs, ran into my room.

"Your life is not safe in this place," he almost shouted at me. "I have orders to move you!"

"I will not go," I told him. "You have taken everything from me there is to take. You can take nothing else."

Horvath left the room. He went to the telephone and called his superiors in Budapest, asking for help. By this time they needed it, for the people of the village had been attracted by his car. First came the children and young people, because they are always first in these things. After them, from the fields, from their homes, from the shops, came several hundred men and women from the village. Many of them carried hoes and other farming tools which they raised as their weapons. These people had known I was in the castle and, on seeing the armored car speed up to the building, were afraid for my life. They assumed the Russians were going to take me away.

Horvath's telephone call to Budapest was intercepted by the Hungarian military unit at Retsag, 20 kilometers away. The officers and soldiers there knew all about the freedom fight in the country. They were not yet in action because there was no need yet. But on hearing Horvath's call for help, they decided this was their time.

(Horvath did not known his message was overheard, and, when his call was completed, left in his car for Budapest. He never got there. The Hungarian soldiers intercepted him on the way and we do not known what happened to him, except that he has not been heard of since that time.)

The AVO soldiers who were left in the house became restless, and I could hear them running from one room to the other and shouting to each other about the demonstrations outside. By this time the people had surrounded the castle and were raising their weapons, calling: "Freedom for Mindszenty and bread for the Hungarian people." Horvath was not gone more than 30 minutes before my guards decided they could not last against the people. They formed a revolutionary council and came to me with humility and presented themselves with great respect before me.

"Sir," said their spokesman, "we have declared ourselves on the side of the people and have decided that you have been kept a prisoner illegally. From this moment on you are free." They spoke not an instant too soon, for then came the Hungarian soldiers in tanks and in armored cars from Retsag . . .

The Hungarian freedom fighters disarmed the AVO guards, but I asked that they not be harmed. Then they went to the cellar, where they found a quantity of machine guns, small-arms, and ammunition, hidden under the coal pile.

The freedom fighters helped me and my secretary pack the few belongings which were ours. Then they brought us down the stairs to the car.

The people cheered as we drove away from the castle in procession. One tank went before us, the other behind. On both of them the red star had been removed and the Hungarian national colors painted on.

Thus we moved to freedom after eight years.

"The Mindszenty Story", New York Herald Tribune (Paris), 16 December

The New Army of "The Glorious Revolution"

Budapest

"Hungarian brethren, comrades-in-arms! A Revolutionary Military Council of the Army Command has been formed. On behalf of every soldier, NCO, officer-cadet, officer and general of the Army, the Revolutionary Military Council approves and considers as its own all decisions and demands of the revolutionary councils of the workers, youth and intellectuals. The Army stands by the people in safeguarding the achievement of the glorious revolution. In the interests of safeguarding these achievements —

(1) We demand the immediate withdrawal of the Soviet Army from Budapest and, within the shortest possible time, from the territory of our country.

(2) We ask the Hungarian people to give us their fullest support in restoring peace and order quickly.

(3) We have dismissed from the Army High Command sectarian forces which were retarding the march of events — for instance, Major Generals Lajos Toth, Jenoe Hazai, Ference Hidvegi and Lieutenant-General Istvan Szabo.

(4) The AVH also kept the Army in a state of intimidation. The Revolutionary Military Council of the Army Command has decided to disarm immediately those AVH formations which are still armed.

(5) The Revolutionary Military Council of the Army Command demands that our heroic Frontier Guards should be intregrated into the Army. We appeal to them to continue to defend the sacred frontiers of our country.

[Signed] On behalf of the Revolutionary Military Council of the Hungarian People's Army: Maj.Gen. Lorenz Konya.

Free Radio Kossuth

A Revolutionary Council has been set up within the National Police Command, the central authority of the National Police Force. We are proud that the entire police force refused to be turned against the people's revolutionary struggle and that it did not fire on the heroic fighters for freedom but fraternized with them and supported their struggle. We have learned, however, that certain AVH functionaries illegally acquired police uniforms. The Revolutionary Council deeply condemns this and is devoting all its energies to unmasking and arresting AVH men dressed in police uniform.

Together with the freedom fighter insurgents we have begun the immediate disbandment and disarming of members of the AVH. We guarantee that criminals will be detained on their arrest until called to account before a court of law. Today, in accordance with our agreement with the armed insurgents' leaders, we have taken into custody 30 AVH men whom they arrested ...

Free Radio Kossuth

The Revolutionary Army Committee of the Hungarian Honved Army is convening a meeting of the leaders of the Budapest Honved Army, Police, and National Guard Revolutionary Army Committees at 2 a.m on 31 October in the Ministry of National Defence. The leaders of the Revolutionary Army Committees of the units of the Third Motorised Army Corps replacing the Soviet troops withdrawing from Budapest should, immediately upon arriving in Budapest, report at the Marko Street entrance of the Ministry of National Defence, to the Revolutionary Army Committee of the Hungarian Honved Army. We request that the emissaries should be supplied with credentials. We request all revolutionary organisations to ensure the arrival of the emissaries.

Free Radio Kossuth

"If I Can Only Get Back Alive ..."

Budapest

We make our way through unknown streets to ... the immense square, vacant and somber in front of the huge dome-shaped house of Parliament. ... Here is the impressive main entrance which I can still remember after seven years. Twice daily then we entered here to attend the sessions of "Youth of the World". Leaning against the stone balustrade, simple Greek girls had stood there, in uniform, partisans from Grammos. In the hall, French delegates had sold albums of

Impressionists to earn money for their return trip. On the staircase smart officers and uniformed activists checked entrance cards. In the galleries one had listened to long speeches in many languages about "defending peace". Whenever Stalin's name was mentioned we had all stood up chanting the two syllables and applauded our own enthusiasm until our hands hurt. After my return I wrote a poem on the subject.

Now the main entrance is closed and silent ... We explain that we are Polish journalists and that we would like to enter Parliament to speak with one of the members of the government ... "For instance, with me?" Our interviewer's name is Geza Losonczy. He is a well-known militant of the Communist left who had been pushed aside and persecuted for many years. Only today did he become State Minister and member of the inner cabinet. With slight irony he tells us that he does not yet have a proper office nor a secretary, nor did he know the building very well which he had opened for us ... Wo wandered throught the dark hallways of purple and gold. There is something both extraordinary and grotesque in that deserted imperial and royal pomposity. Feebly illuminated chandeliers throw ghostly shadows. The rugs absorb the sound of our steps. I feel that if

On a Needle's Point

If Poland nine days ago seemed poised on a razor's edge between Soviet repression and native revolution, Hungary now seems to sway on the point of a needle. Through the last few crucial days the unanswered question has been what was Russia going to do? Would she give a last push and throw Hungary back into the Stalinist gulf hemmed in and held down by Soviet troops? Or would she, by withdrawing in the face of national revolution, allow Hungary to topple forward into an independent democracy of the Western type, with a Government no longer controlled by Communists though probaly committed to socialism?

These questions are still unanswered. Hungary's revolution was unorganised: it has thrown up any number of local powers whose authority runs as far as their words and firearms can carry; but there is no central authority on any side. What picture we can piece together shows chaos in Budapest and in the provinces the calm of anarchy. The security police officially dissolved, seems to be fighting for its own hand; the Hungarian Army has no clear leadership: even the Soviet troops may lack continuous direction. The Government lives on hope. After his many other retreats, Mr. Nagy has now promised to bring down the whole structure of "People's Democracy" and go back to the parliamentary system that was in force right after the war. The old political parties re-enter the Government and none but "National Communists" are to sit beside them. Free elections are promised, and with them the undoing of all Communist wrongs. The Government recognises the local revolutionary councils, it espouses the revolution. The end of it all is "long live Independent and Free Hungary." At last heroism seems to have won its reward. Yet the nagging voice of doubt still warns us that all is not over; the die is not yet cast.

The great uncertainties are two: first, what Russia will decide to do; secondly, how the many forces that have gone to make the revolution will group themselves and with what force they will continue to press upon the Government. From the Russians nothing reliable has been heard, although Moscow Radio said on Tuesday that Russia was ready to reconsider the position of its troops in Eastern Europe. Mr. Nagy said on Tuesday – as he had already said on Sunday—that the troops were withdrawing by agreement. He also repeated that he would at once enter into negotiations with Russia—presumably for the complete withdrawal of Russian troops from Hungary. We still do not know whether the troops are in fact leaving Budapest for their bases, and whether Mr. Nagy spoke with any authority. It seemed on Sunday that Russia might have decided on a "Polish solution". In Poland, after teetering on the brink of force for a day or two, Russia agreed to withdraw its troops to their Polish bases and to accept a "National Communist" Government. This was the price of averting a Polish uprising, and so far the policy seems to have worked. Poland wins some freedom— but under Communist direction – and it wins equal status with Russia in economic and political dealings at the same time.

Does Russia still hope for something like this in Hungary? The attempt, if such it is, comes very late. Revolution has not threatened, it has broken out everywhere: Russian troops have not manoeuvred round the capital, they have killed scores of Hungarians: the Communists are not hanging on, they are struggling to re-emerge with the help of other parties; the Government can hardly find breath to commend the Soviet alliance, it is busy saying that it never meant to bring in Soviet troops. Soviet policy may be to keep Hungary on the needle point until the National Communists secure some kind of hold, however precarious.

But the risk of a fall seems as great as ever; the infamy of final Soviet repression, if it comes, greater still.

Manchester Guardian, 31 October

I turned my head I would notice someone silently following my footsteps—*Man? History?*

Here are large rooms full of tobacco smoke. Members of the government are working and, with them, a number of writers and journalists. People enter constantly. No soldiers jump to attention. There are workers with demands jotted down on note-book paper. Poorly-shaved students. Nobody examines passes. Nobody says, "I shall announce you in just a moment." Everyone heads straight for the person he wishes to see. Conversations are going on everywhere, in the center, in all corners. Someone telephones, someone leans against a pedestal, jotting into his note-book in a large, nervous scrawl. The influx of delegations goes on and on. The comrades who receive them have tired eyes, but they shake the hands of the delegates forcefully to say good-bye and then to receive the next ones.

Our interview is chaotic. ... We talk about everything: about the character of the Hungarian revolution, about the program in the process of crystallizing, about government of national unity, about the demands of the revolutionary committees, about perspectives for the hours and the days ahead. The Government is not yet finally formed; further changes are still to take place to make it more representative. Just a short time before, talks about this were held with Social Democrats. Unfortunately they refused to enter the Government now, declaring they still prefer to wait. But even in the present set-up the basis of the government seems to be widening hourly. Proof of this is the conditional support given by a few of the most important insurgent groups, putting forward demands which the Government is willing to endorse. ... The most urgent of these demands are: the withdrawal of the Soviet army from Hungary, the legalization of political parties, free elections, punishment of those responsible. This is, more or less, the program submitted a moment ago by the revolutionary group of the 8th and 9th districts of Budapest. Their leadership consists of two officers, a few workers and students, a writer and a barber. ...

"Believe me, we are no sadists. But we cannot manage to feel sorry for those Hungarians [AVO-men who were lynched] ..." Then comrade Zoltan Szanto, a member of the Party Committee created a few days ago and a former ambassador to Warsaw, says: "We are living through an immense tragedy.... Crimes have been committed against the people. The Communists have brought guilt upon themselves. The people are right. We must finally go along with the people. It is already very late as far as the Party is concerned ..." Terrible is the grief of this old man who has devoted all his life to this cause and who now

discovers that he was the accomplice of criminals. ...

In the street.... "Halt! Who goes there?" ... Before us a tanned boy with damp, black eyes. After he had checked our identity he seemed to want to chat. He spoke with that characteristic Caucasian accent which does not know the sonorous softness typical of Russian. "Why kill people? One can't make out who is right and who is wrong. If I can only get back to Armenia alive. ..."

Viktor Woroszylski, Nowa Kultura (Warsaw), 25 November, and France Observateur (Paris), 3 January 1957

"Flowers from the Grave"

We can only give hourly news, since we only believe what we see! ... We know that we are responsible for every word we speak. It is with responsibility that we repeat the news we had already broadcast, namely that Soviet troops will leave the country within 12 hours. It is reported from Zahony that one division has already crossed the Tisza. Another has crossed by ferry between the artillery barracks in Zahony and the ford of the Tisza, while other divisions are waiting to cross between Zahony and Tiszadesbo. Freedom Fighters keep us informed by radio. We accept every news report with caution and only broadcast those item which have been checked. We can reassure our listeners that the troops are on their way home! Our listeners should not be restless about the troops which are not returning along the same route as they came. Soviet troops entered Hungary through Zahony and through Beregszasz but are returning by many other roads. This is natural ...

If in the 13th hour the promise were not being fulfilled we should be getting nervous, but there is no need to get nervous now. If we kept calm in the fighting nobody should get restless now.

This evening a tank wandered about in Nyiregyhaza for half an hour. It crossed the city in several directions. As we learned later, road signs had been destroyed and did not point the way to Moscow. But they will find the way. That is certain. This tank left half an hour ago via Nagykallo-Nyirbater to Zahony, or rather to the Soviet Union, and it will be followed by columns of the heavy artillery. There is no need to worry. We must wait with discipline until they go away, until we can give the last soldier the flowers which we send from the graves of our Freedom Fighters to the people of the Soviet Union. Not in anger. Not in revenge. But only a reminder that they too had been misled when the Hungarian Freedom Fighters were abused by Stalinists as counter-revolutionaries. ... *Radio Free Miskolc*

31 OCTOBER

A Yugoslav Finds Unrest and Uncertainty

Budapest

This morning the voice of the Petofi radio station woke us up: "We do not recognize this Government—we demand a provisional Insurgents' Government until elections are held." Radio Gyor—on two kilowatts—was speaking and its program was being run by speakers of the Budapest radio station in Balaton. There are now two radio programs in Budapest: *"Free Kossuth Radio"* broadcasting government declarations, and *"Free Petofi Radio"* transmitting from Gyor. In Gyor a few days ago some revolutionary committee took authority and refused to recognise the Government. This small radio station relayed the program of "Free Europe" for two hours and for another two hours some announcements from Budapest were broadcast. While we are reporting this the station is broadcasting tunes from the film "The Third Man".

Our first glance at the street was focussed on trucks and tanks loaded with civilians, soldiers, and policeman, who were armed from head to foot. The people greeted them. One now feels a general relaxation of tension. People were walking, seemingly carefree and gay, and went into shops where food is being sold. Excitement was introduced only by men selling newspapers, which are in great demand and are completely changed both in headlines and shape.

Rakoczi Street, the main thoroughfare of this city, offers an unusual picture. All shop-windows and walls are full of slogans: *"Russki Haza"* or, in Russian *"Russkie Domoi."* There are many posters, papers, leaflets, or mere notes. There are even poems. About fifteen to twenty various *"movements"* are referred to, various *"revolutionary committees"* and individuals. Everyone is demanding something *"on behalf of the revolution"*, *"on behalf of the people"*. All these demands and these slogans are so different and are so varied that it is hard to find one's way. Many of these demands and slogans are suspicious. Here is a typical poster:

"Hungarian patriots! The government betrayed us again because Soviet troops are withdrawing only from Budapest. We no longer trust the government of Imre Nagy. As a member of the United Nations we demand that the United Nations immediately send international supervisory troops. Let the Soviet troops withdraw from the whole of Hungary! Until then we demand UN troops."

(signed) "Movement of New Hungarian Life"

Citizens read every possible poster, mostly without comment. The walls are covered with slogans: *"Call A Strike," "We Don't Need Communism," "Free Mindszenty." "Free Elections."* These slogans are typewritten or hand-written with chalk, India ink, lead pencils, or are printed on the finest paper.

On a large door in a small street there is chalk-written: *"The Workers Council will be elected at 10 o'clock on Wednesday"*. In the same street leaflets are distributed: *"We don't need Workers' Councils—the Communists have their finger in this pie."*

At a place where traffic is heaviest, a hoarse voice is heard over the microphone: "We won't lay down arms! We shall not be subdued by the Government. We are the Authority until Soviet troops withdraw from the whole of Hungary, until all treaties hitherto concluded are rescinded and new elections take place". This is the loudspeaker of armed troops which even today are outside any control by organised authority. Their representative came to the Parliament for talks with Imre Nagy last evening. Talks have been resumed today. This is Jozef Dudas. It is interesting that this man was once a member of the Communist Party, but he was expelled because of separatist tendencies. After the war he joined the Smallholders Party and belonged to its right-wing.

This morning armed units run by Dudas people attacked Party committees. Armed groups went into the streets carrying all kinds of weapons. In contrast to students and workers who carry out police duties they do not wear badges on their sleeves.

This Dudas group is fairly powerful and numerous. One runs into it everywhere. Their leadership occupied the building and the printing office of the former *Szabad Nep.* ... They call for a provisional government in which they would admit Nagy and Kadar of the Communists, and Bela Kovacs (and not Tildy) of the Smallholders' Party. The movement is called "The Committee of the Hungarian National Revolution". Dudas is even signing permits for free passage through the town. ..

We visited another newspaper *Igazsag*— "Truth," which is the organ of the youth and the army, backing Imre Nagy. It is very hard to find out who is backing whom here, who is behind whom. ....

From everyone with whom we talked we have received the reply that there is no danger of abolishing revolutionary achievements, such as returning factories or land to former owners. It is interesting, however, that all people are predicting a right-wing course in Hungary.

Leftist groups are the least noticeable. First of all, the Hungarian Workers' Party seems not to exist. One has the impression Communists are now seeking suitable organisational forms. This will take a long time. The trade unions were reorganised today. They are abandoning former views, but will ask for Workers Councils.

For the time being the Army is most compact, the best organised progressive force. Although passive for the most part, it was divided in the course of recent events. "Revolutionary Councils" were set up yesterday in the military commands. The commanding officer of the Air Force took the initiative. After being ordered to fire on the masses if they began to march on the headquarters, he refused and "revolutionary committees" were then set up in all services of the Army and even in the Ministry of Defence. Many commanding generals have been dismissed. Today the Army maintained order together with civilians, some wearing badges, some not.

Even today we heard shooting. A real persecution has begun against former officers of the State Security, and today it became a regular frenzy. Groups of armed civilians looked for such officers in various hide-outs. They all defended themselves and were killed on the spot. Crowds gathered around these places and, even more, around mutilated corpses which were displayed in the streets. In front of the building of the municipal Party committee, after yesterday's clashes, a former colonel was detected. Found on his corpse was a note showing that he received a salary amounting to 9,000 florins (the average salary is 800 florins). People tore up the money found on him and pinned it to the corpse. Suspects are identified and if they belong to the Security Service they are simply hanged by the crowd.

From time to time Soviet tanks pass through the streets. Obviously they are withdrawing. They arrived as a hanging was taking place, and stopped for a moment, not knowing why the people had gathered. The crowd dispersed, but the tanks proceeded without interfering. ...

Vlado Teslic, Borba (Belgrade), 1 November

"Ruffians"

Budapest

Hanka speaks of her friends—the insurgents of the group "Dudas". She made their acquaintance when they occupied the huge building of *Szabad Nep* several days ago. They went to the editorial office and said: "We will no longer permit that the people be fed with lies and insults."

Thereupon, the offended editors informed them that they were not willing to converse with ruffians and left. ...

Viktor Woroszylski, Nowa Kultura (Warsaw), 2 December

Vigilance and Concern

Miskolc

Yesterday, October 30th, we were the first to inform the population of the country of Marshal Zhukov's order to the Soviet troops to begin their withdrawal from the territory of Hungary. As reported, the withdrawal of Soviet units has begun. However, for reasons that we and the people of the country do not understand, large Soviet forces — anti-aircraft units, tanks, and troops—have changed their direction and again entered the territory of Hungary from Zahony, in the direction of Nyiregyhaza. The reason for this circular movement of Soviet troops is incomprehensible to us. We observed the movement of Soviet troops all night ... and we informed the President of the Council of Ministers of the happenings during the night. We spoke by telephone with the Minister of State, Zoltan Tildy, and with the Deputy Minister of Defence, and we

earnestly requested them to take up the matter with the Soviet Commanders most energetically. We requested them to obtain the withdrawal of Soviet troops as soon as possible, and to give priority to their answer to Radio Miskolc, so that this answer may immediately be transmitted to the population of the country. At our request the Council of Ministers was called together, and we received the following answer this morning:

"I can reassure you of the creation of an independent, free, and democratic Hungary."

Radio Free Miskolc

Gyor

Hungary will be free, but not before the last Soviet soldier has left our territory and all traces of the Rakosi regime have disappeared. Do not give up your arms, but join the national forces and see to it that all hostile elements are eliminated. Increase your vigilance. The Communists are at this moment adopting revolutionary slogans in order to blunt your vigilance and dampen your enthusiasm. They must be regarded as enemies capable of doing anything. Be careful not to be led astray and deceived. We are proud that we, a small and unarmed nation, have been able to force the greatest military power in the world to retreat. ...   *Free Radio Petofi*

Budapest

Following reports received from the city we announced at 8:00 that all Soviet forces had left Budapest. Since then we have ascertained that this is not so. A number of listeners have also objected. ... There are still Soviet tanks stationed in front of the Ministry of Defence, the Ministry of the Interior, and the Soviet Embassy; doubtless the list is far from complete. According to the latest Ministry of Defence announcement, the remaining Soviet tanks will leave the city during the morning. Through the radio the Ministry of Defence appeals to the population of the capital to refrain, out of sober good sense, from impeding the departure of the Soviet troops by any hostile action, since this would merely lead to further bloodshed. ...   *Free Radio Kossuth [9:06]*

Pal Maleter Appointed
Budapest

The Presidential Council of the People's Republic has relieved Lajos Toth, first deputy of the Ministry of Defense and head of the Honved General Staff, of his office. At the same time the Council nominated Pal Maleter as first Deputy Minister of Defence, and Istvan Kovacs as head of the Honved General Staff.

In order to avoid misunderstanding, we inform you that the Istvan Kovacs who has been appointed head of the General Staff is not the same person as the notorious former First Secretary of the Budapest Party Committee.

Free Radio Kossuth

"Red Star"
Budapest

Many people are now demanding that the red star on the cupola of the Hungarian Parliament building be removed forthwith. Free Kossuth Radio fully agrees with this justified demand by the Hungarian revolutionaries. We have gotten in touch with the Parliament's technical staff, who informed us that the red star is 3½ meters in diameter. It weighs 5 tons and is fixed at a height of 100 meters. Thus considerable technical equipment is required to remove it. Therefore we beg patriots to be patient: the red star will be taken down after technical preparation ensures that no damage will be caused to the building. We have asked that until that time the red star be covered by the national flag.

Free Radio Kossuth

Budapest

The Ministry of National Defence has just now [12:13] informed us that the Soviet tanks surrounding the Ministry withdrew a few minutes ago. ...   *Free Radio Kossuth*

Nagy in Kossuth Square
Budapest

I address you again, Hungarian brethren, with warm and affectionate feelings. ... We are living in the first days of our sovereignty and independence. ... We have expelled from our country the Rakosi and Gero gang. They will answer for their crimes. They tried to besmirch me by spreading the lie that I called in the Soviet troops. This lie is infamous. Imre Nagy, the champion of Hungarian sovereignty, Hungarian freedom, and Hungarian independence, did not call in these troops. On the contrary, it was he who fought for their withdrawal.

My dear friends, today we have started negotiations for the withdrawal of the Soviet troops from our country and for the abrogation of the obligations imposed on us by the Warsaw Treaty. I only ask you to be a little bit patient. I think that the results are such that you can place that much confidence in me.

My dear friends, stand by us, support us in our patriotic efforts.   *Free Radio Kossuth*

This afternoon a large crowd gathered in Lajos Kossuth Square. Imre Nagy came down from Parliament to the Kossuth memorial and made a speech. ... After the Prime Minister's speech, the crowd broke up into smaller groups and expressed its dissatisfaction with the person of the Minister of the Interior, Ferenc Munnich. ...

Free Radio Kossuth

Interview with Nagy

Budapest

Q: What about the Warsaw Pact now? Are you in it or not?

Nagy: At present, we are in it.

Q: Do you wish to leave the Warsaw Pact, if the Hungarian people desire this?

Nagy: Today we have begun negotiations on this matter ...

Q: It will now be necessary to reconstruct Hungary economically. Will you apply to the Western Powers for aid in the reconstruction of Hungary?

Nagy: It seems to me that we will have to count on all economic forces to help us emerge from this situation ...

Q: According to the agreement you have concluded, are the Soviet forces now withdrawing to their original bases in Hungary?

Nagy: At present the forces in Budapest, it seems, have already withdrawn and have returned to their bases.

Q: In Hungary?

Nagy: Yes, in Hungary. I do not know exactly where they came from.

Q: There are also some Soviet forces which came across the border from other countries. Are they also withdrawing to where they came from?

Nagy: I think so, yes. I do not know where they came from, but they will return there.

Q: You said just a few moments ago that you were put under pressure to bring in the Soviet troops, that it was not you who invited the Soviet troops to move into Budapest. Who invited them?

Nagy: It was not I — that I can say. At that time I was not Prime Minister. I was not a member of the Central Committee of the Party.

Q: How then did the impression grow that you invited the troops?

Nagy: I do not know. At that time I was not a member of the leadership. It may have been this way: at first it was said it was the government, and then later on, after two or three days, I was made Premier, and the masses are unable to differentiate. Two days ago or now — it is all the same to them.

Q: But did you not approve of the invitation to the Soviet troops afterward?

Nagy: No.

Q: Did you say it was necessary for the re-establishment of peace and order, or did you not?

Nagy: No, no, no. I did not say such a thing, and I must add that this allegation has caused much damage.

Q: What will now be the first measures of the government? ...

Nagy: We have very grave economic problems. The most important problem is to restore order here, and to re-establish economic life ...

Radio Vienna and Rias (Berlin)

——— *The Negotiator* ———

For a moment we should try to put ourselves in the skin of this man carried to power on the crest of a revolutionary wave. This wave, after having left five or six thousand dead in the streets, had isolated, immobilized and burnt Soviet tanks and was preparing to hunt the others with an irresistible fury. Before negotiating with the Russians, Nagy had to negotiate with these bloodied and victorious insurgents in order to gain their confidence and gain control over them. To do so he had first to be their ally. And that is exactly what Nagy did.

The Russians have accused Nagy of playing a double game. He will certainly be accused of this during his trial, if is true that he will be brought to trial. The accusation is well-founded, but in a diametrically opposed sense. Before entering into official negotiations with them, he had official discussions with General Thikonov. On the night of 31 October, Nagy gave him a frank outline of his program. He told him that, as a Communist, it was his intention to save whatever could be saved of Hungarian Communism, viz., faithful adherence to the Warsaw Pact and the maintenance of the basic economic socialist structure. With regard to the latter, he thought that the solution was easy enough, as the other parties had bound themselves to respect the principle. On the first point he had come up against difficulties and it was

for that reason that he had denounced the Pact. But he intended to bring the question up once more in the next twenty-four hours and to convince even the most violent opponents. I have been told that at that moment Thikonov had proposed that the Soviet troops carry out theatening manoeuvres in order to force the neutralists hostile to the Warsaw Pact to reconsider their position. Nagy is supposed to have accepted and even to have proposed that the frontier with Austria be closed.

All this is possible and even probable. This would very well explain his optimism during Friday when it was learned that the frontier had been closed and that Soviet troops were encircling Budapest in an iron ring. What is certain is that, before the attack, even the most violent opponents of the Pact, Kovacs among others, finished by recognizing the necessity of continued adherence. "Be satisfied with what you have", Nagy said to them. "In offering as a security the Ministry of Foreign Affairs, we shall be able to liberate ten million Hungarians from a concentration camp". And he then added "and it is I, a Communist, who will have to play the role of the imprisoned Minister of Foreign Affairs".

Indro Montanelli, Corriere della Sera (Milan),
29 November

Nagy Asks for Soviet Negotiations
Budapest

The Chairman of the Council of Ministers, Imre Nagy, has informed the Government of the U.S.S.R. that the Government of the Hungarian People's Republic wishes to start immediate negotiations for the withdrawal of Soviet military units from the whole territory of Hungary. With reference to the latest statement by the Soviet Government, declaring the U.S.S.R.'s readiness to negotiate with the Hungarian Government and the other participants in the Warsaw Treaty about the withdrawal of Soviet troops, the Hungarian Government has requested the Soviet Government to appoint its representatives with a view to opening negotiations as soon as possible, and to fix the date and the place of the negotiations.

Free Radio Kossuth [20:00]

Szolnok Delegation
Szolnok

We have had talks with Imre Nagy and Janos Kadar. The Premier asked the factory workers of Szolnok to resume work and production in the interests of the country and the people. We replied that the people of Szolnok are determined to resume work, only if Soviet troops leave the town area and evacuate the Soviet barracks there. Imre Nagy said that as far as he knew Soviet troops would leave not only Budapest but also the town of Szolnok, and would hand over their barracks to the revolutionary committee of the Hungarian Army.

We also asked that the following demand be met: Joszef Mindszenty, the Cardinal Primate, should be set free and enabled to establish direct contact with the Pope. We were told that Cardinal Primate Mindszenty was already free, and that the Government had no intention of hindering him in any way from resuming leadership of the Hungarian Catholic Church. We also discussed the Szolnok workers' demand for immediate liberation of all political prisoners. The answer

to this was also reassuring: the Government has already taken measures in this respect, and was not responsible if in certain places its orders have been disobeyed.

After the talks, Janos Kadar addressed the following message to the workers of Szolnok: "Dear brother workers of Szolnok, on this last day of the old era and first day of the new era of our development, we send out greetings to the workers of Szolnok. Let us join forces with all sincere patriots of goodwill for the restoration of order and the building of a new life."

Free Radio Kossuth

Free Trade Unions
Budapest

Stalinist sectarian leaders have been removed, and factories have now truly and irrevocably become property of the workers. This revolution has also made the liberation of the trade union movement possible, so that, independent of all Party and Government influence, the trade unions can really become an organisation militantly and consistently representing the interests of the workers.

On the recommendation of the Provisional Revolutionary Committee of the National Federation of Free Hungarian Trade Unions, the Praesidium of the National TU Council is dissolved, effective immediately, and, with the inclusion of old and formerly imprisoned representatives of the workers' movement, a Provisional Executive Committee has been set up. The Executive Committee calls on workers, including organised workers who disagree with the composition of the Workers Councils, to hold new trade union elections on the basis of real trade union democracy. ...

We owe it to our youth, workers and army that the factories and workshops have truly become ours. Now it is our turn to defend our factories—if need be with arms—to defend the magnificent achievements of our national revolution.

Free Radio Kossuth

Bela Kovacs in Pecs

Budapest

A meeting for the reconstitution of the Independent Smallholders Party has been held at Pecs. ... Over 100 former members of the party, including delegates of the villages in the County Baranya, attended. Bela Kovacs, the former General Secretary of the party, was invited despite the fact that he is at present under treatment in a Pecs hospital. He was given an ovation and made a speech.

"Today, I have not come among you as a member of the Party. I was expelled in the old days. I have come to greet my old friends and comrades of the struggles of the past. In prison

I wondered how the Hungarian people would receive, and whether they would believe, all the slander which has been heaped on me and on the Smallholders Party during recent years. I see with joy that this campaign of slander has not been succesful. The people trust this party, which, since 1945, alone has really wanted to build Hungary on a basis of independence and liberty."

Of the circumstances in which he became a member of the new National Government, Kovacs said that Istvan Dobi had telephoned him and informed him that Imre Nagy wanted to form a National Government with his participation. In view of the fact that Kovacs had been in touch with Imre Nagy in the past and supported efforts to free the country from Rakosi, Gero, and their like, he had agreed. But since then he has had no communication with the Government.

Kovacs continued as follows: "I was astonished to see on the new Government list the names of several former Communist leaders. Next day I wrote a letter of resignation, in which I expressed my disagreement with the composition of the Government, but my friends persuaded me not to send the letter. I do not know what the Government wants. The prospects are great—in the heroic battles of this revolution our youth has not shed its blood in vain—but I must know the prospects and the Government's intentions. I shall know them only when I have been to Budapest and confered with the members of the Government."

Turning next to the reconstitution and the future activity of the Independent Smallholders Party, Kovacs declared: "The Party has full liberty to reassemble, but the question is whether, on its reconstitution, the party will proclaim the old ideas again. No one should dream of going back to the world of aristocrats, bankers and capitalists. That world is definitely gone! A true member of the Smallholders Party cannot think on the lines of 1939, or of 1945. The last ten years were bitter, but they also provided a useful lesson for the Smallholders Party. We must make use of the lesson learned during this decade and draw up a new party program. We must also change our way of thinking. I cannot and do not wish to define the new program for the Smallholders Party. I must first discuss it with the party leaders in Budapest. ... But one thing is certain; this programme must be based on the creation of a new Hungary. ..."

Speaking of the present condition of the peasants Bela Kovacs declared that they needed their own organisation to protect their interests, in the same way as the working-class and the intellectuals. He said that the old Peasants Alliance should be reconstituted and that he would support this viewpoint in Budapest.

Finally, Kovacs expressed his views on Hungary's foreign policy. "When Hungarian fighters for liberty fought against the Russian tanks," he said, "they fought for the country's independence. This does not mean that we regard the Russian people as our enemies, but one cannot follow a unilateral policy. ... It is necessary to establish relations, based on equal rights, with all nations and one cannot tie the country's fate to one or another military bloc. The Hungarian people want a neutral Hungary."

At the end of his speech, which was received with great enthusiasm, Kovacs, who is still ill, went back to the nursing home.

The delegates to the meeting decided that Bela Kovacs's expulsion from the ranks of the Smallholders Party had been illegal and elected him President of the Baranya County Federation for life. Then they elected the provisional officers of the Federation. ...   *Hungarian News Agency*

A Pole Talks With Prof. Lukacs

Budapest

"...The Communists are also reorganizing," Margit says. A new party must be established, with a new name and new leadership. That is the thing Nagy, Losonczy, Lukacs strive to achieve ..."

"And Kadar?"

Margit grimaces. The young man with the bushy eyebrows makes a gesture with his hands. Anna [Lukacs] asks: "Do you want to visit Lukacs? He will explain more precisely what it is all about, this new party. He is always at home now so that those who want to can find him." ...

Naturally I imagined that, one day, I would meet George Lukacs. If I had asked myself what we would have to talk about, I should have thought of — what do I know? — Hegelian aesthetics, or critical realism, or Thomas Mann. But I never imagined making Lukacs' acquaintance under such dramatic circumstances, or that the first words out of his mouth would be: "Let's leave culture aside, shall we? We have more important questions to settle." ... Lukacs is Minister of Cultural Affairs in the Nagy Government.

The windows of the comfortable apartment look out on the Danube. Walls of many-colored book-covers surround us ... We sit around a large family table and we talk of things more important than culture.

The professor's son, an engineer who was ousted from the Hungarian Planning Commission a year ago, tells how the glory and riches of Hungary — its vineyards — have been ruined. Then, he explains how the mechanism for increasing production in the People's Democracies is seemingly very effective but sterile and ruinous in fact. Mrs. Lukacs questions us on the development of the Polish October. ...

Finally, the conversation turns to the problem of the Party. It seems that in the present leadership of the Party, a bitter struggle is raging between two tendencies. One aims to pursue a slightly more moderate line, but actually it is the same old line. The other is revolutionary, desiring to break completely with the Stalinist traditions of the Hungarian Workers' Party, wanting to create a completely new Marxist party. Professor Lukacs naturally supports the latter tendency.

"Who else?"

"Nagy, Losonczy, Szanto, Donath, Kadar..."

"Kadar, too?" I ask...

The professor does not understand why this name should raise any doubts.

The new Party will not be able to expect rapid success — Communism in Hungary has been totally disgraced. Collected around the Party will probably be small groups of progressive intellectuals, writers and a few young people. The working class will prefer to follow the Social Demo-crats. In free elections the Communists will obtain five percent of the vote, ten percent at the most. It is possible that they won't be in the Government, that they will go into opposition. But the party will continue to exist; it will save the idea; it will be an intellectual center, and after some years or some decades from now, who knows...

But at the moment, one has not yet managed to form it. In an effort to assess the situation incessant discussions are going on. All the other parties are constituting themselves today, and the Communists are again at least 24 hours behind...

Viktor Woroszylski, Nowa Kultura (Warsaw), 2 December

"The Struggle for the Masses"

Budapest

In Budapest, as in the whole of Hungary, a feverish struggle for the masses is under way.... A process of political differentiation is going on. The prevailing majority of those who went into the streets last Tuesday to demonstrate against Stalinism did so to develop Hungarian socialism and to rid it of its shackles....

All parties which have joined Imre Nagy's coalition—the Smallholders Party, the Peasants Party and the Social Democratic Party—have begun to organise themselves. Since in principle a multi-party system has been endorsed, consideration is being given to creating or re-forming some more parties, first of all the Catholic Party, which was formerly very powerful and influential. Thus, it is hard to say what the political outcome of the developments now taking place in Hungary will be.

Disorder still prevails in the streets. In fact there is no real authority as yet, at least not a centralized one. Bloodshed had not yet been stopped. In front of the Opera House, bodies of twelve policemen, members of the AVO who were killed during renewed unrests yesterday, still lie on the pavement. A number of Communists whom I contacted are frightened because more and more often one hears that Communists are being assassinated. ... Today I went to the "Csilaga" printing works. I was told, and not only there, that in Budapest today real anarchy prevails in the publication of newspapers and leaflets. A group of 20 armed men enters a printing shop, taking control of it for a half hour or an hour, and print what they want. ... Of course, there are some people who refuse to leave the printing shops, who occupy them. Thus, a group of insurgents led by Dudas, a former deputy of the Smallholder Party, took full control of the badly damaged building of the *Szabad Nep.*

Nobody can find out what is going on. One paper appears and then is stopped; others are published under new names, or an old one appears with new editors. The picture changes every minute. There are newspapers which appear only once. Today the situation was as follows: for the last two days no copies of the *Szabad Nep* appeared, the organ of the Hungarian Workers Party. It is questionable whether it will be published at all any more. The organ of the United Hungarian Youth Organization no longer appears and the organization itself has been dissolved. At first *Szabad Nep* appeared under the name *Magyar Szabadsag,* but then it was also discontinued when the printing plant was captured.

Today the Communists are said to have succeeded in arriving at an agreement with Dudas to print a Communist paper there. The paper *Magyar Nemzed,* former organ of the People's Front, is still being published, but as an independent paper and organ of a group of progressive intellectual anti-Stalinist Communists. So far the editor-in-chief is a member of the Cabinet, Losonczy, a man who was kept in prison a long time by Rakosi's supporters. The army organ, *Szabadsereg,* has been renamed *Magyar Honved* and it comes out as the organ of the Revolutionary Council of the Hungarian Armed Forces, which was formed yesterday and which has unanimously and decisively sided with Imre Nagy and his present government. ...

For the last two days the streets have been flooded with the *Magyar Fuggetlenseg,* which is being published in the printing works of the *Szabad Nep* and is edited by a group of insurgents around Dudas. This is a paper in which the most varied elements mix....

Very popular, perhaps most popular is a paper called *Igazsag,* published by a group of Communists and progressives who were the first to side with the insurgents. From the very start almost all the insurgents considered the paper as their own because it emerged from their midst and was striving for the abolition of Stalinism in Hungary. This paper is now supporting Nagy.

A paper published by young revolutionary students supporting the platform of national liberation and the revival of 1848 traditions is called *Egyetemi Ifjusag*. Also very popular is *Nepszava*, the traditional organ of Social Democracy. Tomorrow *Kis Ujsag* will reappear the organ of the Smallholders Party, and *Szabad Szo*, organ of the Peasant Party. But they will not be the only ones. . . .

During all this time, the struggle to consolidate the peace of the country is being continued. The key question is how to organize the security forces. A serious step was taken today in the Kilian Barracks, which was one of the centers of the uprising. . . . Representatives of the most important armed insurgents' groups held a joint meeting and formed the Revolutionary Commissariat of Security Forces; they have decided to join their forces — estimated now at about 10,000 men — to the National Guard; together with the regular police and the army, the Guard must secure order in Budapest.

About 100 armed men, mostly leaders of the uprising, were assembled in the hall of the Kilian Barracks. . . . Colonel Pal Maleter seemed to be the most popular among them. He is a former Spanish volunteer, a Communist who, as Commander of the Barracks, joined the insurgents and fought against the Soviet troops. Many people want to see him as commander of the National Guard. Certain differences between individual groups of insurgents were settled at the meeting, particularly those existing between the three most important and most numerous groups assembled. Those led by Maleter; those who fought in the Corvin cinema; and the group from Buda led by Lt. Colonel Marian. A committee of 20 men was formed, including the commanders of the armed groups mentioned, in order to organize their

merger with the National Guard. This was a very serious step toward settling conditions in Budapest. . . .   *Djuka Julius, Politika (Belgrade), 1 November*

"Another Immortal Name"

Budapest

There could be no doubt who held the power in Budapest. The people who held the arms held the power.

And who held the arms? Fascists? No, the people who had done the fighting, the Freedom Fighters, the workers of Csepel and Újpest, the students, teen-age boys and girls, bandoliers over their shoulders, handgrenades stuck in their belts and tommy-guns — "guitars," they called them — in their hands, the soldiers who had exchanged the red star of servitude for the red, white and green ribbon of liberty. They had won a glorious battle, and for a time (how dreadfully short a time!) they rejoiced, even as they mourned their dead and lit candles on the thousands of freshly-dug graves. Even the children, hundreds of them, had taken part in the fighting, and I spoke to little girls who had poured petrol in the path of Soviet tanks and lit it. I heard of 14-year-olds who had jumped to their deaths on to the tanks with blazing petrol bottles in their hands. Little boys of twelve, armed to the teeth, boasted to me of the part they had played in the struggle. A city in arms, a people in arms, who had stood up and snapped the chains of bondage with one gigantic effort, who had added to the roll-call of cities militant — Paris, Petrograd, Canton, Madrid, Warsaw — another immortal name. Budapest! Her buildings might be battered and scarred, her trolley-bus and telephone wires down, her pavements littered with glass and stained with blood. But her citizens' spirit was unquenchable...

Peter Fryer, Hungarian Tragedy (London, 1956)

The Revolutionary Students

London

The Hungarian revolution began as a student movement. This I can say with absolute conviction, having just returned from Budapest, where I discussed the matter with the insurgents themselves. . . .

The events in Budapest on that Tuesday evening had in fact been slightly preceded by uprisings in two other university towns—Szeged and Pecs. There the students had simply called upon the town councils to resign and had re-elected emergency committees from their own numbers. These committees of 15 to 30 members containing professors and students, had a single president, who in more cases than not was an undergraduate. The attitude of the older members of the community was that this was a student movement, and as such should be led by them. That youth

was willing to ask the advice of age was very apparent. This advice was readily forthcoming. Following the student's lead the factory workers took similar action in the non-university towns.

I did not discover whether or not these revolutionary committees are in any way coordinated from one single centre. Gyor, halfway between Vienna and Budapest, claims to be rebel headquarters. Certainly it has a nationalist-held station and is in a good position to press its claim. I was assured by the revolutionary committee of Sopron that they, and for that matter other towns, are not directed by Gyor. . . .

The purpose of these committees . . . is one of maintenance at the moment. In face of the general strike it is up to them to keep the food supplies running. The responsibility with which this has been taken on is fantastic. Where one would expect to find a certain amount of indecisiveness and youthful experimenting, there is in fact efficiency that would do credit to a stable community. Sopron, being one of the distribution centres for supplies coming from Austria, is an outstanding example of this state of affairs.

The student committee of the revolution in Budapest itself seems to be an even more powerful body. Its president, a young man named Josef Molnar, works in constant liaison with Colonel Maleter, commanding the Hungarian Army in Budapest. Almost all the students at this university of technology are armed.

To the older people of Hungary this uprising has come as a surprise—an uprising in spite of the fact that almost all those taking part have had educations doctored by totalitarian methods. The reaction to this now is that nothing said by the Russians is believed. Tito has been condemned by the Russians. In consequence he is on the highest of pedestals in Hungary, in spite of the fact that this revolution aims not only to oust Russian Communism, but even national Communism.

Ian Rankin, The Observer (London), 4 November

Budapest

Appeal by the Revolutionary Committee of University Youth: We regard the present political leadership as temporary. We support Imre Nagy to the extent to which he and his Government meet our demands. To this end, we shall make use of any means in order to rid him of Stalinist influence. We demand therefore that the old Stalinists leave the Government: Antal Apro [Deputy President], Erik Molnar [Minister of Justice], Ferenc Nezval [Minister of Urban and Rural Development], Janos Csergo [Minister of Metallurgy and Machine Industry], and Mrs. Jozsef Nagy [Minister of Light Industry]. On the other hand, we should like to see in the Government Anna Kethly [Social Democrat] and should like Gyoergy Lukacs to be Minister of Education, and Gyula Illyes Minister of Culture. We should also like to see the representatives of youth in the Government ...

We also demand that the Government take steps to arrange for the Soviet troops to begin at once to withdraw from the territory of the country and to complete the operation by 30 November at the latest. If within three days we receive an open and resolute answer to this from the Government then we will do our share in resuming production so that our people should not suffer further material loss. The people of the country and its newly elected revolutionary organs are in agreement with our demands. We do not want either Stalinism or capitalism. We want a truly democratic and truly socialist Hungary completely independent of any other country ... *Free Radio Kossuth*

Budapest

Communiqué from the Revolutionary Students' Committee: "All armed students must return to their posts as soon as possible."

Free Radio Kossuth

"Both Were Then 13 ..."

Budapest

A short lane, narrow and deserted. Only at both ends sizeable groups are gathered, watching silently as armed youngsters wearing tri-colored armbands besiege a house. A few steps away a car is waiting. This is a hunt for hidden AVH-men. We arrive at the very minute when members of the Guard drag two pale men in civilian clothes out of the hallway. Neither the hunters not the hunted look older than twenty.

It is their youth that prompts memories of a Budapest Youth Festival long ago. Every time we had left the house, we were surrounded by a swarm of thirteen-year-old boys, holding out their albums for our signatures and postage-stamps for trading. They shouted: "Szervusz Lengyel!" Most of them were barefoot and in rags, but full of childish vigor. Perhaps I am meeting one of them now. Had I perhaps written "greetings from Warsaw" into the note-book of this tall insurgent with the lined jacket and beret? Or perhaps it belonged to this member of the AVH wearing the black motorcyclist cap, which he has pulled far down to cover his eyes? Both were then about thirteen years old. ...

The insurgents push the AVH-men into the car and get in themselves, surrounding them on all sides. The car starts. Assembled at the far end of the street, the crowd begins to shout and to threaten. The insurgents raise their revolvers, protecting the AVH men from the crowd. The vehicle makes its way through ...

Viktor Woroszylski, Nowa Kultura (Warsaw), 2 November

Picasso's Dove Weeps

Warsaw

The wave of anti-Moscow agitation released here during the Soviet-Polish crisis rolls on, subsiding slowly but maintained by the bloody events in Hungary. Thousands of students met in the Polytechnic Institute to adopt a resolution expressing "full support for the revolutionary forces" in Hungary and protesting against the "participation of Soviet forces in suppressing the uprising."

A number of anti-Soviet speeches were delivered at the meeting. *Trybuna Ludu*, the Polish Communist Party's main newspaper, described the speeches as "irresponsible outbursts against the Polish-Soviet alliance." But this comment reflected a growing fear of the possible effects in Poland of the Hungarian rebellion rather than a criticism of the contents of the speeches. The students were talked out of marching in a protest demonstration to the Soviet Embassy. But other means just as pointed were found to show how they felt.

On the sidewalk outside Warsaw University's Faculty of Fine Arts students placed a huge reproduction of a [Picasso] picture showing robots shooting down men, women and children. An exclamation mark was drawn through the picture. Beside it hung a green, white and red banner of Hungary. Pablo Picasso's "Dove of Peace" was displayed nearby, but with a tear falling from one eye.

All Warsaw buses carried the Hungarian colors and in a hundred and one other ways the Poles were showing their sympathy for the Hungarian fight for independence. ...

Sydney Gruson, New York Times, 1 November

Polish-Russian "Agreement"

Warsaw

The Polish Communist leader Gomulka revealed on Tuesday that high-placed Russian and Polish functionaries have met in Budapest and have reached a full agreement regarding Hungarian developments. On Monday the Polish Communists had demanded that Russian troops withdraw from Hungary. The Russian partners to the discussion included Deputy Prime Minister Mikoyan, and the Polish Deputy Minister of Defense Marian Naszkowski was also present.

Gomulka did not give any details about the Russian-Polish "understanding" on Hungary. Observers recall, however, that on Monday the Polish Communist Party supported the "democratic" program of the Hungarian Prime Minister Nagy. Also attending the Budapest meetings were M. A. Suslow, member of the Central Committee of the Russian Communist Party, and Artur Starewic, member of the Central Committee of the Hungarian Communist Party.

Neue Zürcher Zeitung, 1 November

Laggards

Miskolc

A report from the Revolutionary Councils of the village of Kunmadaras and the town of Karczag: The Szolnok Revolutionary Council is not equal to its tasks. The Szolnok relay-and-broadcasting station is in the hands of the State Security Authority, and Hungarian artillery units in Szolnok have been disarmed by Soviet troops.

Personnel of the Gyorgy Kilian Officers' Academy in Szolnok were isolated from the Revolutionary Council and from the population, because initiative there lay with political collaborators of the Academy's political department who were trying to save their skins at all costs. The Revolutionary Councils of Kunmadaras and

Karczag were trying to contact the officers, students and men of the Academy. The armoured unit at Mezötur had not yet sided with the revolution. The Councils sent an agitator to Mezötur to address a mass meeting. The commanding officer tried to have him arrested. But he was saved by students. Bekescaba had also failed to side with the revolution, although the population supported the revolution. Commanders of certain Hungarian military units and supporters of the Rakosi regime were, however, preventing action, and keeping the soldiers uninformed and isolated. ...

Radio Free Miskolc

Athletes

Budapest

To go or not to go, that was the question put at the railway station yesterday by members of the Hungarian Olympic team ... In our life-and-death struggle, interest in sport has of course vanished ... Hungarian railwaymen announced that they would be unable to take our Olympic team to Prague by rail. Our railwaymen refuse to move a single train as long as there are Soviet troops in our country. After an excited conference, the leaders of the National Sports Committee insisted on the team going, if not by train, then by coach. Excitement reached its peak before departure. The athletes were more concerned with what will happen at home than in Australia. They hastily altered their Olympic uniforms, tearing off the old emblem ...

Free Radio Kossuth

Prisoners

Budapest

The Revolutionary Committee of the Supreme Prosecutor's Office has delegated military and civil prosecutors to control with local revolutionary organs the release of persons detained for participation in the revolutionary movement ... In several places all persons under arrest have been released, including those whose punishment is demanded by the people. The release of persons detained for criminal acts in defence of the Rakosi regime, or who tried to crush the present revolution, as well as of common criminals, must be prevented. The release has been ordered of persons still held prisoners for crimes connected with "public supplies", crimes directed against the Rakosi regime, and crimes connected with land distribution and producer co-operatives. ...

Free Radio Kossuth

Complaints

Miskolc

We call the attention of the population of villages along the border to the fact that from the first moment border guards have been on the side of the people. They cannot be identified with those blue AVH-men whose task it was to preserve the power of the State and who participated in cruelties against the people. Continue to help them, because their task remains very important: to secure the defense of the border.

We are broadcasting this announcement because we have received complaints from the border that the people did not show the respect and trust due to military units who have joined the people....

Radio Free Miskolc

Rebels Seek Leadership in "Complete Communist Eclipse"

Budapest

Now that the Russians have left Budapest no one seems to know who rules Hungary. But everyone is certain it is not the Communists who rule. The Communist party itself appears to be in a state of terror.

The opinion that Budapest might be taken over by a revolutionary mob has not been justified. Order is being kept by the Hungarian Army and by the police, helped out by workers and students. Although members of the secret police have been killed here and there, many more have been captured and spared to be brought before the bar of justice. In Kossuth Square, before the Parliament, a secret policeman in plain clothes was recognized by a crowd that had gathered there. Someone shouted, "Kill him!" and someone else began to beat him. But most insisted that he be handed over to the police. So it is not a mob that rules. It is not fear of the mob that is striking terror into the hearts of the Communists. It is fear of an organized anti-Communist terror, such as followed the short-lived Communist regime of Bela Kun after World War I.

Two prominent Communists who were asked in Parliament whether there was still a Communist party in Hungary said that it had virtually ceased to exist. They did not try to conceal their fear for the future. The two said not only the Communists but the entire Government of Premier Imre Nagy feared that the revolution might turn into another anti-Communist terror. They believed that only Joseph Cardinal Mindszenty, who has just been released, could stop it. For the moment, however, the Cardinal seems concerned with religious affairs. He called a meeting this evening of the heads of the church.

The unique thing about this revolution has been that it was born without leaders and without organization. Such leadership as there was originated among the intellectuals, represented by writers, journalists and students. None had a political experience. Now that the revolution has been miraculously successful, it is looking for leaders and an organization and is wholly uncertain whether it will find them. A pamphlet, issued by a revolutionary committee and signed by Jozsef Dudas, its president, has summoned all national revolutionary organizations to an assembly in the Budapest sports palace. It said only such delegates should be sent who had never supported the

Matyas Rakosi (Stalinist) faction of the Communist party and who had not fought against freedom and progress or on the side of the oppressors.

Mr. Dudas turned out to be a burly man of 45, with a strong personality and evident qualities of leadership. He said he had been a Communist as a young man and belonged to the Communist resistance movement in World War II. He said he had switched to the Smallholders Party after the war and had been arrested at the time Bela Kovacs, secretary of the Smallholders Party, had been denounced by the Russians as a spy. Mr. Dudas said he was held from 1948 to 1954 without trial and was formally rehabilitated only two days before this revolution broke out. He said he controlled the majority of revolutionary groups, including civilian armed patrols and former soldiers, now in the capital. He added that he was in touch with the provisional committees, particularly those in Gyor, Sopron and Miskolc.

Mr. Dudas, who said he had several meetings with Premier Nagy, disapproved of Mr. Nagy's present Government. He will urge that a new provisional government be formed to include Mr. Nagy and Mr. Kovacs, with two or three ministries going to Social Democrats, Smallholders and National Peasants. Other portfolios would be held by the revolutionaries. Mr. Dudas said he had rejected a proposal from the revolutionary committees at Gyor and Sopron to join a new anti-Nagy administration. He explained that there should not be two Hungarian Governments.

While these vital issues are being threshed out, the people of Budapest have been enjoying themselves in the streets, knocking down every Soviet and Communist memorial they can find.

A more important demonstration of the complete eclipse of communism in Hungary is the news from the countryside that the farmers are leaving the collectives, taking with them implements and livestock.

John MacCormac, New York Times, 1 November

"Nothing to Say"

Budapest

Across a poster somebody had written in red pencil: *"Nem Kel Kommunismus!"* We keep encountering this same hand-written inscription. An old gentleman in a worn coat and faded hat, willingly explains ...—this means: "We don't want Communism." Then he adds on his own: "No one in this country wants Communism. From the smallest child to the oldest man, no one wants Communism. We have had enough of it, forever!"

In his voice, I detect hate and satisfaction. I feel sad. I have nothing to say to him. ...

Viktor Woroszylski, Nowa Kultura (Warsaw), 2 December

Dudas Proposes, Replies

Budapest

The daily *Magyar Fueggetlenseg* (Hungarian Independence) — the paper of the Hungarian National Revolutionary Committee, the third number of which appeared this morning — announces on the front page that at 18:00 on 30th October talks were started between Premier Imre Nagy and delegates of the armed forces, insurgents for freedom, the members of the National Revolutionary Committee and the delegates of the revolutionary intellectuals and students. In the name of the freedom-fighters Jozsef Dudas, Chairman of the National Revolutionary Committee, put forward a proposal on the basis of which the talks are progressing in a favourable atmosphere. The insurgents' proposals will be submitted to the Government by Imre Nagy.

The editorial, written by Jozsef Dudas, points out that the armed stage of the revolutionary struggle has been crowned with victory. "Pending the holding of free and general elections by secret ballot, the present coalition Government must be transformed so that alongside Imre Nagy, Bela Kovacs and Janos Kadar, each of the democratic parties is represented in the Government by a Minister. However, these must be chosen from among people who have not lost the confidence of their party."

Magyar Fueggetlenseg welcomes and explains the need for a Congress of the National Revolutionary Forces called by the Chairman of the National Revolutionary Committee for Thursday morning: "The local revolutionary organs which formed themselves spontaneously in Transdanubia, in the Borsod basin, in a great many towns of the great plain, and in all corners of the country, agree in questions of vital importance to the nation, but they still lack a central organisation. Therefore the freedom fighters cannot exert their full strength. They cannot summon the required authority for their position vis-a-vis the Government." The paper calls on various revolutionary organisations to send delegates who, "constantly fighting for the well-being of the people and the fatherland, have always been and remain on the side of freedom and progress. The delegates must not include either men of the anti-popular policy of the pre-1945 regime or zealous supporters of Stalinism. This is a time when revolutionary vigilance is necessary."

The paper also carries a number of appeals calling on the revolutionaries to take action against any excess, to leave to tribunals the task of assessing the responsibility of the former members of the Security Forces, and of punishing looters severely as well as those who dishonour the revolution. "No one has the right to mete out justice on his own." *Hungarian News Agency*

The Soviet Agency *Tass* has accused the revolution of having mobilized the entire Hungarian nation in a shady enterprise in which "reactionary and counter revolutionary forces intend to undermine the basis of the people's democracy regime for the sake of restoring the old capitalist order." Once again, as often before the Soviet Government has falsified reality and presented history after its fashion. The Soviet Government does not want to admit that this struggle, which has created martyrs and heroes, is a sacred struggle. Never before has blood been shed in a cause more just. Here are no sinister agents of reaction and counter-revolution. Our society of labour is firmly determined never to give back factories or land to the old proprietors.

It would not have been inappropriate for *Tass*, before forming judgements, to have sent to Hungary a correspondent charged with submitting a precise and objective account of events for the sake of public opinion. We want to live in peace with the Soviet people, but "news reports" of the kind refered to can only hinder our efforts in this direction. ... *Magyar Fuggetlenseg, 31 October*

Cardinal Mindszenty's Return

Budapest

Here is an important announcement: The Hungarian National Government wishes to state that the proceedings instituted in 1948 against Jozsef Mindszenty, Cardinal Primate, lacked all legal basis and that the accusations levelled against him by the regime of that day were unjustified. In consequence the Hungarian National Government announces that the measures depriving Cardinal Primate Jozsef Mindszenty of his rights are invalid and that the Cardinal is free to exercise without restriction all his civil and ecclesiastical rights.

[Signed]: Imre Nagy, Prime Minister
Free Radio Kossuth

Christian Youth and Burning Candles

Budapest

The Christian Youth League addresses the following appeal to all Christian youth organisations in the world: After ten years of enforced silence, we have formed the first Christian organisation, the Christian Youth League, in the revolutionary days. We are having to contend with indescribable difficulties and therefore we ask you, our sister-organisations abroad, to come to our assistance morally and materially. Our aim is to rally Hungarian Christian Youth into a single camp which would represent the ideals of young masses, on the basis of Christian principles and within the forces guiding the country's political life. Our address is: No. 6 Sandor Nagy Street, Budapest V, Hungary.

The Christian Youth League calls on the population of the country to place a burning candle in their windows on 1 November, All Saints Day, as a sign of mourning for the heroic martyrs of the fight for freedom.   *Free Radio Kossuth*

Small Boys and Their "Guitars"

Budapest

The last Soviet tanks were just moving out of Budapest when we reached the outskirts after a long journey interrupted by innumerable security checks. The tanks had not put out white flags, as the Hungarians had boldly demanded; but they had the air of a defeated army all the same. Their guns were masked. Their turrets were closed, the crews hidden inside. Nobody looked out. Not I think, because they were afraid of being shot at; rather that they could not bear to see the ruin they had caused. It was already dusk. Candles were burning in every window. They were the only lights in all Budapest — the torches not of victory but of thanksgiving.

It had been a strange journey. The road was jammed with convoys carrying medical aid and food. It would have been hard for us to get through without two students, Ferko and Pista, armed with the inevitable "guitars", who acted as our personal bodyguards and helped us to fight our way through the check points manned by Freedom Fighters.

They told us a great deal about the first days of the uprising. The Freedom Fighters, they said, had arrested all the Avos they were able to round up. Many of the secret police had been killed in the process, but only a few had been victims of revenge: most had died in action. The Party apparatus had disintegrated completely on the very first day of the rising, but there had been no massacre of Party officials. "We raided the Party offices, took away their weapons and told them to go home. Only a few were held. In fact, many of them joined us."

They were also very definite about the Jews. There had been reports of pogroms, all the more easy to believe in that so many leaders and officials of Party and police were Jews. "It simply isn't true about pogroms," they cried. "The Jewish community suffered as much as any other. They are all with us fighting for our freedom. Go and see for yourself! You will find thousands of Jewish boys and girls among the Freedom Fighters, especially in Budapest. Hundreds have died fighting."

These two were typical of so many we were to meet — both members of the Communist youth organisation, both totally rejecting everything it stood for, and totally unaffected by the teaching of the Leninist gospel. Their ideas of right and

wrong were a good deal clearer, in spite of the vaunted conditioning process, than one normally meets among the youth of the West. Nor were they perturbed by the future. "There will be no chaos when the Russians leave," they said, "we all know now what we want."

In Budapest, all the same, there was a good deal of chaos. In that autumn twilight we heard mothers calling tremulously and vainly for their vanished children. And we saw the graves. Every park, every garden, every patch of earth had its little cemeteries.

We stopped at one near the Margit Bridge. Small boys in their very early teens were standing guard over the graves, carefully dressed in Honved uniforms which had probably belonged to their elder brothers. Instead of rifles they clutched "guitars" almost as big as themselves. Candles were burning on the newly-dug graves...

These small Hungarian boys, with their devoted, incomprehensible and wholly self-appointed activity, were, for me, the most astonishing and moving aspect of the Budapest scene in those days of brief triumph. Next day, Peter Strasser and I found ourselves guarded not only by Ferko and Pista, our companions of the journey, who would not leave us, but also by a whole gang of small boys, all armed to the teeth, who refused to let us out of their sight and gloried in the privilege of acting as a private army for two middle-aged "foreigners."

A Jew

The youth of Budapest who demonstrated in favor of the people's justified claims have repeatedly been called lately "fascist rabble." The following episode clearly shows that it was no fascist rabble that marched through the streets of Budapest.

Meeting an AVO officer, a raging crowd was about to strike him, but realizing that he was a Jew, several of the armed demonstrators took his defence.

Noble gesture! The soldiers of freedom, those "fascists", rose in the defence of an officer so that their revolution would not be branded as an "anti-semitic and fascist" demonstration.

Igazsag (Budapest), 30 October

They did not belong to Budapest. They had all come in from outside "to see how they could help" — without a word to their parents, without leaving even a note ("*They* know where we are"), they had walked and hitch-hiked into Budapest, begging or stealing tommy-guns and grenades, to do their bit. Alarmed at the multiplicity of weapons, pointed in all directions and treated with the utmost casualness. I asked one of the "gang" why he had to have six pistols: wasn't one enough? "We know how to shoot, Uncle," he replied. "But we don't know how to load."

Lajas Lederer, The Observer (London), 25 November

Three Strikes

Budapest

At 20:00, Free Radio Kossuth broadcast an interview with one Karoly Molnar, who had just been freed from a convict colony of the Csolnok mine in County Somogy. He was sent there to serve a 15-year sentence following conviction in 1953 on a charge of "organising armed opposition to the People's Democracy". He was one of a group of 12 who had a printing press and "a few weapons" in their possession; they wanted "to enlighten the Hungarian people". Molnar was a Debrecen University student of chemistry. The convicts heard about the revolution of Hungarian youth on 23 October and decided to register their sympathy by going on hunger strike: down in the mine 203 convicts took part in it for 96 hours. In sympathy convicts on the surface also staged a hunger strike. Finally, non-convict miners intervened with the competent Ministry to obtain their release, which miner delegates themselves carried out yesterday morning. Beside purely political prisoners, there were ... persons who had hoarded arms and were suspected of wanting to use them for political purposes. "We shall examine their cases and decide whether or not they are fit to be free and to take part in the work of society in a free Hungary", said Molnar.

BBC Summary

Szombathely

The students of the Nagy Lajos Gymnasium will not attend classes as long as Soviet troops have not started withdrawing from the territory of Vas County.... *Radio Free Szombathely*

Budapest

Workers of the Electricity Works join the strike movement of the country's workers and declare that, apart from the needs of the population and of hospitals, they will supply no electricity until Soviet troops evacuate the whole of Hungary. We demand that the Government should do everything to turn Hungary into a neutral State like Austria or Switzerland....

The Revolutionary Workers' Council of the Budapest Electricity Works deems it necessary to draw the attention of the inhabitants of Budapest to the fact that the electricity workers are carrying out the most essential repairs to the electricity network ... and request that this work should not be hampered and that it should not be regarded as an act of strike-breaking. ...

Free Radio Kossuth [20:00]

"Speak Frankly!"

Miskolc

Dear listeners! ... We were the first to announce to our listeners Marshal Zhukov's order on the withdrawal of Soviet troops from Hungary. We were also the first to report that the Soviet Army was carrying out operations in the Zahony area which amounted to going around in circles. At the same time ... we made contact with our present Government. We gave an account of the interview with Mr. Zoltan Tildy, Minister of State, and the Deputy Chairman of the National Defense Committee in our afternoon transmission. During the night, that is, from 2 a.m. until now, we continuously tried to get in touch ... to make inquiries about their opinion of the present situation. All we could get as reply was: "We are negotiating," and again, "We are negotiating," and "Do not worry." Nothing else ...

What can be the reason for this? ... We expect the Government not to strain the people's nerves to the breaking point ... When we announced Marshal Zhukov's order, Free Radio Kossuth resented it half-an-hour later. It resented the fact that we had beaten them to it. Dear Kossuth Radio, if you don't mind, this was not the first announcement with which we came out first. And if you are not up to the mark, we shall try to beat you to it in the future. We turned to the Government, and we expected the Government to understand us, to trust us, and to be pleased, to reply to the County of Borsod ... We have failed to get a reply over the telephone. We are now asking for a reply over the radio to our most important question so that we can act calmly ... in the interest of restoring the Socialist order of our free Hungarian fatherland ...

Barnabas Nagy, Director of Radio Free Miskolc

We demand that the Government speak frankly and without restraint through the allegedly Free Radio Kossuth. We will not stop fighting otherwise. We demand that the Russian troops should actually start to leave the country, immediately, because there will be no order, peace or tranquility on our native soil, sprinkled with precious blood, until they have finally left. We look forward to deeds by the Government and not phrases. [23:35]

The Workers Council Of County Borsod

Radio Free Miskolc

1 NOVEMBER

Mikoyan and Suslov in Budapest

Budapest

During the past few hours I managed to get into the Party office in Akademia Utca. The Hungarian Workers' Party, which is to be reformed very shortly, will soon move to Nador Utca. ... In the foyer with its marble pillars, the chairs are occupied by young men identically dressed in navy blue topcoats and the well-known Russian caps — Mikoyan and Suslov's escorts. Otherwise the building is in the hands of the revolutionary Honved Army.

Janos Kadar asks for a little patience since he is conducting an important discussion. "Whom is he talking with?", I asked one of the Party's leading politicians. "With Mikoyan and Suslov. about the withdrawal of Soviet troops." A short while later Imre Nagy, the Prime Minister, steps out. Apparently the discussion has been fruitless. Now Gyorgy Lukacs is arriving, accompanied by the poet Istvan Boelsci and by a university professor. Their papers were checked in the street and he had to give his word of honour that he really was the Minister of Culture; owing to the great confusion he has had no time to get a new identity card.

Suslov steps out of Janos Kadar's room. On his face we note the smile, well-known from the newspapers. Mikoyan is not nearly as dark as we had thought; his hair and moustache are greying. They are both wearing navy blue top-coats. According to what I have been told, they had already spent a few hours here last week, and now they are back again to obtain a clear picture of what is happening in Budapest and Hungary. People around me are of the opinion that the information Mikoyan provided resulted in the Soviet Government's declaration—which expresses regret that events in Hungary led to bloodshed.

I stand near the doorway, and they shake hands with me as well. We are equals: representatives of the Hungarian press and of the Soviet Government. Mikoyan and Suslov go downstairs, get into a Soviet armoured car, and the armoured convoy sets out for the airport. By the time these lines go to print, they will be on their way to Moscow. ...   *Igazsag (Budapest), 1 November*

Stabilizing Public Order

Budapest

Hungarians! We, the young freedom fighters of the Corvin Circle, have been fighting up to now, not talking. Now that we can speak at last, our first serious word to every Hungarian brother is to maintain order completely and everywhere. And where necessary, restore order! We do not want to provide the Russians with an excuse for remaining in the country on the pretext of maintaining order. ...

According to information from the Revolutionary Committee of the Public Security Forces, in general Budapest had a peaceful night. Discorders only occured in a few places and the forces of public order intervened without delay. Among others, they arrested four people who had been looting hospitals. ...

"Workers of the Mint! The real cause of the revolution is in danger. Arms have been obtained by elements whose objective is not the sacred cause of the revolution but looting and robbery. For the sake of defending the peaceful population, we ask you to mint the insignia of the ... National Guard. .."

Besides the Honved forces and the police only the members of the National Guard are authorized to carry weapons. ... Units and members of the National Guard should isolate themselves from the sporadic trouble-makers. For this reason we shall issue today special gun licenses. From today on the National Guard will wear special insignia and they will obtain ranks identical to those of the Honved forces. The members of the Honved and of the police who remained loyal to the achievements of the victorious national democratic revolution will be provided with an endorsement in their identity cards in order to differentiate them from enemies of the revolution and from the criminals who put on uniforms of the armed forces. . . .

Order of the Revolutionary National Defence Committee and the Minister of Defence:

1. Officers, NCO's and soldiers separated from their units, on leave or otherwise absent should report within 24 hours to local garrisons or the National Guard Command if they are not yet members of units concerned with maintaining order.

2. Military persons who are already members of organized groups participating in the revolution should remain in these groups and help keep order until further notice.

3. Every military person separated from his unit . . . must report his whereabouts to his unit.

The Hungarian Writers Association has issued the following statement:

All honor to the dead of the revolution! The Hungarian writers took part in preparing the revolution. Now it is their duty to guard over the honor of this revolution. That is why they demand that those who are guilty shall answer for their deeds before independent Hungarian courts. But the people should not pass judgement in the streets! We call on everyone to hand over the guilty without harming them, either to the National Guard or to the Honved patrols. Personal revenge is not worthy of us. We are convinced that the Hungarian people agree with its writers in this. The whole world is watching us and recognizes the honor of our revolution. It should not be stained.

(Signed)   *Laszlo Benjamin, Tibor Dery ,Pal Ignotus, Gyula Illyes, Laszlo Nemeth, Lorine Szabo, Aron Tamasi, Peter Veres and Zoltan Zelk*

At a stormy meeting held in the Lawyers' Chamber in Budapest, elements lurking among the ranks of those present, who tried to revive the voice of the past, were promptly silenced with indignation and removed from the Chamber. A new National Commitee of Lawyers and Advocates was elected and it demanded that those members of the corps of lawyers, judges and prosecutors who were party to the illegal and sinister machinations should immediately be removed from their posts . . .

An appeal issued by the Budapest Student Revolutionary Committee declared that the revolution had not yet been ended. "We must remain organised", it continued, "and must continue to fight in order to achieve our freedom in spite of deliberate attempts to mislead us and in spite of the tactics of internal and external

enemies. . . . We guard the independence gained by so many sacrifices. We trust Imre Nagy." . . .

The Revolutionary Committee of the Budapest City Council held a meeting today at the City Hall. It was presided over by the former Mayor, Peter Bechtler [formerly Social-democrat]. Two representatives of each party are members of the Committee. The Chairman announced that the Committee is taking over the ideological and political administration of the municipal authorities. The Committee elected as Chairman Jozsef Kovago, delegate of the Independent Smallholders Party, and as Vice-Chairman, Peter Bechtler. The Committee then discussed problems of close interest to the population of the capital. It was found that the remains of victims of the bloody struggles presented a major problem.

The Committee discussed gas, water and electricity supplies for the capital. The gas works have supplies for 20 days, but the situation with electricity is not so good. In a few days it will be necessary to introduce restrictions. As for water, there is no difficulty at all. Because public works employees struck, great difficulties have arisen concerning garbage collection. The Committee decided to bring these difficulties to the notice of the Government. The situation concerning the capital's food supplies is good. Ninety per cent of food shops and restaurants are open. The county is assisting the population of Budapest on a large scale. . . .

Free Radio Kossuth and Hungarian News Agency

A New, Free Press
Budapest

The ice of eleven years had cracked, and democracy had flooded incontinent into the people's lives.

The most visible aspect of this ferment, and the most exciting, especially to a journalist, was the sudden, explosive advent of no fewer than twenty-five daily papers in place of the five sad, dreary, stereotyped sheets of recent years. Very often the Budapest worker used to find exactly the same announcement, word for word, and sometimes with just the same photographs, in *Szabad Nép*, *Népszava*, *Magyar Nemzet*, *Szabad Ifjúság* and the evening paper *Esti Budapest*. Now he had two dozen papers to choose from (what a field-day the news-vendors had!) with independent editors, clashes of opinion, full-blooded polemics, hard-hitting commentaries, and, above all, news. *Szabad Nép*, the Communist daily, came out for a day and then gave place to *Népszabadság* when the new Communist Party was launched. *Népszava*, the trade union daily, became the organ of the Social-Democratic Party again. The trade unions brought out *Népakarat*. The Smallholders' Party resurrected their *Kis Újság* after six years. The

National Revolutionary Committee brought out *Magyar Függetlenság*. The Revolutionary Hungarian Army and Youth Organisation produced *Igazság*. The Revolutionary Council of Young Workers launched *Magyar Ifjúság*. The Petöfi Party launched *Új Magyarország*. There were *Magyar Világ, Valóság*, and many more.

I went to see the editor of one of these papers in his office at what had formerly been the *Szabad Nép* and *Esti Budapest* building, and which now housed in its warren of offices, more rationally, several newspapers and committees. He turned out to be an old friend of mine, a Communist,

whose journalistic skill was being taxed to its uttermost limits by the sudden but welcome blossoming of new writers, principally from among the youth.

"Wait half a minute, will you?" he asked, motioning me to a chair... It was an hour before he had finished, first correcting a mass of copy, then interviewing a stream of shy but enthusiastic youngsters. "They bring us poems, news items, articles, short stories about the revolution by the score," he said. "Some of them are good, some not so good. But we try to help them. New talent. We never suspected it, never..."

Peter Fryer, Hungarian Tragedy (London, 1956)

Hopes and Fears of the Revolution

Budapest

There was lively activity in Parliament today. In the last two or three days the Parliament has become the center to meet and decide things. Imre Nagy, members of the Government, leaders of the newly formed parties and representatives of "Revolutionary Committees" are constantly present. Arriving every day are delegates with demands of newly-formed authorities from all over the country. The immediate withdrawal of Soviet troops is a common characteristic of all these demands. They have an ultimative character. "Otherwise the strike will continue". And this means the paralysis of communications and the stoppage of all production. ...

This morning we succeeded in getting into the secretariat of Imre Nagy. The Prime Minister was too busy to see us. He was meeting with representatives of many organisations which in these days have seized arms and thus power. They arrived with information on new movements of Soviet troops across the Hungarian frontiers. An astonished representative of the Revolutionary Military Committee asks: "How is it possible that this now happens after we have gone so far towards calming down the situation?" He was very dejected.

Pressure by the newly-established political parties has a strong influence on the decisions of Prime Minister Nagy. But their demands are in harmony with the general atmosphere in the country. Dissatisfaction increased from hour to hour, when it was learned that Soviet troops, after withdrawing from Budapest, have taken up positions at the approaches to the capital. That is why the general strike is still in force in Hungary ... More and more one hears: "We are not moving in a circle but rushing toward a catastrophe. We cannot start production, nor force the people to surrender their arms before foreign troops are withdrawn. And we have coal only for the next two days. This also means that we shall be left without light. The consequences will be felt more

and more. We shall arrive at the brink of economic collapse!"

The hands of the trade unions are still tied. The old T.U. organisation was disbanded. The new one was formed only recently. The new organisations are energetic and clear-headed as far as denouncing everything that was formerly customary is concerned. But they have also made their call on the workers to return to work contingent upon the withdrawal of Soviet troops.

Only the workers' youth organisation is calling for a resumption of work ...

There is acute fear. People are constantly in the streets ... any dramatic news threatens to start riots. Today former members of the secret police are objects of attack, tomorrow others will be attacked as well. A certain psychosis of uncertainty is being born. Today, for instance, long queues formed in front of banks and post-offices — people who want to withdraw their savings ...

But today many more soldiers may be seen maintaining order... They patrolled the streets together with members of the newly-established National Guard — formed from the old police and students. Armed insurgent groups were seen more rarely, and then only in certain districts. This success is undoubtedly due to yesterday's meeting of the representatives of insurgent forces... After many efforts the progressives succeeded in reaching an agreement among them. Among these forces the most important and most positive role is played by Colonel Maleter... Yesterday he was appointed deputy to the Minister of War and is most energetic in the re-establishment of peace and order. An important role is also played by the chief of the police Kopacsi, who during the riots refused to attack the insurgents. Today both are leading members of the Military Revolutionary Committee.

Today various parties have, so to speak, shown their identity cards ... The Smallholders Party and the Social-Democrats ... are energetically defending the idea of a complete neutrality like

Switzerland and Austria. It is intersting that this is also the attitude of all other groups and organisations which have appeared until now, including the most progressive forces among the youth and the workers, who carried the main burden of fighting during the four bloody Budapest days.

The secretary-general of the Social-Democratic Party Kelemen received a group of Yugoslav journalists today. We learned that this party will fight most resolutely for the maintenance of the acquisitions of the working class, and that it will aid Workers Councils ...

At present only the Communists are behind the time. The Party of Hungarian Workers does not seem to exist. It seems that this party is unable to recover from the heavy blow. According to information, the party wants to reorganize itself completely, that is to say, to start again from scratch. Its new name will be "Hungarian Revolutionary Workers Party"...

Vlado Teslic, Borba (Belgrade), 2 November

"Not with a Red Scarf!"
Budapest

The nearer we got to Budapest the more frequently we were stopped by armed guards of freedom fighters. They were young boys, students and industrial workers, very polite and very pleased to see us. These youngsters were carrying their guns not from any joy of fighting but from a deep conviction that they must get rid of Russian domination and Moscow's hated henchmen, the secret police.

"What will happen after your final victory?" we kept asking. And again the answer was surprisingly unanimous, especially as concerted leadership was so obviously lacking: "There should be several parties, and elections as soon as possible." We then tried to find out their views on how far the economic changes of the present regime should be reversed. They left us in no doubt that they certainly did not want the big landlords to come back to their estates but that they also did not want the enforced collectivisation of the peasants on their newly acquired land to continue. And what should become of the big industrial plants which had been erected in recent years and were the property of the state? Certainly, they should remain state-owned and so should all the key industries. But the rest of the economy should go back to its former owners, especially where the small man was concerned.

In Budapest everyone seemed to be out in the streets. Old men and young kids, housewives and workers, gathered in crowds round our cars, eager to talk, eager also to try and get some share of almost forgotten luxuries. As we were passing the crowds on a bridge I pulled off my modestly red scarf to wave it at them and immediately noticed heads turning away. A young motor-cyclist who was showing us the way immediately whispered to me: "Not with a red scarf." ...

We were deeply impressed by the way in which Hungarian youth took up arms against the Communists. In a hospital there were wounded boys of twelve, thirteen and fourteen years of age who had thrown hand grenades and bottles of petrol at Russian tanks or had stood in ambush armed with guns. We were also strongly impressed by the completeness and discipline of the general strike. As long as the resistance movement was in power all essential services were performed without fault. The food shops were open, potatoes, bread and flour seemed to be in sufficient supply; there were no traces of plundering or demoralisation. At the central bus station where I filled up my car with petrol for the return journey they refused to take money — it being state-owned, they could not issue me with a bill! — and would not even accept a tip. No alcohol was allowed to be served, not even with a meal.

When we left Hungary on November 1st we had not seen one single Russian soldier. We were told by people who watched them that the Russians had taken an hour to get out of Budapest. Near Györ a Russian division was in barracks with the gates locked. The fears of Communist officials then may be deduced from the fact that we had to refuse a Hungarian diplomat's plea to take him, his wife and plenty of luggage with us across the boarder. We left with the delusion that the fight had been won ...

Correspondent, The Economist (London), 17 November

Peasant Demands
Budapest

Paraszt Fuggetlenseg [Peasant Independence], the organ of the Hungarian National Revolutionary Committee, published the demands of the Hungarian farming population.

1. Complete rejection and elimination of the Stalinist peasant policy. A decree must be issued which orders the liquidation of weak and forcibly established cooperatives. Peasants must be given the right to have cooperatives if so desired. Peasants will have their land returned, both the property and the animals which they took into the cooperatives. They must be granted state support. The present system of state assistance to cooperatives must be discontinued. Instead state support must be distributed by a cooperative center, the members of which have been elected by cooperative members.

2. An agricultural delegation has to be established from peasant representatives, members of the new parties, agricultural experts and journalists sent to study the system of large-scale farming in Western Europe — in Denmark, Hol-

land, England, in Scandinavia — and in the United States. Their experiences must be used for the benefit of Hungarian agriculture.

3. The present system of machine-tractor stations must be discontinued ...

4. Far-reaching financial assistance must be granted to the individually-farming peasantry.

5. We approve the discontinuation of the compulsory delivery system which exploited the peasantry. But this is only a first step. The extremely high peasant taxes must be reduced immediately and, for the sake of the peasantry, the present system of taxation in Hungary must be revised.

6. The old system of selling and purchasing land must be restored.

7. State farms must be dissolved if their output and profits are unsatisfactory.

8. The Ministry for Collecting Agricultural Produce must be abolished. The Ministries of Agriculture and of State Farms must be consolidated and the overgrown bureaucratic apparatus must be reduced.

9. Peasant Revolutionary Committees must be established in every village. Members should be recruited from the democratic parties, and they should take power until elections are held.

Free Radio Kossuth

"But We Are Alive!"

Budapest

In the name of the provisional leadership of the Social Democratic Party, the secretary, Gyula Kelemen will now speak:

Hungarian Brother Workers! I am addressing you in the name of the Social Democratic Party, which was abolished by force in 1948. Hundreds of our leaders were imprisoned, and thousands interned in labour camps. Men who had devoted their whole lives to the cause of humanity were branded as traitors. Many died in prison following their leader Ferenc Szeder, the old leader of Hungarian Agricultural Workers. But we are alive! Hundreds of thousands of organized workers, who had suffered the bitterness of oppression, are today rebuilding the Hungarian Social Democratic Party. Not even the cruelest capitalism exploited us as have the masters of our country during the last eight years. They lied when they said they were governing in the name of the workers!

We ask every Social Democrat to support the National Committees and to help them in their work. We must develop our youth organizations and build up again our organizations in the countryside. Our peasant members must concentrate their forces in order to prevent any attempt to bring back the large landed proprietors. We ask all families to give us the names of relatives who are political prisoners and who have not yet returned.

Let us protect our liberty, so dearly won, and build up a neutral and free Hungary!

Free Radio Kossuth

Anna Kethly Leaves

Vienna

From Budapest I brought Anna Kethly, leader of the Hungarian Social Democrats, and former vice-chairman of the Hungarian Parliament, to Vienna today by car. She is attending a meeting of the bureau of the Socialist International. This is the first sight of the free world which this gentle and indomitable woman has had since her long years of imprisonment under the Communists ...

The streets of Budapest are strewn with glass and telephone wires, and last night as we drove into the semi-deserted city the only people to be seen were groups of victorious Freedom Fighters checking our documents at every street corner. There are crowds of boys between 16 and 18, armed with tommy guns and army rifles, rather self-consciously got up like revolutionaries in a film. At one corner some of them pointed out a Communist secret policeman hanging dead from a tree on a side walk and insisted on our inspecting the body.

They looked and behaved like people in a film, and yet these are the youngsters who in seven days of desperate fighting forced the monster of world communsim to give way and acknowledge defeat. Later we went to the lobby of the St Margit Palace Hotel where we saw about thirty of these youngsters with caps flung backwards over their heads and hand grenades in their belts sitting in the lobby in an animated discussion with some Hungarian poets and actresses. They were discussing the future of mankind.

By contrast I met the famous woman leader of the Social Democrats at her party headquarters where the Hungarian Social Democratic party was refounded two days ago. She had been trying to fly to Vienna in the morning but Soviet troops had reoccupied the road to the airport and she could not get through. Now she was standing in her black overcoat, grey-haired, receiving delegations of Social Democratic workers from all over the country, "Kethly Anna" as the Hungarians say, putting the surname before the Christian name, is the idol of those thousands of workers who never gave way to communism.

The Hungarian Social Democrats have reorganised their party, and have rigidly excluded all members who have supported the merger with the Communists, such as the former State President, Szakasits. The Social Democrats have not joined the new coalition Government of the "National Communist" Premier Imre Nagy. They may do so later, but that will depend on their own democratic decision.

Manchester Guardian, 2 November

New Parties and "Party Bickering"

Budapest

On behalf of the parliamentary members of the People's Democratic Party, and in my capacity as doyen of the Party, I [Denes Farkas] announce, that the Party has begun its activities. We appeal to the country as a whole, and primarily to those 800,000 constituents who voted for us in 1947 despite terror and the election fraud. The Party stands by its old program. It supports the Government as far as the maintenance of order and protection of life and property are concerned. We refuse to take part in any coalition and ask nothing from the Government except freedom of agitation and organisation. Our flag has remained immaculate ...   *Free Radio Kossuth (2 : 30)*

At a constituent meeting of the Hungarian Christian Party held on 1st November, Karoly Zajgovari was elected Provincial Chairman of the Party ...   *Hungarian News Agency*

Announcement: The Hungarian Independence Party was reconstituted on October 31 ...
          Free Radio Kossuth

So long as the Soviet Government has not withdrawn its troops from Hungary's entire territory, the Petofi Party cannot accept any part in the Government ... The Petofi Party calls for a referendum within three days on the immediate abrogation of the Warsaw Treaty ...
          Free Radio Kossuth

Budapest

A delegation of 28 representing the Workers Council of County Borsod-Abauj-Zemplen [the county's pre-Communist appellation] has called on Premier Nagy and Zoltan Tildy, the Minister of State, to present the demands of the county's workers, miners, undergraduates, peasants, intellectuals and partisans. Among other things they demand the Government set up a National Revolutionary Committee consisting of democratically elected representatives of county and Budapest Workers Councils. This body should replace the present National Assembly.

The Government should concentrate on the restoration of order and deal firmly with all individual acts of terror and illegality. To do this, attention should not be concentrated on a re-formation of parties and the return to party bickering. Emphasis on the organisation of parties is strongly condemned and is considered inopportune by the Borsod-Abauj-Zemplen delegation.

It is also opposed to any attempts to return the property of landlords and capitalists, or to hand over command to Horthyite generals.
          Free Radio Kossuth

Situation Report

Budapest

Reports reaching here said that for three hours early to-day Soviet tanks, guns and lorries were crossing into Hungary at Zahony. Hungarians said there was a flow in both directions, but more entered than went out. Other Russian troops were reported to be digging in to form a cordon around Budapest, from which they withdrew yesterday. They were 15 to 25 miles from the city.

Hungarian troops arriving here from the south-east reported seeing Russian tanks on the outskirts of the city. The insurgents had issued an ultimatum to the Soviet forces to withdraw to the line of the River Tisza by November 15, and completely evacuate Hungary by Dec. 31. If the Russians do not agree the rebels will resume fighting. Workers of Csongrad, South-East Hungary, have decided to stay on strike until Soviet troops leave the country ... Groups of rebels still prowled the streets of Budapest and the city's sewers to-day. They were searching for members of the Hungarian secret police. When they found them in the sewers they shot them and dumped their bodies. Eye-witnesses reported that when the insurgents had shot secret police-men in the streets they poured petrol on the bodies and burned them. Despite pleas by the Government, nobody was back at work in the factories. There was no public transport. Nearly everything was at a standstill.

The Catholic People's party resumed its activities in Budapest. Cardinal Mindszenty, Roman Catholic Primate of Hungary, who returned here yesterday after eight year's imprisonment, said that he would not decide whether to support a broad coalition Government for a few days.

Prince Paul Esterhazy, the Hungarian former landowner, has been released from prison and is back in Budapest, according to press reports. He was sentenced to 15 years imprisonment in February, 1949, for alleged treason and espionage.

Budapest radio reported that Hungarian officers, now attending the Signals Academy in Leningrad, said in a telegram that they were putting themselves at the disposal of the new Government and the Revolutionary Council of the Army. The officers asked the Government to recall them immediately ...

          Daily Telegraph (London). 2 November

Questions in "Fortress Budapest"

Budapest

Soviet tank units which left Budapest yesterday have dug in 10 miles outside the capital and encircled the city, except for a small stretch leaving the road open to Vienna for the medical and food supplies coming in from there. They have also forcibly occupied the large civilian airport at Ferihegy and requisitioned all civilian aircraft. Western military attachés who were able to go there this afternoon confirm the Russian move.

This news, after the relief following the withdrawal of the Soviet troops from the capital, has caused great dismay among the heroic citizens of Budapest. It is not quite clear what this Russian move means; it may be in connection with the flying visit of Mr. Anastas Mikoyan and Mr. Mikhail Suslov — the second in the last seven days — who arrived here this morning for talks with members of the Hungarian Government, including Janos Kadar...

While the Soviet leaders hesitate and may or may not cut their losses in Hungary, Budapest itself, which looked like being lost only 48 hours ago, is now firmly in the hands of the insurgents.

I had a talk today with the commander of the newly-formed Budapest forces, Major-General Bela Kiraly, who is superintending the organising of the army, the police, the workers' brigades and the university students into one unit. He said that they will resist any attempt to undermine the revolution's achievements, whether it comes from inside or outside the country. Their aim is to preserve these achievements intact pending new elections and the formation of a new Government. Budapest is now full of units of the Hungarian Army coming up from the provinces and has taken on the appearance of a fortress...

There is no sign, of jubilation or joy as one might have expected. Are the Russians returning to Budapest or not? Are the Russians going to stay in Hungary or not? Those are the questions which everybody asks in Budapest.

Lajos Lederer, Observer Foreign News Service (London), 1 November

Budapest

The Russians, we heard, were drawing a ring of tanks around Budapest. They had occupied all the airfields and were permitting no foreign plane to land or take off. Soviet reinforcements were rolling in from the east over the Rumanian border. The atomic physicist shook his head. "Why all that, if they intend to pull out? They aren't just going to accept defeat. They'll bring in more men and more tanks and smash the revolution," he repeated again and again. "And what will you do?" I asked. "Fight," he answered simply. "If you knew what it was to live through these ten years of abasement, terror, and treason, you would understand. We can't go back to the way things were, not now. It has nothing to do with heroism; it's much less dramatic than that. It's simply that there isn't a single one of us who wouldn't rather be dead than go through the hell we were living in again." I tried to reassure him. "The Soviets won't dare," I said. "What about world opinion? De-Stalinization? The concessions in Poland? They're only trying to prevent the revolution from getting completely out of hand; the tanks and the reinforcements are a damper, nothing more." This was exactly the sort of thing that the military attachés of the British and American embassies in Budapest were saying to Western journalists. "Nothing that can't be explained by the requirements of an orderly withdrawal..." But the Hungarians knew better. ...

Peter Schmid, Die Weltwoche (Zurich) and Commentary (New York), January 1957

Continuing the Strike

Gyor

The discussions at the meeting of the Transdanubian National Council, which lasted until 2:30 a.m. have been stormy but reasonable. The Transdanubian National Council decided to continue the strike until it was possible to verify that the Soviet troops had started to withdraw, and that some international guarantee was forthcoming. Delegates from Dunapentele ("Sztalinvaros"), Tatabanya, Oroszlany, Dorog, and other mines, and from the South Zala oilfields, declared their firm intention to continue the strike. The power supply, however, would be maintained... *Free Radio Petofi*

Budapest

The guns are silent in Csepel. The glorious revolution has won a victory. But we are keeping our arms at hand. The National Committee has been set up and has taken over. Various political parties have come to life again after a long period of enforced silence. In Csepel the Social Democratic Party and the Smallholders Party have already set up organisations and other democratic parties are in the course of formation. On the political level, therefore, life has begun.

But economic life is at a standstill. Is this expedient? Should several hundred thousand forints' worth of goods be allowed to deteriorate in the Csepel textile factory? We can only answer, no. We cannot allow our property to be spoiled. The point is, the workers of Csepel are on general strike. What, therefore, can be done? The demands voiced in connection with the strike are justified. The withdrawal from our homeland of the Soviet Army is essential ... Nobody wants to betray the revolution.

It is necessary, however, that life begin again. We have our duty to revolutionary youth. Revolutionary Workers Councils must be set up in the factories. Their primary task is to go into the factories and, with the rights we have won for ourselves, to begin carrying out the next tasks. These are to start up those factories where assets are in danger; while the strike lasts, to carry out maintenance work and, when the political situation calls for it to start production. This is the target we must fight for. These are the points that we have to bear in mind. We do not want to hand over the factories to capitalists. Today, in the true sense of the word, the factory belongs to us. Since it is ours we have to take good care of our assets. Until our demands are met, let there be no regular production, but let us repair machinery and tools, so that, when the word is given, work can start without any difficulty.

Jozsef Kiss, Csepeli Ujsag (Budapest), 1 November

Pecs

Miners of Pecs have decided to dissociate themselves from the Baranya County Revolutionary Committee, since it is revolutionary only in name and is actually not doing anything. The miners are firmly determind to go on striking. They protest against the post office, which seeks to isolate them and is not answering telephone calls from the mines ...   *Free Radio Petofi*

Budapest

The Revolutionary Committee of Hungarian Film and Theatre asked us to broadcast the following message to the Modmezonvasarhely Theatre:

We have learned that at the request of the local authorities you want to give a performance of the "*Janos Vitez*" (National Opera). We inform you that this would be breaking the strike that all theaters are holding. Continue with rehearsals and prepare for the first free Hungarian performance!...   *Free Radio Kossuth*

Szeged

The Szeged strike committee, County Csongrad, has called on the workers of the factory of the town to carry on the strike. At Hedmezoevasarhely, where on Wednesday evening a provisional National Committee for Csongrad County was formed,... the Committee decided to carry on with the strike until Soviet forces had withdrawn from the country. ...   *Hungarian News Agency*

Negotiating with Nagy

Gyor

Premier Nagy has taken note of the establishment of the Transdanubian National Council, accepted its demands, and requested its assistance. He said that Soviet troops would leave or had left Budapest on 31st October and that on the morning of 31st October the Hungarian Government has started negotiations with a view to giving notice of its termination of the Warsaw Treaty, and with a view to the withdrawal of Soviet troops from Hungary. ...

The Premier had requested the delegation to call off the strike. Shortly before, he had received a large delegation from the Csepel Iron Works and had succeeded in convincing them, too, of the necessity of calling off the strike. He acknowledged the workers' right to strike as a general principle, and said he would consider it legitimate to stop work in the event of "our demands not being fulfilled or if we were misled".

We asked him, in order to strengthen confidence in him, to tell us with the utmost sincerity about his role in the fight for liberation and the events which have taken place. He said that it was Hegedus who called the Russians into Budapest. He also said that he has already promised the miners of Dorog a general adjustment of miners' wages.

One of our delegates told Nagy that some of the people have no confidence in him and suggested that he should resign in favour of Bela Kovacs. Imre Nagy replied that he felt that he possessed the confidence of the people. However, should he become convinced of the contrary, he would give up his position. At our request he gave a personal pledge that free elections would be held as soon as possible. If he became unable to assure free elections he would resign.

In the course of our talks we handed to Imre Nagy the declaration of the workers of the Varpalota industrial area, demanding that the Government should address itself to the U.N. for the purpose of a just settlement. The workers of the Varpalota industrial area are afraid that the Soviet Union might occupy the whole of Hungary by military force, thus presenting the other Great Powers with a *fait accompli*. Imre Nagy's answer was that the fact that the Government had recalled its U.N. representative was, in the language of diplomacy, tantamount to the most forceful protest...

The Transdanubian National Council requests all Counties and Cities to send two delegates per County and one per City to the Town Hall at Gyor on 1 November at 15:15 ...

Free Radio Petofi

Defiant Miskolc in the Face of "Destruction"

Miskolc

The revolutionary leaders of this industrial center in eastern Hungary reported today the city was at the mercy of Soviet artillery and tanks. The Soviet forces near by were described by the Hungarians as "sufficient to destroy the city in four hours." Miskolc, which with its environs has a population of 200,000, has been controlled by an anti-Soviet council for more than a week after the Communist authorities were driven from power. It has little with which to oppose the Soviet troops. Some Hungarian heavy artillery is drawn up, there are a few infantry men available and youngsters all over the city with rifles and sub-machine guns. The city's position was made even more uneasy by a report received this afternoon from a traveler who told officials he had noted concentrations of Czechoslovak troops on the Czech-Hungarian frontier.

The city remained defiant. The chairman of the revolutionary council, Jozsef Kiss, flew to Budapest this morning to tell the Government that unless it acted to remove Soviet troops from Hungary and denounce the Warsaw Pact the Miskolc area would no longer recognize its authority. The Government did in fact take such a stand this evening.

The Hungarian defiance seemed general. It was typified by two Hungarian tanks drawn up along the Budapest-Miskolc road just east of the town of Gyongyos. "We are here just in case the Russians come back," an officer explained. The Russians in question had passed through the town last night on their way from Budapest. The townspeople reported them to be short on food. Some of the soldiers had offered arms for something to eat.

This morning, about ten miles further east, the Soviet troops, estimated at battalion strength, were stretched along the road for more than half a mile. The major weapons were light artillery pieces. Tired looking and dirty, the soldiers sat back along the roadside staring at the passing traffic. One Western car stopped and the driver, a British correspondent, offered the troops bread. They refused it. One of them broke into a grin and said, "Eat it yourself." The unit was soon joined by another coming from the east toward Budapest with field guns, armored cars, gasoline tanks and field kitchens. They drew off the road and set up camp for the night in the surrounding fields.

Another instance of Hungarian defiance occurred two days ago in Nyiregyhaza, seventy-five miles east of Miskolc. As reported by Miskolc officials, women lay down in the roadway to halt the movement of Soviet tanks. Two women were crushed to death.

In the Miskolc area there appeared to be almost complete solidarity with the Revolutionary Committee. A few districts had not yet accepted its authority, but the committee is confident the districts will be won over. The peasants appear to be joining the anti-Communist, anti-Soviet movement with enthusiasm. Officials said the peasants were delivering their food to the town although not long ago they were telling Communist officials they could not make deliveries because they did not have enough to eat themselves.

Henry Giniger, New York Times, 2 November

Attitudes of Churchmen

Budapest

Cardinal Mindszenty, Primate of Hungary, received Hungarian and foreign Press, radio and television representatives at his Buda palace and made the following statement: "After long imprisonment I am speaking to all the sons of the Hungarian nation. In my heart there is no hatred against anyone. It is an admirable heroism that is at present liberating the fatherland. This struggle for liberty is unexampled in world history. Our youth deserves all glory. They deserve gratitude and prayers for their sacrifices. Our army, workers and peasants have shown an example of heroic love of the fatherland. The situation of the country is very serious; conditions for the continuance of life are lacking. The path of fruitful development must be found as speedily as possible. I am now gathering information, and in two days' time I will broadcast to the nation about the means of achieving this development." *Hungarian News Agency*

Budapest

You will now hear Bishop Laszlo:

The Hungarian Presbyterian Church wishes to express its admiration and homage to the heroes of the national uprising, to students, workers, soldiers, men and women ... The nation is proud of the fact that this was a clean revolution and stood under the protection of our national honour ... He confesses with repentance that the church submitted itself to the pressure of the political power more than it was compelled to do, and because of this it has also caused harm in carrying out its spiritual aims ...

Not only reaction, anarchy also is the enemy of the revolution. Not even in their thoughts should anyone think of the restoration of former regimes. Our objectives must be to safeguard the achievements of the revolution, to develop the same, to correct our mistakes, and to make good for injustices. At the same time we must also protect ourselves against anarchy. The most vital condition for us is restoration of order and peace. It is the duty of state organs and of the independent courts to arrest and to sentence those who committed crimes, and this can never be undertaken by individual actions ... God bless those who are sowing justice and love. *Free Radio Kossuth*

Lutheran Bishops Dr. Lajos Veto and Dr. Laszlo Dezery ... have resigned from their offices. Pending decision by the competent Church authorities, they will carry out no Church services whatever ... Dr. Lajos Ordas has been entrusted with the leadership of the Lutheran Church's Southern District ... The Office of the Lutheran Bishops identifies itself with the heroic fight for freedom ... *Free Radio Kossuth*

Pal Maleter's Press Conference

Budapest

Representatives of Western newspapers called on Maj. Gen. Pal Maleter, military commander of the insurrection and Deputy Minister of Defence, at the insurgents' HQ ... First of all, he informed the foreign journalists that according to military reconnaissance new Soviet forces have entered Hungarian territory during the past few days. "The view of the Hungarian Army", said Maleter, "is that we want to live in friendship with all peoples. Our Army, however, has weapons, and if necessary it can defend itself against the intruders. In the interests of putting the situation in order we stand behind the National Government, behind Imre Nagy and Zoltan Tildy. But the Army makes its further support for the Government dependent on whether the Government fulfils its promises ..."

"What negotiations has the Government entered into up to now with this end in view?" asked the journalists.

"Zoltan Tildy conferred on Wednesday with Mr. Mikoyan, who promised that those troops who are in Hungary not for the purposes of the Warsaw Treaty will be withdrawn from the country."

Question: Does this mean that the so-called Warsaw troops will remain?

Answer: This is out of the question. Tildy has informed Mikoyan that we shall repudiate the Warsaw Treaty in any event, and our Government demanded that negotiations in this respect should begin as soon as possible.

Question: What will happen to those troops now coming to Hungary?

Answer: Naturally, we shall regard them as being outside the Warsaw Treaty and shall treat them accordingly. I must declare, however, that the people of Hungary are mature enough not immediately to regard tardiness in connection with promises made by foreign leaders as an act of provocation. Nonetheless, we shall not throw away our arms before national independence has achieved complete victory.

The journalists then asked Maj. Gen. Maleter to speak about the insurrection, the fighting, and the relations between the insurgents and the Army.

Answer: This insurrection was organised by nobody. The insurrection broke out because the Hungarian people wanted peace, tranquillity, freedom and independence — to which the foreign occupiers replied with weapons. At the beginning of the struggle unarmed single groups, independent of each other, attacked the intruders, and achieved their successes with the weapons they thus obtained. Hungarian youths made their own weapons.

Maj. Gen. Maleter then showed such a weapon. It was an ordinary siphon bottle from the tap of which hung two 15-cm. ribbons. The siphon was filled with petrol which saturated the ribbons. With such bottles many Russian steel monsters were rendered harmless. The burning petrol, flowing from the siphon, set the tanks on fire and burnt them out.

Question: Please tell us something about your part in the battles.

Answer: In the early hours of last Wednesday I received an order from the then Minister of Defence to set out with five tanks against insurgents in the 8th and 9th city districts and to relieve the Kilian barracks. When I arrived at the spot I became convinced that the freedom fighters were not bandits but loyal sons of the Hungarian people. So I informed the Minister that I would go over to the insurgents. Ever since, we have been fighting together and we shall not end the struggle so long as a single armed foreigner is in Hungary.

Free Radio Kossuth

For a Policy of Neutrality

Budapest

In the interests of the development of an independent national Hungarian foreign policy ...

(1) We inform the public that on the morning of 30th October we conveyed to the Prime Minister a proposal in which we elaborated the measures necessary for realising the permanent neutrality of Hungary. In our opinion the recognition of the neutrality of Hungary for all time by the Great Powers and neighbouring States is in the basic interest of the entire Hungarian nation, indeed of the nations of Central Europe at present and in the future.

(2) In the present difficult economic circumstances we consider it important that the Government should turn to the Great Powers and request material aid.

(3) The Revolutionary Committee of the Foreign Ministry demands that the national treasure

of Hungary, bauxite and especially uranium, shall be utilised for creating national prosperity.

(4) At one of the forthcoming sessions of the UN, Hungary must be represented by a delegation that enjoys the confidence of the entire nation. We have taken measures to ensure that the delegation already appointed shall not leave for the General Assembly of the UN and that the delegates Imre Horvarth and Endre Sik are to return to Budapest.

(5) The Revolutionary Committee has prepared a proposal, to be immediately forwarded to the Government, concerning the removal of Stalinist-Rakosi-ist diplomatic representatives. Moreover, measures are being taken for the recall of the unsatisfactory members of the diplomatic service abroad.

(6) We demand that the Hungarian Government informs the Soviet Union that it wishes to initiate negotiations in Budapest for the immediate withdrawal of Soviet troops and for placing relations between the two countries on a footing of complete equality.

Revolutionary Committee, The Foreign Ministry
Hungarian News Agency

The Party Is "Fighting for Survival"

Our Party was forced to make the gravest concessions. It was compelled to consent to the reorganisation of the bourgeois parties. Nevertheless it will never give up its aims and program: we are building a socialist Hungary, an independent, sovereign and socialist Hungary which enjoys an equal status vis-a-vis every country, including the Russian nation. If Moscow wants to restore the confidence of the Hungarian Communists, it will have to make sure that the severest punishment is meted out to all those Russian commanders and officers who were guilty of massacre ...

We Hungarian Communists will make sure what persons and circumstances were responsible for calling in Russian troops. The guilty will meet the fate they deserve—the gallows. It is up to us to see that Hungarian Communists maintain leadership in the coalition Government in accordance with their strength, and it is the Soviet's affair to deal adequately with criminal Soviet officers in the interest of strengthening the Hungarian Communists. Then let each side concern itself with the internal affairs of its own nation ...

The Soviet leaders themselves can see that with bayonets they cannot change the beliefs and firm convictions of our nation. Nor can Hungarian youth be won over to the lofty tenets of Marxism-Leninism by trying to transform them into Russians, by declaring that learning the Russian language is the main thing.

If we Communists request and demand, if the leaders of the Soviet have learned their lesson, and if, following our request, they offer to release us from the Warsaw pact immediately and without delay, then perhaps some Hungarians will restore at least partial confidence in us, and will believe that we Communists also are striving for an independent, sovereign and socialist Hungary.

We demand that Janos Kadar, as temporary chief of the Party, should publicly, immediately, and without delay call upon the leadership of the Soviet Union and the Communists Parties of the Soviet Union and the fraternal People's Democracies, to make them see that the Hungarian Communist Party is now fighting for its life and survival, that it can only survive in the new situation if it serves solely the interests of the Hungarian people ...

Radio Rajk

Interview with Kadar: "The Third Line"

Budapest

Today I talked to Janos Kadar, first secretary of the new Hungarian Communist Party. He told me it was the first interview he had given to a Western journalist. Kadar is 44 years old. He is of medium height, has light brown hair, speaks very slowly, almost in an undertone.

Question: What type of Communism do you represent, Mr. Kadar?

Answer: The new type, which emerged from the Revolution and which does not want to have anything in common with the Communism of the Rakosi-Hegedues-Geroe-group.

Q: This "new Communism," if it can be termed as such—is it of the Yugoslav or Polish type?

A: Our Communism is Hungarian. It is a sort of "third line," with no connection to Titoism nor to Gomulka's Communism.

Q: How would you describe this "third line?"

A: It is Marxism-Leninism applied to the particular requirements of our country, to our difficulties and to our national problems. It is not inspired either by the U.S.S.R. nor by other types of Communism, and I repeat that it is Hungarian National Communism. This "third line" originated from our Revolution during the course of which, as you know, numerous Communists fought at the side of students, workers, and the people.

Q: Will your Communism be developed along democratic lines, if they can be termed as such?

A: That's a good question. There will be an opposition, and no dictatorship. This opposition will be heard because it will have the national interests of Hungary at heart and not those of international Communism.

Q: Prime Minister Imre Nagy, with whom I had an interview yesterday, told me in reply to a particular question, that it was not he who had called

Uranium

The question of Hungarian uranium has been disturbing the public. Hungarian uranium ore is now in Hungarian hands. The Soviet engineers have left with their families, and now revolutionary Hungarian soldiers are guarding the mine of Kovagoszollos. This news prompted our correspondent to bring to the microphone Professor Lajos Janosi, the world-famous Hungarian atomic scientist.

Q: Professor, why haven't Hungarian scientists been permitted to work in uranium mines?

Janosi: Soviet authorities guarded everything concerning uranium jealously. They excluded all scientists and experts; no data came to light. Hungarians were left completely in the dark. For example, as the Vice-President of the Atomic Energy Commission, I was not informed about the existence of uranium in Hungary. I learned about it only through the newspapers.

Q: What do we know about the Hungarian uranium?

A: I know very little ... I do not know what contracts we have with the Soviet Union. Still no great harm can have been done yet, for all uranium mining is only in the initial stage. They cannot have taken much out of the country. The news that 16 tons did go out seems to be true, but that would mean 16 tons of uranium ore. Very little uranium can be yielded from that, and its value is not very great. It is just about enough for experimenting ... At the moment nobody can say for sure how much we have in the country, not even approximately. However, it is likely that the findings are considerable.

Q: What, in your opinion, is the next thing to do?

A: In my opinion the Government should form as soon as possible a national Atomic Energy Comission. It should not work like the old one, but should include experts and disclose the whole situation. It should investigate how much uranium there is, what are the mining prospects, and all other related problems ...   Free Radio Kossuth

Employees in the planning office of the Uranium Enterprise send the following message in order to reassure all Hungarians:

Data and plans for Hungarian uranium ore production are in custody of the Enterprise. With these data, production of uranium can be carried on.

THE TEMPORARY COMMITTEE OF THE
URANIUM ORE PLANNING OFFICE
Free Radio Kossuth

in the Russians to intervene in the struggle. But he told me the name of the person who had been responsible. He mentioned Gero. Is all this correct?

A: I can tell you that Gero perhaps knew of it and gave his agreement to it, but it is Andras Hegedus who called in the Russians.

Q: Did Mikoyan and Suslov really come to Budapest during the insurrection?

A: Yes—they were in Budapest.

Q: And with whom did they confer?

The Minister paused, and then answered: "I don't know."

Q: What will be the future relations between the new Hungarian Communist Party and the U.S.S.R. and Western Communist Parties?

A: Relations will definitely be friendly, but as yet we have not established contact with Western Communist parties. After what has happened, they do not wish to draw closer to us.

Q: What do you think of Italian Communism?

A: The course taken by Italian Communism is definitely the right one for Italian Communists, just as the Marxist-Leninist "third line" is right for us.

Q: What do you think of the widespread Western opinion that after Stalin's death, two different trends of opinion have evolved within the Soviet Central Committee and the Government in Moscow?

A: This is an error which appeals to Western countries. Two different trends exist neither in the ranks of the Party, nor in the Government. There is only one thing that is certain, and that is that the old Stalinists are now adapting themselves to a new Communist tendency, which obviously gives rise to discussions. My own personal opinion, and, believe me, I am right, is that there is no question of two different trends.

Q: What is to be the fate of those Communists who were in the forefront in the days of Rakosi and company and who fought at the side of Soviet troops and the AVO?

A: Our government will take no action against them. But we wish it to be clearly understood that we have nothing in common with these people.

Q: Will you be a participant in the delegation which is going to the U.S.S.R.?

A: The Soviets will definitely extend an invitation, but we do not yet know who will take part or who will lead the delegation.

Q: What do you think of Titoism and what will be your relations with Tito?

Janos Kadar, who had, up until then, spoken through my German interpreter, now said to me in German: *"Sehr gut"* (very good).

Q: Will you accept Western aid if it is offered to you?

A: Yes, we would accept it. We need it, as our country is in a state of economic breakdown.

Bruno Tedeschi, Il Giornale d'Italia (Rome), 2 November

Janos Kadar Forms a New Communist Party

Budapest

Hungarian workers, peasant, and intellectuals! In a fateful hour we appeal to those who, inspired by a desire to serve the pure ideals of socialism, were led to a Party which degenerated into a medium of despotism and national slavery. This came through the criminal policy of Stalinism's Hungarian representatives—Rakosi and his clique. This adventurist policy unscrupulously frittered away the moral and ideological heritage which you acquired through honest struggle and sacrifice of blood in the old days, fighting for our national independence and democratic progress. Rakosi and his gang gravely violated our national decency and pride. They disregarded the sovereignty and freedom of our nation and lightheartedly wasted our national wealth.

In their glorious uprising our people have shaken off the Rakosi regime. They have achieved freedom for the people and independence for the country. Without this there can be no socialism. We can safely say that the ideological and organisational leaders who prepared this uprising were recruited from among your ranks. Hungarian Communist writers, journalists, university students, the youth of the Petofi Circle, thousands and thousands of workers and peasants, and veteran fighters who had been imprisoned on false charges, fought in the front line against Rakosiite despotism and political hooliganism.

We are proud that you have honestly stood your ground in the armed uprising and in leading it. You were permeated with true patriotism and with loyalty to socialism. We are talking to you frankly. The uprising of the people has come to a crossroads. Either the Hungarian democratic parties will have enough strength to stabilize our achievements or we must face an open counter-revolution. The blood of Hungarian youth, soldiers, workers and peasants was not shed to replace Rakosiite despotism with the reign of the counter-revolution. We did not fight in order that mines and factories be snatched from the hands of the working class, or that land be taken from the hands of the peasantry. The uprising either secures for our people the basic achievements of democracy—the right of assembly and of organising, personal freedom and safety, the rule of law, freedom of the press, and humanitarianism —or we sink back into the slavery of the old feudal world and thus into foreign slavery.

A grave and alarming danger exists that foreign armed intervention may reduce our country to the tragic fate of Korea. Our anxiety for the future of our country leads us to do our utmost to avert this grave danger. We must eliminate the nests of counter-revolution and reaction. We must finally consolidate our democratic order and secure the conditions for normal productive work and life—peace, calm, and order.

In these momentous hours the Communists who fought against the despotism of Rakosi have decided, in accordance with the wish of many true patriots and socialists, to form a new Party. The new Party will break away from the crimes of the past for once and for all. It will defend the honour and independence of our country against anyone. On this basis, the basis of national independence, it will build fraternal relations with any progressive socialist movement and party in the world ...

In these momentous hours of our history we call on every Hungarian worker who is led by devotion to the people and the country to join our Party, the name of which is the Hungarian Socialist Workers Party. The Party counts on the support of every honest worker who declares himself in favour of the socialist objectives of the working class. The Party invites into its ranks every Hungarian worker who adopts these principles and who is not responsible for the criminal policy and mistakes of the Rakosi-clique. We expect everybody to join who, in the past, was deterred from service to socialism by the anti-national policy and criminal deeds of Rakosi and his followers. A

Kadar's "Flight"

On the way to the Embassy to telephone to Warsaw, we meet Krzyszlof.

"Have you heard?"

"What?"

"Kadar has fled."

We learn that he left during a meeting of militants of the new party, the meeting where Kadar had spoken in name of the organisational committee. He entered a car headed for a certain embassy. In its neighborhood, the two companions had gotten out and taken seats in another car that was waiting for them and started off immediately at top speed. From this moment, the trace of Kadar and Munnich was lost.

A few days ago Ferenc Munnich, a former ambassador to Moscow, had said: "The only thing that remains to be done is to die honorably." Apparently he has changed his mind. But what about Kadar whose flight literally followed a few minutes after he made his declaration, his public engagement in favor of the new line? Is it possible to deal the Party such a blow unconsciously?

Well, now a good man has stepped out of the game. He has had enough. But what if he is only beginning the game? ...

Viktor Woroszylski, Nowa Kultura (Warsaw),
9 December

Janos Kadar and "Schizophrenia"

The last time I saw him, Janos Kadar was hurrying along one of the corridors of the parliament building in Budapest. It was the middle of November 1956 ... Then I took him for granted. He fitted very well into the dismal landscape, the graveyard of our revolution. But writing now in London, I see him with the eyes of the normal world of human beings ...

Laszlo Rajk was his friend ... In the Spring of 1949, Mrs. Rajk gave birth to a son. In the Soviet-model name-giving ceremony Janos Kadar acted as godfather. A few weeks later Rajk was arrested ... Janos Kadar, the Minister of Interior, declared in speech after speech that Rajk was a despicable spy ... It was Janos Kadar who tricked his best friend and former idol into committing physical and moral suicide by confessing a long series of unlikely crimes at his public trial, promising Rajk that he would not be executed and would live somewhere in the East under a different name ...

In 1951 Janos Kadar himself was arrested ... He was treated with the utmost brutality. After his release he told the Central Committee how he was tortured ... Because he knew from personal experience that promises made to candidates for show trials are never kept, he did not sign the confessions demanded from him ... I saw Kadar after his ordeal. I was a witness at his own rigged trial. But I answered only in generalities ... After my testimony I turned to go out slowly to have a good look at him. The other three in the dock looked at me with friendly approving eyes. In Kadar's gaze there was only misunderstanding and wonder ...

Afterwards he spent nearly two years in solitary confinement. In 1954 Imre Nagy succeeded in releasing from concentration camps and prisons some ninety thousand political prisoners ... After his release from jail, Kadar visited Mrs. Rajk who was just freed after 5 years in prison herself ... He told her that he was the one who on Rakosi's instructions persuaded and tricked Laszlo Rajk ...

"Can you forgive me," Kadar asked.

"I forgive you. My husband would have been murdered anyway ... But can you forgive yourself? ... If you want to live as a decent person, you should inform entire Hungary about the secret of the Rajk trial ..." He left—and did nothing.

In 1956 it was obvious to the Central Committee and Politburo members that they had to sacrifice Rakosi if they wanted to save their own skins. They thought of Kadar as a likely successor. But Rakosi heard of it ... At the next session of the Central Committee in May he made a few remarks about the "unwise behavior of Comrade Kadar in joining some people who demand the punishment of those responsible for the Rajk trial." Rakosi gave a sign to one of his assistants, who brought in a magnetophone tape recording and played it back ... It was a shattering conversation: Janos Kadar persuading his best friend, Laszlo Rajk, not to be obstinate and to confess everything the police and the Russians wanted him to ...

Out of prison Kadar changed into the ultimate type of split personality, a kind of "controlled schizophrenia", a conscious mixture of delusion and cynicism, of obsession and opportunism. Many leading Communists suffer from this. They want and need power. But this naked primitive ambition is deeply unsatisfying unless they self-hypnotise themselves, at times, into that fine fervour of feeling, of fanatical faith which started them on their way. Often they lean on their former public selves, and even on private selves. They exercise double-think and double-speech, but their emotional life is ruled not by double but by treble or quadruple-feeling. In all its varieties, this constitutes the "communist neurosis" ...

On 31 October and 1 November Kadar took part in the work of the Revolutionary Government. But on Thursday evening between 8 and 9 p.m. Kadar and Munnich told their associates that they had to go to dinner, and sneaked out of the Parliament building, where all the Government offices were located during the revolution, and went over to the Soviet Army Command. Their driver returned with the news that they drove to the Soviet Embassy and there got into a waiting car. The driver had the impression that everything was arranged beforehand. I was told about this that very night by one of the most important leaders of the revolt who used to sleep at my flat during those days. He returned late at night very worried. He told me about it with the request to keep it secret. On Saturday afternoon I heard George Heltai, Imre Nagy's foreign policy adviser, who was with Nagy in Parliament the whole time between 26 October and 4 November, tell a friend in my presence about Kadar's disappearance on Thursday ...

By then, probably, Moscow decided to crush Hungarian independence and Kadar offered his services. The Soviet troops were then in a circle around Budapest. On the 1st of November, a few hours before he sneaked away, a seven-men preparatory committee was set up to found the new Communist party. The leader was Kadar. The other six men have since been arrested, deported, or executed ...

George Paloczi-Horvath, Der Monat (Berlin), March 1957

preparatory committee, whose members are Ferenc Donath, Janos Kadar, Sandor Kopacsi, Geza Losonczy, Gyorgy Lukacs, Imre Nagy, and Zoltan Szanto, has been formed to start organising the Party and supervise its operations for the time being ... The Party will publish a paper under the title *Nepzabadsag*.

Workers, peasants, and intellectuals! The new Party, the Hungarian Socialist Workers Party, is prepared to do its share in the fight to consolidate independence and democracy, and it is ready to fight for the socialist future of our people. It is clear to us that there has never before been so great a need for holding the democratic forces together. We turn to the newly formed democratic parties, and first of all to the other workers party, the Social Democratic Party, with a request to overcome the danger of a menacing counter-revolution and intervention from abroad by consolidating the Government. Our people have proven with blood their intention to support unflinchingly the Government's efforts aimed at the complete withdrawal of Soviet forces. We do not want to be dependent any longer. We do not want our country to become a battlefield. I am speaking to every honest Hungarian patriot. Let us join forces for the triumph of Hungarian independence and freedom!

[Signed] Janos Kadar, for the Preparatory Committee of the Hungarian Socialist Workers Party.

Free Radio Kossuth

Imre Nagy and the "Century-Old Dream" of Neutrality

Budapest

At this morning's session of the inner Cabinet of the Council of Ministers, it was decided that the leadership of the Foreign Ministry should be taken over by Imre Nagy, who will also continue in the office of Premier. This change has been made to implement the new direction of the foreign policy of the Hungarian People's Government. The most urgent tasks of this new line are immediate negotiations on the Warsaw Treaty, and the withdrawal of Soviet troops.   *Free Radio Kossuth*

To His Excellency the President of the Praesidium of the Supreme Soviet of the USSR, Moscow:

The Government of the Hungarian People's Republic wishes to undertake immediate negotiations concerning the withdrawal of Soviet troops from the entire territory of Hungary. With reference to the latest declaration of the USSR Government, according to which it is ready to negotiate with the Hungarian Government and with the other member States of the Warsaw Treaty about the withdrawal of Soviet troops from Hungary, the Hungarian Government invites the Soviet Government to designate a delegation, so that talks can begin as soon as possible. At the same time it requests the Soviet Government to designate the place and date for those negotiations.

[signed]   *Imre Nagy*
Hungarian News Agency

Imre Nagy, Chairman of the Council of Ministers, in charge of the Foreign Ministry, today asked Andropov, the Ambassador Extraordinary and Plenipotentiary, to see him. Nagy told Andropov that the Hungarian Government had received authoritative information about the entry into Hungarian territory of fresh Soviet military formations. He demanded that these Soviet military formations be withdrawn at once. He declared to the Soviet Ambassador that the Hungarian Government was giving immediate notice of termination of the Warsaw Treaty, and at the same time declared Hungary's neutrality. The Hungarian Government turned to the UN and sought the help of the four Great Powers in safeguarding the country's neutrality.

The Soviet Ambassador acknowledged the protest of the Hungarian Premier and Foreign Minister and the declaration made by him and promised to ask his Government to give an immediate reply.

In a verbal note the Premier had informed all the heads of diplomatic missions accredited to Budapest of the substance of his conversation with the Soviet Ambassador. At the same time he sent a telegram to the UN Secretary General, informing him of the events and of the decision of the Hungarian Government, and asking that the matter should be put on the agenda of the next UN General Assembly.   *Free Radio Kossuth*

People of Hungary: The Hungarian National Government, imbued with profound responsibility towards the Hungarian people and history, and giving expression to the undivided will of the Hungarian millions declares the neutrality of the Hungarian People's Republic. The Hungarian people, on the basis of independence and equality and in accordance with the spirit of the UN Charter, wishes to live in true friendship with its neighbours, the Soviet Union and all the peoples of the world.

The Hungarian people desire the consolidation and further development of the achievements of its national revolution without joining any power-blocs. The century-old dream of the Hungarian people is being fulfilled. The revolutionary struggle fought by the Hungarian people and heroes has at last carried the cause of freedom and in-dependence to victory. This heroic struggle has made possible the enforcement, in our people's inter-State relations, of its fundamental national interest: neutrality. We appeal to our neighbours, countries near and far, to respect the unalterable decision of our people.

It is indeed true that our people are as united in this decision as perhaps never before in their history. Working millions of Hungary: protect and strengthen—with revolutionary determina-tion, sacrificial work and the consolidation of order—our country, free, independent, demo-cratic and neutral Hungary.

Imre Nagy
Free Radio Kossuth

Breaking with the Warsaw Pact

Budapest

According to *Kis Ujsag*, the Polish Ambas-sador had discussions with members of the Hun-garian Cabinet on the evening of 1st November.

Hungarian News Agency

Budapest

To the official inquiry by Imre Nagy, Ambas-sador Andropov had replied that the rumors were unfounded and that no new troops had entered Hungary. A few hours later, the inquiry was repeated. The answer was: It is only a question of protecting the evacuation of Soviet citizens and wounded soldiers.

In the evening Imre Nagy called a press confer-ence. Only our [Polish] journalists guessed what it would be about. They knew of vain diplomatic efforts to save the situation, the ineffective steps taken. They knew that Nagy had exhausted all possibilities before resorting to the last desperate measure. The press conference was being delayed; western journalists vied with hypotheses about Nagy. Then a short declaration was read, an-nouncing that the Hungarian Government protest-ed against the movement of new Soviet divisions and demanded the withdrawal of all Soviet troops. At the same time, the Hungarian Government renounced the Warsaw treaty and proclaimed the neutrality of Hungary...

Viktor Woroszylski, Nowa Kultura (Warsaw),
2 December

Budapest

Parliament Square was silent and deserted, save for a few weeping women who crossed themselves before the candles under the walls of Parliament. A Hungarian officer approached smiling. I told him I wanted to speak to Nagy or Kadar... Two soldiers, carrying tommy-guns and grinning hope-fully, led me through a maze of rich Byzantine corridors. The incredible thing about Hungary's ten days of liberty was the fact that journalists from all over the world, dashing up and down the Budapest-Vienna road, were the unofficial am-bassadors of the Hungarian government to the outside world.

The two dirty soldiers, in their Russian uni-forms, walking down these golden passages, gave an impression of Russia 1917. After the atmo-sphere of the streets the warm waiting room was

soothing for the nerves, apart from the fact that armed patrols kept passing incongruously across the rich carpets. One of Nagy's assistants spoke fluent English... In the next room Nagy was arguing with Soviet Ambassador Andropov. The assistant told me that in half an hour's time Nagy intended to declare Hungary a neutral country and ask the UN for protection. "Russian troops are pouring in from the Ukraine. They are digging in round Budapest. I am very pessimistic. I hope I am safe in telling you this. But you could not communicate it anyway." There was a swift pass-ing of messages for relatives in the west, a hand-shake, and he advised me to leave Budapest at once...

Bruce Renton, New Statesman & Nation (London),
10 November

Budapest

Had it failed to take this position in the face of the sudden arrival of new Soviet units from the Ukraine and Rumania, the Imre Nagy Govern-ment would, according to its representatives, have remained isolated while the whole country would become involved in the conflagration of new struggles and guerilla war against the Soviet Army. Circles close to the Imre Nagy Govern-ment... say, nothing else can be done but to try in this way to prevent even more serious events tomorrow. They expect that in this way the situa-tion can still be regulated by peaceful means.

As we learned from reliable sources, the Soviet Government had firmly promised no new units would be sent to Hungary, in any case not without the agreement of the Hungarian Government. Mikoyan and Suslov were again here in Buda-pest... Yesterday, before returning to the Soviet Union, they promised that no reinforcements of Soviet troops would be sent and that, pursuant to the statement made by the Soviet Government two days ago, negotiations on a possible withdrawal of Hungary from the Warsaw Pact and on the withdrawal of Soviet troops from Hungary would start immediately between Budapest and Moscow and other interested countries.

We were reliably told that a reply did not arrive from Moscow until late in the afternoon and that the Hungarian Government decided to take this step only now, largely because Ambassador Andropov said that "only certain normal movements of troops were involved." However, we were told here that the Imre Nagy Government has authentic information that what is occurring on the frontiers of Hungary far exceeded "normal troop movements" and that a large number of tank, artillery, and infantry units were crossing the frontier without agreement by the Hungarian Government...

Djuka Julius, Politika (Belgrade), 2 November

Budapest

At close quarters in the Parliament building today, I was able to follow the development of the new phase in the revolutionary history of Hungary. I was in the ante-chamber of the hall, in which a Cabinet meeting of the Government had been called...

The meeting with the Soviet Ambassador was interrupted, and when it was resumed a little later in the afternoon, the Hungarian Government had received information according to which new Russian troops had invaded Hungary over the Rumanian border...

During long hours of agitated debate in the Cabinet chamber, the Hungarian Government was now disputing with the Soviet Ambassador on the question as to whether Hungary should remain in the Warsaw Pact or not. It seems that Moscow has given Hungary the ultimatum to cancel its renunciation of the Warsaw Pact.

But the Government did not waver in its decision, and in a dramatic radio speech tonight Prime Minister Imre Nagy informed the Hungarian population that the Budapest government had renounced the Warsaw Pact...

The meeting of the Government lasted until 21:00 hours tonight. In an atmosphere breathless with excitement officials announced the decision. Tears were in their eyes.

In the headquarters of General Maleter, officers said to me that it might now be a question of Hungary's existence. "Will the West help?" they asked. "Help us, help us!"

Adolph Rasten, Politiken (Copenhagen), 2 November

Budapest

At 11.30 last evening there was some cannonading in Budapest, apparently in the west, and a few bursts of machine-gun fire... The next development was Soviet occupation of the Budapest air field. It is now surrounded by 160 Soviet tanks...

The Government's announcement that the Russians were returning caused a panic in the streets of Budapest. People hurried home to join their families.

A diplomat who visited the Soviet Embassy reported that it was deserted by all of its staff except the Ambassador and a few secretaries, and that boxes and crates were stacked as if for removal. *John MacCormac, New York Times, 2 November*

The Decision to Intervene
London

As far as it is possible to judge—and my contention has been confirmed by several foreign observers in Moscow—it was the October 30 meeting of the Politbureau which decided on crushing the Hungarian revolution by means of force. It is true that the withdrawal of Russian troops from Budapest went on all the next day. Nevertheless, the influx of new Russian troops began on the same day, i.e. on October 31. It was not till November 1 that Nagy made his declaration on Hungary's neutrality, when Soviet tanks had already reached Szolnok. It was not Nagy's declaration of neutrality which caused the Soviet to intervene, it was the threat of intervention that caused Nagy to declare Hungary's neutrality.

In the early morning of November 1—i.e. about ten hours before Nagy declared Hungary's neutrality—Mikoyan arrived in Budapest. He was uninvited and unannounced. He had not come to negotiate with Nagy; he had come to act.

George Mikes, "The Hungarian Revolution" (London, 1957)

Nagy to Hammarskjold
New York

Premier Nagy, in his note to Mr. Hammarskjold, asked today that the Hungarian case be placed as an additional item on the agenda of the "forthcoming Assembly." It was not clear whether this referred to the regular General Assembly session opening Nov. 12, or to the emergency meeting tonight on the Suez crisis.

Whether the matter is taken up at the emergency or the regular Assembly session, United Nations spokesmen said tonight, acceptance would be conditional on a favorable vote by a two-thirds majority, or thirty-nine nations. Twenty votes in support of the Hungarian request are now assured with the arrival of more communications supporting the move made Sunday by Britain, France and the United States to bring the intervention of foreign troops in Hungary before the Security Council.

TEXT OF HUNGARIAN NOTE

Reliable reports have reached the Government of the Hungarian People's Republic that further Soviet units are entering into Hungary. The President of the Council of Ministers in his capacity of Minister for Foreign Affairs summoned (Yuri V.) Andropov, Ambassador Extraordinary and Plenipotentiary of the Soviet Union to Hungary, and expressed his strongest protest against the entry of further Soviet troops into Hungary. He demanded the instant and immediate withdrawal of these Soviet forces.

He informed the Soviet Ambassador that the Hungarian Government immediately repudiates the Warsaw Treaty and, at the same time, declares Hungary's neutrality and turns to the United Nations and requests the help of the four great powers in defending the country's neutrality. The Government of the Hungarian People's Republic made the declaration of neu-

trality on Nov. 1, 1956. Therefore I request Your Excellency promptly to put on the agenda of the forthcoming General Assembly of the United Nations the question of Hungary's neutrality and the defense of this neutrality by the four great powers.   *New York Times, 2 November*

Anguish and the "Mailed Fist"

Budapest

Budapest to-night was a city as intense and embattled as in the cruellest days of the fighting. But the tension and the battle was in men's minds. Those who had fought with arms in their hands— or indeed with bare hands—no longer faced the Soviet troops across the streets and bridges of this city, but faced them in their minds.

For the Russians are out of Budapest, but they are moving on Budapest again. And the question is not "to fight or not to fight"—for it would be an insult to the Hungarian people to-day to suggest that such a question could even occur to them—but how to avoid the extermination of the flower of the nation's youth if it does come to a fight.

Mr. Nagy, the Premier, has suggested a possible solution in his appeal to the United Nations and to the four Powers . . .

Reading History

> I do not suppose that these heroic Hungarians have much time for reading history. If they had, I cannot imagine anything much more apposite to their predicament than a study of the 1848 revolution in Berlin.
>
> On hearing the first rumbles of discontent, that enchanting but wayward monarch, Frederick William IV, summoned the national parliament and granted it the right of being summoned at regular intervals.
>
> Before the month was out, he had ordered his troops out of Berlin, saluted the revolutionary dead, babbled about his "dear Berliners", handed over royal sentry duties to a citizen guard, promised a constitution, ridden through the streets of Berlin wearing a revolutionary cockade, appointed a liberal ministry, and behaved generally in a highly uncharacteristic manner.
>
> Before the years was out, the liberal ministry had been dismissed, the parliament building closed, the constitution forgotten. Before the next ten years were out, the liberals had fled, and all was more or less as before.
>
> Moral: Promises exacted under duress will be kept only so long as duress is maintained.
>
> *Daily Telegraph (London), 1 November*

The details of Soviet troop movements, as disclosed by sources which are usually best informed on these matters, indicate that the military situation is very serious indeed. It is not only that Soviet troops have been observed pouring across the border at Zahony, at the frontier with Russia, or that large troop concentrations have been observed across the border. Strong Soviet columns were known to have reached at seven o'clock to-night the towns of Kissujszallas and Fuezesabony, this side of the river Tisza. Both towns are astride the railway lines to Budapest. And from Miskolc, a stronghold of the revolution in Northeast Hungary, came the news that up to 850 Soviet tanks had been sighted at various strategic points in the area.

Against this mailed fist of Soviet military might the Hungarians can now put up only their indomitable spirits. The anguish in their minds takes them into tortuous byways of speculation, which may well cause pain to those in England who have applauded and admired from afar this nation's courage and, as some might have said, recklessness. For many here believe, wrong as they might be, that in their hour of need, England has betrayed not only her own traditions but also the conscience of mankind by choosing this moment to fish in the troubled waters of Israeli-Egyptian enmity.

Budapest to-night is a city of light and darkness. The light is in the heart of its men and women. The darkness, the terrible darkness of rational fear, born of the determination to fight, is in their minds. Here and there little flashes of hope penetrate the darkness. Perhaps the Russians are bringing in the reinforcements not so that they may fight, but to help in the orderly dismantling of their bases, and to cover their withdrawal from the country against possible attacks by the insurgents? Perhaps.

Mr. Mikoyan, the Soviet Deputy Premier and party praesidium member, is still in town, and he is said to have met some of the Hungarian leaders again to-day. The meeting, as distinct from the tense atmosphere in which Mr. Nagy's message was passed to the Soviet Ambassador, is said to have been in friendly and even light-hearted terms. Perhaps it was. But anxiety still wrings the hearts of Hungarians.

Victor Zorza, Manchester Guardian, 2 November

"Harsh News" and the "Crisis in Moscow"

Moscow

How often have we not heard the hypocritical words of lying bourgeois propaganda concerning the Western Powers' alleged respect for the sovereign rights and independence of other nations and States! How many dirty charges have not been levelled against the Soviet Union in connection with events in Hungary! The Soviet Government has faithfully followed Lenin's principle of respect for other nations' sovereignty and it is far from the very thought of forcing its will on Hungary or of interfering in her national affairs ...

Radio Moscow (in Hungarian)

Moscow

The Soviet Union appeared tonight to be preparing its people for harsh news from Hungary.

The press and radio have given up their effort to picture events in that strife-torn country as being "under control".

An increasingly black picture is being drawn here for Soviet readers of Hungarian development ... Until yesterday reports from Budapest had been carried in most newspapers here under the heading "Failure of the Anti-Popular Movement in Hungary." Then They shifted to simply "Situation in Hungary" ...

New York Times, 2 November

London

The events in Poland and Hungary undoubtedly led to a grave political crisis in Moscow, by far the gravest since Stalin's death. That the Soviet ruling group was divided could be seen even during the Polish crisis, when the leaders of the three main factions came to Warsaw: Molotov and Kaganovich, the Stalinist diehards; Mikoyan, the "liberal"; and Khrushchev, the middle-of-the-roader. Khrushchev's first inclination was to side with the diehards and to use force or at least to threaten it.

Only when the threat failed and it turned out that the Polish upheaval did not after all imperil the Communist regime did Khrushchev reconcile himself to the new situation. The "liberals" in Moscow had won the day. But the Hungarian rising at once aggravated the division. Mikoyan, in Budapest, assisted by Gomulka's envoy on the spot and by Tito's appeals from across the frontier, negotiated for the withdrawal of Soviet troops, while the government in Moscow was preparing the declaration of October 30, in which it virtually committed itself to the withdrawal and openly confessed its errors in treating other countries as satellites. But Zhukov and Shepilov publicly stated on October 29 that Soviet troops would not be withdrawn before the Hungarian

revolt was suppressed. Were perhaps the chief of the Soviet armed forces and the Minister of Foreign Affairs airing their differences with other party leaders?

The Soviet Army, it may be assumed, could have acted with greater vigor and determination at the beginning of the rising, between October 24 and 27, if it had not been hampered by divided counsels in Moscow and contradictory orders. When the army feigned a withdrawal from Budapest on October 30, it probably did so under pressure from the "liberals" in the Presidium who hoped that this would enable Nagy to establish a national Communist regime that would, like Gomulka's regime, still remain aligned with the Soviet bloc. This hope was dashed two and three days later, when the disintegration of Hungarian Communism became evident and Nagy denounced the Warsaw Pact.

The "liberals" in Moscow had suffered a signal defeat. The die-hards of Stalinism and the army dictated policy, and they dictated renewed and more massive intervention. Probably no one in Moscow had the desire or the courage to defend Nagy, whose government was seen as due to be presently replaced by an openly anti-Communist regime—failing Soviet intervention. It was no longer Hungary but the whole of Russia's position in eastern Europe, in Germany, and in the world at large that was at stake. The collapse of Communism in Hungary was sure to increase a hundredfold the anti-Communist pressures everywhere. The Presidium was therefore probably unanimous in sanctioning the new Soviet intervention in Hungary ...

Isaac Deutscher, The Reporter (New York), 15 November

Panslavism

Panslavism is a movement which aims to undo what a thousand years of history have created; which cannot realize itself without sweeping from the map of Europe Hungary, Turkey, and a large part of Germany. Moreover, it must subjugate Europe in order to secure the stability of these results, if they are ever obtained. Panslavism is now, from a creed, turned into a political programme, with 800,000 bayonets to support it.

It leaves Europe only one alternative: submission to the Slavic yoke or destruction forever of the center of its offensive strength ...

MARX AND ENGELS, NEUE ODER-ZEITUNG (BRESLAU), 21 APRIL 1855

Quoted in Forum (Vienna), February 1957

Tension in Poland

Warsaw

Increasing tension in Poland, whose people have been following the events in Hungary closely, was aggravated today by reports of a new Soviet offensive against the Hungarian rebels. In the main cities of Poland, there was growing enthusiasm for campaigns to send aid to Hungary. There has been a new wave of meetings in the largest factories to express sympathy for the Hungarian rebels. In several cases speakers arose to demand immediate evacuation of Soviet troops from Poland.

There is a surface calm in Warsaw, but just beneath it lies a palpable nervousness.

The Polish radio tonight broadcast no news of Budapest after having provided full and speedy reports on developments in Hungary for the last week. Neither the re-entry of Soviet forces nor Hungarian Premier Imre Nagy's withdrawal of his country from the Warsaw Pact was announced here. But news of the events were spread by the many persons who had been listening regularly to Western broadcasts during the last two weeks of emergency.   *New York Times, 2 November*

Ending the Strike with "Unanimous Confidence"

Budapest

Compatriots! In the course of the armed revolutionary fighting every combatant heard with pride that they were supported by the workers' strike. However, as after every battle, the era of peaceful construction must now begin in order to consolidate the achievements of the revolution. The aim of the strike was to weaken the opponent. The present strike, however, weakens not the opponent but ourselves. We must ensure milk for our children, coal for our factories, and regular transport for our workers. Otherwise we shall lose what our revolutionary fighters have won at the cost of so great a sacrifice in blood. Hungarian workers! Strengthen free, independent, neutral Hungary, dear fatherland! Resume work!

Pal Maleter, First Deputy Minister of Defence

Free Radio Kossuth

Miners, power station and industrial communications workers, and intellectual workers! Delegates of the major factories in Budapest have had talks in the Parliament building with members of the Government about the withdrawal of Soviet troops, the country's present situation and getting life started again. The main points of the demands have been fulfilled by the Government. It has asked the UN General Assembly to examine the situation which has arisen in connection with the Soviet Union's military intervention. For its part, the Government has given notice of termination of the Warsaw Treaty. It declared Hungary's neutrality and asked that it be guaranteed by the four Great Powers, the Soviet Union, the USA, Britain and France. The Government has announced that it will make preparations without delay for the holding of free and secret elections.

The economic situation of the country has made it obvious to the delegates that the continuance of the strike would lead to the complete paralysis of the country's life and would undermine our revolutionary achievements. The delegates, however, have also seen that the Government would derive political strength if production were resumed. Since there is unanimous confidence in the Government, this is entirely justified ...

Imbued with deep responsibility towards our nation and revolution, we have decided to resume work immediately in all spheres of life and ask all the workers of the country to respond to our appeal by resuming work.

> On behalf of: Csepel Iron and Metal Works, MAVAG, Ganz Electrical Works, Ganz Wagon Factory, Electrical Works, Lang Machine Factory, Telephone Factory, Hungarian Optical Works, Aron Gabor Iron Foundry and Machine Factory, Heating Appliance Factory, Crane Factory, Lighting Technical Works, Motor Alloy Factory, Small Motor and Machine Factory, Hungarian Steel Works, Siemens Factory, X-Ray and Medical Instruments Factory, Transport Workers, and all workers in Districts Nos. 13, 14 and 4 of Budapest.

Free Radio Kossuth

The National Comittee of the Workers of County Baranya has unanimously decided to begin work in all the factories of the County on 2 November, in the interest of restoring normal living conditions ...   *Hungarian News Agency*

Face to Face

Budapest

The Soviet Embassy in Budapest has announced that airfields of the Hungarian Air Force have been surrounded by armoured forces of the Soviet Army in order to secure air transportation for members of the families of Soviet troops stationed in Hungary and to transport the wounded.

The Hungarian Air Force, in full complement, was ready to defend itself against overwhelming strength. However, fully realising its responsibilities, the Government prohibited the opening of fire. So the troops of the Air Force are now facing the Soviet forces present, without firing and with discipline. They await the departure of the Soviet troops ...

Free Radio Kossuth [23:30]

2 NOVEMBER

"A Great Stride in the Direction of Relaxation"

Budapest

Owing to the strike of workers at the Meteorological Institute no weather report is likely to be issued today. Weather reports will be resumed tomorrow ...

The Ganz works reports that 1,200 men showed up at the factory. The Revolutionary Committee thought it would be best to resume work because the country cannot afford to wait for Soviet troops to leave. The committee considered adequate the guarantee Nagy made last night. However, work could not be fully resumed, since it is not known what contracts remain in force now. Preparations are being made to resume production, and maintenance work is in progress.

Some damage has been done at the "Hungaria" workshop by light automatic fire, but otherwise only minor repairs were necessary.

Life in Budapest cannot start again because of the transport workers' strike ... At present the army is helping to keep buses moving on specific routes ...

The Central National Committee has appealed to county, rural district, village and town National Committees for an immediate resumption of work, since the Government has fulfilled the insurgent people's demands as far as it has been able to do so.

Free Radio Kossuth and BBC Summaries

The neutrality of Hungary, proclaimed by Imre Nagy yesterday, has met with approval. Through their newspapers, political parties and organisations are welcoming the efforts of Imre Nagy at this moment, stressing the unanimity and support of the whole country.

Today Hungary made a great stride in the direction of relaxation. This morning workers from the revolutionary committee of Csepel appealed to all workers of Hungary to end strikes and to return to work ... In many Budapest enterprises work already started today, while return to work throughout the country is expected tomorrow ...

Vlado Teslic, Borba (Belgrade), 3 November

Budapest

The Writers Association started a collection in an unusual manner. This morning huge signs were put up, at the most important points in Budapest, and genuine 1000 forint notes were stuck on them with the following text:

The purity of our revolution permits us to use this method of collection for the families of the martyrs.
THE HUNGARIAN WRITERS ASSOCIATION

Under the signs are placed empty ammunition boxes and these are being filled with money, with 100 and 10 forint notes, and coins. English pounds and Austrian schillings were also placed in the boxes. No one guards them ... In only a few hours this afternoon, the population of Budapest donated 110,000 forints for the families of the martyrs of the revolution. *Free Radio Kossuth*

A picture of the streets in Budapest: ... Traffic is lively. Restaurants and espressos are all open. The newspaper vendors shout about twenty different newspaper headlines ... There are more people in the streets than usual, for some of the workers are not yet back in their factories. The important thing is that more and more factories are starting work. One after the other, the great plants — Ganz, Lang, etc. — announce that they have started up again. Street-cars are already running ... There are still sporadic bits of bad news, such as Soviet troop movements. Then too, somewhere in Buda, there was shooting in the night. We do not know who was firing at whom ... *Free Radio Kossuth*

"Worthy of Confidence"

Miskolc

Statement by Joszef Kiss, Chairman of the National Council of Borsod-Abauj-Zemplen County: On 1 November a 28-member delegation of the Borsod County Workers Council submitted to Imre Nagy and Zoltan Tildy the demands of the people of Borsod County ...

This afternoon the delegation reported to the Borsod County Workers Council on its visit to Imre Nagy. Its main aim was to determine whether Nagy was really worthy of confidence. This could now be definitely affirmed in view of Nagy's declaration of neutrality to the UN and the stand he has taken toward the Soviet Union.

The Workers Council then gave the Government a vote of confidence. Since the Government had conceded the most important demands of the people of Borsod, and since a further strike could only be harmful to the country, the Workers Council unanimously decided to call off the strike. To carry on the strike would not compel the Soviets to quit, but they could be forced to do so if the people refused to give them food, fuel, and accomodations.

Since national unity is now so urgently necessary, the Workers Council resolved to put the formation of parties into the background.

Free Radio Miskolc

Radio Merger

Free Radio Petofi (Gyor) asked listeners to endorse an important step which it had taken. The station's equipment was only suitable for short periods of broadcasting, and had started to wear out. It had therefore been decided to merge with "our bigger brother", Free Radio Kossuth (Budapest). Free Radio Petofi would contribute "its greater revolutionary experience", and Free Radio Kossuth its better technical equipment. As from 3rd November the two stations would co-operate on all their wavelengths under the name of *"Free Radio Kossuth (Budapest) and Free Radio Petofi (Gyor)"* and would broadcast an indentical program, except for five hours in the day, when Free Petofi (Gyor) would broadcast a separate Transdanubian programme.

After this announcement the speaker thanked listeners and friends, especially the miners of Tatabanya, Dorog, and Varpalota, "whose hard fists hit the table when there were voices calling for disturbances" ...

At 22:00 Free Radio Kossuth (Budapest) announced itself as "Free Radio Kossuth Radio and Free Radio Petofi (Gyor)", adding; "This is the first time since the outbreak of the victorious revolution that the great Budapest transmitter and all the provincial transmitters are broadcasting the same programme ... Today we have taken a long step forward to national unity. The fact that the two radio stations, which were developing in opposite directions for some time, have found each other is an expression of this unity. Today Budapest and the provinces, the people and the Government, want the same things ..."

BBC Summary

A Yugoslav Looks for "Fascists ... Socialists"

Budapest

A friend of mine named Endre, a young communist, was talking to me, rather depressed, as we walked along trying to avoid broken glass and torn electric wires ... He complained, quite sincerely, in a comradely way, how the old policy—of Rakosi and Gero's Stalinist methods—had compromised communism and even socialism ... "In fact," he said, "you know, our people, those primitive ones, they do not know that socialism can and must be different, or that what we have had in the last twelve years was not socialism. The policy of oppression, police methods, lies, deception of the people and of oneself, bureaucracy, closing eyes and ears to the wishes and aspirations of the masses, all that was bound to mount up to the events now going on. It's no wonder that the old Party has been dissolved. As soon as peace is restored we've got to start from the very beginning, all over again. We have to gain the confidence of the masses through an honest, truly socialist policy, free of any compromises with old practices ..." He was firmly convinced that that was possible, that the people would support such efforts ... I trusted his words.

We came across a group of young people who were about to paste up slogans on a wall—no unusual scene these days. Watching them was a group anxious to read the slogans as soon as possible. They were typical moderately fascist slogans—a demand to appoint Cardinal Mindszenty Hungarian Prime Minister and to expel the Communists. Only a day or two before, these people might have been hanging Communists if they had a chance. But now they had no weapons. Probably they had been disarmed by the National Guard, which was already confiscating weapons, resolutely and without any compromise, from everybody without an appropriate permit issued by the National Guard Command or the Police ...

I raised the question about the Hungarian future and the aspirations of the Hungarian people. Either it was what Endre had told me or what was stated in fascist slogans—which, of course, called for the liquidation of socialist achievements. Why had the people really gone out into the streets on October 23 and later resorted to an armed struggle?

The next day I obtained the answer at Csepel. I went there to see ... whether they wanted to work, and if not why not, what their views were of the future, etc. They told me to go see Comrade Elek Nagy, the chairman of the Workers Council in Csepel, or the chairman of the Revolutionary Council, the provisional organ of popular authority in Csepel, an old worker called Iranic.

When I arrived both were at a meeting ... They were discussing the "return to work". As soon as they realized that we were Yugoslavs, they graciously let us come into a room where they were convening. They told us that they had decided to go back to work, to back the Government, because the strike was no longer of any use to the insurgents but was detrimental to the Government, which wanted to fulfil the fundamental demands of the workers and the masses. But, they kept saying that, in case they should feel that their requests were being ignored, especially their demand for an energetic repudiation of the old policy and the establishment of full national independence, they would immediately go on strike again.

This is what I wrote in my notebook about this conversation ... "We are not going to give up the achievements of that struggle ... Our Workers' Council has taken management of the factory in its own hands ... The Government should free us from the old Stalinist, narrow-minded, stubborn bureaucrats in the factory, whose work was so harmful ... We are nobody's 'reserve'. We refuse to join any party for now. We are against anarchy. Order and security come first now. Then we'll settle other questions ... There is no use of being granted rights and demands little by little. What we want is to see them all fulfilled without exception ... There has been enough terror exercised in the name of socialism! We want a workers' democracy ... Negotiations should be started with the Soviet Government as soon as possible ... The Government should take most energetic steps for eliminating fascists who have begun to raise their heads in a menacing way ... We refuse to give our factories to anyone, they belong to us ..."

There was no opposition to socialism here. On the contrary. It means as far as popular aspirations were concerned, that Endre, and not the fascists, had been right. For, what had the Rightists been able to offer the workers? ... A rope for hanging progressive people? Horthy and Szalasi? A new terror? The restoration of capitalism? This is what these people have begun to disapprove of ... They want Workers Councils, democratic socialism. In fact, they do not want the old policy pursued by Rakosi, but—for God's sake—I myself would not favour that, I would fight against that, if I happend to be a citizen of Csepel ...

Djuka Julius, Politika (Belgrade), 13 November

The Question of "White Terror"

Moscow

In a dispatch from Budapest, *Politika* notes that the dreadful atrocities and violence committed against Communists by the reactionaries are not stopping in Budapest. The correspondent writes that such acts still continue and that it is a bad sign that the extreme right-wing elements have raised their heads and believe that a favourable time has come for their activities. As is known, during the past few days many bestial murders of Communists have taken place. Further, the paper points out that there are many signs pointing to a sharp intensification of fascist activities ...

Tass, 3 November

Budapest

It is far safer than a few days ago, even than yesterday. National Guard patrols are maintaining order in the Hungarian capital together with military and police units. The Revolutionary Councils, the only practical organs of authority, fully support the Government, and in the provinces they are particularly active establishing order. However, there are still a considerable number of armed groups belonging to none of the parties ... Today National Guard patrols disarmed many people ... All this has helped restore a certain, partial feeling of security among the citizens of Budapest.

Unfortunately all this does not mean that terrible individual incidents of savage violence ceased ... During these last days, there have been many cases of arbitrary killings of Communists, but such cases are less frequent now. We learned that a few people lost their lives yesterday because they wore a certain kind of brown shoes. It is said that the AVO previously distributed such shoes to its members; but they could also be bought elsewhere, we were told ...

Djuka Julius, Politika (Belgrade), 3 November

Moscow

Radio Budapest has broadcast an order by the Hungarian Ministry of the Interior to members of the former Security Service instructing them to surrender to the authorities. The order says that if they do not do so their safety can no longer be guaranteed. The press quotes reports which it is difficult to describe otherwise than as propaganda for the lynching and violence perpetrated by reactionary gangs. One of the latest issues of the newspaper *"Magyar Honved"* contains particularly numerous "graphic" descriptions of lynchings and acts of violence against army men and other workers. The newspaper tries to represent these acts of violence as "popular judgement" ...

Radio Moscow, 3 November

Prague

Rude Pravo today carries another account of the crimes committed by the counter-revolution in Hungary. Istvan Habulin, a Hungarian lieutenant, told a *Rude Pravo* correspondent how the counter-revolutionaries had shot four of his companions and had begun to torture a fifth, who was later taken to hospital unconscious. On the following day, however, he was dragged out of hospital, and a few minutes later his body was swinging from a pole near the church. Another wounded lieutenant, Denes, also in hospital, met the same fate; the counter-revolutionaries tied him up in bandages and dragged him down the stairs until he died in terrible pain.

Such crimes were committed by Horthy officers, by the former district judges and by the landlords, among whom was Szigeti, a Deputy representing the former Agrarian Party. Joszef Szabo, a Communist, described the atrocities committed by the counter-revolutionaries in the town of Rajka, where a list of 76 persons, who were not allowed to leave their homes, was drawn up. On Sunday, 4 November, they were all to be hanged in front of the church so that people leaving Mass could see them. The timely arrival of Soviet soldiers prevented this mass murder. Most of the criminals fled westwards to Austria ...

Czechoslovak Telegraph Service, 12 November

A Soviet Tourist in Budapest

Moscow

We arrived in Hungary on 19 October with other Soviet tourists. We spent four days touring this beautiful country and were everywhere given a most cordial and hearty welcome. On Tuesday, 23 October, on our way to a theatre we saw crowds of people in the streets of Budapest. They were lined up in ranks and carried placards, many of which bore the inscription "Long live Hungary!" ... The students together with members of the intelligentsia and workers were demanding the redress of errors and omissions committed by the Hungarian Government. They were legitimate demands ...

On that first evening I saw from the hotel in which we were staying a man with a rifle appear in the deserted street. He took up a position in one of the drives and, taking careful aim, began shooting out the street lamps. The lamps went out one by one and darkness enveloped the street. What prompted the marksman to do this? Just hooliganism? Hardly. I think he was one of the bright sparks of the reactionary underground who wanted to create confusion and chaos in the city. Quite soon afterwards there were flashes of gunfire and sounds of battle and we saw wrecked and burning buildings in the streets of Budapest, overturned tram-cars and other vehicles. Firing would die down and then flare up again. Hostile elements were aiming at paralysing the city's life but the workers of Budapest were repelling the rebels. Detachments of armed workers tried to restore order in the streets and prevent looting. In many places, including the area around our hotel, workers' patrols were posted ...

One member of our hotel staff, a middle-aged man with grey hair, told us: "Our workers cannot have had a hand in this looting and rioting. It is fascism raising its head." And that is what it was. The counter-revolutionary underground was in action in Budapest. Fascist reactionary elements had arrived there from abroad. The hostile venture was gathering momentum and the Hungarian Government asked the USSR Government for aid. In response to this request Soviet military units stationed in Hungary under the Warsaw Treaty entered Budapest to help to restore order. The overwhelming majority of Hungarians welcomed this move in the hope that life in the city would quickly return to normal. I myself saw in one street how the people were welcoming the Soviet tanks.

One Hungarian, a member of the hotel staff, described the following incident to us. Firemen-volunteers, absolutely unarmed, were putting out a fire in one of the public buildings. Suddenly, from a small house opposite, shots were fired by fascist louts who opened fire on the unarmed firemen. Several of them fell. Our tank was stationed in the street. The tankmen immediately aimed their gun at the house where the bandits were entrenched. This was sufficient to make them run into a side street. Several firemen ran up to the tank and shook hands with the tankmen. This episode gives a good testimony of the attitude of the Hungarians towards the Soviet troops. However, reaction did not cease its activities. When we walked along some of the streets we saw that the walls of houses were thickly covered with counter-revolutionary posters ...

When Soviet troops began withdrawing from Budapest an unbridled White Terror started in the Hungarian capital. We Soviet tourists recall this time with horror. It is difficult to describe the chaos which reigned in the city where public buildings were destroyed, shops looted, and where crowds of armed bandits, obviously fascists, walked along the streets committing bestial murders in broad daylight. I shall never forget what I saw with my own eyes. I think it was on 30 or 31 October. A man in a sports suit walked along the Lenin Boulevard. He might have been one of those who tried to restore order in the city. Several armed ruffians wearing counter-revolutionary tricolours ran up to him. A horrible inhuman cry was heard. A whole crowd of bandits appeared from somewhere. I was unable to see what they were doing with their victim, but in a few minutes he was hanging on a nearby tree with an eye gouged out and his face slashed with knives.

Some time ago I read how the fascists in Germany burnt progressive literature on bonfires. We saw similar things ... A group of some hooligans looted and set fire to the House of Books. Thousands and thousands of books were smouldering in the muddy street. We were there, witnesses of this barbarity. The works of Chekhov, Shakespeare, Tolstoi, Pushkin, and other famous authors were lying in the mud, black smoke rising. We saw an old man who lifted a few books, then carefully wiped the mud with his sleeve, pressed them to his breast and walked slowly away. Many people did the same.

In the Hotel "Peace" the atmosphere in those days was extremely tense. The counter-revolutionaries tore the red star from the front of the hotel and trod it underfoot on the pavement. We were told that the Hotel "Peace" from now on would be called Hotel "Britannia". The person who told us about it looked around and added quietly: "It doesn't matter. It will only be temporary."

More than once we were witnesses of acts which manifested the friendly attitude of the Hungarians towards the Soviet people. This friendly attitude was felt by us Soviet people, when we were leaving Budapest ... In small groups of two or three people we made our way along the devastated streets towards the Danube in order to board a Red Cross steamer. We were accompanied by a worker ... a young girl. She led us from one cross-road to another, fearlessly seeking the safest way. At the pier we heartily embraced her. She said: "Someone in the West wants us to pull their chestnuts out of the fire. Don't believe them, dear friends. We Hungarians are for socialism and we are with you." When we were in Czechoslovakia on our way home, we learned that the counter-revolution in Hungary was routed and that life was becoming normal in the country. Now we are at home in Moscow.

We shall not forget that Hungarian girl who said that the Hungarians were for socialism and that they were with us.

E. M. Bazarina, Radio Moscow, 10 November

"Reactionary"
London

The strikers and freedom fighters were called reactionaries, counter-revolutionaries and Fascists. It is true that in the last days of October some people dragged out their hidden Horthyite uniforms and paraded in them. But those uniforms were seen, not as Horthy-ite, but as Hungarian, as opposed to the Russian fancy-dress Hungarian soldiers had been forced to wear in the last few days. No doubt, reactionary parties smelling strongly of a disreputable past were also reformed in the short period of the victorious revolution. It is a debatable point whether even the most reactionary of these parties was quite so reactionary, retrograde, imperialist and oppressive as the Communist Party. ...

George Mikes, "The Hungarian Revolution" (London, 1957)

"How Rough A Justice ..."
Moscow

Not unnaturally, it was the torture and murder of Communists during the days when power slipped into the streets in Hungary that made the strongest impression in party circles here; and in the new atmosphere of frankness in which people bare their fears and anxieties as well as their hopes and aspirations you can hear many attempts to draw the lesson from the Hungarian events and apply them to the Soviet Union. Ever since the 20th Congress, minds have been opening to take in an idea of the enormity of the mistakes made in the past and of the cost in human suffering, in material and spiritual impoverishment. Discipline, self-deception, self-interest and often sheer ignorance of the truth induced a sort of callousness to the sufferings of others during Stalin's days, but now the leaders themselves are harping on the theme of past mistakes and in every walk of life the surviving victims of those "mistakes" are back from Siberia to tell their horrifying stories. The photographs of Communists hanging head downwards from Budapest lamp-posts have brought home to people here how rough a justice awaits those who leave the correction of "mistakes" too late. Are we going fast enough ourselves? That is a question that many responsible Communists are asking now.

Letter to Kingsley Martin, "from a friend long resident in Moscow," New Statesman & Nation (London), 1 December

"Preserving Revolutionary Purity"

Budapest

The Government of the Hungarian People's Republic calls on members of the State Security Authority and on the security organs of the Interior to report without delay and in their own interests to No. 25 Marko Street, where they will be screened by a screening committee. Those who are not responsible for illegal acts will be free to go home as soon as their case has been examined. Those who are responsible for such acts will be called to account for them in an independent court of law ...   *Free Radio Kossuth*

Nepszava reported that the Social Democratic Party leadership had discussed on 1 November the "regrettable reports it has received concerning the 'popular justice' which is still being practised in several areas." Protesting against summary executions the paper said that the condemnation and punishment of criminals was a task of independent Hungarian courts of justice. The police could detain suspicious elements without resorting to any atrocity. The paper added: "Our revolution will benefit the workers only to the extent to which it proves our humanity, justice and honesty."   *Hungarian News Agency*

...As to the lynchings in Republic Square, it is worth recalling that the mob was eventually driven off by tanks under the Hungarian flag: a *Paris-Match* photographer, bravely getting pictures, was among those fatally wounded by their fire. On the following morning I happened myself to be talking to General Istvan Kovacs (deputy of the newly appointed General Maleter) at the Ministry of Defence, when he was informed by telephone that another crowd was intent on lynching suspected AVH men (political policemen): I heard him give sharp orders for an army unit to intervene and arrest the suspected men ...

Basil Davidson, New Statesman & Nation (London),
8 December

During dinner, Roman tells of his visit today to the camp in which the AVH men are locked up. He spoke to several of them. They are calm and hold absolutely no grudge against the insurgents. On the contrary, more than one owes them his life ... We learned that in the past 24 hours no summary executions took place in Budapest ...

Viktor Woroszylski, Nowa Kultura (Warsaw), 9 December

As one who was not only a witness of, but who also played an active part in, the Hungarian revolution, I would like to reply to some (inaccurate) statements ...

The truth is that the book burning was confined to two book shops, one of which was the "Horizon" book-shop, selling Russian language publications, and the other "Szikra", selling Communist Party publications. The symbolic meaning of this demonstration was identical with the pulling down of the Stalin monument: they expressed the determination of the fight against spiritual oppression inside the country, and against military oppression from outside. These two motives continued to be apparent throughout, culminating in the logical demand for national self-determination. To attempt to assess these as symptoms of extreme nationalism seems to me rather strange. It is even more strange if one wants to reinforce this allegation by citing the demand that Hungarian uranium should be sold to the West and not to the East. The simple truth is that what we asked for was that our uranium should be sold for money ...

I would like to stress that nowhere in Hungary did I see the reappearance of uniforms of the pre-1945 Horthy army. What is even more important, however is the fact that the spirit of the pre-1945 epoch never reappeared ...

Letter of L. H. (Hungarian Revolutionary Council of University
Students), New Statesman & Nation (London), 8 December

A police captain from Cegled begged us to take him with us in the Yugoslav sleeping-car. He was frightened because he still had the five-pointed star on his cap. But he was not so frightened as to take off the badge before receiving strict orders. We gave him Yugoslav brandy and he began to talk. His family was in Budapest, and his wife had a weak heart. He himself was on an official trip.

"Well, then, this should make it easier for you," I said to him rather ruthlessly. "You don't have to make up your mind yet. You can wait to see how things develop."

Making a desparate gesture, he took out of his pocket a photo of his wife and child. "And they?" he asked. "If somebody should break into my flat and kill them? They know that I am a policeman, although this is a profession just like any other. You have police too, don't you?"

He calmed down later on. In spite of the revolution and in spite of the fact that he was far away from home, he was clean-shaven; his hair was grey; his face was not very intelligent, but good-natured.

"I am a Hungarian!" he said. "I am no longer afraid for my own life when so many lives have been lost. But I should like to know at least that I would die on the side of the right people. On

Truth and Propaganda

The argument in favour of Soviet intervention is that there was "White Terror" raging in Hungary, and that for the Soviet Union to have refused to intervene would have been "inhuman." Leaving aside the still uncertain question of whether anyone ever did appeal to the Soviet Union to intervene, let us make quite sure what White Terror is. Just as Red Terror is the organised, systematic repression by a proletarian dictatorship of its counter-revolutionary opponents, so White Terror is the organised, systematic repression by a bourgeois dictatorship of its revolutionary opponents.

Heaven help those ... who call the state of affairs in Hungary on November 1—3 "White Terror" if they ever come face to face with real White Terror. In ten days the Versailles army which suppressed the Paris Commune of 1871 slaughtered between 20,000 and 30,000 men, women and children, either in battle or in cold blood, amid terrible scenes of cruelty and suffering. "The ground is paved with their corpses," gloated Thiers. Another 20,000 were transported and 7,800 sent to the coastal fortresses. That was White Terror. Thousands of Communists and Jews were tortured and murdered after the suppression of the Hungarian Soviet Republic of 1919, and hideous atrocities took place at Orgavány and Siófok. That was White Terror. In 1927 Chiang Kai-shek massacred 5,000 organised workers in Shanghai. That was White Terror. From the advent of Hitler to the defeat of fascist Germany untold millions of Communists, Socialists, trade unionists, Jews and Christians were murdered. That was White Terror.

It is perfectly true that a section of the population of Budapest, outraged to the pitch of madness by the crimes of the secret police, was seized with a lust to exterminate Communists. It is true that the innocent suffered as well as the guilty. This is a painful and distressing fact. But to describe the murder of a number of Communists (which all observers agree was confined to Budapest) as "White Terror" necessitating Soviet intervention is to describe events in Hungary in a one-sided, propagandist way. How many innocent Communists were murdered in Budapest? Twenty? Fifty? I do not know. But certainly fewer—far, far fewer—then the number of A.V.H.men who were lynched. At the "Agony of Hungary" exhibition in London, and in all the hundreds of photo-graphs I have seen, there was not a single one showing a lynched Communist. But there were many showing lynched A.V.H.-men in their uniforms. There was one sequence showing a woman in civilian clothes being molested by a crowd, who accused her of being an A.V.H. spy. The caption stated that the crowd let her go. (On November 14 the Daily Worker published under the head-line "The White Terror in Hungary" a photograph of "the body of a lynched Communist Party member in one of the wrecked Budapest Party offices." Another photograph of the same corpse was in the paper's possession, but was not used, showing clearly that the lynched man wore an A.V.H.uniform.)

Now the only circumstantial evidence for the murder of Communists is that put forward by André Stil in an article translated in World News of November 24. Stil arrived in Budapest on November 12, nine days after the second Soviet intervention. His article was published in Humanité on November 19. Even bearing in mind the assertion of Coutts and others I spoke to that forty of those killed in the Budapest Party headquarters were A.V.H.men, it is impossible to find Stil's account of the treatment of the seven Communists whom he names anything but convincing and horrible. Yet Stil is obviously performing the disagreeable task of a propagandist making the most of a small number of atrocities. His need to have the attack on the Party headquarters begin on October 30 makes him antedate the Soviet withdrawal from Budapest by three days; he describes "the vandals attacking the liberation monument built upon the Gellért Hill," whereas in fact the main figure was not attacked; and, worst of all, he mentions the A.V.H. and its crimes in the following curious and oblique way: "... the attack was directed to the members of a secret police about whom the most unlikely stories were being told." ... The truth about the "White Terror" has been told by Bruce Renton: "In the provinces, only the A.V.H. was physically attacked ... I had seen no counter-revolutionaries. I had seen the political prisoners liberated ... I had seen the executioners executed in the fury of the people's revenge ... But there was no 'White Terror.' The Communists walked free, the secret police were hanging by their boots. Where then was this counter-revolution, this 'White Terror'?" ...

Peter Freyer, "Hungarian Tragedy" (London, 1956)

which side should I die? This is what you should tell me!"

Who could assume responsibility to tell him a thing like that at such a moment? We told him that he was a Hungarian and that he would have to decide for himself. I know we didn't help him much, but we were unable to see things clearly ourselves. The slogans were so contradictory ...

Ivan Ivanji, Mladost (Belgrade), 14 November

Budapest

An Appeal of the National Council, the Command of The United Armed Forces, and The Revolutionary Council of the Chief Attorney's Office:

The Hungarian Revolution was fought by the people rising in a unity hitherto unknown. The heroism, level-headedness, and political maturity of our people has won the admiration of the nations of the world. In order to preserve the purity of the revolution, freedom, citizens' rights, and, in order to assure a humane and completely legal order, an appeal is now made to members of the National Guard and the citizens of our liberated country: continue to preserve the revolutionary purity of our revolution!

Crimes against the state have to be punished. However, this calling-to-account should be left to the organs of legal jurisdiction precisely in order to preserve the revolutionary purity of our fight. Revolutionary Councils formed in the law offices and courts, freed from the agents of the Rakosi-Gero clique, guarantee that court procedures will be started without delay in the legal manner and in public view of all the jealously guarded achievements of the revolution. The culprits will get the punishment they deserve. Therefore, we call on the revolutionary organs of the country to take determined measures against every kind of arbitrariness that might arise. The culprits should be handed over to the local military or legal authorities, who will see to it that criminals are called to account as soon as possible with full adherence to the laws ...

Free Radio Kossuth

Budapest

To excuse the repression of a western-type democracy, the Russians resorted to the story of the "white terror" and "Fascist counter-revolution". They promoted a Budapest street-fighter, Josef Dudasz, to the role of Fascist-Trotskyite leader of the counter-revolution, although outside of Budapest, and in some parts of Budapest itself, nobody had ever heard of this man ...

No greater evidence could be found that this was no "white" revolution than the message of Hungarian Jewry, signed by the Budapest Board of Rabbis, and broadcast by Radio Budapest on November 2.

Hungarian Jewry enthusiastically salutes the achievements of the revolution, pays reverent homage to the heroes, and identifies itself with the free and independent homeland. We appeal to Jewish organizations abroad to give rapid and effective material help to the sorely tried Hungarian people.

The Socialist leader, Anna Kethly, in the first issue of the revived party organ, *Nepszava*, described the nature of the revolution:

The Social Democrat party ... with its own bare hands, has won its chance of living, and it has won this from a regime which called itself a popular democracy, but which in form and essence was neither popular nor democratic. We greet with profound respect the heroes who have made possible this re-birth of the party, thousands of young intellectuals and workers who have fought, starving and in rags, spurred on by the idea of a free and independent Hungary.

At the same time she issued a warning.

Freed from prison, let us not allow the country to become a prison of another colour. Let us watch over the factories, mines, and land, which must remain in the hands of the people.

Josef Dudasz himself — according to Moscow, he was the arch counter-revolutionary — stated in an interview with the Italian *Epoca* on the eve of the Russian attack:

The Communists will be admitted to the elections. We are people with our feet on the ground. We know that Russia is the world's second power, and that this country of 200 million borders on our country of 9 millions ... We want no Danubian Korea. The leaders of the revolutionary forces must have faith in Nagy, even if the people have lost it. This is for the good of the country.

This indeed was a strange "counter-revolution" — in which the leader of the "white terror" called on the people to put their trust in a Communist prime minister.

Bruce Renton, New Statesman & Nation (London),
17 November

"The News on the Walls"

Budapest

The walls of Belvaros [in the centre of Budapest] are plastered with posters, tracts, newspapers, expressing the wishes, the will, the demands of the people. Among hundreds of tracts I found only two serving false propaganda.

The first is in verse; I have forgotten the title but I do remember one line: "And Miklos appeared on a white horse ..." The other is a remark jotted down by some one on the university students' newspaper. A black line is drawn around one article saying that industry and the land will remain the property of the Hungarian people.

Added was the following remark: "Do not read this article. It is a lie."

For the first time in many years opinion may be expressed freely. You can think out loud, publish your opinion in newspapers, etc. Well, I, too, will take advantage of this freedom.

Since 23 October, I have come to realize, a hundred, a thousand times, the true grandeur of our people, of our youth, their strength and their boundless thirst for justice. I admire the keenness of their judgment. Freedom we want, and I believe in the ultimate victory which will give us our freedom. Yes, I believe in freedom, but not the kind that we would gain through people like Miklos Horthy, big landowners and capitalists.

Our struggle is a truly great one. Our flags bear the inscriptions: *Liberty, Independence*. The ruins of our past lie behind us, and we will let no one soil *our* October revolution. We won't stand for a one-party tyranny any longer. We reject Russian oppression; nor do we want big landowners, industrialists, or Miklos Horthys; and still less do we want foreign armies.

Thirsting for liberty, the people of our beautiful country are quite capable of working out their own salvation. The parties which will assume the responsibility of our future are now being formed and are gaining in strength. With them we will forge our own destiny, that of the Hungarian people.

That is how one should interpret the news appearing on our walls.

Magyar Ifjusag (Hungarian Youth, Budapest), 2 November

Kovacs: "With Sincere Pleasure"

Budapest

Dear listeners ... Wednesday, at midnight, Minister of State Bela Kovacs made the following statement to Free Radio Kossuth:

Approximately two or three hours ago I joined the work of the National Government. In this historic situation, I consider it necessary to tell my people, without delay, that our government truly, and with full responsibility, represents the interests of our country. I declare with sincere pleasure that the government has been making, and continues to make all possible efforts for the settlement of our international relations, for the further development, maintenance and strengthening of the present friendly relations. In order to solve the difficult foreign political tasks we must establish national unity, peace and order in our country. Further, it is necessary and of vital importance that, since our peasantry is working in the fields for our next year's bread, industrial workers should also begin production without delay. ...

Free Radio Kossuth

Mindszenty's Press Conference

Budapest

Joseph Cardinal Mindszenty appealed to the West today for political support in Hungary's fight against Soviet domination. He said his appeal was addressed especially to the "great powers" in the West, presumably the United States, Britain and France. He asked also for gifts to relieve the suffering here.

Speaking in German in a strong vibrant voice, the Cardinal told correspondents who crowded his small, almost bare study that "the whole Hungarian people wish and demand that Russian troops leave Hungarian territory." "The people," he added, "want to work for themselves and for the life of the nation."...

The Cardinal said he had received a telegram of blessings from Pope Pius. He said the telegram had contained nothing else. This was taken to mean that he had no political instructions from the Vatican.

As he did just after his release, he avoided a direct answer to the question whether he would take part in a government. He answered that he had not had time to get the full picture of political conditions in Hungary.

Henry Giniger, New York Times, 3 November

Cardinal Mindszenty resumed his role as leader of Hungary's Roman Catholics by receiving [1 November] a delegation headed by Vice-Premier Zoltan Tildy, one of two non-Communists in the Imre Nagy Cabinet. Informed sources said Cardinal Mindszenty told the delegation that he wants the formation of a Christian Democratic party with a voice in the Cabinet and cannot consider supporting the present regime unless this is accomplished. These sources said the Cardinal envisages a party "on the Adenauer line," referring to the West German CDU. But they added that the Hungarian party should embrace "all Christians," including the nation's Protestant Lutheran population. The sources said they believe Cardinal Mindszenty is willing to accept a coalition government including Hungary's "Tito Communists."...

United Press, 3 November

Replying to someone who asked him if he was confident about the future of Hungary, the Cardinal said, after a brief pause "Naturally." The press conference was suddenly interrupted by the Cardinal himself, when a Hungarian journalist asked him to comment on the report that certain political groups wanted to make a Prime Minister of him. The Cardinal stiffened and said in a cold tone: "I am the Primate." After which he left the room.

Although the conference had been called on his initiative, the Cardinal sometimes seemed ill at ease. He avoided certain questions nicely by saying, among other things, "I must ask you kindly to leave me some peace.". . .

But the obvious irritation in which he left us, after the so controversial question of his eventually succeeding to power, shows that he has no intentions at all along those lines. . . .

Giorgio Bontempi, Il Paese (Rome), 3 November

Meeting Joszef Dudas

Budapest

I cross the square where, during the first days of the revolution, the Statue of Stalin was pulled down from its pedestal. More precisely, it was cut down at knee-level with an acetylene lamp. This produced a unique monument: a pair of enormous boots on an elevated platform. From the right boot a straw tuft was frivolously sticking out, inviting a new volunteer to lace the shoes . . .

Tall, colorful, black-haired, a large expressive but repulsive face, with mildly prominent cheek bones. A Tyrolean hat, a coat thrown around his shoulders like a phantasy cape, a gun at the belt, black trousers. He enters the room, surrounded by his following . . .

We ask Dudas to define the movement which he represents. Without much thinking he throws four adjectives at us: "national – revolutionary – democratic – socialist . . . !"

The program of the movement is as follows: The Russians must leave Hungary immediately. The Government must unite with the revolutionary forces, with the Workers, Peasants, and Soldiers Councils, as well as with the centers representing the people. The government should be supplemented with the help of representatives of the traditional democratic parties. But one would not tolerate rightist groupings or Fascists. "It is necessary to preserve socialism at the same time as guaranteeing all citizens freedom of conscience. All economic dogmas should be rejected."

"As our point of departure," he concluded, "we take the conditions of life, social needs, the interests of the workers and peasants, and at the same time we shall adhere to the platform of national unity."

All this was sufficiently general to warrant approval . . . We tried to corner him by asking about his attitude toward existing political parties and whether he intends to found a new party.

"It is now a question of consolidating the gains the revolution has made up to the present day. Later, if the situation develops favorably, I shall probably follow one of the existing parties which pursue our objectives."

"Which party do you feel closest to?"

"Today not one has worked out an economic program. As far as essential political questions are concerned, there is agreement among all the democratic parties, and they are all equally close to me."

"Do you support the present government?"

"Only in part. I could only fully support a coalition government of Imre Nagy, Janos Kadar, Bela Kovacs, Anna Kethly, Sandor Kiss — as well as a representative of the National Revolutionary Committee."

It is not difficult to guess who that representative would be. In the course of the conversation, one feels ever more clearly that, apart from the program — which after all has probably been outlined in a rather sincere way — Joszef Dudas nurtures an uncommon personal ambition. Toward the end of the conversation this ambition reveals itself fully:

"Our most urgent tasks are to form a provisional coalition Government, to establish with the Russians the date for the withdrawal of their troops from Hungary, to fix the date of free, general, and secret elections, to re-establish peace and order in the country. In connection with all these problems I established contact with Moscow last night, and I suggested joint measures to straighten out the situation. I also suggested a government of the kind I just mentioned."

I don't know whether what I just heard had been mere bluff, or whether there was any real basis to it. In any case Dudas' ambitions are not of the most modest. But who is this chief of the National Revolutionary Committee, who publishes his own paper, surrounds himself with an entourage worthy of an ataman, who boasts of a "contact with Moscow" and who, in an interview accorded Polish journalists, proclaims his desire to enter the Hungarian government? Is this really "a Fascist"? What does it all add up to? Is he simply the leader of a gang, an adventurer, a "strong man" pushing for personal popularity and power? And if this is the case — how important is the danger of Dudas threatening the popular revolution? How many more Dudases may there be in the country? . . .

Viktor Woroszylski, Nowa Kultura (Warsaw), 2 December

Budapest

Joszef Dudas can't speak to me; he is suffering from laryngitis, and was being treated by a doctor who speaks French. My four questions are answered with a pencil:

Q: How strong do you estimate the Soviet forces that have entered Hungary?

A: About 500 to 900 tanks have been inundating our territory for the last 24 hours, despite our proclamation of neutrality.

Q: Who is the head of the Hungarian army?

A: Cooperation exists between the Hungarian armed forces under the command of a revolutionary committee. If necessary, the Government will designate a military chief.

Q: What are the relations between the Nagy Government and other committees?

A: The government supports our action.

Q: What military measures have you taken?

A: Hungarian tank units and artillery regiments are moving from the position of Lake Balaton towards Budapest in order to prepare the defense of the city ...

Between 6 and 6:30 p.m. a fight broke out between partisans of Joszef Dudas and revolutionary troops belonging to an opposing group.

According to information we have gathered, Joszef Dudas, the organizer of the [National] Revolutionary Committee wanted to establish his headquarters in the Ministry of Foreign Affairs, located in Buda, on the banks of the Danube. Between this building and the military prison, violent rifle-fire developed ... But we have as yet no information on the outcome of this encounter.

According to unconfirmed sources, this little war can be booked to the account of opposition groups which begin to manifest themselves ... in order to seize power. Certain observers go so far as to say that by radically breaking with Moscow, Imre Nagy has gained a political advantage over his adversaries, and thus will be in a position to group support around him.

"We went too fast", one Hungarian explained to me. "We should never have authorized the parties in our country to reorganize themselves so rapidly. A central military power would have been necessary until order was restored. There would still have been time enough after that." ...

J. J. Leblond, Le Dauphiné Libéré (Grenoble), 3 November

Budapest

Rebel forces representing the Budapest city revolutionary council seized the Foreign Ministry building tonight from soldiers loyal to Premier Imre Nagy ...

The move was reported by Deputy Premier Geza Losonczy, who said the revolutionaries overpowered a handful of Hungarian troops guarding the building. "The men entered the Ministry and terrorized the staff, upsetting work and impeding the Government in the handling of foreign affairs", Mr. Losonczy said.

He said the revolutionaries were taking orders from Jozsef Dudas, chairman of the Budapest city revolutionary council, who has been one of the most outspoken anti-Russian leaders. Mr. Losonczy said no action would be taken against the revolutionaries before tomorrow morning, and he refused to indicate what might be done then.

The so far unexplained take-over had special significance because Premier Nagy is also Foreign Minister.

United Press

Miskolc: "A Middle Way"

Miskolc

Throughout these critical days discipline has been observed in Nyiregyhaza and in the rest of Szabolcs-Szatmar County. One robbery and murder occurred during this period. The culprit was apprehended by the People's Police and will suffer the death penalty. No individual acts of revenge are permissible; any person who commits criminal acts will be prosecuted and judged by the regular authorities. There will be no switching over to the other extreme.

The people have had too much totalitarianism and will never again tolerate systems of government which interfered with family life, religious creeds, or the education of youth. They will never again march in fascist uniforms or cheer in chorus on command. Never again will there be little or big Hitlers or Rakosis. A middle way exists. In its present critical situation Hungary needs the sympathy and assistance of all peoples and cannot refuse assistance from any source.

[The Szabolcs-Szatmar radio then praised the attitude of the local revolutionary leaders of Nyiregyhaza, and stated that reliable citizens should be armed and should patrol the streets of that town. It also transmitted a protest on behalf of small artisans against an appeal that they return to work. The small artisans refused to break the nation-wide strike.]

Radio Free Miskolc and BBC Summary

Gyor: "The Western Pattern"

Budapest

Gyor ... was the center of the provincial as distinct from the Budapest revolution ... The man in charge was Attila Szigeti, a former member of parliament and a personal friend of Imre Nagy. Under the Rakosi regime he had been pushed out of parliament. Now, as the highest political authority in this part of Hungary, his task was to reconcile the viewpoints of his large freedom committee with those of the central government ... One one occasion a man arrived in Gyor purporting to be a new leader sent by the revolutionaries in Budapest. He spoke against

Szigeti, and asked the crowd to appoint him instead. Eventually he was taken to the prison in Gyor, accused of being an AVH agent-provocateur, sent to create anarchy and to frustrate the revolution.

Attila Szigeti maintained his position as leader throughout ... But there were no Communists at all among the Gyor delegates — although there were numerous army officers. Nevertheless there was no intention of abolishing the Communist Party. At Gyor, although there was no place for them in the town hall, the Communists walked about freely. In the provinces, only the AVH were physically attacked ... "If we abolish the C. P. in Hungary," they said, "it would give our adversaries an excuse for saying this was a reactionary revolution. Let the C. P. take part in free elections and we will see how beloved are the Communists." There was also, among these delegates, a feeling against the emigré groups in the West. Those who had spent ten years in America could not hope to return to take up key positions ...

At the Budapest parliament, the spokesmen of "national Communism", the men of Nagy and Kadar, realised that a vast tragedy was approaching ... They already took the Russian intervention for granted. The tragedy, as one of them put it to me in Nagy's office, was that "the revolution has over-rolled itself, and that the government has ended up in the hands of the right-wing" ... By "right-wing", however, my informants meant the Peasants, the Small Peasants, the Social Democrats, and, of course, the embryo Catholic party. Nobody in the Budapest parliament pretended that there was any question of a return to the Horthy regime. The whole point (and it was a questionable "tragedy") was that, instead of Titoism, an all-party coalition system on the western pattern had been set in motion.

It was a question of East or West, and the Hungarian people had clearly said West. This was the fundamental problem for the Russians ...

Bruce Renton, New Statesman & Nation (London),
17 November

Gyor and Miskolc

London

In the provinces, two distinct centers of insurrection sprang into being, at Miskolc in the north-east and at Gyor in the west. In both cities, Communists and anti-Communists were active, and in both cities they soon came to blows with one another. At Miskolc, the insurgents appealed to the country in the Marxist-Leninist idiom, and it was in the name of proletarian internationalism that they demanded the withdrawal of Soviet troops and the restoration of Hungary's sovereignty.

The real headquarters of the rising in the provinces was at Gyor, where after an interval during which Attila Szigeti, a Communist, led the insurgents, the anti-Communists — among whom the clergy were prominent — gained the upper hand. It was no longer de-Stalinization that was the battle cry at Gyor. It was "Down with Communism!"

Isaac Deutscher, The Reporter (New York), 15 November

Releasing Political Prisoners

Budapest

The Supreme State Prosecutor's Office announces that 5,416 detained persons have been freed in the course of recent revolutionary events. The liberation of political prisoners is still in progress in a number of prisons in the province and in Budapest. In Szolnok yesterday, 1 November, the doors of the political internment camp were opened. It was a touching scene as the 600 political prisoners sang the national anthem before the national flag with the government delegates who had released them, as a sign that all were in favour of the Government. The innocent prisoners have already been returned to their homes ...

The Revolutionary Council of the Ministry of Justice, together with the Ministerial Committee for the Drafting of Laws, has already drawn up an amnesty decree providing for the release of political prisoners. The draft will be considered by the Council of Ministers in the near future ... The only exceptions to the release will be those convicted of illegal executions against human beings. Another measure being drafted calls for reduction of punishments inflicted on people for "crimes against property". ...

Free Radio Kossuth

"Poems on Broken Walls"

Budapest

There has been a great deal of loose talk about rapine and looting. I should like to testify that the Budapest rising must have been the cleanest revolution in history. Three things: —

Before the Russians came back there stood in the main thoroughfare large boxes bearing notices: "Give to those who remain alive!" These were full of 100-forint notes. They were unguarded. They were emptied periodcally by small boys sent to collect the contributions. Nobody else touched them. After the battle they were still there.

In the main streets there was nothing but broken shop windows. After the battle the goods were still in the windows, untouched, among the broken glass. Valuable jewels and watches lay there for the taking. Nobody took them ..

The only thing the Freedom Fighters took was food. They had no food. They entered the food shops at night and took what they needed. But they made lists of what they had taken, and left these lists in the shops, together with the money which they thought was due.

One other thing. In all the streets were poems. The most celebrated Hungarian writers had pinned up their tributes on broken walls, in their own handwriting. They did this while the fighting was going on, in short, declamatory verses: —

You are heroes
But not the heroes of our songs of the past
We have no word for you
We shall not rest until we have found the word.

Or: —

Every minute a hero dies
But every minute a new hero is born.

These verses flutter above the graves of the unknown. . . .

Lajos Lederer, The Observer (London), 18 November

The Revolution of Truth

Budapest

On the day I left Budapest — the 2nd of November — most of the foreign journalists crowding the lobby of the Hotel Duna were keenly aware of impending tragedy and disaster. The spokesman for the revolutionary military committee had already forecast, the evening before, the eventuality of "a fight to the death". But on that Friday morning the atmosphere at the office of the Hungarian Writers Association, next door to the Soviet Embassy, had been entirely different. There, everything was intense and hopeful: a moving and strange air of exhilaration pervaded the rooms. Most of Hungary's distinguished writers were there, working and conferring, for their literary centre was functioning as a kind of brainok-trust for Prime Minister Nagy. I listened to the discussions of new plans for reconstruction and education, for various publishing projects, and for a new issue of the literary journal, *Irodalmi Ujsag*, which was due to come off the presses in a few hours.

Through an interpreter (for he does not speak any foreign languages) I talked with Peter Veres, Chairman of the Writers Association, a famous peasant writer and political leader, who stood there with his old-fashioned heavy boots and handle-bar moustache like some Hungarian Gorky. "We have learned that an author must have the right to keep his silence on political issues, as well as the freedom to speak out on behalf of his community ..." As he spoke to me, a peasant from the region of Gyor was announced. He tramped in with mud on his boots. He came to ask Veres to get him a publisher for a long manuscript on which he had spent "many, many nights". Veres told him that this, under the circumstances, would have to wait. There was a brief argument. The farmer went into a corner, sulking and muttering. Veres went on to ask me not to publish any complete verbatim accounts of his remarks because "I am, after all, a writer and it is so rare that the spoken word can have style ..."

On this last morning, I met again the playwright Julius Hay, in whose house I had spent the previous afternoon. Madame Hay, who is a member of one of the Budapest theatre groups, told me how happy she was that her husband's new play, which had been suppressed by the censorship, would be produced as soon as "the patriotic strike of the actors" was over. I asked Hay how it was that he and other "old Bolsheviks" were now openly fighting the Party leadership. He replied: "There were many reasons for the break. The first, I confess, was my instinctive disgust with Stalinism's utter lack of taste and its insensibility in every field of art and letters. As writers, we were all sharply aware of that. Secondly, there was the experience of deep social injustice in our society. A third motive was the glaring failure, even bankruptcy, of our type of economic system. There was finally — and it may have been the most important element — the pressure of our youth ...

"We writers", Hay explained to me, "have always thought of ourselves as the avant-garde in the struggle for freedom. This is a Hungarian tradition of which we are very proud ... I was supposed to be a guide for our youth, but in reality, the youth had become a guide for me. For years I had been lecturing them. I gave interminable ideological answers to every question. I could feel that my young listeners found it all very shallow and boring. At first I thought: how strange and incomprehensible it is that we, the older generation, should work to selflessly to build the future of a happier Hungary for our young people, and that these very young people should not care at all! Why were they so blind, so unfeeling, so cold? Gradually I began to wonder. Were they all, every last boy and girl in Hungary, hopeless reactionaries? Or could it be that we, the old men, were wrong, and that they were right? I began to talk with more frankness. I looked at their problems with more openness. In my public meetings, which were attended by eager thousands, I forced myself to answer every question directly. Some weeks ago, they asked me at a meeting in Gyor, "What is happening in our uranium mines?" I knew the Russians were there, but could only answer: "I just don't know ... But as a Hungarian citizen, I ought to know! And you ought to know! Keep asking! And so they did."

He went on: "And as for me, I keep on asking too. Have we been building in this country a socialist society, marred only by some ugly distortions, or was this not a horrible regime for which I have no name and which was all distortions and no socialism? Even now, I long for the Party which once had our love and loyalty. But its leadership has destroyed it. It is difficult to love a thing which does not exist. I would still support a new and pure Marxist movement. But I would not want to become a Party member ever again ... Was I courageous in speaking for truth, even under Rakosi? The pressure of the young on us all was so great that I can only say, in the words of one of our poets, 'I was too much of a coward to remain dishonest!' ..."

I talked, too, with Tibor Dery, an inspirer of the Petofi circle of Hungarian intellectual dissidents, and a Communist of long standing. I was surprised when he asked me to pass on greetings to one of his closest Viennese friends—a well-known Stalinist functionary who has never deviated from the Party line. Yet Tibor Dery told me, in his halting but perfect French, *"Cette révolution est la plus grande, la plus pure, que vous ayons connue. Peut-être la première révolution victorieuse dans toute notre histoire!"*

Francois Bondy, Preuves (Paris) and Encounter (London), December 1956

Inside Rakosi's Villa

Budapest

Nepakarat, the newspaper of the National Federation of Hungarian Trade Unions, published a very interesting report about the mysteries of the Rakosi villa ... All sorts of documents lay on the desk. It seems that the Rakosis left the villa in a hurry and did not have time to open the last copy of *Pravda*, although the inhabitants of the villa esteemed this paper highly. What do we find among these papers? An envelope generally does not give much information, but this time ... The following was written on one envelope. *"Comrade Rakosi, I want to have these two letters back by eight o'clock in the morning with your instructions. Gabor Peter."*

We wonder what the subject was of the two letters sent by one murderer to another. Who was the unfortunate one now being accused of treason or conspiracy?

He who loses his membership card has to be excluded from the Party, said the severe stipulation worded by Rakosi himself. And now we are filled with consternation at the sight of a membership card on which the signature is Matyas Rakosi. Next to it lies the membership card of his wife. It proves how important the Party must have been to him.

We must say that he did not show up very handsomely as far as his membership fee was concerned. He paid 160 forints and earned 40,000 forints a month. There is convincing evidence here about his enormously high salary ... There is much to be recorded. There were two luxurious bathrooms fitted out with gymnastic equipment and — in case he lost too much weight during his gymnastics — literally drawers full of vitamin pills to which he could turn. A new radio-phonograph — two pianos, apparently in case he wanted to play pieces for two hands — and brilliant white telephones in every room. You push a button and the AVO Guards or the alert squad personnel report immediately in to the parlour or drawing-room. We not only admired the furniture but also the thick Dutch cigars, the French and Spanish and who-knows-what liqueurs, wines, and champagne which we never saw before. We cannot bear to look at it any more, we have to leave!

An immense portrait of Stalin sneers at us, and enthusiastic young National Guards tell us that the house now belongs to the National Government. Every sheet of paper is being most carefully guarded because everything will be needed to establish a full list of the crimes of the genocidist Rakosi ...

Free Radio Kossuth

Russians — "Friendly, Bewildered ..."

Budapest

Whether Russians will ever be willing to leave Hungary was the topic of wide speculation here. One possible motive, it is believed, may be the repugnance that has been shown by members of many Soviet units toward their assigned task of suppressing the revolution.

This correspondent has already related how one Russian officer in the Moritz Zsigmund Square in Buda tried to justify the presence of Soviet tanks to a crowd of students with the statement. "But we have been told you are fascists here." He also recorded the statement of some bewildered Russian soldiers to Russian-speaking Hungarians that "we were told that American troops went to Budapest and have been surprised not to see any."

The Russian-speaking correspondent of the *Times* of London heard a Soviet lieutenant tell some citizens of Budapest Thursday: "Rakosi never told us you did not want us in Hungary. We don't like what we are doing, but what can we do? We are soldiers and we must obey orders."

But the most sensational report of all came from Kecskemet. There, it is said, elements of two Soviet divisions stacked their arms outside the town, entered it and told inhabitants: "We don't want to hurt anybody. We would like some food, but we have money to pay for it."

The Soviet official with the troops is reported to have told some members of the town's Revolutionary Committee that the reason Russian reinforcements had been brought into Hungary was to prevent widespread mutiny among their own troops already there ...

At a press conference a spokesman for the Revolutionary Council of the Hungarian Army said: "West of the Danube Russian units have not really remained neutral but in many cases helped it (the revolution)". It is a matter of history that more than 1,000,000 Soviet army soldiers revolted against communism in World War II. Undoubtedly thousands more would have defected had it not been for the brutality of the Nazis in Russia ...

John MacCormac, New York Times, 3 November

New Soviet Troops on the Move

Budapest

Further information on Soviet troop movements in Hungary particularly in the Eastern Counties: This morning two Soviet armoured trains entered the frontier station of Zahony. After occupying the station, the Soviet troops occupied the line from Zahony to Nyiregyhaza. According to Miskolc University's radio station, a strong armoured unit arrived in the village of Kisvarda on the night of 1 to 2 November. Debrecen also reports the uninterrupted transit of Soviet troops. Units of tanks and self-propelled guns have been moving through Szolnok from east to west. Only supply vehicles had been seen travelling in the opposite direction. Two hundred Soviet tanks which had entrenched themselves for several days between Szolnok and Abony have now started moving westward ... Szolnok denies the report that Soviet troops have occupied the airfield there: Soviet formations are stationed around the airfield but have not yet tried to take possession of it. Nor has the airfield at Pecs been occupied. Tank units arrived in the area of Gyongyos on 1 and 2 November and have entrenched themselves there. Soviet troops are camping in the Nagyrede area. No Soviet soldiers have been seen for years in the above-mentioned places. Soviet armoured units near Dombovar have surrounded the airfield at Taszar a few kilometres from Kaposvar. Soviet reconaissance units advanced as far as the outskirts of Kaposvar. About 20 lorries of Soviet infantry have arrived in Nyreghaza from Zahony on the evening of 2 November. Some units of motorised artillery crossed the Hungarian-Soviet border at Beregsurany. ... *Hungarian News Agency*

Budapest

Only two things seem to be clear in the confused picture of military movements reported throughout Hungary to-day.

One is that Russians intend for the present to reinforce Hungary and to establish an iron grip all along the strategic road and railway links along the line at Budapest—Szolnok—Debrecen—Nyiregyhaza—Zahony. The other is that they wish to have enough tank forces around Budapest to be able to isolate it from the rest of the country if they wish. They could then exercise the strongest psychological pressure on the Nagy regime.

For the first time in a week Soviet tanks were reported to-night to have sealed the main Budapest-Vienna road just inside the Hungarian border. ...

It is still not clear whether the Russians are playing a game of blackmail against the Hungarian regime or whether they are preparing for another bloodbath.

Intelligence reports collected by the Central Revolutionary Committee in the capital say that 304 Soviet tanks were counted crossing into the country yesterday at the Soviet-Hungarian border village of Zahony. Another 301 were said to have entered the same day from Rumania. Of this second force some 250 stayed at Debrecen. The remainder moved on towards Budapest.

All major airfields in the country were by to-day in Russian hands. This morning, according to the same rebel sources, Soviet tanks had moved in to occupy the airfields at Szeged and Kecskemet in Southern Hungary, which they had hitherto left unmolested.

An authoritative independent estimate puts the total strength of Soviet forces in Hungary at the moment at about eight full divisions, mostly armour. This is about four times the size of the permanent garrison and twice the size of the garrison, plus reinforcements, which attempted to quell the uprising.

One thing has been clear throughout. The Hungarian rebels are prepared to fight on to the last man should the Russians renew the attack. Throughout the day Hungarian Army reinforcements have been moving into the capital. The mood of the rebel leaders to-day was grave, but firm. ...

Cardinal Mindszenty said that among those who had risen against the regime had been "very many Russian soldiers." This reference to Soviet troops touches on what may be for the Kremlin the most serious aspect of the whole rebellion: unmistakable signs that the regular Russian garrison in Hungary has become heavily "contaminated." These Red Army demonstrations of sympathy with the Hungarian people have been continuing even after the cease-fire. One report from Kecskemet today speaks of Russian troops stacking their arms in the town and mixing with the townspeople. Some of them are reported to have said that whatever orders they received they had no intention of acting as oppressors. This sort of thing strikes at something more than Moscow's hold on one small satellite. It strikes at the Soviet regime's grip on Russia as such.

Gordon Shepherd, Daily Telegraph (London), 3 November

Budapest

Budapest has been surrounded since Thursday, but so far Soviet tanks have not entered the city. The Hungarian Army has not offered resistance at any point. This is not because it is unwilling to fight but because if there is to be a war the Hungarians want the Russians to take responsibility for starting it. Neither have the Russians fired a shot so far ... All the fighting that has taken place to date has been in Budapest between revolutionists and members of the A.V.H., the Hungarian political police.

The day's political developments in Budapest include the radio announcement that Premier Nagy will reform his Cabinet by withdrawing from it all members who had compromised themselves by collaboration with the Soviet. A second was the arrest of Gyula Alapi, the state prosecutor in the trial of Cardinal Mindszenty. ...

John MacCormac, New York Times, 3 November

Three Notes to the Soviets

Budapest

The Hungarian Government has addressed three verbal notes to the Soviet Embassy in Budapest today.

The first note is a reminder that the Hungarian Government already asked the Government of the Soviet Union last week to begin negotiations immediately concerning the withdrawal of Soviet troops from Hungary. At the time, the Government of the USSR accepted this proposal favorably, and the Soviet Ambassador also made a similar declaration during his visit to the Hungarian Prime Minister. The verbal note goes on to say that, despite these talks, new Soviet formations unfortunately crossed the Hungarian frontier on October 31 and on 1 November. The Hungarian Government has exerted the greatest possible effort to obtain the withdrawal of these troops; however, the steps have proved to be in vain. Indeed Soviet troops even continued to advance, and some units took up positions around Budapest. In consequence of this, on November 1, 1956, the Hungarian Government repudiated the Warsaw Pact.

It is the view of the Hungarian Government that the Hungarian-Soviet relationship must be based on respect for Hungarian neutrality, and on the principles of complete equality, sovereignty, and mutual non-interference in each other's internal affairs. In order to achieve this, the Hungarian Government proposes that negotiations should begin immediately on the basis of these principles, between the Hungarian People's Republic and representatives of the Soviet Government concerning implementation of the repudiation of the Warsaw Pact, with special reference to the withdrawal of Soviet Troops stationed in Hungary without delay.

The members of the Hungarian Government Delegation are: Minister of State Geza Losonczy, as Head of the Delegation, Jozsef Kovago, Andras Marton, Ferenc Farkas, and Volmos Zentai.

The second verbal note deals with the military aspects of the same problem and proposes that a Mixed Committee charged with preparing the withdrawal of Soviet Troops should begin work on November 2, 1956, i. e. immediately, in the Hungarian Parliament building. The Hungarian Government appoints the following delegates to the Preparatory Mixed Committee: Minister of State Ferenc Erdei, General Pal Maleter, General Istvan Kovacs, and Col. Miklos Szvecs.

The third verbal note again protests against the military movements of Soviet troops in Hungary. It states that, today, on November 2 new Soviet units again crossed the frontier, and have occupied railway lines and stations on the way. In Western Hungary, Soviet troop movements can be observed in an east-west direction. This protest stresses that the Hungarian Government considers it necessary to once more inform the heads of diplomatic legations in Budapest about these steps directed against Hungary, and, at the same time, urgently to call attention of the Security Council to these new developments.

Free Radio Kossuth

"Contaminated"

The Soviet troops that attacked [after 3 November] were not the same as those which, during the first intervention, had suffered so crushing a defeat at the hands of young "good-for-nothings" in the Hungarian capital. The troops stationed in Hungary had been relieved between the 28 and 30 October. In fact the occupation army had been largely "contaminated" by contact with the Hungarian population, and scenes of fraternization had been numerous. On October 27th I was brought to the Hotel Royal ... to serve as interpreter between a group of Russian tank men and Hungarians surrounding them. The Russians explained that they wanted to shoot only at the enemies of socialism, and that they could see we were no fascists.

"We won't shoot at you," said one twenty-year-old with flaxen hair.

"Then why remain here?" I retorted. "We are not fighting for capitalism but because we want to let the Hungarian people build its own socialism. We — ours, you — yours."

"Right", said the Russian, and his comrades approved.

The people gave them an ovation. Soon the Soviet car was decorated by a red-white-and-green streamer...

Dezso Kozak, Franc-Tireur (Paris), 25 December

Interview with Tildy
Budapest

The Soviet Government tonight agreed that a joint Soviet-Hungarian commission shall meet in Budapest tomorrow at noon to discuss Hungarian complaints that Russian troops are still rolling in. It will discuss too the ultimate withdrawal of Soviet armour from Hungary ... But in Budapest, however, the news has caused remarkably little reaction ... The main reason is that the members of the new inner Cabinet have their misgivings that this Russian move is just another manoeuvre.

That was the fear of Zoltan Tildy, the silver-haired Minister of State, leader of the Smallholder Party ... "The only real chance of success for these talks," Tildy told me rather sadly, "is that Soviet troop movements pouring fresh armour into Hungary, and their operations inside our country, should stop—at least until the talks begin. The bad, sad news is that the movements have not ceased. According to our incontrovertible information, they are still going on."

Even while we were talking, the new Defence Minister, Colonel Pal Maleter, pulled himself up to his 6ft. 4in. and asked Tildy to step into the corner so that he could give him the latest military report.

During our talk, Mr. Tildy said the Hungarian Government would be prepared to withdraw its appeal to UNO on one condition. "We are prepared," he said, "to withdraw our protest to UNO provided that Soviet troops will immediately cease operations and leave our country."

Tildy, only recently released from eight years house arrest to which he was submitted with his white-haired wife, received me in the very same room in which I had talked with him in 1946, when he was the deputy Prime Minister in the Hungarian Government. Then I found him rather a weak man, waffling, and unsure of himself, giving vague and evasive answers. Today, as he sat there with his wife and two new Smallholder Ministers, I found him strong, firm, and decided.

"From the very beginning the Government," he said, "has wanted to solve this matter by negotiation. But the events which have been taking place since Wednesday afternoon are in contrast to the spirit of the previous negotiation offer that had been agreed ... For our protest to the Soviet Ambassador, our general staff prepared a map showing the exact order of battle of all Soviet military units which are now coming into the country and those which had been formerly stationed here. We insisted that we can tolerate no kind of interference by Soviet troops in Hungary's domestic affairs. Moreover, the Government has declared null and void all declarations made by the former Government concerning the presence of Soviet troops. So there is no legal basis today with which the Soviet Government can justify the operation of troops in Hungary."

Sefton Delmer, Daily Express (London), 3 November

Interview with General Kiraly
Budapest

This correspondent interviewed a man who has played a leading role in the revolution ... Gen. Bela Kiraly, commandant of Budapest ...

The general has had no lack of ups and downs in his forty-four years. He was general under several Communist Governments until he was arrested in 1951 as a conspirator against Matyas Rakosi, then Premier. For four years he remained under sentence of death. His sentence was commuted to life-imprisonment. In August he was released ...

Now he is in charge of restoring order in Budapest while keeping an eye on the Russians. In the Kilian Barracks are still stacked the arms used by its defenders and it remains a fortified center of the revolution. But General Kiraly, a spare, handsome man, who says he learned English in prison, would rather discuss post-revolutionary problems.

"There are 15,000 armed university students in Budapest", he said. "It has been quite a task to organize the little bands that have been fighting all over the city. We have created from them a third force of militia."

The general regretted the lynching of members of the Hungarian political police during the last two days. He said his orders were to turn every man over to the courts. He declared there would be no white terror in Hungary such as Hungarian Communists have said they fear. In this connection he deprecated recent broadcasts by Radio Free Europe and the Voice of America. He said they had been inciting Hungarians to further revolt and to strike, whereas what the revolution now needed was to have the workers return to their jobs ...

John MacCormac, New York Times, 3 November
Budapest

...early in the forenoon of Nov. 2, I got an agitated call from Nagy himself. "My friend Kiraly," he said, "if anyone ever had an important job, you have one now. I have a formal note from the Russian ambassador. He says bands of Hungarians are raging around his embassy. If the Hungarian government cannot control them he, as ambassador, will be obliged to call in Russian troops. I think you understand the seriousness of this demand. If we cannot maintain order, we will offer an opportunity for a second Russian aggression. Drop what you are doing and go there yourself."

I ordered a tank company to proceed immediately to the Square of Heroes, which was near the embassy, and sent a mechanized infantry battalion to join them there ... When I got there the streets were empty and there was no sign of trouble ... I was ushered to the office of Ambassador Yuri Andropov. "I have a command from my premier to check the rioting here," I said, "but I see no rioting." The ambassador appeared embarrassed. He said there had been reports of trouble, but it had stopped. "We Russians don't want to mix in your business," he said. "We understand your troubles and we are on your side." He walked around the desk and said, "Did you know that we have offered to negotiate with your government?" I said I did not. "Our government wants to take its troops out of Hungary immediately, and we want a discussion to arrange the details of the evacuation." I was delighted, and told him so ...

Maj.-Gen. Bela Kiraly, Life (New York), 18 February 1957

Waiting for the West's Reply
Budapest

"Neutrality" is the word today in Budapest. It figures in the notes addressed today by the Hungarians to the Soviet Government, in the message to Mr. Hammarskjold, the Secretary-General of the United Nations, and it crops up in almost every political conversation—and there are few others in Budapest these days.

The model is Austria, not Yugoslavia with its lofty but involved concept of active co-existence, nor Switzerland with its centuries of peace. Ravaged by war, torn by revolution, raped by foreign military occupation, Hungary is sighing for the goal that Austria has achieved: first the withdrawal of foreign troops, then neutrality.

Abstract as this concept is, strange as it may be to the minds of ordinary workers and peasants, it has yet caught the imagination of the nation. "If Austria can do it, why couldn't we?"

Yesterday Mr. Nagy said that he had asked the Big Four to recognise Hungary's neutrality. Hungary is waiting anxiously for their reaction. The people here can understand why Moscow is delaying its reply. But why, it has asked, have the Western Governments not replied immediately that they acknowledge Hungary's neutrality? By delaying its reply, even for a day, the West is making things easier for Moscow. It is, in effect, countenancing the march of Soviet troops on Budapest ...

There is no doubt about the determination both of the people and of the Government to defend the city. "We have had a few days' rest now", said a Hungarian officer, "and we are now ready for them again."

From all areas where Soviet troop movements are proceeding it is reported that the people are joining the national guard in great numbers.

Yet, with all this, it is difficult to believe that the Russians would risk another battle of Budapest. It is most likely that they are trying to intimidate the Hungarians into giving up the city without a fight. They have obviously not learned much about Hungarian mentality.

Viktor Zorza, Manchester Guardian, 3 November

Hungary's "Friends and Neighbours"

Budapest
As of today we are no longer the tool of a colonialism disguised as socialism, nor a figure on the chess-board of some conqueror or other ...

We are extending a friendly hand towards all peoples—to our neighbour, neutral Austria, and to free Yugoslavia which remains outside any blocs, towards Rumania, Czechoslovakia, and the people of the Soviet Union. We hope that their Governments will understand our little nation's thirst for freedom and national life. Such is the message which in these decisive hours we address to the whole world and all its peoples who love freedom. Such is the message which we address to the UN, whose duty is, according to its Charter, to watch over the independence and sovereignty of all its member States and all countries. Such is our message also to the four Great Powers who have paramount responsibility for maintaining

world peace and respect for the freedom and independence of small nations.

Council of Free Trade Unions.
Nepakarat (Budapest), 2 November

From Czechoslovakia and Rumania we heard unworthy commentaries about our people and our victorious revolution ... *Rudo Pravo*, the official paper of the Czechoslovak Communist Party, goes so far as to threaten that the Hungarian people will pay dearly for these days. What are these papers condemning? That our people has shaken off the fetters of Rakosi-Gero tyranny, or that the Hungarians want complete national independence? That they want to live in a country which is truly free and without occupation forces? ... Mikoyan and Suslov have been in Hungary for the last few days and could see with their own eyes what really happened in Budapest. We advise the Rumanian and Czechoslovak newspapers that wrote in an unworthy tone to send their conrrespondents to Budapest and to the other towns and villages of the country to check thoroughly what really happened in Hungary, and afterwards to reveal the truth to the Czech, Slovak and Rumanian peoples ... *Magyar Honved (Budapest), 2 November*

Bucharest

Rumania's Communist regime swore allegiance today to the Soviet Union's opposition to the Hungarian nationalists.

Through their newspaper organs the Rumanian rulers hinted strongly that they were prepared to wage open war against any non-Communist Hungarian Government. They also made clear that Soviet forces would remain in Rumania for an indefinite period ...

Reports of the unrest of a large number of university students have been confirmed. Factory workers and railway employees also were known to have expressed open dissatisfaction with the regime in recent days.

Security measures were being tightened in an effort to discover the sources of disaffection, particularly among university students. The Hungarian section of Cluj University in Transylvania was reported closed today by order of the authorities after rioting among Hungarian-speaking and Rumanian-speaking students during a protest demonstration. The university gives instruction separately in the two languages.

A student boycott against classes in Marxism-Leninism and the Russian language continued...

Rumania's position in the storms now sweeping Eastern Europe was clearly set forth in two major editorials in *Scinteia*, organ of the Rumanian Workers (Communist) party. The paper said Hungary's decision to withdraw from the Warsaw Pact had created "the most serious dangers, not only for the defense and development of the Socialist and democratic conquests of the Hungarian people, but for their very liberty and national sovereignty."

Hungary's new course, adopted with the "connivance of foreign reactionary circles," imperils "the links of friendship, collaboration and mutual aid" between that country and the rest of the Soviet bloc, the Communist paper said. The Communist camp is determined to defend its "Socialist conquests," the paper said, from whatever quarter they might be threatened.

This appeared tantamount to a declaration of willingness to give all aid, including military support, to the Soviet forces in Hungary ...

Welles Hangen, New York Times, 3 November

Berlin

A call to "all democratic and socialist forces" to unite against the "fascist reactionaries" in Hungary was published yesterday in the East Berlin Communist newspaper *Neues Deutschland.*

It was stated in an article that Hungarian counter-revolutionaries were centrally directed "by a general staff, schooled in military affairs", and that the Government under Mr. Nagy was too weak to stop these reactionaries, who were spreading terror and murdering Socialists and Communists.

The East German Premier, Herr Grotewohl, told Parliament today that as long as the countries were divided Russian troops would remain in Germany "to protect the peaceful and democratic work of our people".

There are 22 Soviet divisions in the country. Soviet troops were "doing a great service to our working people and to the entire Socialist camp".

Confessing that there had been provocations by "enemies of socialsm" to persuade East Germans to follow the road of Hungary, he asked:

"Do you wish to destroy all the progress we have made? Do you wish to eradicate ten years of social gains? Do you wish to do away with our achievements? This cannot happen. It must not happen. We must work together and not against each other. I ask our students to understand when I say, with all emphasis, that we will not allow West Berlin students to make themselves at home in our universities and cause unrest". *Manchester Guardian, 3 November*

Warsaw

Comrades, Citizens! The Polish nation follows with great emotion the tragic course of the Hungarian events. From the bottom of our hearts we have always been on the side of the Hungarian workers and all those who fought together with them for socialist democratisation, against the forces which wanted at any cost to maintain in Hungary the old system of government hated by the people.

Incredulity

Budapest

... Telephone connection with Warsaw. We first give all the news—the continued influx of Soviet troops into Hungary, the evacuation of Soviet civilians, Kadar's flight. – Then I dictate my article. The friends at the other end of the line reveal that the article can certainly not appear, for reasons unconnected with the editorial office. Then they ask us curious questions about our safety in the Party hotel, about the "Avenue of the Hanged" (?) etc. When I describe the true situation here, I detect incredulity in their voices.

Viktor Woroszylski, Nowa Kultura (Warsaw), 9 December

When armed clashes occured as a result of a tangle of errors, the former leadership of the Hungarian Workers' Party, instead of immediately taking the path of solutions in conformity with the interests of socialism, with the will of the working class and of the majority of the nation, called for the assistance of Soviet troops. This was a decision which resulted in tragic consequences ...

Lately, the Hungarian events entered a new and dangerous phase. Reactionary elements are ever more clearly gaining the upper hand. The foundations of the socialist system are threatened. Chaos and anarchy are spreading throughout the entire country. Reactionary bands carry out lynchings and bestially murder Communists.

The Polish working class and our whole nation are following this course of events with the gravest concern ... Our Party trusts that the working class and the working masses of Hungary will succeed in uniting and repelling the attacks of reaction.

We are of the opinion that the problem of the defence and maintenance of the people's power and of the gains of socialism in Hungary can be solved by the internal forces of the Hungarian people, headed by the working class, and not by intervention from without ... This opinion is dictated to us by the program and ideological principles of our Party.

It is necessary and indispensable not only from the point of view of the security of the Soviet Union, but also to a still greater degree from the point of view of our security and the inviolability of our frontiers against the schemes of German militarism. For it is known that the Soviet Union has been so far the only one among the four Powers which recognised and which guarantees our western frontiers.

Comrades and citizens! In the course of the last few days the tension of the international situation has increased. The dangerous situation in Hungary and the Anglo-French aggression against Egypt are creating a serious danger ...

This is no time for manifestations and meetings ...
Polish Press Agency

Moscow

The *"Österreichische Volksstimme"* publishes an item under the heading "Squadrons of Aircraft Are Proceeding to Hungary" which says: "Aircraft squadrons are proceeding almost uninterruptedly from Austrian airfields to Budapest. This refers not so much to medicine as official communications are trying to make it appear. With this number of aircraft one could supply medicine to whole continents. Observers have been able to convince themselves that hundreds of Hungarian military men are being sent to Hungary from the West, former officers of the Horthy army, hundreds of Hungarian officers and men who served in the Hitlerite army. Among the aircraft one may see machines of the West German frontier service, British machines and others."
Tass (Moscow), 2 November

Moscow

From the very contradictory reports of the Hungarian press and radio and from the numerous comments in the foreign Press the following can be quite clearly concluded. Various dark forces which do not at all represent the interests of the people have hastened to associate themselves with the just discontent expressed by healthy elements of the Hungarian people in connection with certain shortcomings in the work of the State apparatus of Hungary ... The disorders in Budapest and other parts of the country have been used by direct enemies of the Hungarian working people and by their foreign sponsors. It is they who are now continuing their subversive work, hampering the normalisation of the situation and striving to bring about a rift within the ranks of the Hungarian people and to cause political and economic chaos.

A truth which will be bitter for the Hungarian people must be stated. Unfortunately the enemies of the Hungarian people have to a certain extent been successful. A situation is now arising in Hungary which threatens all the achievements of the Hungarian working people during the years of the people's rule. Friends tell the truth to your face, because they want to help and warn their friends against a wrong step ...

There is every ground for anxiety ...
V. Kartsev, Radio Moscow, 2 November

Wire to Joliot-Curie

Budapest

The Revolutionary Committee of Hungarian intelligentsia, in conjunction with the Hungarian Writers Association, today sent to the World Peace Council, care of M. Joliot-Curie in Paris, the following telegram:

The entire Hungarian people have manifested their completely unified will, insisting that national independence and sovereignty be restored, and that all Soviet forces withdraw from the entire country without delay. The fulfilment of these requirements is an important guarantee for safeguarding peace in Eastern Europe. The Revolutionary Committee of Hungarian Intellectuals in conjunction with the Hungarian Writers Federation, requests the World Peace Council to convene an immediate extraordinary session in Vienna on this matter. We request your early answer to the following address: Hungarian Writers Association, Budapest, Bajza Utca 18.

[signed] Gyorgy Adam, on behalf of The Revolutionary Committee of the Hungarian Writers Association

Free Radio Kossuth

Nagy Appeals to Hammarskjöld for UN Action

YOUR EXCELLENCY: *Budapest*

As the President of the Council of Ministers and designate Foreign Minister of the Hungarian People's Republic I have the honour to bring to the attention of Your Excellency the following additional information:

I have already mentioned in my letter of November 1st that new Soviet military units entered Hungary and that the Hungarian Government informed the Soviet Ambassador in Budapest of this fact, at the same time terminated the Warsaw Pact, declared the neutrality of Hungary, and requested the United Nations to guarantee the neutrality of the country.

On the 2nd of November further and exact information, mainly military reports, reached the Government of the Hungarian People's Republic, according to which large Soviet military units crossed the border of the country, marching toward Budapest. They occupy railway lines, railway stations, and railway safety equipment. Reports also have come that Soviet military movements in an east-west direction are being observed on the territory of Western Hungary.

On the basis of the above-mentioned facts the Hungarian Government deemed it necessary to inform the Embassy of the USSR and all the other Diplomatic Missions in Budapest about these steps directed against our People's Republic.

At the same time, the Government of the Hungarian People's Republic forwarded concrete proposals on the withdrawal of Soviet troops stationed in Hungary as well as the place of negotiations concerning the execution of the termination of the Warsaw Pact and presented a list containing the names of the members of the Government's delegation. Furthermore, the Hungarian Government made a proposal to the Soviet Embassy in Budapest to form a mixed committee to prepare the withdrawal of the Soviet troops.

I request Your Excellency to call upon the Great Powers to recognize the neutrality of Hungary and ask the Security Council to instruct the Soviet and Hungarian Governments to start the negotiations immediately.

I also request Your Excellency to make known the above to the Members of the Security Council.

Please accept, Your Excellency, the expression of my highest consideration.

IMRE NAGY.

U. N. Document S/3726, November 2

UN Session: "Help for Hungary"

New York

The Western powers overrode Soviet objections today and called on the United Nations to take measures against Soviet military action in Hungary.

An emergency meeting of the Security Council heard all nations that spoke, except the Soviet Union, appeal for international action against the reinforcement of Soviet troops in Hungary, where rebel nationalists appear to have taken control. Imre Nagy, Hungarian Premier, asked the United Nations yesterday to guarantee the country's neutralism.

No decision was reached at the two-hour session of the Council tonight. The members will meet again tomorrow afternoon in an attempt to decide on a course of action.

The meeting was sparked by a new message from Mr. Nagy distributed to Council members tonight ... Henry Cabot Lodge Jr., the U. S. representative, laid no specific plan of action before the United Nations.

It had been expected that the United States might put a formal resolution before the Council, which would almost certainly have provoked a Soviet veto, and then pass the question to the special emergency session of the General Assembly called to consider the question of the fighting in the Suez Canal area.

That a Soviet veto could be counted on was made clear in an answer by Arkady A. Sobolev of the Soviet Union. He called reports of Soviet tanks and armored cars moving back into Hungary "utterly unfounded." Soviet planes and armor at Budapest Airport and in the city now are there,

"Not Enough"

Budapest

In front of the Parliament House where the revolution had started ... we saw two tanks guarding the building. As we parked our car, a Hungarian soldier jumped down from the tank, rushed to us, and eagerly asked, looking at the UN Press sticker on our windshield: "Is the United Nations already there?" We were very sorry to tell him that we did not represent the United Nations, but were only members of the UN press corps. "Not enough," said the soldier, and went away with marked disappointment all over his face. Our mood wasn't much different from his ...

Ejaz Husain, Dawn (Karachi, Pakistan), 15 November

he said, solely to assure the removal of civilians and wounded. Mr. Sobolev added that "counter-revolutionary elements" had entered into the Hungarian uprising since its inception. "Hund-reds" of Hungarian Fascists, he asserted, had

UN Debate

New York

MR. LODGE (U.S.A.): *It is sad to state this, but we have heard reports—and they come persistently – that new Soviet troops have entered Hungary, and this makes the situation unclear, if not full of dark fore-bodings.*

It is true that we have had the encouraging news, announced by the Soviet Union on 30 October, of what appears to be a signif-icant modification in the relations of the nations of eastern Europe and the Soviet Union ... With particular respect to Hun-gary, the statement said that the Soviet Union had instructed its military command to with-draw Soviet army units from Budapest as soon as this is recognized by the Hungarian Government to be necessary. It also express-ed willingness to enter into negotiations on the question of the presence of Soviet troops in Hungary with Hungary and other partic-ipants in the Warsaw Treaty ...

There you see the contrast between the statement that I quoted, which is purported to have been made by the Soviets, on the one hand, and the statement of the Hun-garian Foreign Minister on the other ... These reports are known to all of us because they were communicated to all of us last night. ...

M. DE GUIRINGAUD (France): *Who is to believe that a mere handful of fascists suc-ceded in causing difficulties to the Soviet interventionist groups? Who is to believe that it is a small group of fascists that exercises sufficient influence on the minds of Mr. Nagy and his colleagues in the Gov-ernment to persuade them to call for the evacuation of foreign troops? ...*

MR. SOBOLEV (U.S.S.R.): *There is a report today which is being distributed by press agencies which says: "Early today a Govern-ment spokesman said that no new Soviet troops crossed the Russian Hungarian frontier during the night." Mr. Lodge, in his statement, repeated time and again that the situation in Hungary was obscure, but he presented no facts and no evidence to substantiate his allegations against the Soviet Union.*

UN Verbatim Record, Security Council, 2 November

been flown across the borders of Hungary, possi-bly in connection with what he called a "Hun-garian-American center" in Austria, established for that purpose. The Soviet representative was the final speaker at the meeting. Representatives of France, Britain, Nationalist China, Cuba and Peru generally supported the United States' view. None pressed for specific action ...

The debate was opened by Mr. Lodge. The United States view was that the United Nations must take a greater hand in the Hungarian situation, possibly with the establishment of an observation commission that would assure that a Soviet-controlled regime was not brought back against the will of the Hungarian people.

Mr. Lodge asked the Security Council to establish the facts of the anti-Soviet revolution in Hungary. He recalled pledges given by the United States to assist "the brave Hungarian people in their struggle for freedom." Because of the current reports of Soviet action, he said, the United Nations should be prepared, first, to "establish the facts" and then to "take action thereupon." ...

In supporting the United States proposal, the Cuban delegate, Dr. Emilio Nunez-Portuondo, proposed that three steps be taken. These were:

1. An immediate appeal to the Moscow Government to withdraw its troops from Hungarian territory.
2. An expression of the "indisputable right of the Hun-garian people for self-determination by free elections and to establish the type of government under which they want to live."
3. The establishment of "a commission of the Security Council to supervise and report on the implementation of the measures taken by the organization in order to assure the national independence and political freedom of the Hungarian people." ...

Since a resolution condemning the Soviet Union for its moves to repress the Hungarian revolution would surely be vetoed, they could find it more effective, it is felt, to invoke the strong moral power exerted by a majority vote in the Assembly, where the veto does not apply.

The Hungarian situation first was brought before the United Nations last Saturday. How-ever, the major Western powers apparently decided to let the matter rest temporarily while it was determined whether the anti-Soviet revolution had attained its goals or failed.

Lindesay Parrott, New York Times, 3 November

Anxiety

Budapest

Budapest and the entire country is tortured by anxiety over the new Russian menace. Thanks-giving candles are again burning in the windows for the fourth successive evening, but the country is gripped by nightmare fears that the results of their great victory may be lost ...

Lajos Lederer, Observer Foreign News Service (London), 2 November

3 NOVEMBER

"The First Peaceful Day Since ..."

Budapest

The sky above Hungary has been bright today: it was a sunny winter day. The atmosphere in the country, particularly in the capital, was somewhat in accordance with the weather. I think that I would not exaggerate by saying that this Saturday has been the first peaceful day since October 23 ...

Djuka Julius, Politika (Belgrade), 4 November

Budapest

The future of Hungary not only depends on discussions in the UN but also to a decisive extent on Hungarian-Soviet negotiations due to begin very shortly. It is indispensable that a calm atmosphere be established for these negotiations. The cause for the exceptional deterioration of Hungarian-Soviet relations lies in the fact that the Gero-Hegedus clique called Soviet troops into the capital. The revolution is not directed against the USSR as a State. Its main objective is to ensure the withdrawal of Soviet forces. This must be made clear by all possible means ...

Neutrality involves the duty of putting an end to the man-hunt in the country and of using calm and dignified language in regard to our neighbours. We understand the anxiety of our Polish and Yugoslav friends as to the future of the Hungarian revolution. We can, however, set their minds at rest because, after transitory excesses, the situation has in the main been consolidated, and the continued normalisation of international relations can be taken as guaranteed on Hungary's part ...

Our entire position, however, will be decided by the intentions of the 200-million-strong Russian Empire as regards its military forces within our frontiers. Radio reports announce that this armed force is increasing. We are neutral. We are not giving the Russian Empire cause for bloodshed. But does it enter the minds of the leaders of the Russian Empire that we shall esteem the Russian people much more if they do not subjugate us? A country attacked usually curses the hostile attacking people. We did not attack Russia and we sincerely hope for the early withdrawal of Russian armed forces from Hungary ...

Free Radio Kossuth

Austro-Hungarian Frontier

The Austrian frontier at Nickelsdorf was still open when I arrived, and on the other side Hungarian revolutionaries were still in command. But ten kilometers eastwards there were a dozen or so Soviet tanks, lined up alongside the road in the so-called "withdrawal movement." A few last correspondents and diplomats managed to get through; all the others were stopped and sent back to Budapest.

I crossed the frontier and walked two or three kilometers into Hungary. Only a short time ago these fields and woodlands had been dotted with mines and barbed-wire barriers. Now they were cleared and free, as if nature herself were sharing in the national liberation. What no one had dared to believe had actually come to pass: a modern totalitarian regime had been overthrown by a revolution out of the 19th century, with its rifles and barricades and leaflets and angry masses, marching with flags in narrow streets. What sober iron-willed Stalin had built up was destroyed by that stormy popular rebellion of the poor and exploited of which the romantic Marx had dreamed. Had there ever been such a classical example of the rising of the "oppressed masses"? The Hungarian "October Revolution" had just a little in common with the October of Lenin and Trotzky, with "Peace, Land, and Bread", and much more with an idealistically vague notion of freedom, with the longing of a desperate people for a measure of human dignity.

In the wintry cold of this November Saturday everything was still, too still. Unlike a hurricane a revolution has its force and intensity at the centre, and not at the periphery. It was impossible to get on to Budapest, and so I strolled back along the empty lonely highway towards the Austrian frontier, puzzling over the question of the day: would the men in the Kremlin, hesitantly or indifferently, allow this October Revolution to take its course, with the possible risk of a chain-reaction throughout their entire Empire, or would they, with wonted ruthlessness, strike back and be forever branded for murder?

A crowded jeep, filled with armed freedom-fighters and decorated with the national flag (Soviet red star cut out of the middle), came down the road. A man with a machine-gun waved at me and called out, "We've won, we've won, we can hardly believe it! ..." But we wanted to believe it, we had to believe it. Any other prospect was too terrible ...

M. J. Lasky, Der Monat (Berlin), December 1956

A Pole Reports from the Countryside

Budapest

We left at dawn for the north-west, a group of four journalists and two young Dudas followers: the watchful Istvan, who got the car for us, and Bela, the chauffeur, a handsome happy fellow ... From Istvan we learn that Bela used to work as a chauffeur for the Central Committee ...

Despite the early hour there is commotion in the city. People are sweeping away the glass fragments that litter the pavements, repairing street-car rails and righting overturned cars; groups of workers have lunch bags hanging from their shoulders. It is difficult to believe that they are responding so quickly to yesterday's appeal. Istvan is surprised at our lack of confidence. Of course they are going to work—against whom should they continue to strike now? ...

Unexpected gaiety ... We felt as though we had left behind not only the city limits but also the unendurable nervous tension in which we had been living for so long. The rural, calm, monotonous, politically indifferent landscape casually prompted in us a repressed desire to forget the cruel story which we had witnessed ... We begin to gossip about our editorial offices, to tell stale jokes ...

A familiar noise ... We leave the center of the road, turn in to a country inn. The green caterpillar tanks pass on ...

In the inn (the village Ac) there is only wine and bread ... We speak with the workers and peasants.

"How does the revolution look in Ac?"

"Just as it should look. We went out to demonstrate. We organized a committee. There was no shooting. Order was maintained ..."

We ask about the Communists.

"There were not terribly many of them here. About a hundred. But not very agreeable ones. A few are in the committees."

"And the others?"

"Nothing. They keep quiet."

"... A kolchoz?"

"There is one in the village. It has not been supressed. But the peasants don't want it. They are waiting for a Government order to dissolve it."

"And to whom did the land belong before?"

"The landowners. They won't come back. Nobody will permit it."

"But what if they try after all?"

A stocky peasant, wearing a hand-woven jacket, lifts his clenched fist: "Then we will make another insurrection!"

When still in Poland we had heard the most fantastic news of Gyor, the great industrial city in north-west Hungary. It was said that a Horthyite detachment, coming from Austria, had taken over here, that an autonomous government of clear-cut rightist character had been set up, and that it was headed by a fanatic Capucine Monk.

We searched for those Horthyites and the Capucine all over town. We couldn't discover any traces of them. The only creatures from Austria we met were some unbelieveably conceited newspaper correspondents of second-rate Western news agencies. We were not in a position to establish whether they were the ones to whom we owed the sensational stories that have been spread all over the globe ...

The Revolutionary Transdanubian Committee: the atmosphere was the same as in all revolutionary committees I've seen, delegations intruding from all sides, typewriters rattling, noise, tobacco smoke, soldiers, armed civilians.

The president of the committee—a fat man with a moustache—did not behave like anyone who had ever belonged to a religious order. When questioned about the "autonomous government," he answered with a sonorous peasant laugh: "Some initiative in that direction did came from high-school students. We told them: 'That would be a cabaret, but no government.'"

The president's name is Attila Szigeti, a well-known left-wing journalist who has been working with the Communists for years. We asked him about his program ... about his attitude towards the Imre Nagy Government.

"Just today," Szigeti says, "we definitely recognized the Government. Now it's the job of all revolutionary forces to rally around Nagy ..."

"Why 'just today'?"

"Because today the composition of the Government is finally such that we can support it with good conscience."

It appears that this morning the province was informed of a new re-organisation of the Government. Politicians disliked by the people—Apro for example—were dismissed. The Social Democrats, headed by Anna Kethly, entered the Government. General Pal Maleter became Minister of Defence.

"We have news from the entire country," Szigeti says. "All revolutionary committees have proclaimed their support of the Nagy Government. Beginning today this is a truly popular Government ..."

From time to time a young officer with a rosy child-like face throws in a phrase in fairly correct Russian ... I ask: "You were a member of the Party, weren't you?"

The young man is surprised ...

"What do you mean by 'I was'? I am a member of the Party."

"But the Party no longer exists, The seat of the city committee was in this building. You chased them out."

"So what? We chased out the bad leaders. But communists remained. Look here!"—The young man draws his membership card from under his shirt. "Let normal life begin again, and I'll pay my dues again. I was and am a communist."

All this went on in a loud voice, openly, in the presence of some ten members of the revolutionary committee, who are not communists.

As a farewell present we received a leaflet from our young Hungarian officer. It was written in bad Russian with funny mistakes, but its contents were clear and concise:

"Soviet Soldiers! We, the workers from the railroad factory in Gyor, inform you that in our democratic state workers are the guardians of the socialist achievements. That means, with all their might, they are speaking out against returning factories and banks to the capitalists. At The same time, we are against any Rakosite-Stalinist restoration.

We are greatly disturbed by the new entry of Soviet forces into Hungary. For this reason we are neutral in the UNO. We want to defend this neutrality and will prevent every provocation against members of the Soviet Army or their families. Whoever resorts to such means will be treated as an enemy of the just Hungarian cause.

Soviet Soldiers! Don't shoot at Hungarian soldiers!"

How will history one day interpret this document of the Hungarian revolution? As justified optimism? As tragedy? ...

Outside the city, near a bridge, at the crossing of two roads, sunk deep in the moist earth, a tank sits tight ... A man with straight eyebrows and a snub nose is just like thousands one meets in Moscow; sitting beside him is a bald man with a flat nose, rolling a cigarette. Behind them, on the tank, there is a third massive soldier with a peasant's face ... wearing a long trenchcoat, holding a rifle. Around the tank are gathered several dozen Hungarians. The first soldier, bent forward in the posture of an orator, says, "But why destroy monuments? Why burn books? Is that culture?"

"So people have to be killed because of monuments!" a voice speaks up out of the crowd.

The soldier hesitates. — "We know that stone is not worth people. But why destroy monuments to heroes? Monuments to those who died for a sacred cause?"

"At first only Stalin's monument was destroyed."

"We don't recognize Stalin either," the soldier remarks, sadly.

His comrade with the flat nose lights a bulky self-rolled cigarette ... The third soldier makes a brusque movement ... In a loud voice he grumbles: "Enough of these conversations!"

The first pats him reassuringly, and says quickly: "Disperse! Disperse!" And goes back into the tank. ...

The night trip back to Budapest ...

1849

Hungary had tried to win the support of liberal Europe ... These appeals met with a friendly response only from the German national assembly at Frankfurt, and in any case liberal Germany needed support from Hungary rather than being able to offer it. The appeals were now renewed under less favourable circumstances. France, which had failed to do anything for Poland or for Italy, and which was now engaged in suppressing the Roman republic, could not be expected to act for a cause less known and more remote ...

The French intervention at Rome belatedly freed Russian hands ... Of course there were practical considerations behind Russia's action. The greatest of these was apprehension for Poland: many Polish exiles were fighting in the Hungarian army, and its two best generals were Poles. If the Hungarians were victorious, the revolution would spread ... and the whole Polish question would soon be reopened ... The Russians did not wish the

revolutionary example to spread from Hungary to the Danubian principalities ...

The Russian rulers, like the statesmen of other countries, judged according to the moment, not in terms of far-fetched schemes. In 1849 they thought only of Poland and Germany. On the other hand, Palmerston, to whom Poland meant nothing and Germany very little, thought of Austria and Russia exclusively in terms of the Near East ...

The Russian forces entered Hungary in May; they were completely successful by the middle of August. Kossuth and his principal supporters escaped ... The intervention had been carried through without any difficulties from the western Powers, and the Russians could congratulate themselves ... This success was ruined by a Russian blunder, itself caused by an echo from Poland, always Russia's blind-spot ...

A. J. P. TAYLOR, "THE STRUGGLE FOR MASTERY IN EUROPE, 1848—1918."

Quoted in Der Monat (Berlin), December 1956

After passing Gyor and Komaron, we had to get out of the car; it was searched from top to bottom. When we get back in, the patrol chief explains: "From passing cars they were throwing out leaflets signed by the Czechoslovak Communist Party. Disgusting leaflets ..."

We pass a long line of trucks, packed with red meat. We remember the inn of Ac and the indignation of the peasants when asked about the prices of food they sold to Budapest. "We do not let them pay us for food! There, they give their blood ..." Is this meat convoy also an expression of solidarity of the province for the city?

The papers are checked a last time near the hotel on Boot Square ... It is almost 2 a. m. "Until tomorrow!"—We say good-bye to our Hungarian friends—until tomorrow!

In the hotel we wake up our comrades. We share with them our impressions of the trip, and what is more important get Saturday's news. Franciska and Lesze had also gone out into the province, southeast to Szolnok. Their impressions resemble ours. Stabilisation of the country has begun. The Government is bevoming a real government supported by all revolutionary forces.

Budapest was quiet today. As on Friday, there were no cases of summary execution on Saturday.

Innumerable AVO men voluntarily appeared before the committee of inquiry at Marko Street. We tried to estimate the number of lynching victims in the city from Tuesday to Thursday morning. The most likely figure ranges from seventy to eighty persons. There is every indication, in the present situation, that there is no risk of the number increasing ...

Before going to sleep I think of the perspective of the Hungarian revolution as it is taking shape in these days of stabilisation. Naturally I do not know in what type of regime the Hungarian Republic will finally clothe itself. But it seems that we will be able to observe here a curious synthesis: a basic realization of a popular democracy (land in the hands of the peasants, socialisation of factories and banks) and of a pluralism of parties, freedom of the press, and all the other liberties inherent in a liberal democracy. Does not such a regime constitute one of the possible roads—perhaps a very slow one—towards socialism? I am not sure. As for the road along which the Rakosis had led their country, it could not but end in bankruptcy and servitude.

In one way or another, a development begins which will not be resolved in days or weeks. As for me—it is time to return to Poland ...

Viktor Woroszylski, Nowa Kultura (Warsaw), 9 December

Trouble-makers, Intruders, and Objective Trials

Budapest

The armed forces and police are consolidating, and the people, too, should realise that they must avoid splitting up into groups. The time for party struggles has not yet come. Do not forget that the Hungarian Fatherland is in acute danger! Everybody must realise that until the last Soviet soldier has left it is not important what any individual thinks. The important thing now is what unites the people—democracy and neutrality.

Those elements who hid during the revolution are now coming into the open to forward their private aims. The fighters for the revolution oppose these people who camouflage themselves as patriots. The Hungarian people will not allow such people to gain positions as revolutionary leaders. It is the revolutionary's holy duty to remove all these intruders from public life.

It is also the duty of the revolutionaries to take arms away from irresponsible elements ... Elements posing as patriots are stirring up the people by slanders and are inciting lynchings. The revolution fought that law and personal safety might be respected and against the methods of the Stalinist system. It most decidedly condemns and dissociates itself from hooliganism and the rule of lynch-law.

AVH methods are not helpful, and we already have plans for obtaining satisfaction for AVH victims.

In peace as well as in war it is of utmost importance to have a strong Government and a strong defence force. It is, however, impossible to fight for national aims if the supply system collapses. It would only please the Soviet forces were the strike to continue, for this does not weaken them but does weaken the Hungarians. If every Hungarian fulfils his task at his job as heroically as the fighters did in battle, the nation will have solved its task ...   *Free Radio Petofi*

True and false reports concerning certain illegalities committed in Budapest and the provinces are circulating in the country. These reports create an atmosphere of anxiety. We demand the punishment of those guilty of crimes in the past. The terrorists trained and led by Rakosi and his clique have trodden on the law and human rights and have imprisoned innocent people. We demand that all these criminals be brought to account. The best socialist intellectuals have already called for this and it was under pressure from the opposition within the Party that the leadership was forced to celebrate the funeral of the unjustly executed martyrs. Now, after the defeat of the Rakosi-Gero clique, we have the opportunity to climinate the criminals. Let us not allow new illegalities to be committed. Let us see to it that after an objective trial by local tribunals the criminals receive due punishment ...

Nepszabadsag (Budapest), 3 November

The Central National Committee calls the attention of County Revolutionary Councils and National Committees to the fact that suspicious groups appear in county and towns. Referring to certain so-called central organs, these groups say that they have been entrusted with leading and directing revolutionary organisations. These groups are creating confusion and endanger the achievements of our revolution. Trouble-making elements who take the law into their own hands must be arrested. The Central National Committee has sent, and continues to send, only the representatives of the revolutionary university youth to assist revolutionary organs and to help to establish revolutionary order ...

Free Radio Kossuth

"Political Wisdom" for Workers, Mothers, Guardsmen

Budapest

From the editorial, "Let's Not Be Our Own Enemies," in today's *Nepszava,* the Social Democratic paper: Children are hungry, clothing and shoes wearing out, fuel is getting scarce, gas and electricity are getting weaker. The hospitals with all the wounded are endangered ... If the country is paralyzed, if its economy runs down, if it loses strength, it will be more exposed than ever before to the resumption of Stalinist-Rakosist tyranny. We certainly do not want this to happen. We cannot allow this to happen. It demonstrates great political wisdom that almost every worker in Csepel, workers of Mavag, of the Ganz Electrical Works, of the Ganz Car Factory ... and several other big factories, most railroad men and construction workers, have decided to resume work because the continuation of the strike would paralyze the country's economy and would weaken us, not the enemy.   *Free Radio Kossuth*

In an interview by the independent *Valosag,* Jozsef Szilagyi, head of Imre Nagy's office, said that to defend the gains of the struggle for freedom, order must be maintained. He called on mothers not to allow their children, whose heroism in the fighting had been well established, to continue carrying arms, thus endangering their own lives and the lives of others ...

Hungarian News Agency

The Revolutionary Workers Council of the industrial area of Salgotarjan held a mass meeting ... They reserve the right to strike, but will resume work in the mines and essential transport services at once, and in other enterprises on Monday ... To continue the strike would lead to a shortage of goods and other troubles ... The revolution emphasises that they will strike if the Government does not meet the long-term demands. Finally, they state that resumption of work in no way means a retreat. "We continue our national fight for independence and neutrality, if necessary with arms."   *Free Radio Kossuth*

The Committee (of the Forces of Public Order) unanimously elects Major-General Bela Kiraly as commander-in-chief of the National Guard and Sandor Kopacsy, Colonel of police, to act as his deputy. The Committee delegates eight members to the National Guard High Command ...

We shall resist every aggression directed against our independence and neutrality. Pending free democratic elections, we shall help toward the consolidation of order with all our might and shall faithfully carry out Government measures designed to annihilate attempts at restoration by reactionary troublemakers.

Since strikes cause serious harm to our country's defense potential, we recommend that the strike be ended and organized work begun, with the provision that National Guard formations keep their weapons nearby, even while going back to work, so that in case of aggression they can be ready for immediate battle ...

As of today, persons belonging neither to the Army nor the police are permitted to carry arms only if they belong to the National Guard. Persons belonging neither to the Army, the police, nor the National Guard will be disarmed by us in the interest of the consolidation of peace ...

Free Radio Kossuth

Jozsef Kovago, who has been elected Chairman of the Budapest National Committee, made this statement to a News Agency representative: "After six years and six months of imprisonment I have learned with pride of the confidence which the people of the capital have in us. The state of my health does not allow me to occupy this post yet, but the visit I made on Saturday morning to my friend and old colleague Peter Bechtler convinced me that he could conveniently occupy the post in my stead. I intend to ask him to replace me until my return. I hope to be able to present myself soon to the population of Budapest as Mayor and my aim will be to make the capital flourish ..."   *Hungarian News Agency*

Csepel

Budapest

Saturday afternoon I took the trolley to the great Csepel iron and steel works, which employed some 40,000 workers and had emerged as one of the principal centers of the revolution.

Once the plant had been known as the Rakosi Works, but shortly before the revolution, when the dictator fell, the name had been removed from the front gates and now there was only the shadowy outline of the letters to be made out. I was admitted without any fuss and conducted to the manager's office, where I found the new manager talking to a man armed with a tommy gun. Actually he was not the manager, but an engineer and the president of the Workers Council which had taken over the plant, and he shared the office with an old white-haired machinist also representing the Workers Council. Both men told me frankly that they had been members of the Communist party, but that seemed to make no difference to anyone; what mattered was whether you had behaved decently. Even before the revolution everyone had really known where everyone else stood as far as the Russians were concerned. At the first crack of the shots fired by the AVH at demonstrating students on October 23, the ranks of decent Hungarians had rallied as if on signal against the Russians and their creatures.

The old machinist led me through the shops, which were now deserted; in the morning there had been a bit of activity to prepare for the resumption of work on Monday. The floor of the factory was littered with torn-up Communist placards and pictures of Lenin. (By the time the revolution started all the pictures of Stalin had already disappeared). The offices of the Communist party overseers were a shambles: the files lay scattered and torn on the floor. A couple of workers had found their own files in the rubbish, and as they studied the ideological fairy tales that the deposed Communist bosses had woven around them, their faces took on a queer look that was partly made up of the fear they had once felt and partly of a kind of boyish amusement ...

Peter Schmid, Die Weltwoche (Zurich) and Commentary (New York), January 1957

The AVH and Prisoners, Old and New

Budapest

Former AVH members are reporting en masse at the Public Prosecutor's office, asking to be arrested. A report was handed to Dr. Sandor Nemes, the President of the Revolutionary Tribunal of the Public Prosecutor's office showing for example, that in a single district, namely Budapest XIII, 30 former AVH agents reported early this morning. The situation is similar in other districts ...   *Free Radio Kossuth*

Szolnok

The Police Commissariat of the Workers' Revolutionary Council of the Region of Szolnok has just announced that all AVH agents of the region have been arrested. They are regarded as prisoners of war and have been handed over to the Military Command ... The communiqué of the Workers' Revolutionary Council points out that there can be no question of holding them collectively responsible. It appeals to the population of Szolnok not to trouble the families of former members of the AVH ...   *Hungarian News Agency*

Budapest

This morning the Revolutionary Tribunal of the Public Prosecutor's office began the revisions of cases of political prisoners and the cases of common criminals imprisoned in Marko Street Prison. In very many cases sentences were administered which were far too severe in relation to the crimes committed, or such persons were arrested and are still in prison for offenses that are no longer considered crimes. Hundreds were condemned simply because they could not stand the hunger, misery, and the terror which existed under the old regime ...   *Free Radio Kossuth*

The National Revolutionary Committee of Hungarian Lawyers condemned lynch law in a communiqué ... Individuals have been attempting to take revenge for anti-national attitudes or personal grievances. The communiqué emphasized that strictly on the basis of legality Hungarian lawyers protest any action that could imperil in any way the achievements of the National Revolution. The lawyers emphasized that they do not want to exempt anybody from the normal processes of jurisdiction, and they request the people to maintain discipline and moderation ...   *Free Radio Kossuth*

The Party "On the Brink"

It is the duty of the six-member (Party) committee headed by Janos Kadar to go to Moscow immediately to begin negotiations with the Communist Party leadership ... to send telegrams to the French, Italian and German Communist Parties. Let us explain to our Russian and other comrades abroad that there was a time, when the liberating Soviet Army reached the frontiers of Hungary (1944), when at least half of the nation placed its trust in the Communist Party. Let us explain with blunt frankness that, as a result of the behavior of the Soviet Army of occupation, we obtained only one-sixth of the vote in the ensuing free election.

Tell them frankly that, as a result of the past few bloody days and irresponsible mass-murder by Russian officers, our Party today is altogether on the brink of bankruptcy. We (Communists) are worse off than in 1945 when we started. Tell our comrades that a new occupation might assure that Hungary would remain a Russian colony for some time—it would not even be impossible for a new Rakosi, or a new Gero, to report to Moscow that a new Communist Party has been created in Hungary, on paper,—and dues could even be extorted from members at bayonet-point. But the lofty tenets of Marxism-Leninism, of Communism, would have disappeared without a trace from our country ...   *Radio Rajk*

"A Broken System"

Budapest

My friends were mostly at the Writers' Club in Bayza Street. Most of them had gone into gaol during the early months of the Rakosi terror, and emerged only in 1954, during the "liberal period" of Imre Nagy (before they shoved him out again for "rightist deviation", *read* sense of decency and justice).

I shall leave their names unsaid. Yet it is an important fact about the revolt of 1956 that it was encouraged and inspired—like its notable ancestor of 1848 — by men of letters: almost entirely, by radical men of letters. There was no coherent organisation behind the rising of October 23 — not even any preconceived intention; but there was an inspiration. It came from the writings of a score of men who published, week by week and gradually in stronger words, their articles of protest in the *Irodalmi Ujsag*, the "Literary Gazette". As with Petofi in 1848, so these men now.

One of them had lately married. "We met in gaol, as a matter of fact. Met? Well, not exactly. We used to tap out messages to each other. She came out earlier than I did, but she waited for me. They'd given her a bad time. They'd torn-out her toe nails. The usual Rakosi charges: spying, wrecking, all that ...."

One learnt these things with shame.

Counter-revolution? On Wednesday October 31st, this Writers' Club was put in editorial charge of Budapest Radio. Almost to a man they were principled supporters of radical social change ...

And the army?

Many units handed over their arms at once. Others stayed neutral. After the first day, none remained with the Russians and the political police.

Its officers? A mixed bag.

A colonel showed where I could find the office of General Paul Maleter on the day that Nagy made him Minister of War (and the day before the Russians seized him). This colonel was fairly rubbing his hands. He said: "Just think, I've been a colonel for ten years. With my experience, too. I fought on the Russian front, you know — and these Communists wouldn't promote me. You'll see. Now there'll be promotion".

Perhaps; and perhaps not. For Maleter and his fellow-commanders were different. Already famous for his refusal to surrender the Kilian Barracks to Soviet tanks. Maleter impressed one. A tall lean self-confident man: a man of action, a product of Communist training both military and otherwise. He still wore his little partisan star of 1944 (and another Red Star awarded for successful coal-digging by his regiment at Tatabanya) at a time when the whole officers' corps was dragging off its Soviets-style epaulettes. "If we get rid of the Russians" he said to me, "don't think we're going back to the old days. And if there's people who do want to go back, well we'll see". And he touched his revolver holster.

Counter-revolution?

Even the newly-reissued *Sziv* (an authoritative Catholic weekly) wrote that Saturday morning that: "We renounce the nationalised estates of the Church." And Mindszenty's broadcast of the same night — distorted afterwards by those anxious to prove counter-revolution at all costs — was in fact a qualified and yet significant reinforcement of the Nagy Government. Mindszenty, true enough, called that Government "the heirs of a broken system".

That system — the Rakosi regime — did in fact collapse overnight. To defend it, among Hungarians, there was no-one but the political police; and they were only defending themselves.

By Saturday the hunt for these hated hangmen was practically over: in the process, some of the innocent also suffered. Only at the big party headquarters in Republic Square was the chase still warm. There I saw men drilling for a suspected secret "bunker" many feet down. Giant shovels had scooped wide trenches in the Square: fruitlessly.

In the basement they were also drilling. Deep in black miry mud, pastried with filthy sheets of paper, that basement had a long series of stepping-stones that were made of books, bundles of books. We trod on these, wobbling as we went across that gruesome cellar towards the arc-lit din of drilling.

I looked down to see what books had met this fate.

Engulfed in mud there lay the works of Marx and Lenin.

Yes, a broken system ...

Basil Davidson, The Times of India (Bombay),
24 November

Cardinal Mindszenty's Broadcast

Budapest

Nowadays it is often emphasized that the speaker breaking away from the practice of the past is speaking sincerely. I cannot say this in such a way. I need not break with my past; by the grace of God I am the same as I was before my imprisonment. I stand by my conviction physically and spiritually intact, just as I was eight years ago, although imprisonment has left its mark on me. Nor can I say that now I will speak more sincerely, for I have always spoken sincerely ...

Now is the first instance in history that Hungary is enjoying the sympathy of all civilized nations. We are deeply moved by this. A small nation has heartfelt joy that because of its love of liberty the other nations have taken up its cause. We see Providence in this, expressed by the solidarity of foreign nations just as it says in our national anthem: "God bless the Hungarian — reach out to him Thy protective hand." Then our national anthem continues: "— when he is fighting against his enemy." But we, even in our extremely severe situation, hope that we have no enemy! For we are not enemies of anyone. We desire to live in friendship with every people and with every country ...

We, the little nation, desire to live in friendship and in mutual respect with the great American United States and with the mighty Russian Empire alike, in good neighborly relationship with Prague, Bucharest, Warsaw, and Belgrade. In this regard I must mention that for the brotherly understanding in our present suffering every Hungarian has embraced Austria to his heart.

And now, our entire position is decided by what the Russian Empire of 200 millions intends to do with the military force standing within our frontiers. Radio announcements say that this military force is growing. We are neutral, we give the Russian Empire no cause for bloodshed. But has the idea not occurred to the leader of the Russian Empire that we will respect the Russian people far more if it does not oppress us. It is only an enemy people which is attacked by another country. We have not attacked Russia and sincerely hope that the withdrawal of Russian military forces from our country will soon occur ...

This has been a freedom fight which was unparalleled in the world, with the young generation at the head of the nation. The fight for freedom was fought because the nation wanted to decide freely on how it should live. It wants to be free to decide about the management of its state and the use of its labor. The people themselves will not permit this fact to be distorted to the advantage of some unauthorized powers or hidden motives. We need new elections — without abuses — at which every party can nominate. The election should take place under international control. I am and remain independent of any party and — because of my office — also above it. In my authority I warn every Hungarian, after these beautiful days of unity, not to give way to party struggle and disagreement. This country is now in need of many things, but it needs as few parties and party leaders as possible. Today, politics themselves are a matter of secondary importance. The nation's existence and everyday bread is our worry. The successors of the fallen regime have made retrospective revelations which show that a legal accounting has to be made in every field, through independent and impartial law courts. Private revenge has to be avoided and eliminated. Those who have participated in the fallen regime carry their own responsibility for their activities, omissions, defaults or wrong measures. I do not want to make a single denunciatory statement because this would retard the start of work and the course of production in the country. If things proceed decently, according to promises made, this will not be my task. However, I also have to stress the practical framework of things to be done since we want to live in a constitutional state, in a society without classes, and develop our democratic achievements. We are for private ownership rightly and justly limited by social interests and we want to be a country and nation of a strictly cultural-national spirit. This is what the entire Hungarian people want.

As the Head of the Hungarian Roman Catholic Church I declare, just as the Bench of Bishops stated in a joint letter in 1945, that we do not oppose the direction of former progress and that we further desire a healthy development in every field. The Hungarian people will find it natural that we have to care for our institutions which have a great value and a great past. I further mention briefly for the information of the 6.5 million Catholics in the country that in Church life we shall remove every trace of the violence and the characteristics of the fallen regime. This is a natural consequence growing out of our ancestral faith and moral teachings and of laws which are as old as the Church ...

We justly expect the immediate granting of freedom of Christian religious instruction and the restoration of the institutions and societies of the Catholic Church — among other things, her press. From this moment on we shall watch whether the promises and deeds are identical, and the things which can be carried out today. We who are watchful and who want the best for the whole people trust in Providence, and not in vain.

Free Radio Kossuth and Free Radio Petofi

Pal Ignotus: "The Example of Britain..."

Budapest

I recall the day when, 16 years ago, I spoke to you on the BBC. It was a most decisive moment when — half Europe already subjugated, the USA not yet ready, the Soviet Union still engaged in sending war materials to Germany—Britain was left alone in her life-and-death battle. I witnessed then the wonderful unity of a nation which had been accustomed to the free expression of differing opinions... I asked myself: when shall I see the day when my country too would be so welded into unity, so conscious of its task, so brave, so exaltedly determined? Now, listeners, I have seen the day. Such unity is seldom achieved in history, a unity that finds expresion alike in the words of the Roman Catholic Primate and in those of the Prime Minister.

This unity exceeds in wonder even that which Britain achieved 16 years ago. For what we see here was achieved not by a Great Power, not by a nation educated for centuries in free parliamentary development, but by a small country... emerging from dictatorships and semi-dictatorships... that had known man's debasement and the loss of a nation's conscience. This national unity is mirrored in that international sympathy towards the Hungarian freedom fighters which has united American capitalists and Chinese Communists, Christians and freethinkers, conservatives, liberals and socialists, east and west of the Iron Curtain.

But you must not think that the struggle is over. In the work of reorganization — while houses are in ruins, shops closed, and offices groping towards new life — we shall need unity more than ever before. We need resolutely to preserve the cohesion of the people and the world's sympathy. We might easily lose the things we have gained so wonderfully...

Atrocities and torture must be condemned... Those responsible for crimes of the past — as members of the Security Police — must be punished by courts at long last truly free... But no true soldier of the revolution should ever take part in illegal revenge; there is no place for the man-hunt. I have known both fascist persecution and the prisons of the Rakosi terror; I could say much about the cruelty and humiliating treatment meted out by Rakosi, Gero, Mihaly Farkas, and Gabor Peter. But just because I had so much cause to learn to hate them, I hate even the idea of acting now from a desire for vengeance, however justified... We must not risk the international success of our national revolution with passionate outbursts which might create the impression of a man-hunt in the eyes of those unfamiliar with the situation.

We also owe it to our national revolution to resume work; cessation of work can only help our enemies. And here again I recall the Britain of 16 years ago, when, in a country where the right to strike is most jealously protected by the worker, in the face of national danger, this right, in spite of some opposition, was voluntarily surrendered...

The unity into which Hungarians were welded by their fight for freedom does not mean the renunciation of different parties, or of the individuality of persons with different viewpoints... Many different forces met in the revolution; this is the strength, not the weakness, of the revolution... For what we want is truly the order of freedom, and this implies different approaches. The time for that will come too, but now the united effort and victory of the nation must be our sole desire.

Free Radio Kossuth

Announcement of Government Changes

Budapest

The Presidential Council of the People's Republic, for the purpose of complementing and consolidating the National Government, has appointed the following:

Anna Kethly [Social Democrat]
Gyula Kelemen [Social Democrat]
Jozsef Fischer [Social Democrat]
Istvan B. Szabo [Smallholder]
Istvan Bibo [Petofi Peasant]
Ferenc Farkas [Petofi Peasant]
Pal Maleter

The Presidential Council has relieved the following from their posts at their own request:

Imre Horvath, Minister of Foreign Affairs; *Dr. Ferenc Muennich,* Minister of Interior; *Karoly Janza,* Minister of Defence; *Istvan Kossa,* Minister of Finance; *Erik Molnar,* Minister of Justice; *Janos Csergoe,* Minister of Metallurgy and Machine Industry; *Sandar Czottner,* Minister of Mining and Electricity; *Gergely Szabo,* Minister of Chemical Industry; *Mrs. Jozsef Nagy,* Minister of Light Industry; *Ferenc Nezval,* Minister of Urban and Rural Development; *Miklos Ribianszky,* Minister of State Farms; *Jozsef Bognar,* Minister of Foreign Trade; *Janos Tausz,* Minister of Internal Trade; *Rezsoe Nyers,* Minister of Food Industry; *Antal Gyenes,* Minister of Produce Collection; *Antal Apro,* Minister of Building; *Gyoergy Csanady* Minister of Communications and Post; *Gyoergy Lukacs,* Minister of Popular Culture; *Albert Konya,* Minister of Education; *Antal Babits,* Minister of Health; *Antal Apro,* Deputy Chairman, Council om Ministers; *Jozsef Bognar,* Deputy Chairman, Council of Minister; *Ferenc Erdei,* Deputy Chairman, Council of Ministers.

With the exception of the Foreign Affairs and Defence portfolios, the Presidential Council leaves all Ministerial portfolios vacant. The Presidential Council will instead appoint Deputy Ministers to be in charge of the Ministries concerned. It will be the duty of these to exercise leadership over the functioning of the Ministries and their Governmental and economic activities, and to do so on the basis of decisions and measures taken by the National Government.

On the basis of the above decisions, the composition of the National Government is as follows:

Imre Nagy, President of the Council of Ministers and Minister of Foreign Affairs; *Zoltan Tildy*, Minister of State; *Bela Kovacs*, Minister of State; *Istvan B. Szabo*, Minister of State; *Anna Kethly*, Minister of State; *Gyula Kelemen*, Minister of State; *Jozsef Fischer*, Minister of State; *Istvan Bibo*, Minister of State; *Ferenc Farkas*, Minister of State; *Geza Losonczy*, Minister of State; *Janos Kadar*, Minister of State; *Pal Maleter*, Minister of Defence.

Members of the National Government, as Ministers of State, will, in groups to be defined by the National Government, discharge the leadership of the Ministries through Deputy Ministers to be appointed ...   *Free Radio Kossuth* [13:25]

The Petofi Peasant Party

Miskolc

We resolve now to lift up again the glorious and spotless flag of the National Peasant Party, and to continue our political movement under the name: *Petofi Peasant Party*.

The Petofi Peasant Party believes in private property and advocates free production and marketing. In the field of religion we advocate the fullest freedom of conscience, freedom of religion and institutional protection of the activities of churches true to the spirit of Christ. The Petofi Peasant Party announces that it will not retreat from its demand to give to peasant children and peasant youth more education. We declare that we accept fully the 1945 Land Reform Law, that we will not return land now in the possession of our peasantry, that we will fight relentlessly against any attempt which would try to challenge the rightfulness of that great national achievement, against anyone who would dare attack land reform measures. But we deem it necessary to re-examine all illegalities in this field that have been committed from 1948 until our national revolution. While fully respecting the right of peasants to sell their products without restrictions, we consider it necessary to maintain existing agricultural cooperatives until peasant-cooperatives are set up on a sound basis ...

Radio Free Miskolc

Budapest

An editorial by the writer Laszlo Nemeth was published by the Petofi Party organ. He said the big strides along the road to socialism made by Hungary in the last few years must not be for-gotten. He knew of no writer or thinker opposed to socialism, but differences had existed as to whether Hungary's socialism should be a copy, or adapted to her own circumstances. The decision had now been taken—not against socialism, but against a form that was alien to the nation. Hungary had proclaimed her neutrality. But she must not alienate socialist states, such as Poland and Yugoslavia, or States advancing towards systems akin to socialism, such as India, by a return, even if superficial, to bourgeois democracy. Nemeth called for what he said would be a political system of historic importance: a multi-Party system based on a common fundamental principle, combining the force of an ideologically-based social system with the elasticity of a parliamentary system ...   *Hungarian News Agency*

Austria Denies

Budapest

Imre Nagy received the Austrian Minister Dr. Peinsipp, at noon on 3 November. Dr. Peinsipp gave him the following aide-memoire:

My Government has authorized me to take the most energetic stand against allegations that the Austrian Government enabled armed or unarmed Hungarian emigrés to infiltrate into Hungary through Austrian territory. The Austrian Government has ordered the establishment of a closed zone along the Austrian-Hungarian frontier. Only authorized persons, such as local inhabitants, Red Cross auxiliary personnel who are staying there officially, and journalists are entitled to enter it. The Minister of Defence has inspected this zone in the company of military attachés of the four Great Powers, including the USSR. The military attachés were thus enabled to make sure of the measures which have been taken in the frontier zone with a view to protecting the Austrian frontier and Austrian neutrality.

All precautions have also been taken on Austria's western frontier to prevent emigrés from infiltrating. Visas are granted to emigrés only with the consent of the Minister of the Interior. The Austrian authorities have requested the former Premier Ferenc Nagy, who arrived in Vienna unexpectedly on Monday, to leave Austria's territory immediately. This is known also to the Soviet authorities ...   *Free Radio Kossuth*

Foreign Aid

Budapest

The following gift consignments have arrived in Budapest by air in recent days: 20 plane-loads from Poland, 26 plane-loads from Vienna, nine plane-loads from Switzerland, seven from the [East] German Republic, two from Bulgaria, two from Czechoslovakia, and one each from Rumania, Yugoslavia and Belgium.

Free Radio Kossuth

Communist Reporter Protests, Resigns

Vienna

Franz X. Philipp, 41-year-old Austrian representative of the Soviet-Zone German News Agency, has resigned. His editors in East Berlin have for weeks now been either suppressing or distorting his reports about the events in Hungary and Austria. They even went so far as to attribute to him articles which had been entirely invented to disseminate Soviet propaganda.

Philip is a veteran Austrian communist. Taken prisoner by the Russians in May, 1943, he worked in the Moscow "Committee for Free Germany". He was considered so trustworthy that, together with the Red Army, he arrived in Berlin in May 1945. For ten years he worked as the deputy foreign editor of the *Taegliche Rundschau*, the official Soviet daily in Eastern Germany. There had been, Philipp told me, repeated quarrels with East Berlin since the outbreak of the Hungarian revolution, especially after the second intervention of the Red Army in Hungary, because ADN had been arbitrarily changing his reports. "The

chief reason for my break is that I wrote about the Hungarian tragedy in the only way any decent human being can write of it. I told my friends that the Soviet intervention was a *Schweinerei* that had nothing whatsoever to do with socialism."

He also cited to press representatives dispatches which appeared in the ADN Service under his signature without his ever having written them. This applied particularly to the slanders against Austria for her alleged violation of neutrality and support of the revolutionaries.

One of Philipp's interesting statements is that in East Berlin the name of Janos Kadar was crossed off the list of ministers included in his report of November 3rd, relating the reorganization of the Nagy government which was just then taking place. Philipp said in this connection: "*They* were already aware of Kadar's treason one day before the Russian attack, and of his rôle as the leader of Budapest's puppet Government." H. G. Rambousek, *Die Welt (Hamburg)*, 3 December

"The Ideas of Proletarian Internationalism"

London

Soviet news on the situation in Hungary remained very sparse until 2nd/3rd November, when reporting from Budapest, combined with reports from the Vienna Communist press and an expurgated report of an appeal by the PZPR (Polish Communists), began to suggest that a new menace had arisen in the otherwise quiescent state of affairs in the shape of a resurgence of "black reactionary elements" encouraged or dispatched by primarily U.S. subversive interests from outside the country ... *BBC Summary*

Moscow

The declaration of the Government of the U.S.S.R. on the foundations for the development and further strengthening of friendship and co-operation between the Soviet Union and other socialist States has been received in all socialist countries with warm approval ... The democratic public of the whole world notes that this is a document of tremendous historical importance permeated with the ideas of proletarian internationalism ... *Pravda (Moscow), 3 November*

Prague

Dear friends, comrades! I am addressing you on behalf of our Communist Party and the Government of the National Front of Czechoslovakia. Events of far-reaching importance and significance are developing at present around us ... It is necessary to express a clear attitude towards these events.

In neighbouring Hungary a counter-revolution has been raging during the past few days. It has unleashed a fascist white terror against the workers. Its hands are soiled with the blood of thousands of murdered workers and ordinary people of all classes. Hungarian reaction, hand in hand with the Western imperialists, has begun to implement a plan, prepared long ago, directed not only against the people's power in Hungary, but ultimately against all socialist countries, against world peace.

Now returning to Hungary are reactionary elements, war criminals, aristocrats, fascists and other emigrés from the West who in 1945 ran before the advancing Soviet Army or later fled from the people's anger. Horthyite fascist officers are active in the army. Exploiters are re-emerging from the ranks of large estate owners and capitalists, whose power had been broken by the working-class and the people. The old bankrupt political parties are being re-established with the aim of dividing the nation into hostile factions. These groups are fighting each other for posts in the Government; and everyone is being removed who attempts to defend the interests of the working people and of socialism ...

The declaration of Imre Nagy, whose Government has not been confirmed by Parliament, concerning the withdrawal of Hungary from the alliance of socialist States under the Warsaw Treaty, his negotiations with capitalist countries, confirm clearly all I have said. We are confident that the Hungarian working class and the Hungarian people will not give up their socialist achievements. We believe that the workers will not return the factories to the industrialists, or that the farmers will return their land to the big estate owners. A person who has lived in freedom even for a single month will not voluntarily accept capitalist fetters again. The Hungarian people will not voluntarily submit to enslavement.

In this endeavour we all shall stand by the side of the Hungarian working class, of the working people. We stood by their side during the time they were building their socialist State, and also during the past few days when they defended it heroically in bloody combats with bourgeois reaction ...

President Zapotocky, Czechoslovakian Radio

East Berlin

Nobody wants to hide the fact that mistakes have been made in people's democratic Hungary. But it was an even greater mistake to permit for months on end the so-called oppositionists of the Petofi Circle to focus the attention of the whole people on the past and to do everything to undermine the Workers' Party and the State Power. These people of the "opposition" in the Petofi Circle were incapable of working out a constructive political and economic policy themselves; they diverted attention from their own shortcomings by disseminating propaganda of hatred against the Soviet Union ...

What the capitalist press wants is not the independence of Hungary but her dependence on monopoly capitalism ...

The people must be watchful. Anyone who makes the slightest concession to reaction will, in the end, pay with his life ...

*Walther Ulbricht, Communist Deputy Prime Minister,
East German Radio, 3 November*

Sofia

The workers already understand that the "democratic" and "revolutionary" slogans of the counter-revolutionaries were a cynical deception ... The tragic events of Hungary are a grave lesson, and not only for the Hungarian people. They have once again shown that international and internal reaction are not dead, and that nation-wide vigilance must be maintained. The Bulgarian people will, therefore, rally their Fatherland Front around the Bulgarian Communist Party, today stronger, more monolithic, and more prepared for battle than even before.

Otechestven Front (Sofia), 3 November

Negotiations

Budapest

On Saturday morning, in the Parliament building in Budapest, negotiations began between representatives of the armed forces of the Soviet Union and of Hungary. The negotiations are taking place between Ferenc Erdei, Hungarian Minister of State, Maj. Gen. Pal Maleter, Maj. Gen. Istvan Kovacs and Col. Miklos Szucs for Hungary, and Gen. Malinin, Lt. Gen. Stepano and Maj. Gen. Shchelbanin for Soviet Russia. These talks are still in progress and their results will be known only late in the afternoon ...

The mixed committee of the Hungarian and Soviet Army Commands met this morning and both parties have explained their points of view as regards the technical problems of the withdrawal of the Soviet troops. The mixed committee has agreed to study the respective explanations and to meet again at 22:00 tonight. Meanwhile, the Soviet delegation has promised that no further trains carrying Soviet troops will cross the Hungarian frontier ...   *Free Radio Kossuth*

UN Security Council Postpones Hungarian Question

New York

There can be no real freedom of choice for the Hungarian, or any other Eastern European, people so long as Soviet troops remain on their soil. Premier Nagy has appealed to the United Nations to defend Hungary's neutrality against the threat of renewed Soviet military domination. No less than the problem of the Middle East this appeal presents a challenge to the United Nations. If the Security Council, because of the Soviet veto, cannot meet this challenge, then it is imperative that the General Assembly, now meeting in emergency session, take up the problem at once.

New York Times, 3 November

THE PROCEEDINGS IN THE U.N.

General Assembly

In emergency session at 8 p.m. Assembly debated Egyptian complaint against British-French aggression in Egypt.

Security Council

Council continued debate on joint complaint of Britain, France and United States against Soviet intervention in Hungary. Debate will be resumed on Monday at 10:30 a.m.

New York Times, 4 November

New York

Ambassador Lodge laid before the Council a resolution "deploring the use of Soviet military forces to suppress the efforts of the Hungarian people to reassert their rights." The resolution proposed also that United Nations members furnish food, medicine and relief supplies to the people of the Central European state. The resolution failed of immediate passage. By a vote of 10 to 0, with one abstention, the Council voted to postpone consideration of the Hungarian question until 10:30 a.m. Monday.

But a series of speakers from the West, including Latin America, made plain that they looked with grave doubts on Soviet good faith in negotiations reportedly in progress in Budapest for withdrawal of Soviet forces. An initial proposal by Yugoslavia for postponement of discussion while the negotiations proceeded found no support.

The British delegate set the keynote in a warning to the Council that, "as a matter of history," many nations had had experience in negotiations with the Soviet power which "have ended in misfortune." Louis de Guiringaud of France reminded the United Nations of the "Soviet coup in Prague eight years ago", when Czechoslovakia "became a satellite in the Soviet orbit."

Dr. Donald Walker of Austrialia, Victor A. Belaunde of Peru, and others, voiced similar doubts. Finally, an attempt by the Western powers to get a statement from the Soviet representative regarding the Hungarian situation brought scant success.

This Security Council session continued the discussion of the Hungarian situation begun at a meeting of the international body Friday night. The session was called at the request of Britain, France and the United States.

The United States resolution proposed that the United Nations "affirm the right of the Hungarian people to a Government responsible to its national aspirations and dedicated to its independence and well-being. These rights and fundamental freedoms, the United States pointed out, were guaranteed to Hungary by the Allied and associated powers of World War II in the peace treaty signed in Paris, Feb. 10, 1947. The Soviet Union was a signatory.

Seated at the Council table was Dr. Janos Szabo, the new representative of Hungary to the United Nations. On Friday objections had been raised to Dr. Szabo's presence as an observer, replacing the previous Hungarian Minister, Dr. Peter Kos, who was relieved from duty by the new Government of Premier Nagy ... The Secretary General reported that credentials for Dr. Szabo had been received by cable from Budapest ... (and) that these credentials were considered adequate.

The Council met some uncertainty regarding the immediate situation in Hungary. Dr. Joza Brilej of Yugoslavia told the group that negotiations already had been begun between the Nagy

UN Debate

New York

Mr. Sobolev (U.S.S.R.): *A request has been made to me to comment on the report concerning the continuation of negotiations between Hungarian and Soviet representatives with regard to Soviet troops in Hungary. I can confirm that such negotiations are in progress ...*

Mr. Janos Szabo (Hungary): *I should like to thank the President and the members of the Security Council for giving me the opportunity to take part in the Council's discussions as a representative of the Hungarian People's Republic.*

In reply to the question of the representatives of the United States and Yugoslavia, I should like to inform the Council with satisfaction about the following promising information received from Budapest today; the leaders of the Hungarian and Soviet Armies met today at noon, and both parties expressed their views on the technical questions of withdrawing the Soviet troops. They agreed that they would study each other's proposal and they would meet again at 10 o'clock tonight, Budapest time. According to the Soviet proposal, no more troops will cross the border until an agreement is reached ...

M. de Guiringaud (France): *Can we believe the contentions, when we bear in mind the c o u p which took place in Prague eight years ago? Some of us here can remember Mr. Jan Masaryk. At that time, Soviet troops concentrated on the frontiers of Czechoslovakia and imposed capitulation upon the Czechoslovak Government, a capitulation which made Czechoslovakia a satellite in the Soviet orbit. Is not that exactly what Soviet forces are now trying to accomplish in Hungary? Is it not another attempt in Budapest to repeat the c o u p which was successful in Prague? If the Soviet Union does wish to negotiate with Hungary, then it can certainly withdraw its troops. Why should it need tanks and troops for negotiations? For all these reasons, the representative of the Soviet Union cannot come here and submit that the situation is a highly confused one and that, consequently, the Soviet Union must await some clarification of the situation before taking action. It is just because the situation is confused that we must act ...*

UN Verbatim Record, Security Council, 3 November

regime and the Soviet authorities, looking toward the removal of Russian troops from the country. This information, he said, came to him from his Government.

Lindesay Parrott New York Times, 4 November

Budapest

At the editorial office of the journal *"The Truth"*, where I have set up shop, news came in that a UN delegation composed of sixteen persons was expected at the Ferihegy airport in order to open negotiations with the Soviet authorities.

During twelve hours of rain and fog Budapest has been stagnating while the rest of the world went about its business, and the UN appear as the supreme hope of the strangled city.

At 3 p. m. I went to the airport. Some hundred meters short of it, I ran into an armed Soviet patrol; behind, tanks threatening the suburbs of Budapest ... The tri-colored press card gave me access without difficulty. But on the rain-battered and deserted runway, no plane was landing. Hope was put off until tomorrow. Another night of restlessness is beginning, but one knows now that the free world is alerted ...

J. J. Leblond, Le Dauphiné Libéré (Grenoble), 3 November

Hungary and Suez

London

The connection between Russia's decision to crush the Hungarian revolution and the Anglo-French attack in the Middle East is, and will be, keenly debated. What effect did the Anglo-French attack in Suez have on the Soviet attitude to Hungary? Would Hungary have been crushed if the Israeli attack on Egypt had come, say, a month later?

My own answer is that the Anglo-French attack did in fact play a large part in persuading Russia to intervene in Hungary and I believe that had the Anglo-French ultimatum been sent to Egypt a month later, Hungary would be a second Poland today ...

World opinion has always counted for much with the Russians in spite of all appearances to the contrary. They were not keen to appear lone ruthless aggressors and flouters of the authority of the United Nations and be sermonised by the West from a high pulpit ...

George Mikes, "The Hungarian Revolution" (London, 1957)

"Partial Agreements"

Budapest

I left the Hungarian News Agency and my editorial office at *Igazsag* and went out again to gather news. Budapest seemed to justify optimism ... It no longer showed the excitement of the last days ...

How many jokes there were that morning! The people were relieved, the people were jesting. In a shop window, I saw three "mannequins", each wearing a sign with the inscription "Gero", "Rakosi", "Apro" ... At the Soviet propaganda headquarters "Horizon," a huge inscription: *"Store for Rent"*. The motion picture theater *Nap* advertised a Czech film: *"Irene, Please Return Home."* A facetious hand had crossed out the name of Irene and had written in *"Russki"*. The Bastya theater announced a French film *"The Escaped"* ... Jokers had added a subtitle: "Gero, Hegedus, Apro." Stalin Square, where only the bronze boots were left of the enormous statue of the dictator, was re-baptized "Boot Square". People joked about the defeated AVH ... which only a fortnight ago tried to prevent groups of more than three people from walking in the streets. Their call to order at that time was said to have been: *"Proletarians of the world, unite! But not in groups of more than three!"* ...

At five o'clock in the afternoon I was present at the memorable press conference held by the government in the Parliament building ... In another group — under the mantle of secrecy — important and well-informed personalities — gave "off the record" accounts about the negotiations being conducted with the Soviets. They said agreement had "partly" been reached on four points:

(1) Soviet troops would completely evacuate Hungarian territory and the Government would make it clear, in the solemn farewell, that this was not a matter of "occupation troops."

(2) Damaged monuments erected in commemoration of the Red Army's battles against Hitler are to be restored, and the Hungarian Government would be responsible for their further up-keep.

(3) A financial reimbursement would be made corresponding to the value of Soviet property in Hungary, and indemnities would be paid for losses inflicted upon the Red Army during the insurrection.

(4) Hungary would become a neutral country, with a neutrality, as in Finland, oriented towards the East, and not oriented towards the West, as in Austria ...

Dezso Kozak, Franc Tireur (Paris), 23 December

As for the Russians, [Bela] Kovacs thought that their pride had run away with their common sense. "When Pál Maléter reported about his first contact with the Russian high command only yesterday, he said the Russians made just three demands— the restoration of destroyed Red Army memorials and desecrated Russian cemeteries, a guarantee that the resting places of Soviet soldiers would in future be respected by the Hungarians, and finally that the Soviet Army when leaving Hungary should be accorded full military honors."

The Nagy government had felt that these demands were reasonable and that their fulfillment was a small price to pay for getting rid of the Russians. Yet when Maléter had gone to meet again with the Soviet commanders later that Saturday evening, he had never come back ...

Leslie B. Bain, The Reporter (New York), 13 December

Hope, Propaganda, Tension

Dunapentele

We received information proving that propaganda supplied to the Soviet radio and Soviet troops tells of "fascist massacres" in Hungary. As it is feared that many Soviet soldiers will believe these slanders, we urge every free Hungarian radio station to start regular broadcasts in Russian and Hungarian to counteract these false rumors.... *Free Radio Rakoczi*

Budapest

According to information from the Ministry of Defence, members of a Soviet battalion in the Gyongyos area have handed their arms over to the civilian population, stating that they do not wish to fight the Hungarian people. Since handing over their arms they have been camping at the outskirts of the town.... *Free Petofi Radio*

Bekescsaba

A member of the Revolutionary Council of Bekes County ... gave the following information to a correspondent of the Hungarian News Agency about Soviet moves in the neighborhood: There is a Soviet motorized unit stationed southwest of Bekescsaba and another south of Szarvas. As far as I can see they intend to surround the city. The Soviet commander was surprised when I asked him to avoid populated areas, for the people are in a very excited mood and an armed conflict might ensue. The Soviet commander said that his troops had been sent with orders to fight fascists, people who want to bring back the fascist order. The negotiators explained that there was no question of this. They also told the Soviet commander that Rakosi's anti-people's regime had brought the population in a difficult position. The Soviet officers, having been informed of all this, declared that they would never fire on the Hungarian people. ... *Free Radio Szombatheley*

Gyor

The soldiers who have arrived at Gyor said that ... they were told that the Americans want to attack Hungary and that they must defend the Hungarian workers ... The Soviet soldiers are unaware of the true situation and, on seeing the enthusiasm of the people, they are more and more convinced that the Hungarian people is fighting for the independence of its fatherland and the well-being of the workers.... *Hungarian News Agency*

Tanks are approaching ... No one is in the streets except Soviet troops on patrol. Nyiregyhaza has been surrounded ... Every part of the county has been occupied ... The situation has reached maximum tension. .. *Radio Free Miskolc*

The "Ghost Army"

Budapest

The 12 Soviet divisions which have been coming into Hungary in the past two days were by noon to-day in full command of all strategic points in the countryside. But there is not a single Russian soldier to be seen in Budapest ... As far as the town population is concerned, Hungary is occupied by a ghost army.

But this is a substantial ghost, made up of six divisions of armour, and six divisions of mechanised infantry. Its tentacles spread from the railway centre of Miskolc in the north-east down to the Yugoslav border in the south and to Hegyeshalom on the Austrian frontier in the west. Russian tanks have also occupied all the military airfields, but they have refrained from any attempt to expel the Hungarians from them. The airfields, like the roads, are shared in an uneasy and strained partnership between the Soviet and Hungarian armies. Strong Russian reconnaissance units are scurrying back and forth along the main lines of communications. ...

The orders from Budapest, where the Hungarian Regular Army and the regular units of the Freedom Fighters are now acting under a unified command, are: "Stand by and do not, for the present, provoke the invaders." Apart from a few isolated clashes there has been no fighting. But the Hungarian forces are ready to fight as soon as Budapest gives the order.

The sinister and ruthless demonstration of Soviet military might has shocked the Hungarians, accustomed as they are to Soviet duplicity. Only a few days ago they had been solemnly told by Moscow Radio that the Soviet Government was ready to consider the complete withdrawal of its armed forces from Hungary. They now believe that the Soviet promise was only a trick to gain time in which to carry out a military regrouping. They see how the Soviet leaders, in stark defiance of treaties, of their own promises, and, indeed, of the firmly expressed wish of the whole Hungarian nation and its Government, are getting ready to crush the nation and to close again the gates of the prison-state, which have only just been broken open with such immense courage and sacrifice.

One has only to drive around Budapest — as I have in fact done — and to talk to the people in the streets, and to the Freedom Fighters at the many posts with which the city is dotted, to realise how this great drama of liberty versus slavery may end. I have met no man or woman, young or old, who, when it came to the test, would not sacrifice life for liberty. If the Russians strike, they will face 10 million Hungarians, who will fight to the bitter end, however long it may take.

Every town, every village, every house, and every flat will be a stronghold. And when these are demolished, the fight willl still go on. The Russians ought to know from their own experience what partisans could do to a hated and despised army of occupation.

In fact, it is by no means certain that the Soviet Army is prepared to face this great risk or that the Russian soldiers will fight the Hungarians as readily as they fought the Germans in the War. A report has just come in from Vac, some 50 miles north-west of Budapest, that the crews of 15 Russian armoured cars have gone over to the Freedom Fighters, together with their full equipment.

Aware of these and other considerations, Western observers in Budapest are not quite as alarmed as the Hungarians. They believe that the Russians will not force the issue and will not actually occupy the towns and interfere with the people's newly won freedom. They believe that the Russians will eventually leave Hungary. But before doing so, they may wish to prove to the Hungarians and to the world that they are not leaving because they were forced to leave by the Hungarians, but because they have decided to give all countries the freedom to choose "their own road to Socialism."

Lajos Lederer, The Observer (London), 4 November

Budapest

For the third time in five days, the Government has been reconstructed. Now it contains no more than three Communists. Imre Nagy, Janos Kadar, and the new Minister of Defence, Pal Maleter ... Janos Kadar's presence and participation at the cabinet meetings shows that the future president of the "revolutionary government of the workers and peasants" had not — as he has since claimed — broken with Imre Nagy as early as November 1st. The truth is that he stayed with Nagy to the end. As late as 3 November the newspaper *Nepszbadsag* (organ of the new Hungarian Socialist Workers' Party) published two articles (one of which was probably edited by Kadar himself) in which it declared itself in full agreement with the Imre Nagy Government and with the decision of the latter to ask the United Nations to guarantee the status of the country. ...

Saturday evening, State Minister Losonczy received 250 special representatives of the foreign press in the Parliament. The atmosphere is heavy. Most disquieting reports keep coming in. It is learned that the delegation headed by Maleter, charged with negotiating the withdrawal of Soviet troops has given no sign of life ... I heard the telephone ring in the office of Premier Nagy: new Soviet reinforcements continue to arrive by way of Zahony. Losonczy, his face bathed in sweat, gives final directions. The tanks are heading towards Szolnok. They are occupying the road from Budapest to Vienna. The capital is thus surrounded.

But the Hungarians who are far away from Parliament and do not see the worried looks of Nagy, Losonczy, and Boldiszar, are not aware of the danger. ...

I spent the night of 3-4 November with some Hungarian friends in a private apartment near the Duna Hotel. The atmosphere was certainly not gay, but everyone remained optimistic about the country's future. ...

Thomas Schreiber, Le Monde (Paris), 7 December

Press Conference with Ministers Tildy and Losonczy

Budapest

A press conference held by Zoltan Tildy and Geza Losonczy at the Parliament building was attended by Hungarian and foreign journalists and photographers.

A Dutch radio correspondent asked whether the Austrian-Hungarian frontier was still open.

Tildy: We do not know at present how the situation is at the Austrian-Hungarian frontier. Some incidents along the route to Vienna have just been announced.

A journalist asked about the result of talks held on 3 November between the Hungarian Prime Minister and the Soviet Ambassador.

Tildy: I was not present at this meeting. The purpose of the meeting was to bring to the attention of the Soviet Ambassador the reports which the Hungarian Chief of Staff has received concerning the movements of the Soviet forces in Hungary and to ask for an explanation. It was also to discuss the date and place of negotiations which must start between the two States, and the technical problems connected with the withdrawal of the Soviet troops.

The BBC correspondent asked for information on talks which took place today between the representatives of the Hungarian army and the Soviet army.

Tildy replied that negotiations had begun that day and would continue that night; nothing could yet be said about results.

Losonczy: The talks have already yielded some results; we hope more will come. One can perceive a certain *détente.*

Tildy then said that he had information according to which the Soviet military delegation had promised that no new convoys of Soviet troops would cross the frontier.

In reply to a question about the Soviet reply to demands put forward on Thursday (1 November) by the Hungarian Premier concerning withdrawal of the Soviet troops, Zoltan Tildy replied that Soviet replies given so far were not satisfactory.

A foreign journalist asked the number of Soviet units stationed in the country.

Tildy: Our Chief of Staff possesses precise data, which I will not divulge.

New York Post correspondent: Does the fact that the Russians agreed to negotiate on the technical questions connected with the withdrawal of their troops imply that they agreed to withdraw?

Tildy: I believe that if a person is inclined to argue about a problem it means that he thinks this problem may eventually be solved.

The France-Soir correspondent asked whether the Soviet troops had closed the frontiers with Yugoslavia, Czechoslovakia, and Rumania.

Tildy: I do not know; but this does not pre-occupy us at the moment.

A Stuttgarter Nachrichten correspondent asked whether the Soviet side would approve setting up a committee to discuss, at a political level, the withdrawal of Soviet troops.

Tildy: We have proposed sending a delegation which would also discuss certain political problems. The Soviets have accepted in principle, but they have not given a specific answer.

A correspondent asked whether, on the conclusion of an agreement for the withdrawal of Soviet troops, the Hungarian Government would demand an immediate withdrawal.

Tildy: We desire that the Soviet troops withdraw with the least possible delay.

The Manchester Guardian correspondent asked whether the Hungarian Government knew that the Polish Government supported this demand for the withdrawal of Soviet troops from Hungary.

Losonczy said that the Polish Government considered that Hungarian questions should be settled without foreign intervention.

A Newsweek correspondent asked whether the Soviet Government had sent a responsible delegate to Hungary to examine the question of withdrawal of Soviet troops.

Losonczy replied that high-ranking Soviet officers were at present in Hungary. Asked whether Marshal Zhukov was at present in Budapest, he said he could not reply.

A French journalist asked about the arrival in Budapest of a UN delegation.

Losonczy: I was informed this morning about the arrival in Budapest from Prague of a UN delegation. I have had no information since. I heard that it had actually arrived, but I have not yet met it.

An Observer correspondent put questions about the stay in Hungary of Mikoyan and Suslov.

Losonczy: As far as I know, the two Russians came to Budapest in the course of last week. According to reports they left a few days ago.

A Paris-Presse representative said that according to his information the two Soviet statesmen had talks at the central seat of the Hungarian Workers' Party with several leaders of that Party, Imre Nagy, Kadar ... etc., following which they had left, accompanied by an armoured formation.

Losonczy stated that in his opinion these reports corresponded to the truth. He added: They left on Tuesday or Wednesday, and I do not know exactly with whom, but it is probable in view of the present situation that they were accompanied by armoured vehicles when they left town.

Losonczy — asked about the formation of the new Hungarian Government — emphasized that it was not a question of forming a new Government; the existing Government had been completed. Hitherto, certain democratic parties of the coalition had not been represented in the Government; neither had the armed forces of the national insurrection. The Government had been completed and strengthened by three representatives of the Social Democratic Party ... and by one representative of the armed forces of the insurrection. Hence it was not a question of a new Government but of a reinforcement of the existing one.

Tildy — asked whether there was a possibility of a clash between the Soviet and Hungarian armed forces — replied that the Hungarian troops had received orders to abstain from all hostile acts: "I consider that a clash as tragic as that could not take place. It would be tragic from the point of view of the Hungarian people and of the Soviet Union, and for the whole world, and I think that this will not happen." Asked whether the Hungarian Government had received, in the course of talks, a guarantee from the Soviet side that this would not occur, Zoltan Tildy replied that in the notes exchanged by the two sides there were no guarantees of this kind.

The Observer correspondent asked whether the Soviet Government had informed the Hungarian Government about the dispatch of reinforcements to Hungary.

Tildy: That is a good question but it has to be divided in two. The first part relates to the period when the preceding Government was in power.

This Government, which was still influenced by Rakosi, really asked for intervention in the internal affairs of Hungary and for aid against the insurgent nation. This situation was brought to an end when the Government directed by Imre Nagy came to power. This Government declared on the very first day that it annulled the demand of the preceding Government and asked for the immediate recall of the Soviet troops involved in our internal affairs. This denuded the interference of the Soviet troops of all judicial or political basis. From the very first hour of Imre Nagy's Government we have sent a whole series of notes to speed up the withdrawal of the Soviet troops. We have not received any satisfactory reply.

Tildy continued: The Soviet Government and the leaders of the troops which have come to Hungary did not inform the Hungarian Government in advance concerning their action. I can say in the name of the entire Government that in spite of all that has happened we aspire to create a true friendship with the Soviet Union. The foundation for this friendship must be the total recognition of Hungarian independence, in principle and in practice.

A journalist then asked whether the Soviet Union had made any conditions regarding the withdrawal of the troops.

Tildy: The re-establishment of national independence cannot be linked to conditions. It is only after the re-establishment of this independence that one can re-establish friendly relations.

Losonczy: We consider that the counter-revolutionary forces are rather important in the country. The Government has declared unanimously that it will not make any concession as far as the positive achievements of the past twelve years are concerned; for example, the agrarian reform, the nationalisation of factories, and the social legislation. It demands also that the conquests of the present revolution remain intact, notably national independence, equality of rights, and the building of socialism not on the basis of a dictatorship but on the basis of democracy. The Government is determined not to tolerate the restoration of capitalism in Hungary.

I wish to emphasize in this grave situation that the Hungarian Government desires to settle questions in dispute between the Soviet Union and the Hungarian People's Republic by means of preliminary negotiations and does not desire tension between the two countries. We do this not only because we are a country much smaller than the Soviet Union, but also because we wish to maintain and even deepen our good relations with the Soviet Union and the countries building socialism. I underline this, for even in the socialist countries we encounter opinions which recognize the character and the policy of the present Hungarian Government.

Free Radio Kossuth and Hungarian News Agency

Budapest

... Any optimism was dissipated, however, when Mr. Tildy, after absenting himself some minutes, declared on his return:

"The answers to our protests against the influx of Soviet reinforcements have been unsatsfactory. This Government from its first days had demanded the withdrawal of Soviet troops. With this any legal or political basis for their presence disappeared. We demanded their withdrawal in innumerable notes. We have never received a satisfactory reply. Neither the Soviet Government nor the military commanders have ever informed us what points they want to occupy, or the direction or purpose of their military movements."

His replies strengthened a belief widely entertained here that the Russians, in their customary fashion, were dragging out the negotiations for the withdrawal of their troops to gain time to widen their occupation.

John MacCormac, New York Times, 4 November

On the Eve

Budapest

On the evening of the second, the people of Budapest went to bed convinced that the authorities had been wrong in banning the international football match between Hungary and Sweden due to take place at the Nepstadion on the following day. The opinion was that they were being over-cautious and everyone regretted that it would not be possible to acclaim the rescucitated Puskas, not only a great player and captain of the national team, but also a hero of the insurrection.

At that moment the whole country was under Soviet control, but no one believed it ...

At six in the evening, the general optimism was to some extent confirmed by an official announcement. The most difficult item in the negotiations had been settled. Soviet troops would leave the country in three weeks, and two months at the maximum. I shared a gay dinner with Hungarian friends ...   *Indro Montanelli, Corriere della Sera (Milan), 13 November*

Budapest

Crowds of housewives were lined up at the food stores, and they did not limit their purchases to immediate needs. Women who had scraped up enough money were struggling home from the market with a goose in each hand, against the uncertain days ahead.

An even longer line had formed in front of the municipal pawnshop. In impoverished Hungary one pawned one's winter wardrobe in the summer and one's summer things in the winter; now people flocked by the hundreds and thousands to redeem their winter clothes. "In 1944 the Russians looted all the pawnshops," someone in the queue told me. "So we're taking our things out now before it's too late." Women coming out of the shop staggered under the bundles of clothes and the valises they had to carry home . . .

Peter Schmid, Commentary (New York), January 1957

Budapest

. . . The planes flew toward Russia. Russian tank columns moved ostentatiously through the city, asking directions for the best way out of town. Then the Russians asked to have the evacuation talks postponed to the 3rd. By then I had been removed from the negotiation committee; Nagy felt I should remain in command of the troops. General Pal Maleter, who had replaced Janza as minister of home defense, remained on the committee. On the afternoon of the 3rd I went to parliament and caught Maleter coming out of the committee room. "How are things going?" I asked. "In fine order," he said.

I came back at 6 that evening and cornered another member of the committee, General Istvan Kovacs, the army chief of staff. I asked the same question. "It is practically agreed," he said. "First, Russia will evacuate all her armed forced from Hungary. Second, to avoid disrupting transportation, the Russians want to leave by degrees. A committee of experts will be set up to arrange a time table. Third, the Hungarian garrisons must cease denying the Russians food and fuel. Fourth, the Russians are not prepared for a winter movement and Hungary must be patient; the troops will not be able to lave until Jan. 15. Lastly, they say the Russian army did not want to attack the Hungarians but only did what the Hungarian government asked. Therefore the evacuation must be not only peaceful but friendly. The troops must leave in a festive air, and the Hungarians must cheer them as they leave."

In effect, said General Kovacs, the committee had agreed to all the Russian demands, even the friendly farewell, but insisted that departure date be stepped up by a month. The meeting was to be continued that night at 9 p.m. at the Russian military headquarters at Tokol, on Csepel Island . . . As late as 11 o'clock on the night of the 3rd, the Russians, negotiating with the committee on Csepel Island, suggested Maleter call me and say that everything was in good order. This he did. We both believed it. I told my staff, "Now I will sleep. Tonight, for the first time, I will sleep

myself out. I must not be disturbed before 9." I went to bed at the house of a friend . . .

Maj. Gen. Bela Kiraly, Life (New York), 18 February 1957

Budapest

. . . We thought Hungarian heroism had won the day, that the country was in fact free. Such was the opinion of half the Soviet experts known to me, and of Geza Losonczy and Zoltan Tildy, two members of Nagy's last cabinet, at a press conference six hours before the Soviet aggression. It was the writer's own opinion—I will not forget that when I saw my first Soviet tanks west of Gyor on November 2nd. I said, "Ah, Soviet tanks; we needn't be frightened of them." A majority of the ordinary Hungarian people thought otherwise. These saw that it wasn't a question of ideology but of simple imperialism and military prestige. How else, speaking with hindsight, could the Red Army have reacted? It had lost Poland a fortnight before, and seen its proconsul there humiliated; and now it had been defeated by school-children in Hungary. Its whole satellite empire was crumbling . . .

Peter Wiles, Encounter (London), January 1957, and The New Leader (New York), 11 February 1957

Negotiations for the withdrawal of the Soviet troops were in fact commenced on 3 November in the Parliament building and continued during the night at Soviet headquarters at Tokol on Csepel Island. In a further cable to the United Nations, Mr. Nagy confirmed his previous communications. According to the evidence of General Kiraly, an agreement for the withdrawal of Soviet forces was signed at 6 p.m. and the subsequent discussions at Soviet headquarters related to technique and timing; contact was maintained with the Hungarian military delegation until just past midnight, when communication was broken off; the Hungarian military delegation, headed by General Pal Maleter, was then placed under arrest.

Interim Report of the Special Committee on the Problem of Hungary. UN General Assembly, 20 February 1957.

"*Without the Slightest Delay*"

Moscow

Imre Nagy turned out to be, objectively speaking, an accomplice of the reactionary forces. Imre Nagy cannot and does not want to fight the dark forces of reaction . . .

The Soviet Government, seeing that the presence of Soviet troops in Budapest might lead to further aggravation of the situation, ordered troops to leave Budapest, but ensuing events have shown that reactionary forces, taking advantage of the non-intervention of the Nagy Cabinet, have gone still further . . .

The task of barring the way to reaction in Hungary has to be carried out without the slightest delay—such is the course dictated by events.

Pravda (Moscow), 4 November

4 NOVEMBER

The Attack at Daybreak

Budapest

Attention! Attention!
Attention! Attention!

Now Imre Nagy, President of the Council of Ministers of the Hungarian People's Republic is going to address you! [05:19]

This is Imre Nagy speaking, the President of the Council of Ministers of the Hungarian People's Republic. Today at daybreak Soviet forces started an attack against our capital, obviously with the intention to overthrow the legal Hungarian democratic Government.

Our troops are fighting.

The Government is in its place.

I notify the people of our country and the entire world of this fact.

[The announcement was followed by the National anthem, and then repeated in English, Russian, and French, and German.]
Free Radio Kossuth

Attention! Attention! Attention! [05:56]
Premier Imre Nagy calls Minister of Home Defence, Pal Maleter, the chief of our General Staff, Istvan Kovacs, and the other members of the military delegation who went yesterday at 22:00 hrs. to the headquarters of the Soviet Supreme Command and who have not returned until now, to come back without further delay in order to take over their respective offices.

Free Radio Kossuth

Attention! We read now an important announcement! [07:14]
The Hungarian Government requests officers and soldiers of the Soviet army not to shoot. Avoid bloodshed! The Russians are our friends and will remain our friends in the future!

Free Radio Kossuth

This is the Association of Hungarian Writers speaking to all writers, scientists, all writers' associations, academies, and scientific unions of the world. We turn to leaders of intellectual life in all countries. Our time is limited. You all know the facts. There is no need to expand on them. Help Hungary! Help the Hungarian writers, scientists, workers, peasants and intelligentsia. Help! Help! Help!

Free Radio Kossuth [07:56]

[The message was repeated in German and Russian After the writer's appeal, music was played until 08:10. Then the signal was discontinued, although a silent carrier wave could still be detected until 09.45 ...]

SOS! SOS! SOS!...
Free Radio Kossuth [08:24]

Budapest

...everything happened at once. Russian tanks streamed into the city... They moved to the Kilian Barracks and the Corvin Theater, two main freedom-fighter strongpoints, and started shelling. I grabbed my direct phone to the premier. It was about 4 a.m. I told him the city was being invaded and begged for orders to open fire... "No, no," Nagy said. "Calm down. The Russian ambassador is here in my office. He is calling Moscow right now. There is some misunderstanding. You must not open fire." I hung up, bewildered... About a half hour later I heard him on the radio... The nation was at war.

Maj.-Gen. Bela Kiraly, Life (New York), 18 February 1957

The Battle Rages

Budapest

From my windows I saw the horizon light up with sinister flames. The ground shook and for three hours one explosion followed upon the other. The Russians entered into Budapest without any difficulty. The roads leading into the town were merely guarded by a total of about thirty Hungarian tanks.

The battle raged right in the midst of a town of one million. Dwellings, factories, barracks, and streets just like those in Paris served as battle lines. The principal resistance centres were workers' districts. The targets which the Soviet attacked with particular rage and fury were the metallurgical factories in the "red outskirts" of Budapest, districts inhabited by workers, groups of workmen's dwellings and factories where the Hungarian Communists had their strongholds and their most active militants.

It was they — the young Hungarian Communists, the metal workers, the workers with grimed hands, who fought the most fiercely against Soviet armoured cars ...

Michel Gordey, France-Soir (Paris), 13 November

Counter-Atacking

It could not have been more than five in the morning when we were roughly awakened by our colleague Saporito who rushed into our room after having hastily put his overcoat over his pyjamas. "There is shooting!" he said. "Can't you hear it?" And, indeed, from afar a mournful rumbling could be heard, like the noise of a distant avalanche. I got up immediately, asking Matteotti to do the same. He was rubbing his eyes, trying to justify his desire for sleep by optimistic remarks that were immediately repudiated by the approach of the cannonade.

As I rushed to the telephone switchboard, the whole hotel was in uproar. I met a poor woman, quite pale, who said to me: "I left the concentration camp last week. I was in for seven whole years." ...

Now ten armoured divisions were advancing on the capital. They entered at 6:15 with a terrifying clash of steel. Arriving from all directions, always accompanied by the muffled rumbling of artillery, they dispersed in threes along the main avenues towards the centre of the city, their cannons pointing before them, and machine guns attached on every side. At every crossroads, one tank halted, while the others continued on their route ...

On the part of the Hungarian insurgents, this extraordinary battle was carried out without the slightest attempt at dissimulation. They all knew perfectly well that sooner or later their ammunition would be exhausted, they would have no other arms, and they would be at the mercy of police repression. But no one troubled to take an assumed name. ... None of them tried to grow beards, to wear glasses, to change their address. Their action was co-ordinated and orderly. ... This could be noticed by the number of messages arriving at the students' headquarters which I was visiting. ... The basic order was that armoured columns should not be attacked; they had to be followed and note taken of single vehicles which, for some reason or other, remained behind, and where they were to be found. Then groups left to attack. ... Soon the Russians began to avoid posting isolated tanks at any spot but always left them in pairs, one protecting the other ...

Indro Montanelli, Corriere della Sera (Milan), 13 November

"Help Us!"

Budapest

I woke suddenly—from the heights of Buda, Soviet tanks had opened fire on the city ... The telephone rings. It is one of my Hungarian friends, a long-time Party member who had joined the freedom-fighters: "We are ready to battle to the last cartridge ... It's up to you Westerners to help us!"

A few minutes later another telephone call. A high official of the Ministry of Foreign Affairs implores me, a French journalist, to intervene with my Government: "Send us arms!" All my colleagues received similar appeals. (And those who sent them were not "fascists" or "counter-revolutionaries," but well-known communists.) ...

The dawn is fresh. The streets are literally swarming with Soviet tanks and arms. Guards have been posted at street-crossings. Shots are fired from all sides.

At Bajcsy-Zsilinsky Avenue, I can see a tank column maneuvering in the direction of Alkotmany Street ... probably towards Parliament, where Imre Nagy had sent out a desperate appeal ... The Hungarian News Agency at Feny Street has been partially destroyed by Soviet artillery. All communication with the outside world has been cut off. The bridges connecting Buda and Pest have been occupied by the Russians ...

Thomas Schreiber, Le Monde (Paris), 7 December

Waiting for Disaster

Budapest

It was Sunday, the fourth of November. For three days Budapest had gloried in its triumph. But now the storm was coming back. The Russians, they said, were on their way in; and this time in strength.

All day and all night I had resisted the implications of these rumours and more than rumours. I myself early on Saturday morning had seen Soviet tanks moving into position outside Budapest. I had talked to a Hungarian staff officer who had himself interrogated a captured Russian tank commander; and the Russian had said that the attack was planned for dawn on Sunday.

I had been told a few hours earlier by a senior member of Nagy's Government that there was no hope. But I still allowed myself to hope, in spite of all.

And now it was Sunday. I got back to my hotel, shaken and exhausted, at 2 a.m., only a few hours before the avalanche began. I had a last look at my young friends — some thirty wounded boys — who were quartered in an improvised field-hospital in the hotel — the Gellert. They were all wide awake. And they waited for inevitable disaster.

They knew the Russians were coming back. They did not wish to be consoled. They only regretted that they were not fit to fight ...

After that I had joined a handful of Hungarian intellectuals, who had lost their homes and found refuge in the hotel, to listen to the B.B.C. news.

They were the *élite* of Hungarian cultural life. The news was chiefly about the Anglo-French action in the Middle East, which seemed very far away and irrelevant. From their bitter but restrained comments it was clear that they felt that Hungary had been "let down".

At 2.30 a.m. I had a telephone call from London —a friend asking who was in charge of Hungarian relief—where and to whom to send medical supplies. This was the last call from London.

Though I had hardly slept for a fortnight, I could not sleep now. Instead, I sat on the balcony of my room, looking out over the city. It was a grey dawn. With flickering candles in the windows, the city was deathly quiet ...

Then, suddenly, there was the rattle and rumble of tracked vehicles. A Hungarian artillery formation, with medium guns and anti-tank guns, was moving past to take up defensive positions on the southern outskirts of the city. It was 3:30. Not much longer to wait. Soon the skies were flickering with the flash of gunfire, and the roar of guns shook the air. The Battle of Budapest had begun.

The hotel entrance hall was packed with people, mostly women with tiny children. They were waiting for an important announcement to be made by Premier Nagy ...

We crossed the Ferenz Jozsef Bridge at 6.30, just before it was closed by a tank unit of the Hungarian Regular Army. We stopped to make sure that they really were Hungarians, for the Hungarian Army is equipped with Russian-made T-54 tanks, and its uniform is very similar to that of the Soviet Army. They were Hungarians all right. They had taken up their positions covering the bridges on the Pest side of the Danube. And they were supported by truck-loads of infantry ...

Before we got to the British Legation we saw a strong formation of Soviet T-54s moving swiftly towards Parliament Square. There was no doubt this time about their being Russian. Their blind firing, with hatches battened down, right and left at every building as they roared down the avenue made this quite clear. They had reached the centre of the city much earlier than the Hungarians had expected. As I heard later in the day, they had broken into Budapest through the northern suburbs from the Vienna road ...

Lajos Lederer, The Observer (London), 18 November

"If You Have Any Answer, Pass It On"

Budapest

[Hungarian News Agency message by teletype line to the Associated Press bureau in Vienna.]

Russian gangsters have betrayed us. The Russian troops suddenly attacked Budapest and the whole country. They opened fire on everybody in Hungary. It is a general attack ...

I speak in the name of Imre Nagy. He asks help ... Nagy and the Government and the whole people ask help.

If you have anything from the Austrian Government, tell me. Urgent, urgent, urgent ...

Long live Hungary and Europe! We shall die for Hungary and Europe! ...

Any news about help? Quickly, quickly, quickly! ...

The Russian attack was started at 4 a.m.

Russian MIG fighters are over Budapest. Russian MIG fighters are over Budapest. Gyor is completely surrounded by the Russians. Szekesfehervar does not answer.

Associated Press Vienna, if you have something, please pass it on to me. The Government waits for your answer!

We have no time to lose, we have no time to lose! ...

The news of the capture of the Hungarian military leadership was confirmed by the Government spokesman, Mr. Hamori.

Mr. Nagy is at a safe place now. Mr. Zoltan Tildy is in the Parliament now.

The time is 5:45 and the Russians stopped their fire for a minute. The street-lamps are on and the town shows a peaceful sight, but everywhere Russian tanks are in the street. A Russian infantry division is going toward the Parliament.

Nagy is speaking to the people on the radio. He said some elements tried to overthrow our lawful Government. Our troops are in a fight with the Russians.

Pecs was attacked by the Russians at 2 a.m. They tried to seize the uranium mines and the airfields, but the Hungarians stopped them. Now the town is in their hands, but all the highways are ours ..

If you have any answer, pass it on. Any answer, pass it on. Imre Nagy personally asks help. Nagy personally asks help. And diplomatic steps, diplomatic steps ...

[A series of teletype messages to The Associated Press from the office of the Budapest newspaper *Szabad Nep*.]

Since the early morning hours Russian troops are attacking Budapest and our population ...

Please tell the world of the treacherous attack against our struggle for liberty ...

Our troops are already engaged in fighting ...
Help! — Help! — Help! —
S O S ! — S O S ! — S O S ! —

The people have just turned over a tram to use as a barricade near the building. In the building, young people are making Molotov cocktails and hand grenades to fight the tanks.

We are quiet, not afraid. Send the news to the public of the world and say it should condemn the aggressors.

The fighting is very close now and we haven't enough tommy guns in the building. I don't know how long we can resist. We are fixing the hand grenades now.

Heavy shells are exploding nearby. Above, jet planes are roaring, but it doesn't matter . . .

[8.30 a.m.] At the moment there is silence. It may be the silence before the storm. We have almost no weapons, only light machine-guns, Russian-made long rifles and some carbines. We haven't any kind of [heavy] guns.

People are jumping up at the tanks, throwing hand-grenades inside and then slamming the drivers' windows. The Hungarian people are not afraid of death. It is only a pity that we can't stand for long.

A man just came in from the street. He said we should not think that because the street is empty the people have taken shelter. They are standing in the doorways, waiting for the right moment.

One Hungarian soldier was told by his mother as she said goodbye to him: "Don't be a hero, but don't be cowardly either!"

[A little later] Now the firing is starting again. We are getting hits.

The tanks are getting nearer and there is heavy artillery. We have just had a report that our unit is receiving reinforcements and ammunition. But it is still too little. It can't be allowed that people attack tanks with their bare hands.

What is the United Nations doing? Give us a little encouragement.

[There were between 200 and 250 people in the newspaper building with him, the reporter wrote; about 50 of them were women.]

[9 a.m.] The tanks are coming nearer. Both radio stations are in rebel hands. They have been playing the Hungarian National Anthem.

We will hold out to our last drop of blood. The Government has not done enough to give us arms. Downstairs there are men who have only one hand grenade.

[At 9.15 the first Russian bombers were reported over Budapest. There were about 15 planes accompanied by fighters. Occasionally, the reporter would tap out a quick note.]

I am running over to the window in the next room to shoot. But I will be back if there is anything new, or you ring me.

Don't be mad at the way I am writing. I am excited. I want to know how this is going to end. I want to shoot, but there is no target so far. I will file to you as long as possible.

[He continually inquired what the United Nations was doing. When informed of a Washington despatch that Cardinal Mindszenty had taken refuge in the United States Legation in Budapest, he asked: "Is that all they have achieved?"]

[Then] A Russian plane has just fired a machine-gun burst. We don't know where, just heard and saw it.

The building of barricades is going on. The Parliament and its vicinity is crowded with tanks .. Planes are flying overhead, but can't be counted, there are so many. The tanks are coming in big lines.

Our building has already been fired on, but so far there are no casualties. The roar of the tanks is so loud we can't hear each other's voices.

[He broke off typing] Now I have to run over to the next room to fire some shots from the window. But I'll try to be back if there is anything new.

[When he returned he wrote] They just brought us a rumour that the American troops will be here within one or two hours.

[Then, in the midst of the fighting and as bullets hit his own building, he asked the Associated Press to transmit for him a personal message to a relative in Britain which said: "Sending kisses. We are well and fighting."]

The tanks are now firing toward the Danube. Our boys are on the barricades and calling for more arms and ammunition. There is most bitter fighting in the inner city.

[9.45 a.m.] Now things are silent here, except for a few rifle shots. The tanks rolled away from our building and have gone somewhere else.

[10 a.m.] A shell just exploded nearby. Now there is heavy firing in the direction of the National Theatre, near us in the centre of the city.

In our building we have youngsters of 15 and men of 40. Don't worry about us. We are strong, even if we are only a small nation. When the fighting is over we will rebuild our unhappy country.

We hope the U.N. meeting won't be too late.

Send us any news you can about world action in Hungary's behalf. Don't worry, we burn your dispatches as soon as we have read them . . .

[10.50 a.m.] Just now the heaviest fighting is going on in the Maria Terezia Barracks. There is heavy artillery fire . . .

[Five minutes later the connection was cut. The reporter did not come back. — A. P.]

Associated Press, 4 November; New York Times, 5 November; Daily Telegraph (London), 5 November

Russians Veto UN "Censure"

Budapest

Dear listeners, here is an important announcement [07:55]:

AP reports from New York . . . that early this morning the USA asked the UN Security Council to hold an extraordinary meeting on Sunday to discuss the Soviet offensive in Hungary. The request was submitted by the US delegate Lodge less than an hour after the news agencies reported large-scale Soviet attacks all over Hungary. The Security Council had discussed Hungary on Saturday night and adjourned the debate until Monday morning. Lodge, however, requested the

Chairman of the Security Council to convene the meeting earlier should the situation deteriorate. The Austrian delegate Ronald Walker, speaking in the General Assembly on the situation in Hungary, read out a telegraphic dispatch from the rostrum and called for an unofficial meeting of the 11 members of the Security Council to discuss what steps to take. This closed meeting is to take place at 08.45 on Sunday morning ...

Free Radio Kossuth

New York

The Soviet Union early today vetoed a United States resolution proposing Security Council censure of the Russian military attack on Hun-

gary. Nine nations favored the United States proposal and one abstained, Yugoslavia.

The veto was at 5:15 a.m. [11:15 a.m. Hungarian time].

Henry Cabot Lodge Jr., United States representative, immediately moved for an emergency session of the General Assembly to take up the Hungarian crisis. The Assembly already was in permanent special session over the French-British intervention in the Suez Canal area.

Angrily, Mr. Lodge told the Council that the will of the world organization had been "thwarted" by the Soviet veto and that the eleven-nation body had been prevented from fulfilling its re-

UN Debate

MR. LODGE (U.S.A.): *Shortly after midnight I requested a Sunday meeting of the Security Council to deal with this agony of the Hungarian people. Five minutes later the fact of this request was broadcast by Radio Budapest. That shows how quickly what we say and do here affects the people of Hungary in their struggle ...*

MR. NUNEZ-PORTUONDO (Cuba): *... At the very moment when the permanent representative of the Soviet Union was telling us here that negotiations were in progress between Hungarian and Soviet authorities, at the very moment when, in the General Assembly, the Soviet representative was speaking so highly in favour of the principle of self-determination and in favour of non-intervention in the internal affairs of States, Hungary was attacked by surprise and invaded by Soviet armed forces. This brings shame on the Moscow Government and is a reason for a strong and vehement protest by all the free peoples of the world ...*

MR. TSIANG (China): *... We must immediately ask the Soviet Union to withdraw its forces from Hungary and to cease its intervention in that country. This, I believe, is the least we can do.*

MR. SOBOLEV (U.S.S.R.): *The most recent events of this last week in Hungary have shown that there was a counter-revolutionary movement directed against the wishes of the overwhelming majority of the Hungarian people. Reactionary elements, taking advantage of the situation, prevented the Hungarian people from learning what was actually happening. Those elements confused the Hungarian people and engaged in provocation. As a result, the people were deceived by propaganda containing nothing but lies ...*

It is therefore my submission that the United Nations and particularly the Security

Council have nothing to do in this matter. Interference by the United Nations and by the Western countries in the Hungarian events might only lead to complications, and it goes without saying that such interference would be unlawful and contrary to the principles of the Charter.

We know why the United States, the United Kingdom and France are placing this matter before the Security Council. We know that the purpose is to conceal, behind speeches full of demagoguery, the action that has been taken by Israel, the United Kingdom and France against Egypt. They are trying to conceal those activities by raising this provocative question of Hungary in the Security Council ...

MR. LODGE (U.S.A.): *In connexion with the Soviet representative's attack on United States activities regarding Hungary, I will merely say this. He would apparently have us believe that our American programme, which aims to fill the people's stomachs with food, is somehow inferior to a Soviet programme which fills their stomachs with lead, as this night's tragic dispatches all too plainly and poignantly attest ...*

MR. SOBOLEV (U.S.S.R.): *I have already indicated that there was no justification whatsoever for the consideration of the Hungarian situation in the Security Council, since that would be interference in the internal affairs of Hungary. This can also be said about the proposal that has been made to refer the question to the General Assembly. The only purpose served by referring the question of the situation in Hungary to an extraordinary session of the General Assembly would be that of further complicating a situation which is already complicated enough ...*

UN Verbatim Record, Security Council, 4 November

sponsibilities. In this "grave situation", he said, Assembly action was required. The Council adopted the United States resolution for reference to the Assembly by a vote of 10 to 1. This ballot came at 5:21 a.m. The Assembly meeting was set for 8 o'clock tonight. The Council adjourned at 5:24 a.m.

The Council's action, marking the Soviet Union's seventy-ninth veto, was taken after the United States had called the group together at 3 a.m. to protest against the reoccupation of Budapest by Soviet troops ...

The Soviet representative, Arkady A. Sobolev, after prodding by Western delegates, had explained that "negotiations are in progress" between the Hungarian Government of Premier Imre Nagy and Soviet military authorities. These talks were supposed to lead to the evacuation of Soviet troops. Mr. Sobolev's statement, Mr. Lodge commented, displayed a "total lack of candor and indifference to human suffering". The Soviet representative's remarks were made just as the Hungarian radio went off the air, with a final appeal by Premier Nagy to the United Nations ...

Mr. Lodge told the Council the Hungarian capital was "flooded" early today by Soviet forces that met no resistance. He called attention to recent Soviet protests against alleged aggression by France and Britain in the Middle East. Then he added:

"How far can actions and words be apart?"

Lindesay Parrott, New York Times, 4 November

"40,000 Aristocrats"

Budapest

It was dawn ... the day the Russians struck again.

We were awakened by the roar of heavy guns. The radio was a shambles. All we got was the national anthem, played over and over again, and continual repetition of Premier Nagy's announcement that after a token resistance we must cease fighting and appeal to the free world for help.

After our ten days' war of liberty, after the pathetically short period of our "victory", this was a terrible blow. But there was not time to sit paralysed in despair. The Russians had arrested General Maleter, head of the Central Revolutionary Armed Forces Council. The Army had received ceasefire orders. But what of the fighting groups of workers and students?

These courageous civilian units now had to be told to put up only token resistance in order to save bloodshed. They had been instructed not to start firing.

I called up the biggest group, the "Corvin regiment." A deputy commander answered the phone. His voice was curiously calm:

"Yes, we realised we should not open fire. But the Russians did. They took up positions around our block and opened fire with everything they had. The cellars are filled with 200 wounded and dead. But we will fight to the last man. There is no choice. But inform Premier Nagy that we did not start the fight."

This was just before seven in the morning. Premier Nagy, alas, could not be informed any more. He was not to be found.

The situation was the same everywhere. Soviet tanks rolled in and started to shoot at every centre of resistance which had defied them during our first battle for freedom.

This time, the Russians shot the buildings to smithereens. Freedom fighters were trapped in the various barracks, public buildings and blocks of flats. The Russians were going to kill them off to the last man. And they knew it. They fought on till death claimed them.

This senseless Russian massacre provoked the second phase of armed resistance. The installation of Kadar's puppet government was only oil on the fire. After our fighting days, after our brief span of liberty and democracy, Kadar's hideous slogans and stupid lies, couched in the hated Stalinite terminology, made everyone's blood boil. Although ten million witnesses knew the contrary, the puppet government brought forward the ludicrous lie that our war of liberty was a counter-revolutionary uprising inspired by a handful of Fascists.

The answer was bitter fighting and a general strike throughout the country. In the old revolutionary centres — the industrial suburbs of Csepel, Ujpest and the rest — the workers struck and fought desperately against the Russian tanks.

Posters on the walls challenged the lies of the puppet Government: *"The forty thousand aristocrats and fascists of the Csepel works strike on!"* said one of them.

"The general strike is a weapon which can be used only when the entire working class in unanimous — so don't call us Fascists," said another.

Armed resistance stopped first. The Russians bombarded to rubble every house from which a single shot was fired. The fighting groups realised that further battles would mean the annihilation of the capital. So they stopped fighting.

But the strike went on.

The Workers' Councils, the Writers' Association and the Revolutionary Council of the Students decided at last that the general strike must be suspended if Hungary were not to commit national suicide ...

George Paloczi-Horvath, Daily Herald (London),
12 December

Budapest

I went down to the police station to ask for weapons. There I heard about a group of revolutionaries from Buda who had drawn back to the hill where the old royal palace was located. Numerous armed insurgents were effectively guarding the approaches to the palace castle and trying to parry Russian artillery with their strange collection of light weapons.

Among us were a number of soldiers who had escaped from their barracks. They told me that,

with a remarkable coordination revealing a well-laid plan, the Russians had struck at all the barracks simultaneously in a surprise attack supported by a strong enforcement of armoured vehicles. Their superiority in men and arms had been so great that in certain places after brief resistance they succeeded in disarming the Hungarian soldiers. But at that time they were not yet organised for taking prisoners, and a large number of soldiers managed to escape and join insurgent groups fighting in the city . . .

Dezso Kozak, Franc-Tireur (Paris), 25 November

Minister Bibo's Final Statement

Budapest

[10:30] The foreign correspondents were invited to a press conference in Parliament. The Soviet Ambassador, M. Andropov, offered the advice, through our interpreter, Michel Gordey, not to attend . . . *Agence France Presse (Paris), 15 November*

Budapest

From Parliament came a call summoning correspondents to a press conference with Istvan Bibo, Minister of State in the Nagy Government. Asked to supply safe conduct through the Soviet lines, he replied sadly that he could not . . .

We decided to go to the United States legation. En route we saw a white sheet hung outside Parliament to signify surrender.

But Mr. Bibo had not surrendered. At 9 o'clock he dictated a statement to the secretary of the United States Legation. This said:

"Premier Imre Nagy went to the Soviet Embassy when the Russians started their attack at dawn today and was unable to return. Only Ministers of State Zoltan Tildy, Istvan Szabo and Istvan Bibo were able to attend an extraordinary meeting of the Cabinet called to consider the new situation.

"When the Russians ringed the Parliament, Tildy, to avoid further bloodshed, agreed with them that Soviet troops should occupy it on the condition that civilians be allowed to leave freely. In accordance with this statement Tildy left, convinced however that he was going to his death."

Only Bibo remained as representative of the legal Hungarian Government.

"In this situation I state that Hungary has no intention of following an anti-Soviet policy. I reject the slander that Fascist or anti-Semitic actions have stained the glorious Hungarian revolution. The entire Hungarian nation participated in it, without class or religious discrimination.

"The attitude of the people who rose up was moving and wonderful. They turned only against the oppressing foreign army and against their gangs of henchmen.

"My orders to the Hungarian nation are not to consider the occupying army or the puppet government to be set up by this army as legal authorities and to use all weapons of passive resistance against them.

"I am not in the position to give orders for armed resistance. I joined the Government only one day ago and it would be irresponsible on my part to allow that the precious blood of the Hungarian youth should flow further. The people of Hungary have sacrificed enough blood to show to the world their tenacious attachment to freedom and justice. Now it is the turn of the world powers.

"It is my conviction that now when the liberation of East European countries has been almost realized, in this historical moment, the only means by which world peace can be insured is by taking the risk of a world war. On the other hand, deferring the decision endangers the policy of the free world and makes certain the outbreak of a world war at a later date, just as was the case in the past in two instances when Western isolationist tendencies and the policy of appeasement towards the aggressor prevailed.

"I appeal to the great powers of the world for a wise and courageous decision in the interest of my enslaved nation and of the liberty of all Eastern European nations. God preserve Hungary." . . .

Bibo was one of the left-of-center brilliant intellectuals who disliked those who rallied behind the Smallholders Party after World War II and established the National Peasant Party in 1945. When it turned out that the Peasant Party was nothing but a communist-sponsored political party, Bibo retired from active political life and returned to his professorship at the University of Szeged . . .

On the way to the legation we had noted that all Danube bridges were blocked by Soviet tanks. Others commanded Budapest's main streets. Armoured cars and self-propelled guns had taken up battle positions, particularly in streets leading to Parliament, which we knew had become headquarters not only of the Hungarian Government but of the Budapest radio.

One correspondent who had crossed the Danube before the bridges were blocked reported he had seen youths rushing to assembly points in Zsigmond Moricz and Moscow Squares with rifles over their shoulders. Others were bricking up entrances to old air-raid shelters.

"We are going to fight the Russians," they said.

Near Astoria Hotel on Lajos Kossuth Street in the heart of Pest, other youngsters were making "Molotov cocktails" and prying up paving blocks for barricades.

Later in the day came the news that the Army barracks, despite the heavy battering it had received earlier in the revolution, had again become the chief strong point of the revolutionaries in Pest. As night fell, the volume of fighting rose ...

John MacCormac, New York Times, 12 November
and United Press, 13 November

Mindszenty's Escape

Budapest

Early on Sunday morning Mindszenty had awakened, as we all had, to the sound of cannonading. A few minutes later Mindszenty was called to the telephone. An excited voice told him that Nagy and his Cabinet were meeting in Parliament. Could he come immediately?

The Cardinal and Turchanyi slipped quickly into their cassocks, summoned several other aides and left in two cars. As they crossed the Danube and turned into Liberty Square they were confronted by the Soviet tank ring around the Parliament building. A Russian-speaking priest in the lead car explained to a Soviet officer without mentioning the Cardinal's presence, that the Hungarian Government had requested them to appear. The officer smiled tauntingly and said, "I am afraid we are in control here, not the Hungarian Government."

The alarmed Turchanyi suggested that he reconnoitre alone. He entered the building after receiving permission from the officer. No sooner was he inside than two blue-uniformed members of the dreaded A.V.H.—Hungarian Communist Security Forces—rushed towards him with drawn revolvers. Turchanyi wheeled and ran from the building. As he panted towards Mindszenty, the pursuing A.V.H. men held their fire for fear of hitting Russians.

Mindszenty ordered the driver to start the car. He held open the door for Turchanyi, who leaped inside as their chauffeur drove the car around the square at full speed. Turchanyi directed him to the bank building where a temporary refuge could be found. The Cardinal and his secretary dashed inside as the car roared down the dark street to throw off any pursuers.

By telephone and through trusted intermediaries Turchanyi immediately started negotiations with the American Legation to grant the Cardinal asylum ...

"But in taking refuge with the United States, won't you be separated from your people?"

"No one can separate me from my people, not

even the entire armed might of the Soviet Empire. If I seek temporary asylum I do so as a last desperate measure."

Leslie B. Bain, Daily Express (London), 7 December

Budapest

The cardinal stayed at his residence until the early morning of Nov. 4 after the Russians had already started their movement into the city. At that time he was asked by Premier Nagy to come to the Parliament building, about one mile away across the river.

As he left his residence to cross the Chain Bridge in the car which the soldiers had left for him, there was already shooting near the Fortress. This is what the hill is called on which there are several government buildings and his residence.

As the Russians approached, a group of young Hungarian soldiers dashed to the Museum of Military History on the Fortress. There they loosened the cannon which had been used in the revolution of 1848 and ran the guns out through the ramparts. Through the same portholes they fired their own rifles and pistols and the Russians, thinking it was cannon fire, were delayed.

The cardinal was not long in the Parliament building. He attended a dramatic session of the Cabinet and it was clear that everything was lost. He talked with Nagy and others of what should be done. The Russians were approaching the building.

"You must flee", said Nagy.

"Where?" asked the cardinal.

"To the nearest diplomatic mission — the American Legation" was Nagy's answer.

The cardinal rolled up his cassock so he would not be recognized and put on his overcoat. Then three young Hungarians who had been in the building led the way. Three others walked behind him. They shielded him from the eyes of the Russians who were milling around the building. Their quick thinking probably saved his life ...

Father Josef Vecsey, "The Mindszenty Story",
N. Y. Herald Tribune (Paris), 10 December

Kadar: "Smash the Sinister Forces!"

Attention! Attention! Comrade Janos Kadar speaking [06:00]:

The Hungarian Revolutionary Worker-Peasant Government has been formed. The mass movement which started in our country on 23 October had the noble aim to remedy the anti-Party and anti-democratic crimes committed by Rakosi and his associates and to defend national independence and sovereignty. Our socialist achievements, our people's State, our worker-peasant power, and the very existence of our country has been threatened by the weakness of the Imre Nagy Government and the increased influence of the counter-revolutionary elements who edged their way into the movement. This has prompted us, as Hungarian patriots, to form the Hungarian Revolutionary Worker-Peasant Government. I will now give the composition of the Government:

Janos Kadar	Premier
Ferenc Munnich	Deputy Premier and Minister of the Armed Forces and Public Security Force
Gyoergy Marosan	Minister of State
Imre Horvath	Foreign Minister
Istvan Kossa	Minister of Finance
Antal Apro	Minister of Industry
Imre Dogei	Minister of Agriculture
Sandor Ronai	Minister of Commerce

The other portfolios remain unfilled for the time being. These portfolios must be filled, after the restoration of the country's legal order, by representatives of other Parties and non-Party persons loyal to our People's Democracy, who are ready to defend the achievements of socialism ...

Our nation is passing through difficult days. The power of the workers and peasants, and the sacred cause of socialism are in danger ... The counter-revolutionaries are becoming more and more impudent. They ruthlessly persecute the followers of democracy ... We know that many questions are still awaiting a solution in our country and that we have to cope with many difficulties. The life of the workers is still far from what it ought to be in a country building socialism ... The Rakosi and Gero clique has committed many grave mistakes and gravely violated legality. All this has rightly made the workers dissatisfied ... Horthy's gendarmes and prison wardens, the representatives of the hated and cursed oppressive system, have already set out to sit on the neck of the people. Had they won, they would not have brought freedom, well-being and democracy, but slavery, misery, unemploy-

Radio Monitoring

The "Budapest I" medium wave transmitter (539 kc/s) ... changed its name from "Kossuth Radio" to "Free Kossuth Radio" in the course of the revolution. Up to 07:10 [GMT] on 4 November this station remained in the hands of the Nagy Government. It was not heard thereafter until 10:00, when a brief fragment of speech, referring to "counter-revolutionaries," was intercepted. The transmitter was again lost until 21:00 when for a few minutes it relayed a special broadcast originating from Moscow ... From this time on, the radio has been in the hands of the new "Revolutionary Worker-Peasant Government," and has been announcing itself as "Kossuth Radio" ... The material carried by the Kossuth transmitter since it became audible again at 21:00 on 4 November has contained much local material concerning the town and country of Szolnok.

Until the evening hours of 4 November the new Government's main mouthpiece was a transmitter normally used for the Hungarian radio's foreign services on 1,187 kc/s and situated in Balatonszabadi. The Kadar Government also appears to have obtained control of all other local transmitters on 4 November, an isolated exception being a transmitter using one of the frequencies of

the "Free Petofi-Gyor" group, which broadcast an appeal for help to the West as late as 13:34 ... *BBC Summary*

It was stated by the technical experts of the Voice of America that the broadcasts of the Kadar Government (addresses of Kadar and Munnich) are transmitted on 1187 kilocycle, through the Balkan Radio station of Radio Moscow ... *Radio Free Europe (Munich)*

At 14:05 on 4 November an unscheduled broadcast was intercepted on the Moscow radio frequencies of 15,130, 11,715 and 15,220 kc/s. This consisted of announcements of the program of the "Revolutionary Worker-Peasant Government" of Hungary, broadcast in Bulgarian, Albanian, French, Hungarian and Czech. From 17:00 until 21:05, when the service closed down without any announcement, it was heard on the 11,715 and 11,770 kc/s Moscow radio frequencies. Between 18:46 and 21:05 the output consisted of unannounced music, interrupted on three occasions for further readings in Hungarian of the Kadar Government's program. Between 21:00 and 21:05 the music broadcast on these Soviet frequencies was relayed on the Budapest I (Kossuth Radio) frequency ... *BBC Summary*

ment, and ruthless new oppression. Exploiting mistakes committed during the building of our people's democratic system, the reactionary elements have misled many honest workers, and in particular the major part of the youth, which joined the movement out of honest and patriotic intentions... With deep sadness and a heavy heart we see into what a terrible situation our beloved fatherland had been driven by those counter-revolutionary elements, and often even by well-meaning progressive people, who willy-nilly abused slogans of freedom and democracy and thus opened the way to reaction.

Hungarians, brothers, patriots, soldiers, citizens! We must put an end to the excesses of the counter-revolutionary elements. The hour of action has struck... The interest of the people and the Nation is to have a strong Government... That is why we formed the Hungarian Revolutionary Worker-Peasant Government. The program of this Government is as follows:

(1) To secure our national independence and our country's sovereignty.

(2) To protect our people's democratic and socialist system against all attacks. To protect our socialist achievements, and the guarantee of our progress along the road of building socialism.

(3) To end fratricidal fighting and to restore internal order and peace. The Government will not tolerate the persecution of workers under any pretext whatsoever for having taken part in the most recent events.

(4) To establish close fraternal relations with every socialist country on the basis of complete equality and non-interference. The same principle is to govern their mutual economic relations and mutual assistance agreements.

(5) Peaceful co-operation with every country, irrespective of its social order and form of government.

(6) To raise quickly and substantially the standard of living, in particular that of the working class. More houses for the workers. Factories and institutes must be enabled to build apartments for their workers and employees.

(7) The modification of the Five-Year Plan, changing the methods of economic management, taking into consideration the capacity of the country, so that the population's standard of living may be raised as quickly as possible.

(8) The elimination of bureaucracy, and broad development of democracy in the interest of the workers.

(9) On the broadest democratic basis, workers' management must be realised in factories and enterprises.

(10) To develop agricultural production, abolish compulsory deliveries, and grant assistance to individual farmers. The Government will firmly liquidate all illegalities in the sphere of the co-operatives and redivision of land.

(11) To guarantee democratic elections in hitherto existing administrative bodies and the Revolutionary Councils.

(12) Support for retail trade and artisans.

(13) The systematic development of Hungarian national culture in the spirit of our progressive traditions.

(14) The Hungarian Revolutionary Worker-Peasant Government, acting in the interest of our people, working class and country, requested the Soviet Army Command to help our nation smash the sinister forces of reaction and restore order and calm in the country.

(15) After the restoration of peace and order, the Hungarian Government will begin negotiations with the Soviet Government and with the other participants to the Warsaw Treaty about the withdrawal of Soviet troops from Hungary.

Workers, peasants, intellectuals, youth, soldiers and officers!... Support our nation's just struggle, defend our people's democratic system! Disarm counter-revolutionary gangs! Organised workers, line up behind the Hungarian Revolutionary Worker-Peasant Government! Resume work without delay. Working peasants, defend the land! Fight shoulder to shoulder with your worker-brethren for our common cause, for our people's democratic system. Working youth and students! Do not allow yourselves to be misled. Your future can be guaranteed only by the People's Democracy—defend it!...

Workers, Hungarian brethren: Truth is on our side. We will win. *Kadar Government Radio*

Munnich: The "Initiative" of 1 November

Statement by Ferenc Munnich:

This is an open letter to the Hungarian working people, compatriots, our worker and peasant brethren. We the signatories, Antal Apro, Janos Kadar, Istvan Kossa, and Ferenc Munnich, Ministers, former members of the Imre Nagy Government, announce that on 1 November 1956, we severed all relations with that Government, left it and took the initiative to form the Hungarian Revolutionary Worker-Peasant Government.

We were prompted to take this responsible act by the realisation that, within the Imre Nagy Government, which became impotent under the pressure of the reaction, we had no opportunity whatsoever for action, in face of the ever-growing strength of the counter-revolutionary threat...

Esteemed time-tested champions of the working class movement have been murdered: Imre Mezoe, Secretary of the Greater Budapest Party Branch; Comrade Kalamar, seasoned fighter of the labour movement in Csepel; Sandor Sziklai, the director of the Museum of War History; and other widely-respected sons of the working class and the peasantry have been exterminated *en masse*.

We could no longer stand by idly as members of the Government, incapable of action, while under the cover of democracy counter-revolutionary terrorists and bandits were bestially murdering our worker and peasant brethren, holding our peaceful citizens in terror, dragging our country into anarchy, and putting our entire nation under a counter-revolutionary yoke for a long time to come... *Kadar Government Radio*
Szombathely

Bayonets

Hungarian workers!... The counter-revolutionary government resigned. They did not succeed
in delivering our country to the Western capitalists. They could not succeed because the Hungarian workers and working peasants reject the
Fascist dictatorship. We do not want the old
system with its gendarme bayonets...
Workers, peasants, the power is ours!
We are building the country of the people...

Radio Szombathely

Communists! Comrades! Fascism has not succeeded in ruling us. The heroic fight of the working class ... has overthrown the outrageous
attempt of counter-revolutionaries. The glorious
fight for freedom was led by our Party, just as it
always has led our peaceful constructive work.
Always Communists have been in the forefront.

The past twelve years of people's democratic
rule have left lasting marks on our people and
that fact cannot be changed by no matter how
great a treachery. Comrades, the Communist Party
has again proven that it is the reliable leader of
the people ... The Party has won! The Hungarian
people has won!

Comrades, take the lead into your hands again,
in battle and in work alike! Stabilize again your
organization in the entire country! Be very resolute in your actions against even the slightest
sign of any reactionary element. Explain to workers that it is impossible to overthrow the regime
of the people...

Comrades, prove again and again that you are
worthy of the heroic traditions of our Party! That
you are worthy to be called Communists! This
will be the last fight!...

Radio Szombathely

"Our Situation—Tragic, But Not Hopeless"

Dunapentele

This is the Free Radio of the Dunapentele
National Committee on 36 short wave meter band.
[08:30] The treacherous occupation forces attacked Budapest and several other cities in the
country! The battle is on in Pecs, Szekesfehervar,
Dunafoldvar, and Veszperem. Hungarian Honveds are fighting as one man against the intruders
and will keep on fighting for the sacred cause of
Hungarian Revolution to their last drop of blood!
The situation of our nation is tragic but not hopeless. Our anti-aircraft artillery has been put into
action in every line. The fight is going on everywhere against the intruders!

Hungarians, do not let the Russian troops carry
out massacres in our precious country! Take up

your arms and stand together ... The fight is still
on, but we must win, for this is demanded by
every single honest Hungarian patriot! The garrison troops of Dunapentele will hold out up to
the last man! Death to the Soviet occupiers!

Doctors, nurses and hospital workers, report
immediately to your places in the hospital. Soldiers and civilians who know how to handle guns
should come immediately to the Bela Bartok
House of Culture. Those under 18 and over
61 should return immediately to their homes...

Radio Free Dunapentele

All Budapest bridges have been occupied by
Soviet troops. Ujpest has fallen. The Army units
and freedom fighters at Csepel continue to hold
out. Soviet light bombers continue to enter the
southern area of Trans-Danubia. Soviet armored
units and artillery assisted by the air force are
heavily attacking the bridge at Dunafoldvar (south
of Budapest)...

The Revolutionary Council of the Miskolc Garrison Troops has declared a state of siege for the
city. A Hungarian air bomber unit has started a
big attack against Soviet troops crossing the Tisza.
The Hungarian bombers are bombing the Soviet
pontoon bridges built across the Tisza... The
miners of Pecs have armed themselves and have
joined the Army troops fighting the Soviets...

Trans-Danubian Free Military Radio

This is Hungary calling! This is Hungary calling! *[13:55]* The last free station. Forward to the
United Nations. Early this morning Soviet troops
launched a general attack on Hungary. We are
requesting you to send us immediate aid in the
form of parachute troops over the Transdanubian

Lincoln
Dunapentele

*In the important Gettysburg speech Abra-
ham Lincoln said: "Four score and seven years
ago our fathers brought forth upon this continent a new nation conceived in liberty and
dedicated to the proposition that all men are
created equal. We are now engaged in a great
civil war testing whether that nation or any
nation so conceived and so dedicated can
long endure."*

*People of the United States, these words
are more than ever true today! We are now
fighting for these important principles today
— but not in a civil war. We are fighting for
freedom. ... We are fighting for you, too.
This is not the time for diplomats to argue
over trifles. This is the time for action...*

Free Radio Rakoczi [19:15]

provinces. It is possible that our broadcasts will soon come to the same fate as the other Hungarian broadcasting stations ... For the sake of God and freedom, help Hungary! ...   *Free Radio Rakoczi*

Civilized people of the world, listen and come to our aid. Not with declarations, but with force, with soldiers, with arms. Do not forget that there is no stopping the wild onslaught of Bolshevism. Your turn will also come, if we perish. Save our souls! Save our souls! ...

Civilized peoples of the world! We implore you in the name of justice, freedom and the binding moral principle of active solidarity to help us. Our ship is sinking. Light is failing. The shadows grow darker every hour over the soil of Hungary. Listen to our cry, civilized peoples of the world, and act. Extend us your fraternal aid. SOS! SOS! — May God be with you!
Free Radio Petofi [14:34]

Urgent! Urgent! ... This is the Hungarian Army radio ...

If you are receiving our broadcasts, acknowledge to Radio Rakoczi. We are breaking off, *[15:35]* for we are in immediate danger!

We ask urgently for immediate help!
Free Radio Rakoczi

We announce in the name of the Hungarian Army troops, that they will not put down their arms. Should the combat troops bleed to death, then the older generation will continue the fight ... *[15:00]*   *Radio Free Gyor*

The Revolutionary and National Councils of Borsod refuse to accept the appeal issued by the [Kadar] government to lay down their arms, until such time as there are no Soviet troops within the country. *[16:45]*

The Revolutionary Councils of Counties Borsod, Szatmar, and Szabolcs have come to an agreement with the Soviet Military Command on a cease-fire and mutual troop withdrawal in a radius of three to four kilometers. *[17:11]*
Radio Free Miskolc

Stevenson to Eisenhower

Libertyville, Illinois
DEAR MR. PRESIDENT:
I have been following the developments in Hungary throughout the night, and, like all Americans, I am shocked and gravely disturbed over this brutal, treacherous attack. I would like to be as helpful as I can, and, with this in mind, may I respectfully urge upon you a course of action that might offer protection or relief to the satellite nations which are now under attack, or the threat of attack, by Soviet Russia.

Premier Nagy of Hungary has already appealed to the United Natioans for help. May I there-

fore recommend that you at once set in motion machinery to activitate the Peace Observation Commission with was created in 1950 under the Uniting for Peace resolution. This would make it possible for the United Nations to mobilize large teams of official observers and fly them into Hungary, or at least the still-free parts of Hungary, and also into any other satellite nations, such as Poland, that might welcome or consent to their presence.

I believe that this step, expressing through action the will of the United Nations, might help to save Poland from a fate similar to Hungary's. These U.N. teams, representing the whole world, not only should be a restraining influence, but their presence in Hungary, if they can be gotten in, might also benefit that suffering country.

My understanding of the peace commission is that it can be used to observe and report on the situation in any area where there exist international tensions the continuance of which is likely to endanger maintenance of international peace and security. My further understanding is that the Peace Observation Commission can be activated by either the General Assembly or the Security Council, and hence is beyond veto by the Russians. It then merely requires the invitation or the consent of the state in whose territory it is to go. The Secretary General of the U.N. has the authority to provide the necessary staff and observers.

It may be, Mr. President, that some better plan will occur to you, but I earnestly hope you will receive this suggestion from me in the spirit in which it is sent. If you think well of it, may I respectfully urge that you ask the United Nations to put it into effect as soon as possible.

Sincerely, ADLAI E. STEVENSON
New York Times, 5 November

Eisenhower to Bulganin

Washington
President Eisenhower, in an eleventh-hour move to save the freedom of Hungary, sent an urgent and personal message today to Marshal Nikolai A. Bulganin, Premier of the Soviet Union ... The President's statement read as follows:

"I feel that Western opinion, which was so uplifted only a few days ago by the news that the Soviet Union intended to withdraw its forces from Hungary, has now suffered corresponding shock and dismay at the Soviet attack on the people and Government of Hungary.

"I met today ... to discuss the ways and means available to the United States which would result in:

"1. Withdrawal of Soviet troops from Hungary.

"2. Achieve for Hungary its own right of self-determination in the choice of its Government.

" I have sent an urgent message to Premier Bulganin on these points ..."

The President's feelings of shock and dismay were echoed at all levels of official Washington. Some officials had suggested several days ago that the United States could have exerted some deterrent influence on the Soviet Union by some demonstrative movements of the Strategic Air Force, and by cancellation of military leaves. But these ideas did not gain Administration favor, and there was no evidence that they were discussed at President Eisenhower's conferences during the day.

High-level informants were inclined to the view that the ways and means the United States would use to influence events in Hungary would be largely confined to appeals to world opinion.

Among these informants two major ideas were in circulation about the origins of the sudden Soviet shift from negotiation with the rebels to forceful repression.

One was the British-French attack on Egypt had provided a moral smoke screen behind which the Soviet leaders found it convenient to operate.

The other was that the switch in Hungary meant that Nikita S. Khrushchev, First Secretary of the Soviet Communist party, author of the Soviet Union's liberalization policies, had finally lost out to the authoritarian Stalinist wing of the party headed by Vyacheslav M. Molotov.

The tragedy of the Hungarian rising against Soviet domination, was that it moved so far so fast, diplomats widely remarked. If, as had the Polish revolt, it moved through a Titoist stage, the Soviet crackdown might have been avoided, they said ...   *New York Times, 5 November*

Radio Moscow: "Crushing the Conspiracy..."

Moscow

This morning the forces of the reactionary conspiracy against the Hungarian people were crushed. A new Hungarian Revolutionary Worker-Peasant Government, headed by the Prime Minister Janos Kadar, has been formed. The Government has appealed to the Hungarian people to ally its forces in defence of the victories of the people's democratic system and for a final rout of the reactionary conspirators headed by Horthy officers who served in the Hitlerite army.

The Revolutionary Worker-Peasant Government has appealed to the Command of the Soviet troops for assistance in the suppression of the insurgents who were recently protected by the remnants of the Imre Nagy Government, which has disintegrated as a result of the resignation from it of honest Hungarian patriots.

The counter-revolutionary bands nesting in public buildings are being successfully smashed and are capitulating ... [21:05 GMT]

...Many Hungarian workers who were deceived by the insurgents' propaganda have had their eyes opened. They have seen how the enemies of the people's regime, who tortured and hanged the finest representatives of the Hungarian people, tried to re-establish the authority of the capitalists and landowners of Hungary. In Budapest and other Hungarian towns order is being restored, the resistance of neglible groups of insurgents in Budapest is being crushed with the active participation of the Hungarian population ...

[15:10 GMT]

During 4 November events have led to a complete defeat of the forces of counter-revolution ... The proclamation of the new Revolutionary Government in Hungary has found a lively response among genuine patriots ... [21:10 GMT]

Radio Moscow

The UN, "Last Citadel of Hope"

Near Budapest

Attention! Attention! [16:20]

To all U.N. members and delegates! Delegates of the peoples!

In the coming hours you will decide about the life or the death of this nation. While your sons are at peace and happy, we sons of the Hungarian nation are falling under the cruel fire of Soviet tanks and bombers. Our country has been attacked from abroad. We turn to you. You are our last citadel of hope.

Exercise the opportunity which your nations

have given you and save our country from destruction and slavery! We are asking for immediate and effective help. Save us from further bloodshed and give us back our neutrality. Show that the U.N. can carry out its will, and thus achieve that our country again be free! We appeal to your conscience and call on you to act immediately ...   *Free Radio Csokonay*

Attention Radio Free Europe: We heard your acknowledgement of our message to the Secretary-General of the U.N.

Mourning for the Dead . . .   *. . . and Flight*

We now interrupt our broadcast for an indefinite period. *[17:15]*

Long live freedom, long live the free Hungarian people! *Free Radio Csokonay*

New York

The General Assembly voted today for a United Nations investigation in Hungary.

The seventy-six-nation body deplored the use of force by the Soviet Union to crush the Hungarian revolt and called on the Soviet Government to desist from intervention in Hungarian affairs. The Soviet Government was asked to withdraw its forces "without delay".

The Assembly ... requested Secretary General Dag Hammarskjold to send his representatives into the central European state. The resolution instructed the international investigators to look into the situation brought about by "foreign intervention" and proposed means to end it. It asked the new Government of Hungary and the Government of the Soviet Union to allow the observers to travel freely. They will report to the Secretary General ...

The vote came just after 8 p.m. Fifty nations favored the resolution. Eight were opposed and fifteen abstained. The Soviet bloc made up the whole opposition ...

Lindesay Parrott, New York Times, 5 November

Telegram to Dag Hammarskjold, U.N. Secretary-General:

The Hungarian Revolutionary Worker-Peasant Government hereby confirms the mandate of Dr. Peter Kos or, in his absence, of Janos Szabo as the permanent representative of the Hungarian People's Republic in U.N. ...

The Hungarian Revolutionary Worker-Peasant Government states that the appeal made by Imre Nagy to the U.N. organisation requesting that the Hungarian question be discussed in the United Nations has no legal force and cannot be regarded as an appeal sent by Hungary as a State. The Revolutionary Worker-Peasant Government categorically opposes the discussion both by the Security Council and the General Assembly of the above-mentioned question since this question lies exclusively within the competence of the Hungarian People's Republic.

(signed) *Janos Kadar, Prime Minister of the Hungarian Revolutionary Worker-Peasant Government; Imre Horvath, Foreign Minister.*

Radio Kossuth [23:48]

Diary of "A Sordid Crime"

Budapest

[12:30] Violent fighting in the Szena-Ter section of Buda. Regrouping of Hungarian forces in the interior of Pecs. Soviet artillery are bombarding Csepel ...

[13:55] The Russian occupation of the East Station. Szolnok has been bombarded by Soviet aircraft. Fighting continues in the Gellerthegy part of Buda.

[14:15] Four Soviet armoured cars followed by trucks near the [French] Legation.

[15:00] Soviet troops, coming from Czechoslovakia, are passing through Komaron and Gyor.

[15:15] According to a Hungarian source, Zoltan Tildy was arrested this morning by Russians occupying Parliament. On the other hand, three "Nagy-ist" writers who were inside Parliament at the time got away: Erosi, Gyula Hay, and Lajos Tamasi.

[15:25] Fighting continues around the railroad stations.

[15:40] Soviet aircraft are flying over the city. Artillery fire on the heights of Buda.

[16:00] A battle around the Astoria Hotel, 5th city district.

[16:15] Acker, whose observation post is on the Embassy roof, reports fires burning in the 15th district. Violent fighting near the Austrian and French Embassies in Buda. Mortars and violent explosions nearby.

[16:30] Two sixteen year-olds are ambushed behind the Duna hotel and one of them attacked a tank with a hand-grenade. He was slightly wounded. This is news from Chatelot. Girard furnishes details on the battle at Hotel Astoria. His car came up against two Soviet tanks. Bombs and shells bursting two hundred meters in front and three hundred meters behind. Numerous bottles of gasoline thrown on the tanks ... The avenue is in flames.

[17:50] A violent explosion near the Legation. Soviet leaflets about "the liberation" distributed by troops in the streets.

[18:00] Soviet mortars installed near the Legation are firing on the city.

[18:20] A Hungarian source: Battle raging around the National Theater between the 7th and 8th city districts ...

[19:00] Violent engagements between the Soviets and insurgents in the Krisztinavaros quarter ...

[21:15] The Russians are occupying the Buda citadel which overlooks the city.

[21:30] No more electricity in the 5th district (southern portion). Soviet armoured cars are withdrawing toward the suburbs in order to avoid being taken by surprise in the center of town by teams of dynamiters during the night ...

[22:20] New explosions . . . a violent exchange of machine-gun fire . . . The approach of tanks makes the walls shake . . . Street being torn up by the tread of tanks has been renamed twice. Formerly called Andrassy Road. It became Stalin Road. Then after the insurrection, covered with blood, it became the Street of Hungarian Youth. Will it be changed again?

Soviet tanks are concentrated around the two buildings that house the Soviet Embassy . . . It is bitter and ironical to hear the East Berlin radio broadcast on the intentions of "patriots to liquidate the counter-revolutionaries." Never has so much affrontery been associated with so sordid a crime . . . And the drama is only beginning . . .

[Midnight] The insurgents retire to positions in the South Station. The Russians attack with armoured cars. The Varhogy district was bombarded at regular intervals by artillery . . .

Agence France Presse (Paris), 15 November

Budapest

To achieve their purpose the Red Army launched elementary maneuvers, taught in all the military schools throughout the world: how to take a hill. The Russians are good pupils. First an artillery barrage, followed by the attack of tanks with supporting groups in the rear, then followed by infantry encirclement at the bottom of the hill, in order to pick up survivors attempting to escape.

But this classic plan was to be upset by a child's trick. The "children" poured oil on the narrow roads leading to the castle. The tractors skidded and the tanks had to give up. There were a few hours of respite.

But then files of "Molotova" lorries could be seen advancing to the attack on the left, up a road behind the hill. At 6 p.m. the fate of the War Ministry was sealed. Thirty survivors who came out, hands raised above their heads, were shot on the spot, one after the other . . .

Alain de Sédouy, Paris-Presse, 16 November

Budapest

Just before midnight we heard the rumbling of heavy Soviet tanks, some of them passing our buildin the direction of nearby Andrassy Street. There they were concentrating and making a laager for the night. The whole street was floodlit to keep snipers at bay. It was a fantastic sight.

But the precautions were in vain. The temptation was too great. Thousands of freedom fighters moved into an extemporised attack before dawn. This attack on the tanks led to one of the heaviest battles. I watched it from my window. More than thirty tanks were destroyed. And after that the Soviet tanks never stayed in the centre of the city at night. Every night, before midnight, they moved out, to come back at dawn . . .

Lajos Lederer, The Observer (London), 18 November

Last Interview with Bela Kovacs

Budapest

Late in the evening of Sunday, November 4— a night of terror in Budapest that no one who lived through it will ever forget—I met Bela Kovacs, one of the leaders of Hungary's short-lived revolutionary government, in a cellar in the city's center . . .

Kovács, as a Minister of State of the Nagy régime, had started off for the Parliament Building early that morning, but he never reached it. Soviet tanks were there ahead of him. Now he squatted on the floor oposite me, a fugitive from Soviet search squads . . .

A hunched, stocky man, with a thin mustache and half-closed eyes, Béla Kovács was only a shadow of the robust figure he once had been. Now in his early fifties, he had risen to prominence after the war as one of the top leaders of the Hungarian Independent Smallholders Party. Back in 1947, when Mátyás Rákosi began taking over the government with the support of the Soviet occupation forces, Kovács had achieved fame by being the only outstanding anti-Communist Hungarian leader to defy Rákosi and continue open opposition. His prestige had become

so great among the peasantry that at first the Communists had not molested him. But then the Soviets themselves stepped in, arresting him on a trumped-up charge of plotting against the occupation forces and sentencing him to life imprisonment. After eight years in Siberia, Kovács was returned to Hungary and transferred to a Hungarian jail, from which he was released in the spring of 1956, broken in body but not in spirit by his long ordeal. After what was called his "rehabilitation," Kovács was visited by his old enemy Rákosi, who called to pay his respects. Rákosi was met at the door by this message from Kovács: "I do not receive murderers in my home."

So long as Nagy's government was still under the thumb of the Communist Politburo, Kovács refused to have anything to do with the new régime. Only in the surge of the late October uprising, when Nagy succeeded in freeing himself from his former associates and cast about to form a coalition government, did Kovács consent to lend his name and immense popularity to it. He himself had not been in Budapest when the revolt broke out, but at his home in Pécs, a southern city near the Yugoslav border. In fact, he told me, he was made a member of the new Nagy government before he had even a chance to say "Yes" or "No," but, understanding the situation and what Nagy was trying to do, he had agreed to go along. The name of Kovacs among the Ministers of State was to many Hungarians a guarantee of a new era in which the government would carry out the mandates of the victorious revolution.

At about six o'clock in the morning of November 4, when Soviet tanks were already pouring into the city, Kovács had received a message from Nagy calling an immediate meeting of the Cabinet. When he reached Parliament Square the Russians had already thrown a tight cordon around it. One of Nagy's new Ministers, Zoltan Tildy, who had been ousted from the Presidency in 1948, came out of the building and told Kovacs that he had just negotiated a surrender agreement with the Russians whereby civilians would be permitted to leave the building unmolested in exchange for surrendering the seat of the government. However, Tildy reported, State Minister Istvan Bibo refused to leave and had entrenched himself with a machine gun on the second floor. Tildy begged Kovacs to get in touch with Bibo by telephone and order him to leave. Then Tildy himself left.

Kovacs called Bibo from a nearby phone and tried to persuade him to leave. He was unable to move the aroused Minister, whose argument was that if the Russians moved against him, this would serve as a clear demonstration before the world that Soviet forces had been employed to crush the independent Hungarian government. Bibo declared that the Russians intended to install Janos Kadar and his clique as a new government, and by not yielding, he wanted to demonstrate that the exchange of governments was accomplished by armed force.

I told Kovacs that as late as four in the afternoon, I had been in touch with the beleaguered Bibo by telephone. He was still holding out, but an hour later his private line did not answer. By that time Premier Nagy himself was in custody, and the Ministers who had not been arrested were in hiding. Kovacs voiced his admiration of both Bibo and the Premier. "My fondest memory of Nagy," he said to me, "will always be his transformation from an easy-going, jolly, studious professor into a flaming revolutionary."

"What do you think caused the Russians to change their tactics and come in again?" I asked Kovacs.

"Two things. First, we went too fast and too far, and the Communists panicked. Second, the Russians felt deeply humilated." He went on to explain that he felt that all the goals of the revolution could have been attained if there had been a way to slow down the process. In a free election, he estimated, all the left-of-center parties would not command more than thirty per cent of the vote. But a free election was what the Communists were afraid to risk.

"Wouldn't such an election have brought in the extreme Right and possibly a new reign of White Terror?" I asked.

Kovacs admitted there might have been a possibility of that, but he was convinced it could have been checked in time. He went on to say that in his estimation there was no chance of reconstituting large land-holdings in the hands of their former owners or of the workers permitting the return of the mines and factories to their former owners. "The economic salvation of Hungary lies in a mixed economy, combining capitalism, state ownership, and co-operatives," he said. Politically, there had been the likelihood of a strongly rightist development, but, in the absence of economic power, after a few short months the extremists would have been silenced ...

I asked Kovács whether he felt the Nagy government's declaration of neutrality had aroused the Soviet leaders to action. No, he thought that the decision to crush the Hungarian revolution was taken earlier and independently of it. Obviously the Russians would not have rejoiced at a neutral Hungary, but so long as economic co-operation between the states in the area was assured the Russians and their satellites should not have been too unhappy.

In that regard, Kovács assured me, there was never a thought in the Nagy government of interrupting the economic co-operation of the Danubian states. "It would have been suicidal for us to try tactics hostile to the bloc. What we wanted was simply the right to sell our product to the best advantage of our people and buy our necessities where we could do it most advantageously."

"Then in your estimation there was no reason why the Russians should have come again and destroyed the revolution?"

"None unless they are trying to revert to the old Stalinist days. But if that is what they really are trying—and at the moment it looks like it— they will fail, even more miserably than before. The tragedy of all this is that they are burning all the bridges which could lead to a peaceful solution."

Sympathy

The Russian intervention provoked the indignation of the entire world ... I trust I am right in saying: it has hardly ever happened in the history of the world that a nation's fight for freedom excited greater sympathy than ours. We fought by ourselves, cut off from the world.

LAJOS KOSSUTH, REGENT OF HUNGARY, 1849

Quoted in George Mikes, The Hungarian Revolution (London, 1957)

He went on in the semi-darkness to say that after today there would be no way to bring about a rapprochement between Hungary and the Soviet Union. The wound the Russians were inflicting on Hungary was so deep that it would fester for generations. "Yet we can't pick up Hungary and take it somewhere else. We have to go on living with our ancient neighbours who are now in the Soviet grip."

We discussed the revolution itself. Kovác's somber eyes lit up. "It has brought modern history to a turning point," he said. "It has exposed totalitarian fallacies more sharply than any event before. Our people were beaten, cowed, and for years lived in abject surrender, yet when the hour struck they all streamed out of their homes, Communists and non-Communists alike, to regain their self-respect by defying their tormentors. And look what happened to the Communist Party! It disappeared overnight—not forced to dissolve, but by common consent! Have you ever heard of a ruling party voting itself out of existence? Once the revolution touched them, all became Hungarians—all except those whose crimes were too many to be forgiven. These are the ones who now serve their Russian masters."

As to Janos Kadar, the Russian favorite just being installed as Premier, Kovács was reserved. He was not sure that Kadar agreed with all that his masters had dictated. Kovács knew, as we all did, that on Friday, November 2, while still serving the Nagy government, Kadar had disappeared from Budapest. All efforts to locate him failed, and it was widely thought that he had been kidnaped by the Russians. Whether this was true was hard to say in the light of subsequent developments, but Kovács thought he might still be acting under compulsion. "Compulsion or no, he has an impossible task ..."

How much truth was in the Russian assertion that the revolution had become a counter-revolution and that therefore Russian intervention was justified?

"I tell you," said Kovács, "this was a revolution from inside, led by Communists. There is not a shred of evidence that it was otherwise. Communists outraged by their own doings prepared the ground for it and fought for it during the first few days. This enabled us former non-Communist party leaders to come forward and demand a share in Hungary's future. Subsequently this was granted by Nagy, and the Social Democratic, Independent Smallholders, and Hungarian Peasant parties were reconstituted. True, there was a small fringe of extremists in the streets and there was also evidence of a movement which seemed to have ties with the exiled Nazis and Nyilas of former days. But at no time was their strength such as to cause concern. No one in Hungary cares for those who fled to the West after their own corrupt terror régime was finished—and then got their financing from the West. Had there been an attempt to put them in power, all Hungary would haven risen instantly ..."

"What of the future?" I asked. After some hesitation Kovács said: "All ist not lost, for it is impossible for the Russians and their puppets to maintain themselves against the determined resistance of the Hungarians. The day will come when a fateful choice will have to be made: Exterminate the entire population by slow starvation and police terror or else accept the irreducible demand—the withdrawal of Soviet forces from our country ..."

Leslie B. Bain, The Reporter (New York), 13 December

"The Last Minutes of the Revolution"

Sopron

In this small town, the most westerly in Hungary, the last minutes of the revolution ran out to the rattle of machine-gun fire, the rumble of Soviet tanks, the screams and tears of women, and the singing of the Hungarian National Anthem.

Until 3 p. m. no Russian troops had entered Sopron, but they were known to be all around it, in the hills and woods. I arrived at Klingenbach, the nearest point in Austria, at three o'clock and decided to go in and have a look for myself. Approaching Klingenbach I saw streams of Hungarian refugees, walking in little groups along the road, carrying their worldly belongings on their backs, or on oxcarts, handcarts, bicycles, or wheelbarrows. The refugees, a look of sorrow and resignation on their faces, trudged in an unending stream to political asylum in Austria. Austrian officials said 5,000 had already arrived, and all the time more were coming.

On a short drive from the frontier to Sopron, I passed several groups of student-partisans. They were armed to the teeth, with rifles and "guitars" —the familiar name for the Russian-type submachine gun carried slung around the neck—and up to a dozen hand grenades stuck through their belts.

The men at a Hungarian artillery barracks nearby had previously decided to resist the Russians and had positioned some field guns in the hills overlooking the town, pointing in the direction the Russians were expected to come. But their crews had gone and the untrained students were trying to find out how to fire them.

We drove into the town and saw people standing around in little groups at street corners and in doorways. Just as we reached the main square and got out I heard the rattle of distant machine-gun fire. Everybody looked at each other. This was it. We walked along and within two minutes I heard screams. Some men and women came running around the corner. "They're here, they're here," they yelled. "Four Russian tanks have entered the town."

A sudden panic gripped everyone. We were swept along in a scurrying crowd of men, women, and children, some weeping, some screaming, some yelling senselessly. We stopped at our car and waited. Everyone else disappeared from the streets. In a few seconds Sopron had become a ghost town. Only here and there a head peeped from a basement window or doorway.

I waited apprehensively. The engine of our car was ticking over. All was ready for a quick get-away. But I wanted to see the Russians enter. Soon we heard them. The roar, screech, and rumble of tanks on concrete; then the first vehicle, an armoured car, round a corner. Three T-34 tanks followed it. They did not pass us but turned down another street which led to the university. They seemed to know the way well. I saw no infantrymen.

We made for the frontier. On the way out my chauffeur recognised a man who had been one of the leading revolutionaries in the town and we gave him a lift. He told me that, according to last-minute feverish telephone calls around the country, Sopron seemed to be the last town in Hungary to be taken by the Russians.

At every other telephone exchange the operator either cut him off or indicated carefully that the "Revolutionary Council" no longer existed. "I am sorry, that number is temporarily out of order," an operator had told him from Veszprem.

On the first hills outside the town we stopped and took a look back. I heard the chatter of a machine-gun. Otherwise there was silence. The sun was setting in a darkening sky over the fields lightly covered with snow.

On the way back to the frontier we passed the Hungarian artillery pieces we had seen on our way in. They were completely deserted now. The stream of refugees had vanished. Only here and there a straggler made his way towards Austria. We picked up an old woman and her fourteen-year-old granddaughter. Their possessions were in an untidy bundle hardly larger than a lady's handbag. The old woman was weeping bitterly.

At the Hungarian frontier post three lorryloads of refugees stood, looking back towards Sopron. A number of Austrian gendarmes and other officials, journalists, and cameramen, and a crowd of curious sightseers stood around. Suddenly, a hoarse male voice lifted above the hubbub and started singing the Hungarian national anthem, "God bless the Hungarians . . ."

Others joined in. Soon all the Hungarians present, perhaps a hundred in all, were singing. Many had tears in their eyes. Everything came to a complete standstill. Austrian gendarmes saluted. Men took off their hats. An old man knelt and prayed. When the anthem ended, there was a long silence, broken only by the sobbing of the old woman beside me in the car and of many other women in the crowd.   *Peter Howard, Reuters, 5 November*

A Cry of Wailing

Austro-Hungarian Frontier

Hope had been so deceptive. Shouldn't we have known better? We were awakened by the news on the blackest Sunday of modern European history, shattered, speechless. In Vienna the people seemed almost to be paralyzed by the red headlines of the extra editions: "*Ungeheures Verbrechen! Der gemeinste Verrat aller Zeiten! Sie greifen an!*" All day, and half the night, as we drive from frontier post to frontier post along the Hungarian border, we hear the news in our car radio, in the jammed saddened inns along the way . . . The Austrian Red Cross, with surprising and heartening efficiency, has moved in to take care of the thousands of refugees now pouring across. Camps, barracks, refugees. In the eleventh year of peace. Once again women and children running for their lives like hunted animals. Once again the same old folding cots, the same field-grey blankets. How often had one seen this—the Alsatians fleeing from the battles of the Rhine in the winter of '44, the Jews from the concentration camps, the DP's trying to make their way home, the liberated prisoners-of-war, the expellees from Poland and Czechoslovakia, the Soviet-zone refugees in West-Berlin . . . Near Hegeshalom an Austrian nurse tries to calm a group of children; a little boy begins to tremble and scream, for some one had opened a window and the traffic of the street sounded as if a battle were still raging . . . In Eisenstadt we listen to the news: the UN General Assembly is altogether likely to meet again soon; a hundred people in the crowded café stand up, wave their hands angrily, helplessly, and walk out. I talk with a student from Sopron who mumbles. "We shouldn't have burned the Russian books, Tolstoy was among them . . ." In Klingenbach we run into an Hungarian lieutenant and six of his men, embarassment and bad conscience in their eyes, who tell us that the Soviet attack had cut them off; but who is to sit in judgement, even if they had run away? At the border crossing at

Drassburg a foreign car manages to come over: "We thank you," says a Hungarian, rifle still slung across his shoulder, "we thank you for sharing our suffering with us!..." Somebody else cries out: "But why don't you help us? Don't give us words or food, give us munition!" And a third: "In the name of betrayed Hungary, come back to us!"... On the road back to Nickelsdorf we listen to the Viennese radio: a variety program called *"Take It Easy."* Radio Budapest, we are told, has come on the air again, with music, "Alexander's Ragtime Band." In Margersdorf: a few radio men who are still monitoring messages from Gyor, the last SOS-calls of the dying October Revolution...

From every side, from the excited students, from over-wrought women, from confused young officers in their clay-brown uniforms, one hears the stories, "atrocity stories" if you will. In the epoch of primitive war propaganda a whole generation learned to mistrust all tales of atrocities; then came the generation, in the era of the Gestapo and the GPU, who came to know the truth of even the wildest most unbelievable inhumanities. How could one distinguish, along this panicky fear-ridden frontier, history from hysteria? A pale young girl tells of tanks running over children; students relate how their university buildings in Sopron had been set afire; a lieutenant reports how officers and soldiers had been executed along the road of the Soviet offensive. But then two old men tell touching anecdotes of Russian soldiers who "fraternized," and of a few who deserted because "the cause of Hungarian freedom was also the cause of the Russian people"...

At the end of the day of the brutal Soviet counter-attack I looked out of the window of a little Hungarian frontier check-point at the "Stalin" tanks which had moved up to cut off the flight of soldiers and civilians. Everything had become quiet. And I thought of a passage I had once read in Xenophon, describing how, one night in 405 B. C., people in Athens heard a cry of wailing, making its way up between the long walls from the Piraeus, and coming nearer and nearer as they listened. It was the news of victory and disaster.

"And that night no one slept. They wept for the dead, but far more bitterly for themselves. For they knew that they would suffer the same fate they had inflicted on others..."

Melvin J. Lasky, Der Monat (Berlin), December 1956

IV

AFTERMATH

"The times of that superstition which attributed revolutions to the ill-will of a few agitators have long passed away. Everyone knows nowadays that, wherever there is a revolutionary convulsion, there must be some social want in the background which is prevented by outworn institutions from satisfying itself . . . Every attempt at forcible repression will only bring it forth stronger and stronger until it bursts its fetters."

Karl Marx

"This was the flash [the Kronstadt revolt, 1921] which clearer than all else illuminated reality . . ."

Lenin

"It is not for nothing that the proverb says, 'An obliging bear is more dangerous than an enemy' . . ."

Stalin

AFTERMATH

"Orders to Crush and Exterminate"

Budapest

The new day broke in the deadly roar of tanks. They were coming in much greater force than on the day before. I watched them moving up to surround the University strongpoint near the National Museum. And each tank was accompanied by a small detachment of the M.V.D. Their orders were to crush and to exterminate.

This was the hour of horror and brutality. My window overlooked the Karoly Boulevard, which led to the avenue where the Budapest students had their strongpoint. The Soviet tanks shelled every house in this boulevard with total savagery. This was the order of the day. And reports came in all that morning saying that the same sort of thing was going on in many other places.

By evening there was scarcely a building in the main boulevards of Budapest which had not been torn open by Soviet shells. People swarmed to the Legations all day, hundreds more telephoned, imploring the Great Powers to intervene.

"Tell the world what they are doing to us!" they cried. And we could do nothing. The outside world was busy elsewhere, in Suez. We were ashamed. We could offer nothing but a promise that we would do our best to tell the world about these horrors ...

Lajos Lederer, The Observer (London), 18 November

Budapest

During the first twenty-four hours, Russian tanks and cannon-fire crushed the principal resistance centres. The Hungarians had very little artillery and could not retaliate. Soon the resistance centres fell, one by one. There was silence. The Kilian barracks and the Budapest strongholds were silenced by artillery fire.

But the young Hungarians continued to fire on the Russians from the windows and house-tops of their dwellings, and this marked the beginning of the repression. The Russians answered each rifle shot with tank fire. The tanks, in a roar of thunder, bore down upon the houses from which shots were being fired, pointing their guns first at the ground floor, then at the first floor, the second, and the third. Six, eight, ten cannon shots ... The houses were blown apart and crumbled; the inhabitants were either killed, or lay wounded on the ground ...

Any minute now we expected the Budapest telephone exchange to be destroyed, or simply paralysed, by the Russians. But nothing happened. During all the next day of the horrible week, the telephone functioned for town calls. And we received telephone calls from Hungarian friends, or foreign journalists sheltered in their legations:

"Two tanks have been destroyed next to our house!"

"The Russians have just destroyed the school opposite by mortar fire!"

"They are shelling in the direction of this-or-that army barracks."

"I cannot speak to you any longer, they are shelling too hard. I am going to take shelter in the cellar. Call you again later ..."

"Later" sometimes meant some 12 or 24 hours, especially in those parts of the town that were hardest hit.

The other miracle was the electricity, which never went off (except in two districts where the electricity works or principal supply lines were severely damaged). It was thanks to the light that one could live through these hours of terror, that the sick could be operated on in the hospitals and that we who were left, and who were cut off from the rest of the world, could listen in to foreign transmitting stations on the radio — our only source of information from the outside world ...

Michel Gordey, France-Soir (Paris), 14 November

A student, aged 27, explained: "The arrangement was for the women to stand in doorways with machine-guns. The men threw the Molotov cocktails into the tanks. If the cocktail did not go off, or if any Russian soldiers escaped, the women shot them down. We took most of our arms and ammunition from the Russians. One thing we were short of was bottles for filling with petrol to throw into the tanks. Although food was so short, the housewives emptied out the tomatoes they had bottled so that we could have the empty bottles." *Manchester Guardian, 21 November*

Budapest

The defenders of the city are without command. They have no plan of defense, and no arms except machine guns, grenades and gasoline bottles. Is it possible to hold a city with such forces? The aggressors have artillery, armored cars, tanks.

Above their units patrol jet plane squadrons. But they have no infantry in Budapest; perhaps they have reasons not to throw infantry into action ...

From the Soviet side, only fresh troops brought from the far end of their continent are taking part in the fighting. Time and again we can personally verify that fact, and the observations of all our informants confirm it. Very young men in dark grey coats (the age group most often encountered: 1937) who still do not know where they have been led, who speak a poor Russian, but who are always convinced of one thing: that in this city they are fighting vile fascist traitors.

And on the other side? All in all they are the same ones who demonstrated in front of the Parliament on October 23rd, who then repulsed the first intervention and organized the national guard. But they are more numerous than before: the worker and student youth has now been joined by older workers, who previously had supported the revolution passively. Now, weapon in hand, they have mounted the barricades of Csepel and Kobanya.

Franciszka and Marian went today into the cellars of the defenders. They spoke with the head of one detachment — a miner with a severe leg wound — and with other soldiers. They came back convinced that the Hungarians will fight to the end ...

Viktor Woroszylski, France Observateur (Paris), 3 January 1957

"Fortress of the West"

We request every Western station which is able to receive our message, to transmit this in English, German and French!

We need help!

The population of Budapest has no food! For lack of medicines and military help many persons are dying! We ask for food and arms! ...

Severe fighting is going on in the 8th District of Budapest. The Russians have encircled the district and the population is digging trenches and making barricades. Russian Army transports are arriving at Budapest airfields. Nepliget district and the East station are crowded with Russians.

Hungarian youth will fight to their last breath. Hungary was always the fortress of the West. The situation becomes more difficult by the hour. Only military help can save us. The whole nation pleads for help.   *Free Radio Roka, 5 November [18:30]*

Dunapentele

At the moment fighting is going on in the capital. Csepel and the railway bridge are entirely in the hands of the freedom fighters. Some Russian tanks only dare to move in formations. In many places they have built barricades along the roads. Desperate fighting is going on. The Hungarian Honveds stood their ground with honor ... In Dunafoldvar the Russians hold the barracks and have dug themselves in ... News

from Kecskemet says that the Russians have occupied it. In Veszprem there is sporadic street fighting ... Inota is in the hands of the Hungarian freedom figthers. It was calm Monday morning ...

Free Radio Rakoczi, 5 November [15:10]

Dunapentele

Please, forward our request to the Vienna Red Cross! They should help!

Several hospitals are in flames! ... Kossuth Radio is in the hands of traitors! ... Food and ammunition is becoming scarce! Russians are launching extremely strong attacks! When will UN delegates arrive? ...

Free Radio Rakoczi, 5 November [17:08]

We have very little to say to the Soviet masters. They have convinced not only the whole world, but also all Communists, that they do not care for Communism, that they simply prostituted Communism ... to Russian imperialism.

We also want to speak of the traitors ... the Janos Kadars, who play the dirty role of colonial governors ... We send them the message that we consider them all traitors to Communism ... [Kadar's] crime and that of his accomplices is clear and the sentence has already been pronounced. We Hungarian Communists will see to it that the sentence is carried out. ...

Free Radio Rajk, 5 November [17:30]

Vac

All Hungarian radio stations are in Muscovite hands ... They have become mouthpieces of the Muscovite Government. ... We want free elections! We had enough of the Muscovite trickeries!

We want free elections under international control ... The Government of Imre Nagy and Imre Nagy himself ... are now in prison ... We shall continue fighting ... We will broadcast again tomorrow.

Free Radio Csokonay, 5 November [21:15]

"Too Late"

To The West

You still want to come?
Too late, too late.
We are cut and fallen
like wheat in the reaper ...

Hungarian Student, † 5 November

Süddeutsche Zeitung (Munich), 15 December

Keep fighting! Keep fighting! Do not believe Communist and Soviet broadcasts! This is the radio of the national freedom fighters. Do not surrender your arms!

Insurgent Broadcast, Wave-length 12, 6 November [11:50]

Dunapentele

Russian soldiers! The Hungarian nation rose against its occupiers, against tyranny. With us fight no fascists but the whole nation for freedom. You do not know that you fight against workers. ... Do not shoot! ... You are our friends, and will be our friends. This is not propaganda. This is the truth. We will die for our freedom.

Free Radio Rakoczi, 6 November [12:00]

We appeal to the conscience of the world! England and France cannot be indifferent to a possible loss of the Suez Canal, since they immediately asked for policing action from the United Nations. A loss of liberty for the world — of a little country which throughout thousands of years maintained this liberty with sacrifice and loss of blood — why are only the interests of the great powers important? Why are not our hospitals, schools and national churches important, and why can these be easily sacrificed to bombs and fire? Why can't you hear the call for help of our men, women and children? People of the world, hear the call for help of a small nation ... We have seen the atrocities committed under the slogan of commands "down with fascism". We are not fascists. We can prove this to an independent committee, but we will not prove it to those who reply with phosphorous bombs. Help! For under the guise of slogans of democracy, they are taking away the last possibility for democracy. ...

Free Radio Rakoczi, 6 November [14:50]

Vienna

The refugees include many unaccompanied children with labels round their necks, saying "Look after our children; we stay to fight to the last." ...   *Manchester Guardian, 6 November*

"The Resistance Continues"

Budapest

The shelling was heavier than ever Tuesday. The main points of resistance were the Var fortress in Buda, the army barracks, Moscow Square in Buda, the Csepel automobile factory and the Obduda Post Office ...

John MacCormac, New York Times, 12 November

Budapest

We managed to get out into the streets. Some of us went as far as the intersection of Terez Boulevard and Kiraly Street, one of the strongpoints which the Russians had been unable to take. There were Soviet tanks at every corner of the boulevards; but they had now stopped firing. Freedom fighters skirmished among them.

I saw small children standing by the tanks and cursing the crews for what they had done.

"Do you really believe," one little girl was asking, "that you have come to liberate us from a handful of Fascists?"

"You unspeakable swine", another shouted. "You won't get away with this!"

It was the first time the compulsory learning of Russian in Hungarian schools had paid a dividend. The young Hungarians could tell the Russians what they thought of them — and in their own language ...

The tank crews themselves looked tired. They were dirty and bewildered. At first they would try to argue back; but in the end they gave up. They themselves were hardly more than boys, some of them obviously of Mongol blood. They were shabby in the extreme — shabbier than those I met in Budapest and Vienna at the end of the war.

Dumbly, they put up with being spat at and cursed. Their expressions seemed to say that they knew they deserved nothing better. They sat motionless by their machine-guns in their turrets, but they did not shoot. This day marked the end of the really heavy fighting in Budapest.

Lajos Lederer, The Observer (London), 18 November

Dunapentele

Fighting has flared up in Kecskemet, Mohacs and other towns. ...

... Now Dunapentele is being attacked from several directions ... We are asking for immediate armed help ... Please forward this appeal to President Eisenhower. Please forward it to Anna Kethly. We are fighting against overwhelming odds.

Possibly our radio will soon be annihilated. We shall continue to fight a partisan war. We ask for urgent ... help. We ask for armed help for Hungary. [13:05]

... On November 6, 1956, delegates of the Soviet Command in Kecskemet handed the following notice to the town's National Committee and

"All Honorable Men"

Prague

It goes without saying that the Hungarian workers deeply appreciate the help which the Soviet Government gave the Hungarian people in stopping the raging counter-revolution. This help is also appreciated by the population of our own Republic and all the other friendly countries as well as all honorable men in the entire world ...

Rude Pravo (Prague), 5 November

Military Command:

"I call on the garrison forces of Dunapentele to lay down arms. All officers, NCOs and soldiers who lay down their arms will preserve their lives, their liberty and their political rights. If the garrison does not lay down its arms, the Soviet Command will take the city by force. After the fighting is over, all those who carried arms — soldiers and civilians — will be treated as POW's."

The Military Command of Dunapentele and the National Committee answered:

"Dunapentele is the foremost Socialist town in Hungary. The majority of residents are workers and power is in their hands. After the victorious revolution of October 23, the workers elected the National Committee ... The Military Command of the town is in close collaboration with the National Committee ...

"The population of the town is armed ... The houses were all built by the workers themselves ... The workers will defend the town from Fascist excesses ... but also from Soviet troops ...

"We are prepared to live in peace with the Soviets so long as they don't interfere in our internal affairs ...

"The majority of factories and plants are working. There are no counter-revolutionaries in the town ...

"We suggest further negotiations in a neutral zone..." [13:30]

An appeal to the UN:

The battle in Dunapentele has continued since morning with unflagging violence ... Intervention urgent. According to the last reports, partisan fighting against Soviet troops has started again in Kecskemet and Kalocsa ... We beg you to send urgent help ... Dunapentele is being attacked by tanks from several directions. The people of the town are armed and will defend the town ... to their last drop of blood. If Soviet troops do not enter the ten kilometer zone around the town they will not be attacked. If they come nearer, they will be fired on ...

We beg to send urgent help to Kecskemet, Kalocsa, and Dunapentele ... [13:40]

Soviet tanks and planes are attacking Dunapentele. Soviet tanks and planes are attacking Dunapentele.

The battle continues with unflagging violence. ... We interrupt our broadcast for an uncertain period. ... [14:53]   *Free Radio Rakoczi, 7 November*
Budapest

During a pause in the fighting I jumped over torn cables, broken pavement and shattered glass to reach the other side ... A Hungarian captain described the situation to me: in the Kilian-Barracks there were about 1200 freedom-fighters, facing Soviet tanks that had drawn up; another 1000 Hungarians were at their rear, trying to relieve the embattled barracks ...

An assault group, equipped with hand-grenades,

machine pistols, and bottles of gasoline, were just reporting to the captain. A very young soldier leads the group. I asked permission to join them ... Through back-yards and broken walls, from cellar to cellar, we worked our way toward the Soviet positions. In the cellars were frightened women and children; some embraced the young fighters.

Suddenly we were in the bar of a small hotel. An iron shutter protected the room from the street. In front of the window were Soviet tanks, firing. A Hungarian, with a mustache right out of a novel, was bouncing madly about, shouting orders that I couldn't grasp, waving a bottle of gasoline in the air. The assault unit prepared to break out.

I can't remember what happened next. I woke up toward evening on a mattress in the hall of a Hungarian hospital ...

Next day I decided to leave ... I wandered from street to street ... dodging time and again into a doorway for safety. I spoke to a Hungarian with a wounded arm who turned out to be the leader of the 9th Budapest city district. He wanted to reach a foreign embassy to get help for 150 children in a hospital that is under Soviet fire ...

On Thursday the sound of fighting eased off. I went towards the Kilian Barracks to search for my car, which I'd left in a side street. It is a strange war. The streets are crowded with people. On the corner a line of people stand waiting for food. A street further Soviet tanks are battering a house to pieces. Suddenly someone put his hand on my shoulder. I recognize him as the adjutant of Dudas, the freedom-fighter leader ... He says: "We only have munition until morning. Then it will be all over." And: "Where are our western friends? Alas, Hungary doesn't have a Suez Canal." ...

Early next day the return trip to Austria was to begin. 40 cars were assembled on Freedom Square ... All the flags of the western world were represented. Desperate, pleading questions: "Are you the UN Commission?" For the first time I hear a Hungarian begin to curse us: "Where were you when our youths were dying? For years your radio stations have promised us everything, and now?" ...

... We are taken to the Soviet Kommandatura ... I'm called into a room. Sitting before me is a thick-set, tall Soviet officer with a seedy face; next to him a small civilian. They check my papers. Then the officer asks: "So, and what's your real name?" I name it. The Russian laughs, and then: "What's your real name?" This is repeated five or six times. Then the Russian says: "I'll tell you. Your name is Poschek and you're a Polish spy. You've been fighting with the Hungarian Fascists." ...

Hans Germani, Der Spiegel (Hamburg), 21 November

Kadar, "Humanism and Honour"

Kossuth radio (the "Budapest I" wavelength) continued broadcasting [5—8 November] from Szolnok, and to carry much material of interest to that area, until 13:00 on 8 November, when it was explained that transmissions had hitherto come from Szolnok but would henceforth emanate from Budapest. The station has now reverted to the pre-revolution identification formula of "Kossuth Radio, Budapest". Much of the material heard from Kossuth Radio and the Balatonszabadi transmitter during the period was repeated by Tass or Moscow Radio in Russian only a quarter of an hour or so after being broadcast from Hungary. In some instances, items were heard from the Soviet source a quarter of an hour or so before they were intercepted from a Hungarian station ...

BBC Summary, 13 November

We greet the Soviet Union which has for the second time liberated the Hungarian people. ...

Radio Kossuth, 6 November

In factories, plants and in the streets people are vividly discussing the new government program, and its realization. The Hungarian people are backed by all Socialist states, the true brotherly solidarity of all those who fight for peace, democracy and for socialism. ...

Radio Kossuth, 6 November

Szolnok

... Imre Nagy's Government tried to eliminate the counter-revolution peacefully, by political manoeuvres. But it achieved a diametrically opposite result. The policy of procrastination only helped the counter-revolutionaries. They voiced slogans of independence, legality, and democracy while they were killing innocent people by the hundred. We, the Communists in Imre Nagy's Government, could not stand by and let this happen. We left his Government on 1st November. There was complete turmoil in the country. Anti-popular forces were committing atrocities with impunity. It was in these circumstances that the Hungarian Revolutionary Worker-Peasant Government addressed a request to the commanding officer of the Soviet troops in Hungary to help liquidate the counter-revolutionary forces and restore order and peace. The Government agrees with the demand that the Soviet troops should leave Hungary as soon as order and calm is restored, and will start negotiations with this end in view. ...

Janos Kadar, Szabad Nep, 6 November

How brutal and inhuman it was that in the past days simple party men had been attacked only because they were party members. Could that be called a humanist attitude! No! ... It was the revenge of a few wicked persons ...

It has to be said clearly and firmly that nobody is permitted to commit illegalities in these days. We address you on behalf of humanism and honour ... Let us remain sober and honest ...

Szabad Nep (Szolnok), 6 November

Police squads are to be set up in the seats of district courts. The members of these squads shall carry weapons on the basis of permits issued by the Soviet Military Command. The Ministry of the Interior shall organize a police action for the purpose of starting preliminary arrests. All those who took a leading role in the organization of the Social Democratic, the Smallholders, and other civilian parties shall be put under preliminary arrest. All individuals who injured or killed AVH members or aided in such acts also shall be taken into preliminary arrest in accordance with the instructions of the Government. These preliminary arrests will be made by the police squads of the workers' and peasants' revolutionary councils assisted by the Soviet Military Police. ...

Unidentified Soviet-controlled Radio, 6 November [09:30]

Crushing the Octopus
Neues Deutschland (East Berlin)

The Thirty-Nine Years

Moscow

Comrade soldiers and sailors, sergeants and petty officers! Comrade officers, generals and admirals! Working people of the Soviet Union! Our dear foreign guests! ...

I greet and congratulate you on the occasion of the 39th anniversary of the Great October Socialist Revolution! ... Rallied closely behind the Party and the Government, which are resolutely implementing Lenin's behests, the Soviet people will spare no efforts or creative energy in the struggle for the continued flourishing of our socialist homeland ...

In its foreign policy, the Soviet Union has invariably proceeded from the principle of the peaceful co-existence of countries with different social systems, from the great aim of preserving world peace ...

However, the enemies of socialism, the enemies of peaceful co-existence and friendship of the peoples, proceed with their actions designed to undermine the friendly relations between the peoples of the Soviet Union and the peoples of other countries, to frustrate the noble aims of peaceful co-existence on the basis of complete sovereignty and equality. This is confirmed by the armed aggression by Britain, France and Israel against the independent Egyptian State and by the actions of the counter-revolutionary forces in Hungary aimed at overthrowing the system of people's democracy and restoring fascism in the country. The patriots of people's Hungary, together with the units of the Soviet Army called in to assist the revolutionary workers' and peasants' Government, firmly barred the road to reaction and fascism in Hungary ...

Long live our mighty Soviet Homeland! Long live the heroic Soviet people and its armed forces! Long live our Soviet Government! Glory to the

Lenin

"The words of our leader and teacher, the immortal Lenin, take on special force to-day..."
M. A. SUSLOW

"We may not use force to compel other nations to ally themselves to Russia. Only a really voluntary, a really free agreement may be used, and this is impossible if there is no freedom to repeal the agreement. Only equals can come to an agreement. The parties must have equal rights, if the agreement is to be real, and not a conquest marked by phrases."
V. I. LENIN
Quoted in Der Monat (Berlin), February 1957

Communist Party of the Soviet Union, the inspirer and organiser of all our victories! Hurrah!
Marshal Zhukov, Tass (Moscow), 7 November

Moscow

It will be just as Vladimir Mayakovsky wrote: "Live to be a hundred without getting old." ...

Soviet democracy, born of the October Revolution, is a democracy of a new type. Distinct from the false and restricted democracy of capitalist States, democracy for the rich, Soviet socialist democracy is democracy for the working folk, for the people.

The profound democratic nature of the Soviet system consists in the fact that the policy of the State is based on the interests and will of the working classes, precisely the classes which under capitalism are the most oppressed and with whose interests the bourgeois Parliaments and Governments reckon least of all. ...
M. A. Suslow, Radio Moscow, 7 November

Budapest

November 7, 1956, has been declared a working day, because this year the anniversary of the Great October Revolution coincides in our country with the extraordinary situation caused by the counter-revolution. ...
Radio Kossuth

Szombathely

On this great holiday of the world proletariat it is not easy for us, Hungarian Communist journalists, to find true words. Sober, calm and thoughtful words are needed. ...
Radio Szombathely

Budapest

The Hungarian workers value the determination of the Soviet Union. ... The Hungarian workers are conscious that the interests of this nation and also the interests of peace demand the firm unity of all Socialist countries and on the anniversary of the Great October Revolution refute every misleading attempt and swear loyalty to Soviet brotherly solidarity and to the steadfast friendship between the Hungarian and the Soviet people. ...
Szabad Nep (Budapest), 7 November

Moscow

The resumption of the jamming of BBC broadcasts in Russian early in the Hungarian crisis was widely interpreted as the first step back to the rigours of Stalinist isolation. Then, on the eve of the November 7 celebrations, there was an unexplained interruption in the sale of foreign newspapers in a number of cities and there were wild scenes at the kiosks in Leningrad when the Polish and Yugoslav papers eventually arrived ...

Speakers at lectures on the international situation were bombarded with questions about Hungary. On several occasions their repetition of the official version angered the public so much that foreign students present were called on to answer, a role many of them undertook with zest. According to reliable sources, the discontent of rank-and-file party members at being kept in the dark was reflected in the results of elections to party committees and bureaus held at local branches on the eve of the November 7 holidays. A sharp, ill-tempered note was discernible in the tone which students and workers at some institutions adopted in voicing grievances. At one Leningrad college a discussion of the new method of distributing grants according to need — a progressive measure, in the opinion of most — ended by the students staging a demonstration in which they carried a picture of Gomulka.

It was, no doubt, to such youthful effervescence that Krushchev was referring at his Sports Palace speech on November 8, when he indirectly reminded Soviet students that if they did not approve of the regime they had no right to be studying at the expense of the factory workers. There was plenty of room for them at the benches, he said, and others were ready to replace them in college.

Correspondent, New Statesman & Nation (London),
24 November

Dunapentele
Appeal to Soviet soldiers in Hungary:

Soldiers! Your State was achieved at the price of bloody revolution so that you could enjoy freedom. That revolution has its 39th anniversary today. Why do you want our freedom to be oppressed? You can see that it is not the factory owners, landowners and bourgeoisie who are taking up the fight against you, but the Hungarian people who desperately fight for those rights for which you fought in 1917. Soviet soldiers, you showed at Stalingrad how to defend your country against foreign aggressors. Why are you surprised that we defend our country? Soldiers, do not fight against the Hungarian nation!

Free Radio Rakoczi, 7 November [11:12]

New York
The thirty-ninth anniversary of the Bolshevik Revolution was celebrated in Moscow in the atmosphere of moral degradation created by the Soviet crimes in Hungary. The Soviet troops in Hungary marked the anniversary by killing still more Hungarians battling for their freedom and independence. Thus was the "humanitarian" nature of Sovietism "proved" again.

It was fitting that Mikhail A. Suslov was chosen to deliver the keynote anniversary speech. He had, after all, gone to Hungary last June to reaffirm Matyas Rakosi's hold on power in Budapest. He was in Budapest, too, last week, gather-

ing the information on the basis of which he and his colleagues decided to unleash the Hungarian blood-bath. It was appropriate that the man who thus signed the death sentences for innocent Hungarians should be permitted personally to incarnate the Bolshevik Revolution's nature on its thirty-ninth anniversary.

But what cannot be accepted are the gross lies and slanders he heaped upon the heroic freedom fighters of Hungary. The Hungarian revolution, he said, represented a "revival of fascism." He gave great place in it to "Hitlerite forces" and to "Horthy's Fascist Army". Mr. Suslov lied. The Hungarian revolution was the spontaneous national liberation revolution of the Hungarian people seeking to end Soviet enslavement. The present butchery being performed by the Soviet Army is the real reactionary counter-revolution.

One more point by Mr. Suslov deserves attention. He says baldly that Hungarian Communists established their own "government" and called in the Red Army. Now we have out in the open what is meant by the "peaceful transition to socialism". In Hungary the precedent has been set. Mr. Suslov has now warned us that if French or American or Indian Communists set up a "government" and call on the Red Army, it will respond to the call. Dare we ever relax our guard in the face of this warning?

New York Times, 8 November

"We Accuse"

Budapest
Resistance forces of the city's Ninth District distributed a leaflet entitled, "We accuse." It contained the following charges:

"On Nov. 7, 1956, you shot at and wounded or killed eleven civilians who were not taking part in the fighting but proceeding to a bakery for bread.

"On Nov. 6 Soviet soldiers broke into stores on Ulloi Ut and looted them, then on Nov. 7 permitted the same opportunity to the famished population, which had been taking refuge in cellars, and then photographed them with the evident intention of camouflaging their own (Soviet) robberies. The same thing happened Nov. 8 at the corner of Rakoczi Ut and Berzsenyi Utca in a clothes store.

"Col. Nikolai Mashirevich, interpreter of the Soviet Embassy, has called us bandits and Fascists and declared that all the acts against the city and its population of which we have accused the Soviet troops were perpetrated by the revolutionaries. It appears, therefore, that we destroyed the city.

"We make Col. Nikolai Mashirevich, Janos Kadar, Marshal Zhukov and every member of the Soviet Embassy responsible for the destruction of our people and for supporting this destruction, for

Anniversary

"The most indubitable feature of a revolution is the direct interference of the masses in historic events. In ordinary times the state, be it monarchical or democratic, elevates itself above the nation, and history is made by specialists in that line of business—kings, ministers, bureaucrats, parliamentarians, journalists. But at those crucial moments when the old order becomes no longer endurable to the masses, they break over the barriers excluding them from the political arena, sweep aside their traditional representatives, and create by their own interference the initial groundwork for a new regime . . ."

*

"The revolution is terrifically chaotic . . . Everywhere aimless movements, conflicting currents, whirlpools of people, individuals astounded as though suddenly gone deaf, unfastened trench coats, gesticulating students, soldiers without rifles, rifles without soldiers, boys firing into the air, a thousand-voiced tumult, hurricanes of wild rumor, false alarms, false rejoicings. Enough, you would think, to lift a sword over all that chaos, and it would scatter apart and leave never a trace. But that is a crude error of vision. It is only a seeming chaos. Beneath it is proceeding an irresistible crystallization of the masses around new axes. These innumerable crowds have not yet clearly defined what they want, but they are saturated with an acid hatred of what they do not want. Behind them is an irreparable historic avalanche. There is no way back . . ."

*

"The revolution begins a search for enemies. Arrests are made all over the city—'arbitrarily,' as the Liberals will say reproachfully later. . . . 'we are witnessing the death of a great country' . . . The great country, which had no intention of dying, marched by these people of the past, stamping its boots, clanging the butts of its rifles, rending the air with its shouts and stepping all over their feet. A revolution is always distinguished by impoliteness, probably because the ruling classes did not take the trouble in good season to teach the people fine manners."

*

"Lawyers and journalists belonging to the classes damaged by the revolution wasted a good deal of ink subsequently trying to prove that what happened was essentially a petticoat rebellion, backed up afterwards by a soldiers' mutiny and given out for a revolution. Louis XVI in his day also tried to think that the capture of the Bastille was a rebellion, but they respectfully explained to him that it was a revolution. Those who lose by a revolution are rarely inclined to call it by its real name. For that name, in spite of the efforts of spiteful reactionaries, is surrounded by the historic memory of mankind with a halo of liberation from all shackles and all privileges. The privileged classes of every age, as also their lackeys, have always tried to declare the revolution which overthrew them, in contrast to past revolutions, a mutiny, a riot, a revolt of the rabble. Classes which have outlived themselves are not distinguished by originality."

*

"The similarity in the action of revolutionists in the twentieth and eighteenth centuries would be striking, were it not outweighed by a more striking similarity in the slanders peddled by their enemies . . . The history of all revolutions and civil wars testifies that a threatened or an overthrown ruling class is disposed to find the cause of its misfortunes not in itself, but in foreign agents and emissaries . . . Political slander is so poor and monotonous . . ."

*

" . . . It was not always easy to tell who was shooting or where. One thing was clear: the past and the future were exchanging shots."

LEON TROTZKY, HISTORY OF THE RUSSIAN REVOLUTION.
Quoted in Forum (Vienna), December 1956, and Preuves (Paris), February 1957.

on Nov. 7 at 3 o'clock they declared their unwillingness to deal with us and told us to negotiate with the military command.

"We accuse the alleged premier Janos Kadar, who lent his name to all this and for the second time invited the Soviet Army and thus caused all the unrestricted and barbarian 'Fascist' mass murder. We accuse him of destroying the people and demand that he immediately take steps for the withdrawal of Soviet troops.

"Should you fail to come to your senses you will have to accept the consequences and sentence that will be carried out by the people and pronounced by history.

"For the Ninth District Armed Revolutionary Youth. *(Signed)* Istvan Angyal, Commander."

John MacCormac, New York Times, 12 November

The Battle of Budapest

On 4 November large-scale fighting took place throughout the day all over the country. The following outline is based on the evidence of General Király, confirmed or supplemented by broadcasts from both Soviet-controlled and other stations with Hungary. The principal objective of the Soviet forces was the capture of Budapest, and the fiercest fighting occurred in the centre of the city and in the suburbs. By evening, organized armed resistance by the Hungarian forces had been broken, except for groups which continued fighting in the Bakony Mountains in the centre of the Transdanubian area and in the Vértes Mountains—a connecting mountain chain between the Bakony Mountains and Budapest. It would appear that after nightfall all cities within the country, with the exception of the industrial centre of Dunapentele, had come under the provisional administration of the local Soviet Military Command. Armed resistance of smaller groups of army personnel, of members of the National Guard, and of "freedom fighters" continued in the centre of Budapest until 6 November; and for several more days, possibly until 9 November, in the Eighth District of Budapest, in some of the industrial sectors of Greater Budapest, in the mining area around Pécs, in the Szabolc-Szatmár area, and in the cities of Gyor, Kalocsa, Kecskemet and Mohacs. In Dunapentele the organized resistance continued for four days and was overcome only after the use of Soviet tanks with the support of the Soviet tactical air force ...

UN General Assembly, Interim Report of the Special Committee on the Problem of Hungary, Document A/3546, 20 February 1957

General Kiraly disclosed that the Soviet command on Nov. 4 opened up on the helpless city of Budapest the most massive artillery barrage since the Soviet Army had hammered Berlin in the last days of World War II ...

Soon, General Kiraly said, it became evident he could not defend Budapest.

General Kiraly had at his command a force of about 400 men and eight tanks. He led them from the police building headquarters across the Danube River to Liberty Hill to the west of Budapest.

The tiny force hit Soviet units as they came in to reinforce the garrison in the city. After four days of attempting to organize guerrilla resistance, General Kiraly and his men moved to the old castle at Nagy-Kovacsi, about ten miles west of the capital. For days the general and his men were pushed from village to village in the Vertes Mountains. They would be given food and shelter by the peasants only to be discovered within a few hours and forced to flee again.

As the party neared the border, they broke up into small groups and set out separately for the frontier.

United Press, New York Times, 30 December

Budapest

People are watching the movement of tanks through the corner of their windows. In the streets they avoid Soviet patrols. This is certainly not the army that millions of workers in every country of the world have hailed as the bastion of the ideas of social progress.

To-day the town is in the hands of an army, in full occupation. Tracts signed by General Grebennyik, commander of the armoured forces, are being distributed in Russian and Hungarian. It is the first proclamation of the occupying military authorities ... The power of the Hungarian authorities is non-existent. The Government is sending out messages through the Budapest Radio appealing for calm and asserting that the situation is returning to normal. But can one speak of "normal" in a city where the roar of cannon still echoes, where dead lie in the streets, their faces covered by a handkerchief or a sheet of paper, where barricades of burnt-out trams block streets ...?

During the day, fighting diminished in intensity and became concentrated in specific districts. Buildings at important road crossings, where insurgent snipers had been installed, are no longer anything more than walls pitted with yawning gaps. The hospital has been seriously damaged, the agricultural museum burnt, and in the evening from the roof of the Italian Legation a large fire reddening the western part of the neighbouring park can be seen. Desolation is increasing. Thousands of families are without shelter. Entire streets have been destroyed. Where insurgent troops have attacked Soviet tanks the reaction has been violent, and the buildings in the neighbourhood have suffered cruelly. Nearly every house has had its windows shattered ... And the wounded!—the wounded for whom there is no longer space in the hospitals and who must be transported to private flats, the wounded for whom there is no medicine and not enough doctors ...

While I write these last lines, written during the battle in the Hungarian capital, I should like to emphasize one last fact, namely, during these twenty days so filled with horror and violence, I spoke to many workers and students in Budapest. I did not take their faces to be those of fascist troublemakers. These workers and these students urged me to report exactly what I had seen. I have tried to stick to my promise as far as I am capable of doing, for I felt that at a moment so painful I was under a moral obligation to do so ...

Luigi Fossati, Avanti (Rome), 13 November

Budapest

The Russians are now in control of the Capital. General Grebennyik, Budapest commandant, is the single authority giving orders to the population. Only yesterday he threatened that houses where military weapons were found would, in retaliation, be demolished by Soviet armour. At the same time, he urged the workers to "go back to work" and to "defend the revolutionary régime of the workers and peasants."

All appeals by General Grebennyik (which were distributed in leaflet form, and broadcast over the radio) have been ignored, with the exception of the curfew. At 7 p.m. life stops in Budapest, and until 7 a.m. there are only tanks and armoured cars in the deserted streets. Bursts of gun-fire are heard in the night. Then complete silence, heavy and sinister.

The patriots have been defeated. I have seen Soviet lorries full of young people, driving into the barracks occupied by the Russians: prisoners of the Five Days' War. I have also seen black flags hanging beside the Hungarian green-white-and-red flag in every window in Budapest, mournful but at the same time defiant. I saw the people finally emerge from the cellars and the rubble, filing along the highways, blocking cars in Rakoczi Street, Budapest's main thoroughfare, which is completely in ruins, with trolley-bus wires hanging all over the place, tram rails torn out of the ground, broken shop-windows, hotels in ruins, holes on the sidewalks. And, perhaps the most horrible sight of all: faces haunted by fear and hatred ...

One of the Soviet officers with whom I had an opportunity to speak during the last few days, expressed the opinion: "It is both disagreeable and inconvenient for us to be in Budapest." He was telling the truth. Even though they may be completely taken in by their propaganda, the Russians realise that the Hungarian tragedy has destroyed their whole ideological program. They have a foreboding feeling that Hungary will bring serious repercussions in the Communist world. Under our very eyes Polish and Italian left-wing colleagues openly denounced Soviet folly and the grotesque comedy of the "government" of Budapest, put into power by Russian tanks ...

Michel Gordey, France-Soir (Paris), 14 November

Conversations with Russians

Budapest

When listening to the radio, I suddenly heard two husky Russian voices calling to each other in a military tone:

"Moon, where are you? Moon, answer me. This is River."

Two Russian officers were exchanging radio messages which were hardly coded.

"Moon, by 6 p.m. tonight you are to prepare a precise account stating your trophies, how many of the enemy have been killed, your exact losses and damage sustained. Understand?"

"I understand perfectly. It will be done by 6 p.m."

So the Russians are beginning to count their losses ... According to reports received over the telephone, they are supposed to have lost at least a hundred tanks in five days ...

Walking from one office to another, the hours passed and we waited ... I talked to Russian sentries who told me: "We want to go home again. The war is over, here. The Fascists have been beaten. We shall be leaving soon."

I spoke to a young captain who began to tell me the official version of the Fascist plot, but finally stopped talking, and clearly showed his embarrassment. The same day, a lieutenant repeated the same explanation to me, almost word for word. Clearly, they must all have been given the same official explanations by their political commissars ...

These Russian officers are usually rather friendly, always polite, a little sardonic. One of them, a lieutenant-colonel, said to me on the last morning, just when he was signing the passes: "Can you hear the bells ringing? That Church is holding services again. Perhaps your compatriots would like to go to Church to pray before their trip from Budapest to Vienna." This remark was accompanied by a wave of the hand, as if it were a friendly invitation. And a few minutes later, with a false air of sympathy: "Petrol is rationed in France. What a shame! Soon you will be unable to balance your budget if you continue your aggressive policy in Egypt."

I answered: "Will your own budget remain stable if you continue your policy in Hungary?" He laughed ...

When a lorry full of young Hungarian civilians drew up in the courtyard of the Kommandatura in Budapest, I caught a Russian soldier nudging another standing beside him, and whispering:

"Just look how many they are, and nearly all of them workers ..." The expression on his face was sad and utterly crushed.

During my last conversation with passers-by in Budapest, who crowded round our car marked with tricolor flags, they all said to me: "When you get back, tell them that the men who have been fighting were workers ..."

Victor Zorza, Manchester Guardian, 15 November

A conscript in the Hungarian Army who had fought against the Russians near Budapest told the story which more than all the details of physical suffering and separation summed up for me the tragedy of Hungary's October revolution. They had captured a young Russian soldier and asked him if he knew what he was fighting for. He was fighting, he said, to drive the English and the German Nazis into the English Channel. The Nazis were the ordinary people of Budapest. The English Channel was the Danube.

Manchester Guardian, 29 November

Budapest

The people laugh only when they read the posters or talk of the Russians. When they turn away the grimness returns. Some Russians, curiously enough, have been seen to laugh too, sheepishly, it is true, but genuinely. The officers, however, pursuing the Moscow line to the Hungarian are one thing. The private soldiers with a working class or peasant background who have had it drummed into them for years that they are the "protectors of workers and peasants," and who are unable to comprehend the intricacies of the new party line, are another thing altogether. They are told that they are here to fight the Fascists. But the people who argue with them at street corners are obviously ordinary workers.

Many of the Russians understand perfectly well what it is all about and they feel very uncomfortable about it. A Russian sentry who stopped me in front of one of the public buildings volunteered the information as soon as he had discovered that I spoke Russian that he was heartily sick of the whole thing and that he had only one wish: to go home.

He admitted that he was angry with the Hungarians — and so, he said, were many of his comrades — for the simple reason that if it had not been for the present trouble some of them would by now have been on their way home, to civilian life.

Another Soviet soldier took me confidentially aside and asked for advice on how one would go about leaving one's unit if the fighting broke out again. He had taken me for a Russian who had done exactly this in the earlier fighting. Suspecting the possibility of what the Russians call "provocation", I showed him my passport and explained that I was not qualified to offer advice on a matter of that nature.

But it is clear that some Russians do in fact feel like this about the prospects of the resumption of the fighting and that most of the remainder, while they would not go as far as to desert their units, would fight with a very heavy heart indeed — if they fight at all.

Victor Zorza, Manchester Guardian, 15 November

Budapest

A small crowd of citizens had in the eerie light of a blood-red sunset gathered around a stationary Soviet T-54 tank and were engaging one of the crew sitting on the hull in earnest conversation.

It was the Russian, a simple soldier, sitting there in his black rubber crash helmet, battle weary and nervous, who seemed to be the one cornered. "Look what you did to our houses with your tanks, with your cannon, with your heavy mortars," a young man exclaimed bitterly. Had this been necessary when the freedom fighters had used only small arms?

Knitting his brow the Russian replied that it was true that "mainly automatic weapons" had been

"Let's Go Wash Our Hands in the Canal ..."
Express (Bombay)

used against them. "But how do you think we felt, cooped up in a tank, with people dropping bottles of liquid fuel, grenades, and anti-tank mines on us from the houses?"

And in any case he was not the tank commander, but had to obey orders. Why had the Russians entered Budapest in the first place, someone else demanded. Because they had been asked to come and intervene by the Hungarian Government. "What Government?" "The Kadar Government" the Russian replied amid derisive laughter. He offered cigarettes to those standing nearest him. One or two reluctantly accepted the offer, others turned away in disgust. The Russian's attempt to argue that he had been fighting "reactionaries and counter-revolutionaries" met with a reply from the crowd that though there may have been some people of this type among the freedom fighters, "most are just ordinary Hungarians."

This incident illustrates, perhaps, both the present feeling of the Hungarians and the embarrassment felt by at least some of the Russian soldiers at what has been going on—the first stirrings of conscience perhaps among the Russian people at the crimes of their Government. Another Russian soldier went so far as to say that he knew very well what the present operation in Hungary was really all about and he wanted to get out of it all as quickly as possible.

However, whether such views are widespread or not among the Russian soldiery, it has not made them any the less ruthless when ruthlessness was the order of the day.

The Times (London), 13 November

"The Revolution Can't Die"

Budapest

I visited the partisan unit at the East Station several times; after three days of fighting their casualties came to only 18 dead and 28 wounded out of a total strength of 250 men ...

They felt the free world's impotence as a betrayal. Almost overnight, from Tuesday to Wednesday, the élan of the rebels seemed to fade away ... The engineer-commandant had to spend hours arguing with subordinates who no longer wanted to obey his orders. "That is the tragedy of us Hungarians," he said bitterly. "We are a nation of heroes, but only as individuals. When we need to make a common effort, we immediately split up into factions. Maybe I'll give up my command tomorrow." I spent the night in an atmosphere of foreboding and left the command post early Thursday morning. It was a good thing I did: a few hours later the Soviet tanks zeroed in on it ...

But on that Wednesday evening I met someone who revealed to me the hope that still burned fiercely at the heart of the revolutionary movement. Late at night the editor of *Truth* slipped in with one of his co-workers. The editorial office, located below us on the Ring, had been under fire all day long from eighteen Soviet tanks, and it was only by heroic sacrifices that they had managed to print the last edition of 15,000 copies and carry it out through subterranean passages. The copies were now piled up ready to be distributed through the city by "ambulances" the next day. The man accompanying the editor, a young poet (one of his poems took the place of a lead article in the paper) and a colleague of the Marxist philosopher Georg Lukacs, was one of the leading spirits among the insurgent intellectuals. He had spent the whole day conferring with his group, and he reported that, in view of the enemy's overwhelming strength and the pitiably scanty supply of food and fuel for the civilian population, they had given up any idea of resistance to the death. It would be better, they thought now, to save the lives of the freedom fighters who could then carry on the struggle by other, political, means. Had not the general strike already shown itself to be a more effective revolutionary weapon than the tommy gun? At the moment of crisis a new insight and a new source of strength had come to this young poet.

It seemed to me that he represented an interesting new type that was appearing in considerable numbers among the young people not only of Hungary but also of the other satellite countries. He had grown up a Marxist under the Communist regime and it was the Marxist in him, not any convert to liberalism, capitalism, or Western democracy, that had rebelled against Communist despotism. The Communists, he argued, were bad Marxists if they believed that they could suppress a historical development like the satellite freedom movements by the violent methods of colonialism. "As a true Marxist I believe in the inevitability of historical processes," he told me. "We know perfectly well what a wave of terror and Stalinist repression will be let loose on us. But repression cannot cancel the laws of history, which are working in our favor." "Then will you surrender?" I asked quietly. "Surrender?" he laughed. "We don't need to do that. You know how the revolution broke out—spontaneously, without any kind of preparation, when the police fired on our students; leadership and organization sprang up over night. Well, we'll scatter now just as spontaneously as we came together. We'll bury our weapons and those of us who haven't exposed ourselves too much can change back into civilians and lose ourselves in the crowd. The revolution can't die; it will play dead and await its moment to rise again. Right now, there's no longer any chance of winning."

I will never forget that midnight moment in the partisan headquarters. The tired commanders with their bloodshot eyes were still insisting that they could hold out to judgment day. But there was this sparkling young face, full of genuine faith in the strength even of the weak. The majority of the young Hungarian rebels were like that—never for an instant suggesting pathos, buoyed up by an intractable idealism, calmly heroic, as if what they were doing was the most natural thing in the world . . .

Peter Schmid, Commentary (New York), January 1957

We are both writers, both Communists. He is older and has rendered incomparably greater service . . .

This was how two Communist writers from two People's Democracies had to meet in Budapest on 10 November 1956. I arrived by car in a street agreed upon and blew the horn near a paint-shop. An old woman whom I met for the first time got into the car . . . She led me into an apartment which neither I nor the one whom I was to meet had ever entered before.

We talked about the Hungarian situation and the international situation. If, before the second intervention, he saw some prospect of saving socialism, he could not picture it now . . .

For some days people in Budapest had been influenced by appeals framed in tri-colored stripes, pasted on walls, and signed jointly by three organizations: The Revolutionary Committee of Students, the Revolutionary Council of the Army, and the Association of Hungarian Writers. My friend collaborated in composing these appeals. He was busy working out the text of the next one: "Because enemy action is mainly causing the civilian population to suffer, it is necessary to put an end to desperate armed resistance. It is necessary to follow a course of passive, moral resistance . . ."

"This appeal will appear tomorrow."

"Will they listen to you?"

"We are the only ones that they are listening to."

Before leaving we remind each other of the precautions to be observed . . . "Tell me, can one really live in such a fashion?"

Viktor Woroszylski, France Observateur (Paris), 3 January

The General Strike, "a Murderous Weapon"

Budapest

The fighting in Budapest is over. The streets are crowded. It is at once a city at peace and a city at war. The crowds in the streets, the workers of the factories, have no thought of resuming work. The people filling the city's main thoroughfares are part of a huge silent demonstration of protest. In an unending line they file past the damaged and destroyed houses, silently point to the shell holes and heaps of rubble that were once walls, and pass on.

The workers are streaming back to the factories but only to collect their pay—in most cases 50 per cent of their wages—and then go home. Sometimes they assemble for mass meetings in their factories, where resolutions are passed demanding an immediate withdrawal of Soviet troops, the formation of a Government under Mr Imre Nagy, the admission of United Nations observers into the country, the establishment of a neutral Hungary, and free elections—though this last point is omitted in some resolutions. No work will be done except by public facilities and food services, the resolutions say, until the workers' demands have been conceded.

Leaflets, some of them printed, some cyclostyled, spread the texts of these resolutions through the city. Government posters calling for a return to work are plastered over with these leaflets and with smaller handwritten posters calling for a continuation of the general strike.

The fighting in Budapest is over but the fight is on. And it is a grimmer fight than during the days when shells were whizzing past and boys and girls with Molotov cocktails were throwing themselves at Soviet tanks . . .

For, while limited supplies of food are available, the refusal of the fathers to work means starvation both for young and old and death for the weakest. Indeed, the youngest and the oldest and the infirm, deprived of the minimum food they need and of the medical attention that goes in the first place to the wounded freedom fighters, are dying in greater numbers than in more normal times. These deaths, like the deaths resulting from the actual fighting, are the logical consequences of the decision taken by the whole nation to carry on the fight.

The general strike through which this fight is now carried on is a murderous weapon both for those who use it and for those against whom it is directed. For the Kadar Government, supported only by Soviet tanks, is being killed as effectively as if each of its members were strung up from a lamp-post. The people taking part in this strike realise full well that what they are doing is madness, that they are not harming the Russians by their strike but only themselves. Yet there is method in their madness. They cannot believe that the West will stand by and witness passively the slow suicide of a whole nation . . .

Manchester Guardian, 14 November

Janos Kadar Argues with the Workers

Budapest

A 19-member delegation of the Central Workers' Council went to the Parliament building to call upon Janos Kadar, Chairman of the Presidential Council, to put to him the demands of the workers of Budapest's main enterprises and of several great enterprises in the provinces. These demands were expressed in several points agreed to by the Central Workers' Council, and stated that the Workers' Council strictly adhered to the principle of socialism, and defended social ownership of the means of production, but demanded, among other things, that Imre Nagy should take over the leadership of the Government; that there be a multi-party system of several parties, but that only parties based on socialism should be allowed to function; and that free elections by secret ballot should be held after a certain lapse of time.

Janos Kadar made a thorough examination of these demands. First he made known the Government's point of view in connection with Imre Nagy. He said that Imre Nagy was at present on the premises of a legation of a foreign State in Budapest, where he had asked for political asylum. In these circumstances we had no opportunity to confer with him and, naturally, he could not become Prime Minister. If, however, Imre Nagy should give up his extra-territorial position and return to Hungarian soil, it would be possible to consult and reach an agreement with him.

Janos Kadar then spoke about the question of Parties, and he said the following: "Let us consider the monopolistic position of the Party. We want a multi-party system and free honest elections. We know that this will be no easy matter, because not only by bullets, but also by the ballot can the workers' power be killed. We have to take into account that we may be thoroughly beaten at the elections, but if we take on the election fight, the Communist Party can have the necessary strength again to obtain the confidence of the working masses. The Communist Party has faults, and mud is now being flung at it, but the Party is not identical with those who have abused its name; 900,000 honest men used to be members of the Party ..."

He further pointed out that the crowding out of Communists from Parliament would necessarily lead to the overthrow of socialism and the people's power, and continued: "We have no reason to doubt the statements made by honest middle-class politicians that they want socialism; only, after an election defeat of Communists these politicians could be set aside by their own Parties. There is no middle-class politician, however well-intentioned he may be, who could defend the factories and the land, without the help of the Party of the working class."

After this he turned to the question of the Soviet troops and said that we were compelled to ask for the intervention of Soviet troops, declaring: "It has been made clear by the events of the past weeks that we were threatened with the immediate danger of the overthrow of the people's power. This, of course, is not understood by many, nor is it all easy to assess the events of past weeks. We have all witnessed the transformation within two hours of a proper student demonstration, which had set out with justified demands, into a fight in the course of which they captured the radio, the building of *Szabad Nep,* military warehouses, the Joseph Telephone Exchange, and the Central Telephone Exchange. It is impossible that this was a spontaneous act on the part of students, for such actions do not denote inexpert organisation. In the course of later events we witnessed demonstrations by workers demanding a strike. We realised that this whole movement could not be described as a counter-revolution, but we would have been blind if we had ignored that, apart from the deep indignation felt over grave mistakes and the just demands of the workers, there were also counter-revolutionary demands ..."

In connection with the State Security Authority (AVH), Comrade Kadar, on the basis of his own prison experiences, related that he knew several members of the AVH personally. In spite of that, he counselled the need for moderation in that respect ... The AVH has disintegrated, we have smashed it; nor is there any need for it. "The ordinary recruits among the young men of the AVH, however, must not be persecuted. But at the same time former AVH members must be prevented from regaining positions of privilege."

Comrade Kadar then turned to the question of strikes. He asked members of the delegation to think the situation over, and said that when they had given it consideration they would realise that further strike action would only lead to inflation and famine. There was not much more time left. Within a week or two we shall become the beggars of the world ...

Members of the delegation then went on to negotiate and argue with Comrade Kadar at length ... One problem was that of neutrality. Comrade Kadar stressed that that is a highly understandable demand; however, the issue was not a simple one of desire and aspiration, so long as there were people who did not want the same thing, whose interest was not in neutrality, but in war. The matter was not a simple issue of writing down on a piece of paper: "We want neutrality"; it required a balance of power, an international situation which lent reality to the demand ...

In reply to another question, Comrade Kadar definitely confirmed that no one would come to harm because of his participation in the great popular movement of the past few weeks. He also emphatically stressed that agreement had been reached with the competent Soviet authorities that no one would be deported from the country ...

Nepszabadsag (Budapest), 15 November

"The Tanks Now Face Westwards"

Budapest

To-day Budapest is a city both of grimness and of laughter. There is laughter at the street corners where Soviet officers, half-hidden in the turrets of their tanks, lamely dispute with nonchalant groups the rights and wrongs of the Russian presence in Hungary.

A few days ago it was only the concluding words of the Russian argument — "we are here to defend you against the Fascist bandits" — that evoked laughter from the Hungarians. To-day any Russian references to the Hungarian "Government" that had called them in, or to the "treaty of friendship and mutual assistance" which makes their presence in Hungary "legal," produce merriment among the Hungarians, and this in turn produces embarrassment among the Russians.

The stern posters, calling for a continuation of the strike, are more plentiful to-day, but a new kind of poster has also made its appearance. One of these is in the form of a police notice, which warned Hungary's population of ten million that "ten million counter-revolutionaries are at large in the country." It goes on to parody the puppet Government's political line by announcing that:

"Former aristocrats, cardinals, generals and other supporters of the old regime, disguised as factory workers and peasants, are making propaganda against the patriotic Government and against our Russian friends."

Another "police notice" promises a reward to anyone who can find one supporter of the Kadar Government in a population of 10,000,000. Yet another lavishes generous praise on Kadar — "the only person who has succeeded in uniting the Hungarian nation ... in hatred of Kadar." Yet another goes like this:

"Wanted: Premier for Hungary. Qualifications: no sincere conviction, no backbone; ability to read and write not required, but must be able to sign documents drawn up by others. Applications should be addressed to Messrs Khrushchev and Bulganin."

Another proclaims:

"Lost — the confidence of the people. Honest finder is asked to return it to Janos Kadar, Premier of Hungary, at 10,000 Soviet Tanks Street." Victor Zorza, Manchester Guardian, 15 November

...We had to silence our enemies ... The Soviet Union is sending us everything, helping us with everything ... The tanks now face westwards ...

Radio Nyiregyhaza, 6 November

...Truth will triumph. Its force springs from reality and life itself will triumph over death ...

Radio Moscow, 14 November

News Chronicle (London)

Budapest

In Budapest, Russian resistance continues stubbornly. This is not a slip of the pen. It is the Russians who are now resisting in the Magyar capital. By day they are the masters, but at night they go to earth in their shelters and in the barracks, practically leaving the town in the hands of the patriots. They do not venture into the countryside except in long armoured columns, in order to protect each other against insurgent ambushes. Even their artillery has not been able to stop the strike. Nowhere have they succeeded in appointing a single mayor or town clerk. They cannot even have their presence recognized by the official organ of the Communist Party, the only authorized newspaper in Hungary which, to ensure some circulation, has to protest in its turn against the occupation, even if gingerly and in general terms. On the roads, road-blocks and patriot controls persist. The Russians cannot buy an egg or a piece of bread. They day before yesterday a Russian armoured car approached a Yugoslav frontier post and begged the customs officials for a kilo of potatoes. Hunger may have even compelled some units to offer arms to the Hungarian peasants in exchange for a little food. In fact, these arms are the only currency the Hungarians will accept in such a transaction ...

Indro Montanelli, Corriere della Sera (Milan),
21 November

Hungarian workers declared a two-day "total strike" after Russian tanks and troops had tried to break up a national workers council meeting [21 November]. The strike had been called for this morning, but when news of the Russian intervention spread through Budapest trams and buses stopped at once and passengers had to get out and walk.

It is estimated that at least 70 per cent of Hungarian workers are maintaining the general strike, now in its fifth week, to try and force the withdrawal of Soviet troops, and an end to the deportation of Hungarian youths to Russia.

The meeting of the National Workers Council—the supreme body representing the nation's workers—had been set for yesterday morning at the

─────── *Rakosi* ───────

A frequent guest in our Moscow Embassy is Matyas Rakosi, chief defender of the hated Stalinist period.
What are his aims? Is it only information he gets? Does he also give instructions? With whom does he talk by phone in Hungary? Maybe he is giving advice to his faithful followers to work their way back ...
Nepakarat (Budapest), 22 November

sports hall of the National Stadium. When reporters arrived they found the way blocked by Russian tanks, guns, armoured cars and troops, and some Hungarian troops and police. A Russian captain told the journalists to leave at once.

Later it was learned that the national council also had been refused entry to the stadium. Members of the council then adjourned to the Budapest transport building. They were followed in by Hungarian troops and police. An Army officer ordered them to break up the meeting and said the Hungarian Government had received information that they were planning to set up an anti-Kadar Government, distribute arms and resume street fighting.

When told that this was merely a meeting of workers' delegates the officer apologised and ordered troops and police to withdraw. In protest the national council called the strike, beginning this morning ...

Correspondents who visited the big Dorog coalmines, 35 miles west of Budapest, found work at a standstill except for maintenance operations. The twelve mines normally employ 10,000 men and have an output of 6,500 tons daily. A meeting of the Miners Council was going on when Western reporters arrived, and they were loudly applauded as they entered. Members of the council said they were determined to keep up the strike until the Russians left.

A group of six Russian T-54 tanks arrived at a near-by churchyard and parked there while the miners' council met. The Russians did not, however, attempt to break up the meeting.

Western correspondents yesterday were shown a note thrown from a train near Szolnok in Hungary on Monday reporting that 2,000 people aboard it were being taken to Russia. The note said:

> *We were arrested on the same day in Budapest by the A.V.O. (secret police) and handed over to the Russians. We were taken by lorry to Vecsec, where we were put on the train.*
> *We are being taken to Russia. Please inform our parents and the International Red Cross.*

The note was signed with five names, all of which were seen by reporters ...

A girl, one of a group who were returned to Budapest, said they were warned that if on the way they tried to make distress signals to Hungarians they would immediately be shot. The girl said a number of the other girls had been raped by Russian soldiers.

It was reported in Budapest that a workers' delegation called on Mr. Kadar, the Premier, on Sunday and demanded the cessation of deportations to Soviet Russia. He was alleged to have replied: "The Russians cannot be deflected from their purpose ..."

Reuters and British United Press, 21 November

Peking, Reykjavik, Bombay, Warsaw...

Peking

I was in Peking listening to the BBC on October 23, when the Hungarian rising began. For five days no report at all appeared in the press, and when it did no mention was made of Russian action, although later it was reported that Russian troops had withdrawn from Budapest, and great prominence was given to the Soviet declaration on "the principle of equality among nations."

Next day, announcing that Nagy had formed a coalition Government which "would defend the fruits of the socialist revolution," and admitting that "past errors of chauvinism and incorrect thinking" had caused the present unrest, the *People's Daily* suddenly sprung on its readers the news that Hungary was in "a chaos of anarchy."

So far the Peking Government had not committed itself either way. Its attitude changed overnight when Nagy demanded the abrogation of the Warsaw Treaty. "The just discontent" of the workers became "The White Terror"... "Celebrate the Great Victory of the Hungarian People!" sang the *People's Daily* on November 5 as Russian tanks rolled back into Budapest and "the gallant Soviet people shed their own blood to save Hungary from Fascist slavery." ...

For the next ten days, as far as China was concerned, life in Hungary was "returning to normal." ... Tito's speech, the censuring of Russia by the Bandung Powers, Nehru's condemnation, the general strike, all passed by unrecorded.

"Hungary and Egypt," Vice-Premier Teng. Hsiao-ping explained to me, "are two entirely different problems. The one is a case of naked aggression, the other a case of defending Socialism from capitalist and reactionary forces." ...

I was staying at the same hotel as the members of Moscow Circus and the Hungarian Army Ensemble. The Hungarian were living in the shadows of uncertainty and fear, enduring sleepless nights, acting their parts in a nerve-strung charade of peace and friendship and Socialist solidarity, with no news of their families.

The only news they would trust was what they could get from the BBC, but all wireless sets had been removed from the hotel on their arrival. I began to supply them with BBC bulletins; and I was not greatly surprised when my hosts informed me—politely but without warning—that I must move to another hotel...

Michael Croft, The Observer (London), 6 January 1957

Warsaw

Glos Pracy (organ of the Polish Trade Unions) published on October 30 an attack on Louis Saillant's appraisal of the situation in Hungary. After expressing agreement with Saillant's confidence in the ability of the Hungarians "by themselves to frustrate the schemes of home and international reaction", *Glos Pracy* stated: "But ... his horrible accusation against honest people who want to build socialism free from Stalinist injustice are a painful surprise to us ... The appraisal made by Comrade Saillant in his letter is hasty, to say the least. It differs from the attitude of the trade unionists and the working masses not only of Poland, but also of other countries. For instance, in its communique on the events in Hungary, the Secretariat of the C.G.I.L., among whose members is Comrade Di Vittorio, General-Secretary of the C.G.I.L., and President of the W.F.T.U., has by no means appraised the situation in the same manner ..."

Polish Press Agency (Warsaw), 30 October

Rome

While the Stalinist group of the Party leadership has demanded that Signor Di Vittorio, secretary-general of the C.G.I.L., the Communist-dominated Confederation of Labour, should be severely reprimanded for issuing a statement on behalf of his organisation sympathising with the Hungarian rebel workers, the anti-Togliatti section demands that he should replace Signor Togliatti as secretary-general of the party. *Unità*, the party's official organ has been flooded for days now by thousands of letters ... protesting

"Bah! Counter-revolutionaries!"

Daily Mirror (London)

against Signor Togliatti's attitude to the Polish and Hungarian uprisings. Today, 120 intellectuals, the Communist Party's *élite,* addressed a manifesto to *Unità* which the newspaper refused to publish ... Even within the editorial staff of *Unità* there is a clash of opinion. Signor Lajolo, editor-in-chief of the Milan edition, was suspended because he published an outspoken criticism of Hungary's Communist Government ...

The Times (London), 31 October

Copenhagen

At a meeting yesterday, the executive committee of the Danish Communist Party joined protests of several party locals and communist-directed trade unions against the Soviet military intervention ...

Berlingske Tidende (Copenhagen), 31 October

The Soviet intervention in Budapest called forth world-wide protests and demonstrations of sympathy for the Hungarians.

Vienna: About five hundred delegates of an Austrian Socialist youth congress—carrying red banners draped with black crêp—staged a silent march past the Soviet Embassy.

Copenhagen: About a thousand Danish students demonstrated outside the Russian Embassy.

Berne: A wave of popular indignation swept Switzerland ... Associations of all kinds met to pass protest resolutions.

Paris: Police dispersed about a thousand students, carrying the Hungarian flag at the head of their procession, who marched towards the Soviet Embassy.

Bonn: Flags on Government and other buildings flew at half-mast. The West German Trade Union Federation called on its six million members to stand silent for three minutes to-day.

Berne: Students followed up protest meetings by distributing buttonholes in the Hungarian national colours. Thousands of people signed a petition demanding a break in Switzerland's diplomatic relations with Russia.

The Hague: Angry crowds attacked the Soviet commercial building in Amsterdam during the night, bombarding it with stones. More than 60,000 Catholics marched "in silent prayer" through the streets. Rotterdam dock workers refused to unload two Russian ships. A Dutch travelling agency cancelled its co-operation with the Russian Intourist bureau. An Amsterdam v. Red Army football match, due to have been played on November 28, was cancelled.

Rome: Big forces of police surrounded Communist party headquarters to protect it from thousands of student demonstrators. Signor Togliatti, the Communist party leader, was meeting his lieutenants in the building to decide whether to issue a formal statement on Russia's action. The Vatican City newspaper *L'Osservatore Romano* said that "no pretext justifies the Russian intervention in its enormity."

Oslo: Norwegian MPs stood as the Speaker opened the day's sitting with a short speech of sympathy for Hungary. The Government handed the Soviet Ambassador a note urging his Government to allow a Norwegian Red Cross mission into Hungary.

New York: The *Daily Worker,* organ of the American Communist party, sharply criticised the Soviet Union's use of force. Socialism, it said, could not be imposed on a country by these means.

Jakarta: Two Government party leaders in Indonesia, Mr. Mohammed Natsir and Mr. I. J. Ikasimo, condemned Russia's action as aggression, but a Foreign Ministry spokesman said Indonesia should adopt a "wait and see" policy.

Reuters, 4–5 November

Tokyo

It is no exaggeration to conclude ... that the Soviet Union will not merely not tolerate the existence of any regime which attempts to escape her control, but is also prepared to destroy it by armed force. The problem is different in nature from the British and French military operations against Egypt, and far more important.

Even if the new government in Hungary has "requested" this aid, it is still indisputable that the Soviet Union is trying to overthrow a legitimate regime by arms. This action is worse than intervention in internal affairs and makes a mockery of the "independent relations between nations" and "equality" constantly being preached by the Soviet Union. How will the Soviet Union explain her "five peace principles" to the world now?

Asahi Shimbun (Tokyo), 5 November

Berlin

An impassioned crowd of West Berliners marched tonight to the Brandenburg Gate on the border of the Soviet sector of East Berlin ... The demonstrators lighted oil torches and stood facing the gate shouting anti-Soviet and pro-Hungarian slogans. Across the gateway, which leads to Unter den Linden, the East Berlin people's police stood with rifles pointed at the crowd ...

Willi Brandt, president of the city government's Assembly, finally induced the agitated crowd to "end this day of mourning for Hungary" by singing "The Song of the Good Comrade." The singing rose with tremendous volume. It was a dramatic moment against the theatrical backdrop of the massive Grecian gateway to the Communist world.

Harry Gilroy, New York Times, 6 November

Rome

"The blood of the Hungarian people cries to the Lord," Pope Pius XII said today in an encyclical letter to the Roman Catholic episcopacy. For the third time in ten days he asked all Christians to join him in prayer.

Addressing directly those who "bear responsibility for these grievous events" in Hungary, he asked them to remember that "the just freedom of peoples can never be drowned in blood." The Pontiff also told them that God, "as a just judge, often punishes the sins of private persons only after their death, but sometimes, as history teaches us, strikes governors and even nations during their lifetime for their injustices."

The encyclical is understood to have been written personally by Pope Pius. It was one of the shortest encyclicals, running to less than 500 words. It was printed tonight in the Vatican newspaper *L'Osservatore Romano*.

The Pope said his soul had filled with "most painful bitterness" when he learned that "the cities and towns of Hungary are again running with the blood of citizens who from the bottom of their souls desire just freedom." He said his duty commanded him to protest, "deploring these painful facts which cause bitter sadness and indignation not only in the Catholic world but also among all free peoples." The pontiff recalled the words addressed by God to Cain: "The voice of thy brother's blood crieth to me from the earth" (*Genesis* IV, 10).

"May the most merciful God touch the hearts of those responsible so that at last injustice may cease, every violence may be calmed and all nations, pacified among themselves, may again find the just order in an atmosphere of serene tranquility."

Arnaldo Cortesi,
New York Times, 6 November

Rome

The Soviet Government has become entangled in the web of contradictions resulting from a policy that, while preaching de-Stalinization, is still using Stalinist methods. They cannot take away with one hand what they give or offer with the other ...

To-day — and no propaganda whatever can alter this fact —, the Soviet Union has not defended the cause of Socialism either in Hungary or anywhere else. It has defended solely the political system and methods of government of the People's Democracies, born with the cold war and conceived by Stalin ...

Avanti (Left-wing Socialist daily, Rome), 6 November

Brussels

Thousands of university students demonstrated outside the Soviet Embassy here today against Russian action in Hungary. Forty demonstrators and about twenty policemen were injured, some seriously.

The Brussels headquarters of the International Confederation of Free Trade Unions, the world's largest non-Communist labor movement, called on its 11 affiliates in eighty-three countries to stage a five-minute strike Thursday in protest against the suppression of freedom in Hungary and the military events in the Middle East.

Luxembourg

Anti-Communist demonstrators broke into the Soviet Embassy tonight and burned part of its furniture, two automobiles and portraits of Russian leaders.   *New York Times, 7 November*

"Fascist and reactionary elements have been crushed..." · *Soviet-controlled*
Budapest Radio

Daily Mirror (London)

Paris

In the moment when, happily, the counter-revolution is being defeated with a clean sweep in Hungary, a certain set of newspapers (*Franc-Tireur* and *Le Populaire* join the chorus of *l'Aurore* and *Le Figaro*) is trying to present the Hungarian counter-revolutionaries, the murderers of militant workers, as "fighters for freedom". It is not for the first time. In 1921, in Kronstadt, the Soviet Government had to face an insurrection which recalls in many ways the dealings of reaction in Hungary ...

L'Humanité (Paris), 7 November

Reykjavik

The misfortune which has befallen the Soviets in Hungary is for me, Icelandic socialist, a thing of great sadness ...

I am a member of the World Peace Council ... There is nothing more contrary to the World Movement for Peace than armed action on the part of foreign armies against smaller countries ... If I were to accept the events of the last few days in Hungary, I should feel that I was never again entitled to protest against the activities of foreign armies in other countries ...

Halldór Laxness (Nobel Prize), Thjodviljinn (Reykjavik), 7 November

Paris

To the last words from the Revolution set in motion by the students and the writers of the Petofi Circle, there has been no response. We could not reply, and they knew it. In spite of this they appealed to us, and we understood their message. [see p. 228] They want their fight to outlive their defeat.

This appeal must be heard and made known to the entire world. Each of us must now reply. Each of us must take action.

Those who in any way support the monstrous crime of Budapest are beyond the realm of humanity. This is the first thing that must be said. But practical conclusions must also be drawn. For our part, we are thinking of what must follow.

Henceforth, to shake the hand of a Western Communist who "freely" approves of his Party, is to salute an accomplice in the crime of Budapest. To publish his writings is to aid the type of intellectual propaganda which led to the crime of Budapest. To reason with him is to forget that he must of necessity "justify" the massacres of Budapest. To continue cultural exchanges with the Soviet Union under the false banner of the "thaw" which has just shown its true colors in Budapest, is to walk into a trap. To receive and to fête troupes of pretty artists and subservient intellectuals sent to us by the Moscow regime and at the same time to forget the voice of the martyred writers who appealed from Budapest, is to betray their testament.

Let each one search his heart and determine freely what action he intends to take in his personal or public sphere of influence, against those who applaud the crime, who will try to make us forget it, or who will look for an excuse.

Let all free men who want to associate themselves with the international action of the Congress for Cultural Freedom know that they will find men here who do not forget the appeal of the writers of Budapest, who will not allow it to be forgotten, and whose entire efforts are directed toward responding to their appeal.

Denis de Rougemont, Figaro Littéraire (Paris), 10 November

"NO HONOUR, NO PITY, NO HUMANITY?"
"NOTHING BUT **THIS**"

Comradeship   *Manchester Guardian*

Delhi

We Socialists have persistently urged that foreign troops should not be allowed to be stationed in a country without the consent of the government concerned, as they would inevitably give rise to tension in the particular area. But for a big power to station its troops without the consent of a small country and, what is still worse, to suppress people and to impose on the helpless government its own puppets and stooges, is the most despicable form of colonialism. Yet this is

exactly what has been happening in Hungary, who has now appealed to the United Nations for help. *U Ba Swe, Prime Minister of Burma, at 2nd Congress of the Asian Socialist Conference,*
Janata (Bombay), 11 November

Rome

News reached Rome to-day that Signor Matteotti, secretary of the Social Democratic party, has been allowed to leave Hungary. He arrived in Vienna to-day with a group of Italian correspondents, after being confined in the Italian Embassy at Budapest for eleven days.

Signor Nenni, leader of the Socialist party, has made it known that he intends to give the sixteen million lire (£ 9,600) of his Stalin prize to the families of fallen Hungarian patriots. The gesture is a protest against the massacre of the Hungarian insurgents.

Paris

Two Parisians have died of injuries received during the demonstration and riots of Wednesday and Thursday. Both of them were apparently Communists.

Meanwhile anti-Communist demonstrations continue in many parts of France. At Bastia (Corsica) the local Communist leaders were besieged for some hours until released by the police. In Toulon the Communist newspaper office had to have police protection, and in Marseilles the office of a Communist cell was sacked by students. In Bordeaux demonstrators marched past the Communist headquarters carrying the Hungarian flag; they tore down the street sign of the Place Stalingrad and renamed it Place Budapest.

The Communists continue to react by counter-attacking. Communist demonstrations at Nice ended in a battle with the police in which fifty people were injured; four of them are in the hospital.

There is no indication at present of any change in the structure, outlook, or leadership of the French Communist party, but all the efforts of its leaders to break down its isolation have been nullified. One observer comments that the party is now as isolated as it was after the signature of the Ribbentrop-Molotov pact in 1939.

Manchester Guardian, 12 November

Bombay

The trend of our foreign policy in the past few days has seriously disturbed me... To Egypt Mr. Nehru's reaction was immediate and firm and righteous... But for many days there was not even a whisper heard from New Delhi about Hungary. Then, one fine morning, the papers reported Mr. Nehru's chief adviser on foreign policy, Mr. Krishna Menon, as having stated that the Hungarian question was a domestic affair of the Hungarian people. It was an astounding statement that left me aghast ... Then came the anti-climax. The Russian army swooped down and set the seal of doom upon that unfortunate country ... It was at that last stage, when the curtain was being rung down on the last act of the Hungarian tragedy, that Mr. Nehru spoke out at the Unesco Conference. It was a futile gesture because it was too late ... Mr. Nehru did not break his silence till November 5. It took him two weeks to make up his mind ... But the Unesco speech seems to have been the product of a passing mood ... When the first resolution on Hungary was adopted by the UN, India surprisingly enough had abstained ... Krishna Menon subsequently ... revealed that the abstention was deliberate. Then came Mr. Nehru's astonishing speech at Calcutta. Evidently Mr. Nehru had second or rather third thoughts and revised the opinion expressed earlier at the Unesco Conference. Finally came the crowning piece of this shameful story, namely India's opposition to the second resolution on Hungary. ... A more perverse and false view of the situation could have hardly been imagined. As an Indian I hang down my head in shame that a spokesman of my country [Menon] should have gone so far in cynical disregard of the truth and the fundmental principles of freedom and peace that are said to guide our international conduct ...

Jayaprakash Narayan, Bulletin No. 1 of the Indian Committee for Solidarity with Hungary (Bombay), 13 November

The Conqueror of Budapest   *Daily Mail (London)*

Djilas on Hungary and Yugoslavia

Belgrade

The experience of Yugoslavia appears to testify that national Communism is incapable of transcending the boundaries of Communism as such, that is, to institute the kind of reforms that would gradually transform and lead Communism to freedom. That experience seems to indicate that national Communism can merely break from Moscow and, in its own national tempo and way, construct essentially the identical Communist system. Nothing would be more erroneous, however, than to consider these experiences of Yugoslavia applicable to all countries of Eastern Europe ...

The resistance of the leaders encouraged and stimulated the resistance of the masses. In Yugoslavia, therefore, the entire process was led and carefully controlled from above, and tendencies to go farther — to democracy — were relatively weak. If its revolutionary past was an asset to Yugoslavia while she was fighting for independence from Moscow, it became an obstacle as soon as it became necessary to move forward — to political freedom ...

Yugoslavia supported this discontent as long as it was conducted by the Communist leaders, but turned against it — as in Hungary — as soon as it went further. Therefore, Yugoslavia abstained in the United Nations Security Council on the question of Soviet intervention in Hungary. This revealed that Yugoslav national Communism was unable in its foreign policy to depart from its narrow ideological and bureaucratic class interests, and that, furthermore, it was ready to yield even those principles of equality and non-interference in internal affairs on which all its successes in the struggle with Moscow had been based ....

The Communist regimes of the East European countries must either begin to break away from Moscow, or else they will become even more dependent. None of the countries — not even Yugoslavia — will be able to avert this choice. In no case can the mass movement be halted, whether it follows the Yugoslav-Polish pattern, that of Hungary, or some new pattern which combines the two ...

Despite the Soviet repression in Hungary, Moscow can only slow down the processes of change; it cannot stop them in the long run. The crisis is not only between the USSR and its neighbors, but within the Communist system as such. National Communism is itself a product of the crisis, but it is only a phase in the evolution and withering away of contemporary Communism ...

Just as it is compelled to be national in its forms, in essence Communism is one and the same, with the same historical origins and the same destiny. The events in one Communist country necessarily affect all other Communist countries, as in one and the same living organism. And just as Yugoslav Communism, separating itself from Moscow, initiated the crisis of Soviet imperialism, that is, the inevitable birth of national Communism, in the same way the revolution in Hungary means the beginning of the end of Communism generally.

As in all other great and decisive historic events, the Hungarian fighters for freedom, struggling for their existence and country, may not have foreseen what an epochal deed they had initiated. The world has rarely witnessed such unprecedented unity of the popular masses and such heroism. The unity of the popular masses was so strong that it appeared as though there had been no civil strife, as though a ruling class had not been wiped out overnight as if it never existed. And the heroic intoxication was so high that barehanded boys and girls were stopping the tanks of the interventionists who, like the Cossacks of Nicholas I in 1848, tried to suppress their liberty and enslave their country.

This event will probably not be repeated. But the Hungarian Revolution blazed a path which sooner or later other Communist countries must follow. The wound which the Hungarian Revolution inflicted on Communism can never be completely healed. All its evils and weaknesses, both as Soviet imperialism and as a definite system of suppression, had collected on the body of Hungary, and there, like festering sores, were cut out by the hands of the Hungarian people.

I do not think that the fate of the Hungarian Revolution is at all decisive for the fate of Communism and the world. World Communism now faces stormy days and insurmountable difficulties, and the peoples of Eastern Europe face heroic new struggles for freedom and independence.

Milovan Djilas, The New Leader (New York)
19 November

Hamburg

In all three cities (Amsterdam, The Hague, Rotterdam) stones were thrown at the buildings of the Dutch Communist Party. People shouted in chorus over and over again: "Away with the Communists and the murderers!" Many resolutions called for the breaking off of diplomatic relations with the Soviet Union.

Die Zeit (Hamburg), 15 November

London

Not since the Spanish War has England seen so popular a revulsion of feeling as over the Hungarian tragedy. I suppose the Russians will think that the workers who have demonstrated and the students who volunteered to go and fight or, as in Cambridge, collected £ 1,000 almost overnight for Hungarian relief, are Fascist dupes. They may be more impressed by the rapid disintegration of the Communist Party ...

Kingsley Martin, New Statesman & Nation, 17 November

Paris

There are circumstances in political life when discreet expression becomes intolerable. One feels the need to say all one has to say, or rather to cry out one's feelings and one's thoughts. Far from feeling ashamed of the emotions that affect us, we would be angry with ourselves not to feel them. Even if, when some time has elapsed, we can look at things with a clearer head and we put the merits and blame on other shoulders, we will never regret that today's judgment was clearly defined.

In the course of the first few days of November we reached the depths of political despair. The fact that France and England were accused by all the nations of the world whilst Soviet tanks massacred the people who claimed the right to live in freedom, and that Europe's protest was half smothered and half disqualified by the landings in Egypt, represents an historical disaster, for which we shall feel remorse for a long time to come.

Let us be blunt: everything that we have since learned leaves no doubt in our minds as to the hypocrisy of the Russians when they resolved to repress the rising. The evacuation of Budapest was only a war stratagem and the tanks which left then occupied strategic positions. Russian troop movements had begun before the Franco-British ultimatum ... Yes, but Hungarians coming from Budapest told me: "When we learned of the Franco-British ultimatum, we knew that we were lost." Throughout the world, millions of people continue to ask themselves: "Would they have dared if ..." This question, even if we do not hesitate over the answer, will torture our consciences. I admire those who are not troubled by it.

Raymond Aron, Demain (Paris), 22 November

Paris

The French Communist Party is still busy with its policy of tightening up, and has begun to take disciplinary action against those members who have advocated a more liberal attitude towards events in Hungary ...

In his speech to the party's central committee yesterday, M. Thorez, the secretary-general, sought to distract attention from Hungary ... To try to explain events in Hungary without first taking into account the existence and activity of the class enemy was to turn one's back on historical truth. He denied that there had ever been such a thing as "Stalinism" ... It was a term invented by the enemies of Communism.

The Times (London), 23 November

Warsaw

We stand shocked before the tragedy of Hungary, before the tragic account which in the eyes of the world must be paid for the grave sins and crimes of the Stalinist period. It is impossible to sum up at present, perhaps we should even lack the courage to do so. But one thing is certain: if the Hungarian tragedy does not become for the international workers' movement a lesson equally effective as that provided by Poznan to the Polish movement, then we are faced, on the international scale, with the same fate as that of the Hungarian working class ...

Roman Jurys, Zycie Warszawy, 23 November

Madrid

Leaflets have appeared in Madrid calling on Spain's students to show "active solidarity with the heroic students of Hungary who are fighting for liberty against tyranny."

Protest

Stockholm

Eight Nobel Prize winners, in a sharply-worded telegram to Soviet Premier Nikolai A. Bulganin, protested against the Russian quelling of the Hungarian anti-Communist rebellion. Among those protesting was the Spanish-born poet Juan Jiménez, this year's literature Prize winner.

The telegram, sponsored by the Swedish Committee for Cultural Freedom, said:

"In the name of humanity we condemn and protest against the Soviet Russian oppression of the freedom efforts of the Hungarian people. The events in Hungary form a flagrant crime against human rights. The Soviet Union should immediately withdraw its troops from Hungarian territory and entrust the re-establishing of free, settled relations to the United Nations."

"John F. Enders, Nobel Prize for Medicine, 1954; Juan Ramon Jiménez, Nobel Prize for Literature, 1956; Hans Adolf Krebs, Nobel Prize for Medicine, 1953; Fritz Lipmann, Nobel Prize for Medicine, 1953; Linus Pauling, Nobel Prize for Chemistry, 1954; Frederick C. Robbins, Nobel Prize for Medicine, 1954; Thomas H. Weller, Nobel Prize for Medicine, 1954; Fritz Zernike, Nobel Prize for Physics, 1953."

United Press, 1 December

All countries of the civilised world [says one such clandestine appeal] *have condemned Soviet aggression in Hungary. By showing their solidarity with the Hungarians they have re-affirmed those freedoms which are the heritage of honour: freedom of religion, freedom of opinion, freedom of association, freedom of expression ... Spanish students! Support the Hungarian students who are fighting for those very ideals for which we are struggling. In the East and in the West there resounds a un-animous call to liberty. Down with tyranny, down with police states based on terror and the rule of silence! Down with all dictatorship which debase religion and culture, which falsify the law and falsify the truth with their con-trolled press! Down with Soviet tyranny! Down with all tyrannies!*

Correspondent, *The Economist (London), 24 November*

Moscow

Soviet leaders are known to feel that youth, at least some segments of it, and especially those of the most privileged class and students in higher institutes, have become divorced from the working class and from reality ...

There was no way to measure how much this growing official concern with Soviet students is a reaction to the role youth has played in the revolts in Poland and Hungary. Soviet leaders are aware of the great curiosity of Soviet youth about recent events inside the Communist orbit.

Meetings of *Komsomol* (the Communist Youth League) have broken up in disorder when questions about Hungary were raised ...

William J. Jorden, *New York Times, 25 November*

Warsaw

You will ask, what did the World Federation of Democratic Youth (WFDY), whose head-quarters are located in Budapest, do in those tragic days?

We are very sad about this, and truly ashamed. The Federation played no role whatever. It turned its back on youth. There was, it is true, an attempt to define an attitude, but the draft resolution declaring the solidarity of the WFDY with the struggle of Hungarian youth, paying tribute to the dead and calling upon member organisations to bring assistance to Hungary, was signed with determination only by two Englishmen ... and by a Pole ...

This fact shows clearly how remote from life and corroded by the mistakes of the past period are the Federation and its leadership.

Another voice: Those who know the truth find it easiest to lie.

Radio Warsaw, *25 November*

Warsaw

Once the attitude one took toward the Paris Commune was decisive. Later, the attitude to the country of the Soviets. Tell me what you think about Hungary and I will tell you who you are ...

Zycie Gospodarcze *(Warsaw), 26 November*

Warsaw

[Interview with Jaroslaw Iwaszkiewicz, Chairman of the Polish Peace Committee, by Wladyslaw Zralek, representative of AR (Worker's Agency) on the subject of the World Peace Council resolution]

Q: Why did representatives of the Peace Movement [in Helsinki] speak up so late concerning the events in Egypt and Hungary?

A: ... [because of] divergencies in appraising the Hungarian problem which appeared both in the WPC and in the national Peace Movement organisations ... I do not want to go into details about those stormy debates. They lasted 24 hours. Nevertheless it can be stated that the most marked difference of opinion was between the Chinese delegation and part of the French delegation on the one hand, which maintained that what was happening in Hungary was the internal affair of

"Revolutionaries"

"Refugees"   *Krokodil (Moscow)*

that country, and the Italian delegation on the other. The Italians demanded that the Soviet intervention in Hungary should be condemned. As far as the attitude of the Soviet delegation is concerned, one can define it as conciliatory.

Q: What was the attitude of the Polish delegation?

A: In my speech at Helsinki I discussed certain aspects of the events in Hungary, warning the delegates, among other things, against an over-hasty definition of the insurgents as "fascists." The Polish delegation was, however, against any theoretical controversies ... Instead, we strove to arrive at the adoption of a practical resolution

Paul Ignotus Replies

Was the Hungarian revolution supported by the whole population?

The rising was started, as far as I could see, by two centres of intellectuals: (1) the Hungarian Writers' Association, in which Communist authors such as the novelist Dery had for a long time fought Stalinism very bravely, and (2) the association of Communist undergraduates, the Petofi Club. It was they who, inspired by the Polish example, went into the streets and proclaimed that the Hungarian people must act decisively to bring about Socialist democracy and liquidate the remnants of the Rakosi dictatorship. These were joined by people of all sorts and especially the industrial workers. The latter were in fact most intransigent in their fight against Muscovite rulers, and since then they have continued to fight, either with arms or with strikes and sabotage, although other sections of the population seemed ready to accept a fait accompli. In the democratic national revolution which started with the rising the whole population took part ...

Do you then completely discount the stories of a "counter-revolution?"

I must make clear what I mean by "counter-revolution."

If one means by it that the people wanted to set up a parliamentary democracy such as exists in Finland, with which the Soviet Union seems to maintain very friendly relations, then it is no secret that this is what the Hungarians wanted. If one means a restoration of landed property and a return of huge industrial concerns to private owners, then the fear was less because, although there might have been persons hoping for it, I am sure that the great majority of the Hungarian people would have rejected such an attempt. If one means an attempt by some former military officers and other embittered and dispossessed elements to indulge in white terrorist acts and eventually to establish their own dictatorship, then again they would have met the resistance of the overwhelming majority of all classes. It is true that spora-

dically there were such excesses. One of the most grotesque of them was characteristic, perhaps, of a country in which the national rising was started by poets and novelists. An ultra-nationalist poet of the Horthy regime, Gyula Somogyvary, in the city of Gyor, took a detachment of soldiers armed with tommy-guns to the radio station in an attempt to compel it to broadcast his poetry. But this, as well as other similar attempts, was foiled by the supporters of Imre Nagy and the coalition government, which was on the way to establishing order when the Russians marched into Budapest once again. As for the Russian fear of Hungary becoming a jumping-off ground for anti-Soviet military action, this would certainly have been prevented by an understanding (a) with the Hungarian government, which wanted to avoid war at all costs, (b) with the governments of Yugoslavia and Poland, which were keen to avoid both the restoration of Stalinism and the establishment of "white" rule, and (c) with the big powers which dominate the U.N., for these, I think, would also have been satisfied with a really neutralised Hungary.

Was the reaction of the West to events in Hungary well considered? ...

The Hungarians are, and have to be, grateful to the West for the expressions of sympathy and appreciation which they have received. But there are two things which they have missed. (1) A statement on behalf of the leading western powers to the effect that they would consider any attack on the independence of Hungary as an act of aggression, and that they would help Hungary by all means in their power if such an aggression occurred. (2) It should have been made clearer that the West would condemn the restoration of former fascist or semi-fascist methods no less than a restoration of Stalinism, and that Hungary was by no means expected to sacrifice the very existence of her people for the sake of an anti-Bolshevik crusade ... Paul Ignotus, New Statesman & Nation (London), 8 December

which would help the Hungarians as much as possible ... putting forward the demand for the withdrawal of Soviet troops on the basis of an understanding between Hungary and the USSR ... calling for full respect for Hungary's sovereignty ...

Q: The resolution states in a general way that it has been signed by members of the WPC Bureau, but mentions only the names of Joliot-Curie, Ostap Dluski, and your own. Did all participants in the conference sign the resolution?

A: The resolution was not signed by the Italian Socialists ...

Polish Press Agency, 28 November

London

I was in Hungary from October 28 until November 11 ...

Now I am sure — what I did not know before, but ought to have suspected or found out — that the Rákosi regime was a bloodstained tyranny

beside which Horthy's pre-war regime pales to a tolerant and liberal democracy. I ought to have suspected or found out because radical friends of mine, in Hungary, have now told me how they suffered under that terror; and I am one of those who owe them such amends as one can make for not having bestirred myself in their behalf. What is clear and certain now is that the Stalin-Beria system was exported and imposed on Hungary, after the end of 1948, "down to the last chip." Thereafter Hungary was a Soviet colony, "Socialist and peace-loving" on its propaganda façade, murderous and bankrupt in reality. The British *Daily Worker*, I notice, is still loyal to the propaganda façade: with a dishonesty as silly as it is cynical, it is still talking about the "mistakes" of the Rákosi regime. But murder is not a mistake. Fake trials are not errors. Criminal perversions of everything that Socialism is thought to mean are not malpractices. This, of course, is the language of the morally bankrupt ...

Basil Davidson, New Statesman & Nation (London),
8 December

Moscow: Hungarian Writers and "the Western Wind"

Budapest

This is not an idle question, it is a legitimate one which comes from the heart: On whose side do you stand, Hungarian writers? This is a friendly question dictated by the conviction that at a moment when the struggle for life, for smoke to rise from the factories, for children to receive schooling, for books to be published, for order, peace and tranquility to be consolidated by the joint efforts of millions of people is in progress in all spheres of Hungarian social and economic life, the place of a writer is in the midst of the people, among those who defend democracy and socialism.

This question is all the more appropriate because, as is well known, bourgeois ideology, the western wind, which is permeated by the miasma of corruption, has long ago swept over the Hungarian writers. Many of them (many!) long before the events in October, openly opposed the Leninist principle of the party spirit in literature, disseminated nihilistic ideas about the state and society, aesthetic and philosophical conceptions which are alien to socialism, under the false disguise of "the freedom of thought" and "freedom to create". These writers have spread serious ideological confusion and embarassment among the intellectuals, students and youth.

The situation became graver because, as we were told, long before these events the leadership of the ideological front slipped out of the hands of the old party and state leadership. Month

after month open propaganda against the party and government was conducted in newspapers, magazines, and on the radio, in the guise of criticism of inefficient leaders. Some writers took part in this campaign who long ago had broken away from the people and sold themselves to the West.

Undoubtedly, criticism of the leadership of that time was necessary and it contained much that was correct. But more and more often the truth was drowned in fabrications and inventions; chauvinism and anti-socialist moods were insistently pushed to the fore. It was even asserted that the working people of Hungary "do not want socialism" at all. And strange to say, workers on the ideological front did not cut themselves off from these statements, did not open the eyes of the people to their sources and their true meanings. Moreover, it seemed that officials of the ideological front were making way for such statements.

And even now, when times have changed completely, the work of the organized Hungarian intelligentsia still contains much that is not clear, that is immature and gives rise to serious misgivings.

Where and on whose side did Hungarian writers stand during these tragic days? What did they think and what do they now think of the events of the past weeks? Did they help and are they helping their people, the Revolutionary Workers' and Peasants' Government to stop reaction, to restore order and legality in their country?

It should be stated with profound regret that an objective study of the role of the Union of Hungarian Writers in the Hungarian events does not give grounds for any positive judgements. Moreover, we can now state quite responsibly that some writers have acted as secret allies of reactionary forces in these events. And once reaction was crushed, without their help, they took a false, ambiguous and essentially anti-government position.

We met the Hungarian writers and talked to them in their club. In a cold building filled with smoke, people scurried up and down, they argued about something, dozens of young people shouted something.

The secretary of the Union, Gyula Fekete, invited us in the next room. We were introduced to Istvan Erkeny, Sandor Nagy, Mihaily Gorgy, Derdye Mate, Peter Kutcka, Endre Vesi and other writers. The room was filled to overflowing with pseudo-literary young people who were notable for their extremely bad manners.

Vesi, Erkeny, Kutcka, Fekete, spoke about recent events. The others were either silent or nodded approval. The writers spoke differently, each giving his own opinion but unfortunately, in their speeches, we did not feel that human sincerity which comes from the heart; we did not observe open or pure views.

Istvan Erkeny bombastically tried to prove what cannot be proved. He asserted that the threat of counter-revolution in Hungary either did not exist at all, or at least had been over-estimated in panic.

We asked on behalf of what ideas were books of the classical writers of Marxism and the works of Lenin and Gorky, Chekhov and Hugo, Dreiser and Sholokhov publicly burned? Why were museums set on fire, monuments to Soviet warrior-liberators destroyed and profaned? With what intent had more than 4,000 Horthyite officer-emigrés come back into the country from abroad? We waited, but we received no reply.

If the threat of counter-revolution was "overestimated", on whose behalf did Cardinal Mindszenty speak on the radio, describing his impudent program, and in whose interests did Count Esterhazy claim to participate in the political life of the country?

Perhaps, we asked, gallows were not set up in the Square of the Republic, mass executions of communists, party activists, rank and file members of the public security forces did not take place, perhaps there was no destruction of the buildings belonging to party organs? Perhaps the ardent heart of Col. Astalos, which was cut out of his breast by the Hungarian "Black Hundred" is beating as before? What was this — a "mass peaceful" movement or rampant black

reaction, counter-revolution? And we received no answer to these questions.

Kutcka changed the subject; he, so to speak, attempted to explain "theoretically" what had happened by breaking it down into "stages". He spoke the words "the nation", "consolidation", "deportation". And each of these words is a lie, because each was used only to try to turn rumors into facts, fabrication into evidence, to by-pass

Culture and Truth

Moscow

If those who reproach my people with unreasonableness and cruelty were to talk to the mother of any one of our soldiers who laid down his life during the dramatic events of October and November they would understand the rashness of their premature judgment ... That lad, like the Hungarian workers and every Hungarian patriot, faced a common enemy ... enemies of culture ...

Do you think we are blind or callous? Do you think the men of culture in our country are deaf to the beating of humanity's excited heart? Don't think that, because it's wrong. We are not blinded by hatred ... We cannot allow ourselves to be deceived ... We have closely observed the events in Hungary. We have tried to analyse everything carefully and then pronounce our judgment. No, we cannot allow the rampage of fascism ...

Arkady Perventsev, Radio Moscow, 25 November

Paris

The Communist chiefs have just learned a truth which was horrifying to them and utterly astonishing to most of the world: There exists in each human being an inalienable part which is immune to enslavement and invulnerable to the most frantic propaganda. It is never really conquered by the most humiliating terror. In it the sense of liberty and the need for truth find a refuge. We have just seen the youth of Hungary, subjected since childhood to the monopolistic propaganda of the totalitarian regime, rise up against their oppressors with an ardor which inflamed the entire nation to the point of making it forget all fear of death. And this youth fought for the rights of man, against all lies, against all forms of dictatorship. Let the Communists and their accomplices slander them and call them fascists; the Khrushchevs know that, wherever they hold power, they are protected only by guns and tanks against the revolt of truth, which, when it takes hold of the masses, becomes the immense force of which Marx spoke ...

Manes Sperber, Demain (Paris), 8 November

what is known to the whole world and to legitimize as self-evident truths the most base fabrications of the defeated Horthy-fascist underground.

We discussed the United Nations debate on the Hungarian question. And suddenly it became clear that among Hungarian writers there are not only sympathizers but even people who support the Cuban delegate who introduced the forgery about genocide for discussion in the General Assembly. In any case, the dirty slander which was piled on the heads of the Hungarian people at the plenary meeting of the General Assembly by the Cuban delegate was not condemned by Zoltan Fabian and Gyula Fekete.

Thus, for three hours, as though through a primordial forest, we fought our way through contradictions in the evaluation of Hungarian events by Hungarian writers.

One of them, who called himself a Communist, muttered something about a "crisis of Marxism". Another pseudo-literary young man who was present began to shout about his "hatred for the Russians". The atmosphere was by no means that of a friendly conversation.

But the heckler was removed and the talk was renewed . . .

Returning to the hotel through the dark and quiet streets of Budapest, we reflected that the ideological poison which has affected many Hungarian writers evidently is seriously hindering them from defining swiftly their position under new conditions.

We sincerely regret that Peter Veres, Gyula Ilyes, Bela Illes, and Gyula Hay did not take part in this talk. We would not have been sorry to met György Hamos — the editor of the Hungarian *Literary Gazette,* the position of which in the period preceding the events was often ambiguous, to say the least. We learned later that at the time, these writers were discussing in the competent bodies their desire to aid the

Revolutionary Workers' and Peasants' Government appeal to the working people to start work and to normalize life — promising to raise this question at a meeting of the board of the Writers' Union.

Unfortunately, we do not know what happened at this meeting, but the discussion was evidently fruitful. Soon afterwards, we read in *Nepszabadsag* a statement by the union of writers "On Public Security, the Commencement of Public Work and the Freedom to Speak the Truth." This document did not express everything fully, openly and correctly. Some of its theses prompted objections or puzzled questions. But the core of the document, its basic ideas, were undoubtedly encouraging.

The social and economic system of Hungary, the document said, "should be socialism built by democratic means, taking into consideration the nation's future, and preserving the land reform of 1945 and the nationalization of the factories, major enterprises, mines and banks."

The statement of the writers convincingly confirms that among the creative intellectuals, as well as in other groups of the working people, the rallying of forces which are faithful to socialism continues. These forces are gaining the upper hand. The future belongs to them.

But the question: "On whose side do you stand, Hungarian writers?" can not yet be disposed of. It is an open question. The people, the government, the party of the working class, all honest people fighting for socialism and peace still await from Hungarian writers a definitive and clear answer, a reply to this question in deeds.

Time does not wait. Time presses. It is necessary to answer and to answer today, without fail. The Hungarian people need a rallying and inspiring message from its writers at this difficult time.

A. L. Romanov, *Literary Gazette (Moscow), 1 December*

A Hungarian Reply to the Soviet Writers

Budapest

Three Soviet writers and some people from the Soviet Embassy visited the Writers' Association in Budapest [in November] for "a friendly talk about grave problems." At first they behaved in a "hail-fellow-well-met" manner, were rather too cheerful for the occasion, and talked down to their Hungarian colleagues as superior "Soviet people" talking to mere Hungarians. We Hungarians present were not as cheerful as "our guests," who cracked stale jokes and then roared with laughter. We sat there, thinking of Budapest in ruins, our homes, cold and without windows. We could not laugh.

At last our guests graciously began a serious conversation and asked us about recent events. Istvan Erkeny, the novelist, was the first to answer. Erkeny had been a prisoner of war in Russia for years, and had written a friendly book about the Russian people. He speaks Russian. Beginning with his experiences as a prisoner of war in Russia, he talked about the friendly spirit which had developed there between simple Hungarians and simple Russians. He said there had been no chauvinistic Russo-phobia in the Hungarian people, nor any hatred of the Russian people later on, not even during the revolution. The common people of Russia and Hungary got on rather well,

Erkeny said, and during the revolution those Russians who refused to fight against Hungarian workers and peasants, were treated as beloved friends.

The Soviet writers present did not like this at all. Erkeny explained that frequently during the revolution a Russian commander saw in the street that he was only dealing with peaceful demonstrators and hence did not give orders to fire. On such occasions the Russian troops were cheered. Romanov's summary of all this was that Erkeny attempted to "prove the unprovable." But it is a fact that a great many Russian soldiers joined our revolution.

Erkeny and Endre Vesi after him spoke at length about the so-called "Jewish question." Vesi said that in Hungary every counter-revolutionary movement or episode was always connected with outbreaks of anti-Semitism. During the Hungarian October revolution there were no signs at all of any anti-Semitic tendencies, although the Rakosi-Gero clique's "cadre-policy" did a lot to enrage people in this direction. In spite of all this our revolution remained pure in this respect. All this was said by two Hungarian writers who themselves are members of Hungarian Jewry, so they cannot be accused of trying to hide anything.

After this Romanov asked us a series of questions. He said in his article that he received no replies to his questions. All who were there know very well that every one of his questions had been answered—only not in the way he wanted. According to Romanov the answers of the Hungarian writers would have shocked the Soviet people, but I think they would only shock some of their leaders.

In a booming voice he asked who could have set the Hungarian National Museum and the National Archives on fire if not counter-revolutionaries? . . . This rhetorical question was intended to prove that in Hungary counter-revolutionary acts had taken place.

To this the Hungarian writers present replied: they agree that these were counter-revolutionary acts—acts to crush a revolution. But they were committed by *Soviet* tanks and *Soviet* cannons. *They* set fire to the two buildings in question. Everyone in Hungary knows this ... Thousands of people saw Russian tanks and cannons firing on the National Museum and the National Archives. There were no insurgent fighters in these two buildings, the Hungarian writers explained to their Soviet guests, so this firing was just unprovoked aggression, similar to the firing which, even according to the official *Nepszabadsag*, destroyed 40,000 homes.

Romanov and his colleagues raised the question of the bonfires built with Soviet books. The fact is that the propaganda bookshops of "Mezhdunarodnaya Kniga," called *Horizon* in Budapest,

were attacked by the revolutionaries *after the Soviet intervention* against the Hungarian revolt. The contents of the bookshops were thrown out in streets and huge bonfires were built. Now Romanov did not talk about that; he only asked: "Why were the books of Tolstoy, Chechov, Gorki and others burnt in Budapest?" The Hungarian writers explained what happened. They said that they, of course, do not agree with the destruction of books. But they said that the anger of an oppressed people in revolt against tyranny does give rise to excesses that are historically justifiable and humanly pardonable. Angry people burnt the entire contents of the Soviet propaganda bookshops, translations of Hungarian and Western novels alike, not to speak of gramophone records of troubadours, and Lehar, Liszt, Kalmann etc. The whole action had symbolical meaning for these people; it was a symbol of protest against the monopoly of Stalinism over Hungarian cultural life. This is proven by the fact that no other bookshops were touched—not even Party bookshops with window displays of the works of Stalin, Molotov, Vishinsky, Zhdanov, etc.

As the Hungarian writers explained, they were fully aware that it was difficult for their Soviet guests to understand this; they judged everything "from above," from the standpoint of power.

Actually they did not understand it, or at least they pretended not to understand, and kept harping on "the fact that great classics were destroyed, and such acts can be inspired only by extreme nationalism and fascism." The Hungarian writers again explained with great patience that the book-burning affair was the elementary protest of a small people against big-power chauvinism, and against the cultural monopoly which had been imposed on them by force. The Hungarians pointed out that there had been a rebellion, that enraged people protested against Soviet-backed tyranny and, as it happened, some protests perhaps took an unfortunate form.

Mr. Romanov chose to forget these explanations. But scores of Hungarian writers present remember well how this single "unanswered question" had been answered for nearly twenty minutes.

One of the questions raised dealt with the lynching of AVH (security police) people and of some communist leaders. This question was also answered clearly, and in detail.

The Hungarian writers stated that they were and are most definitely against lynchings. They had warned and protested, in pamphlets, in newspapers, over the radio, in speeches and declarations. In the "revolutionary issue" of the *Literary Gazette* (published on 2 November), there was a special declaration of the Hungarian Writers' Association protesting against the law of the mob, against lynching. Thanks partly to these protests and thanks to the way the people sobered up during the last two days before the second Soviet intervention, these atrocities stopped. But the writers did not only talk about the atrocities and the stand they had taken against them. They explained how the Hungarian people felt about the AVH. And this was the decisive factor.

Colonial rule and the monopoly of Soviet might in Hungary was forced on the Hungarian people by the pampered, over-paid, over-dressed, over-fed and thoroughly corrupted special army of thugs called the AVH. Without the AVH the Hungarian people would have chased out Rakosi and lived the way they want to; they would have been permitted to be loyal to those Hungarian traditions to which the Soviet leaders only paid lip-service and at the same time did everything to suppress... Tens of thousands of innocent people were deported and imprisoned by the AVH. In 1954 it was officially announced that many thousands of innocent people were tortured and killed. The AVH was the organ of terrorism

and suppression. Not communism but, in reality, an imperialist regime of colonisation was based on the AVH. The Hungarian people suffered the rule of the AVH for 10 years. The only way to get rid of the AVH was to disband it. Naturally a great many people craved revenge. Revenge is a terrible thing, but the craving for revenge was there in the hearts of millions. There were ten years of horror to revenge, and there were those women who were queuing up for bread and milk during the revolution and had been machine-gunned by the AVH. The AVH wanted to stop people getting food, because they thought that this way they could put an end to the revolt...

"Yes, yes"—the Hungarian writers said—"some dozens or hundreds of AVH officers and men were killed during the revolution. But what about the many more killed by them during the revolution? What about the hundreds of unarmed women and children they killed during the revo-

---

Exchange

Paris

The undersigned who never harbored unfriendly feelings to the U.S.S.R. and socialism, today consider themselves justified in protesting to the Soviet Government against the use of guns and tanks to suppress the uprising of the Hungarian people and its striving to independence, even taking into account the fact that some reactionary elements, which made appeals on the rebel radio, were involved.

We consider and always will consider that socialism, like freedom, cannot be carried on the point of a bayonet. We fear that a government, imposed by force, will soon be compelled, in order to stand its ground, to resort to force itself and to the injustices against its own people which ensue from this...

We are equally opposed to the hypocrites ... We deny the right of protest against Soviet intervention in Hungary to those who kept silent, or even expressed approval, when the U.S. drowned in blood the freedom won by Guatemala...

The first and principal demand which we address to the Soviet Government ... is the demand for truth. Where truth triumphs, crime becomes impossible; where truth is suppressed, there can be neither justice, nor peace, nor freedom.

JEAN-PAUL SARTRE   VERCORS
ROGER VAILLANT   CLAUDE ROY
SIMONE DE BEAUVOIR   CLAUDE MORGAN
(AMONG OTHERS) ...

France-Observateur (Paris), 15 November

Moscow

Yes, what has taken place in Hungary is grave and tragic. But you see only one side in this... You are mistaken! You do not see the whole truth!

The people of Hungary was dissatisfied with the situation in the country... We think that a share of the responsibility is ours... We know that our country adopted measures [to help Hungarian leaders correct "grave mistakes"], but what has happened forces us to think that these measures were inadequate... Are there no other paths for correcting mistakes except the unleashing of counter-revolutionary fascist forces seeking the liquidation of the people's democratic order and the formation in Hungary of the centre for a new war?...

Many of us met you, Vercors, Roger Vaillant, Jean-Paul Sartre, Simone de Beauvoir, Claude Morgan, in Paris, in Moscow, and in other cities of the world. Many of you showed courage in difficult times, took part in the armed resistance to fascism. Then you saw the truth. Look it in the face now too... We do not wish the black memory of 1933, the year of the coming-to-power of fascism, to be repeated again in history. Not in Hungary, nor anywhere else!

And we want you to know this and to think about it.

M. SHOLOKHOV   K. FEDIN   V. KATAYEV
V. PANOVA   K. SIMONOV   B. SMIRNOV
A. KORNEICHUK (AMONG OTHERS) ...

Literary Gazette (Moscow), 22 November

lution? And what about those ten thousand whom they murdered during the last ten years?"

All this should be remembered, they pointed out, and something else too. When some workers arrested AVH people, workers, whose average monthly wage was about 900 forints, when they searched AVH officers, they found in their pockets tens of thousands of forints ... and sometimes even more.

Such a lynching mob felt they were killing traitors, thugs, and murderers. Is it any wonder?

The Hungarian writers also asked questions. But their questions were definitely *not* answered by their Soviet guests.

It would take up too much time to mention everything about a conversation that lasted more than two hours. But two things ought still to be discussed.

One of them is a speech made there by Peter Kutcka. Romanov wrote with a superior sneer that Kutcka tried to give an "ideological justification" of the recent events. We who listened to Kutcka felt that he not only tried but really justified everything that has happened. He explained that the working people wanted really to secure in their own hands the means of production. They were not satisfied with owning everything according to the words of the constitution. They wanted to put the constitution into effect. The workers wanted to be masters of the factories. In order to realise "worker's rule," the workers had to fight against the Hungarian State, for this state was simply the colonial organ of the Soviet Union. On 23 October some might still have doubted this statement. But on the next day the Soviet tanks convinced everyone that this "state" was just an organ of oppression in the hands of the Kremlin rulers. Kutcka said that only through revolution could the Hungarian people cut the umbilical cord of the "Hungarian" state. This umbilical cord connected that state apparatus to the Kremlin leadership. Hence social and national factors were bound together. If the working people wanted to rule themselves, they had to fight for national independence.

Kutcka talked about this. He emphasized the fact he is a Marxist and as such he can definitely state what happened in Hungary was revolution and *not*, repeat *not*, counter-revolution. It was a revolution which wanted to take away the means of production from state monopoly and make it really public property, operated by the people for the people. It was the revolution of a people who wanted national independence. Kutcka said that a revolution remains a revolution whatever atrocities have been committed while it occurs. But actually during the Hungarian revolution very few atrocities were committed. All the journalists who had been present, including Polish colleagues,

called the Hungarian revolution clean. Many communist journalists stated this; at first Mr. Kadar's newspaper did not deny this. On the whole, Kutcka said, there was a pretty general agreement in the world that the Hungarian revolution was one of the cleanest revolutions in history.

Why does not Romanov deal with these arguments in the *Literaturnaya Gazeta?* Why does he impute to us statements which were never made? It is true, of course, that in order to argue against a statement, you first have to quote it, and Mr. Romanov could not afford to do that.

But it was a curious feeling for the writers present later to read that Gyula Fekete and Zoltan Fabian "did not denounce" the "slanderous" debate in the General Assembly of the UN, and especially the slanders of the Cuban representative. They could not "denounce" all this because during the conversation that debate and those "slanders" had never been mentioned at all. On the other hand Fabian has stated that cannon and machine guns are not proper tools to make propaganda for an ideology. Furthermore he stated that Soviet tanks shot to smithereens in Hungary belief and trust in the Communist Party.

But the saddest epilogue to this conversation was the fact that Gyula Fekete, one of the officers of the Hungarian Writers' Association, was arrested shortly after this conversation. Fekete had been very prudent during the conversation. He tried to state all the facts in the most civilized terms possible. He summarized the views of the Hungarian writers quietly, intending to inform and not to insult. Do the Soviet writers, and especially Romanov think that the best way to convince their Hungarian colleagues is to have them arrested? ...

During the debate, true enough, one of our young colleagues got enraged by the superior attitude and sneering manners of Romanov and his Soviet friends, and he started to raise his voice to say: "Yes, I don't like you! Yes, I fought against you!" He even showed with gestures that he had fought. The Hungarian writers quieted him down; but they never pretended that they were exactly grateful for the Soviet intervention.

Romanov closes his article with the question: what line will the Hungarian writers take in the future? I think the Hungarian writers proved to the world that they are "taking the line" of the Hungarian people, of the revolution. We think there is one other "open question": what line will the Soviet writers, the *Literaturnaya Gazeta* and its writers, take in the future? Will they dare to face facts? Will they ever dare to face their own conscience?

A Representative of the Hungarian Writers Association
BBC (Russian Program), 25 January 1957

What Happened to Imre Nagy

At 8 p.m. this evening [November 23] Radio Budapest broadcast a Hungarian Government statement giving the official version of what happened to Imre Nagy and his companions the moment after they were taken last night to an unknown destination by agents of the Soviet security service ...

> *Imre Nagy, the former Prime Minister, and a number of his associates, as is known, sought and were given asylum 4 November in the Yugoslav Embassy in Budapest, which ended 22 November. Over two weeks ago, Imre Nagy and his companions sought permission from the Hungarian Government to pass from the territory of Hungary to the territory of some other socialist country. With the agreement of the Government of the People's Republic of Rumania, Imre Nagy and comrades went 23 November to the territory of the People's Republic of Rumania ...*

It is striking that Government circles told us as late as 7 p.m. that they "had no idea" about the whole matter.

The central question in Budapest this evening is whether it is at all possible to assume that Nagy had voluntarily gone to Rumania, since it is known that the agreement provided for his remaining in Hungary. In Kadar's letter to our Government it is expressly said that their free return to their homes was guaranteed and that no reprisals would be taken.

During the past few days your correspondent had the opportunity of personally talking with Imre Nagy and his associates, and not once did Nagy express even the idea of going to Rumania or to "some other" People's Democracy. He talked only of remaining in Hungary, or, were this not possible, of going to Yuogaslavia. However, the agreement reached between the Yugoslav and Hungarian Governments, and the written guarantee given by the Hungarian Government, gave the appearance that it was possible for them to remain in Hungary.

This evening we talked with the official spokesman of the Hungarian Government, Tardosz, asking him to reply to a number of questions ... Tardosz was unable to reply to a single question put to him. He said that he could only keep to the framework of the official statement, that he did not know anything else.

Here are some of the questions I asked him: If Imre Nagy and his comrades decided to go to Rumania voluntarily, why then did the Soviet security agents appear, contrary to the agreement, in front of the Embassy? Why did Imre Nagy, as well as the Yugoslav diplomats, protest against this? Why did Imre Nagy even come out of the omnibus once and only climb in again when the Soviet officers had removed themselves, so that one of them had to jump on when the omnibus had started to move? Why has nothing been heard of them for over 24 hours? How is it that they went to Rumania without anyone first going home to pack? A departure for Rumania is obviously a long journey—and we know that while they were at the Embassy they only had on the clothes they were wearing, no underwear, and no toilet articles?

Why did no one report home and say where he was going? Their families knew nothing of their departure, and the families of some, like Julia Rajk, were waiting at home for them as late as this evening, hoping that they would still come? Although the young Tantzosz couple have a small child, who was not with them at the Embassy, how could they go without taking their child with them?

How does all this fit in with the dry words of explanation, which leave the impression of an idyllic holiday excursion. Why does the Government's statement say that the asylum had "ended" without mentioning the agreement between the Governments of Yugoslavia and Hungary about the circumstances under which Imre Nagy and associates freely decided to leave their place of asylum, believing they had received a most decisive guarantee that they could remain in Hungary?

We did not get a reply to a single question which would throw some light on this matter, or which could show that the official statement is based on true facts ...

No wonder unprecedented excitement exists here. It is felt that the agreement between the Yugoslav and Hungarian Governments has been grossly violated, and that Imre Nagy, his associates, and their families have simply been taken to Rumania against their will. This explains why the Soviet officers received orders last night to "take over the omnibus."

Special Correspondent, Politika (Belgrade), 24 November

... Imre Nagy and his colleagues thanked the Yugoslav Government for the asylum which was granted to them. Yesterday at 18:30 hours, they entered the bus which was sent by the Hungarian authorities to take them away and which was supposed to take them home. However, already in front of the building itself, of our Embassy, at the corner of Heroes Square and the former Stalin Street (which is now called Youth Street), a Soviet officer managed to get into the bus. Yugoslav diplomats protested to the Soviet officer that this was interference by a third power, which was not party to the agreement concluded between the Yugoslav and Hungarian Governments ... A car, with Soviet security agents on board, stopped in front of the bus, and another behind it. The small convoy proceeded directly to the headquarters of the Soviet Command Headquarters in Gorki

Boulevard. The two Yugoslav diplomats in the bus, who again protested against the action of Soviet officials, were simply thrown out into the street in front of the building of the Soviet Command.

When they said that this action violated the agreement, the Soviet officer replied that the agreement was no concern of his, and that he had been instructed to take possession of these people. Two armoured cars replaced the police cars, and the bus, with Imre Nagy and others aboard, was taken away in an unknown direction ...

Borba (Belgrade), 24 November

In the process of settling the asylum question, a proposal was also submitted to the government of Yugoslavia that Nagy and certain other persons from his group be given asylum in Rumania, and that they remain there until the situation in Hungary had been normalized. In a letter dated 18 November ...: "The Government of Yugoslavia has nothing against Imre Nagy and others leaving for Rumania, but this depends entirely upon their acceptance of the proposal."

Imre Nagy and the other persons in the Yugoslav Embassy considered the proposal that they remain in Hungary the most acceptable because they wished, above all—as they declared in the Embassy—to remain in Hungary in the interest of the situation there and in order to take part in the normal life of the country ... They expressed this wish and readiness with the provision that they receive a guarantee for their personal safety; and in case this was impossible, all of them expressed the wish to take asylum in Yugoslavia ... For a long time the Hungarian Government was not ready to settle the matter on this basis, insisting on solutions that practically would have meant extraditing Nagy ... Of course the Yugoslav Government could not accept this, and so the negotiations continued ...

On 16 November ... an agreement in principle was reached between the two governments ... The Hungarian Prime Minister was ready to give such guarantees in writing, and on this occasion he declared that he thought that Nagy and the others could already leave the Yugoslav Embassy on 17 November ...

However, on 17 November the Hungarian Government unexpectedly raised new conditions for the settlement of this question. Their essence was that Imre Nagy and Losonczy should resign their posts in the Government, issue statements recognizing the fight of the Hungarian Government against the counter-revolution, do public self-criticism of their earlier activities, and give guarantees that they would not do anything against the Hungarian Government. The Hungarian Government also asked that, until the situation in Hungary was normalized, Nagy and the others should take asylum in some East European socialist country.

This proposal was not accepted by Imre Nagy and the others ... *Politika (Belgrade), 2 December*
Budapest

Spreading like wild-fire is the news of the disappearance from their homes of the world-famous Marxist philosopher Gyorgy Lukacs, Zoltan Santo, and Zoltan Vas. They had also sought asylum in the Yugoslav Embassy, but they left earlier than the Nagy group of their own free will, before the Yugoslav and Hungarian governments had reached the agreement which was later flagrantly violated. They were detained for one day, interrogated, and then set free. Now they have also been taken away. Karol Kiss, committee member of the Hungarian Socialist Workers Party, confirmed this at a meeting yesterday of party activists. He added that most probably they were where Nagy is, that is to say, in Rumania ...

Djuka Julius, Borba (Belgrade),
29—30 November, 1 December

Yugoslavia Officially Protests Kidnapping of Nagy

On November 18, 1956, the Government of Yugoslavia addressed a letter to the Government of Hungary on the subject of asylum granted by the Government of Yugoslavia in its Embassy in Budapest to the following persons: Imre Nagy, Geza Losonczy, Ferenc Donat, Gabor Tanczos, Sandor Haraszti, Ferenc Janosi, Georgy Fzekas, Janos Szilagi, Szilard Ujhely, Miklos Vaserhely, Julia Rajk, as well as 15 women and 17 children.

For the purpose of settling this question, the Government of Yugoslavia, on November 19, instructed the Under-Secretary of State for Foreign Affairs, Dobrivoje Vidic, to go to Budapest, where he handed the letter of the Government of Yugoslavia to the Prime Minister of the Revolutionary

Workers and Peasants Government of Hungary, Janos Kadar, and held several meetings with him.

The Yugoslav Government considered that the question could be settled in one of the two following ways: (a) either the persons concerned would be given guarantees of their personal security, in which case they might return freely to their homes, or (b) the persons concerned would be allowed to leave Hungary and seek refuge in Yugoslavia. We emphasize that the above-mentioned persons, Imre Nagy and others, expressed their desire to take refuge in Yugoslavia if the first of the two above-mentioned suggested solutions of the questions could not be secured.

In his reply of November 21, 1956, to the letter of the Government of Yugoslavia of November 18, 1956, the Prime Minister of Hungary, Janos Kadar, with the approval of the Hungarian Revolutionary Workers and Peasants Government, accepted the first above-mentioned Yugoslav suggestion, and this is clearly seen from the following section of his letter to the Government of Yugoslavia:

> *"In the interest of settling the matter, the Hungarian Government, accepting the proposal contained in the letter of the Yugoslav Government of November 18, 1956, page 3, par. 8, addressed to me, avails itself of this opportunity of reaffirming in writing the statement which has already been given verbally on several previous occasions that it has no intention of taking punitive action against Imre Nagy and members of his group because of their past activities. We understand that this discontinues the asylum granted to the group concerned, that they themselves will leave the Yugoslav Embassy, and that they will return freely to their homes.*
> *"In view of the fact that the Hungarian Government accepts the solution of the problem as suggested by the letter of the Yugoslav Government, and which the Under-Secretary of State for Foreign Affairs of Yugoslavia, Dobrivoje Vidic, also set forth verbally, — we are convinced that the question which arose between the Governments of the two countries in connection with asylum granted to Imre Nagy's group has now been settled in a way which serves the common interests of the two countries."*

On the basis of such full agreement reached between the two Governments and on the basis of guarantees granted in respect to Imre Nagy and other above-mentioned persons, they left the Yugoslav Embassy of their own accord on November 22, 1956, at 18:30 hours, and boarded a bus which was placed at their disposal for the purpose of returning home by the Vice-Premier and Minister of Armed Forces and Public Security, Dr. Ferenc Munnich.

It should be stressed that it was only on that condition, i.e. that Imre Nagy and other above-mentioned persons would be allowed to return freely to their homes and on the basis of above-mentioned guarantees, that the Government of Yugoslavia was willing to settle the question of asylum in the spirit of the Hungarian-Yugoslav agreement, which was confirmed by the sections of the letter of the Prime Minister of Hungary to the Government of Yugoslavia of November 21, which are quoted above.

However, according to information received from the Yugoslav diplomatic mission in Budapest, when the above-mentioned persons boarded

Guests

Budapest

Imre Nagy and his party have travelled safely to the Rumanian People's Republic. Holding regular residence permits, they can move freely about the country, like any other citizen. The Rumanian Government will make a statement in due course on the presence and state of health of the Hungarian guests. Neues Deutschland (East-Berlin), 25 November

the bus, Soviet military agencies intervened claiming that they were instructed to take away the persons in the bus, and one of the Soviet military organs, in spite of strong protests by the Yugoslav Minister in Budapest, boarded the bus. The Yugoslav Minister then instructed diplomat Georgijevic and Military Attaché Milan Drobac to accompany Imre Nagy's group so as to see for themselves whether the persons concerned would be taken to their homes.

However, the bus was taken to the Soviet Command Headquarters in the town, where a Soviet Army Lt.-Colonel forced M. Drobac and M. Georgijevic to leave the bus. When Military Attaché Milan Drobac protested, the above-mentioned Soviet Lt.-Colonel stated that he was carrying out the orders of his Command. After that, the bus with the above-mentioned persons, accompanied by Soviet armoured cars, was taken to an unknown destination.

The Yugoslav Minister in Budapest, Daliber Soldatic, informed by telephone the Vice-Premier of Hungary, Dr. Ferenc Munnich, of all that happened, and protested against an obvious breach of the agreement reached between the Government of Yugoslavia and the Government of Hungary, and the Vice-Premier, Dr. Ferenc Munnich, in reply to the protest, promised that he would investigate the whole matter.

According to information received by the Government of Yugoslavia, Imre Nagy and other above-mentioned persons have not yet returned to their homes.

On November 23, 1956, the Under-Secretary of State for Foreign Affairs of Yugoslavia, Dobrivoje Vidic, received the Chargé d'Affaires of the Embassy of Hungary in Belgrade, J. Kuti, and on behalf of the Government of Yugoslavia asked the Government of Hungary for urgent information as to why the above-mentioned persons had not returned home as the agreement concluded between the two Governments on November 21 stipulated.

Up to this moment, the Yugoslav Government has received no official information from the Government of Hungary on the above question.

The Yugoslav Government regards the above-mentioned action as a flagrant breach of the existing agreement. The fact itself that the act of breach was committed immediately following the conclusion of the agreement throws a special light on the matter.

The Government of Yugoslavia can by no means accept the version suggesting that Imre Nagy and other above-mentioned persons went to Rumania of their own will, for it is well acquainted with the desire of the same persons to remain in their country, as well as with the fact that the persons concerned, while in the Embassy of Yugoslavia in Budapest, rejected a suggestion that they should go to Rumania.

The Government of the Federative People's Republic of Yugoslavia hereby addresses its strongest protests to the Government of Hungary because of the violation of the agreement reached on November 21, and asks the Government of Hungary to carry out the agreement forthwith.

The Yugoslav Government is convinced that any action which would be contrary to this cannot fail to have negative effect on Yugoslav-Hungarian relations, to say nothing of the fact that the breach of the agreement, which was thus committed, is entirely contrary to the generally recognized norms of international law.

The Government of the Federative People's Republic of Yugoslavia expects to receive an answer from the Government of the People's Republic of Hungary to this Note.

The State Secretariat for Foreign Affairs of the Federative People's Republic of Yugoslavia avails itself of this opportunity of conveying its respects once again to the Embassy of the People's Republic of Hungary ...

The Under-Secretary of State for Foreign Affairs, Dobrivoje Vidic, then also received the Counsellor of the Soviet Embassy, N. Grjaznov, and handed him a Note of the Government of Yugoslavia to the Government of the U.S.S.R. which quotes the text of the Note addressed to the Hungarian Government and says:

> *"Informing the Government of the U.S.S.R. of the above, the Government of Yugoslavia cannot but express its surprise to the Government of the U.S.S.R. over the fact that Soviet organs in Hungary prevented the carrying out of the above-mentioned agreement which should have settled, in a friendly way, the question at issue between the Governments of Yugoslavia and Hungary.*
>
> *"Because of this, the Government of Yugoslavia refers to the Government of the Union of Soviet Socialist Republics hoping that it will do all that is necessary to enable the abovementioned agreement to be carried out.*
>
> *"The State Secretariat for Foreign Affairs of the Federative People's Republic of Yugoslavia avails itself of this opportunity of conveying its respect to the Embassy of the Union of Soviet Socialist Republics."*
>
> *Borba (Belgrade), 25 November*

General Kiraly's Comments

New York

A knowledgeable report and evaluation of Soviet military capabilities and strategy has been presented to the free world by a high-ranking professional Hungarian Army officer, once a Communist and now a refugee from communism ... Gen. Bela Kiraly, now in the United States, testified before the special United Nations committee on Hungary Jan. 29 ...

General Kiraly's report, highly technical and detailed, is considered by military experts to be one of the most important first-hand studies of Soviet military power and its exploitation of satellite countries as forward bases for projected attacks on Western Europe and Yugoslavia.

In an exclusive interview, he disclosed that in war exercises last year, atomic weapons were used in Hungary as tactical weapons for offensive purposes. These war exercises, involving the general staffs of Czechoslovakia, Poland, Hungary, Rumania, and Bulgaria, were under the personal command of Marshal Georgi K. Zhukov, Soviet Minister of Defense. During the games, Marshal Zhukov addressed the general staffs and disclosed plans for reorganization and mechanization of Soviet and satellite armed forces and new training methods for high-ranking officers.

What was General Kiraly's estimate of the Soviet soldier? Very low, morale bad, he said, "and remember, we (Hungarians) fought them practically with our bare hands."

"Contrary to what the West believes," he said, "the first evacuation of Budapest by the Russians was not for political reasons but for military reasons. The Russian troops could have been annihilated on the streets of Budapest. They evacuated only so that they could have time for reinforcements and overwhelming superiority."

General Kiraly emphasized that the Soviet Army he knew in Hungary was equipped with "obsolete weapons," either dating from World War II or else manufactured from designs used in that war. Only Soviet jet fighters and bombers are new.

What did he think of the Soviet general staff officer?

"I have seen," he said, "German and Italian staff officers and Russian officers. Most general staff officers are the same the world over. They speak the same military language, but not the Russians. They are all specialists, the Russians, according to their service. The artillery, for example, has a special general staff. The Russian general staff officers are divided according to their services, their specialties, and there is no general military knowledge, as it is all over the world" ...

"Since the Russians expect," he said, "that tactical atomic weapons would be used against them, they have made certain changes — there is a higher engineer ratio in their ground forces; they are thinking of greater entrenchment and they are increasing forces in rear areas but they are still thinking of massed troops, the same features of their World War II tactics." ...

How motorized are Soviet and Hungarian troops?

"Very badly," said General Kiraly. "You normally move troops by truck, train, or plane, but not the Russians. The soldier on foot is still the backbone of the Red Army ...

"We are all surprised how badly the Russian soldier behaved, as a soldier, during the rebellion.

They are not badly trained with their obsolete weapons but they were only able to subdue us with armed superiority. They beat us, not with the quality of their weapons or the quality of their manpower, but with their quantity. Something was wrong with the Red Army in Hungary. For example, they didn't dare enter the Vertes Mountain forest where our underground army was concentrated. We felt so safe we slept out in the open."

To demonstrate the weakness of Soviet troops in Hungary, General Kiraly offered this evidence based upon his knowledge of the Soviet order of battle:

Before the revolution, the 2nd and 17th Mechanized (motorized) Divisions were stationed in Hungary with a strength of about 20,000 men and 600 tanks. The 2nd Division was moved into Budapest to choke the revolt while the 18th was moved into western Hungary.

The Soviet 32nd and 34th Mechanized Divisions were moved from Rumania Oct. 23 and thrown into battle Oct. 24. At the same time, sub-Carpathian and Ukrainian-based divisions were alerted, moved into Hungary, battle ready. By Nov. 3, the Soviet Union had seven divisions and about 2,500 tanks.

It was with such overwhelming force that the Soviets were finally able to crush the rebellion, he said.

Arnold Beichman, Christian Science Monitor (Boston),
6 February 1957

A German Military Analysis

Munich

In Budapest on 25 October Mikoyan and Suslov attempted to intercept developments. They returned to Moscow on the next day. The decision fell there during the night of 26 to 27 October, at the very latest. Hungary was not to be sacrificed; the revolution would be suppressed by force. Soviet Armed Forces stationed in Hungary were far too weak for this. Delaying tactics would have to be pursued until an attack by an overwhelming military force could be executed. Whereas in the coming days Prime Minister Nagy promised to satisfy all the insurgents' demands, at the same time his complete helplessness in the decisive point was obvious. He could not bring about the withdrawal of Soviet troops. The promised negotiations served only to camouflage Soviet intentions. As the revolution strode from victory to victory in the following days, its fate was already sealed ...

At first only two Soviet divisions were stationed in Hungary. Whereas one of them attempted to hold, or rather to retake, important positions in Budapest, the other remained passive. It was withdrawn between Raab (Gyor) and Komorn where it could control rail and road connections between Vienna and Budapest. It did not involve itself in the fighting. Its task was quite clearly to hinder a possible intervention by western troops. As protective cover it had the Czech border at its rear. In the night of 30 to 31 October Soviet troops evacuated the Budapest city area, thus seeming to satisfy the Hungarian demands. Actually they occupied positions of approach for a general attack against the city later ...

By relieving or, as in other cases, by reinforcing Soviet armoured divisions with infantry divisions, at least 35 Soviet divisions participated in defeating the revolution and breaking the general strike. That is one fifth of the entire active strength of the Soviet Army. Despite propaganda and sup-

pression of news it would have been impossible to withhold from the Soviet population knowledge of what actually occured in Hungary. The effect on Soviet soldiers of the situation with which they were actually confronted will be all the more lasting because it contrasted so rudely with what these soldiers had been led to expect when they marched into Hungary. Reliable sources reported that they had expected to find American armed forces in Budapest and that some of them believed they were in Egypt. Incidents of Soviet defection in the first days of the revolution again prove, as the examples of Poznan and of the Soviet Occupation Zone in Germany show, that the most intensive political training cannot be absolutely successful if it stands in sharp contradiction to the influences of the world around it ...

Soviet armed forces began to encircle Hungarian airports on 28 October. At the same time, especially in Eastern Hungary, the most important facilities for traffic by rail and road were put under guard. On 1 November, Soviet tank divisions suddenly began to move in across the Soviet as well as the Czechoslovakian and Rumanian borders of Hungary. The Hungarian Armed Forces, which openly joined the revolutionaries on 30 October, waited for the Soviets to begin hostilities in order to deny them the slightest possible legal excuse for an attack. Thus they could be hopelessly outmanoeuvred. In the night of 3 to 4 November Soviet troops began their attack on already encircled cities. The borders, especially to the West, were blocked off. The massacre took its course. Freedom fighters who capitulated were shot down or herded to collection points where they were packed into rail wagons and transported to the East.

Eight days passed between the Kremlin's decision and the second intervention in Hungary. This is a remarkably short time; even if the decision were to be dated back two or three days

[24-25-26 October], which is possible, the fact remains that the Soviet General Staff did not require more time to plan and open its attack than did the German Army for its unforeseen attack against Yugoslavia in 1941. Western general staffs should not ignore this fact. Yet the perfection of the Soviet military machine is not as great as the villainy with which higher Soviet officers deceived their unfortunate victims. Marshal Zhukov told western correspondents on 29 October that the Soviet Union was prepared to recall all Soviet troops from Hungary if the Hungarian Government and other members of the Warsaw Pact declared this was necessary. As a first step the evacuation of Budapest was ordered to take place just as soon as the Hungarian Government wished. On the evening of 3 November the Hungarian officers who had been invited to Soviet headquarters in Hungary to negotiate the withdrawal of Soviet troops were deceitfully arrested. On 5 November the commander of Soviet forces operating in Hungary appealed over Budapest radio to "the comrades" of the Hungarian army to "protect the Hungarian People's Democracy ... shoulder to shoulder with the Soviet troops ...

The Soviet Union made an example out of Hungary and thereby prevented a rapid disintegration of the satellite empire. The price was high ... Violence won a victory in Hungary, but the Hungarian revolution inflicted the greatest political defeat Soviet policy has yet suffered.

A German Analyst, "Wehrkunde"
(Journal of Military Affairs, Munich), December 1956

Could the West Have Helped?

London

Few people in Hungary desired Western armed intervention to help the country to win its freedom. At the same time most of them realised that, however great their blood sacrifice, their country's freedom was forfeit without active Western help to regain it. Therefore if "active" was not to mean "armed" help they expected the West to use every means short of war to compel a Russian withdrawal.

They realised that the only language the Kremlin understands is that of force, and that, failing the use or the threat of force, the Russians would not withdraw. But the threat of force, to be effective, had to be real, and a real threat of armed intervention would be as good as armed intervention itself—which, however, they did not desire because it would carry with it the threat of a world war.

This then is the dilemma both of Hungary and of the West. That it was insoluble the Hungarians realised from the very start. But they went on fighting, hoping against hope and against reason that the blood they shed—their own rather than the Russians'—would somehow help to solve the dilemma.

Were they wrong to believe this? They have achieved their desperate purpose, which was to awaken the conscience of mankind. Some thirty thousand lives—Mr. Nehru's conservative estimate—are on the debit side of the ledger. Are they balanced on the credit side by the "awakened conscience of mankind," by the universal recognition of Hungary's heroism, by the condemnation of the Soviet action, by the millions of dollars and pounds contributed to Hungarian relief, and by the eloquent speeches at public meetings and at the United Nations?

Every one of these lives was given consciously, willingly, and readily so that Hungary might live again. The mother of a 17-year-old student told me:

"He came home during a break in the fighting to get his first hot meal in three days. 'Don't go back, my little son.' I said to him. 'I wouldn't stop you. I really wouldn't, if there were any hope that we may win. But there is no hope for us, there is

R. F. E.

Much has been heard in recent weeks about the alleged partial responsibility of Radio Free Europe, the unofficial American station—broadcasting to the satellite peoples from Munich under German licence—for the Hungarian tragedy. It was to be expected that the Soviets would try to blame the popular rising on RFE "counter-revolutionary incitements" but many Hungarian refugees too, complain that these broadcasts raised false hopes of western help.

In fact those who have made a careful analysis of RFE output so far are satisfied that it never called for a rising and never promised western assistance. But oppressed people listening to a foreign radio station may easily mistake the voice of sympathy for the promise of practical help to come: after the war we found numerous anti-Nazi Germans firmly convinced that the BBC had promised them all sort of things which it had carefully refrained from doing. The truth is that the western powers have felt a moral obligation to inform and encourage the enslaved peoples so as to keep alive the hope of regaining freedom but have never thought out how to assist them by realistic diplomatic moves ... The Observer (London), 2 December

only death for you if you go, my little son.' 'There is hope in death, little mother,' he replied.

"That night he was shot dead. I did not believe all this talk about hope in death. A good Catholic would not have spoken so (the boy was a convinced Communist). To speak like that was to speak of suicide. God rest his soul. But I must believe it now, and may God forgive me. I must believe that there is hope in his death, just as there was in Our Lord's. How else can I go on believing in God, or in man? Please, please tell them this when you get out of Hungary. Every Hungarian mother, wife, child of a dead hero believes this. Please, tell them. They must not, they cannot betray us."

What was the good of explaining to her the nature of the dilemma? "Of course, the world will not betray you." I said, and as I spoke I felt I was lying. So, too, I have been swapping lies like this, ever since I came out of Hungary, with people who keep saying: "There must be something the West can do."

Yes, there is something the West might do. Tell the Russians they must get out of Hungary, or else. But that is just what the West cannot and will not do. They cannot risk a world war just because some Hungarians died so that their country may be free. Western statesmen could threaten and bluster—just like the Soviet leaders did—only nobody would believe them.

They could announce that Western "volunteers" were getting ready to go to Hungary's assistance, just as Moscow and Peking announce that their "volunteers" would be available to help Egypt. Of course, neither Moscow nor Peking would have taken the risk of actually sending the "volunteers" and thus provoking a world war, but they thought—and rightly so—that to utter the threat was worth while.

Would they have gone through with it? Not unless they were prepared to risk the destruction of the world and what is more important to them, of the Communist system. But in the West the threat was taken seriously. The West could, conceivably, have threatened the Russians in the same way when they were murdering Hungary, and the Russians, too, might have taken the threat seriously.

What little I have learned, as a "Student of Soviet Affairs,"— and before that in Russia—has taught me that no Soviet official, except perhaps Stalin, was ever prepared to accept ultimate responsibility. And, even if there are some people in the Kremlin willing to call what they might have regarded as the West's bluff, there would have been other members of the "collective leadership" who would not quite so readily play with fire. They are as aware as the statesman of the West of the danger of blundering unwittingly into war. But, because Western leaders are more susceptible to the pressure of public opinion, they could not risk even appearing to play with fire ...

Victor Zorza, The Manchester Guardian Weekly
20 December

V

EPILOGUE

"The workers have been beaten, but they have not been defeated. History will prove that it was quite others who suffered defeat . . ."

MARX

"That power which needed two hundred thousand Russian bayonets to pick itself out of the dust into which God's justice and the strength of my mortally wounded country had pushed it—that power has crushed all rights, all laws, all liberties in my unhappy fatherland so worthy of a better destiny . . ."

LOUIS KOSSUTH

"A new revolution is only possible in the wake of a new crisis. But one is as certain as the other . . ."

ENGELS

EPILOGUE

The Kadar Government had been entrusted with the task of organizing a national administration in Hungary which would accept the presence of the Russians and, at the same time, re-establish the Hungarian State. The government's primary objective could scarcely be the vain pursuit of popularity; that was indeed impossible, or at least possible only if Kadar and his associates made a point of preserving to the utmost the gains achieved by the October revolution. Instead, their chief concern was the creation of machinery for administration and repression:

> It is in some respects more important and easier to reconstruct the machinery of the State Police than to reorganize the shattered Communist Party on a mass basis.
>
> *(Nepszabadsag, 8 February)*

The only possible basis for this machinery was in fact the Communist Party and the political police. But the Party had actually ceased to exist and was an object of hatred, even in the eyes of its own former militant members. The Rakosi era could no longer be restored, yet Kadar, pressed by events, could only turn back to the old order, try to rebuild its institutions and do his utmost to salvage some of its supporters:

> The last days had brought about an almost ghostly situation, which my [Hungarian] companion described to me as follows: "Suddenly, they were all there again. They seem to creep out of the cellars like rats and to be suddenly in power again at their desks. And they stare at us threateningly, at us who, meanwhile, have been desperately trying to defend the cause of Socialism and to save what could yet be saved."

"They were so small,"—and my worker companion made a gesture with his thumb and finger to indicate how small they had been—"when the revolt first broke out. But now that the Russians have mastered the situation again, they are resuming their normal rat size!" I must stress that the man who made this remark to me was an old-guard Communist.

Still impressed by the qualms of conscience of my companion, I met many of these rats who had returned in the wake of the Russians when I visited a number of offices in the Ministry for Foreign Affairs. I had gone there in order to register as a foreign correspondent, as was required, and also to fetch my passport which I had been forced to hand in, a day earlier, for examination. A woman received me with a friendly smile. An old Communist, she had worked for many years here at her desk in the Press Section. She showed me the marks of shots on the wall behind her desk and remarked, with relief, that the windows were now fitted with new panes. During those "terrible days," for a short while "other people" had obtained control of the Ministry of Foreign Affairs, but everything was now "in order again"...

> *(Joachim Steinmayr, Süddeutsche Zeitung, 11 December)*

Those Communists who shared the ideas of Nagy and had fought for freedom on the side of the rebels could no longer be employed by the Kadar government. The "neutrals" who had waited now found themselves caught between the pressure of the government and the hostility of the workers and other broad sections of the people. Therefore they no longer dared commit themselves. Except in the case of civil servants who could keep their jobs only if they registered as members of the "Socialist Workers Party," and also in the case of those who had formerly belonged to the "privileged classes," a policy of immediate expediency and opportunism scarcely worked in favor of the Kadar government. As for "boring from within" in the factories, the villages and the intellectual groups, this could be achieved but very slowly and superficially.

Even the government radio and its own inspired press reflected the most contradictory points of view and revealed the sincerely critical opinion of

---

FRANCOIS BONDY, the author of this Epilogue, is a well-known Swiss journalist who was in Budapest during the Revolution. He is the editor-in-chief of a French monthly, "Preuves," in Paris.

those who worked there, among whom one no longer found any writers or journalists of repute, only anonymous pens and voices. Official propaganda tried desperately to prove that the fragments of the Communist Party that had been brought back to power at the point of the Soviet bayonets were the nation's only possible leadership. At the same time, this propaganda argued that the two main wings of the Communist Party, "the Rakosi clique" and "Imre Nagy's gang," only represent two different "diversionist and criminal" trends.

During the first five months of its existence, the Kadar Government was characterized by uncertainties, contradictions, and denials. In one breath, it would criticize the Rakosi era, in the next it would glorify it. At one moment, it would seek to explain the October revolt as a justified popular outburst:

> I repeat, and unequivocally declare, that the solemn promise made in our Government's appeal of 4th November remains valid, that no worker will come to harm as a result of his participation in the mass movement initiated on October 23rd. (*Kadar, Radio Kossuth, 26 November*)

At another moment, the government would nevertheless condemn this uprising as a "counterrevolutionary putsch." Those who had fought for freedom were thus alternately reassured and threatened. Since there was absolutely no attempt to present the Kadar government as legitimate—the Nagy government had not even resigned—the Hungarian Parliament was not even summoned to meet, and a delegate from the provinces even asked whether Parliament might "be given a chance to establish contact with the Government" (*Nepakarat, 13 December*).

Actually, this government tried for a while to strike some balance between the real powers, represented by the Workers Councils and the Soviet forces, but gradually it began to shift from a spirit of compromise to outright repression. The same attitude could be detected in the government's relations with writers and journalists, whose organizations were dissolved or placed under a kind of trusteeship. Kadar even made a number of attempts to inveigle into his government certain political leaders who were not considered Communists, although he was careful to exclude Social Democrats of every shade.

The leaders of the democratic parties, however, immediately made specific demands. The London *Times*, for instance, reported on January 3rd:

> ...Most active in this respect has been the Petöfi Party, whose leader, Mr. Istvan Bibo,

now in hiding, produced a memorandum in the early days of November while Budapest was still filled with the sound of Russian shot and shell. In this he discussed means of safeguarding the gains of the Hungarian revolution while also ensuring that Russian strategic interests in Hungary were respected. Mr. Bibo had been one of the three members of the Petöfi Party to join in Mr. Nagy's short-lived Government.

A series of other memoranda followed, prepared by other parties and organizations, some of which are believed in one way or another to have been conveyed to the Russians. Their common assumptions are that assurances are being given to the Russians concerning their interest in this part of the world, that provision is made for the phased withdrawal of their troops from Hungary, that Socialism as a social system for Hungary is accepted, but that provision is made for a gradual progress towards genuinely democratic forms.

Actually, Kadar was not so desirous of finding political partners, as hostages; none of the leaders whom he contacted agreed to cooperate with his régime. Hence he now began to make numerous formal concessions to national sentiment: the Honved, for instance, was to be allowed its old uniform, and the Russian language ceased to be required as a subject in all schools.

The *Süddeutsche Zeitung* reported (2 February) that:

> 90% of all students in Hungary's institutes of higher education and 60% in its secondary schools have expressed their preference for German as a foreign language. The alternative offered them was Russian.

The *Neue Zürcher Zeitung* added (2 February):

> An article published in *Nepakarat* stresses the fact that a knowledge of Russian remains absolutely necessary for our younger generations. Russian is indeed a language that brings us closer to the world of Socialism, to our neighbors, and assures us contact with progress, culture and a richer and brighter future. Wise parents, who recognize the importance of the languages of the Western World, will have to take these factors too into consideration.

Die Welt, on the other hand, reports (5 February):

> In the advertising sections of the daily newspapers one finds announcements like the following "German instructor requested for home study", "German and French taught by instructor trained abroad", "English, French and German short-hand and typing", "German conversation taught by native Austrian teacher",

"Study German and English at the Gorky Cultural Center" ...

The government then found itself forced to take steps in order to maintain Russian as a subject in school curricula. The *United Press* reported (2 February):

The Hungarian Minister of Finance, Istvan Kossa, made a statement on Tuesday to a group of Communist Party Activists: "It is absolutely false that children between the ages of ten and twelve will henceforth be allowed to make any decisions of this kind on their own."

On December 24th, "Father Christmas" or Santa Claus had been allowed to appear again in public ... The Stalin Avenue had already been renamed Avenue of Youth. The *Manchester Guardian* (7 January) reported that religious freedom had again been granted and that "artists would be allowed to create what they liked. Every progressive line in science and art would be free to develop ..." The London *Times* (8 January) also reported the following:

In the main square of Keszthey stood a rough monument—three pillars of bricks surmounted by a plaster statue of a youth with a banner—recently erected in honour of the uprisings. The inscription on it reads: *"In memory of those who died for freedom in October 1956, and of those who die for freedom in the future."*

But even these somewhat superficial concessions to public opinion were not respected for long. The new police still wore the hated red star on their caps. The same old red stars were repainted on the entrances of all factories, where workers had removed them. In February, the Russian language was reinstated as a required course in all grade schools.

Everywhere Soviet Russians were to be seen, both in Budapest and in the mining-towns, and in all provincial administrative centres. Whenever there were strikes or public demonstrations, the Russians appeared as the major and most necessary force to maintain order. The Soviet Union neglected no effort in order to recover its hold on Hungary and thought that it endowed Kadar with some prestige when it decided to hold in Budapest a conference of the leaders of all the more faithful People's Democracies, on the occasion of which the Chinese Minister Chou En Lai was also present. It was indeed imperative for the Russians to demonstrate the irrevocable nature of the restoration of the old order in Hungary.

Kadar tried however, to achieve a balance between this return to totalitarianism in politics and a vague hope of economic liberalization. He thus offered some advantages to independent craftsmen, to small traders, and tolerated for the time being the redistribution of collective farms. But the contradiction between a policy that could not trust any spontaneous expression of opinion and an economy which founded its hopes on individual initiative soon appeared to be insoluble. Actually, Kadar's Hungary was destined to be a régime that relies on the presence of a foreign army and foreign subsidies, while almost two per cent of its population (including an important share of its intellectual and technical élite, of its students and skilled workers) chose the paths of exile. This veritable exodus indeed constituted a gigantic and moving plebiscite. Kadar's only reply, after having first promised, then denied, general elections and even trade union elections, was an original formula, the so-called "plebiscite of work": all those who returned to work in Hungary proved thereby that they supported the government.

The Hungarian resistance—with no hope of victory, but sure of the justice of its cause and of the support of the nation—found itself pitted against a terrified and isolated government that had no solid administrative structure and no real ideology. After the "Unanimous Revolution" of October—the first revolution of a whole people that history has yet recorded against a totalitarian dictatorship—the Soviet Army could only restore a system without "myth," imposed as a superstructure on a people that refused to accept it, deprived of all the habitual supporting themes of modern totalitarian propaganda. The Kadar régime presented the ultimate paradox of contemporary Communism: a "People's Government" resolutely opposed to the people, a "Worker's State" in bitter class conflict with the workers.

The Kadar régime succeeded in destroying one by one all the organs of democracy that had survived the October Revolution. The strikes of the workers turned out to be a two-edged sword in the hands of the opposition, since they were undermining the very substance of the nation's economy. The need to enforce "order" so as to ensure the very physical reconstruction of the country thus strengthened the régime in the long run and worked against resistance. At first active, the strikes now become passive. The people remained silent, and the strike of the writers was the national symbol. Kadar even ceased to be the mask of a foreign occupation and revealed himself as its very face. His government symbolises

Interview with Anna Kethly

KETHLY: *It is not true that reactionary counter-revolutionary or fascist groups prepared a conspiracy against the People's Republic of Hungary, nor that the popular rebellion developed into an anti-socialist counter-revolution ... The real cause of rebellion was, in fact, that the régime and the people, the Communist Party and the working-class, became absolutely alienated from each other. The wrath of the people grew from day to day ... Some months before the 23rd of October, I warned a Communist functionary that "the longer you postpone reforms the greater the danger of a terrible bloodbath" ... He told me that it would be too difficult to undo the national network of the régime. There are about 200,000 major and minor functionaries, AVO-men, et al., whose lives are bound to the régime ... But it became more and more inevitable for the Communists to surrender their absolutist reign. In a reformed socialist state, it would also be impossible for them to retain a position of supremacy. In fact, their best hope would have been to be eased out of power bloodlessly, and to cooperate in a democratically elected government, which would guarantee socialist achievements ...*

Wouldn't this be difficult for the functionaries to accept?

KETHLY: *Still, there were some Communists, especially intellectuals and writers, poets in Budapest, students, scholars, but also Communist workers, who accepted it ... But the top leaders of the party could not go along and were not ready for it ... In fact, there existed in the Communist Party a very serious division between the old Stalinists and those for a new Party line. The reformers grouped themselves around Imre Nagy and hoped that he would succeed in giving leadership in a desperate situation. But Rakosy was in the way. Rakosy was also in the way of the Stalinists, because his name was forever coupled for the people with the reign of terror.*

In other words, among the Communists themselves there was an opportunistic opposition to Rakosy. They wanted to win over Nagy, a very popular figure. This question arises: how did it come about that Nagy, shortly after the beginning of revolution, asked for the Soviets to help?

KETHLY: *Nagy n e v e r asked for Soviet help! He never had a reason to do so. He was brought into power by popular demand, against the resistance of Gero. Finally, even the party leaders decided for Nagy against Gero ...*

And the Russians?

KETHLY: *The Russians, too, were ready to negotiate with Nagy — at least they gave that impression.*

Did Nagy really have a popular majority behind him or only the majority of the Communist Party?

KETHLY: *All patriots saw in Nagy the only chance to avoid the worst. All democrats knew that they had to support him against the Gero clique in order to help him along.*

You, — I mean the democrats — supported Nagy, but meanwhile you submitted requests and demands which the Communist Party could not realize, but which pressed him to reform his government along more national and democratic lines.

KETHLY: *Yes, this could only be attained step by step, and each step forward only under the pressure of the national democratic revolution. The people brought Nagy to power and the people alone could support him in power ... Only the people could give him the strength and authority he needed for negotiations with the Russians.*

And because of that the rebels resisted the Russians, asked them to leave Hungary, and demanded more and more concessions from Nagy?

KETHLY: *Yes, this was the very basis of the position of the insurgents in Budapest, where the Socialists were in a majority. The popular resistance was our only strength; the people had to go out in the streets and onto the barricades to make the government's position secure.*

—And afterwards, this became quite difficult to control by the government or even by the revolutionary councils?

KETHLY: *That's the way things happen. The strength of revolution lies in its spontaneous mass character. An organized "putsch" would have been impossible. In spite of that the revolution was by and large very disciplined. But revolutions cannot stop half-way. The people wanted both freedom and independence. There was simply no getting around that.*

Don't you think that middle-class and peasant elements had a different conception of freedom from the Socialists?

KETHLY: *Everybody supported the Revolution.*

Did they all support the Communist Imre Nagy?

KETHLY: *The majority, yes. People wanted land and bread and freedom. Nagy had promised it. What one could call "middle-classes elements" went along with the workers, and the peasants were with the workers too. The new parties which* were formed — even the non-socialist parties and groups — were united in recognizing and guaranteeing the socialist achievements of 1945, or rather 1947.

What was behind this? A thing for the moment ... or with an eye on the outcome of free elections?

KETHLY: *The Communists would, of course, have been most certainly defeated in free elections, and would have been reduced to a minority party. Everybody knew that. But the Social Democrats were there and the Smallholders party—which had been the majority party earlier. These two parties were clearly committed to the socialist state. Other parties—the peasants, the democratic and liberal-minded groups,— declared themselves for maintenance of the socialist conquests ...*

— Excuse me, but ...

KETHLY: *Look here: everybody understood that the peasants who, after the war, had received the land or big owners, wanted nothing more than the end of forced collectivization, but not the return of dispossessed proprietors. For example: Prince Esterhazy, after his release from prison, sent the peasants of his former estates packages of food to help them. In spite of hunger and real need, the peasants sent everything back and protested against his intervention in their affairs. They wanted nothing of him. The same held true for the workers in relation to the former factory owners. The working class wants a just socialist order with liberty and democracy, but not the return of the factory owners, bankers and foreign investors.*

— So you didn't see any serious opposition to socialism in Hungary?

KETHLY: *None at all. Reaction has no chance at all in Hungary. Even the bourgeois parties, which stand for private property and free trade, have respect for social peace and social achievements.*

—What do you mean by "social achievements" besides the expropriations of landed estates and factories?

KETHLY: *Nationalisation of factories, banks, transportation, public services; the railways were already nationalised before the war. Yes, and natural energy resources and the mines.*

What was Cardinal Mindszenty's position?

KETHLY: *Cardinal Mindszenty intended to re-establish the Christian-Democratic party which existed in the post-war period; this party, like the other non-socialist parties, would also have accepted the nationalisation, land-distribution, etc. ...*

He was not able to take part in the liberation of Hungary, and for good reason: he was absolutely cut off from the outside world and was in no position to judge the political situation clearly.

But didn't just this lead him to commit some serious errors?

KETHLY: *He supported the revolution and he never intended to give it a reactionary character. He did not want to bring back Horthy and the capitalists. He was loyal. When he talked to American journalists at the American Embassy, he declared in so many words that he supported Nagy ...*

Wasn't Mindszenty's hesitation reflected in the attitude of the insurgents? Why didn't they put down their arms before the 31st of October? ...

KETHLY: *They could not and would not surrender their weapons so long as they had no security that Russians would withdraw and there could be no Stalinist counter-attack.*

This position was also that of the Social Democrats. When did you and your party come into Nagy's government?

KETHLY: *On 31st October, when all our conditions were accepted: The withdrawal of Russian troops from Hungary—and this seemed to be going on. The termination of the state of emergency and martial law—and this was done. A firm commitment to free elections—which was given. The legalisation of the Social-Democrat party—which was approved.*

How did it happen, then, that Nagy, when the negotiations with the Russians were still going on about troop evacuations, declared that Hungary was cancelling the Warsaw pact, proclaiming neutrality, and placing the country under the protection of the United Nations?

KETHLY: *It was the demand of the entire people and also the wish of Nagy himself. It was also a demand of the Social-Democrats.*

Was it one of your conditions for entering the government?

KETHLY: *Yes, it was.*

Could you really trust and believe that the Russians would fulfil these conditions?

KETHLY: *We believed in the honesty of the Russian promises that Hungary would be able to take her own path to socialism and independence. We did not reckon with the intervention of Russian troops to restore the oppressive old regime.*

Lothar Ruehl, Der Spiegel (Hamburg), 12 December

the physical defeat of Hungary, even more the ultimate humiliation of Communism. A defeat that cannot be lasting, it is true, but a humiliation that is final.

The Government vs. the Workers

The Kadar government has never insisted as much on its *national* character as on its character as an authentic government of *the workers.* Janos Kadar reminded his listeners in many speeches that he is himself a former mechanic and that his opponents cannot pretend that he represents the "capitalists" or the "landed gentry." Within the framework of the resistance of all classes to a Communist government in the shadow of a foreign power, the most significant factor remains Kadar's permanent conflict with the workers and, at the ideological level, it is this that embarrasses him most. It has indeed been the working class that, all along, has most violently opposed the government.

The history of the first months of the régime's existence remains to a great extent the history of its struggle against the Workers Councils. During a preliminary stage, in November, strikes remained the immediate form of expression for all those who were fighting the occupying power and who, to all intents and purposes, ignored the very existence of the Kadar government.

Nepszabadsag, on November 14th, could only express surprise—

Why is there still a strike? What political end does it serve? Who is responsible for the fact that in many Budapest factories work has not begun again? Let us answer the second question first. The pompously-worded leaflets plastered on the walls of Budapest streets assert that the continuation of the strike is an expression of the united determination of the Hungarian working class ... This is not so. This is a barefaced lie.

Honest workers ... want to work. They want to work not only because their pride commands them to live from their own labor and not on charity, but also because they know that the inflation, into which irresponsible elements are ready to drive the country, would affect their own wives and children ... The strike merely delays still longer the withdrawal of Soviet troops and postpones the democratic political development that must take place in our fatherland.

Kadar then began to multiply assurances, to promise new elections, liberation from the secret police, the inclusion of the various other parties in his government, a promise that those who had fought for freedom would not be persecuted nor imprisoned, etc... On elections, *Nepszabadsag* still quoted him on November 14th as follows:

It is possible that we may suffer a resounding defeat in the elections, but we shall participate in the struggles of the electoral campaign because the Communist Party will thus be able to regain the confidence of the mass of the workers.

At that moment, Kadar was thus rejecting only those demands that concerned Hungary's relations with the outside world at the international level, i.e., the country's neutrality and the withdrawal of Soviet troops. Even concerning Imre Nagy, Kadar then said that "he would be able to participate again in the political life of the nation ..."

In the course of a second period, the Workers Councils tried to cooperate in a resumption of production and in the reconstruction of the nation. The 48-hour general strike that began on November 21 came as a result of the Government's veto of the national conference of Workers Councils, scheduled to take place in the Sports Palace. As for the deportations of young people to Soviet Russia, contradictory declarations made by Government spokesmen indicated that the Government itself was ill-informed about the local actions of the Soviet troops.

Satirical posters have made an appearance in Budapest and are causing the Communist administration great difficulties: *"Applicant required for the position of Minister President for Hungary. Requirements: a heavy criminal record and Soviet citizenship."* Or else: *"Ten million Fascists are at large in Hungary. They consist mainly of former Cardinals, nobles and officers of the Horthy army, and have spent the last few years disguised as workers in the factories on Csepel Island."* Again: *"Applicants sought for membership in the Hungarian Communist Party. As soon as there are more than ten applicants, a mass demonstration will be organized."* ...

(*Der Tagesspiegel, Berlin, 11 November*)

The newspaper *Nepszabadsag* admitted that the strike had not been organized by "terrorists" and that it expressed the dissatisfaction of the workers and their thirst for freedom and independence. Faced with the success of the strike, the Government shifted its policy from one of brute force to one of reasoning, and Radio Budapest then declared that only the Workers Councils could persuade the workers to return to work. These councils "can now be assured of the complete support of all sectors of the administration." On November 15th, the Councils had submitted eight demands. But Kadar's speech of November 2?th left no possible illusions about his willingness to accept them:

It would be extremely unwise to pursue the path of concessions made to the will of the counter-revolutionary forces. Our opinion is that one cannot placate a tiger, and that one can tame it and make it peaceful only if one beats it to death.

The most dramatic confrontation between the two political powers occurred on November 25th in the Hungarian Parliament. A number of ministers, including Kadar, Marosan, and the Minister for Industry, Antal Apro, as well as some delegates of the Workers Councils, technicians, factory managers and trade-union leaders, held a conference which was discussed at length that same evening at 7 p.m. on Radio Budapest. Apro opened the meeting with a long speech on the necessity of resuming work:

I must say openly that many people are of the opinion that to produce, to construct and to create new values are very unpopular things today, and that only those people are popular who draft memoranda, write pamphlets, draft various demands in paragraphs or, out of a spirit of revenge or servility, draw up lists of persons who should be dismissed from office. These internal strikes must be stopped in all Ministries, national offices and national concerns ... Everybody must declare on whose side he stands, whether on the side of democracy or of the counter-revolution. He who sides with the counter-revolution must take his hat and go. We do not need vacillators and opportunists. Everybody must now work and create in the interests of the people. Those who have a heart, a mind and an honest attitude, must prove this through creative work ...

Apro then went on to explain that the Government had received the visits of the delegates of hundreds of Workers Councils. He expressed admiration for the central Council of Unions which, "unlike the Workers Councils, is directed by functionaries who are nominated by the Party"; at the same time, however, he made complimentary remarks about the Budapest Workers Councils: "I have recently conducted negotiations with the Budapest Workers Councils. I must say that the comrades who work in that Council have given us valuable support in the task of restoring

order and discipline and of resuming productive work. The actual political situation in the country proves that order, normal life and productive work now prevail throughout over eighty per cent of the nation's territory."

Kadar's address began by justifying at length the Soviet intervention which had immediately followed the events of October 23 and which "cannot possibly be defined as a counter-revolution," though he was destined, on November 30th, to affirm the contrary. To the first demand of the Workers Council of Greater Budapest for the "withdrawal of the Soviet troops," Kadar replied that this condition should be taken up last: "First we must restore order."

The speech of Sandor Bali (who was arrested a few days later) remains an historic reaffirmation of the power of the workers.

The Hungarian working class developed these Workers Councils quite spontaneously ... We are well aware that they cannot be political organisations. We are fully aware of the need for a political party and a trade union. But in view of the fact that for the time being we have no practical opportunity to set up such organisations we are compelled to concentrate all our forces ... We should not and we cannot talk about trade unions before Hungarian workers have built up the unions from below and delegated to them our right to strike.

Sandor Bali denied that the Workers Councils wanted to assume governmental powers. The independence of the working class in its relationship with the State was, in his view, the most important of the gains achieved by the October Revolution:

We know that the Workers Councils will become organs directing the country's economy. This is exactly what we want them to be. We do not want to commit the same mistake as the Party did in the past, namely, when it was, at the same time, master both of the country and of the factories and also the organization which represented the interests of the workers. If we commit this mistake, we shall again be where we were in the past. We want the Workers Councils to direct the country's economic affairs, and the Trade Unions to have the right to strike and to manage all affairs relating to the protection of the interests of the workers. We shall do everything in our power to achieve this. And we shall do it in a healthy and Hungarian way ...

Sandor Bali's urgent question was: "Why doesn't the Government help us to restore the morale of the workers?"

Why didn't a single member of the Government come to talk to us. If he was afraid he should have come under the protection of armed guards. Why did they expect the members of the Budapest Workers Council to sit here until midnight and even 2 in the morning waiting for the various members of the Government?

We know you are very busy, and are engaged in international discussions. But, in our opinion, Hungarian home affairs, the affairs of our workers and peasants, are the most sacred things today. Everything should have been put aside in order to face these. I think that the duty of the Workers Councils in connection with striking and working is quite clear to you ... The workers also know that you here in the Parliament will not catch cold as soon as their children in their homes.

Another delegate, representing the Ganz factory in Csepel, stated:

A fortnight ago we conducted fairly thorough discussions with the Government on this matter. These talks were attended by Comrades Kadar, Apro, and Kallai. I mention Kallai because he was present throughout the talks though he did not speak once. We were given the assurance that the demands of the workers would be met. Up to the present, no steps have been taken in this matter ... Another demand of the same nature was that units of armed guards must be organized for the factories, because it is not only the government which wants guarantees from the working-class to the effect that it will not allow the return of Fascism in Hungary; the working class, too, wants guarantees that, through its being armed, no other force will be able to pervert the original and true aims of the revolution and abolish the successes that it has so far attained.

A chemical engineer, a member of the Workers Council, complained that time was being wasted in mere talks: "The ministers now seem to spend all their time receiving delegations, and the delegations leave these meetings without having achieved any results."

Minister Apro, who had opened the meeting, closed it with the assurance that the Government had no intention of dissolving the Greater Budapest Workers Council. This is, however, exactly what the Government did in its decree of 9 December.

The Yugoslav Minister Kardelj had already noted the "paradox of a Workers Government that is afraid of Workers Councils."

On 11 December, the two most outstanding labor leaders, Racz, President of the Greater Budapest Workers Council, and Bali, were both arrested, as announced in a communiqué issued by the Budapest Police Command and broadcast at 19:00 on 12 December:

Sandor Racz, the former Chairman of the proscribed Greater Budapest Workers Council, and Sandor Bali, one of its members, were called on 9 December to appear at the Budapest Police Command. Since they failed to comply, on 10 December a warrant was issued against them. On 11 December the police succeeded in tracing them. They have played a primary part in turning the Budapest Workers Council into an instrument of the counter-revolution and have striven with all their might to obstruct the restoration of order, calm, and peaceful work. They were the leaders of an illegal organisation. They organized provocations and used misled youths for leaflets against the Government. By their threats they sought to intimidate honest workers, youths, and others. In the last few days they organized an illegal conference on a national scale for which they recruited not only members of the Workers Councils, but also counter-revolutionary elements who have nothing to do with the Workers Councils. On the last occasion they called for the overthrow of the Government and, despite the sober views of the honest workers and technicians present, pushed through the provocative 48-hour general strike call. The said persons maintained close contact with the subversive "Free Europe" Radio and with Western press correspondents whom they misinformed deliberately in order to compromise the Hungarian working class and the Revolutionary Worker-Peasant Government. All these factors have made their detention necessary.

(Signed)   *The Chief Constable of Budapest*

They had, at first, been able to avoid the police, but had then agreed to go to a new meeting scheduled in the Parliament building. As they entered the Palace of the Parliament they were arrested, just as Colonel Maleter had been when he had gone to negotiate with the Russians, and as Imre Nagy and his friends had also been when they had left the Yugoslav Embassy.

The arrest of these two Labor leaders immediately led to a new wave of strikes. *Borba* published on December 12th the following dispatch from its Budapest correspondent:

...Anyone who, this morning, went out in the streets in Budapest could see that the underground was not running, and that there were no buses. In the afternoon, only one trolley-bus, of the 75 line, passed crowded with passengers across the Square of the Heroes. Later, that trolley-bus too disappeared from the streets. We were told that somebody had fired at it. On the line to Kispest, a street-car was running under the protection of military escort. In Budapest, I saw one train running on a local line; it departed, but did not return. It was alleged that the line had been blown up in one place ... In some towns demonstrations occurred. In Eger, at noon on Monday, some two thousand people marched through the town. Soviet armored cars appeared in the streets but were later withdrawn. The demonstrations continued and the masses called on the Government to repeal its latest decisions. Today, the demonstrations are continuing, as a number of new arrests were made yesterday. Several thousand people gathered in front of the Soviet High Command and demanded that all arrested workers be released. They were released, and the demonstrators went home ...

The *Manchester Guardian* of December 10th published a Reuter's despatch:

Their statement said that the arrests of the Chairman and of members of the Council were continuing. Therefore the Council resolved to order a strike to begin at midnight tonight and to last until midnight on Wednesday. The strike, it said, was in protest against the Kadar Government's "activities directed against the people and the workers." The Resolution added: "We request all members of Trade Unions to support the Hungarian workers in their fearless struggle for life and for personal freedom by organizing simultaneous strikes to express solidarity."

The strike began in the Beloyannis plant, where the arrested leaders had worked. In repressing this strike, the Russians intervened directly, as reported on December 15th in the *New York Herald Tribune*: "At the huge iron and steel works on Csepel island, south of Budapest, a Kadar Government commission and a group of Russian officers, including two colonels, seized formal authority today ... The commission declared: 'The Workers Council no longer represents the Csepel workers ...'"

In Moscow, *Pravda* wrote on December 12th: "The situation in Budapest has become somewhat more complex." This was indeed an under-statement. The order for a general strike had been followed throughout the country; the railroads were no longer functioning; and international telephone communications may have been interrupted by order of the government in order to keep the extent of the strike from being known abroad. During these days, arrests and deportations continued, according to reports gathered from refugees who flocked to Austria. Often, crowds intervened and managed to liberate the prisoners from the Russians. The most serious incident occurred at the Salgotarian mines.

At 19:00, on December 9th, Radio Budapest broadcast the following communiqué concerning the occurences:

In Salgotarjan, unfortunately, the provocation partly succeeded. Under the pretext that they wanted to set free Lajos Gal of Kisterenye, who was arrested that very same morning and who distributed anti-democratic leaflets and incited the miners to strike, and Tibor Viczian of Cuppstak who had been sentenced to 12 years' imprisonment for armed organisation against the People's Republic, they organized a demonstration against the police. They drove the workers out of the factories by force. In front of the Police HQ and the County Council the counter-revolutionary provocateurs opened fire with machine-guns and tommy-guns and threw hand grenades into the assembled crowd and at the forces of public order. This provocation caused several deaths, and several people were wounded. The counter-revolution, with similar aims in mind, has also made attempts at provocations in the past few days in Tatabanya, Bekescsaba and Battonya ...

Hungarian police riding on top of Russian armored cars fired into the crowd and there were about a hundred persons killed, among them ten women.

The dissolution of the Workers Councils and the proclamation of martial law stressed the existence of a state of open warfare between the Government and the forces of Labor and provoked a new wave of strikes. On Monday De-

---

Tactic

The tactic of "*arrest by invitation to negotiation*" is a standard Communist tool. In the aftermath of the revolution (on December 11, 1956) the chairman of the Budapest Central Workers Council, Sandor Racz, and his deputy were arrested after accepting an invitation to confer with Kadar in the Parliament building. A similar and notorious instance of the postwar era took place in March 1945 when the 16 leaders of the Polish Underground Army were arrested and taken to the Lubianka Prison in Moscow after responding to an invitation in Marshal Zhukov's name to enter talks "in an atmosphere of mutual understanding and confidence" (See Z. Stypulkowski, *Invitation to Moscow*, Thames and Hudson, London, 1951, p. 211). ...

R. L. Garthoff, *Problems of Communism* (*Washington, D. C.*), Jan.-Feb. 1957

cember 10th, the Government lauched a radio appeal "to all persons who back the regime, to place themselves immediately at the disposal of the Government in order to break the counter-revolutionary offensive." For the first time, Budapest was now without any electrical current and without postal services. "The workers are being terrorized by counter-revolutionary strikers," the Radio explained. Minister Marosan also spoke of "the writers who are terrorized by their colleagues who are in prison."

It was on 11 December that the Hungarian Delegation to the United Nations walked out of the General Assembly in protest against the "slanderous statements" made there about the Kadar Government. On 31 December, this delegation, led by Imre Horvath, quietly returned to its seats, but continued to boycott all discussions in which Hungary was mentioned. On 14 December, it was reported from Miskolc that bloodshed had occurred in the course of encounters between Russian troops and Hungarian workers.

Kadar received delegates from the Workers Councils in the various plants, and explained to them that the Workers Council of Greater Budapest "had engaged in politics" and "had raised questions concerning the political order and had thus, in the natural course of events, effectively come into conflict with the power of the State. That is why," concluded Kadar, "we are now opposed to regional Workers Councils." This was reported on 11 December by Radio Budapest, and *Nepszabadsag* commented on the event as follows:

> We do not at all doubt the existence of important elements of the Hungarian working class who are lucidly aware of the implications of the situation. But these elements have been paralyzed by the pomp and the crimes of the past few years, by the divorce between words and deeds. In the situation that has thus arisen, even honest men can find no moral foundations on which to take a stand openly. These elements, besides, are today still on the defensive, since they face masses which are undergoing the influence of chauvinistic and pseudo-democratic slogans ... It would have been completely unreasonable and contrary to the basic interests of the people to hand over political power to the Workers Council of Greater Budapest for the sole purpose of temporarily appeasing the mood of the workers...

Kadar also declared that he could not understand why the workers should demand the existence of several political parties.

> ... Some people make it appear, as one of the workers' demands, that we should permit the free functioning of all sorts of parties. I never knew that in the heart of the working class is a lively and ardent desire that these bourgeois parties should function freely ... The multiparty question must be resolved so that in our political life every honest person who wants socialism should participate. A foreign visitor who was in Budapest recently said to me that he had met many people and he was pleasantly surprised that everyone without exception told him that they wanted socialism. I said in reply that the essential point was what the person in question meant by socialism. Hitler and his followers, too, professed that they wanted socialism—but National Socialism. The Hungarian people have experienced on their own skins what that turned out to be. There are people whose conception of socialism is a thing without Communists. This, however, means a national socialism amounting to Hitlerite fascism ...   (*Radio Kossuth, 11 December*)

Scarcely had the general strike come to an end, when the workers of the Csepel steel-mills proclaimed a sit-down strike as an expression of solidarity with other strikers in a dozen Budapest plants and in order to demand again the liberation of Racz and Bali. The leaders sent an ultimatum to Kadar: "All persons arrested must be liberated, all persons deported must be brought back to Hungary. Soviet equipment must be replaced by Hungarian equipment of a better quality within six months ..." The London *Times* reported (on December 17) that: "The ultimatum then gave a table of graded increases of production according to the number of demands met. Thus, if the police and troops were evacuated from the mines within 48 hours, work would resume up to 25% of normal; if prisoners were set free in a further 48 hours, work would go up by another 33% and so on, reaching 100% when all the demands were met ..."

The Hungarian newspaper *Nepakarat* reported that 20,000 out of 84,000 miners had definitely abandoned their jobs and that, of those who remained, more than a quarter had not yet turned up for work.

The Government continued to pursue a policy of threats and promises, repression and concessions. It abolished the Stakhanovist system in the factories, promised to build ten thousand new housing-units for miners, re-established March 15th as the National holiday (in word-of-mouth propaganda, this date, which commemorates the Revolution 1848 was interpreted as forecasting the next great revolt). On 18 December, the Unions announced the repeal of collective agreements according to which the workers committed themselves to achieving a given level of production; new advantages were promised to technicians, including freedom to travel abroad. The London *Times* reported on 29 December:

The newspaper *[Nepszabadsag]* ... proposed that technical information centres should be opened in Budapest by technically developed countries, including the United States as well as Russia

But the workers continue to think of their October gains. Kadar's press could not avoid mentioning them frequently. The abolition of the "Confidential File" on each worker, entrusted to

The Women of Budapest

Budapest

The newspaper "Nepszabadsag" carried a leader entitled "Women". The writing of the article was necessitated by the major and minor demonstrations which took place in Budapest on 4 December. Women and girls were the participants ... The purpose of the demonstrations—according to the leaflets calling for them—was for relatives to pay homage to the memory of those who have fallen in the course of the fighting and to place candles on their tombs. The article states that probably the majority of the demonstrators marched into the streets with that intention. Further, however, the paper deplores yesterday's demonstrations because they only tend to aggravate the pain caused by the open fighting which came to an end some weeks ago ...

Hungarian News Agency, 5 December

Budapest

Yesterday afternoon and this morning proclamations were glued on walls calling on "Hungarian Mothers, Girls and Wives" to appear on Heroes Square at 11 a.m. today to place flowers at the Unknown Warrior's Tomb. Men were warned not to participate in the processions, and even not to appear in the streets so as to "avoid any provocations." The objective of that silent demonstration was (according to small typed and unsigned notes): "Protest against slanders calling our beloved dead 'counter-revolutionaries' and our Hungarian revolution 'fascist' ..."

The first groups of women arrived on the Square from various directions about half past ten. In columns, two or three in each line, they walked silently, calmly, carrying national and black flags. They were of all ages. Most of them wore old clothes. Many of them had baskets with food. All of them, without a single exception, had flowers in their hands.

At the same time a large number of Soviet armoured cars appeared in the streets leading to the Square. From a number of these cars which had blocked the Road of Hungarian Youth, soldiers and officers, with their weapons aimed at the women, began to push them back ...

Soviet officers called on the women to disperse. They protested. They shouted that their demonstration was peaceful, that they merely intended to pay tribute to victims of the uprising. They were again called upon to disperse. Some of the armoured cars moved in their direction, and soldiers jumped out of the cars. A shot was fired in the air. Many of the women ran back, but they soon halted again ...

Soviet officers began to talk to the women. They told them that they were not enemies. But their words could not be heard under the noise of protests. I tried to listen to the stormy dialogue, but women warned me (as well as other men who were there) that this was their, women's business, and that we should not intervene. Finally, they turned back, and returned to Andrassy Street, protesting and saying that they would demonstrate again ...

It was obvious that the Soviet troops wanted to refrain from provoking any clashes. However, during the day, reports came from all parts of town that the Soviets abducted a number of citizens. At the Kossuth Club, on the Museum Boulevard, a meeting was held of young intellectuals. Reports from various quarters indicated that a number of youths were taken away ...

... In the late afternoon, in front of the American legation, where I myself was a witness—this was at 16 hours—demonstrators sang the Hungarian anthem and Petöfi's poem about Lajos Kossuth. Soviet tanks stood at some distance and refrained from intervening. A car arrived; in it was the Indian Ambassador, Menon, visiting Budapest as a special envoy of Premier Nehru. The crowds began to shout: "Long Live Menon!" "United Nations Must Help Us!" When some people shouted "Russians Go Home!", others silenced them. Menon struggled to make his way through the crowd of demonstrators who were finally dispersed by a unit of Hungarian police ...

Borba (Belgrade), 6 December

the Personnel Section of each enterprise, had been one of these gains. *Nepszabadsag* discusses this matter on December 18th as follows:

> How many people have trembled, spent sleepless nights at the mere thought of that File, trying to guess what it might contain, the best means of finding out still being to observe whether the all-powerful chief of the Personnel Section still answered one's greetings ... Now it has been revealed that factories and offices function just as well without Personnel Sections and individual files, and there is no reason to expect that they will be reinstated. It is regrettable that such tragic events were necessary in order to come to this conclusion, but better late than never ...

It is interesting to note how this Kadar editorial formally recognizes that only the October Revolution had been able to abolish one of the most hated institutions of Rakosi's Hungary, one that represented, in the eyes of the workers, the intrusion of the political police in their daily life. And how weak the link was between actual workers and the "working-class power" of the Government is revealed by the following:

> Miners, metal-workers, unskilled laborers and skilled workers are condemned to heavy prison sentences for harboring weapons, hand-grenades, sub-machine guns, etc.... Severe sentences are pronounced in loud tones in our law-courts. For these workers, now seated on the bench of the accused, besides bums, men who evade every civic duty, pimps and plain criminals, their sentences are the first step in a long calvary that must last many years. And it remains a calvary, even if our prisons, since 1956, can no longer be compared to those of the era of Rakosi, Farkas, and Peter ... Before history, it is not the miner from Kesztölc, not the laborer from Kecskemet, who are responsilbe, but truly

---

"Name-calling"

A few weeks ago, one was given to understand, surprising as this was, that all those who had taken up arms were heroes. And today, though it is no less surprising, one is given to understand that those who then fought were all fascists. Can one truly say that the Workers Councils that have meanwhile been dissolved were all acting against the interests of the people? Can one really treat as fascists the leaders of the Workers Councils, who were known to thousands of their comrades as honorable and decent men? The moment has now come when one should stop this kind of name-calling. Tell us the truth! Mai Nap (Budapest), 18 December

---

those who have been their leaders and have brought them to this predicament ...

It is in the daily life of this working class that the explosion of October 23rd occurred. And during the days of actual fighting, one was able to observe that the industrial citadels defended with great tenacity, not the counter-revolution or the revolution, but *their own conception of revolution* ...

Many of us have been surprised to observe, in the course of this vast popular upheaval, that thousands of workers had tolerated with indifference all sorts of objectives that tended to destroy the power of the working class. But it is not because these men, women and young people did not want the power of their class, but rather because they had never felt that the regime in Hungary, of which they were destroying all the emblems, on the silk of its banners and on the pediments of its buildings, was truly a Workers' Government.

(*Nepakarat, Budapest, 19 December*)

The Workers Councils continued to consider themselves the real masters of the factories. Deprived of the support of free trade unions and of any political responsibility, they quite naturally accepted the responsibility of securing a living for the workers. Kadar accused them of wasting goods and equipment by selling them illegally, and thus of making part of the nation's production disappear into a black market. Even the semblance of democracy was abandoned. On 8 December, *Nepszabadsag* reported that the leaders of the unions had reversed the decision of the secretariat to hold elections.

In order to protest against the meddling of the Government in its own affairs, the Workers Council of the Csepel steel-mills resigned and invited the Councils of neighboring factories to follow suit. This was described as an "act of provocation," and Kadar's militia was sent to guard the entrances of the factories.

Two workers were killed by the Militiamen, and the mass firing of office employees of the Csepel concern was one of the causes of demonstrations witnessed by the last foreign correspondents left in Budapest. News of the executions fanned indignation. The East-Berlin Communist daily *Neues Deutschland* commented: "This led to considerable demonstrations by Fascist elements, which were defeated by the police." On 13 December the death-penalty was instituted for "inciting strikes." Special tribunals, composed of one judge and two jurymen, were set up in all provincial administrative centres, and Justice Minister Nezval declared: "This decree will remain in force until the honest workers have unmasked all counter-revolutionary agitators and destructive elements."

At the same time, the Government continued to carry on negotiations in order to broaden its base. But Bela Kovacs, the popular leader of the Small-holders Party, announced on 14 December that he was retiring from political life. Offers made to party leaders (with the exclusion of the Social Democrats) only served to make Kadar's isolation appear more obvious.

The correspondents of the press of the free world who had seen the workers of Csepel demonstrate with cries of *"Down with Kadar! Long live Nagy!"* were now expelled from Hungary. John MacCormac of the *New York Times,* Raymond Hörhager of the *Süddeutsche Zeitung,* the Indian journalist Emery Ray, of International News Service, and Michael Weigal of Reuters, were all expelled, and the Hungarian journalist Endre Marton and his wife, who represented the Associated Press, obtained exit visas to leave the country. From Vienna, Marton wrote in the *New York Times* (25 December):

...Mr. Kadar made his first bid for popular support when he sought conferences with Mr. Nagy. The ousted Premier was in asylum in the Yugoslav Embassy in Budapest, after the Soviet Army's sneak attack of Nov. 4 forced him from office. Mr. Nagy smuggled out a penciled message to Western correspondents to tell the world that he would have nothing to do with Mr. Kadar.

Another who snubbed Mr. Kadar then was Prof. Gyorgy Lukacs, a Marxist philosopher. He refused to become Minister of Education and preferred to accompany Mr. Nagy into exile.

But Mr. Kadar gets his biggest rebuff from the workers. This correspondent has talked with hundreds of former Communist party members—in the Csepel steel works, in the Dorog coal mines. Will they join Mr. Kadar's new party? The almost unanimous answer is no. Intellectuals give the same reply ...

The Communist press was full of lamentations:

We have to clench our fists when we hear of the dismissal of workers who sided from the beginning with continuation of work, protested against the strike and called it a folly ...

It should not be allowed that honest workers, party or non-party members, should be dismissed, leaving the loudest sharks of the counter-revolution on jobs. *(Vas Nepe, 6 January)*

A *Nepszabadsag* reporter paid a visit to the Budapest Electricity and Cable factory and reported on Party life within the factory:

The Workers Council is against the Party's organisational work. It puts obstacles in the way of the Party getting rooms in the factory. It does not invite the Party organisation to its sessions. It does not even acknowledge the existence of the Party ... They dismiss and persecute Communists, and practically force the local organisation of the Hungarian Socialist Workers Party into illegality ...
(Nepszabadsag, 23—24 January)

The refusal of workers to cooperate with the Party was described as a kind of "reign of terror and the silence of the writers, whose last manifestoes still circulated in the factories, was called "intolerable."

Finally, before the members of the Party in the 21st district of Budapest, in a speech broadcast on December 31st by Radio Budapest, Kadar openly attacked the autonomy of the Workers Councils, though this autonomy had been guaranteed time and again.

...The Workers Council of Csepel which has recently resigned had been working for the counter-revolution and not for the workers. The Workers Councils were set up during the Revolution, but certain counter-revolutionary elements joined them. We accept the institution of these Workers Councils in principle, but they must all be directed by Communists." Kadar stressed the necessity of a reconstruction of the Party which must occur as soon as it is practicable, "because the working class cannot exist without the Party." The Party, during the events in October and November, had not been able to assume its proper place, because of the presence of traitors in its ranks ...
(Neue Zürcher Zeitung, 2 January)

One can well understand why the population of Budapest commented humorously on Marosan's latest boast. On 2 February he threatened: "We are organizing a tough police force, capable of breaking every hope of a revolt, and, if necessary, I warn you, *we will arm the workers.*"

The government, in fact, had only one worry: how to disarm them.

The Resistance of the Intellectuals

Those writers who had still dared speak of freedom under Rakosi did not allow themselves now to be intimidated under Kadar. On 21 November 1956, a "Hungarian Revolutionary Council of Intellectuals" was constituted. *Nepakarat,* the newspaper of the unions, published its membership on the 27th. The famous composer Zoltan Kodaly had accepted the chairmanship, Professor Georges Markos had been nominated

Secretary, and the other members of the Presidium included the writer Tibor Dery, the Academician Dezso Keresztury, the Academician and University Professor Laszlo Gillemot, the actor Ferenc Bessenyei, the economist Ferenc Fekete, the architect Mate Major, and the Professors Tomas Nagy, Endre Nizsalovsky and Deszo Pais.

The most sacred right of literature and arts which has been achieved in the revolution is freedom and the right to tell the truth. We shall protect this right and, led by a sense of responsibility towards our people, we will avail ourselves of it and will take part, in the future, in press work, including the radio, only if its guiding principle is truthfulness and the service of the people. We shall submit this resolution to those organisations of the intelligentsia which signed the joint declaration of 12 November and we will call on them to join us.

(Signed) THE HUNGARIAN WRITERS ASSOCIATION

On 24 November a *"New Manifesto of the Hungarian Intellectuals"* was published:

"We, the intellectual workers of Hungary, desirous of remaining worthy of our great forebears, declare that we associate ourselves completely with the heroes who are pursuing the battle for the freedom of Hungary. We accept all the consequences that our acts or our words may bring upon us: prison, deportation, and, if necessary, death."

In these terms, the manifesto signed by 110 leading personalities in the cultural life of Hungary affirms the will of the nation's intelligentsia.

"We declare our solemn protest: do not deport our men, our young heroes. We demand that those who have already been arrested be released.

"We declare that we fully approve the actions of which they are accused as if they were crimes: we too, we are fighters for Hungary's freedom and independence.

"This decision to deport our compatriots is in flat contradiction with the dictates of common sense. In a free and strong Hungary, the Soviet Union would be able to maintain the relations of a good-neighbor. With an occupied or enslaved Hungary, this would never be possible.

"We do not want the restoration of the old social order. We do not want and will never tolerate the counter-revolution. We shall have the strength to defend a régime of the farmers and workers of the country, and it is with them that we wish to share in common the life that lies ahead of us in the future."

The manifesto then concludes:

"Conscious of the truth of our ideals, we appeal to the writers, artists and scientists of the Soviet Union and of the entire world."

This document was drafted on 17 November. Its publication was postponed, pending a meeting of the members of the Executive Committee of the Writers Association with the representatives of the Soviet High Command, scheduled for 20 November.

As a result, a few writers who followed the Stalinist line published a declaration in which they stated that the meeting had "positive results." This led all those who had signed the manifesto to decide to publish it in protest.

Among the 110 names of those who signed it, we find the most famous writers, artists, musicians and scientists of the country, including: the composer Zoltan Kodaly, Peter Veres, President of the Writers Association, the poet Geza Kepes (Secretary-general of the Hungarian PEN Club), the novelists Louis Kassak, Kolzsvari Grandpierre, Ladislas Nemeth, Tibor Dery, the dramatist Julius Hay, the essayist Paul Ignotus, the poet Gyula Illyes, the sculptor André Beck, the conductor Janos Ferencsik, the architect Georges Janossy, the singer Judith Sandor, and a considerable number of members of the Hungarian Academy and of professors of the various faculties of the University of Budapest.

On 31 November, the students had published their demands. The Journalists Club published a declaration of solidarity with the Writers Association, after which its premises were raided by the police.

The article—and it is the center of an affair which is symptomatic of the present situation in Hungary—has the headline: *"What We Do Not Agree With"* and the sub-heading *"Remarks on An Article* in *the Moscow 'Pravda'"* ... and it is a critique of Pravda's attack on the speech of Comrade Tito held in Pula ...

Every day a second, third and fourth "milder variant" of the article had been prepared. Every day there were new comments from the highest leaders of the party, with the promise that the article would be printed. The day before yesterday Janos Kadar definitely promised the publication of the article. A short notice in yesterday's number informed the public that the article was to appear. However, yesterday evening, after the Party committee had approved the article, but before the paper was printed, the information arrived that the article is definitively prohibited.

The paper's entire staff and many typographers were so embittered that they went home. The paper was not printed at all. The editorial rooms remained empty.

(Politika, Belgrade, 25 November)

On 12 December, the Writers Association protested against the arrests of writers and journalists —Dajos Tamasi, a poet, who was released soon after, Gyula Obersovsky, who had edited in October the newspaper *Igazsag*, and Zoltan Molnar. One of the rare "Rakosist" writers, Bela Illyes, who had been a colonel in the Red Army and became a Soviet citizen, had given a statement to André Stil, editor of *L'Humanité*, then in Budapest, in order to declare that he did not share the views of the majority of his colleagues and supported, on the contrary, the Kadar régime. The same Bela Illyes wrote, however, in the Christmas issue of *Nepszabadsag*, an open letter to Minister of the Interior Ferencz Munnich, which was ignored by the French Communist press, though the latter had widely publicized his earlier letter. In his second open letter, Illyes pleaded on behalf of his arrested colleagues:

In the course of the night of 1 November, when the Soviet troops had already evacuated Budapest, I had a telephone conversation with Gyula Illyes, who knew that I was in disagreement with him on a great number of matters, but realized that I believe firmly in the cause for which I work and that I was at that time in a very difficult position, threatened even with death. He offered me money, food and, within the limits of his means, his protection. He explained to me why he was particularly anxious to come to my assistance, as he felt himself bound to do so in the light of his devotion to democratic ideals. This conversation taught me many things. But others, besides myself, can learn much from Illyes. We Communists, we cannot allow ourselves to be outdone by anybody in the matter of humanitarian ideals. We cannot allow ourselves to be behind our friends in this respect, as we would then lose our right to act on behalf of the people ... A few Hungarian writers and journalists have been arrested by the Hungarian authorities. I do not know what they are accused of, but I know them as men. They are no enemies of ours! The real enemy is indeed pleased to see that the authorities, instead of concerning themselves ʾth him, are now wasting their time on a few writers. It is not as an appeal to sentiment that I demand the release of these writers and journalists, but in order to serve the interests of the government ... We do not have the right to condemn a writer as an enemy simply because he can see but one half of the truth and of reality, or even less. If we act in this manner, we harm ourselves as much as him. Comrade Munnich, you know that a reprieve, if well administered, strikes a harder blow at the adversary than all energetic measures that are questionable or doubtful ...

In the same issue, the Minister answered this appeal and explained: "There exist no privileges for counter-revolutionaries whose profession happens to be that of writing."

The appeal launched by the Hungarian writers in favor of George Lukacs, who had been deported with Imre Nagy, was picked up by Yugoslav writers:

We have been informed through an appeal on the part of the Hungarian Writers Association, which was sent to us from Budapest a few days

Escape

Towards the end of November, members of the Central Revolutionary Council and the leading writers were driven underground. Our ranks were already decimated by arrests and deportations. Further arrests occured daily.

It was decided that some of us should try to escape and speak up abroad for our people. I was one of those chosen.

In the last days of November the frontier was already crammed with Russian tanks and AVO monsters. The problem was how to escape with my wife and year-old son. I could not risk challenge by Russian or AVO guards on the route. We had to choose a swampy region of the frontier where even the Russians do not like to wade about. We made a fur sack for the baby. A doctor gave us medicine to make him sleep during the long frontier passage. We were joined by my friend and former prison-companion Paul Ignotus — another writer — and his wife.

It was a stormy night when a group of thirty-three of us entered the swampy frontier region. We waded knee-deep in mud and water. The Russians kept sending up flares. Machine guns rattled in the distance. Each step was an enormous physical effort. With my son on my shoulder, and my wife at my side, we struggled on for hours. At one point, all our strength was gone and we lay down on a drier piece of land, where the mud was only ankle deep. There I lay, holding my little son in my arms and looking up at the stormy sky in despair. After an hour or so, we gathered enough strength to start wading again.

By now we were alone in no man's land. Then we saw swiftly-moving shadows: another group of escapees. They helped us on.

We struggled with the swamp for another two hours. Then, at last, an Austrian flag — and a haystack! We collapsed.

George Paloczi-Horvath, *Daily Herald* (London), 12 December

ago, that the distinguished Hungarian philosopher and writer, whose works are valued throughout the world as a contribution to contemporary culture and progress, "has been deported to an unknown place." We are concerned about his fate... His age makes his deportation still more incomprehensible... We demand that Lukacs be set free as soon as possible.

We believe that it is the duty of Yugoslav authors to make this appeal, the more so because Lukacs has been taken away immediately after he left the Yugoslav Embassy of his own free will [November 18], where he had taken refuge on November 4...   *(Borba, 14 December)*

The "sit-down strike" of the Hungarian writers who had remained silent and refused to publish anything since November was felt by the Government to be an other act of "provocation."

At a meeting in Pecs, Hungarian Minister of State György Marosan warned students against allowing themselves "to be exploited by counter-revolutionary elements in order to achieve reactionary aims." The demands of the students for the freedom of the Universities were unnecessary, as the Government was already doing everything in its power in order to promote the interests of the schools and institutes of higher education of Hungary...

Marosan then attacked the writers and journalists and declared that the Government would break every form of resistance without the slightest hesitation. The Government had waited long and been patient, in the hope that some writers might yet modify their opinions and recognize at last the dangers of the Counter-revolution. Some of them, however, had interpreted the Government's patience as weakness, and this was why the Administration would now have to adopt sharper counter-measures. The Minister then stressed the fact "all counter-revolutionary, bourgeois, nationalistic and anarchistic tendencies in Hungarian publications would be ruthlessly repressed." This was a necessity, and the Government would guarantee freedom and its protection only to those writers and journalists "who work in the spirit of Socialism and on the basis of a People's Democracy." The writers should at long last free themselves from the "spiritual terror" of their colleagues who were under arrest...

(Süddeutsche Zeitung, 29 December)

What the "literary strike" meant can be observed by examining the press of the Hungarian capital; it published only obscure names and anonymous articles. The Kadar government felt that its prestige was seriously affected by this silence. The Writers Association, meanwhile, did not hesitate to publicize its disapproval of the régime imposed on the country. The Communist weekly *Lettres Françaises* thus published on 27 December a letter to this effect. The Paris weekly added a long and embarrassed commentary, remarking on "the extreme confusion that exists at the present time in relationships between the writers of our two countries."

In a closed session held on 28 December, the Hungarian Writers Association condemned the Soviet intervention in their country as an "historic mistake." Of 250 writers, only eight opposed this resolution. The Association's Secretary, Sandor Erdei, observed that six writers were still in prison, and expressed the gratitude of the country's writers towards the farmers who had continued to supply them with food while they were striking and earning no pay.

The time will come, declares the Hungarian Writers Association of writers, when the USSR will regret its error. On Friday in Budapest, at its first meeting since the Revolution, over two hundred Hungarian writers participated. After unanimously adopting several resolutions that only six members opposed, the Association approved a manifesto that declares, among other matters: The Revolution of October 23rd is the spring that surged from the sufferings and the desire for freedom of the Hungarian people. It is with bitterness that we now affirm that the Soviet Government committed a grave and historic error when it polluted with blood the waters of this spring. We dare proclaim that the day will come when this mistaken power will repent its error...   *(Le Monde, 30 December)*

On 17 January 1957, Minister Munnich announced the "temporary" dissolution of the Writers Association; this was followed by the seizure of the Journalists Club. Other writers were arrested, and threatened with the heaviest martial law penalties. Here is an incomplete list of writers and journalists arrested between 4 November 1956 and 24 January 1957:

Zoltan Molnar, Gyula Fekete, Secretary of the Union of Writers, Aneras Sandor, Joseph Gall, Miklos Obersovsky, Julius Hay, Zoltan Zetzk, Tibor Tardos, Balazs Lengyel, Domokos Varka, Sandor Novobaczky.

François Fejto published this list in *France Observateur* (24 January) and noted:

This strike still continues. One seeks in vain the signature of any reputed writer in all the official newspapers and periodicals. The voluminous Christmas issue of *Nepszabadsag* was published without a single article or poem or story by any known living writer...

The Government then declared war on the writers. The Minister of Agriculture, Dojei, declared, as reported in the *Neue Zürcher Zeitung,* that "the majority of Hungarian writers has chosen the path of treason." Kadar announced "a well-deserved punishment".

A few days earlier, the leaders of the Hungarian Students' organization Mefesz had been arrested, and this organization had been prevented by the police from any further activity. A new Youth Association that had never been heard of previously suddenly appeared to publish resolutions condemning the attitude of the students.

The Communist press of the other Soviet satellites continued to rage against the Hungarian writers. East Berlin's *Neues Deutschland* published, on 31 January, an interview of its correspondent, Werner Kolmar, with Bela Illyes, "On the Present Situation in Hungarian Literature":

Bela Illyes declared:

... Now, five weeks later, we must admit that Comrade Munnich was right. During all this period, it has become clear that appeals have been published illegally, in the form of leaflets, inviting the workers to strike and to commit acts of sabotage. The paper for these leaflets had been supplied by the Writers Association, and the texts had been drafted by some of the leading members of the Association. But this is not the whole story.

Some members of the Association, including myself, had defended the Kadar Government in French newspapers and had published there rebuttals of certain foul and fantastic lies broadcast by the Free Europe Radio and by the B.B.C. The Presidium of the Writers Association protested against our explanations, although it knew perfectly well that everything that we had published in France corresponded to the truth. The same Presidium, on the other hand, found no necessity to protest when a number of Hungarian writers who had fled to the West declared, in a Radio Munich broadcast, that the Hungarian writers—not a few Hungarian writers but all of them—were fighting against Communism, against Soviet Russia, and against the People's Democracies. Of course, these people are forced to utter such lies, according to the demands of their American masters ...

I would like to add a few words about the situation in publishing. The program for the publishers for 1957 had been worked out during the critical days of October and still reflects the picture of those days. The so-called 'Revolution' removed from this program all Soviet authors, nearly all Hungarian Communists, and all the best representatives of literature from the People's Democracies. To replace them, they discovered a whole series of 'new' works and of disgraceful commercial literature. Sholokhov was suppressed, but replaced by Vicki Baum; Gorki was suppressed, but the Tarzan books published in his stead. And such is the real face of this 'Revolution,' which has provoked so much enthusiasm among a few writers in the West ...

Bela Szabo, the Government Commissar who henceforth managed the affairs of the Journalists Association, declared that it would continue its activities: "Only its autonomy is temporarily abolished."

In February, the University of Budapest finally opened its doors again.

Radio Budapest broadcast on Sunday night a declaration of the Hungarian Minister of Education Albert Konya concerning the reopening of the Hungarian Universities. All the Universities of the nation resumed their activities on Monday morning for the first time since the Revolution of 23 October.

The Deputy Minister for Education, Gyula Kallai, who is also a member of the Executive Committe of the Communist Party, added another declaration, stating that the Universities would be closed again at the first sign of any disturbance. Those students who had caused difficulties would immediately be dismissed. And all students who instigated disturbances in the future could no longer be considered to have merely been led astray ...

(Neue Zürcher Zeitung, 5 February)

The atmosphere in the schools was described as "deplorable." The few children of Communists had to face the hostility of the other children; and those who failed to follow religious instruction were placed in "moral quarantine." According to *Nepszabadsag* on February 2nd:

An atmosphere hostile to teachers prevails throughout the country. Many local organizations, even some local leaders of the Hungarian Socialist Workers Party, believe that every teacher was a counter-revolutionary and that the teachers staged the revolution ...

The commentator Gyorgy Kalmar described, in *Nepszabadsag* of 6 February, the inextricable confusion that existed:

One has experienced more than once that there are persons who did not learn from the old bitter mistakes and did not understand that dictatorship of the proletariat can not consist only of dictatorship. When will they get rid of this dangerous one-sidedness which keeps away so many people from the Party?

When will they understand that the counter-revolution did not do the most serious damage with weapons? *The most difficult and complicated thing is to undo and clean the almost inextricable ruin and disturbance caused in the mind.*

A New Party?

As the Kadar Government had not obtained the recognition of the Hungarian Parliament, and as it was not founded on the revolutionary Workers Councils which, when the new government was imposed, provided the real leadership in the country, some kind of appearance of legitimacy was needed to allow the government to assume the leadership of the masses. It was therefore urgently necessary to reconstitute a political party. As Minister Marosan explained (as reported by the *Neue Zürcher Zeitung* on 2 February): "The reconstruction of the Party constitutes the fourth phase of the return to normalcy." The first three phases were (1) armed repression of the Revolt, (2) the renewal of contacts with the other Communist nations, and (3) the reorganization of the Police.[1]

The name of "Hungarian Workers Party" had been abandoned. The new party was called "Socialist Workers Party." Its membership is open to all those who recognize Marxism-Leninism as their doctrine and who want "a brotherly unity founded on equality with all Socialist nations."

> The Hungarian Socialist Workers Party builds its activity first and foremost on the basis of former members and organizations of the Hungarian Workers Party ...

Exceptions were made in the case of those who committed "serious political mistakes under the Rakosi clique or who have persecuted honest Communists in October." This excluded active supporters of Rakosi, and all the supporters of Imre Nagy. Kadar wanted, above all, a smaller and more compact party, but his Government was soon forced to bring pressure to bear on civil servants to make them join the new Party if only to keep their jobs. *Nepszabadsag* commented on 12 December:

> The Communists in Pecs have a difficult task. They have to face mass feelings, and even among the Communists every individual has to be won over individually, as the past twelve years have made the workers sceptical.

It was difficult to convince the sceptics.

> Communist workers are organizing demonstrations in which they proclaim their support

of the Government, but their slogans, and the rare echoes that they rouse, remain weak. All ask why it is necessary to paint the devil on the wall. Why is every demand for freedom called counter-revolutionary diversionism?

> (*Bronislav Dadic, "Nin", Belgrade, 16 December*)

The complications mounted. *Nepszabadsag* reported on 10 January: "Many people join the new Party in the hope of thus avoiding the loss of their jobs or, if they still lose their jobs, in order to blame this loss on anti-communist persecutions." Others made a point of refusing to enter the Party for fear of being called opportunists or cowards.

We have already had occasion to denounce the disgraceful situations that arise as a consequence of the attitude of certain Communist leaders who use the threat of firing a man as an enticement in order to recruit him as a miltant member of the Party. They force men who have no political convictions at all to enter the Party, and they thus justify the view according to which the new party is already using the methods of the old one. ...

On 31 December, *Nepszabadsag* reported that 12 % of the members of the former Workers Party have been recovered by the new party and that party organizations have already been set up in 42 % of the nation's villages. This amounted to admitting that the Party still did not exist at all in a majority of villages. The new Party was generally considered to be still-born, and an Italian correspondent described it as such:

> Not only will Kadar have to do without the cooperation of other parties such as the Smallholders Party, but now he lacks even the cooperation of his own party. As a result of a careful check made in the past few days, it has been observed, for instance, that out of one hundred and twenty organizations registered with the Central Committee of the Hungarian Communist Party, only eighteen have now registered with the new Communist Party. And out of these eighteen, at least two-thirds may turn out to be definitely Rakosi-minded. Even in the restricted circles of the members of his own government, Kadar cannot move with much ease. Ronai, the President of the National Assembly, at present Minister for Commerce, has several times tried to offer his resignation. As much can be said of the Minister of Finance, Kossa. The new Kadar Party has simply not yet come into being.

> It is known that the workers in some factories have until now prevented the posting of all declarations and communiqués of the new party. Of the three thousand workers in the

---

[1] On 23 March, in Csepel, Marosan claimed that he had been "the man who asked for the intervention of Soviet troops" on 4 November.

Questions and Facts

London

To the Editor of PRAVDA

We, the undersigned members of the British Parliamentary Labour party, who in the past have always worked for a better understanding between our two countries, are deeply distressed at the use of Soviet armed forces in Hungary. We therefore ask for this opportunity to express our view to Soviet readers and to put certain questions to you about the events in Hungary.

First of all, your newspaper has portrayed the Hungarian uprising as "counter-revolutionary." May we ask exactly what you understand by this expression? Does it include all systems of government which permit political parties whose programmes are opposed to that of the Communist party? If, for example, the Hungarian people were to choose a parliamentary system similar to those in Finland and Sweden, would you regard that as counter-revolutionary?

Secondly, you said on November 4 that the Government of Imre Nagy "had in fact disintegrated." Did you mean by this that it resigned or that it was overthrown? If it was overthrown with the help to Soviet arms, does this not amount to Soviet interference in Hungary's internal affairs?

Thirdly, do you consider that the present Government of Janos Kadar enjoys the support of the majority of the Hungarian people? Would it make any difference to your attitude if it did not? We ask this question because on November 15, according to Budapest radio, Janos Kadar said that his Government hoped to regain the confidence of the people but that "we have to take into account the possibility that we may be thoroughly beaten at the elections."

Fourthly, we recall that the Soviet Union has repeatedly advocated the right of all countries to remain outside military blocks. Does this right to choose neutrality extend, in your view to members of the Warsaw pact?

Finally, you have said that the Hungarian uprising was planned long in advance by the West and you have in particular blamed Radio Free Europe. Are you seriously suggesting that masses of Hungarian workers and peasants were led by these means into organising mass strikes aimed at restoring the power of feudal landlords and capitalists?...

Fenner Brockway, Barbara Castle, George Wigg, Dick Crossman, Anthony Wedgwood Benn

Moscow

Gentlemen, the nature of the majority of the questions put in your letter in connection with recent events in Hungary is such that, in our opinion, you should write not to the editor of "Pravda" but to the appropriate Hungarian organisation...

The counter-revolutionary nature of the rebellion in Hungary was noted, before it was so described in our newspaper, by the then leaders of Hungary... In the days that followed, the counter-revolutionary nature of the rebellion was revealed and pointed out in the speeches made by Janos Kadar and others... It was not a question of establishing a "parliamentary system similar to the one in Finland or Switzerland," but of the restoration of the Fascist regime in Hungary. This became obvious in the course of events when Horthyist officers dreaming of a military dictatorship, land-owners demanding the return of land nationalised by the people's regime, and capitalists who wanted once again to take into their own hands enterprises which had become the property of the people, came to the forefront...

On November 1 the former members of the Imre Nagy Government, that is, Antal Apro, Janos Kadar, Istvan Kossa, and Ferenc Munnich, broke with this Government... When this group of Ministers left the Nagy Government, this Government in effect ceased to exist as such and disintegrated...

It is well-known that declarations of support for the Kadar Government were also made by Hungarian trade unions, workers' councils at enterprises, workers' youth organisations, Army officers, and others. These are facts which are difficult to refute... The facts which came to light in the course of the Hungarian events revealed the machinery of subversion against the Socialist nations which had been set in motion with the hope of American dollars...

Your letter betrays a manifest intention to present matters in such a way as if the Hungarian people had sided with the counter-revolutionaries. This was not so. The working masses of Hungary, far from supporting the counter-revolutionaries, came out against them with determination... We hope that a more careful study of the facts connected with the Hungarian event may help you to discard harmful misconceptions...

The Editorial Board of PRAVDA
*Pravda (Moscow), 10 February 1957;
Manchester Guardian, 11 February 1957*

largest rubber works in Hungary (situated in the Kerepetsi Street in Budapest) not one worker has registered as a member of the new so-called Hungarian Socialist Worker's Party. ...

(*Corriere della Sera, Milan, 16 January*)

The situation of the Kadar communists, in the face of this general moral quarantine, was vaguely discussed by the Hungarian press, which expressed, or pretended to express, its consternation over this state of affairs. In *Magyar Ifujsag* of February 2nd, for instance, a woman teacher from Budapest complained to an interviewer that, since she joined the party, her colleagues all boycott her: "If I go into the teachers' Common Room, they all stop talking. An ice-cold, impenetrable dividing wall rises between us. I know why they turn away from me. It is because they have found out that I have joined the Party. I am the only Communist teacher in our school. I walk among my colleagues like someone who has been branded ..."

A New Justice, a New Police

On 26 November Kadar broadcast the following statement on Radio Budapest:

Recently we have frequently heard about the demand for a life without fear. We wish and we work for the speedy and complete restoration of legal order throughout the country and in all spheres of life. The primary conditions already exist for this. We feel that with the support of all law-abiding honest citizens who desire public order that in a short time we shall be in a position to say: We have resolved this task. And we shall also be able to say that we have ensured for all law-abiding citizens in the Republic a life without fear. I must frankly say that it is not quite the case today. ...

Kadar added in this very same declaration:

In the interest of the working people and in the defence of the State order of the People's Republic, the Government considers it a primary task, and will carry through without wavering, the *hunting up, rendering harmless and bringing to justice of all counter-revolutionaries, counter-revolutionary inciters and persons who have committed ordinary criminal acts, who may yet be in hiding.* In this question we will not yield or bargain, as this would mean a deadly sin against our people and our State. ...

Thus, the regime came to rely mainly on the reorganized police force and on special decrees applied by a somewhat reticent judiciary, often blamed for its untimely humanitarianism. In an interview with the Public Prosecutor Geza Szenasi (broadcast on 23rd November):

I see the greatest change in that their duty of prosecuting crime will not contradict the priciples of deep humanitarianism. The prosecutors' work of general supervision must be extended because we want to give legal aid to the whole population in all domains of life. We shall systematically visit places of work, and take immediate steps against those who commit illegal acts. We rely in our work on the working people's sense of justice and on the rule of law ...

Our most important duty is to set free, as soon as possible, those people who were arrested by mistake during the counter-revolution. Apart from this, we have elaborated an extensive Amnesty Bill in association with the Ministry of Justice, and submitted it to the Presidential Council ...

Several months later, on the occasion of his official assumption of duties as public prosecutor, Geza Szenasi made a public speech (reported in *Nepszadsag* on 2 February):

The militia should make it clear to fascists, either summarily or in the course of a court procedure, or even in the streets, that it is not good business for them to oppose the militia ...

He also spoke about arrested would-be refugees:

All those who were arrested for illegal border crossing will be handed over to the courts. What we hitherto called humanitarianism would become a harmful liberalism from now on. Till now we did not apply our laws — out of indulgence — but from now on these laws will be applied. ...

Martial law had been proclaimed as early as 9 December, in two decrees signed by President Istvan Dobi, who at the same time dissolved the Workers Militia units that had until then existed in the factories. On 12 December, the Budapest Radio broadcast an amendment to one of these decrees:

If the accused is declared guilty by the summary court of justice on any of the charges falling within the categories of martial law, the verdict at the same time involves the imposition of the death sentence. The amendment comes into force at the time of its promulgation. ...

On 14 December, all public meetings were subjected to police authorization. On 20 December, the police was again granted the authority to intern at will in concentration camps for periods up to six months. A request made on 17 December by the British Bar Association to the Hungarian government for assurances that adequate defence would be guaranteed to all persons accused, was not considered worthy of an answer.

Leaders who had become prominent during the October Revolution, Joszef Dudas and Janos Szabo, were executed at dawn on 19 December. The official communiqué stated that all the witnesses at the trial, including those summoned by the accused themselves, had proven their guilt without question. At first, the idea of "tolerance" had not been entirely foreign. There had been some talk of an "amnesty" for actions undertaken during the turmoil of October. True, a just retribution had also been promised for the worst henchmen of the Rakosi regime, in particular for the police officials Gabor Peter and Farkas, father and son; but the Hungarian press now reported that these police officials received visits in their prison cells and that the preparation of their trial was proceeding very slowly. They at least were able to appreciate the humanitarian spirit and the concern for scrupulous legality that animated the Government.

Nor was the trial of Matyas Rakosi mentioned any longer, though *Nepakarat* had stressed on 21 November its extreme urgency.

The new political police was called *Karhatalom*, and the régime seemed to be only too willing to change the names of institutions rather than to modify the institutions themselves. The newspaper *Nepakarat* condemned, on 19 December, this tendency to perpetuate methods that had been in force under Rakosi.

> Our editorial offices receive many of our readers who visit us in order to report to us grievances that we cannot ignore. . . . Managers of factories solicit our help in order to find out what has happened to some of their colleagues. After complicated enquiries, we find out that the missing persons are in the prisons of Marke Street or of Fö Street, that they have not yet been given a proper hearing days after their arrest, and that nobody has shown them a warrant for their arrest. Lawyers also come to tell us that they cannot manage, for weeks on end, to obtain an interview with their imprisoned client, and that the authorities pretend to be ignorant even of the place where these clients are held incommunicado. . . .

In March arrests of Protestant ministers and residents of student dormitories were reported. Thousands were being detained in concentration camps. On 19 March the "Official Gazette" of the Kadar Government published an order for the banishment of citizens considered "dangerous." On 15 February the Government announced that

21 executions had taken place; a month later the Commissioner of Justice stated that by 23 February there had been 40 death sentences, but a former government official who escaped testified that more than 200 persons had been executed by the end of March. A show trial in Budapest, during which defendants stubbornly refused to recant on their views of the revolution, ended on April 8 with three death sentences and prison terms ranging up to ten years. In restoring the arbitrary methods of a terror regime, no pretence was made to distinguish them from the Rakosi system from which they were copied.

The Army also played its part in repressions, which constituted the only conceivable form of enforcing public order for the time being. Every officer had to sign an oath of loyalty to serve the Kadar regime. According to Major-General Geza Uszta, 80 % of the officers had signed it. The judges were constantly criticized for not applying rigorously enough the new legislation. Among the many persons imprisoned, one finds, in addition to writers and journalists, more than four hundred members of the Workers Councils, as was reported in the London *Times* on 21 January. Many homes were searched after dark by the police, and all private mail was again subjected to censorship. On 2 February the London *Observer* reported:

Girl of 20 Hanged

BUDAPEST. — Two people, one a girl of 20, were hanged to-day for organising and leading armed bands during riots in December, reported the newspaper *Esti Hirlap* this evening. The same paper also stated that 10 Supreme Court judges have been relieved of their posts. No reason was given.

Under such conditions, it seemed entirely superfluous when Minister Marosan took the trouble to announce that a reign of terror was about to be instituted by the Government. The amnesty promised to the Freedom Fighters was annulled and the Public Prosecutor declared: *"We have two paths ahead of us, a merciless government or a state of chaos."*

Actually, terror and chaos were not alternatives that excluded each other; instead, they conditioned each other. Kadar wanted to rule Hungary, or had to rule it, according to the very methods that led to the October outbursts. His Government had invented no new methods, and he found no new personalities to work with him but, first and foremost, the police officials and the boondogglers whose very existence was bound even more closely than before to the perpetuation of the Soviet occupation of their fatherland. The country was not yet pacified, as shown by the military precautions which had to be taken to prevent popular demonstrations on the March 15th anniversary of the revolution of 1848. Kadar's secret policemen still ran the risk of being shot down in the streets, and on 16 and 17 March *Nepszabadsag* was still complaining bitterly against the continuing boycott of communists in many offices and factories.

Hungary: The Open Wound

An attempt to impose on a whole nation a regime that no fraction of its people was willing to accept could only lead to serious international repercussions. In the eyes of the free nations, Hungary remained an occasion for remorse and a permanent tragic reminder. In the Communist world, observers began to detect the infectious progress of a "Hungarian disease" that affected, above all, the younger generation of intellectuals. From Moscow, Dresden, Sofia, Bucharest, and even Prague, there came proofs of a new ferment at work in the minds of people. The Communist Parties in the democratic nations were, meanwhile, going through a crisis as they lost more and more members, especially among the intellectuals and in those Labor Unions on which they had once exerted a stranglehold. The Hungarian revolution posed clear problems to which the Communist regimes (except in Poland) proposed only answers derived from the past. In Yugoslavia, Milovan Djilas, the former Vice-president, was condemned to three years in prison for having dared to write, in the New York periodical *The New Leader*, that the Hungarian revolt revealed a crisis in the ruling bureaucratic class of all Communist States. At the same time, manifestos published by writers and students circulated in Madrid and Barcelona and demanded democracy for Hungary — and for Spain! ...

Within the United Nations, an increasing number of Asian and African nations voted in favor of resolutions which condemned the Soviet intervention in Hungary. On 3 December, in the General Assembly, the delegate of Ceylon, Mr. Gunewardene, asked whether "Marshall Bulganin, who suggests the recourse to armed force in order to drive the aggressors out of Egypt, would likewise allow United Nations forces to drive the aggressors out of Hungary." Imre Horvath, Minister of Foreign Affairs in the present Hungarian Government and chief of the Hungarian delegation to the United Nations, accepted in principle the forthcoming visit to Budapest of the Secretary-General of the Assembly, Dag Hammarskjöld, even fixing with him the date of 16 December. But the Budapest Government immediately cancelled this visit and, on 6 December, the official Hungarian News Agency, MTI, declared: "Mr. Hammarskjold will not come to Budapest on December 16th as this date is not convenient to the Hungarian Government."

On 10 December, in further discussions in the United Nations, the delegate of Peru spoke of the "curtain of blood" that had now replaced the Iron Curtain. The chief of the Indian delegation, Krishna Menon, invited the Russians to withdraw their troops from Hungary, "because such a move would be in conformity with the wishes of the majority of the Hungarian people." He also asked the Soviet leaders to understand that "the power of the USSR in Europe depends on the willing cooperation of its neighbors, whereas their refusal to cooperate is capable of breaking the most powerful domination." Menon subsequently voted against the resolution which condemned Soviet Russia and proposed an amendment to this resolution, in agreement with Burma, Ceylon and Indonesia.

On 12 December, the resolution condemning Soviet Russia was accepted by 55 delegations out of the 76 that took part in the vote. Burma and Ceylon voted in favor of the resolution, Menon having previously withdrawn his amendment.

Concerning the proposal made by the Indian Minister, to the effect that a Secretary-General of the Assembly be entrusted with the mission of mediating between Moscow and Budapest in order to eliminate the "non-cooperation" that continued to characterize the crisis between the Hungarian government and the people of Hungary, the Danish delegate Jakobsen declared: "What you define as non-cooperation, I call outright murder!"

On 12 December the Hungarian delegation, led by Mr. Horvath, walked out of the General Assembly, declaring that the Hungarian Government has been "deeply offended" by speeches that were "incompatible with the dignity" of the Hungarian nation. The Western press became more and more outspoken in its criticisms of Mr. Hammarskjöld and of his failure to undertake any greater effort in order to make his own mission or that of a team of observers possible in Budapest.

The Swiss newspaper *National-Zeitung*, of Basel, and the *New York Herald Tribune* both asked why Mr. Hammarskjöld did not simply inform the Hungarian Government of his forthcoming arrival in Budapest on a specific date. The feeling that the free world and the United Nations were not doing all that they could to help Hungary was expressed in December by the entire non-Communist press of the Western world.

Pandit Nehru, on 13 December, submitted new information to the Indian Parliament, based on reports received from the Indian representatives in Hungary, P. K. S. Mennon and Dr. Khosla. There was no doubt, he said, that the revolution in Hungary was a national movement, in which the great majority of industrial workers and students took part in the city of Budapest and elsewhere. That was a basic fact. It appeared that 25,000 Hungarians had died in the fighting. The damage in Budapest was as heart-rending as the damage which occurred in wartime. Mr. Nehru concluded that "so long as foreign troops remain there it is difficult for the local people to come together and function properly."

From January 4th to 7th, a mission of the United Nations led by Philippe de Seynes was in Budapest to undertake an enquiry into the country's economic situation and its need of assistance. On 8 January, a resolution, proposed by the United States and by 23 other governments, suggested that a committee of five be set up to hear the testimonies of Hungarian refugees. Two days later, this committee was created by a vote of 59, with 8 opposed and 10 abstentions. The five members selected were: Australia, Ceylon, Denmark, Tunisia, and Uruguay.

Philippe de Seynes submitted his report on 18 January. In his opinion, assistance of some thirty million dollars was urgently needed, and the food situation threatened to become serious in the spring.

Before the new Committee of Five, Mrs. Anna Kethly appeared as a witness on 29 January, and again asked to be recognized as Hungarian delegate to the United Nations, as a member of that country's last legally constituted government. The former Mayor of Budapest, Mr. Kovago, then appeared on 30 January and expressed the bitter disappointment of his compatriots; and General Bela Kiraly, who had been commander-in-chief of the Hungarian National Guard during the October uprising, submitted information on how Hungary had been prepared as a base for aggression against the Western world.

The Hungarian government, in a memorandum of eleven pages on February 6th, protested against "tendentious" information disseminated by exiled Hungarian anti-Communists. The U.S. representative declared:

"If the Hungarian Government complains that only one side of the case is being presented, why doesn't it ask the Committee to come to Budapest and talk to the people there?"

(New York Times, 7 February)

Meanwhile, Soviet Russia and the "reliable" People's Democracies gave Kadar their full support. Between the 1st and the 4th of January, a Conference was held in Budapest, with the participation of the Ministers and Party chiefs of the USSR, Hungary, Bulgaria, Rumania and

---

The Pose and the Mask

We do not speak of a Hungarian Revolution. We speak of the Hungarian agony. From the moment when the Communist regime in Budapest fired upon an unarmed crowd and turned its quarrel with the Hungarian people from a political quarrel which it could not win into an armed revolt which, with Soviet aid, it could not lose, the suppression of the Hungarian resistance was inevitable. The world seemed to feel that it had no choice, short of atomic war, but to sit back and watch, in horror and disgust, the brutal, methodical destruction of an angry people by overwhelming force and conscienceless treachery.

It is understandable, certainly, that we in the United States should feel shamed by our inability to act in this nightmare. Nevertheless, we should not forget, in all the suffering and pain, that we owe the people of Hungary more than our pity. We owe them also pride and praise. For their defeat has been itself a triumph. Those Hungarian students and workers and women and fighting children have done more to close the future to Communism than armies or diplomats had done before them. They have given more and done more. For what they have done has been to expose the brutal hypocrisy of Communism for all of Asia, all of Africa, all the world to see. So long as men live in any country who remember the murder of Hungary, Soviet Russia will never again be able to pose before the world as the benefactor of mankind. The Hungarian dead have torn that mask off. Their fingers hold its tatters in their graves.

ARCHIBALD MacLEISH, *Time-Life Supplement (New York), 10 December*

The Students of Storkow

Berlin

Fifteen senior students from Eastern Germany fled to West Berlin over Christmas as a result of having demonstrated their sympathy for the Hungarian revolution. For this they were expelled from the school by the Communist Minister of Education, Fritz Lange (SED), and their class was dissolved. Except for five girls (who also took part in the demonstration) the entire class has fled the Zone. The students were to take their final Abitur-diploma in several months; all were members of the FDJ (Communist Youth organisation).

Two of the high-school students, interviewed in a West Berlin refugee camp, related how it occurred.

The twenty students, fifteen boys and five girls, of the Kurt Steffelbauer High-School in Storkow, a small town in Mark Brandenburg, knew that Soviet tanks had intervened in the Hungarian fight for freedom when they went to school on Monday, 5 November. They had the news from a West-Berlin radio broadcast. As the history teacher Mogel entered the room to begin a lesson about Germany's "November Revolution", in 1918, the large clock on the front class-room wall showed 9:45 a.m. When the clock struck 10, suddenly the class froze still.

For a while, the teacher continued, ignoring the unusual silence of his students, but when he noticed forty eyes fixed on the clock, he turned to the secretary of the FDJ group: "What's the silence all about, Gisela?" The girl kept mute until the hand of the clock reached five minutes past ten. Then she answered: "Nothing."

After this the lessons took a normal course.

In the absence of a teacher the next day, Tuesday, 6 November, the class had to manage for two hours on its own. A new demonstration began ... A discussion followed, first about the "Halbstarke" (Teddy-boy) problem, and then about political events. This discussion was calm and disciplined, the refugees said; they condemned the assult of Soviet tanks in Hungary just as they did the Anglo-French intervention and Israel's invasion of Egypt. In addition, Walther Ulbricht was called a "ridiculous figure" ...

Nothing happened for several days ... Then on 10 November, seven members of the class were summoned, one by one, into the principal's office. "Who was the ins-

tigator of the fascist provocation?" None of the seven answered. Later the school-inspector, the principal, and the history teacher appeared in class. One very excited student greeted them with the charge that the cross-examinations had seemed pretty much like "Gestapo methods". In the name of the class, he said, he had to condemn this ... The principal answered aggressively: "That's enough of that. You no longer have the floor. Sit down. That's no way to talk to your principal. We'll come back to you later."

The SED (Communist Party) Central Committee and the Minister of Education Lange had heard of the incidents, and on 13 December, Lange made an unexpected appearance in Storkow. The Minister talked for four hours with the twenty students about "what really happened in Hungary", using tactics of "friendly persuasion" and "enlightenment", in vain ...

In an uncontrollable rage Lange shouted at the students: "If times should change – and I were to be hanged – you wouldn't only stand around – you'd all tug on the rope!" Finally, he gave the class an ultimatum: "In a week I will come back. If by then you don't reveal the names of the instigators, the whole class will be excluded from the Abitur."

A week later, four SED functionaries appeared at the school. The class-speaker stood up and said: "We all participated. We will all take the consequences ... We are naming no names." Next day, 22 December, the students were to appear in school at 4 p.m. before seven SED-functionaries. The names of three students were read. They were to be expelled from the school as "the ones guilty of the provocation, the ringleaders and spokesmen" ...

Once again each of the students was cross-examined ... They all stood fast. Whereupon the "judgment" was revised. All twenty students were expelled. The class was dissolved. In a unit the students left the class-room.

Next day the boys met on the Storkow sport field and decided to flee. During the Christmas holidays, by ones and by twos, they made their way illegally to West Berlin. On 28 December the last of the fifteen Storkow students had registered in refugee camps ...

Der Tagesspiegel and Der Kurier (Berlin), 31 December

Czechoslovakia. (Poland was not represented.) The agenda included the subject of the struggle against all forms of "National Communism". It was at the close of this conference that Kadar announced the long-awaited program of his Government which reaffirmed "the conquests of the past twelve years", in fact the heritage of Rakosi. The Czechs, if one is to believe the press of their country, were the most violent in refusing any concession to democratic demands. Yet the "Hungarian disease" continued to be felt in all centres of the Communist world and also affected Czechoslovak intellectual circles. In January, the Prague organ of the Party, *Rude Pravo*, did publish an article by K. J. Benes, criticizing the official interpretation of the Hungarian uprising. The editors of the paper condemned this article and described its author as a "confused intellectual" clinging to his own "conscience". The editor-in-chief, however, was subsequently obliged to publish apologies for having granted space at all to this article. A Professor of Philosophy at the University of Brno also wrote in the literary journal *Literarny Novitny*:

> The same kind of confusion exists in the minds of our young people as in the minds of the youth of Hungary. We have before us a younger generation, and we do not really know what kind of young people they actually are.
> *(Die Welt, 31 January)*

On 9 March the youthful Wolfgang Harich, one of East-Germany's most prominent Communist intellectuals (and Professor at the East-Berlin University) began serving a ten-year sentence for "counter-revolutionary activities"; he had been convicted of maintaining "conspiratorial connections" with the Petofi Circle and George Lukacs in Budapest.

The Chinese Prime Minister, Chou-En-Lai, met with Janos Kadar in Moscow and was in Budapest in his company on 17 January. He expressed his "complete approval" of the repression of the Hungarian revolution by the Soviet Army. The Chinese Premier and Mr. Kadar then made a common appeal to the Hungarians "to place themselves firmly beside Soviet Russia, the leader of the Socialist camp."

But Kadar's regime needed material help as much as political support. As early as October, Russia had offered 100 million rubles to Hungary as well as to Poland. Now it was a matter of much more substantial sums, and the other Popular Democracies were also called upon to make an effort.

Marshall Tito's government seemed to be ready to pass over the unpleasantness of the kidnapping of Imre Nagy and his group. The spokesman of the Belgrade Ministry of Foreign Affairs refused to make any further comment on the Nagy case and declared to foreign journalists who questioning him: "Our relations with Hungary are normal."

But it was towards the Yugoslav frontier that more and more Hungarian refugees were fleeing at this time. This mass exodus suggested at the very least that there was no "return to normalcy".

On the political and diplomatic level, there was a return to earlier "abnormalities." During the Hungarian "state visit" to the Soviet Union in late March, Janos Kadar, fervently welcomed as "a true friend", denounced "national communism" as a slogan which was only "a late-born twin of Hitlerite National Socialism", and Marshal Bulganin went on to note that it was "no accident" that "the conspirator Nagy" had sought asylum in the Yugoslav Embassy.

Exodus

On Sunday, 4 November, the flight to Austria began. By 30 November, the number of Hungarian refugees in Austria had passed the 100,000 mark. Close on a quarter of them, in fact 23,700, had already, by that date, been transported to other countries; 56,000 remained in Austrian transit camps. The League of Red Cross Associations then informed the Austrian government that it was ready to assume the responsibility of looking after 20,000 refugees in ten Austrian camps, supplying them with food and clothing. A Vienna correspondent wrote on 2 December:

> We went out into the fields again, this time almost as far as the frontier posts. A small stream flows among bushes through the fields. Suddenly, we heard from the far bank a slight sound. We called out: "Austria!" A joyful reply was shouted back: "Austria? O. K.!" Out of the darkness heavily muffled figures appeared, five of them, ten, even more. They embraced us and greeted us heartily, patted us on the back. They are nearly all young men, with only two or three women among them; most of them are young miners from the Balinka collieries near Stuhlweissenburg. They were driven from their homes by the fear of being deported to the East, or being subjected to other Russian reprisals. At first they had believed that Kadar would pursue a relatively moderate policy of national reconciliation, but

his threatening speech of last Monday had made them understand that the Russians were not prepared to allow the Budapest puppet cabinet any freedom of action at all ...

(Neue Zürcher Zeitung)

The Austrian government then sent out urgent appeals to world opinion for other nations immediately to accept a majority of these refugees.

Air-lifts had to be organized to transport a maximum number of refugees immediately to the United States, England and Ireland. The United Nations High Commission for Refugees collected 600,000 dollars for the organizations which were looking after the Hungarian refugees. Among the nations that contributed to this fund, only those of the Western world are listed.

Disturbing reports began also to come in from Yugoslavia. No foreign correspondents were allowed access to the refugee camps that had been set up there. Hundreds of refugees were being driven back across the frontier into Hungary. A Hungarian newspaper printed in Györ, *Hazank*, published a report about this situation, and there were also the testimonies of refugees who had been sent back from Yugoslavia but who had subsequently been able to escape again to Austria.

In December, the Kadar government launched a campaign to encourage the return of the Hungarian refugees. The Communist leaders had begun to realize that such a massive flight had assumed the nature of an indisputably unfavorable plebiscite, and that Hungary was also losing an élite of teachers, technicians, artists and skilled workers and miners, that the country could not possibly replace.

A majority of the refugees wanted to go overseas, to the Americas or to Australia. President Eisenhower permitted the immediate immigration of 15,000 Hungarian refugees to the United States under his emergency powers. Canada similarly undertook to accept immediately 9,000 redeployed immigrants who had been provisionally placed in Western Germany, Belgium or Great Britain and who, after leaving Austria, were now experiencing difficulties in obtaining admission to other overseas nations. In Great Britain, this problem of immigrants who thought they had come to that country only in transit, and then found out that they had thereby compromised their chances of admission to the United States, was already becoming acute. Many refugees were refusing to accept work in order to avoid what they believed might further compromise their chances. Reports published in the

English press discussed this situation with great sympathy. The *Times*, on 19 December, published a important letter from Arthur Koestler on the subject. Close on half of the 11,000 Hungarians accepted in Great Britain seemed to want to emigrate overseas.

The Vice-President of the United States, Richard Nixon, visited in person, late in December, the Hungarian frontier and a number of Austrian refugee camps. On 1 Januar 1957, he submitted to the President his "Report on the Hungarian Refugees".

The large majority are young people — students, technicians, craftsmen and professional people. There are many family units, including a large number of children. The majority of the refugees who have been interviewed say that they left Hungary because of fear of liquidation or of deportation. The number of floaters and of those who left Hungary purely for economic reasons is relatively small.

The majority of those who have been interviewed to date have expressed a desire to return to Hungary in the event of a change of government which would make it safe for them to do so.

In his report, Mr. Nixon also discussed the problem of re-emigration:

Another factor which must be taken into account in analyzing the total problem is that some of the 73,000 who have gone to other countries did so with the understanding that they were going there temporarily and would eventually have the opportunity to go to the United States.

The President has stated that the United States would accept within this country those who went to other countries with such an understanding.

While the total number of refugees in the above categories can not be estimated with any degree of certainty, there can be but one conclusion. The United States and other free nations must take substantially more refugees than they have agreed to take up to this time ...

In conclusion, it is essential that in our necessary and understandable concern over the immediate problem of providing for the needs of refugees we not lose sight of the historical significance of this mass migration of people from an area of slavery to an area of freedom. The Communist leaders thought they were building a new order in Hungary. Instead they erected a monument which will stand forever in history as proof of the ultimate failure of international communism. Those people, both inside and outside of Hungary, who had the courage to expose by their actions this evil ideology for what it is, deserve all the gratitude and support which we in the free world are so willingly giving today.

Everywhere, great efforts had been undertaken to make it possible for Hungarian students to pursue their studies. In Oxford University, English students had assumed the initiative of setting up a "Hungarian Students Scholarship Fund" and collected four thousand pounds sterling.

On 14 January, the Austrian government launched a new appeal in order to accelerate the redeployment of refugees:

> The slowdown has produced a growing unrest among the refugee population that has already resulted in several incidents, the Government said.

> Despite this plea, sent to Western nations and the United Nations High Commissioner for Refugees, there were indications that the overseas movement of Hungarians would have to be delayed because of financial problems.

> The immediate cause of concern was an unannounced decision by Washington to end tomorrow all financial support for refugee transport by the State Department ...

On 19 January, the Intergovernmental Committee on European Migration published the following release:

> The number of Hungarian refugees evacuated from Austria in the last twelve weeks went over the 100,000 mark today ... 100,253 of the 168,056 fugitives received thus far by Austria had been resettled elsewhere, at least temporarily. Nearly 24,000 Hungarians have now been admitted or cleared for admission to the United States; 15,000 have gone to Britain; More than 11,000 to Germany, and more than 10,000 to Switzerland ...

The Hungarian Government then protested on 15 January to the United Nations.

> In a memorandum to the Secretary-General, the Hungarian Government asked particularly that runaway children who had joined the refugee flood be returned to their parents.

> It also charged that adult refugees were being prevented from returning, if they wanted to, or were being discriminated against in the countries where they chose to go.

> Hungary asked that her citizens be treated in accordance with international law in the countries where they have taken refuge, and that Hungarian Government representatives be able to try to persuade some of them to go home.

A Hungarian Repatriation Commission arrived on 16 January in Austria. By January 19th, of the more than 160,000 refugees who had fled to Austria since the start of the Hungarian revolution, only 1,360 were known to have returned to their native land. The Austrian government had, moreover, declared that it was prepared to provide prompt transportation to the border for all who inisted on going back to Hungary.

Meanwhile, the police of the Kadar government had sought to seal ever more tightly the frontier with Austria; refugees were beginning to seek escape more frequently via the Yugoslav frontier, which is twice as extensive. The representative of the United Nations High Commissioner for Refugees, Amir Hoveyda, went to Belgrade and reported that 3,189 refugees, out of the 7,958 officially listed in that country, had expressed the desire to emigrate further to some Western nation. The attitude of the Yugoslav authorities seemed to have become more cooperative, as far as the refugees are concerned. The Yugoslav Minister of the Interior, Mr. Stefanovitch, declared on 16 February that his country

Refugees

Status Report as of Dec. 31, 1956, 0700 hours

Total influx into Austria Oct. 28, 1956, to date – 155,085.
Total number residing in Austria 67,008.

COUNTRY	QUOTA	CUMULATIVE TOTAL MOVED
1. Switzerland	10,000	10,300
2. Germany	13,552	10,934
3. Netherlands	5,000	2,920
4. France	Unlimited	8,395
5. Sweden	4,000	3,993
6. United Kingdom	Unlimited	12,866
7. Australia	5,000	1,055
8. Canada	Unlimited	7,635
9. U.S.A.	21,500	19,668
10. Belgium	3,000	3,019
11. New Zealand	1,000	66
12. Ireland	1,000	530
13. Luxembourg	200	189
14. Italy	4,000	3,451
15. Spain	—	—
16. Denmark	1,000	1,000
17. Brazil	3,000	—
18. Colombia	1,000	—
19. Chile	1,000	47
20. South Africa	500	148
21. Norway	1,000	528
22. Argentina	2,000	20
23. Iceland	—	52
24. Israel	—	756

Daily average of arrivals in Austria by weeks for December:

	No. Per Day
First week	2,532
Second week	1,724
Third week	1,185
Fourth week	866
Last three days	714

(1437) *There were the Hussites in neighboring Bohemia ... Our rising started all over Transylvania and in northern Hungary. After a little while we thought that our lords would make peace ... So we had a meeting to discuss and agree on our demands. We sent five serfs with our offer of peace as our negotiators. We said: "The lords tread underfoot even our smallest right, and load us with unbearable burdens. For this reason we have gathered here on the Babolna hill in Alparet to regain and re-establish our liberty ... and to shake off our heavy encumbrances after reciprocal consultation, and through our delegates we humbly request our lords to remove the unbearable yoke which enslaves us and to recognise our liberty ..."*

These were our demands. Mind you, we were armed and very strong. But we still kept a civil tongue in our heads while addressing our lords. After we had "humbly requested them" to be human to us, we waited hopefully. Of our five delegates only one returned. He brought back in his satchel the heads of the other four.

This was the answer of our lords ...

(1440) *We felt pretty desperate. As our lords demonstrated to us that they did not keep their word, we demanded that this new treaty should be sanctioned by the King-Emperor Sigismund. While the delegation went to him we remained armed.*

Our lords did not wait for the return of the delegates. They again attacked us; in great force. In 1440 they finally beat us, torturing to death Antal Budai Nagy and the other leaders ...

(1514) *We were eager to fight the Turks. But our lords grew alarmed ... Dozsa gave the order to rise against our lords. He saw he had to beat them before he could turn against the Turks ...*

The people's revolution became a people's war. Our lords sent armies against us. The first armies were beaten. Then they went to get foreign help. (They always do this.) ...

We do not want to bore you with the story of our battles. For a long time we were victorious everywhere. Then we lost a battle or two. Then the nobles and bishops played their usual treacherous tricks on Dozsa. They sent their agents into our armies. They started to parley, and then broke their word. And at long last the mighty armies of Szapolyai beat us in armed combat ...

(1849) *So we were punished again. A regime of terror started all over Hungary ... Kossuth was exiled. Thirteen of our generals were hanged. More than ten thousand of us were executed.*

Petöfi died fighting against the Czarist armies ... Our newspapers were stopped. Our schools were controlled ...

In July 1849, two hundred thousand Russians invaded Hungary. Kossuth asked for help from "free Europe". He did not get it ...

(1850) *"Buda-Pest is a dead city. The victors can be seen everywhere ... In the coffee-houses the agents are watching. People do not talk. For a while they tried to whisper to each other in the coffee-houses, but they gave it up because the police arrest everyone who whispers. One gets up every morning with an awful feeling, knowing full well that one will hear terrible news, streams of it. News of fresh executions, fresh orders. One never knows when the police will knock. Whenever the bell rings the family exchange glances and wonder if they are seeing each other for the last time. The dangers and uncertainty of the future and the terrors of the present lie heavy on everybody. Buda-Pest, the gay and lively city, has become a prison-city sentenced to death ..."*

(1937) Hundreds of our villages were destroyed ... This was our last defeat. Of course the fight was not so simple. There was blood. Men get mad if their houses are destroyed and their wives and children are chased out into the cold and rain. But we don't want to overdo our complaining; this, our last defeat, we mention only so that you should not despise us for being so humble. We are not.

Some district is always at boiling point. Some district is quiet. It is the aftermath of one of our defeats. To fight we need strength. To have strong emotions we need strength.

Have you seen the old type of oil-lamp which our rich peasants use? It makes a bright light if it is turned full on. But if it is only half turned on, to save oil, the light barely flickers. Well, you see, after one of our defeats, after heavy losses and much hungering, our bodies are just like these half-turned-down oil-lamps. Life is barely flickering in our bodies. Our minds are dull. We can be slapped in the face, we can be kicked, we cannot do anything.

Then time passes. There is a better year. Somehow we can eat more. We put on weight. Life returns to us. We start to think, to want things. Slowly we get up enough strength to start a new fight — the fight for land, for food, for the good things ... In some districts we are barely flickering, in others we are just preparing ...

(1938) Centres of resistance were created under the camouflage of regional literary societies and cultural clubs. The writers became very active. In Hungarian politics the important things have been done chiefly by writers. The 1848 revolution was created, organised and led by the young and ardent poet Petöfi. When the great lords and their politicians betrayed the country by collaborating with the Habsburg, the Turks, Metternich or Hitler, the writers became the politicians of Hungary ...

(1942) Torch-singers in night clubs, university professors, actors, writers and lecturers carried on more or less open anti-Hitler propaganda, and on March 15th, the anniversary of the 1848 anti-Habsburg revolution, there was a country-wide anti-Axis demonstration. The slogan was "Petöfi-1848". People wore badges with Petöfi's profile and the date 1848. Naturally every Hungarian child knows what Petöfi stands for ...

(1943) Do you know how they make us dance when one of our revolutions fails? They take a pistol and start to shoot at the ground on which we are standing. They make us jump. Bullets come from all sides, and we move our feet mighty quick. The behaviour of our lords during this period reminded us of this dance. But for once they did the dancing, and history did the shooting ...

(1944) It is cold now. We—all the workers of factories, estates, workshops—sit about in cold rooms. We are hungry and discouraged. About a hundred thousand of us are out in the East. Our leaders are anxious and nervous. They still say that we must think. We must think clearly and effectively. We must understand well this confusing situation. Our only chance of salvation is to understand and to think, to be firm and enthusiastic.

But we are worn out and confused. You know our history. You know that we inherited a great weariness. We inherited hopelessness ...

Our lords are armed to the teeth against us. Those men who can talk hope into us, who can awaken us to action, are mostly in prison or abroad.

Go ahead and punish us ...

G. PALOCZI-HORVATH, "IN DARKEST HUNGARY" (London, 1944)

Quoted in Der Monat (Berlin), December 1956

bore at that date the responsibility for 17,254 refugees, of whom 976 had subesquently returned of their own free will to Hungary and only 384 were willing to remain in Yugoslavia. He asked the nations of the Western world to release Yugoslavia as rapidly as possible from this heavy load that exceeded by far the nation's means. However, all in all, only 869 refugees had left Yugoslavia for Western countries in another month's time.

The way in which the refugees were being handled in the Western world was described by Hungarian propaganda as a "vast kidnapping enterprise" directed in particular against Hungarian children. At the same time, all help received by Hungary from the Red Cross and from other donors was constantly attacked in a campaign that has much in common with the Chinese one on "bacteriological warfare".

In Budapest, new emergency decrees defining expatriation as a crime were promulgated. Persons engaged in organizing clandestine emigration were subject to penalties of imprisonment ranging from six months to five years, and persons who failed to denounce a clandestine frontier-crossing that had been planned or put into effect were subject to penalties of imprisonment up to two years.

In spite of all official and private efforts to help, and to offer asylum, work and a home to the refugees, Austria continued in February to bear the disproportionate load of some 70,000 refugees, of whom the country was able to absorb definitely only 15,000. In the third week of March Austria and Yugoslavia were still caring for about 60,000 refugees. In April, when the original U.S. quota of 30,000 had been filled, there was much desperation and a wave of suicide attempts; there were, however, assurances from Washington that further immigration would be facilitated. But this is not the place to discuss the problems and the personal tragedies of these thousands of Hungarians who have chosen the paths of exile, nor to estimate the total amount of human effort and of good-will that this great drama has inspired.

For the majority of these refugees, their escape from Hungary represents a ballot cast against the land of Soviet Kommandaturas and of the Kadar government, the most tragic but also the clearest of all possible plebiscites. More than 200,000 Hungarians had left their own country. In itself, this figure should suffice to keep the Hungarian tragedy, the despair and the hope of a whole nation, well in view of world public opinion.

François Bondy

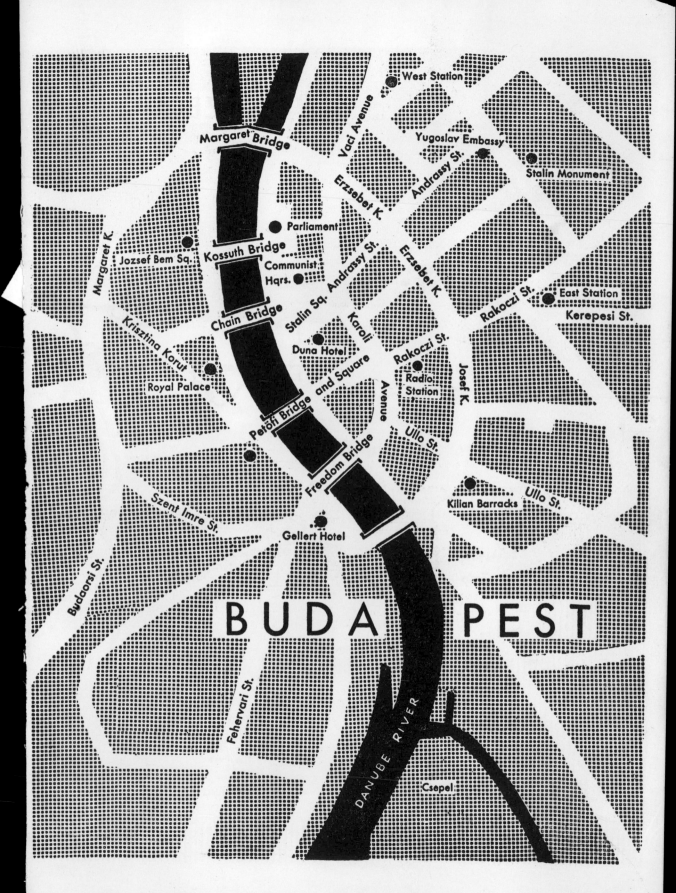

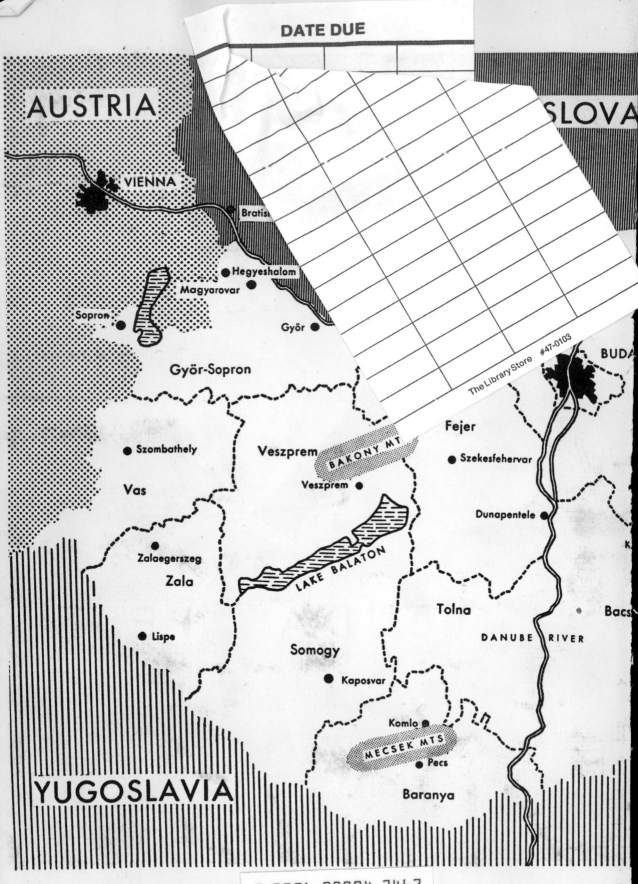

AUSTRIA

VIENNA

Bratis

DATE DUE

SLOVA

The Library Store #47-0103

BUDA

Hegyeshalom

Magyarovar

Sopron

Györ

Györ-Sopron

Fejer

Szombathely

Veszprem

BAKONY MT.

Szekesfehervar

Vas

Veszprem

Dunapentele

Zalaegerszeg

Zala

LAKE BALATON

Tolna

Bacs

DANUBE RIVER

Lispe

Somogy

Kaposvar

Komlo

MECSEK MTS

Pecs

YUGOSLAVIA

Baranya